TO THE PROMISED LAND

To the Promised Land

A HISTORY OF GOVERNMENT AND POLITICS IN OREGON

Tom Marsh

Oregon State University Press   Corvallis

To the Promised Land is dedicated to
Katherine and Brynn,
Meredith and Megan,
and to Judy, my wife.

Publication of this book was made possible in part by a generous gift from Thomas E. Clark. The Oregon State University Press is grateful for this support.

The paper in this book meets the guidelines for permanence and durability of the Committee on Production Guidelines for Book Longevity of the Council on Library Resources and the minimum requirements of the American National Standard for Permanence of Paper for Printed Library Materials Z39.48-1984.

Library of Congress Cataloging-in-Publication Data

Marsh, Tom, 1939–
    To the promised land : a history of government and politics in Oregon / by Tom Marsh.
    p. cm.
    Includes bibliographical references and index.
    ISBN 978-0-87071-657-7 (pbk. : alk. paper) – ISBN 978-0-87071-658-4 (e-book)
    1. Oregon–Politics and government. I. Title.
JK9016.M36 2012
320.795--dc23
                        2011052977

Oregon State University Press
121 The Valley Library
Corvallis OR 97331-4501
541-737-3166 • fax 541-737-3170
http://osupress.oregonstate.edu

Contents

Preface and Acknowledgments xi

Introduction. 1

1 "WHO'S FOR A DIVIDE?" THE OREGON COUNTRY, 1834-49 8

The Death of Ewing Young / Decision at Champoeg / No Taxes, No
Liquor, No Negroes / 1844: New Blood / A Government Gone
Broke / Oregon's First Newspaper / The Whitman Massacre and the
Cayuse War / Men Go South, Gold Comes North

2 FROM TERRITORY TO STATE, 1848-59 19

Meet Joe Lane / Two Houses Instead of One / Samuel Thurston and the
Donation Land Act / Counting Noses / Daily Life in Territorial
Oregon / Congress Pays the Bill / Go Home, John! / Where Should
Our Capital Be? / Rival Legislatures / Asahel Bush and the Oregon
Style / The Salem Clique / Temperance and the Challenge of the
Know-Nothings / The Democratic Landslide / Hurrah for Stephen
Douglas! / Slavery as a Political Issue in Oregon and the Nation /
Republicans Appear / Democrats Dividing / Free State or Slave State? /
Oregon's Constitutional Convention of 1857 / Democrats: A Two-Headed
Party / Were Oregonians Ready for Statehood?

3 EARLY STATEHOOD AND THE CIVIL WAR ERA. 48

1860: A Year of Decision / Civil War / Oregon's Union Party Takes
Charge / Lincoln: Reelection and Assassination / Arguing Over
Reconstruction / Oregon's Union Party Unravels / Dumping James
Nesmith / The Return of the Democrats / Growing / Woman of the
Century

4 JOHN MITCHELL AND OTHER TALES OF CORRUPTION, 1868-73. . . 65

Ben Holladay, Wheeler-Dealer / Land Scams / The Railroads /
Something Is Rotten in Oregon / The Lowdown on John Hipple
Mitchell / No Love Lost / Getting "Guts" Gibbs / The Era of
Democratic Domination Ends

5 MONEY, CORRUPTION, AND THE REFORMERS, 1882-1902. 77

The Big Three: Power in One Place / Weeding Out Political Corruption /
The Legislature of 1885 / Governor Grover and the Chinese Issue /

Sylvester Pennoyer Rockets into Power / Regulation and Abuses / Harrison Yes, Cleveland No / Reformers in Oregon / Populism Takes Root in Oregon / The Campaign of 1894 / Mountains of Money / The Hold-Up Legislature of 1897 / Joe Gets His Wish / A Winning Strategy / The Vote for Women? / The Oregon System Is Born / George Chamberlain Steps Up

6   GEORGE CHAMBERLAIN AND THE OS WEST EXPRESS, 1903-13 . . . 106

More Disappointment / What's in It for Me? / Oregon's Infamous Land Fraud Trials / Reform Continues with the 1905 Legislature / Enter Dr. Harry Lane / Chamberlain Gets Another Four Years / Testing the Direct Primary Law / The Campaign and Election of 1908 / The Contest for Governor / Governor Oswald West / West and Bowerman Lock Horns / The Woman Suffrage Victory of 1912 / The 1913 Legislature: A Shining Star and a Punch / Progressive Reforms / Os West Saves Oregon's Beaches / America 1912-13

7   OREGON DURING WORLD WAR ONE, 1914-20 133

Governor James Withycombe / Oregon's First Women Legislators / The Election of 1916 / An Issue of Race / The 1917 Legislature / Senator Harry Lane Votes Against War / Oregon, the Great War, and Unbridled Patriotism / Intolerance Runs Amok / Oregon's 30th Legislature / Violence By and Against Labor / A Special Session / The 1920 Senate Race

8   THE ELECTION OF 1922, THE KU KLUX KLAN,
    AND GOVERNOR WALTER PIERCE, 1921-27 145

The Klan in Oregon / The Klan and the Governor's Race of 1922 / Walter Pierce Is Inaugurated / The "Yellow Peril" / Walter Pierce Hammers Away at Tax Reform / Pierce and the 1925 Legislature / The 1926 Senate Race / Isaac Patterson

9   TWO DEATHS: 1927-33 163

Many New Faces / A Special Election / Mr. Smith, Mr. Hoover, and the Election of 1928 / Wall Street Trembles / The Legislature of 1929 / Republican Scramble / A Crusading George Joseph / A "Rich Boy" for Governor? / Other Results in 1930 / Oregon Slips into the Great Depression / Oregon's First Depression-Era Legislature / Politics Undergoes Fundamental Change / Oregon Is Dead Broke

10 FDR, OLD IRON PANTS, AND THE POLITICS
    OF UPHEAVAL, 1933-38 177

FDR and the New Deal / The Ugly Reality of Deepening Depression / Election of 1934; General Martin Runs for Governor / Portland's 1934 Dock Strike / Oregon's Second Depression Legislature / Labor Strife Resumes / The Election of 1936 / Man Is a Fighting Animal / Charles Martin Out, Charles Sprague In / Republican Resurgence / A New Capitol Building

11 HOW THE WAR CHANGED OREGON, 1939-48 194

Governor Charles Sprague / The 1939 Legislature / The World Lurches
Toward War / 1940 Election / Pearl Harbor! / Frustrated Democrats /
Charles Sprague's Defeat / The 1942 General Election / The War's
Impact on Oregon's Economy / Lawmaking in Wartime: The Legislature
of 1943 / Oregon's Isolationists / Senator McNary's Death /
Republican Shuffle / Governor Earl Snell / The Legislature of 1945 /
The Nation's Leading Lumber State / Oregon Elections of 1946 /
The 1947 Legislature: Milestones Galore / Death on a Mountaintop /
The Primary Election of 1948

12 OREGON AT MID-CENTURY, 1948-55 217

The Election of 1948 / Oregon at Mid-Century / The Election of
1950 / A Fistful of Stars / Richard and Maurine Neuberger / Oregon
and the Nation in 1952 / Mr. McKay Goes to Washington / The 1953
Legislature / Wayne Morse Talks On, and On, and On / 1954: A Year to
Remember / Colliding Titans / Edith and Tom / Growing Pains /
Rising Racial Tensions

13 RAGING BULLS, 1956-59 238

A Silent Death / Phone Calls in the Night / The Campaign of 1956 /
Senate Showdown / Other 1956 Election Results / Trouble Ahead /
Governor Robert Holmes and the Legislature of 1957 / What to Do
with $70 Million? / The Campaign of 1958 / Wayne's Big Blunder /
The Legislature of 1959: Oregon's 50th

14 WHEN TOM BLEW THE WHISTLE, 1960-62 257

An Untimely Death / John Fitzgerald Kennedy / The Contest for the
Senate Nomination in 1960 / Nixon, Neuberger, and Appling / The 1961
Legislature / Morse Ascending and the Election of 1962 / Tom McCall
Makes a Big Splash / Organized Confusion / New House and Senate
Districts / Dallas, November 22, 1963 / An Election to Remember /
The 1965 Legislature / Maurine Neuberger Leaves the Senate /
Tom Makes His Move / A Republican Juggernaut / The Governor's
Race / Mr. Dellenbeck Goes to Washington

15 THE TOM McCALL YEARS, 1965-75 279

Goodbye Mark, Hello Tom / McCall Swings into Action / Tax Relief
and the 1967 Legislature / Celebrity / Wayne Morse Wants a Fifth
Term / The Special Session of 1967 / 1968: Primary Politics in Oregon /
Murder in the Kitchen / Tom and Monte / The 1968 General
Election / Trouble in Paradise / A Progressive Legislature / Too Many
Eggs in One Basket / Citizen Chambers / McCall Takes on the
Establishment / Vortex / The Election of 1970 / The Legislature of
1971 / The 1972 Oregon Primary / The 1972 General Election /
Changing of the Guard / Tom McCall Pushes Tax Reform / Dueling
Democrats / A Landmark: Senate Bill 100 / More Precedents /
Catching Up with History / Campaign and Elections of 1974

16   BOB STRAUB—LIVING IN TOM'S LONG SHADOW, 1975-78. 320

A Democratic Legislature / A Full Plate / Other Accomplishments
of the 1975 Legislature / The Election of 1976 / Turmoil in Salem: The
1977 Legislature / Issues Facing the 1977 Legislature / The May
Rebellion / The Author's Interpretation / No Safety Net / Staggering
to the Finish / A Record of Solid Accomplishment / Straub Behind the
Scenes / Economic Woes / Politics in 1978 / Another Democratic
Legislature / The End of an Era

17   GOVERNOR VICTOR ATIYEH: SAVING A SINKING SHIP, 1979-86 . . . 340

The Legislature of 1979 / A Decade of Change / The Election of 1980 /
Bob Packwood Goes for Another Term / The November General
Election / Meanwhile, Back in Oregon / Governor Victor Atiyeh /
The Specter of a Taxpayer Revolt / The 1981 Legislature / Three
Special Sessions: Back to Salem / The Election of 1982 / The 1983
Legislature / The Death of Tom McCall / Strapping on the Boots /
Never Had a Prayer / 1984: Time to Elect a President / Kitz and Katz
and the Legislature of 1985 / The Campaign of 1986 / Neil or Norma?
The Governor's Race / Money, Money, Money / Victor Atiyeh's Legacy

18   NEIL AND BARBARA, VERA AND JOHN, 1987-94 364

Back on Track / Oregon's 66th Legislature / What the Legislature
Did / One Cost of Rapid Population Growth / Election Year
1988 / Kitz and Katz and the Legislature of 1989 / Goldschmidt
Drops a Political Bomb / Oregon Changes Direction: The Election of
1990 / Ballot Measure 5 / Kopetski vs. Smith / Governor Barbara
Roberts, 1991-95 / The Challenge Posed by Measure 5 / Big Budget /
Sales Tax? / The Election of 1992 / The Packwood-AuCoin Senate
Contest / Elizabeth Furse Goes to Washington / President Clinton /
The Ballot Measures / How Measure 9 Changed Oregon / 207 Days /
Packwood in Trouble / Barbara Bows Out / Mike and Bob Come
Home / A Republican Stampede / Barbara Roberts: Too Tall a
Mountain?

19   CHOOSING SENATORS, 1995-96 395

A Republican Legislature / The Folly of the Rule of Eighteen /
An Interesting Mix / "The most difficult vote I ever cast" /
More Blood-letting / Knocking the Train off the Tracks / What Did
the 1995 Legislature Accomplish? / Kitzhaber Calls a Special Session /
The Packwood Scandal / The Campaign to Replace Bob Packwood /
Ron Wyden in a Photo-finish / A One-Day Special Session / Oregon
Holds Its Presidential Preference Primary / More Elections /
The Battle for Mark Hatfield's Senate Seat / Other Key Political
Contests / Wester Shadric Cooley / The 1996 General Election /
The Smith-Bruggere Senate Race / A Democratic Sweep / Stirring
the Political Pot: Oregon's 23 Ballot Measures / Money and PACs

20 JOHN KITZHABER AND THE REPUBLICANS, 1997-99 421

Lynn Lundquist and Brady Adams / Bill Sizemore in the Spotlight /
"Blood will splatter" / Confrontation at the Capitol / Governor
Kitzhaber and the Republican Leadership / Feuding Republicans /
Breaking the Logjam / Doctor-Assisted Suicide / The 1997
Legislature / The High Cost of Growth / "Dr. No" / Doctor-Assisted
Suicide: Round 2 / The 1998 May Primary / PACs, Lobbyists, and
Oregon Politics / The Rise and Influence of the Christian Coalition /
Wanted, Dead or Alive: Moderate Republicans / Turn Off the Spigot! /
Yawn, Yawn, Yawn / Kitzhaber's Landslide and Ron Wyden, Again /
Congressional Races / Which Party Will Control the Next Legislature? /
The Ballot Measures / Lynn Out, Lynn In / $$$ for Schools /
Locking Horns: Kitzhaber and the Republicans / Snodgrass Backpedals /
What the 70th Legislature Accomplished / Dr. No: Round 3 /
Keisling Resigns / No Friend of Assisted Suicide / Looking Forward to a
New Century and Millennium

21 INTO THE FUTURE, 2000-11 451

January 1, 2000: The Dawn of a New Millennium / Exhausted
Voters / Focus on Legislative Elections / Poverty in Oregon /
The Fall Campaign of 2000 / Who's In, Who's Out / The Contest for
President / Eight of 10 Oregonians Voted / Trying to Get Along:
The Legislature of 2001 / Gene Derfler / Mark Simmons /
John Kitzhaber / The Issues / A Smooth Start—and Rebellion /
The May Economic Forecast / The Challenge of Redrawing the
Political Map of Oregon / The Big Walkout / Salem 2001: Grinding
to a Halt / John Kitzhaber, Politician / A Troubled 2002 /
Five Special Legislatures / The Election of 2002 / Money, Mountains
of Money / Another Democratic Governor / The Legislature of 2003 /
The 2004 Elections / The Campaign of 2006 / And They Kept
Coming / The Election of 2008 / Money Woes, Again / Oregon's
Contest for Governor, 2010 / Where Is Oregon Headed?

Notes 479

Index 497

Preface
Politics in the Pursuit and Exercise of Power

"Somebody should write a book." As it turned out, *I* was that somebody.

For nearly thirty years I taught high school in the Beaverton School District. One challenge I repeatedly faced when preparing curriculum for my Oregon government classes was the dearth of published materials on the subject. It didn't take long to realize that I'd have to do my own research and writing. These experiences reinforced my belief that someone needed to write a general history of government and politics in Oregon appropriate for high school and lower division college students and their teachers, as well as for those Oregonians having an abiding interest in our state's history. *To the Promised Land: A History of Government and Politics in Oregon* is the result.

This book is unique. *To the Promised Land* is a history of the Oregon Legislature, our governors and their administrations, our United States Senators and Representatives, and our political campaigns—over a span of nearly 200 years. In some respects it is a textbook, while in others it is a gigantic drama of people and leaders, played out in a state where issues and large personalities stand out vividly.

Coupled with my teaching background is my personal experience in state government: I served two terms in the Oregon House of Representatives, 1975-79. In addition, I have been a Democratic precinct committeeman and been active in numerous political campaigns over a span of fifty years. In short, I have been an *insider*, a campaigner, an elected officeholder, volunteer, and advisor who has experienced state and local government firsthand.

Why, the reader may ask, did I choose the title *To the Promised Land*? There are two reasons: First is the obvious biblical meaning, the Promised Land being either heaven, the land of Canaan promised to Abraham and his descendants, or simply a place believed to hold final happiness. Second, Americans wanted to come to Oregon because of the promise of free land.

In the late 1820s, New Hampshire-born and college-educated Hall Jackson Kelley embarked on a crusade. Kelley believed that God intended him to organize and lead a movement of Americans across the continent to settle the remote Oregon Country. The New Englander barraged Congress and newspaper editors with letters and petitions pressing for the colonization of Oregon by Americans. In 1829, Kelley organized an association of like-thinkers: the American Society for Encouraging the Settlement of the Oregon Territory.

Historian Malcolm Clark, Jr., put Kelley in perspective when he wrote: "Kelley proposed to bring salvation to the savages, and at a profit. There would be opportunities in the Promised Land for merchants as well as missionaries. A settler might, at his option, work either in the Lord's vineyard or his own."[1] Joining Kelley and other enthusiasts for the American settlement of Oregon were two Missouri senators: Thomas Hart Benton and, later, Dr. Lewis Linn.

Hall Kelley made it to Fort Vancouver—the Hudson's Bay Company's outpost on the Columbia River—in October 1834, after a perilous two-year crossing that included traversing the length of Baja and Alta California. In March 1835, Kelley sailed to the Sandwich (Hawaiian) Islands. He never returned to Oregon. Although Kelley realized his dream of going to Oregon, he failed in almost every other aspect of his vision. Suspicious and all too ready to blame others for his failings, he drifted into an unhappy life, overcome by his growing paranoia. Although Kelley lived long enough to witness (from afar) the largest human migration in North American history—the cross-continent journey of 330,000 Americans (including thousands of recent European immigrants) to the Pacific Coast and Far West—he did not achieve his dream of *personally* leading these emigrant crossings or serving as an important American leader in Oregon. Rather, Hall Kelley's place in Western history is this: he was one of the first champions of the idea that Oregon was a place where Americans should go to live, where the dream of heaven on earth was to be found. Indeed, the Protestant and Catholic missionaries and the capitalists, merchants, tradesmen, and craftsmen, along with the great body of farm-folk who settled here in the mid-19th century did so because most of them believed the ideas that Hall Kelley was selling.

Senator Lewis Linn began introducing bills in Congress in 1838 to bring the Oregon Country, still jointly occupied by Great Britain and the United States, into the exclusive domain of the United States. For five years Linn pushed legislation to establish a permanent American military presence in the Oregon Country. In 1842, Linn introduced a new (and highly publicized) bill: the granting of a section of land (640 acres) to every white man who emigrated to Oregon. And, said Linn, the land was to be a gift—it would be free. Federal law then in effect normally required a payment of a minimum of $1.25 an acre in order to acquire public lands.

According to historian Robert C. Clark, the emigrants who moved to Oregon after 1838 had been encouraged by Senator Linn's bills. "None of these bills had ever become, it is true, a law, but they were considered as a promise that each settler would receive a section of land."[2] In 1843, Oregon's first provisional government enacted a land law based on Lewis Linn's idea, providing 640 acres of land free to each white male settler. This law was in effect at the time the Oregon Boundary Question was settled in 1846 and in 1848, when Oregon officially became a territory of the United States.

In 1850, Congress passed the controversial Oregon Donation Land Law, at the behest of Oregon's delegate in Congress, Samuel Royal Thurston. This Act confirmed the system of land ownership in Oregon that had been in place for seven years, legitimizing Oregonians' land titles. "Backed by the authority of the federal law, settlers would no longer need to rely upon voluntary organizations to protect their lands from claim jumpers. For Oregonians it was a matter of extreme concern whether the Congress would recognize the land laws of its provisional government as the claims of its early settlers."[3]

The title *To the Promised Land* poses two basic questions: What effect did the Oregon Country, as a Promised Land or even as a land of promise, have on the imaginations of ordinary Americans? And why did the promise of free land lure so many Americans into moving halfway across North America to start their lives over on the raw and remote Oregon frontier?

Acknowledgements

One of my goals when researching and writing this book was as much as possible, to write history from a personal point of view. I've drawn on my knowledge and experiences as a high school history and government teacher, my involvement in state and local government, and, most importantly, my dozens of conversations with Oregonians who were personally involved in "making history." It is this latter group that I want to acknowledge.

Two gentlemen, now deceased, were of particular help to me, each going overboard to assist in any way he could. Cecil Edwards and Monroe Sweetland both participated in and observed state government (especially the legislature) for over sixty years. I was fortunate to have spent a dozen hours in the early-1990s talking with Cecil Edwards, historian of the Oregon Legislature. Cecil Edwards personally observed every legislature from the early-1930s to the 1990s. He served as a governor's chief-of-staff, as legislative committee staff, legislative historian and several other capacities in and around the Capitol. In short, Cecil Edwards was a walking encyclopedia of Oregon politics and government. Edwards was most helpful when he discussed how the legislature evolved from the Depression-era through World War II and forward into the 1970s—when the Legislative Assembly began to reform itself by opening the doors to the public, welcoming Oregonians to actively participate in the work of their government. His stories and anecdotes were priceless—and I think I have written a better book because Cecil Edwards is so much a part of it.

I am forever indebted to Monroe Mark Sweetland for his friendship, generosity, wit, wisdom, and deep firsthand knowledge of Oregon's political and government institutions. A newspaper publisher, editor, lobbyist, Democratic Party leader and activist, national committeeman, a veteran legislator, and, most important, a longtime friend and advisor to dozens of Oregon politicians, Monroe Sweetland's ninety-seven-year-long life was one of extraordinary accomplishment. Beginning in 1946-47, Sweetland, along with Howard Morgan, was responsible for resurrecting the modern Democratic Party of Oregon.

I was fortunate to have had conversations over a period of months with Sweetland in 1998. Like Cecil Edwards, Monroe Sweetland had a remarkable memory rooted in hundreds of personal relationships over a period of nearly seventy years in Oregon. No Oregonian knew as much about 20th-century politics in Oregon as Monroe Sweetland. His keen observations about such leaders as Maurine and Richard Neuberger, Mark Hatfield, Wayne Morse, Edith Green, Robert Holmes and Tom McCall were invaluable to me.

Several individuals were very helpful in the early stages of my work. I spent an afternoon with Portland historian E. Kimbark MacColl, learning about the history of Portland politics and the graft and corruption associated with Oregon's legislatures of the 1890s. The late Jim Klonoski, professor of political science at the University of Oregon, was an enthusiastic early backer of this project.

I spent an afternoon with the late Travis Cross in July 1994. Cross was a longtime friend and advisor of Mark Hatfield's. As a Republican Party leader, Travis Cross was familiar with GOP politicians in the 1950s, '60s, and '70s. His insights into the personality of Tom McCall were a great help to me.

Veteran lobbyist, Dave Barrows, who has worked in every legislative session beginning in the late-1950s, was another helpful source, particularly when he shared his insights into how the legislature has evolved and how politics in Oregon has changed over the past fifty years.

The late Robert Y. Thornton, former attorney general and justice of the Oregon Court of Appeals, shared with me his experiences as a politician, from his time in the Oregon House to his sixteen years as Attorney General.

The Honorable Victor Atiyeh, a twenty-five-year veteran of the legislature, and governor of Oregon from 1979-87, was most generous with his time and comments. I am indebted to the governor for critiquing two chapters of my book and for allowing me to interview him on several occasions. His friendliness, encouragement, and candor are most appreciated. His personal experiences, freely shared, were of inestimable help to me.

Veteran legislators Grattan Kerans and Clifford Trow were important contributors to my research. I have known both men since the mid-1970s, when we served in the legislature together. They remained in the assembly long after I returned to teaching. Cliff Trow was a state senator for twenty-eight years, 1975-2003. His knowledge and first-hand experiences over that period were offered with special clarity and insight. Senator Trow's observations about the Kitzhaber-era (from Kitzhaber's time as president of the Oregon Senate to his eight years as governor) were important to my understanding of that period.

Grattan Kerans served in both the house and senate; in 1983 Kerans was house speaker. In addition to sharing his experiences and observations with me, Kerans helped me to better understand the personalities and inner-workings of the governorships of Victor Atiyeh, Neil Goldschmidt, Barbara Roberts, and John Kitzhaber. Kerans critiqued a couple of my chapters—for which I am most appreciative.

Early in my efforts I relied heavily on the writing talents and knowledge of several friends and colleagues. All critiqued early chapters and assisted me in developing my writer's voice. Thank you Rod Craig, Dave Robbins, and Joan Johnson. And, to my daughter, Megan Thomas, thank you for editing and typing the early chapters of my manuscript. And, to daughter Meredith Marsh thank you for devoting so many hours assisting me in assembling the historical photographs featured in the book.

The library staff at these institutions were very helpful, particularly the staff at the Oregon Historical Society, Reed College, the Oregon State Archives, State Library, and Secretary of State's office in Salem.

To my longtime friend Tom Clark for his generosity and support, a special thank you.

Adair Law's assistance in revising my original manuscript is very much appreciated, as are the suggestions and critique offered by one of my oldest and wisest friends, Professor Kenneth Lockridge.

And a final THANK YOU to my wife, Judy, whose patience and encouragement have supported me over the years it has taken me to write *To the Promised Land: A History of Government and Politics in Oregon.*

Tom Marsh
Salem, Oregon

Introduction

Oregon has been shaped by hundreds of forces over the span of its history. No factor, however, has had as much impact on Oregon as this one: most Oregonians live within a two-hour drive of one another in the Willamette Valley. Two-thirds of Oregon's land area lies east of the Cascade mountain range. Yet only a fraction of the population live there. Today four out of ten Oregonians live in just three counties: Multnomah, Washington, and Clackamas. In fact, the 2.5 million people who reside in Oregon's six most populous counties is more than the population of Oregon's remaining thirty counties by a ratio of two to one. This lopsided population distribution continues to shape all aspects of life in Oregon: the economy, social trends, educational opportunities, and politics. A mere eight of Oregon's sixty state representatives are from districts east of the Cascades. District 60, for example, which includes Harney, Malheur, and Baker counties, and part of Grant county, is so vast (23,200 square miles) that it is larger in land area than nine U.S. states and nearly as large as Massachusetts, Connecticut, and New Hampshire *combined*. Thus, the vastness of eastern Oregon belies the fact that this part of the state has to work doubly hard to have its economic and political interests considered by the "westerners" who typically dominate the state legislature and the governor's mansion.

Historically, eastern Oregonians, as well as those living along the state's long coastline, and those in far southern Oregon, have often felt like step-children, who, like Cinderella, are assigned menial tasks, sleep in a gloomy room, and eat left-over food. This feeling has, throughout state history, led those who live outside the Willamette Valley to resent Portland and her affluent suburbs. Modern politics in Oregon—her statewide ballot measure campaigns, presidential, and gubernatorial elections, as well as the state's clout in Congress—is dominated by how Multnomah, Washington, and Clackamas counties vote. Over the decades, then, Oregon's political leaders have had to balance the interests of a more urbanized and economically diversified metropolitan Portland with the interests of Oregon's other regions.

The history of state government and politics in Oregon is far more complex, controversial, and colorful than the typical citizen realizes. Historically, Oregonians have displayed a willingness to take great political risks (the Oregon System, Bottle Bill, and doctor-assisted suicide) while maintaining a basic conservatism when it comes to spending money or taxing themselves.

For most of her history Oregon has been a modified one-party state. Between 1880 and 1934 the Oregon House of Representatives was controlled by Republicans, as was the state Senate from 1880 to 1956. Not until 1950 did Democratic voter registration, for the first time in the 20th century, exceed Republican. Yet Democrats, despite their surge in popularity, continued to have trouble getting their candidates elected to high public office. Only five Democrats were elected to the United States Senate between 1950 and 2008 (Wayne Morse, Richard and Maurine Neuberger, Ron Wyden, and Jeff Merkley), and only one Democrat was elected governor between 1938 and 1973 (Robert Holmes). When it comes to voting for president, Oregonians voted for a Democrat only six times between 1860 and 1984. But between 1988 and 2008 Oregon favored the Democratic nominee for president every time.

Until 1952, when reapportionment of the Oregon Legislature occurred, the rural minority elected a majority of members in both houses and non-Portland legislators were elected as speakers of the House and presidents of the Senate. There is an unwritten rule in the legislature that its leaders should represent the state's more rural areas. Only twice in the 20th century (1913 and 1935) were both the Senate president and House speaker from Portland.

Throughout their history, Oregon's Republican and Democratic parties have suffered from internal ideological differences so divisive that the opposition was able to elect their candidates. This disunity has been particularly true of the Republican Party (in the period 1876-1920, the 1930s, and the 1980s and '90s). Beginning in 1902 voters took matters into their own hands: they adopted the Oregon System. By introducing the initiative, referendum, and recall, and the direct election of U.S. senators, Oregonians gave themselves the power to pass laws, refer laws passed by the Legislature, and the power to recall or vote an elected official out of office. Adoption of the initiative, referendum and recall was a turning point in Oregon's political history. What may have made little sense to people and politicians in other states made perfect sense to Oregonians. For a generation Oregonians had lived with widespread political corruption and unresponsive politicians. By 1902, Oregonians had had enough. The tide of change was here and there was little politicians could do to stop it.

William U'Ren, Oregon's leading political reformer, and his legions of dedicated followers, had pushed politicians (and their monied friends) into a corner:
either you get aboard and support the Oregon System or voters will see you as
part of the problem. The movement to adopt the initiative and referendum in
Oregon was one of those moments when the people came together to answer
this fundamental question: what do we want state politics and government to
be like?

Voters have utilized the initiative hundreds of times over the past century.
This habit has engendered a political activism unknown in many states and it has
led to an important political tradition in Oregon. Besides the three branches of
state government established in the Constitution of 1858 (executive, legislative,
and judicial), there is a fourth branch: the people. Time and again, Oregonians
have gone around their elected leaders, using the initiative and referendum to
pass laws popular with voters.

Many Oregonians have traditionally voted in a non-partisan way, for the individual candidate, not for the party label she or he represents. Several successful Oregon politicians have downplayed their party affiliations to campaign on
their character and political beliefs. For example, governors Sylvester Pennoyer,
George Chamberlain, Oswald West, Walter Pierce, Charles Sprague, Tom
McCall, Bob Straub, and Victor Atiyeh all appealed to voters not so much as
Republicans or Democrats but as men who had lots of ideas and took positions
on issues important to Oregonians.

Before Statehood

Many of Oregon's most cherished political values and traditions are rooted in
the frontier period. Starting in 1818, the United States and Great Britain jointly
occupied a vast region (285,000 square miles) known as the Oregon Country.
Today we call this area the Pacific Northwest. From 1825 to 1846 the Oregon
Country was also part of a huge trading empire based in British Canada, the
Hudson's Bay Company (HBC). Between 1824 and 1845, Dr. John McLoughlin,
Chief Factor of the HBC, was the most powerful man in the Oregon Country.
Locally, the HBC was headquartered at the newly rebuilt Fort Vancouver, with-
in walking distance from the north shore of the Columbia River, across from
modern-day Portland. Prior to 1840 only a couple of wagonloads of Americans
lived in the Oregon Country, almost all of them south of the Columbia River.
In 1841, 1843, and 1845, the American settlers established provisional governments, but it was not until 1846 that President Polk and the Senate agreed to a
British proposal to divide the Oregon Country with all lands below 49 degrees

The Oregon Country, 1818-1846
Between 1818 and 1846 the United States and Great Britain jointly "owned" and occupied a vast area of 285,000 square miles known as the Oregon Country. Present-day Oregon is shown in the lower left corner. The boundaries of the Oregon Country extended from the Pacific Ocean on the west to the crest of the Rocky Mountains on the east, south to 42 degrees and north to the 54th parallel. Future American states of Oregon, Washington, Idaho, western Montana and a portion of Wyoming as well as the British-Canadian provinces of British Columbia and part of Alberta comprised the Oregon Country.

north becoming part of the United States. In 1849, the first Oregon Territorial Legislature convened. In 1853, Congress divided the U.S. portion of the Oregon Country into two regions: the area north of the Columbia River and basically east of the Snake River was to be the Washington Territory, with the area south of the Columbia to remain as the Oregon Territory. By the time Oregon joined the Union as a state in 1859, over 52,000 Americans were residing here. Most of the emigrants had walked here via the Oregon Trail from in and around Missouri. Why had they come? Why were they willing to leave their more established, settled lives to risk a 2,000-mile walk to a place so far away from their reality that they could only dream about it?

Oregon was a popular topic among eastern writers and promoters throughout the 1820s, '30s, and '40s. Dozens of articles, letters, pamphlets, and books were written about Oregon and the Pacific Northwest. Beginning with the published journals of William Clark and Meriwether Lewis, a body of work evolved which, over time, created a mystical Oregon, a place so idyllic that some writers characterized Oregon as a paradise on earth. Thus was a vision born: Oregon took on the mystique "of a land biblical in scale; this was not just the next unclaimed territory, but a Promised Land, or even an Eden."[1] Indeed, Oregon was, in a sense, a mythical vision before there were any Oregonians at all.

Throughout the early 19th century, Americans believed their young nation was destined for greatness. Many Americans believed their culture should be spread across the North American continent. In a span of forty-five years (1803-48) the land area of the United States quadrupled. In 1844, John Quincy Adams, then a congressman, made an eloquent plea on behalf of Oregon. America claimed Oregon for a noble purpose: "To make the wilderness blossom as the rose, to establish laws, to increase, multiply, and subdue the earth, which we are commanded to do by the first behest of God Almighty."[2] In the mid-1840s this idea that God had a plan for the United States was given a name: Manifest Destiny. The idea of Manifest Destiny remained a potent political force in America for the rest of the century. And it was an idea that explains why so many Americans and their political leaders were so eager to create a new society in a place called Oregon, a Promised Land, an Eden. Eden or not, it became Oregon.

The emigrants who flooded into Oregon between 1843 and 1854 had a lot in common. Most of them were repeating a life-cycle familiar to the young American nation; these people, in traveling to Oregon, were merely doing something that they fervently believed in and had done before, over and over. These emigrants (who some called "movers") were in the habit of leaving their homes, farms, or trades, packing their possessions, and moving to a new place farther west.

For millions of Americans the frontier was a mystical place. The frontier represented opportunity, an environment where a person could renew him or herself, a place to start over. Life in 19th-century America was hard. Most Americans were farmers, as were their fathers and grandfathers. Life was short, cut down by disease, famine, back-breaking labor, natural disasters, debt, loneliness, and poverty. Few farmers knew anything about crop-rotation or the practice of leaving parts of one's land fallow for a year or two. Because of these practices many farmers found that, no matter how hard they worked, their harvests got smaller and smaller. For many Americans, then, farming where they were had led them down a dead-end road. So, when the opportunity presented itself, many Americans simply pulled up roots and headed west where new territories were opening up. And what was best about this frontier was that much of this land was free (though it can be argued that the lands had been stolen from the Native Americans, who had lived on them for generations).

Historian Malcolm Clark, Jr., said it best in his book, *Eden Seekers*, when he wrote: "On the frontier, however, there was nothing to prevent a man from walking away from failure, or from successive failures, drawn along by the conviction that something better would turn up farther on. In this way the Westerners pushed back the West, going at it in stages, the whole process of a continental crossing taking years and even generations. They were not called pioneer, but movers. Restlessness was their dominant trait. The gene of it was passed from father to son as a part of the act of procreation. The frontier was constantly reproducing itself." Oregon, like other frontiers, attracted many people who had been unsuccessful where they were. Although a majority of emigrants who came to Oregon after 1844 were family people, there was also a rowdy minority of single men here, as well. "A substantial number of emigrants were social misfits—the rebels, the restless, the adventurous, the unruly—and more than one was a social outcast. That they were crass and coarse-fibered does not mean they were ineffectual. Nor were they simple," wrote Malcolm Clark. [3]

The Panic of 1837, the worst economic depression in 19th-century America, caused widespread hardship. The depression lasted for several years. Particularly hard hit were farmers in the Mississippi River basin. Faced with higher shipping costs, a shortage of currency, and mounting debts, thousands of Midwestern farmers saw Oregon as an opportunity to, once again, start over.

But for many emigrants, the lure of Oregon was different. The myth of Oregon as an Eden was really part of the American Dream. For many emigrants, Oregon was a vision. Oregon, with its fertile Willamette Valley and temperate climate, long growing season, giant trees, and fair winds, represented hope. Oregon, like other frontiers, attracted people who wanted to improve their lives and the future of their children.

Thus it was that early Oregon, even with its share of misfits, eccentrics, and dreamers, evolved in its own unique way, with its own sense of values, of time and place and experience. Cut off by their isolation, Oregon's pioneers, on their own, reconstructed a civil society on this raw Pacific frontier. Over the next five generations it would become apparent that their descendants had a conservative and, at times, an eclectic and astonishingly innovative view of what state government might do for them.

Keep it in mind

Because this is a history book it will be helpful to remember these facts as you begin to read.

- Until 1912, politics was a man's business in Oregon. Women could not vote nor hold office except in local school elections. Nationally, women were not granted the vote until ratification of the 19th Amendment in 1920. Oregon men, however, beat Congress to it, giving Oregon women the vote in 1912.

- Between 1789 and 1913, United States senators were elected by their state legislatures—not by popular vote. It was not until the 17th Amendment was ratified in 1913 that the direct election of senators began. Again, Oregon led the way; as early as 1906, Oregonians had, by initiative petition, passed a law which was intended to bind the Oregon Legislature to elect the U.S. Senate candidate who had been voted the "people's choice" in the previous election.

- Oregon's early history was shaped by its extreme isolation. Oregon was among the last places in North America to come under the influence of outsiders. Situated halfway between the Equator and North Pole, Oregon was "on the edge of nowhere." Separated from Asia by the Pacific Ocean, and from western Europe by the North American landmass and the Atlantic Ocean, Oregon in her first century was dominated by this one fact: her acute isolation. Until the early 1880s, the fastest overland route to Oregon from the east took up to six months to traverse. The first transcontinental railroad did not reach Oregon until 1883, when track was completed through the Columbia Gorge. Until then, Oregonians were linked by rail to the trans-Mississippi east only if they first went south to California.

- Oregon's early isolation was compounded by the fact that communication, as well as transportation, was so slow. Until late in the Civil War, news typically reached Oregon by going through California first. The impact of this was that (prior to 1870) Oregonians were among the last Americans to know what was going on in the rest of the nation and world.

- Another important impact of Oregon's isolation was the effect it had on the values and psychological makeup of early settlers: a take-charge, make-do, self-reliant independence took hold in Oregon early.

Chapter 1
"Who's for a Divide?"
The Oregon Country, 1834-49

It took a decade (1834-45) for the American population south of the Columbia River to reach 2,000. Throughout this period, the Methodists (originally led by missionaries Jason and Daniel Lee) dominated valley society. The Methodists prized law and order and as early as 1838 anticipated controversies that might arise between themselves (or between other Americans) so they elected a justice of the peace and a constable at their mission.[1] The mission's court of justice was based on the power of public opinion. The Methodists had now placed their society on both a more orderly and a legal footing. Though they had little personal need for law (their vows as servants of their church provided them with the law and order required in daily life), Methodist leaders quickly recognized the benefits of living in a place where American law was in effect. Jason Lee and his followers drafted an 1836 letter to Congress urging them to take possession of Oregon, thus extending both United States law and military protection to American settlers in the Willamette Valley. Congress did not respond. Two years later, in 1838, Lee's group drafted a more formal document, a Memorial to Congress, signed by 36 settlers, including nine French-Canadians, again, pleading with the U.S. government to take formal and speedy possession of Oregon.[2] Four similar petitions were drawn up and sent to Congress between 1840 and 1847. Senators Lewis Linn and Thomas Hart Benton dutifully introduced them in Congress. These petitions reminded Congress and the president that thousands of Americans were living in a distant corner of the Pacific Northwest. The documents also helped to shape public opinion when the idea of Manifest Destiny was catching hold of the American imagination.

What had motivated these Oregon pioneers to send so many petitions to Congress? There wre several reasons. First was the absence of U.S. law anywhere in the Oregon Country. As emigrants from the United States, these settlers desired to live under institutions with which they were familiar back "home." There were no U.S. courts or judges, no marshals, and no military protection. Another factor was their feeling of extreme isolation and vulnerability. Because most Americans had traveled overland to Oregon—a hazardous journey of five or six months—they were acutely aware of how remote and isolated they were from the territory of the United States. The dominance of Fort Vancouver constantly reminded Americans of the organized presence of the HBC and the British law it was empowered to impose on its citizens. Like their sisters and brothers east of the Mississippi River, the Oregon pioneers held the belief that the United States had a destiny to continue her westward expansion all the way to the Pacific Ocean.

The Death of Ewing Young

Ewing Young settled in Oregon in 1834, taking a land claim in the Chehalem Valley in the northwest corner of the Willamette Valley. In February 1841, Young died, having amassed the largest American fortune in the Oregon Country. But he had no heirs. How was Young's valuable estate to be settled? This predicament motivated settlers to call a mass meeting at the Methodist mission on February 17 and 18, 1841. In those meetings a committee was appointed to draft a code of laws. A supreme judge with probate powers, a clerk and recorder, a high sheriff, and three constables were selected and held office for two years. "The supreme judge was instructed to act according to the Laws of New York until a code of its own was adopted by the community. The people now had the machinery for making arrests, punishing offenders, and settling disputes, more elaborate and efficient than they had possessed before."[3]

The American settlers were genuinely concerned about Ewing Young's property and their "respect for property rights became a keystone for Oregon's first government."[4] Because of Ewing Young's death a crude American government had been established. A new era, the provisional period, 1841-49, had begun in Oregon. During this period Americans in the Oregon Country established three governments: in 1841, 1843, and 1845. The rudimentary government of 1841 was not based on a written constitution. But the few men empowered to serve the community did so because the settlers so desired. The people were in control—and the ultimate power resided with the people. Because the Americans had no code of laws of their own, the settlers chose to live under the laws of New York State. Now a degree of formal structure and order came into a community where only casual ways had existed before.

Decision at Champoeg

In the fall of 1842, one of the Methodists, Dr. Elijah White, returned to Oregon. He'd departed two years earlier after clashing with the Rev. Jason Lee. Now he had a title: Sub-Agent of the Oregon Indians. No one, including White, seemed to know exactly what his authority was. He was arrogant and boastful, and was disliked by many. He claimed his office gave him broad powers, including those of a governor. While the settlers wrestled with his claims, another problem was surfacing. A serious dispute was brewing between Chief Factor John McLoughlin and Methodist leaders at Willamette Falls (soon after named Oregon City). A third problem surfaced that demanded immediate attention: Wolves! Valley farmers' livestock was under constant threat from these predators. Meetings were called in February and March, 1843, to discuss the wolf threat. Disappointed with Congress for ignoring their written requests, the settlers took matters into their own hands. Because Congress had done nothing to answer the Oregon Question, or to extend its authority into the Willamette Valley, American settlers realized that if they were to improve their lives they would have to establish a better government for themselves.

The "wolf meetings," as they were known, in fact had two purposes. Besides predators, the men also wanted to discuss the idea of establishing some kind of government south of the Columbia—but they did not want John McLoughlin to know about it. After adopting a dozen motions pertaining to predators, the men approved a motion to establish a committee of twelve "to take into consideration measures for the civil and military protection of the colony."[5] The committee was to report at a May 2, 1843, meeting at Champoeg, the site of the first HBC warehouse on the Willamette River south of Oregon City.

Assembled in the Champoeg grain barn on May 2 were 102 men. Fifty were American, 52 were Canadian. Most Canadians opposed the idea of establishing a local government and they intended to kill the American proposal. The committee of twelve gave their report, which recommended that a committee of nine be chosen to draft "a code of laws, for the government of this community, to be presented to a public meeting on the fifth day of July next, for their acceptance."[6] The motion appeared to lose. Joe Meek, a former mountain man, broke the stalemate when he stepped dramatically forward, bellowing, "Who's for a divide? All in favor of the report follow me."[7] The Americans, voting as a bloc, were joined by two French Canadians, Etienne Lucier and Francis X. Matthieu. The vote to approve Meek's motion passed 52-50. Most of the Canadians stormed out of the meeting. Those remaining went into action. Civil offices were established and nominees selected, including supreme judge, sheriff, four magistrates, four constables, a treasurer, recorder, a major, and three captains. A legislative committee of nine was appointed. The committee was to submit its report on a proposed government at a July meeting. Committee members would be paid $1.25 a day for up to six days. The wheels were now in motion. Americans were determining a government for themselves. The Champoeg meeting was a turning point in Oregon history. The government they were about to establish, with later revisions, served them for the next six years.

No Taxes, No Liquor, No Negroes

Americans reassembled at Champoeg on July 5, 1843. The special legislative committee gave its lengthy report, a blueprint for a provisional government. What became known as the Organic Law, consisting of 17 articles, quickly passed. The Organic Law established three departments of government: executive, with an elected committee of three; legislative, a committee of nine, representing various districts according to population; and judicial, comprising a supreme court (consisting of a supreme judge and two justices), a probate court, and justices of the peace.[8]

The settlers enacted other important pieces of legislation: a bill of rights, which provided for the freedom of religious belief and worship, *habeas corpus*, trial by jury of one's peers, proportionate representation, judicial procedure according to common law, and moderate fines and reasonable punishment. Also included were statements about the importance of establishing schools, a ban on slavery and involuntary servitude (except for the punishment of a crime). White men of 21 and over could vote; and males 16 and females 14 and older were granted the right to marry (with parent or guardian consent if either spouse was under age 21). The Americans also moved to organize a battalion of soldiers, and they passed an important land provision that allowed settlers to take individual claims of 640 acres.

The provisional government of 1843 was a stop-gap, intended to be temporary. The Americans assumed that Congress would soon answer the Oregon boundary question and install a territorial government, but until that happened, Americans would make do with their Organic Law.

The government of 1843 was hobbled by two handicaps: it originally had no authority to levy taxes, and there was no governor, only an executive committee. Problems quickly surfaced.

Emigrants were flooding into the Willamette Valley via the Oregon Trail in the fall of 1843. Would these 875 newcomers, who doubled the population of the valley, abide by the Organic Law, and be ruled by its officers and laws? They had had no voice in creating the government. The last problem was that none of the past or present employees of the HBC fell under the jurisdiction of the Organic Law. And where did the French Canadians, the American missionaries living east of the Columbia River, and the British living at Fort Vancouver fit in?

The Organic Law of 1843, despite its shortcomings, tells us a lot about what early Oregonians believed. Above all, the American settlers valued personal liberty (articles one and two are a listing of individual rights); they were jealous and distrustful of executive authority (not only did they limit executive power, they also distributed it among three men); they disliked taxes, a power they denied their new government (voluntary contributions were accepted); and they did not like slavery and involuntary servitude.

1844: New Blood

Oregon's first general election took place on May 14, 1844. All three executive committee members were replaced. Seven of the nine legislative members were also turned out. Five of the new legislators were recent arrivals:. outsiders quickly became insiders, part of the political establishment. When the legislative committee convened at Willamette Falls in June 1844 it passed two controversial laws: one was about alcohol, the other about Negroes. The first prohibited "the manufacture, introduction, and the sale of ardent spirits."[9] A strong temperance group had appeared in Oregon as early as 1836. These foes of liquor were white men, especially the Lees and their Methodist brethren. For years, the Methodists tried to keep liquor out of the hands of all inhabitants, white and Native American. In 1845, the legislative committee passed a similar law and ran head-on into the recently appointed provisional governor, George Abernethy. The governor, a Methodist, was personally opposed to the consumption of alcohol. Yet Abernethy vetoed the 1845 act, the only veto he cast in four years. He believed the legislative committee had overstepped its authority when it prohibited alcohol. The Organic Law did not grant the committee a power to "regulate" so the governor said the legislative body had acted improperly. Voters, by a seven-vote margin (of 1,393 cast) approved a prohibition law again in 1848. The presence of a vocal, well-organized temperance element remained an active social and political force in Oregon until the 1930s.

The other controversial act of 1844 banned the entry of free Negroes into Oregon. Oregonians did not want people of color here, free or slave. Many settlers recognized the volatility of the "Negro Question." Many had immigrated to Oregon to distance themselves from the tensions common where Negroes (free or slave) lived. By 1844, the abolitionist movement was growing in most

George Abernethy

George Abernethy was a native of New York who arrived in Oregon, age 33, with his wife and two children aboard the *Lausanne* (via Cape Horn) on June 1, 1840. A Methodist, Abernethy had come to Oregon to assume financial management of Jason Lee's mission colony on the Willamette River north of Salem. The Abernethys settled here at a time when fewer than 100 Americans lived in the Oregon Territory.

Oregon's only Provisional-era governor, Abernethy owned and operated a mill and mercantile store in Oregon City near Willamette Falls. The flood of 1861 destroyed Abernethy's properties and nearly ruined him financially. Abernethy Island in the Willamette River near the Falls at Oregon City, is named for its former owner.

George Abernethy was governor during a time of explosive growth in western Oregon. The American population doubled during his term. The Provisional government was hard pressed to keep up with demands of this population explosion. The need for roads, bridges, ferry service, schools, jails, land surveys, courts, and law enforcement, coupled with military protection against sometimes hostile Native Americans, put a lot of pressure on Oregon's fledgling government. And, always, there was the nagging question of how all of these services were to be paid for. George Abernethy's steady hand steered Oregon through these troubled waters. Abernethy was the first Oregon governor to use the veto—which the legislature overrode.

George Abernethy died in Portland in May 1877, several months short of his 70th birthday.

northern states and was increasingly outspoken and confrontational. Early Oregonians chose not to confront the dilemma of defining and maintaining race relations between white and black. Their solution was to not let any Negroes into Oregon. Thus began a policy of Negro exclusion in Oregon. Slavery would be the top political issue in the United States in the 1850s, an issue that deeply divided Oregonians, as it did the rest of the nation. Indeed, the development of Oregon's two-party political system was an outcome of how Oregonians felt about slavery.

A Government Gone Broke

Wagons bearing the possessions of over 1,400 Americans lumbered into the Willamette Valley in the fall of 1844. Valley society was wrenched by the social and economic stresses caused by the arrival of these hordes. Food shortages and skyrocketing prices affected everyone. The severely under-financed provisional government could not cope with the rising demand for roads, courts, the processing of land claims, or for more law and order in general. The week before Christmas, the legislative committee drafted amendments to the Organic Law of 1843. The legislative committee evolved into a larger body, a one-chambered legislature consisting of a House of Representatives. Politically, the summer of 1845 was busier than usual. Voters made several critical decisions in June and July. The newly established office of governor was filled by George Abernethy, a prominent Oregon City merchant and Methodist. He was Oregon's only provisional governor (serving 1845-49). Voters passed a revision of the Organic Law of 1843; and the more comprehensive Organic Laws of Oregon (1845) were approved easily, 255 to 22.

The selection of Francis Ermatinger, chief trader of the HBC post at Oregon City, as treasurer was notable. John McLoughlin and his longtime assistant, James Douglas, agreed to become a party to the revised Organic Laws. On August 18, 1845, the legislative committee created the Vancouver District ("district" was later replaced by the word "county") out of the Oregon Territory north of the Columbia. The next day, lawmakers elected HBC officials James Douglas and Charles Forrest as district judges for Vancouver. The HBC and the thousand or so British subjects under its jurisdiction were now wedded to the provisional government established by American settlers in 1843. The government now served "all the people of the Oregon Country by their common consent and acquiescence and without regard for their allegiances."[10]

Early Oregonians grappled with the problem of paying for their provisional governments. Money was scarce, most people were poor, and, in the early 1840s, there wasn't a lot of high-value property. As noted, the problem worsened as thousands of emigrants arrived in western Oregon and Washington after 1843. Joseph L. Meek, sheriff of the provisional government, collected Oregon's first taxes in 1844, a total of $353.81. There was a poll tax of fifty cents for each male adult and a levy of one-eighth of one percent on property valued at $218,000 or more. These were the first American taxes on the Pacific Coast. The legislative committee enacted a new tax on June 25, 1844, on merchandise brought into the Oregon Country for sale, improvements on farm lots, mills, pleasure carriages, clocks, watches, and livestock. There was no tax on farmlands, or on merchandise previously brought in.[11] The four most valuable categories of taxable property in 1844 were cattle, horses, town lots, and grist/sawmills. Both the poll and property tax were originally optional with a penalty for nonpayment. Men who didn't pay the poll tax couldn't vote. A man declining to pay his property tax was denied use of the courts. Of 400 property owners in 1844, several dozen refused to pay the property tax. Some were too poor to pay any tax.

The legislative committee also set license taxes on merchants, lawyers, on ships, and set court fees. But it was a losing cause. By the time Oregon became a U.S. territory in August 1848, a $100,000 debt had been amassed, the result of infrastructure costs for government buildings such as jails, legal fees for drafting and printing documents, legislative and court expenses, and salaries—which Congress paid in 1849.

In September and October 1845, 3,000 American emigrants swarmed into western Oregon and Washington. A stable government, established on the principle of the consent of the governed and in which British subjects had already joined with Americans, was securely in place. The chaos that could have resulted from the arrival of so many people never occurred. With Gov. George Abernethy, an elected legislature, a court system and law enforcement officers, as well as a compulsory tax to pay for all of it, settlers looked forward to a period of stability and prosperity.

Oregon's First Newspaper

The first American newspaper published west of the Rockies, *The Spectator*, appeared at Oregon City on February 5, 1846. An outgrowth of the Oregon Lyceum or debating society, *The Spectator* played a part in the founding of Oregon's first political parties. Readers enthusiastically welcomed the newspaper even if most news was six months old.

On May 12, 1846, Congress declared war on Mexico. Oregonians did not hear about it until early fall. On June 15, the U.S. Senate approved a treaty with Great Britain, settling, at long last, the Oregon boundary question. Nearly six months later, Governor Abernethy announced the news that American settlers had waited a decade to hear: the Oregon Country—south of 49° north latitude—was now part of the United States.

Oregon men conducted a spirited election in the spring of 1847. Governor Abernethy stood for reelection to another two-year term. He won, but by only 17 votes out of 1,056 cast. Running as a non-sectarian candidate (not church-affiliated), Asa Lovejoy lost his bid to be governor to the Methodist-backed Abernethy. The still single-chambered legislature expanded to 18 members. The uncertain status of land claims in Oregon continued to worry valley residents.

The Whitman Massacre and the Cayuse War

Ghastly news reached Oregon City on December 8, 1847. Dr. Marcus and Narcissa Whitman along with twelve other Americans had been murdered at Waiilatpu, the Whitman mission near Walla Walla. Cayuse Indians were responsible. Governor Abernethy told the story to a stunned legislature. Word quickly spread. Volunteers, armed with their own rifles, astride their own horses, answered the call for an army to march east. The legislature, however, was broke! With only $43.72 in the treasury and debts of over $4,000, legislators had to perform some financial magic. "Commissioners were appointed to raise $100,000 against bonds secured only by the good faith of the territory and the general expectation that the federal government would eventually assume the obligations. The governor was authorized to raise a regiment of not more than 500 volunteers, each recruit [would] receive $1.50 each day in promises."[12] The legislature then declared war on the Cayuse.

As angry settlers prepared to march to Walla Walla, two Americans were headed to Washington, D.C. Governor Abernethy had appointed the Supreme Judge of Oregon, J. Quinn Thornton, to lobby Congress to pass an Oregon territorial organization bill. Thornton had departed by ship in October. Within days of the Whitman Massacre, the legislature chose Joseph Meek, Oregon's sheriff, to travel overland to the Capitol to notify Congress that Americans in the Willamette Valley had declared war on the Cayuse Indians. With a petition in hand, Meek tried to persuade Congress to send aid to the hard-pressed Americans. Foremost in the minds of President Polk and Congress, however, was the conclusion of the Mexican War and the annexation of as much of Mexico's northern frontier as possible. Oregon would have to wait a little longer.

The provisional government ran up a bill of over $109,000 to fight the Cayuse War, a huge sum for so small and so poor a community.[13] Eventually, five Indian fugitives surrendered. Tried and found guilty of the Whitman murders, they were hanged at Oregon City on June 3, 1850.

Smaller clashes between Native Americans and settlers occurred in southern Oregon in 1848. Beginning in 1850, Congress appointed commissioners (backed by funds) to arrange treaties with various tribes west of the Cascades. Slowly the threat settlers felt from the Native Americans faded. But, in carrying out the Cayuse War, the legislature had put Oregon in deep debt. Their solution was simply to leave Congress holding the bag.

Men Go South, Gold Comes North

In a span of eight months between July 1848 and March 1849, three events occurred that changed Oregon history. A ship, the *Honolulu*, anchored at the village of Portland in late July 1848. Her captain told the locals that a great gold strike had occurred on the American River in northern California. Three weeks later, on August 14, President Polk signed the Oregon territorial organization bill. On March 3, 1849, newly arrived Gen. Joseph Lane declared the territorial government in effect, and himself governor. The provisional period had ended and the territorial period began. Meanwhile, the electric words "Gold! Gold on the American!" ignited the California Gold Rush of 1848-49.

Over the next two years, 100,000 men poured into California. Rumor was that a man could earn $100 a day panning. Not only were Oregon men among the first to hear of the strike, they were also the closest American population outside of California. An estimated two-thirds of Oregon men went south. Some, foreseeing an increase in prices in Oregon, stayed put and reaped their own harvest in gold through trade.[14] Fortunately, valley farmers had produced bumper crops in 1848. California's hungry hordes wanted every bushel, bale, box, and barrel of produce that Oregonians could send. Prices soared. Basic food exports such as wheat saw 200 to 300% price jumps each year between 1848 and 1851. Flour prices rocketed. Wages in Oregon were up to $5 a day.

Oregon men began to return early in 1849, some $30,000 to $40,000 wealthier. By January 1849, $500,000 worth of gold dust had filtered into Oregon's economy, by December, $5 million. Because of a lack of money in circulation, local trade had always been complicated and the economy had been almost exclusively based on credit. With the flood of California gold into the Willamette Valley, a fundamental change in business practices took place. A suitable currency and accessible markets had been the Oregon Country's greatest need. Gold dust stimulated import trade and the life of the community changed radically. "Farmers were equipped with better tools; mills with better machinery; new and better means of transportation were introduced; roads were built and bridges took the place of ferries; [and] the agitation for railroads now began."[15]

A special session of the legislature met at the home of Walter Pomeroy in Oregon City on February 5, 1849. It would be the last meeting of Oregon's Provisional Legislature. The session lasted eleven days. In order to attract coin to the area, the Provisional Government passed its own coinage law. "The Oregon Exchange Company was organized for the express purpose of weighing and stamping gold. Dies for both $5 and $10 gold pieces were improvised. Altogether some $58,500 in $5 and $10 gold pieces were minted during 1849."[16]

The Oregon Boundary Dispute, 1845-46: Settling the Oregon Question

The American presidential campaign of 1844 featured the jingoistic slogan of "54-40 or Fight! Democrat James Knox Polk was elected, in part, because many Americans were caught up in a nationalistic fever known as Manifest Destiny. What did Polk's campaign slogan mean? Polk meant that the United States should press its claims to ownership of the entire Oregon Country, all the way north to the 54th parallel...even if it meant war with Great Britain. Calmer heads, however, prevailed, and, in 1846, the so-called Oregon Question was settled when the U. S. Senate ratified an Anglo-American treaty in which the Oregon Country was divided at the 49th parallel, all lands north of that latitude becoming part of British Canada and all lands south of 49 degrees becoming part of the United States.

As of 1845 (as shown on the map) Britain insisted that

the Oregon Country be divided at the Columbia River, with the United States taking the area below 45/46 degrees north latitude, and Britain taking the area above that line. So, as of 1845-46, the area between the Columbia River and 49 degrees was the main source (the crux) of disagreement between the two governments: The 1846 Treaty settled the ownership question once and for all.

Popularly known as Beaver money because of the likeness of a beaver on the coin, the coinage circulated for several years. With gold dust remaining as a medium of exchange, Oregon finally had an adequate money supply.

The legislature adjourned on February 16, 1849. Two weeks later, Gen. Joseph Lane of Indiana arrived to take over as Oregon's first territorial governor. On March 3, in Oregon City, Governor Lane proclaimed the end of Oregon's provisional government. Oregon's experiment in self-government had turned out far better than many could have imagined.

Happy to again be living on American soil, Oregonians still didn't care for the idea that, except for their local legislature, they were now governed by outside men over whom they had little control.

Chapter 2
From Territory to State, 1848-59

Oregonians welcomed their new territorial status with mixed emotions. Oregonians knew that, as territorials, they could expect the U.S. government to provide new services*; what tight-fisted Oregonians liked most about these new services and facilities was that Congress would pay for them. Congress would also foot the bill for the salaries of Oregon's legislators, governor, marshal, judges, postmasters, librarian, Indian agents, secretary, district attorney, and customs collector. Oregonians loved the idea of eating their cake without having to pay the baker.

But American citizens living in the Oregon Territory had no voting representative in Congress. They couldn't vote in national elections for president and vice president. Congress legislated in significant matters affecting the territory and it had the (seldom-used) power to declare territorial legislation null and void. The territory's only part in national affairs was through their elected delegate, who could speak, but not vote, on their behalf in Congress.[1] The only major officials directly elected by the settlers were their legislators and the delegate to Congress. Otherwise, all territorial officers were appointed by the president and were part of the national patronage system. Oregonians were skeptical: Would appointees be honest, competent, genuinely concerned about what was best for Oregonians? Or would the territorials suffer at the hands of unscrupulous, self-serving politicians? Designated Chief Justice William B. Bryant was one of the first appointees to arrive. He reached Oregon City in April 1849 with an empty wallet and left for good six months later with a bulging one. He departed Oregon in November, without

---

* These new services included military protection for settlers and emigrants (U.S. Army units would be stationed locally as well as along the Oregon Trail); construction of lighthouses to aid navigation and harbor improvements; establishment of regular mail service; and construction of territorial buildings such as a capitol (to include a legislative hall), a penitentiary, and an asylum for the mentally ill.

The Oregon Territory, 1849

Congress, in 1848, officially made Oregon a United States Territory, extending the arm of the federal government into the area. Future Washington state was part of the Oregon Territory until 1853--when Congress separated it from Oregon, establishing Washington as a separate U.S. Territory. This map shows the first political/governmental subdivisions in the two areas: counties.

authority to do so, and collected his salary for a year and a half. Luckily, Territorial Governor Joseph Lane turned out to be the most popular politician in Oregon in the 1850s.

Meet Joe Lane

When Indiana's 48-year-old Joseph Lane finally arrived at Oregon City on March 2, 1849, the territory's crudeness and isolation shocked him. Oregon City was half-deserted because so many men had gone south for California gold. Two dozen houses stood empty. Gardens were unattended. It was a town of mostly women and children. Yet the locals celebrated Lane's arrival with a party and reception in his honor.

Scarcely 9,000 people could be found in all the Oregon Country that spring. But even with several thousand men and boys gone to California, the area was active. The Willamette, from the Columbia River to the falls at Oregon City, had never seen so much traffic. Fifty ocean-going ships came into the river that year with 20 anchored in Portland at one time. Barges, flatboats, and canoes loaded with lumber, wheat, flour, and vegetables dotted the waterways. Each week saw more gold in circulation, forever changing the way Oregonians did business. With workers in such short supply, daily wages soared to $5.

Would Oregonians be able to overlook Governor Lane's status as an outsider and accept him as their governor? A consummate politician, Joe Lane quickly made himself known to the locals. With 24 years of service in the Indiana Legislature, Lane, at 45, had volunteered for military service when the Mexican War erupted 1846. At war's end (1848), Lane was both a hero and a general. He was a Catholic, a devout family man and father of ten children. Blessed with common sense, an even temperament, and an easy friendliness, Joe Lane naturally drew people to him and his wartime heroics played well with frontier Oregonians. He was accorded a level of respect and affection attained by few 19th-century Oregon politicians. His later fall from favor matched the swiftness of his rise to popularity in 1849-50.

Two Houses Instead of One

Governor Lane called for a June 6 special election to elect members of Oregon's new territorial legislature, and the lone delegate to Congress. The August 14, 1848, act of Congress that had created the Oregon Territory had significantly revised the legislative assembly. The legislature now became a two-chambered body, consisting of a nine-member House of Representatives and a Council (Senate). The number of members of the house could be increased but could not exceed 30. Legislators were popularly elected, vacancies were to be filled by special election, and the legislative sessions were limited to 60 days.[2] The first Territorial Legislature met at Oregon City on July 16, 1849, with Samuel Parker as President of the Council and Asa Lovejoy as Speaker of the House of Representatives. Members were in session, off and on, for 54 days, but they did nothing bold. The session was a trial run, a chance for new lawmakers to get familiar with each other and with a second chamber; two bodies had to learn to work together where only one had existed before.

Samuel Thurston and the Donation Land Act

The main candidates in a hotly contested race for delegate to Congress were Judge Columbia Lancaster, a Whig, and Samuel Royal Thurston, a Democratic legislator. Both men had immigrated to Oregon in 1847. With no organized political parties in Oregon, the candidates' political labels did not have much to do with the outcome. With most men still in California, or, if returned, too busy putting their lives back together, only 30% voted. A Maine native, Thurston was a graduate of Bowdoin College. At 33 he was ambitious, haughty, and intelligent, and shrewdly linked himself to former Gov. George Abernethy and what remained of the Methodist interests. With Methodist backing, Thurston scored a narrow victory.[3] Delegate Thurston took a non-partisan approach to the job. Once in Washington, D.C., Thurston focused his energy on a land law for the Oregon Territory. His crowning achievement as a delegate to Congress was the passage of the Donation Land Law of 1850, which had more impact on Oregon than any other law passed by Congress before 1859. Congress gave Oregon settlers something very special: free land! Prior to 1850, Americans wanting to settle on public lands in the territories were required to pay for the property, usually $1.25 per acre. Citing Oregon's long record of sending petitions to Congress, Thurston convinced the U.S. House and Senate that, because they'd been occupying the territory, Oregonians had helped ensure its possession by the United States. Surely, said Oregonians, they deserved special consideration from Congress.[4]

The Oregon Donation Land Law was an almost unique piece of federal legislation.* The law was passed both to reward Oregonians (the act also applied to western Washington) for planting an American presence in the distant Pacific Northwest and to encourage further settlement of the region. There were several interesting features and significant consequences of the Donation Land Law. It allowed wives the privilege, uncommon at that time, of holding real property in their own names, thereby recognizing the part women played in the task of pioneering. This double allotment for married couples led to an increased number of marriages. Since single women were scarce in Oregon, very young girls suddenly became marriageable when the Oregon Legislature lowered the age for females to 12.[5]

The Donation Land Law worked as it was intended and sparked a human stampede to Oregon. The generous terms of the Donation Land Law proved irresistible to land-hungry Americans, who sold, gave away, bartered, or simply abandoned their property and set out for Oregon. In the last six months of 1850, five thousand emigrants arrived in Oregon. Another 2,500 entered in

---

* It granted a half section, or 320 acres, to every settler over the age of 18 who was a citizen or declared his intention to become one before December 1, 1851, and who had occupied and cultivated the land for four consecutive years. The offspring of mixed white / Native American marriages were included in the offer. If a settler married by December 1851, his wife was granted a like amount to be held in her own right. This covered the claims of those who had settled Oregon before 1850. To qualify for 160 acres, those settling between December 1851 and December 1853 had to be white male citizens of 21 years of age. Wives of such qualified settlers were entitled to a like amount. In February 1853, an amendment extended the expiration date of the act to 1855, and permitted settlers to patent their claims after two years' occupancy and the payment of $1.25 an acre. Congress had never enacted a law that gave away public lands to individuals (except in the case of Florida when Congress, in 1843, granted settlers 160 acres free). Thus, the act of 1850 was an exception in federal land policy. See Johansen and Gates, 291.

1851, followed by 15,000 in 1852 and 8,000 in 1853.[6] From just over 13,000 inhabitants in 1850, the Oregon Territory exploded to over 35,000 by the end of 1853. But there was a downside to the law. Because so much land, particularly in the Willamette Valley, was claimed by married couples, large tracts were gobbled up early. These huge "farms" tended to isolate the settlers, and slowed the growth of towns and the diversification of occupations, industry, and crops. It also increased a growing tendency in Oregon's pioneers toward provincialism and localism.[7]

Counting Noses

The Oregon Territory was included in the Federal Census of 1850, which revealed that 13,294 people (excluding Native Americans) lived in the territory. About 1,000 of them lived north of the Columbia River in western Washington. Almost all of the remainder lived in western Oregon and nine of ten residents in the Willamette Valley. Marion, with 2,749 souls, was the most populous county, followed by Washington at 2,652 and Clackamas with 1,859. Portland, with 821 residents, was the largest town, followed by Oregon City at 697.[8] There were two males for every female. Half of the males were aged 20 to 49 and most of the rest were boys.

The most common occupation was farmer, followed by laborer. There were 2,374 families in the territory, along with nine churches, 45 physicians, 29 lawyers, and three newspapers. Three of four inhabitants had been born somewhere else in the United States. About 2,500 of the children had been born in the territory. One in 11 persons was foreign-born. More emigrants came from Missouri than any other state, and four of 10 had come from only three states: Iowa, Illinois, and Missouri. One adult in five had been born in Kentucky or Virginia.[9] The issue of slavery, which, in the 1850s and 1860s, caused severe social and political tensions in Oregon, was hiding just below the surface of the 1850 Territorial Census: 47 of every 100 adults had come to Oregon from a slave state.

Slightly more adults than children lived in Oregon in 1850: nearly half the children had been born in the Oregon Territory. Overall, the population was youthful. The most important fact to be gleaned from the census, however, is that "only a small percentage of the people were having their first experiences of pioneer life, [a] condition which continued until well after the Civil War.[10] Most Oregonians of 1850 were frontier people who had moved the rest of the way west from their most recent homes near the Mississippi River. These settlers had pulled up their shallow roots before. They were used to starting over. Like most frontier folk, Oregonians were independent, proud, opinionated, hard-working, optimistic, self-reliant, stubborn, and dreamers. It was the lure of a better life that drew people to Oregon and they continued to come for that reason.

Daily Life in Territorial Oregon

What was Oregon like during the 10 years of its territorial period, 1849-59? How well did Oregon's pioneers get along with Congress and the federal officials sent to Oregon? In what ways did Oregon change during this decade? And what did Oregonians do to get themselves ready for statehood?

Oregon's population increased by nearly 300%—40,000 people—during the territorial years. Of this increase 16,534 were born in Oregon and 30,474 migrated here from other states (some moved elsewhere or died). There were fewer foreign-born emigrants in Oregon than in any other northern state. The influx to Oregon was mainly from Missouri, Illinois, Ohio, Indiana, Kentucky, New York, and Iowa.

Joseph Lane

COURTESY OF THE OREGON STATE ARCHIVES, GOVERNORS PHOTOS

Lane served as the first territorial governor of Oregon (1849-50, and May 1853), as territorial delegate to Congress (1851-59), and as U.S. Senator (1859-61). He was a founder of the Democratic Party of Oregon (1852-53) and was a candidate for vice president of the United States (1860). Lane County is named for him.

Joseph Lane was born in North Carolina in 1801. He immigrated to Indiana in 1821 and embarked on a political career, and was elected to the legislature, only months after his arrival. Indeed, over the next 24 years, Joseph Lane was a fixture in the Indiana House and Senate.

When the Mexican-American War began in 1846, Joseph Lane jumped at the chance to serve; he was commissioned colonel of an Indiana regiment. Although he was 45 years old, he quickly moved up through the ranks, achieving the status of major general when the war ended in 1848.

President James Polk, a Democrat, appointed Joseph Lane as the first governor of the new Oregon Territory in 1849. Lane arrived at Oregon City on March 2 and took office the following day. Lane made a good first impression and remained the most popular politician in Oregon for the next 10 years.

Oregon's first territorial delegate to Congress, Samuel R. Thurston, drowned (on April 9, 1851) when the ship on which he was a passenger sank off the coast of

In terms of developed infrastructure, Oregonians accomplished little during their territorial years. In 1856 there were only two steamboat mail routes in the territory, both of which were out of Portland. Territorial "highways" were really unimproved roads—muddy in winter and spring, plagued by gaping potholes and protruding tree stumps the rest of the year. There were only a few bridges anywhere in Oregon. People and products crossed rivers by ferryboat. Steamboats made their appearance on the Columbia and Willamette rivers in the early 1850s. By 1860, dozens of these vessels were anchored at Portland and Astoria. The stagecoach also appeared during this decade, though most people got about by pack-train, wagon, on horseback or, on foot. There were only 3.8 miles of railroad track (around the rapids at Celilo Falls on the Columbia) in all of Oregon in 1856. And as late as 1860 there were no organized banks in Oregon.[11]

Towns were few and far between in territorial Oregon and only a few had more than several hundred residents. Because most settlers were farmers,

Mexico as he was returning home from his term in Congress. Sam Thurston's death opened a door for Joe Lane: he was elected territorial delegate to Congress, taking office on June 2, 1851. Oregon men reelected Lane in 1853, 1855, and 1857. Indeed, Joseph Lane represented Oregon in Congress until she was admitted to the Union as the 33rd state on February 14, 1859.

Joe Lane and newspaperman Asahel Bush were the most prominent and powerful Democrats in Oregon between 1852 and 1859. In 1853, President Franklin Pierce, a Democrat, re-appointed Lane governor of the Oregon Territory. Lane, however, resigned after three days in office (May 16-19), preferring to return to Congress as Oregon's territorial delegate.

In 1858, the Territorial Legislature elected Joe Lane as one of Oregon's first U.S. senators. But because it took Congress so long to finally enact the Oregon Statehood Bill, Lane had to wait until statehood took effect, on February 14, 1859, before being sworn in. His term ended in March 1861.

The legislature did not reelect Lane. Senator Lane's outspoken support for slavery (remember that Lane was a Southerner by birth) turned the majority of Oregon voters against him. Indeed, Lane's political credentials, coupled with the fact that he was a senator from a northern state who favored the Southern position on slavery, made him an attractive choice when Vice President John C. Breckinridge, a Southern Democrat, split from the regular Democratic Party to run for President in 1860. Lane was Breckinridge's VP running mate.

After Lane's fall from power, he led a life of obscurity as a Roseburg-area farmer. He died in Roseburg in April 1881 at the age of 80. His grandson Doctor Harry Lane became mayor of Portland and U.S. senator, 1913-17.

Oregonians tended to live isolated lives. Neighborly calls were out of the question because the Donation Land Law, by virtue of the size of the "farm," kept farm houses far apart, even in western Oregon and Washington.

Congress Pays the Bill

One of the main benefits of being a U.S. Territory was that Congress paid most of the bills. Oregonians paid a total of $85,000 in local property taxes (farms were exempt) and fees during the territorial era, as a result of laws passed by Oregon's elected legislature. There was no federal income tax in 19th-century America, so the taxes that Oregonians paid went for such things as schools and road improvements. Otherwise, Congress picked up the tab. Congress paid for military protection, harbor and lighthouse improvements, construction of government buildings, and the salaries of most government officials, including the salaries of the Territorial Legislature, its staff and supplies. Congressional funds also covered the salaries of the governor, treasurer, warden of the penitentiary, customs officials, land agents, Oregon's delegate to Congress, and the courts. The biggest congressional expense was the federal military presence in Oregon during the 1850s. This included U.S. military posts located at Fort Dalles, Fort Lane (near Jacksonville), and Fort Orford on the southern Oregon coast. Smaller installations were set up near Dayton and at Rhinelands (near Fort Orford) in 1856. By 1859, additional forts were established at Fort Yamhill, Fort Hoskins (40 miles west of Corvallis), and Fort Umpqua, near the mouth of the Umpqua River. Native American wars broke out in the Rogue Valley and along the Snake River in 1853-54. Though these fights were short, they were costly: hundreds of U.S. soldiers, their equipment, and housing had to be paid for. The regional Native American wars of the mid-1850s cost the federal government over $6 million.[12]

Another source of government revenue came from the sale or lease of congressional land grants set aside for educational purposes. Two of the thirty-six sections (each equal to one square mile) in each township were designated for educational purposes. Part of the land was reserved for siting public schools. Local officials had the option of selling or leasing all or part of the remaining land, placing the money in a common school fund. It was the sale of all or part of these two sections of public land that produced the third source of government revenue during Oregon's territorial years.

Go Home, John!

Joseph Lane was a political appointee of outgoing Democratic President James K. Polk. The majority of Oregon men were Democrats. As emigrants from the

Midwest, an area long devoted to Andrew Jackson, Oregonians had brought their Democratic loyalties west with them. Polk's strong appeal to western men in the election of 1844 and his successful resolution of the Oregon boundary question in 1846 made him hugely popular in the territory. Thus, when Polk's man, Joseph Lane, arrived, Oregonians were inclined to like him, too.

The day after Lane officially began his term—March 4, 1849—Gen. Zachary Taylor, a Whig, was inaugurated President of the United States. It was assumed that Taylor would remove Lane in favor of a fellow Whig. With Taylor's Whig appointee as governor, John Pollard Gaines, and other Whig officials en route to Oregon, Democrats decided it was time to organize as a political party. On May 4, 1850, Democrats in Marion County met in Salem to "nominate officers for [the] County, including members of the territorial legislature."[13] Ten days later Democrats met at Oregon City, where the legislature was in session, and passed resolutions praising Governor Lane and condemning President Taylor for replacing him.

John Gaines had two strikes against him when he arrived in Oregon in August 1850. He was an unpopular Whig and a "foreigner." Where Lane was informal and friendly, Gaines was stiff and reserved. Described as "pompous and aristocratic in bearing, he was tactless in action and over-zealous in exerting his authority." For Oregonians used to governing themselves, to be governed by a man like Gaines was "positively galling."[14]

Where Should Our Capital Be?

The second regular session of the Territorial Legislature met on December 2, 1850, at Oregon City. Two days later and a few miles down river, Thomas Jefferson Dryer printed the first edition of the *Weekly Oregonian*. Dryer was a died-in-the-wool Whig and intended his newspaper to be a voice for the Whig point of view. Dryer would become a founder of Oregon's political party system.

Meanwhile, legislators were wrestling with a thorny question. Which town, Salem or Oregon City, should be Oregon's capital? Lawmakers tried to strike a political compromise by proposing a so-called location bill. Corvallis was to get a university, Portland the penitentiary, and Salem the capital. The bill passed both houses by a total of 16-11. Governor Gaines criticized the measure, but because the governor at this time had no veto power, he could only protest to the legislature. The legislators, who were already suspicious of executive authority, bitterly resented Gaines' interference. They disliked him and his politics and defiantly passed the bill without his suggested changes.[15]

It was the controversy over the capital location that goaded Democrats and Whigs to form territorial political parties. Governor Gaines and his fellow Whigs favored Oregon City, while Democrats liked Salem. Throughout 1852, and a dozen years after that, the issue was a hot potato tossed back-and-forth between Democrats, Whigs, and Republicans; the legislature and the governor; and between Oregon and Congress. Oregon Democrats made political hay out of the issue, using it as a glue to bind members together into a cohesive party.

Rival Legislatures

A bizarre set of events unfolded in the Willamette Valley in December 1851. Split along emerging party lines, the legislature met on the same date in two different towns. Governor Gaines and the two Whig Supreme Court Justices set up their offices in Oregon City. They were joined by the four Whig members of the House of Representatives and the lone Whig Council member. Each morning this rump legislature called itself into session and immediately adjourned for lack of a quorum. Finally conceding that their Democratic foes were never going to join them, the Whigs ended their holdout on December 17 and went home. Meanwhile, the Democrats (with a quorum) conducted their legislative session 30 miles away in Salem. Justice O. C. Pratt, a Democratic leader, disagreeing with his Supreme Court colleagues and Governor Gaines, presented a lengthy legal opinion supporting the Democratic claim that Salem, not Oregon City, was the legal capital of the Oregon Territory. The controversy ended up in the lap of Congress. In its 1852 session, Congress confirmed Salem as the legal capital and recognized the Democrats' December 1851 meeting in Salem as the legitimate legislative session of that year. For now, Democrats had carried the day. Disorganized and declining in number, Oregon Whigs never came close to matching the power and influence of the Democratic Party.

Asahel Bush and the Oregon Style

Asahel Bush slipped quietly into Oregon in early 1851. A lawyer and journalist from Massachusetts, Bush came to Oregon at the urging of Samuel Thurston, for the purpose of establishing and editing a Democratic newspaper. Thurston had bought the press Bush was to use to publish the *Oregon Statesman*, the first edition of which appeared on March 28, 1851. Thurston, who was still in Washington, D.C., as Oregon's congressional delegate, was bright and keenly ambitious, and planned to establish an Oregon Democratic Party with himself as leader, and with higher office in mind. The *Statesman* quickly became the official voice of the Democratic Party. The paper's circulation exceeded the *Weekly Oregonian* and Oregon City *Argus* combined. The vast majority of Democratic homes sub-scribed to the *Statesman,* making Asahel Bush the most widely read journalist in the territory. As such, he became one of Oregon's most powerful political leaders over the next 10 years. Bush could (and did) break politicians at will.

Early in May 1851 the *Statesman* wrote that Sam Thurston had died aboard a ship off the coast of Mexico. Thurston was returning to Oregon from Washington, D.C., to seek reelection. His untimely death opened the way for Joseph Lane. Asahel Bush penned an endorsement of Lane's candidacy. With only token opposition, General Lane coasted to victory. For the next eight years (until statehood), Joseph Lane was both Oregon's man in Congress and the ter-ritory's most powerful politician.

Writing in the *Statesman* on June 13, 1851, Bush called for a convention of Democrats to meet on July 4 in Salem, hoping to formally organize a Democrat Party in Marion County. In their July meeting, Democrats resolved that political parties were inseparable from a free government. Anticipating statehood, they served notice of their intention to construct a state organization to enable them to elect Democrats to office.

In the fall of 1851, Asahel Bush turned his acid pen on both Tom Dryer, editor of the *Weekly Oregonian,* and Gov. John Gaines. Dryer had editorialized against organizing political parties, arguing that parties tended to divide people and keep them from working together on common problems. Bush scorned Dryer's posi-tion, and in attacking Dryer, established a brand of journalism known as the Oregon Style. For the next 10 years this brand of journalism dominated territorial newspapers. Dryer himself and, later, William Adams of the Oregon *Argus* were also practitioners of the Oregon Style, which consisted of heaping written abuse upon one's foes, name calling, sarcasm, and ridicule. "Bush was called 'bushy' in the *Oregonian,* 'Ass of Hell' in the *Argus.* Bush called the *Argus* the 'Airgoose' and T. J. Dryer 'Toddy Jep.' Whatever group Bush opposed was barraged with biting editorials and scathing criticism. Editor Bush called Tom Dryer 'Sewer Man.'"[16]Bush made lots of political enemies. Writing in the *Jacksonville Herald* in 1858, Col. James K. Kelley called Bush "a monster of cruelty and oppression, an editor who impaled his victims on the point of his pen."[17]

The emergence of these partisan newspapers also contributed to the de-velopment of political parties in Oregon Territory in the 1850s. Indeed, politics and party allegiance was serious business in early Oregon.

Antebellum Democrats dominated Oregon territorial politics because they were both numerous and, more often than not, were organized as a tightly knit party. The hundreds of men who regularly participated in party activities took their affiliation seriously, considering it both a civic and patriotic duty. The party had its roots in local communities. "Organized from bottom to top in a system of precinct caucuses and county, territorial (or state), and national conventions, these men became part of what the Democrats called 'the Democracy' through participation in the winter-to-spring round of ceremonies that punctuated the seasonal cadence of their lives as farmers. The calendar of antebellum politics, marked by Jackson jubilees, Jefferson-Jackson dinners, Fourth of July bonfires, precinct caucuses, county conventions, and legislative sessions, made up the public life of individuals otherwise isolated from one another."[18]

Not all Oregon men, of course, were Democrats. For the thousands who were not, the anti-Democrats, most were drawn either to temperance or to the nativist movement of the 1850s. Other anti-Democrats included those who disliked the imperious Asahel Bush and his coterie of powerful political friends, as well as old-time Whigs, a fading national political party. Indeed, it was the fractured nature of Oregon's anti-Democrats that explains why these disparate factions never coalesced as a party to rival Oregon's Democrats.

The decade of the 1850s was a time of constant change in Oregon, due mainly to the arrival of thousands of emigrants every year. Oregon's fledgling institutions were challenged to keep up with the demands of this growing population. Newcomers were expected to attach themselves to either the ruling Democrats or to one of the elements comprising the anti-Democrats.

As the decade progressed, the question that most defined Oregon's political debate was: Where do you stand on the issue of slavery? "Far from being abolitionists, anti-Democrats opposed slavery, though for a different reason: slavery degraded white labor ... Freedom's survival depended on the protection of free soil—that is, on slaveless western territories. Free soil, unencumbered by slavery, was the foundation of free labor and the guarantor of free men."[19]

The Salem Clique

Democrats had cleverly turned the capital-location squabble into a hot political issue. Coupled with the fact that the territory was governed by the unpopular Whig outsider Gov. John Gaines, Democrats had two emotional issues to help build their party. Asahel Bush, James Nesmith, and O. C. Pratt were among the earliest party leaders and they made the Democratic Party the most powerful political force in Oregon prior to the Civil War.

Democratic legislators caucused in January 1852 and chose Oregon's first party central committee and gave it the task of organizing a party, county by county. Local conventions met and most passed resolutions stating that political parties were the best way to select faithful and competent Democratic office-holders. The modern Democratic Party of Oregon traces its origins to these 1852 meetings. The Democrats' early success at party building explains their domination of Oregon politics in the 1850s.

Asahel Bush wore many hats: newspaper publisher/editor; behind-the-scenes Democratic Party organizer and manipulator; and, from 1851 to '59, the territorial printer. In this latter role, Bush published all legislative documents and court records, and the official papers of the governor.

With the capital relocated to Salem, Bush moved his presses to that city in 1853. The Democratic Party was soon headquartered there. Besides Judge Pratt, Asahel Bush gathered an inner circle of powerful Democrats, dubbed by opponents the Salem Clique, to run the party. The Salem Clique reads like a Who's Who of early Oregon politics: James Nesmith, U.S. senator, 1861-67, and U.S. representative, 1873-75; Reuben P. Boise, Oregon Supreme Court Justice, 1858-70 and 1876-80; LaFayette Grover, governor, 1870-77, and U.S. senator, 1877-83; and Benjamin F. Harding, U.S. senator, 1862-65. Stephen F. Chadwick was secretary of state, 1870-78, and governor, 1877-78; and Matthew Deady, Supreme Court Justice, 1853-59, and U.S. District Judge for Oregon, 1859 to 1893.* The remaining clique members, Bush and Joseph W. Drew, never held high public office. As a group, these men molded the Democratic Party in their image. Asahel Bush took over the clique and the Democratic Party, which he preferred to call the "Oregon Democracy." Bush's *Oregon Statesman* was the official voice of the Democratic Party and for a decade he was the political boss of Oregon. The rule of Bush and the clique was absolute and imperious. Plans were made and orders issued for the rank-and-file to obey without questions. "If a Democrat forgot this he was disciplined. If he persisted, the wrath of the *Statesman* was turned upon him and he was destroyed politically. Bush was absolutely uncompromising, took offense easily and the fear of his terrible invective was potent in maintaining party discipline." In short, Asahel Bush was the "most influential and feared man in the territory."[20]

Not all Democrats went along with Asahel Bush and the clique. As early as 1851 there were dissident Democrats who resented Bush and his autocratic style. As the years passed, more disaffected Democrats (called "Softs" by the clique, or "Nationals" by the dissidents) appeared. By 1855, volatile national issues (the expansion of Negro slavery and popular sovereignty, for example) had begun

---

* Deady and Asahel Bush were close friends and political allies for most of the 1850s. Deady became a Republican after his break with Bush.

Asahel Bush

Asahel Bush, like many of Oregon's early pioneer leaders, was a New Englander. Born in Westfield, Massachusetts, on June 4, 1824, Bush arrived in Oregon Territory in 1851. He was 27. Bush's father had died when he was 15; consequently, Asahel was apprenticed to a printer in upstate New York. After a decade, Bush returned to Westfield and began to study law. He passed the Massachusetts Bar in 1850. Soon after, the young attorney set out for Oregon.

Traveling by ship to Panama, Bush crossed the Isthmus to the Pacific and caught a ship to San Francisco, before sailing on to Astoria and Portland. Bush set up shop in Oregon City on March 28, 1851: he founded and began publishing one of Oregon's first newspapers, the *Oregon Statesman* (using the printing press he had shipped around Cape Horn). From the beginning, Bush made the *Statesman* the voice of Oregon Democrats. In 1853 he moved his home and newspaper to Salem, where he lived the rest of his life.

Ashael Bush was a founding member of the Oregon Democratic Party in 1851-52. Indeed, Bush and fellow Democrat Joseph Lane were the most powerful politicians in Oregon between 1852 and 1863 (the year Bush sold the *Statesman*). Bush headed a band of influential Democratic politicians based in Salem. Known as the Salem Clique, these Bush-Democrats maintained an iron grip on their party throughout the 1850s. Bush made sure that no Democrat could run for political office without the

to creep into party politics, threatening Democratic unity. And there was also the personal agenda of Democrat Joseph Lane, Oregon's Territorial Delegate to Congress. Lane wanted to be a U.S. Senator once statehood was achieved.

In April 1853, Democrats held their first territorial Democratic convention in Salem. Participants re-nominated Joseph Lane as delegate to Congress. They also adopted a series of resolutions, several of which dealt for the first time with national issues.[21]

Governor John Gaines' term ended in May 1853. Democrats celebrated when word came that President Franklin Pierce, a Democrat, had appointed a new governor for Oregon: Joseph Lane. But Lane had other ideas. Three days after his appointment, he resigned to run for another term as Oregon's delegate to Congress. He easily won reelection.[22] Democrats also won most legislative contests, sweeping all the Council seats, and 22 of the 26 House positions.

Clique's approval. As the decade passed, Asahel Bush found himself increasingly at odds with the most popular politician in the territory, General Joseph Lane, Oregon's delegate to Congress.

Eventually, Oregon Democrats, like their brethren in the rest of the country, split, largely over the volatile issues of slavery and states' rights. The fateful presidential election of 1860 found Bush backing Illinois Senator Stephen A. Douglas—while Joseph Lane became the running mate of the pro-slavery faction of the Democratic party led by presidential candidate John C. Breckinridge. Indeed, once the Civil War erupted in 1861, Asahel Bush was one of Oregon's leading pro-Union voices.

In 1868, Bush joined with Portland businessman William S. Ladd to establish the Ladd-Bush Bank in Salem. Bush became sole owner of the bank in 1882 and ran it until 1910, retiring at age 86. The bank, as well as other business interests, made Asahel Bush one of the wealthiest men in Oregon.

Never one to shrink from tackling a difficult task, Bush took the job of superintendent of the state penitentiary in 1878, a post he held until 1882. During his tenure at the penitentiary, Bush overhauled the budget and cut costs in half. This prison job followed, by many years, his service as Oregon's only territorial printer and, in 1859, as Oregon's first state printer.

Asahel Bush died in 1913, age 89. Historian Robert C. Clark, in his *History of the Willamette Valley, Oregon* (1927) wrote this about Asahel Bush: "For over six decades he commanded general recognition as one of the ablest and most public-spirited citizens in Oregon."

Asahel Bush's legacy can be seen today in the form of his longtime home (owned by the City of Salem and open to the public) and surrounding Bush's Pasture Park, along with the Ladd-Bush Bank building in downtown Salem.

George Curry, an Oregon pioneer and secretary of the territory, became acting governor when Joe Lane resigned to serve another term as Oregon's delegate to Congress. Curry served until December, when the new governor, John Davis, arrived. Like Joseph Lane, Davis was from Indiana. A former Speaker of the U.S. House of Representatives and twice a national chairman of the Democratic Party, Davis flopped as territorial governor. Oregonians were unhappy about having another outsider foisted on them. Democratic leaders urged President Pierce to replace Davis with an Oregonian and then launched a nasty campaign to drive Davis out of Oregon. They gave Davis the silent treatment, keeping a chilly distance between the new governor and themselves. Asahel Bush led the assault by circulating unflattering and untrue rumors about Davis, with critical comments cascading from his pen. After nine months of abuse, John Davis resigned in disgust and left Oregon forever. President Pierce replaced him with George Curry, and he held the job longer than anyone during the territorial period, serving over four years (November 1, 1854 to March 3, 1859). The Salem Clique had finally got its way.

Oregon Whigs, stinging from their crushing defeat of 1853, began to talk about organizing as a political party. Editor Tom Dryer focused on Whig issues in his *Weekly Oregonian*. He declared that Whigs favored a national program of internal improvements (roads, railroads, ports) funded by Congress. Whigs met in Portland in March 1854 to decide on party organization and slowly patched together a territorial organization. Some counties (Washington, for example, a Whig stronghold) quickly established a party apparatus. Whigs in other counties were not as successful.

Temperance and the Challenge of the Know-Nothings

While Whigs toiled to build a party equal to the Democrats, two short-lived political movements exploded on the scene. The first was a temperance movement. The Oregon Territory Temperance Association formed at Salem in April 1854. They wanted Oregon to adopt the Maine Law of 1851 that banned the consumption of alcoholic spirits. Association folk set to work to nominate and elect pro-temperance candidates to the legislature. Desiring to capture as many seats as possible, these prohibitionists allied themselves with the Whigs, a rocky partnership. Asahel Bush sprang into action. Throughout the campaign of 1854, he waged war in the *Statesman* on the Maine Law Party, opposing its doctrine of prohibition and its alliance with Oregon's Whigs. Whigs often ran against Maine Law candidates as well as the better organized Democrats. Consequently, temperance candidates ran poorly, as did more established Whigs.

Another political force surfaced in Oregon, and Asahel Bush and the Democrats recognized its potential for success. The movement was the American Party, whose members called themselves Know-Nothings. The American Party set its sights on winning the presidency, control of Congress, governorships, and state legislatures.

Know-Nothings were an element known as "nativists." Nativism was a potent force in America in the 1850s and it has reappeared at various times and places, throughout America, up to the present day. The Know-Nothing outburst in Oregon was part of a national movement. Nativists hated foreigners and Catholics. Native-born white men ("true Americans," they called themselves) feared that the United States was being overrun by German and Catholic immigrants. Nativists believed the Roman Catholic Church was corrupting American institutions. Know-Nothings resented the fact that "foreigners" could vote and hold political office in the United States. The nucleus of the American/Know-Nothing Party was a secret fraternal lodge, the Order of the Star-Spangled Banner, founded about 1850. Their name came from the stock answer to the question: "Are you a member of the Order of the Star-Spangled Banner?" The response was: "I know nothing."

In 1854 rumors were rife in Oregon that local Know-Nothing chapters, or "wigwams," were organizing in several communities. Due to the party's secrecy rule, the public couldn't tell how many Oregonians were Know-Nothings and who they were. Asahel Bush vowed to expose the nativists. A Bush acquaintance joined the Salem wigwam and smuggled membership lists and copies of Know-Nothing rituals and oaths to Bush. The lists confirmed Bush's suspicions: Whigs (and even a few Democrats) had joined the Know-Nothing crusade. Bush turned his *Statesman* into an attack dog. For over six months, in editorials and stories, he exposed the Know-Nothings, calling them "the most ridiculous piece of bigotry, intolerance and stupidity grown persons were ever engaged in."[23]

Bush published membership lists. In edition after edition, he kept the pressure on, and threats of bodily harm didn't stop him. Then Democratic legislators set a trap. In the December-January (1854-55) legislative session, they forced through the viva voce ballot law, which passed in a close vote (5-3 in the Council, and 14-12 in the House). The law required that every ballot cast in a general election be read aloud, so all present would hear how each individual voted—including, of course, whether or not the ballot was for a Know-Nothing-backed candidate. Between Bush's relentless attacks in the press and the viva voce bill, Democrats discredited the Know-Nothings, thwarting their political ambitions in Oregon.

But the Democratic assault on the Know-Nothings energized Oregon's lethargic Whigs. On April 18, 1855, delegates from most counties met in Corvallis in what was to be the only Whig convention held in the territorial period. Whigs nominated former Gov. John Gaines for delegate to Congress to oppose Democrat Joseph Lane. The next day, Oregon's American Party met in Albany and endorsed Gaines' candidacy. Asahel Bush branded Gaines a Know-Nothing. Faced with an unusual collection of opponents (Maine Law folk, American Party/Know-Nothings, and Whigs) Democrats redoubled their efforts to organize their party.

The Lane/Gaines campaign was ugly. On a platform in Polk County, the candidates got into a fist fight. Bush and Dryer printed one caustic political salvo after another. Whigs in Multnomah County met and openly declared themselves in no way tied to Know-Nothingism. Other Whigs continued to ally with the nativists. Bush droned on, calling this unholy alliance a "corrupt and wicked coalition," the "dregs of fanaticism," "dens of darkness," and "midnight assassins."[24]

The Democratic Landslide

Democrats scored an overwhelming victory in the 1855 election. General Lane was reelected delegate by a margin of 2,149 votes. The legislative lineup in the House was 28 Democrats and two Whig/Know-Nothings; in the Council, it was seven Democrats and two Whig/Know-Nothings. Bush knew that victory was the result of a well-organized and thoroughly drilled Democratic Party. Late to organize and erratically led, the Whig Party quickly faded from the political scene in Oregon and the nation. In 1856, a new national political party, the Republicans, ran John C. Fremont for president, while the American Party nominated former President Millard Fillmore. Democrats picked James Buchanan. Nationally, the Whig Party was dead. From 1856 to 1860 major political realignments took place nationally and in the Oregon Territory. During these years, four events of great political significance occurred in Oregon: Oregon's Democrat Party split over the issue of slavery; the new Republican Party appeared in Oregon; voters approved Oregon's first constitution; and Congress passed and President James Buchanan signed the Oregon Statehood Bill.

Hurrah for Stephen Douglas!

Until 1854, Oregonians were "very willing to let slavery alone."[25] Then, in May 1854, Illinois Senator Stephen Douglas dropped a bomb by guiding his Kansas-Nebraska Act through Congress. The shock waves from this law rocked the nation for years. Douglas had upset a delicate balance that had been in place since 1821. The Missouri Compromise of 1821 had prohibited the spread of slavery north of 36° latitude (except for Missouri, which was admitted to the Union as a slave state). Douglas's act established the territories of Kansas and Nebraska, granting to the people who settled there (as well as those living in older territories) the power of "popular sovereignty." This meant that territorials, by a majority vote, could decide what they wanted to do with slavery, either legalize it or prohibit it. Popular sovereignty was, not surprisingly, wildly popular in Oregon as well as throughout the rest of the western frontier. Since becoming a U.S. territory, Oregonians had petitioned Congress to grant them the right to choose their officials from among local men. Oregonians, and especially Democrats, favored local control. They resented the president's and Congress's power to choose their leaders. Popular sovereignty put power in the hands of the people directly, removing the president and Congress as decision makers. Let the people decide for themselves!

Slavery as a Political Issue in Oregon and the Nation

Initially, Democrats did not view popular sovereignty as a means by which to bring slavery into Oregon (it was already against the law to do so), but merely as a way to achieve local control over governmental matters. Later, realizing that many members of the party favored slavery, Democratic leaders feared that popular sovereignty could be used to reopen the Negro question in Oregon. So, when some Democratic leaders in Oregon tried to create sentiment in favor of the Kansas-Nebraska Act, they were met with stiff opposition. In April 1855 Yamhill Whigs repudiated and condemned the Kansas-Nebraska Act as "a wanton and unnecessary renewal of the slavery agitation." The Oregon Whigs belonged to the Northern wing of the party and denounced the principle of popular sovereignty. They declared the right and duty of Congress to exercise sovereignty in the territories. The Oregon Whigs could be counted on to resist pro-slavery aggression.[26]

Oregon's first anti-slavery convention met at Albany in June 1855. Delegates laid plans to build a broad organization to stop the expansion of slavery into the Pacific Northwest. They urged the support of anti-slavery newspapers, county meetings to arouse public sentiment against the growing evil of slavery, and the election of anti-slavery men to office. The Albany meeting sparked several vitriolic outbursts. Asahel Bush referred to the delegates as a "collection of old grannies." He called the anti-slavers "nigger-struck dames" and "stale fanatics."[27]

The 1855 election contest between Joseph Lane and John Gaines for delegate ignored the recent Kansas-Nebraska Act. Neither candidate touched this potentially explosive issue. Over 60% of Oregon voters were Democrats and they were divided over the question of slavery in their territory. Party managers would not permit any discussions of the question in Oregon and took no party action whatever.[28]

Two events, each linked to slavery, rocked the nation in 1856-57. Though far from Oregon, these events shook its political institutions to the core. One event occurred on the prairies of Kansas, the others in Washington, D.C. Kansas Territory was gripped by civil war in 1856. In just two years (since the passage of the Kansas-Nebraska Act) Kansas had become a battleground. With the principle of popular sovereignty in effect, those who settled there would decide whether Kansas would permit or prohibit slavery. With interference from pro-slavery neighbor Missouri, those favoring slavery had gained control over Kansas' Territorial Legislature. A second, anti-slavery legislature formed to oppose the pro-slavery body. The pro-slavery government drafted a proposed state constitution legalizing slavery; likewise, their anti-slavery foes wrote a constitution banning it. Violent attacks on people and property resulted in several hundred deaths by 1856. Oregonians were horrified to learn of the unfolding of these grisly events. Many feared the same thing could happen in Oregon.

James Buchanan, a conservative Democrat, was elected president in November 1856. Two days after Buchanan's inauguration (March 4, 1857), the U.S. Supreme Court, under Chief Justice Roger B. Taney, handed down the infamous *Dred Scott* decision. The Court ruled that Negroes were not citizens and never could be. The Court said that, in passing the Missouri Compromise in 1821, Congress had acted unconstitutionally because Congress had no authority to deny a slave owner his right to use his Negro property anywhere he chose. Congress had violated the Fifth Amendment property rights of slave owners—because it had prohibited slavery north of 36° north. Justice Taney ruled that Congress could do nothing to stop the spread of slavery. To do so would violate the Fifth Amendment rights of America's slaveholders. The South was jubilant. The rest of the nation was dumbfounded. Did the *Scott* decision mean that popular sovereignty was dead, that even if a majority of settlers in a territory or state wished to ban slavery, there was no legal way for them to do so? Ironically, Oregonians were preparing to vote on a proposed state constitution in which they would decide on whether slavery would be made legal in the new state of Oregon and whether free Negroes would be welcome to live here.

Republicans Appear

A new political force appeared in Oregon in 1856, the Republican Party. Founded in the summer of 1854 in Jackson, Michigan, the party had been born as a reaction to the passage of the Kansas-Nebraska Act. Most Republicans rejected the idea of popular sovereignty. They viewed it as a ploy through which the slave states could spread slavery where it didn't exist. In this respect, Oregon's Republicans differed from their national party: they endorsed popular sovereignty and the Kansas-Nebraska Act. Oregon's first Republican meeting was held in Jackson County in May 1856. Agreeing with their Democratic opponents, these early Oregon Republicans stated their belief "that the people are the rightful source of political power and that officers should be chosen by a direct vote of the people."[29] Delegates also enthusiastically endorsed a resolution calling on the federal government to prohibit slavery in all regions outside of the South. In August, Republicans met in Albany to lay plans for building a party organization in the Oregon Territory. Delegates adopted a party motto: "We fling our banner to the breeze—Free Soil, Free Labor, a Free Press, a Free State and Fremont" (the 1856 Republican presidential nominee). Oregon Republicans wanted slavery restricted to the South. The rest of the nation (and its millions of acres) must be preserved for white people only.

Oregon Republicans continued organizing their new party into the fall of 1856. On November 1, William Adams, the fiery editor of the *Argus* in Oregon City, announced that his newspaper would serve as the official voice of Oregon's newest party. Asahel Bush blasted the newcomer party. Snarling, he dubbed them "Black Republicans," the "mongrel opposition," the Party of Disunion. Whig Tom Dryer answered Bush, announcing that his *Weekly Oregonian* would also oppose slavery. The passage of the Kansas-Nebraska bill had set in motion a complete political realignment. A state Republican organization seemed to promise the only security against the possibility of bloodshed as had happened in Kansas.[30] In February 1857, delegates from eight counties gathered in Albany to write a Republican platform. They endorsed a Free State Constitution for Oregon and announced themselves as the Free State Republican Party of Oregon. Members also adopted a resolution urging the federal government to undertake an extensive program of internal improvements on the Pacific Coast. They urged immediate construction of a central Pacific railroad and river and harbor improvements paid by Congress. The Republicans then attacked the Democrats, in particular the Salem Clique. They accused the ruling party of wasting public funds, of enacting the oppressive *viva voce* law, and of keeping the state capital question inflamed.[31]

Democrats Dividing

Cracks big enough for all to see appeared in Oregon's Democratic Party in 1857. Since the Salem Clique had taken control of the party in 1853, a group of dissident Democrats calling themselves National Democrats had opposed them. They deeply resented the clique's stranglehold on the party. The clique was too autocratic, said the Nationals, and honest disagreement was not tolerated. Asahel Bush and the clique insisted that a good Democrat kept his mouth shut and did what he was told.

A Democratic Party caucus met on January 20, 1857, while the Territorial Legislature was in session. The rancorous caucus revealed the Democrats' deep divisions. The clique introduced a resolution condemning a small newspaper, the

Democratic Standard, which was the voice of the dissident National Democrats. The clique wanted the caucus to rebuke the newspaper for challenging the clique's authority and its iron grip on the party apparatus. They claimed that the *Standard* undercut party unity, threatening the Democrats' grip on local government and weakening the party. Bush likened the *Standard* to a "rotten limb" that had to be "cast off" if the healthy body was to be protected. The resolution condemning the newspaper was approved, but only by a vote of 15-12. Three months later (on April 13), Democrats held their territorial convention in Salem. Delegates passed two important resolutions: the first was intended to coerce all Democrats to pledge their unwavering allegiance to the party and its candidates (or face excommunication from the party); in the second, delegates took on the volatile issue of slavery and its expansion. Regular Democrats pushed through a motion to direct future delegates to a constitutional convention to not address the issue in a constitutional draft. It was suggested that the slavery question be put to voters in a separate measure, to be voted on in addition to the constitution. For the time being, Regular Democrats had removed the slavery issue from the party agenda. They wanted the issue off the table because it could tear the party apart.

Voters made three critical decisions in the June 1857 election. First, they reelected Gen. Joseph Lane to a fourth term as Oregon's Territorial Delegate to Congress. Lane, who still considered himself a Regular Democrat, defeated G. W. Lawson, an independent, free-state Democrat, 5,662 to 3,471 votes. Everyone knew Joe Lane favored slavery and its spread into the territories. But in 1857 it didn't seem to matter; Lane's personal popularity was as high as ever. Second, voters overwhelmingly approved a resolution calling for a convention of elected delegates to draft a state constitution. Third, voters elected their territorial legislators. Here, the voting was closer. Democrats won a one-vote majority in the smaller Council, while 10 non-Democrats won seats in the larger House. In addition, 21 of the delegates elected to the constitutional convention were also non-Democrats, leaving the Democrats with the other 39 seats.

Free State or Slave State?

There were eight weeks between the June election and the August 17 constitutional convention. In the interim, the lively debate of whether Oregon would be a free state or a slave state grabbed the public's attention. Oregon's newspapers, politicians, and political parties joined ordinary citizens to debate the consequences of becoming a pro- or anti-slave state. Most supporters of slavery were Democrats, most prominent being congressional Delegate and former

Governor Gen. Joseph Lane, Judge Matthew Deady (later a Republican), and John Whiteaker, gubernatorial candidate (and Oregon's first state governor), as well as a dozen territorial legislators and three dozen delegates to the constitutional convention. As the slave debate intensified during the summer and fall of 1857, there was ample reason for uneasiness about the direction Oregon voters would take.

The *Oregonian* and *Argus* were staunch Free Staters. The *Argus*, voice of the Republicans, made it very clear where Oregon's newest party stood. In February, the Republicans had declared themselves "as the Free State Republican Party of Oregon and as such will fight the political battle of freedom."[32]

At least two territorial newspapers endorsed slavery in Oregon: the Jacksonville *Sentinel* and the *Occidental Messenger* in Corvallis. J. C. Avery, a prominent Democrat, owned the *Messenger*. Avery began publishing in summer 1857 and by fall the *Messenger* was the territory's most radical pro-slavery newspaper. L. P. Hall, whom Avery had brought to Oregon as editor, wrote that slavery was "a divinely appointed institution."[33]

Asahel Bush and his Democratic *Oregon Statesman* remained neutral. For the time being, Bush, a Free Stater, seemed satisfied to raise but one question: Will slavery pay?[34] After the June election, Bush announced that the *Statesman* would provide a forum for anyone who wanted to submit a signed letter on the subject of slavery. On July 28, 1857, he published an extraordinary letter from the Hon. George Williams, a letter that changed the direction of the slavery debate in Oregon.

Chief Justice George Williams, a lifelong Democrat, disliked the tone of the slavery debate. He was no friend of slavery, nor did he like the idea of free Negroes living in Oregon—positions held by a majority of whites in the Territory. The tide seemed to be moving in favor of the pro-slavery position. Someone had to push the debate into a new direction. So Williams wrote a letter that appeared on the front page of the *Oregon Statesman* on July 28, 1857, in which he focused on the economic reasons why slavery would not work here.

Williams took his readers through a step-by-step examination of how difficult it would be to adapt Negro slavery to conditions in the Northwest. As a system of labor, could slavery be successfully integrated into Oregon's social order and economic activity? Here are several of Williams' arguments:

> Negro slaves other than house servants would be perfect leeches upon the farmers during the long, rainy winters; the risk and expense in transporting slaves to distant Oregon and the ease of escape into

the sparsely settled, wooded and mountainous country, would render investment in slave property altogether too hazardous; escaped Negroes would find refuge and consort with Oregon's Indian enemies and become an added menace to the people; introduce slavery, and free white labor will become degraded, if not impossible to secure altogether; and, can Oregon afford to throw away the friendship of the North—the overruling power of the nation—for the sake of slavery?[35]

The issue of free (white) labor was central to why so many early Oregonians feared the introduction of Negro slavery. Many of the men and women who emigrated to Oregon did so because they did not want to live in a slave state (Missouri or Kentucky, for example), nor in a place where significant numbers of free Negroes lived. For white working men, Negro slave labor was a threat; unpaid slave workers could jeopardize the jobs of white workers (and their ability to earn a living wage). And free Negro workers usually toiled for lower wages than whites; why hire a white man for $4 a day when you could get a free Negro to do the same job for $2.50 a day?

Reading this letter will likely raise a red flag for the contemporary reader. The existence of slavery in nearly half the states, coupled with the fact that hundreds of thousands of free Negroes lived in the more northern states* and territories, meant that many whites lived near Negroes. The prevailing attitude of whites in America in the 19th century was that Negroes, as a race, were inferior to white people. The majority favored the separation of the races.

The greatest challenge for students of history is to overcome the temptation to judge those who lived in the past by contemporary standards. When Williams used charged words like the "degrading" of free labor, he was reflecting the prevailing attitude of the day, warning whites lest they be brought down to the inferior level of Negroes—an attitude most Americans would find offensive today.

Another important argument that Williams raised pertained to Oregon's future as a state. He warned Oregonians to think twice before applying for statehood as a slave state, as this might jeopardize their chance of being admitted to the Union when Congress took up the Oregon statehood bill. Williams understood how volatile the issue of slavery and its expansion was in American politics. Indeed, he could foresee a time when the Union might be torn apart by this issue. Surely, he argued, Oregonians did not want to end up on the side of the slaveholding minority in America.

---

* New York and Pennsylvania, for example.

Williams' letter had an electric effect. Public opinion began to swing away from the pro-slave position. George Williams had shaken the majority out of its lethargy. Oregon would become a Free State. But perhaps for the reasons that Williams suggested, voters approved a Negro exclusion clause in the constitution, a clause that remained in the Oregon Constitution until voters finally removed it in 1926. Oregon was the only state admitted to the Union with such an exclusionary clause in its constitution.

Oregon's Constitutional Convention of 1857

The convention was held at the Salem courthouse from August 17 to September 18, 1857. The Democrats dominated the convention of 60 delegates; Yamhill's J. R. McBride was the only Republican delegate. Thirty-nine votes were cast for Judge Matthew P. Deady for president and 15 votes for Martin Olds, the opposition. Delazon Smith was the principal orator of the convention.[36] Other delegates included the territory's Supreme Court justices George H. Williams and Cyrus Olney. Fifty-one of the delegates were either farmers or lawyers. Most delegates were acquainted; many had served in the legislature or in other government offices. "Attached to place and favored with good health and long lives, these men left an indelible mark on the politics of their state in the 1860s and 1870s . . . at least thirty-five held office after 1857."[37] *Weekly Oregonian* editor (and a delegate) Tom Dryer kept the public informed about convention proceedings in his editorial, calling "attention to the fact that no delegate opposed to the Salem clique had been placed at the head of a committee and declar[ing] that every committee had a pro-slavery majority."[38]

All suggestions and resolutions on the subject of slavery were referred to the appropriate standing committee—where they were buried. Democrats kept both the slavery question and the admission of free Negroes off the table, assuring that each issue would be voted on separately by the people. The delegates approved the final draft of a constitution but not by a very wide margin, with only 34 of the 60 voting to approve. Eleven voted against and 15 were either absent or did not vote. The vote was strictly along party lines, with some "soft" (National) Democrats either in the "no" or "not voting" category. Citizens had until November 9—the date of the territorial vote—to make up their minds about the constitution. Meanwhile, the campaigns for and against the document shifted into high gear. Four newspapers opposed ratification: the *Weekly Oregonian, Argus, Standard,* and *Messenger.* Dryer hissed that the constitution was like a "huge viper, with poisonous fangs, a legion of legs in its belly and a deadly sting in its tail."[39]

The main discussion focused on the two side issues that would also be voted on: should Negro slavery be legalized in Oregon and should Oregon remain off-limits to free Negroes? If these measures were approved, they would be incorporated into the new state constitution as additional articles. The November 9 vote ratified the constitution 7,200 to 3,200. The question of whether to allow Negro slavery in Oregon was defeated, 7,700 opposed to 2,600 in favor. And the issue of whether to permit free Negroes to live here also lost, 8,600 against to 1,100 in favor. Following these votes, it would take Congress another 16 months to debate and pass the Oregon statehood bill.

Democrats: A Two-Headed Party

Opposition Democrats bolted in February 1858. After five years of bickering and intrigue, the minority "Softs" (or Nationals) had decided to pull away from their clique-dominated party, attempting to build a rival Democratic Party that better represented what they believed. James K. Kelly and James O'Meara, editor of the Democratic *Standard*, "launched the National Democrats of the State of Oregon, a new political party."[40] The party breach was based on local issues. "Although Democrats had split over the domination of the Salem Clique, both wings were united as far as national policy was concerned. The fight was simply between the 'ins' and 'outs'—the fundamental issue in this quarrel was who would get the [political] offices."[41] The separation was complete by the spring of 1858, with both wings scheduling conventions and nominating a full slate of state officers.

As the critical election of 1858 approached, the Republicans were also in disarray. Because their party was dead nationally, hundreds of loyal Whigs had to decide where they fit in. Many distrusted the Republicans, seeing them as "Negro worshippers." Tom Dryer, in his *Oregonian*, opposed the new Republican Party, arguing that the principles of the Whig Party were still important and timely. Like many Whigs, Dwyer was a man without a party. Some Whigs simply did not vote in 1858, while others joined hands with the National Democrats. This Whig-National Democrat coalition backed E. M. Barnum for governor. The Regular Democrats chose a compromise candidate, a little-known Lane County farmer named John Whiteaker, who favored slavery. Considering that Asahel Bush and other clique leaders were personally anti-slavery, Whiteaker seemed like a strange choice, but he was the only candidate that all the Regulars could agree upon. The Regular Democrats proved that they were still popular with voters. Whiteaker was elected Oregon's first governor, defeating Barnum 5,545 to 4,407. The June election was a complete victory for the pro-slavery faction of the Democrats, despite the decision that had earlier been taken on slavery.

Lafayette Grover was sent to Congress. And pro-slave Democrats won a majority of seats in the legislature as well.

Oregon's popular delegate to Congress had been busy behind the scenes quietly strengthening his base in the Democratic Party. Through his power to dispense federal jobs (patronage), Gen. Joseph Lane remained the most influential Democratic politician in Oregon, with many Democratic friends who owed him a favor. The big decision for legislators in 1858 was to elect Oregon's first two U. S. senators, anticipating that Congress would soon act on the Oregon statehood bill. Pro-slavery Democrats, who had taken control of the 1858 Territorial Legislature, elected Lane and another clique insider, Delazon Smith, a native New Yorker who had moved to Oregon in 1853 and served in the Territorial Legislature and as a delegate to the constitutional convention.

By early 1859, Asahel Bush was condemning Senator Lane for building his own "Lane Party," further weakening Democratic solidarity. Now another issue exploded onto the scene, further dividing Democrats. Senator Stephen A. Douglas, one of the nation's most popular Northern Democrats, publicly broke with Pres. James Buchanan. Douglas continued to support his controversial doctrine of popular sovereignty, while Buchanan disagreed. Douglas condemned the *Dred Scott* decision of 1857, saying that it threatened popular sovereignty. President Buchanan supported *Scott* and the pending pro-slavery constitution of Kansas; Senator Douglas favored a rival, free-state document. The rupture between Douglas and Buchanan crept into Oregon politics. Lane sided with the President, as did Oregon's National Democrats. Asahel Bush and the clique-led Regular Democrats favored Douglas. Pro-slave Democrats, led by Joseph Lane, took control of the National Democratic wing of Oregon's · dominant political party.

Judge Matthew P. Deady, a longtime political ally of Bush, broke with the Regular Democrats, declaring himself pro-slavery and for Joseph Lane as party leader. Meanwhile, Lane was consolidating his control over the Democratic Party. He had federal officeholders in Oregon who were Douglas loyalists removed from office. By spring 1859, "all the influential federal offices in the territory were filled by Lane men."[42] General Lane's final victory over the clique came at the Democrats' first state convention in April 1859. Lansing Stout was Lane's choice for U.S. Representative. The clique's choice, Lafayette Grover, lost a bitter contest to Stout for the Democratic nomination, by a seven vote margin. The party platform also represented Lane's views and those of the National Democrats. The party was now the instrument of Joseph Lane; the

Bush-Douglas Regular Democrats were now a splinter group and the clique had disbanded.

While Democrats slashed at each other, Republicans closed ranks and planned a vigorous 1859 campaign. They blasted abolitionism but favored stopping the further spread of slavery. They declared themselves a "white man's party," and condemned the idea of racial equality.[43] David Logan, an 1849 immigrant to Oregon, emerged as a new Republican leader in 1859, and was nominated for the U.S. House against Lansing Stout. Logan lost the election by 16 votes and his impressive showing was a measure of the growing popularity of Oregon's new Republican Party. The surprising Republicans were only months away from a power-sharing arrangement that would make them Oregon's dominant political party for the duration of the Civil War.

Were Oregonians Ready for Statehood?

For Oregon to qualify for statehood, the population had to be at a level to convince Congress that there were enough people here to develop a modern state. The Oregon Territory population was under fifty thousand in 1858 and it was argued there were too few people to develop a state with a land area of nearly 100,000 square miles. Yet, the population argument didn't block Oregon's 1859 admission to the Union. By 1859, Oregonians had had nearly fifteen years of experience in self-government. They had fought wars with Native Americans by raising their own militias, established an agrarian and trade economy with California, and had generally lived ordered and peaceful lives.

Statehood was not achieved simply because Oregon men approved a constitution in November 1857. Congress had to approve Oregon's action by passing a bill that admitted the newly formed state into the Union. And because of the question of slavery, Congress was slow to act. Pro-slavery congressmen didn't want to disturb the balance of power between slave and free states with the admission of another free state.[44] Southern Democrats wanted to block the admission of any more northern free states. Congressional Republicans were also in a bind. Oregon voters had sent contradictory signals to Washington. In November 1857, voters overwhelmingly approved the state constitution. At the same time voters defeated, by an even bigger margin, proposals to permit slavery in Oregon and to allow free Negroes to live here. Yet, only seven months later, the pro-slavery Lane-National Democrat faction won a majority of seats in the legislature. Voters also elected two pro-slavery Democrats, John Whiteaker as governor and Lafayette Grover to the U.S. House of Representatives. The new legislature then elected Joseph Lane and Delazon Smith, both of whom favored slavery, as Oregon's first U.S. senators. How could voters adopt a free-state constitution in one election and then, in the next, elect virtually all pro-slavery candidates to state and federal office?

The Oregon statehood bill did not glide through Congress. After months of wrangling, the Senate finally passed the bill on May 18, 1858, 35-17. But Oregon was left hanging when Congress adjourned in June 1858, before the House voted on the bill. The issue was resolved early in the congressional session of 1859 when the House narrowly approved the bill, 114 to 103. President Buchanan signed the bill on February 14, 1859; and Oregon's two new senators were sworn in that day.

The news of Oregon's admission to the Union was carried by pony express from St. Louis to San Francisco in only 24 days. The steamer *Brother Jonathan* arrived in Portland from San Francisco on March 15, with the good tidings. Governor John Whiteaker called a special session of the legislature to meet in Salem on May 16, 1859.[45]

The May legislature made a terrible mess of things. Although Oregon had been in the Union only three months, lawmakers had to choose a new U.S. senator. Oregon entered the Union midway in a two-year election cycle. The U.S. Constitution requires that the six-year Senate terms be staggered, so that only one-third of senators face reelection every two years. As the newest state in the Union, Oregon was given two shortened Senate terms, the shortest one lasting only until the end of that current session of Congress, March 3, 1859. Delazon Smith drew the short term and served 17 days in the Senate. Senator Joseph Lane's term ended two years later, in March 1861. Because of the split in the majority Democratic Party, legislators could not agree on Smith's replacement; consequently, Oregon had only one senator during its first two years as a state. It was not an auspicious beginning for the Union's newest member.

Chapter 3
Early Statehood and the Civil War Era

1859. It seems like ancient history, doesn't it? Considering that 32 states were already in the Union when Oregon was admitted on February 14, 1859 and only 17 states entered the Union after, Oregon is a relatively young state. Looking at it another way, the span of time between 1859 and the present is about equivalent to the lives, back to back, of two 75-year-old people.

To many, early Oregon is a mythical place, a primitive colony of mountain men, wagon trains, and rugged pioneer families, with primitive farms and log cabins and huge forests, an Eden half a continent away from frontier states like Iowa and Minnesota and Texas. Yet there were plenty of signs in 1859 that America was pushing westward. California had been a state since 1850, and, next door, Nevada was about to become a territory (and, in 1864, a state). Still, ominous clouds hovered over the land. The Union was in danger. The issues of slavery, abolition, and states rights, along with the balance of power in Congress and the actions of a few fanatics, were deepening the divisions between America's regions and her people. If there was war, where would Oregon's loyalties be? Living in a new state, Oregonians would be sorely tested during a period of national crisis. Fortunately, Oregonians of 1859 had lived in relative harmony for two decades under a government and laws that they had created for themselves. When the Civil War started in April 1861, Oregon already had the necessary institutions in place to carry her through this awful American tragedy.

Oregon celebrated its first birthday as a state on February 14, 1860, with citizens who were optimistic about the new decade. Thousands of emigrants entered the state every summer and fall. The white population of Oregon in 1860 was 52,465. Males outnumbered females about three to two. Just under 50% of the men were between ages 20 and 49. The economy was healthy and jobs were plentiful. Portland was Oregon's largest town with 2,874 residents. Weekly stagecoach service linking Oregon City to Jacksonville began that spring. Portland had daily stagecoach service to Sacramento, via Roseburg and

Jacksonville, beginning in September. But it would be another four years before Oregon was linked by telegraph to California: Portland was connected to Yreka and from Yreka the telegraph linked to Marysville and transcontinental service. Slowly, Oregon was emerging from its extreme isolation.

1860: A Year of Decision

Americans everywhere recognized the importance of the 1860 presidential campaign. Slavery—and the super-charged emotions it aroused—was the foremost political issue of the day. Senator Stephen Douglas, darling of Northern Democrats, was the leading presidential candidate. New York's William Seward appeared headed for the Republican nomination and Abraham Lincoln of Illinois was preparing to challenge him for it. Oregon's delegates were committed to Joseph Lane, their popular U.S. senator, who had repeatedly surfaced as a prospective presidential candidate with a small but vocal following in Democratic ranks. Rumor had it that Joe Lane was President James Buchanan's choice.

Republicans met in Chicago. Abraham Lincoln's managers packed the galleries with his fans and he was nominated on the fourth ballot. Republicans were confident that he would take them into the White House.

A new party, the Constitutional Union Party, nominated John Bell of Kentucky. Pro-slavery Democrats chose John C. Breckinridge, Buchanan's vice president, as their presidential candidate, and Joe Lane was picked to be his running mate.* The convention of Northern Democrats adopted a popular sovereignty plank in their platform and nominated Sen. Douglas for president. Badly broken, the Democratic Party seemed destined to defeat in November.

Oregonians fell in behind Douglas, Breckinridge, or Lincoln; the Bell people had no state organization here. The June legislative election was fiercely contested. Douglas-Democrats realized that they had no chance of capturing enough seats to have a majority. Republicans knew they had the same problem. So, a marriage of necessity was made to assure that, together, they would control the next Oregon Legislature. This coalition of Northern Democrats and Republicans held together for seven years. Known as the "Union Party," it controlled Oregon government through the Civil War and for two years after. Oregon was the only state to have such a coalition during the Civil War.

The legislative campaign centered on the popular sovereignty issue. The coalition rested on it, clinging to the principle that the people, through their

---

* Joseph Lane in 1860 and Charles McNary in 1940 (vice presidential candidate on the GOP ticket with Wendell Willkie) are to date the only Oregonians chosen by a major political party as candidates for president or vice president.

elected representatives, should control their own government and laws. As far as frontier Oregon was concerned, this right to representative self-rule was sacred.[1] The coalition swept to victory in June, although 19 Breckinridge men were elected to the legislature. The Union Party had 31 seats in the House and Senate combined (18 Democrats and 13 Republicans).

Lansing Stout, a Lane Democrat, had been elected Oregon's first congressman in 1859, his term complete in March 1861. Democrats refused to re-nominate Stout and tapped George Shiel, a Lane-Breckinridge-Democrat, instead. Shiel squeaked to a 103-vote victory over Republican David Logan. Many challenged the election's legitimacy because Oregon's constitution had no provision for choosing a congressman in June—November was the time to elect. So, in October, Douglas men nominated A. J. Thayer for Congress. Breckinridge men boycotted the election. Running unopposed in November, Thayer got 4,099 votes, went to Washington, and was officially seated in the House on July 4, 1861. Shiel also went and filed a challenge, claiming he was the rightful Representative. The House reversed itself, removed Thayer, and put Shiel in his place. Thayer had served for twenty-two days. Shiel completed the term, serving until March 1863.

When the legislature met in Salem on September 10, 1860, Douglas-Democrats organized the House, electing Marion County's Ben Harding speaker. The Senate, however, slipped into chaos. Six dissident (Lane) senators went into hiding to keep the 15-member body from having a quorum. Without a quorum, the Senate could do nothing. Absent for two weeks, the senators returned when Gov. John Whiteaker (also a Lane Democrat) asked them to do so. Once organized, the Senate joined the House to tackle the biggest task facing the 1860 session: the election of both of Oregon's U.S. senators. Because the 1859 Legislature had refused to fill the short-term seat originally held by Delazon Smith, that position was still vacant. Senator Joseph Lane's term would end in March 1861.

The choice of senators was complicated by the upcoming November election and the possibility that Republican Abraham Lincoln would be elected president. Would Lincoln's election cause slave-holding states to revolt? If Oregon elected two pro-slave senators, would this upset the delicate balance between pro- and anti-slave forces in the U.S. Senate? Should Oregon vote as the northern, anti-slave state it was? One thing was certain: Joe Lane would not be reelected. Breckinridge-Lane Democrats (and their pro-slavery views) were now a minority in the legislature. Oregon would have two new senators.

John Whiteaker

John Whiteaker was Oregon's first governor after she became a state in 1859. Whiteaker was born in Indiana in 1820. He had little formal schooling and, like his predecessor, George Curry, was self-educated. As a married father of six children, Whiteaker made a living as a carpenter/cabinetmaker. In 1849, he joined the flood of prospectors going to the California Gold Rush. Whiteaker made enough money in California that he could return to Indiana, gather his wife and children, and set out for the Willamette Valley on the Oregon Trail in 1852.

The Whiteakers settled on a farm in Lane County and he plunged into Democratic Party politics. He was elected judge of the probate court for Lane County in 1856 and, a year later, he was elected to the Territorial Legislature. In June 1858, after Oregon men had ratified a state constitution, John Whiteaker was elected governor and was inaugurated on July 8, 1858. But Oregon's new governor could not take office until the Oregon Statehood bill had been adopted—which happened eight months later when President James Buchanan signed the legislation. John Whiteaker officially took office as governor on March 3, 1859.

By the time the Civil War started in April 1861, Governor Whiteaker had painted himself into a corner. Whiteaker's strong pro-slavery, pro-confederacy views had alienated him from the majority of Oregonians; he left office without fanfare on September 10, 1862. Whiteaker's political career revived after the Civil War ended. He was elected to three terms in the Oregon House, serving in the sessions of 1866, 1868, and 1870. His personal popularity returned quickly, as he was elected House Speaker in 1868. Whiteaker was elected to a state Senate seat in 1876 and was immediately elected Senate president for the 1876 and 1878 sessions.

In 1878, John Whiteaker was elected to Oregon's lone congressional seat; he served one term in the U.S. House, 1879-81. Whiteaker's last political position was that of collector of internal revenue in Oregon, a job to which he was appointed in 1885; he held the position until 1889.

John Whiteaker died in Eugene in 1902, age 82. He had enjoyed a political career spanning 33 years, 1856-1889. Oregon's first state governor, John Whiteaker, a self-educated pioneer of the Oregon Trail, had contributed to the early development of his adopted state in ways that only a few men had.

James Nesmith, a longtime Democrat leader, was elected to the six-year Senate term and Edward Dickinson Baker was elected to the shortened term. Baker, a friend of Abraham Lincoln and one of the founders of the Republican Party in California, was an eloquent and charismatic orator who would play a short but colorful part in Oregon's early political history. Fifteen Douglas-Democrats voted with the Republicans to elect Baker, whose election signaled a realignment of Oregon's political parties. Republicans now shared power with Douglas-Democrats and had helped elect Oregon's first Republican senator. It was a remarkable achievement considering that Republicans held only 13 seats in the legislature. Except for Congressman Lansing Stout and Gov. John Whiteaker, the National or Lane-Democrats were without power. The Oregon Legislature dealt Joe Lane's chances of being elected vice president on the Breckinridge ticket a mortal blow.

November election returns revealed the depth of the nation's political divisions. With only 40% of the popular vote (and 180 electoral votes out of 303) Abraham Lincoln was elected president, carrying every northern state, including Oregon and California. A united Democratic Party would have easily carried Oregon in 1860.

The six-month period following Lincoln's election was a critical time for the country. From a Southern viewpoint, the election was interpreted as a threat that struck at the very heart of the Southern social system. And they were quick to act on what they saw. Seven slave states of the Deep South adopted ordinances of secession and by the first of February 1861 they were out of the Union.[2] Abraham Lincoln's inauguration in March 1861 came after the formation of the Confederate States of America. Jefferson Davis of Mississippi was sworn in as president of the Confederacy three weeks before Lincoln took office. When Confederate forces attacked Fort Sumter, South Carolina, on April 12, 1861, Oregonians displayed their devotion to the Union.

Oregon was a solid Union state, but there were thousands who sided with the Southern cause. Because they were a minority, they tended to keep a low profile, but they didn't always keep quiet. For a while, several pro-South newspapers were published in Oregon. Chapters of a national anti-Union organization called the Knights of the Golden Circle also popped up at various Oregon locations. Rebel flags were occasionally unfurled, as well. The presence of Confederate sympathizers could have led to acts of violence in Oregon, but few such episodes occurred. Confrontations typically occurred in the form of newspaper editors taunting one another, or when a shouting match or fistfight broke out. Bloody noses, bruised knuckles, and damaged egos were Oregon examples of Union vs. Confederate expression. An incident in Portland was typical of how Oregonians disagreed. "A party of mounted men rode down Front Street along the Willamette last night, hurrahing Jeff Davis, cursing Abe Lincoln, and defying any person who should cheer Lincoln."[3] Marshal Hoyt and his deputy gave chase but failed to apprehend the boisterous bunch.

Civil War

Responding to the Confederate attack on Fort Sumter, President Lincoln called for 75,000 Union volunteers. Dozens of Oregon men left to serve, some joining the Confederacy, but most hitching up with the Union military. In May 1861, deposed Sen. Joseph Lane came home. Lane's large family and a few old friends and political allies welcomed him. But his strong popular following had deserted him, disgusted by his pro-Southern views. Lane quietly lived out his last 20 years on his Winchester farm near Roseburg.

Governor John Whiteaker, in an "Address to the People," spoke in favor of reconciliation and compromise. Although he personally favored slavery, Whiteaker was appalled by the fighting and urged an end to the bloodshed.

In July, the nation was stunned by news of the gore at the First Battle of Bull Run. Americans now realized that a single battle would not end the war. Julia Ward Howe, pen in hand, composed the Union classic, *Battle Hymn of the Republic*. Reluctantly, the nation settled into war.

Senator Edward Baker had left for Washington, D.C., in October 1860. Sworn in during December, Baker was on hand in the Capitol when war came. Early in the new year, he delivered several passionate Senate speeches against secessionists. When fighting began, Senator Baker joined the Union Army. October 21 found him leading a Union charge across the Potomac near Balls Bluff, Virginia. Gallantly, he led his men directly into Confederate fire. The senator, gray-haired and conspicuous in his officer's uniform, was shot and killed. Edward Dickinson Baker was the only member of the Union Congress to die in battle during the Civil War. Elected senator only seven months after moving to Oregon, Baker died only 10 months after taking his Senate seat. A Union hero was born. For several weeks after his death, Baker's body, dressed in its full officer's uniform, was on display in various cities, attracting thousands of sympathetic mourners, who, in turn, contributed thousands of dollars to the Union war effort. The 1862 Oregon Legislature named a new county in eastern Oregon for Baker, and, a couple of years later, Baker City was born.

Oregon's Union Party Takes Charge

One year into the war, the Union Party held its convention in Eugene in April 1861. Addison C. Gibbs, a Douglas-Democrat, was nominated for governor and John R. McBride for the U.S. House. A week later Breckinridge-Democrats met in Eugene and picked A. E. Wait for Congress and John F. Miller for governor.

The Union Party dominated Oregon's June election. Gibbs was elected governor with 67% of the vote. The legislature met on September 8 for its usual 45-day session. Governor Gibbs was sworn in two days later. The chief task before the assembly was to fill Edward Baker's U.S. Senate seat. Governor Whiteaker had appointed Democrat Benjamin Stark to replace Baker. Republicans thought that one of their party members should have been appointed to the seat, since Baker had been a Republican. Ben Stark was unpopular, had no following in the legislature and he hadn't even been nominated for the seat—and Stark had been appointed by outgoing governor Whiteaker, not elected by the legislature. So, legislative Democrats led a drive to nullify Whiteaker's action, electing their Senate choice, Benjamin Harding, a Douglas-Democrat. Sen. Harding served from September 1862 to March 1865.

While Oregon legislators wrestled with choosing senators, a turning point in the Civil War occurred at Antietam Creek, Maryland, in September 1862. The Union victory allowed President Lincoln to issue the Emancipation Proclamation. Throughout Oregon and the Northwest, white men expressed disgust that Negroes should be freed. If there was anything Oregon and Washington whites disliked, it was the idea of Negro emancipation. Most Northerners fought the Civil War to preserve the Union, not to necessarily end slavery, or to provide equal citizenship to Negroes, free or slave. Only their loathing of abolitionists could match their contempt for Negroes.[4]

Asahel Bush sold the *Statesman* in March 1863 but remained active in the Democratic Party for another five years. Bush embarked on a second career in banking and became one of the wealthiest men in Salem. In the same month, the Union Party nominated J. H. P. Henderson for the U.S. House at their convention in Albany. Six Lincoln delegates were also chosen to attend the Republican National Convention. Democrats nominated James K. Kelly to oppose Henderson.

The June election resulted in a stunning Union Party victory. Henderson rolled over Democrat James Kelly for Congress by over 2,600 votes. Only seven Democrats were elected to the fifty-six-member legislature (two in the Senate and five in the House).

As usual, the legislature convened in Salem in September. Members got right down to business. Who would succeed Senator Ben Harding?[5] George Williams, once a Democratic leader, but now a Union Republican, was elected. The assembly then recessed for a week so members could attend the State Fair in Salem.[6] Watching the judging of cows and sows at the fair was, some members thought, a lot more fun than choosing a United States senator. After their recess lawmakers established two new counties in eastern Oregon, bestowing on them the patriotic names of Union and Grant.

Lincoln: Reelection and Assassination

Abraham Lincoln stood for reelection in 1864. The Republican Party chose pro-Union Tennessee Senator Andrew Johnson, a Democrat, as Lincoln's running mate. Meanwhile, disgruntled Democrats adopted a controversial platform at their national convention. Declaring the war a failure, Democrats demanded a cease-fire. They then nominated Union General George B. McClellan for president.* About 50 men and boys marched through sleepy La Grande, Oregon on the night of February 27, 1864. Carrying torches and signs they chanted "Union, No Free Negroes, and McClellan!"[7] Oregon was afire with political activity. And, as if public order was not already volatile enough, it was time for the legislature to elect a senator.

The fall presidential campaign was unusually emotional. Exhausted by three years of war, a large minority in Oregon and the North wanted to end the war immediately. Many Union-Democratic leaders, including Asahel Bush, James Nesmith, Ben Harding, A. J. Thayer, and Lafayette Grover, returned to the regular Democratic fold and voted for McClellan in November. Despite the defection of these key Democrats the Union coalition stood up well in the election. President Lincoln, who had carried Oregon by only 270 votes in 1860, beat George McClellan by 1,431 votes (out of 18,345 votes cast) in 1864. Oregon's unswerving loyalty to Lincoln and the Union remained the dominant force in Oregon politics.

Portland was home to six thousand residents in 1865. The forest line had been pushed a half-mile west from the Willamette. Streets were unpaved. Boardwalks helped pedestrians stay above the oozing mud during rainy spells. Stray cows and horses were a daily sight, as were chickens, pigs, and dogs. In April, young Harvey Scott took over as editor of the *Oregonian*. Until his death in 1910, Scott was Oregon's most influential newspaperman. His older sister, Abigail Scott Duniway, would soon emerge as the Northwest's leading suffragist.

As a divided nation welcomed 1865, it had one thing on its mind: when would the war be over? With General Sherman still ravaging the Deep South and General Robert E. Lee's army pinned in by General Grant's superior

---

* Lincoln had removed McClellan as commander of the Union Army for failing to follow his orders to engage Confederate troops in battle.

numbers, the end seemed near. On January 31, Congress passed and referred to the states the 13th Amendment to abolish slavery.

Inside a span of six days in 1865, two events occurred in the East that dramatically altered the course of American history. On April 8, Robert E. Lee surrendered to Ulysses S. Grant at Appomattox, Virginia. Officially, the Civil War was over. Celebrating the Union victory on the night of April 14, President and Mrs. Lincoln went to Ford's Theater in Washington, where Lincoln was fatally wounded by the deranged actor, John Wilkes Booth. Oregonians, recently linked by telegraph to the rest of the country, got the terrible news the next morning. Lincoln's death caused an enormous power vacuum. Troubled days were ahead both for Oregon and the nation.

Arguing Over Reconstruction

Addison C. Gibbs, Oregon's popular war-time governor, called a special session of the legislature for December 1865, to ratify the 13th Amendment. Breckinridge-Democrats, led by the *Statesman*, vigorously opposed the amendment. Once Negroes were freed, they asked, what would they demand next? Citizenship? Equal rights? The vote? Would they want to live where whites lived, and compete for white jobs? The *Statesman*, claiming that Negro suffrage was the "most important question of the day" wrote, "We do not believe that any democratic or republican form of government can successfully govern two separate and distinct races in large numbers with equal political rights to both races."[8] While many Union men privately shared these concerns their actions did not reflect those views. After all, Oregon's Negro population was so tiny there was nothing to worry about, was there?

All 43 Union Party legislators voted for the 13th Amendment; the seven Democrats voted no. The 15-day session ended as Oregon slipped into one of its coldest winters ever. The Columbia River froze at its confluence with the Willamette. Great ice blocks backed up the river for miles. The bitter winter foretold the political weather ahead.

Oregonians, like their Union siblings, were torn by the great political and social questions facing the nation in 1865-66. How were the rebel states to be returned to their proper alignment in the Union? What punishment, if any, ought to be imposed on Confederate leaders? What was to become of the Negro? Did government have a role in assuring Blacks their safety and their rights?

Oregon's Union Party Unravels

Since 1860, Oregon had been governed by the Union Party, a political coalition, a fusion of Douglas-Democrats and the youthful Republican Party. What bonded this unusual coalition together was the desire to hold power. It was the overarching reason why the coalition was formed and why it lasted as long as it did. Coalition members were bound by loyalty to the Union and its war effort. Preservation of the Union was as sacred to these men as it was to Abraham Lincoln. Breckinridge-Democrats survived the war years, too, although they were fewer in number and without power. Undaunted, these Democrats continued to hold their annual state convention and regularly nominated candidates for office. Once the war was over, these Democrats came roaring back with a vengeance.

The 1866 election saw Oregon's Union coalition hold together one last time. All Union candidates for major office won with slim margins of victory. George Woods of The Dalles was elected governor, besting James K. Kelly, Democrat, by only 277 votes out of over 20,000 cast. Legislative returns were surprising. After holding 43 seats in 1864-65, many Union men were defeated by Democrats in 1866. Democrats captured 28 seats, a gain of 21. These returns showed that Oregon's war-time coalition was fast unraveling. The Democratic Party—which had controlled Oregon government until 1860—was alive and it was close to regaining power. At their April convention Democrats had adopted 11 resolutions that told much about 1866 party beliefs. First, they stood squarely behind President Johnson in his battle with Congress, which led to his impeachment by the House in 1868; he escaped removal from office by a single vote (both Oregon senators voting for removal). They condemned the protective tariff, national banks, and the squandering of public funds by state officers. They sealed all this with a resolution ridiculing Republicans for trying to turn the Civil War into a party triumph, and for supporting "a war for the Negro instead of the white man."[9] On the other hand, Oregon's Union Party platform of 1866 "pledged to preserve the general government and to support the right of the states in their domestic affairs. The Party also resolved that the so-called Democratic Party is antagonistic to the perpetuity of the Union and destructive of the peace, order and prosperity of the American people."[10]

These platforms reveal the bitter animosity between parties. Democrats charged Republicans with promoting war for selfish purposes as well as for the benefit of Negroes over whites, while Republicans slammed Democrats as the party of disunion, death, and depression. Oregon politics was again turning ugly.

Dumping James Nesmith

The 1866 Legislature fought a lot and little important legislation was passed, with the exception of the approval of the 14th Amendment. Members voted along party lines, the 13 Senate Republicans for ratification, the nine Democratic senators against. In the House, 25 Republicans voted for and 22 Democrats against. The largest appropriation approved by the assembly was for $85,000 "for the support and treatment of lunatics and idiots."[11] The session spent most of its time electing a U.S. senator. Democrat James Nesmith's term was to end in March 1867. Nesmith's record was solid. He had served the state and nation with distinction and had steadfastly supported the Union and Presidents Lincoln and Johnson. He used his influence to frame some very important measures, some of which passed because of his one Democratic vote.[12] He was the only Democrat in the Senate to vote for the 13th Amendment to abolish slavery.[13]

But Oregon Republicans disagreed with Nesmith. The senator had supported George McClellan's presidential bid in 1864, stood by President Andrew Johnson, and did not share Republican views on rights for freedmen. Democrats were also unhappy with the senator, but for different reasons. He was disliked politically for his support of the war and they held a grudge against him because of his 1860 alliance with the Republicans that sent him to the Senate and led to the overthrow of the Oregon Democratic Party.[14] James Nesmith was doomed. Instead, Gov. Addison Gibbs got the nod from the legislature and appeared headed to the Senate. Gibbs needed 35 of the 36 Union Party votes. But John H. Mitchell and several others voted against him, opening the way for Henry Corbett, a former state chairman of the Republican Party and one of the richest men in Oregon, to be elected senator on the 16th ballot. Republicans had a new U.S. senator. They had sacrificed party unity to achieve victory. The 1866 Senate election was the first in a long series of political intrigues that have become part of the history of Oregon's Republican Party and have made the state known for its senatorial vendettas and deadlocks.[15] The personal hatreds aroused in Henry Corbett's 1866 Senate election disrupted Republican unity for the next 40 years. Despite the great numerical majority that Oregon Republicans enjoyed after 1880, their constant internal bickering occasionally doomed their candidates to defeat. Then came the election of 1868.

The Return of the Democrats

In 1868, Oregonians chose state officers and legislators in June and presidential electors in November. Slashing personal attacks and vicious partisan charges marked both campaigns. The question of Negro suffrage and equality was discussed vociferously. Democrats accused Republicans of standing for universal Negro suffrage and battered them with such pungent and ugly questions as "Do you want your daughter to marry a nigger? Would you allow a nigger to force himself into a seat at church between you and your wife?"[16] Pounding away at Negroes and taxes, Democrats succeeded in attracting some Republican votes and swamped their Republican foes in June. From 28 seats in the 1866 Legislature, Democrats surged to 43 seats in 1868. In four years the Democrats had roared back from being a shadow party to being the majority party.

Two factors account for this Democratic resurgence. Hundreds of Democrats hadn't voted in the 1862 and 1864 elections, turned off by the war, Abraham Lincoln, and the Union Party coalition. With the war over and Lincoln gone, in 1866 Democrats returned in large numbers to the polls and did so again in 1868. In the last year of the war, 1864-65 (and in 1866-67), hundreds of Border State Democrats from around Missouri immigrated to Oregon, swelling Democratic ranks by 1868. The racist Democratic platform appealed to many voters. When they added charges of Republican corruption and extravagant spending in state government, the combination was irresistible for many Oregon voters.

Now back in control for the first time since statehood, Democrats flexed their new muscle in the 1868 legislative session. Virtually every action they took was intended to embarrass Republicans. They passed a resolution requesting Republican Senators Williams and Corbett to resign. (The U.S. Senate returned the resolution without comment.) They then overturned Oregon's earlier ratification of the 14th Amendment, drafted by a Republican Congress. They refused to ratify the 15th Amendment, which prohibited states from denying a citizen the right to vote based on the citizen's race, color, or previous condition of servitude. Republicans in retaliation blocked all legislative action. The session was prolonged, and on the 43rd day the Republicans withdrew, leaving the legislature without a quorum. Appropriation bills failed, and the state departments had no funds for two years.[17] In November, Democrat Horatio Seymour carried Oregon in the presidential election. Oregon was one of only three northern states to vote Democratic in 1868.

The 1870s found Democrats with such a tight grip on state government that the era was called the Democrat Decade. For most of the decade Democrats held the governorship, the offices of secretary of state and treasurer, controlled the legislature, and—except for John Mitchell's election to the U.S. Senate in 1872—held Oregon's other Senate seat and lone U.S. House seat. Yet it was also a time of political re-alignment in Oregon. Despite the Democrats' dominance, the Republican Party attracted thousands of new members. By 1880, Republicans would be ready to take and hold power again.

Building on their 1868 victory, Oregon Democrats won big in the election of 1870. LaFayette Grover was elected governor, Stephen Chadwick was elected secretary of state, and Democrat James Slater replaced Joseph S. Smith in the U.S. House. The 1870 Legislature filled Republican Sen. George Williams' seat with Democrat James K. Kelly.

The Legislature of 1870 was bitterly partisan. Democrats, standing on a state party platform condemning the 14th and 15th amendments, again refused to ratify the latter and adopted a resolution blasting it as an infringement on states' rights. Democrats established a three-man committee to investigate charges of official misconduct in the preceding administration of Republican Gov. George Woods. The committee also investigated claims of possible malfeasance in the office of Secretary of State Samuel B. May, where a shortage of several thousand dollars was found.[18] (May was indicted and stood trial in

LaFayette Grover

COURTESY OF THE OREGON STATE ARCHIVES, GOVERNORS PHOTOS.

LaFayette Grover was Oregon's fourth governor and the first chief executive to be reelected to a second term. LaFayette was born in Maine in 1823, the son of a prominent surgeon and politician. In an age when many Oregon politicians were self-educated, LaFayette Grover was an exception. He graduated from Maine's Bowdoin College before going to Philadelphia to study law, and was admitted to the Pennsylvania Bar in 1850. But, like so many ambitious young adults of his day, LaFayette Grover could not resist the lure of California and the Pacific Northwest. So, at the end of 1850, Grover boarded a ship bound for San Francisco, a nine-month journey around Cape Horn.

Within weeks of his arrival in San Francisco, Grover decided that greener pastures awaited him in Oregon. Arriving in Salem in fall 1851, Grover hung out a shingle, announcing that his law practice was now open. Within months, however, he took the job of clerk of the U.S. District Court, before returning to private practice. From this point, Grover began to mix his law practice with holding government jobs while also embarking on pioneering business ventures. A founder and director of the Willamette Woolen Manufacturing Company in Salem, Grover was instrumental in the company's growth between 1856 and 1871. A man of boundless energy, LaFayette Grover next went into the wheat/flour business.

Marion County in 1873; he was acquitted 11-1 by a jury that included some of his acquaintances.) Republicans bristled at these Democratic actions, charging they were merely partisan attempts to embarrass and discredit their party. They retaliated: Democrats were the party of war and disunion! Republicans are the saviors of the Union. The only way to safeguard peace and prosperity is to put Republicans in power everywhere.[19] The old Civil War wounds remained open and raw.

Democrats ran incumbent LaFayette Grover for governor and George La Dow for Congress in the June 1874 election. With 38% of the vote, Governor Grover was reelected by a 550-vote margin over Republican J. C. Tolman. La Dow also won, but he died in early March 1875 before taking his seat, leaving it unfilled until October 1875.

An Independent Party candidate for governor, T. F. Campbell, pulled 25% of the June vote. The Independent Party attracted thousands of reform-minded citizens. Their candidate for Supreme Court, John Burnett, was elected, as were

Wheat was one of Oregon's most important export crops and Grover was right in the middle of the action. From 1867 to 1871, he managed the Salem Flouring Mill, Oregon's first wheat-exporting company. Grover was a 42-year-old bachelor when he finally married in 1865.

Grover's political career had taken-off shortly after his arrival in Oregon in 1851. In 1852, he was elected prosecuting attorney for the 2nd Judicial District of Oregon. He was elected to the Territorial Legislature in 1853 and reelected in 1855; he was House speaker in 1855-56. Grover was elected Oregon's first U.S. representative, a position he would take once Congress finally passed the statehood bill. Grover's term in the House lasted only 17 days, February 15-March 3, 1859. Grover devoted himself to his business enterprise during the 1860s.

LaFayette Grover was elected governor in 1870, defeating Republican Joel Palmer by 627 votes. He was reelected in 1874 with 38% of the vote, due to the presence of a popular third-party candidate. Grover resigned on February 1, 1877, after the legislature elected him to the U.S. Senate, where he served until 1883.

LaFayette Grover was the first Oregon governor to make fish a political issue. A conservationist, he was the first politician to propose establishing a state fish commission and the need to build a fish ladder at the Oregon City Falls. Grover was also a vocal critic of Chinese workers and wanted to stop them from settling here. Gov. Grover called for establishing a state university (the University of Oregon was founded in 1876) and an agricultural college (Oregon State University today).

LaFayette Grover ranks as one of early Oregon's most influential politicians and business visionaries. His long, eventful life ended in Portland in 1911; he was 88.

a number of Independent candidates for the legislature. The appearance (and minor success) of an Independent Party in Oregon in the mid-1870s was not unusual. A handful of splinter or third party groups were active throughout the decade. Farmers and small-businessmen were unhappy with high freight rates (ship and rail), low crop prices, high interest rates on loans, and a shortage of currency in circulation. Ordinary citizens were upset with alleged corruption and cozy relationships between politicians, government employees, and wealthy businessmen. With so much discontent Oregonians sometimes turned away from the established Democrat and Republican parties, joining, for brief periods, various reform groups seeking political answers to their economic and social problems. One such organization was the Patrons of Husbandry, better known as the Grange. Founded in 1867, the Grange was a secret society primarily for farmers. Its chief purpose was to provide a social outlet for members as well as educational programs. The Grange quickly spread westward, especially taking hold in the Midwest. The first Grange chapter was established in Oregon in 1873 in Clackamas County. By 1875 there were 11,000 Grangers (including women) belonging to 112 Oregon chapters. It was Grange men who subsequently became the backbone of various third-party political movements in Oregon over the next 30 years.

Growing

Oregon's population grew from 91,000 in 1870 to 175,000 in 1880. Because the fertile Willamette Valley was filling up, newer settlers were forced to take lands east of the Cascades, or along Oregon's Pacific shore. Small towns became big towns. Villages became small towns. Portland was Oregon's only true city, growing from about 9,000 inhabitants in 1870 to 21,500 residents in 1880. Salem, East Portland, and Astoria ranked next in size with populations of 4,100, 3,900, and 2,750.

Oregon continued to establish and expand its manufacturing-industrial base. Flour milling, lumbering, salmon canning and packing, and wool spinning and weaving were growing industries. Agriculture remained king, with wheat becoming Oregon's most valuable export crop. Raising sheep and orchard crops were also profitable pursuits. Most Oregonians were self-sufficient farmers, people who grew their own food, and either made or bartered for their basic necessities, such as tools, seed, and clothing. They were a practical, rural folk, often skeptical, and fiercely independent.

Oregon's economy remained insulated from the national economy in the 1870s. Aside from markets in northern California, Washington and Idaho territories, and a growing wheat and flour trade with Europe, Oregon was trapped by her remoteness. This isolation motivated farmers, merchants, and investors to expand Oregon's transportation system. Steamboats regularly plied the Willamette River from Eugene to Portland, and the Columbia from Astoria all the way inland to the Snake River. Smaller vessels linked remote areas to the Willamette via its many tributaries. The railroad reached Eugene from Portland in 1871. Rail service expanded in the Columbia Gorge from Portland inland to Walla Walla and beyond. Roads were built throughout the Willamette Valley and over the Cascades and Coast Range. Nonetheless, small businessmen, like farmers, were unhappy with Oregon's poor transportation system. There were too few roads and not nearly enough railroad track (there were only 159 miles of track in Oregon in 1870). The coastal region and the vast eastern lands were remote and physically cut off from the bustling Willamette Valley-Portland economy.

Woman of the Century

Farmers and small businessmen were not the only disgruntled Oregonians. Women were awakening to their predicament of being politically, socially, and economically second-class citizens. Women had few legal rights and they could not vote (except in school elections) or hold public office. In 1871, a pioneer wife and mother of six set out to change women's status: Abigail Scott Duniway launched the women's suffrage movement in Oregon and the Pacific Northwest.

"Converted early to the women's movement, Abigail Scott Duniway began writing letters to the editor of the *Oregon Argus* as a twenty-four-year-old farm wife in 1858, declaring for the equality of the sexes."[20] When her husband, Ben Duniway, was disabled in a wagon accident, she became the family breadwinner. By 1870, Duniway had experienced discrimination in many forms. At the time, married women had no right to their own earnings, no property rights other than as donation land grant brides, no right to guardianship over their children, and no legal recourse against husbands who might gamble or drink away family savings or desert their wives.[21] As a businesswoman she became even more aware of the legal, economic, and social obstacles she faced as a woman.

In 1870, Abigail Duniway made her first public speech in favor of women's suffrage. She and two other women formed the Equal Rights Society in Albany. For Duniway suffrage was the key to women's equality. "Her ideas and her tactics guided Oregon suffragists through four of their six campaigns. In fact, her control of the state suffrage association was for years so complete that only those women who supported both her ideas and tactics held positions of power in the organization."[22] Abigail Duniway and her supporters faced enormous hurdles. They lacked political influence and access to power, and were faced with the task of educating and persuading people around the state. The Oregon suffragists used the two free sources of public communication available to them: the lecture hall and the newspaper. They delivered hundreds of speeches, planned public events to attract press coverage, wrote innumerable letters to the editors of state newspapers, and started their own pro-suffrage weeklies. In May 1871, Abigail Duniway published the first edition of her suffrage newspaper, *New Northwest*. It was the first—and during almost 16 years the only—woman suffrage newspaper in the Pacific Northwest.[23] "Without press discussion of the suffrage issue, the movement could not hope for success at the polls."[24] Despite the tireless efforts of Duniway and her small band of supporters, it would be many years before women in Oregon gained the right to vote.

Chapter 4
John Mitchell and Other Tales of Corruption, 1868-73

Oregon was six years old when the Civil War ended in 1865, its infant institutions still rough and ill-formed. Traditions were forming, yet change was the rule. It was during these formative years that a sinister force took hold in Oregon. For the next 40 years Oregon's politicians and government were captive to political corruption. Unprincipled, greedy men lusted for political power—and all too often gained it. Oregon was riddled with graft. Common attitudes were "If you want to do business with me, it will cost you," or "How much are you willing to pay for my vote?" Oregon's political institutions were the tools by which a few advanced their narrow interests. Among the corrupt were governors, secretaries of state, U.S. senators and congressmen, city and county officials. Corruption knew no limits, as both Republicans and Democrats were caught in its web.

Not all officeholders were corrupt. Many dedicated and honest men held office during this period. Yet among state legislators, many were as likely as not to take a bribe. Others were willing to sell their vote for a promise of a job or contract for themselves, a friend, business partner, or family member. For such men political power was a ticket to riches and influence. It was an age when politics was played for intensely selfish purposes.

Bribes, usually in the form of a $20 or $100 bill, were the most common type of political corruption. Cash bribes were regularly offered to legislators on two occasions: when a vote on a key bill was pending (especially if there was a lot of money to be made), or when the legislature was voting on the office of U.S. senator. Indeed, Oregon's most notorious episodes of political corruption occurred during the election of two U.S. senators. In virtually every senatorial vote between 1872 and 1906, thousands of dollars (on one occasion, $300,000) flooded the State Capitol as eager candidates and their rich backers vied for votes among legislators. In the late 1890s, Republican lawmakers demanded $4,000 for their senatorial vote; minority Democrats got $3,000.[1]

Ben Holladay, Wheeler-Dealer

Benjamin Holladay, the "Stagecoach King" moved to Portland from California in August 1868. Within days, he had a new friend and ally, John H. Mitchell. Mitchell was Ben Holladay's lawyer, advisor, mouthpiece, and henchman. For five years, the Holladay-Mitchell team rattled Oregon's fragile political institutions to their foundations.

Ben Holladay was a shrewd, bold, sometimes reckless capitalist. A self-made millionaire, he was known for his ruthless business ethics. He had lots of money that he spent liberally. Ben Holladay was the man who introduced Oregon to big-time political corruption.

Many Portlanders wondered why such a successful businessman would forsake California's many riches in favor of doing business in Oregon. Oregon, after all, was a crude and isolated backwater. The answer was simple: Ben Holladay intended to be on the ground floor of Oregon's budding railroad age. His goal was to build Oregon's first railroad line from Portland into northern California. Holladay relished challenges. And what could be more of a challenge than directing the building of a railroad across nearly 300 miles of raw Oregon frontier? The financing, engineering and grading, the laying of track, the construction of bridges and trestles, and the opening of new markets—these were the challenges that drew Ben Holladay to the Willamette Valley. For those bold enough to take big risks, the reward could result in a life of influence, fame, wealth, and comfort. It was the potential for huge profits, made quickly, that attracted Ben Holladay and others like him to Oregon in the 1860s and 1870s.

Land Scams

Oregon's greatest resource was land, millions and millions of acres of it just waiting to be claimed. Across the land, roads and rail track could be built, on it stood vast coniferous forests, representing billions of board-feet of valuable, quality lumber, and beneath its surface lay rich mineral deposits. The men ready to compete for the title to Oregon's public lands would capture the great wealth that the land represented. Men like Ben Holladay, Henry Villard, S .A. D. Puter, John Ainsworth, Simeon Reed, Henry Corbett, Joseph Gaston, and John Mitchell set out to take title to as much of Oregon as they could. This is how they did it.

Over half of Oregon's land area of 97,000 square miles consists of what is called the "public domain." Lands in the public domain are "owned" by the federal government; these lands technically belong to the people of the United States and are held in trust by our national government. In Oregon the federal government made these lands available to the public in two ways. "Under various acts, 4.47 million acres were sold by the federal government, 4.8 million acres donated to the railroads, and 2.5 million acres were given to military road companies. Second, the federal government granted land to the states for internal improvements and educational purposes. Through this policy, Oregon received [an additional] 4.2 million acres of land."[2]

The state of Oregon, primarily through the legislature, was a major player in deciding which companies would get title to nearly 6.8 million acres of public land. This awesome responsibility fell to a few dozen lawmakers. In the end, those who got the titles to Oregon's valuable public lands were those individuals and groups who most successfully influenced the state's legislators and governors. Here is where corruption entered Oregon politics in a big way. To those who coveted these lands money was no object. Buy a vote, buy a legislator—it was worth it. The legislatures were besieged by railroads and land companies seeking special favors. Most legislators and officials chose not to maintain their integrity and succumbed to pressure. Large portions of the public domain fraudulently passed into the hands of land syndicates and a few transportation companies, many of them bogus.

The military road (or wagon road) companies were the first in Oregon to benefit from government land grants. The state legislature would incorporate a company for the purpose of road construction and then petition Congress to grant the necessary land.[3] Between 1856 (when Oregon was still a territory) and 1869, Congress donated 2.5 million acres to five Oregon road companies. The state legislatures were even more generous, with each session petitioning Congress to grant more public lands to additional road companies.* When grants were not forthcoming, the legislatures came to the aid of the companies with large grants of state money.[4] Congress made no further grants to Oregon road companies after 1869. Legislatures, however, kept right on requesting such grants for another decade. By 1869 it was already clear that the so-called military road companies were working a swindle. Most of them were not constructing roads, but were using the lands solely for the purposes of re-selling their land donations to the highest bidder. In essence, they were real estate companies rather than road companies.[5]

Oregon Gov. George L. Woods was implicated in The Dalles Military Road Company scam. In 1869, Woods certified that The Dalles group had, in fact,

---

* The five military road companies were: Oregon Central, Corvallis and Yaquina Bay, Willamette Valley and Cascade Mountains, The Dalles, and the Coos Bay Military Road Company.

completed 10 continuous miles of road, making it eligible for a hefty federal land grant. Woods lied. No such road was built and Woods knew it. He lied in order to protect the economic interests of friends. In doing so, Woods helped set a pattern of land fraud that lasted in Oregon until after 1900.

The Railroads

Congress, in 1866, had given the Oregon Legislature an important task: choose a company to build a railroad connecting Oregon to California. The company the legislature picked would receive a 3.8-million-acre land grant—right through the heart of western Oregon. Two rival groups sought the legislature's approval. The politicians chose the Oregon Central Railroad Company (OCRC). The OCRC's competitor did not, however, give up. Instead, the rival group also incorporated, under the same name. Both companies began construction, one as the West Side Company, and the other as the East Side Company (named for the side of the Willamette River each occupied).

Guess who bought a major interest in the East Side Company in 1868? Newcomer Ben Holladay. Holladay knew that his East Side Company would fail if it did not wrestle the land grant away from his West Side rivals. Holladay "arranged to finance more construction through purchase of the railroad's heavily discounted bonds, and recruited such prominent non-Portlanders as Asa Lovejoy, Asahel Bush, and Governor George L. Woods as [company] directors."[6] Holladay also hired the ambitious John Mitchell as his lawyer. Mitchell served as Holladay's bagman during the 1868 legislative session. Holladay wanted the East Side's land grant and he would do what it took to get it. He wanted lawmakers to reverse themselves, taking the charter away from the West Side Company and transferring it to his East Side line. Like locusts, the Holladay gang descended on the legislature when it convened in September 1868.

Most legislators were farmers, and they had never seen anything like the Ben Holladay machine. Holladay admitted shelling out $35,000 to influence them. After six weeks of parties, promises, and flowing cask and cash, legislators voted to take the 1866 land grant away from the West Side railroad group and give it to Holladay's East Side Company. Ben Holladay had bought himself a legislature. By 1870, Holladay gained controlling interest in the East Side line and changed its name to the Oregon and California Railroad. "Holladay then issued $10.9 million in bonds guaranteed by the lands he expected to receive from the federal government."[7] He subsequently sold all the bonds. In so doing, however, he assumed huge interest payments, which started his financial ruin three years later.

But between 1868 and 1873, Ben Holladay was the most powerful man in Oregon. He selected candidates, both Democrat and Republican, for the legislature. As rail baron he set the stage for what followed: an age in which railroad companies wielded more political muscle in Oregon than any other interest group. These companies were among the most corrupt influences to ever enter Oregon politics. The railroads controlled Oregon's political parties, its legislatures, its U.S. senators and representatives. Even mayors, sheriffs, and other local officials were under the influence of the railroad bosses. Exactly how did Ben Holladay and his competitors get so much control over Oregon's public officials? Basically with money and free rail passes. Holladay began the practice of providing free annual rail passes to Oregon's officeholders. For legislators, a rail pass was like money in the bank. Lawmakers, when traveling on official business, were reimbursed at the rate of ten cents a mile. With a free rail pass, most lawmakers submitted their expense vouchers anyway, thus collecting money to which they were not entitled. The free pass was the first brick in the structure through which a candidate for U.S. Senate built support in the legislature.[8] Legislators had no trouble getting rail passes, giving them as favors to friends. It was good business and smart politics to have a friend close to a railroad executive.

Something Is Rotten in Oregon

The 1868 Legislature did more than just make Ben Holladay happy. It also lavished gifts on a coterie of prominent fellow Democrats, presenting a classic example of bald-faced political favoritism. These shady dealings sparked a bitter political controversy that raged in Oregon for ten years. Here's what happened.

Back in 1862 a group of Willamette Valley investors, fed-up with the Oregon Steam Navigation Company's monopoly on the Willamette River, had formed the People's Transportation Company (PTC). Through stock sales the company purchased and ran several steamboats on the river. In 1865, the PTC began to construct improvements at Willamette Falls, long an obstacle to inland traffic. Without government aid, the company spent $100,000 to build a 1,000-foot dam and breakwater above the falls, and a huge warehouse and inclined railway. These projects had a dramatic effect. Passengers and freight were now moved from one ship (either above or below the falls) to another vessel in only ten minutes. Considerable time and money was saved. But there was more to be done.

By the time legislators convened in September 1868, there was growing public support for a canal and locks at Willamette Falls. Responding to

John Hipple Mitchell

John Mitchell was the most influential politician in Oregon for 40 years. He was also the most corrupt and immoral. Mitchell was an adulterer, wife beater, and bigamist. Within weeks of arriving in Oregon, Mitchell was Portland's new city attorney. Two years later he was elected to the state Senate and was immediately chosen president of that chamber. By the end of the decade John Mitchell was Ben Holladay's attorney—Holladay was a corrupt transportation baron. Mitchell's law partner was Joseph Dolph. The law firm of Mitchell and Dolph became the seat of Republican Party power in Oregon. In 1872, the Republican Legislature elected John Mitchell to  the U.S. Senate. Mitchell won the coveted Senate seat by identifying and backing Republican legislative candidates who supported him, and by bribing lawmakers. With Ben Holladay's money, Mitchell had bought a Senate seat. Over the next 30 years, Mitchell was reelected three times (in 1884, 1890, and 1900). Altogether, Mitchell served in the Senate for 22-years.

John Mitchell was charming and charismatic, a man noted for his spellbinding speeches—qualities which served him well. With his long, neatly trimmed beard, wire spectacles, and "senatorial bearing," John Mitchell, along with his nemesis, Joseph Simon, controlled Oregon politics with an iron grip. Bribery was not the only tool Mitchell used to retain power. He also made promises to powerful backers, and relied heavily on his power to dispense government jobs (patronage) to his friends and their relatives.

Political corruption was common in Oregon and the rest of the nation in the late 19th century. John H. Mitchell just happened to be one of the cleverest and most corrupt politicians ever spawned in Oregon. Finally, in 1905, John Mitchell was indicted for accepting a bribe of $2,000. A Portland jury (of all white men) found Mitchell guilty as charged. The judge sentenced Mitchell to six months in jail and fined him $1,000. Senator Mitchell appealed the verdict, remaining free while his case made its way through the courts. In December, Senator Mitchell died while in a diabetic coma induced during a dental procedure in Portland. He was 71 years old. His trial re-energized Oregon's political reform movement, which in 1902 had passed the initiative and referendum. In 1904, voters passed a Direct Primary Law—giving them the power to nominate candidates for public office—thus bypassing the political cliques that had dominated Oregon for years.

popular will, lawmakers decided to award a grant of $150,000 to a company it would choose to build the proposed locks and canal. The public assumed the PTC was the logical choice to get the state's construction subsidy. With its own funds, the PTC had already done much to enhance river travel. Its service was efficient, though its rates were high. But the legislature awarded the subsidy not to the PTC, but to a brand new company. On the same day the legislature convened, September 14, six prominent Oregonians formed a new corporation called the Willamette Falls Canal and Locks Company (WFCLC). The established People's Transportation Company was ignored—despite its offer to construct the project for $125,000, which was $75,000 less than the WFCLC said it needed to do the job. The Democratic Legislature had caved in to its friends. Several of Oregon's leading Democrats were partners in the new company, including company president Bernard Goldsmith (mayor of Portland, 1869-71, and later state party chairman), Col. James K. Kelly (Democratic U.S. senator, 1871-77), Capt. John F. Miller (former Democratic nominee for governor), and wealthy Democratic businessman Joseph Teal, Sr. David P. Thompson and Judge Orlando Humason, both Republicans and OSN stockholders, were the other major partners. Behind this deal was a story of corruption. To make matters worse, the Democratic Legislature of 1870 increased to $200,000 the canal-locks bill it had passed two years before. Public outrage grew. Fanned by a newspaper assault on Democratic lawmakers, citizens demanded an investigation of the alleged wrongdoing. The *Oregonian*, in its May 21, 1872 edition, charged that "first and last it cost the company [WFCLC] between $25,000 and $30,000 to get the legislature fixed up to its liking."[9] This sensational revelation came on the eve of the June legislative elections. For the only time between 1868 and 1880, Democrats lost their House and Senate majorities.

In the final days of the 1872 session Republicans passed two resolutions. For the first time ever in Oregon a legislative investigation committee was set up. The first was to look into Democratic charges of widespread corruption in the administration of Republican Gov. George L. Woods, 1866-70. The second resolution, according to the *House Journal of 1872*, established a Select Committee of Five to investigate allegations of legislative corruption in the 1868 and 1870 sessions.*

---

* No reference to such a body appears in either the *1874* or *1876 House Journals*. As far as can be determined the Select Committee never materialized. Two subsequent legislative investigation reports were published, one in 1873 and the other in 1879. Neither contained allegations of bribery or other forms of illegal behavior in the granting of the lock and canal subsidy to the WFCLC in 1868 and 1870. Both reports, however, did unearth extensive corruption in the Woods administration. Charged with a host of crimes was Samuel E. May, secretary of state from 1862 to 1870. Also implicated in wrongdoing were the warden of the state penitentiary, the state treasurer, and May's successor, Stephen Chadwick, among others. May was indicted in 1873 and stood trial in Salem.

After building the locks, the Willamette Falls Canal and Locks Company began running boats on the Willamette. The PTC sold out in 1873 to Ben Holladay, the other competitor in the Willamette Valley. The OSNC bought out the WFCLC in 1875 and reorganized it under the name Willamette Transportation and Locks Company. Soon after, all major transportation in the Willamette Valley passed into the hands of Henry Villard. In 1878, Villard took over Holladay's holdings and, in 1879, bought the OSNC and its subsidiary, the Willamette Transportation and Locks Company.[10] So ends one sordid chapter of political favoritism, legislative corruption, and unmitigated greed. Unfortunately, similar episodes were to follow.

The term of Oregon's Republican U.S. senator, George Williams, ended in March 1871. Ben Holladay and his trusty bagman, John Mitchell, spent huge sums trying to buy enough legislators' votes to save the seat for Williams.[11] With Democrats controlling the legislature, Williams had no hope of reelection. Democrats chose one of their own, James K. Kelly, to replace him. George Williams consoled himself by accepting President Ulysses Grant's offer to be Attorney General of the United States, a position he filled from 1871 to 1875.

Portland held a city primary election in May 1872 and Ben Holladay's money flowed once again. Holladay recruited agents to make the rounds of hotels and boarding houses, promising to pay residents a $2.50 gold piece to vote. Many voted several times, taking another coin each time. A traditionally Democratic precinct went Republican for the first time. At day's end, Holladay had helped reelect three friendly city councilmen."[12]

The Lowdown on John Hipple Mitchell

John Hipple Mitchell was the most powerful politician in Oregon between 1872 and 1905. He was also the most corrupt. From his arrival in Portland in July 1860, until his peculiar death in December 1905, John H. Mitchell connived to get himself elected and reelected senator. Seven times Mitchell ran for the position. On four occasions Oregon's Legislature elected him (1872, 1885, 1891, and 1901).*

The all-male jury included acquaintances of the defendant. The jury voted eleven to one to acquit May. Legislative investigators determined that over $96,000 in state monies had been illegally spent or stolen by state officials between 1864 and 1871. The aroma of political corruption was to linger in Oregon for the next thirty years. See *House Journals*, Oregon State Library, Salem.

* In total John H. Mitchell served twenty-two years in the U.S. Senate, a record not duplicated until Republican Charles McNary reached the midway point in his fourth term in 1939. McNary's record of longevity was surpassed by Sen. Mark Hatfield, also a Republican, who served five full terms, between January 1967 and January 1997.

Whether he won or lost, Mitchell's campaigns were notoriously corrupt and the money spigot was always wide open. If bribery didn't coax a reluctant lawmaker, he resorted to other tactics. Mitchell, forever courteous and quick to flatter, would wine and dine the solon, often extracting the man's vote after a beef steak and a bottle or two of whiskey. If these methods failed then there was the promise of favors (such as a government job for the politician's friend or relative). As a last resort Mitchell was not above making threats. More often than not John Mitchell got his way. He used his personal charm, "generosity," and striking appearance (he had a long, well-trimmed beard that grew whiter as he aged), along with a direct, forceful way of talking to make him "a favorite son for a majority of Oregonians until the end of his life."[13]

John Hipple was born in Pennsylvania in 1835. In 1855 he took a teaching job in Butler County, Pennsylvania. The next spring, Sarah Hoon, one of Hipple's 15-year-old students, gave birth to his child. Hoon's father threatened to press charges against Hipple—who relented and married Miss Hoon. Over the next three years Hipple studied law and opened a local practice. Sarah bore him two more children. During these years Hipple was brought to court for wife beating. After relatives intervened, Sarah Hipple agreed to withdraw the charges and the case was dropped. Meanwhile, Hipple began an affair with Maria J. Brinker, and moved her into his home. When Sarah protested, Hipple threatened to kill her if she ever again complained about Maria.

In early 1860, John Hipple stole $4,000 belonging to clients of his law firm, packed up his four-year-old daughter, Jessie, and his mistress, Maria, and fled to California. Sarah and the other two babies were left penniless. In July 1860, John Hipple arrived in Portland— with Jessie but without Maria, who, like Sarah, he had abandoned. Hipple introduced himself in Portland by an assumed name, John Hiram Mitchell. He joined the new Multnomah County Republican Party. A month later Mitchell was appointed Portland's first city attorney. In 1862, Mitchell formed a law practice with an ambitious newcomer from New York, Joseph Dolph. Mitchell also married Mattie Price of Oregon City and won a state Senate seat in the legislature. Mattie gave birth to six children. Until 1869, Mitchell had two wives and at least seven children. In 1871, Mitchell fell in love with his sister-in-law and began a torrid seven-year affair.

Prior to 1872 no one in Portland suspected John Mitchell was really two men. Most saw him as a prosperous attorney, a Republican Party leader, a former state senator, and Ben Holladay's personal lawyer. Mitchell's enemies were, however, about to expose him.

No Love Lost

Republicans faced a tough decision in 1872. Their U.S. senator, wealthy Portlander Henry W. Corbett, wanted a second term. But Corbett faced a serious challenge from John H. Mitchell. With $20,000 of Ben Holladay's money, Mitchell went to the state Republican Convention in spring 1872 to meet Henry Corbett head-on. When the battle was over, 37-year-old Mitchell had emerged with his party's nomination. From that spring of 1872 until his death in 1903, Corbett never forgave Mitchell; he made Mitchell his political enemy for life. The Republican Party had split, with Mitchellites pitted against Corbettites. This GOP schism lasted for nearly 40 years. And it became one of the most distinctive features of Oregon politics until after 1900. As long as both men lived, Republican unity was impossible. When the legislature met in fall, it elected John Mitchell U.S. senator. So began the long and checkered Senate career of Oregon's most notorious politician.

Henry Corbett was not, however, done with John Mitchell. In October, Corbett bought a controlling interest in Henry L. Pittock's financially strapped *Oregonian* newspaper. Portland city councilman William Lair Hill was hired as editor. Hill began to dig into Mitchell's past. In spring 1873, Hill wrote and published a detailed and vivid account of John Mitchell's bigamous life, naming names and retelling the story of his flight from Pennsylvania and abandonment of his young wife and their two infants. Mitchell's marriage to Mattie Price, while still wedded to Sarah, was exposed. Oregonians were dumbfounded. Corbettites gloated. Mitchell protested. The senator branded the *Oregonian* story a pack of lies. Counterattacking, Mitchell accused Hill and Corbett of trying to get even for Corbett's recent defeat. It was nothing more than a case of sour grapes, said Mitchell. The wily Mitchell then appealed to Republican legislators to decide whether or not he was telling the truth, whether he was worthy to be their United States senator. When Republicans met in their annual state convention in 1873 they adopted a resolution pardoning Mitchell for any past "indiscretions" and confirming their support for him as both a man and a Republican politician. It seemed, over the next 33 years, that whatever John Mitchell did, no matter how dishonest, how immoral, or how corrupt, he always seemed to have enough friends in the Oregon Legislature to be reelected senator.

Getting "Guts" Gibbs

Joseph G. Smith was elected Oregon's new congressman in November 1872, but died before taking office. Republicans chose another Smith, Hiram, of Linn County, to replace him, while Democrats picked their popular former U.S. senator, James "Nes" Nesmith, as their U.S. House candidate. John Mitchell and

Ben Holladay tried to rig the Portland election in Smith's favor by funneling money into vote fraud activities. They also padded their campaign treasury by assessing federal officeholders such as postmasters, marshals, customs officials, people whose jobs were held at the pleasure of Oregon's senators. Vote buying and repeat voting occurred on such flagrant scale that the *Oregonian* estimated that one-quarter of Portland votes cast were illegal.[14] Yet Nesmith overcame Holladay's skullduggery and was elected with 57% of the vote statewide.

With so many rumors and editorial charges of vote fraud in Portland, federal officials decided to investigate. Because the contest was a federal election, charges of wrongdoing brought it under U.S. District Court jurisdiction. Matthew P. Deady, U.S. District Judge, presided over the legal proceedings. Representing the Department of Justice was Addison "Guts" Gibbs, U.S. Attorney in Oregon. Gibbs, former governor of Oregon, was honest and incorruptible. Deady presented the grand jury with a strong charge of illegal voting and the corrupting of the voting procedure. Yet the jurors refused to vote for indictments even in those cases where the proof of guilt was overwhelming. Gibbs investigated quietly and found that unnamed but obviously interested parties had arranged for sympathetic men to serve on the grand jury. Gibbs asked Deady to discharge the grand jury and order another. Judge Deady obliged, with the instruction that the new list of potential jurors be drawn by selecting one hundred and fifty at random from the assessment rolls. Mitchell had already discovered Deady was untouchable, so he demanded of Attorney General of the United States, George Williams, an Oregonian, that Gibbs be either forced to desist, or be removed. At the time Williams was awaiting Senate confirmation as Chief Justice of the United States. His was an unpopular appointment and Mitchell threatened to withdraw his support if Williams did not halt the prosecution of the bribery cases. All the while Gibbs continued presenting evidence and securing indictments. But he wasn't given the opportunity to reach the people at the top. Gibbs was charged with insubordination and Williams summarily removed him.[15]

Senator John Mitchell played hardball. The truth about vote fraud never came out. Mitchell had saved his own hide and that of Ben Holladay's, too. Over the ensuing years Senator Mitchell became a master manipulator, using his Senate powers for personal and political benefit.

The Era of Democratic Domination Ends

Democratic control of the Oregon Legislature ended in 1880 when Republicans won a majority in both houses. For the next 77 years the state Senate would remain in Republican hands, as would the Oregon House for the following 55 years.

Three future governors were among the 90 members of the 1880 Legislature: Zenas F. Moody (who was House speaker in 1880), George Chamberlain, and Theodore Geer. Chamberlain, a Mississippi transplant, had arrived in Oregon in 1876. Geer remarked on his friendly, personal approach to politics: "At the end of the first week [of the session] he [Chamberlain] knew Jim from eastern Oregon and Tom from [Jackson] well enough to slap them on the shoulder and walk out of the State House arm-in-arm with them, thus laying the foundation of [his future] popularity."[16]

Chapter 5

Money, Corruption, and the Reformers, 1882-1902

The issue of money was a hot political potato in America for several decades after the Civil War. Indeed, it was as divisive an issue as there was, except for the issue of White-Negro race relations.

What types of money ought the U.S. Treasury to produce? Paper bills, gold coins, and silver coins? Should a gold coin have more gold in it than a silver coin has silver? Should the value of paper money be backed by (that is, be redeemable/in) gold or, by both gold and silver, or by neither? And just how much paper money should be in circulation? These were the types of questions with which all Americans and their political officials wrestled in the latter third of the 19th century.

Businessmen, especially those at banks, financial interests, and large corporations, wanted a limited supply of paper money in circulation, paper money backed by gold. Indeed, Big Business preferred the Gold Standard—they believed that the paper currency of the United States should be backed by and redeemable in gold, a large supply of which would be kept in federal gold depositories. These people were called "Goldbugs."

More ordinary Americans (farmers and debtors, in general) wanted a large supply of paper money in circulation to make it easier to pay their bills/debts. They also believed that silver should be elevated to the status of gold, so that a person could take a bag containing $100 in paper bills into a large bank or Treasury office and exchange them for $100 worth of silver bars or coins, or $100 worth of gold coins or gold bars, or a mixture of gold and silver. These people were known as "Silverbugs" or silverites, or, later, Silver Republicans. Silverbugs wanted the Treasury to purchase silver ore from western mines and convert it into silver coins at a ratio of 16-to-1; that is, silver coins would have 16 times more silver in them than the gold content of a gold coin.

The issue of money tended to divide people along economic, social, sectional, and regional lines. The issue caused deep political divisions in both Oregon and the nation between 1870 and 1910. Indeed, the appearance of the Greenbackers in the 1870s, and the Populists and Silver Republicans in the 1890s, as well as the rupture of the National Democratic Party under President Grover Cleveland, and the rise of William Jennings Bryan are all manifestations of this money issue.

The Big Three: Power in One Place

After 1880, when political power shifted from Democratic to Republican control in Oregon, railroad, timber, mining, and banking interests became identified with the Republicans. In fact, the three men who dominated the Republican Party between 1872 and 1905 were prominent Portland railroad attorneys. This triumvirate—Joseph Dolph, John Mitchell, and Joseph Simon—exercised a degree of political control not seen since in Oregon. When John Mitchell left Oregon in 1873 to take the U.S. Senate seat he had won the previous year, Joe Dolph, with whom Mitchell shared a law practice, took on two new partners. One was his brother, Cyrus. The other partner was a precocious 23-year-old named Joseph Simon. For the next 30 years, the firm became the virtual governmental headquarters of the state, managing Republican policy, ruling the legislature, making and unmaking U.S. senators. Year after year, bankers, editors, and businessmen of Oregon who had paid huge sums for the honor of being elected to Congress were played for suckers. "Four members of the firm—Mitchell, Dolph, Simon, and John Guerin—served in the office of senator, in the aggregate, forty-one years. [Mitchell] used his influence with his patronage power as a senator to further land and timber frauds and protect the interests of the corporations. Up to 1892, the firm of Dolph, Bellinger, Mallory and Simon acted as counsel to the Southern Pacific Railroad, besides dominating state politics."[1] John Mitchell and Joe Simon remained dominant political figures well after 1892.* Mitchell and Dolph (though no longer law partners) both represented the Northern Pacific Railroad Company as early as 1886. Joe Dolph, in fact, "became the vice-president of the Oregon and Transcontinental Company which controlled and financed the Northern Pacific, Oregon Railway and Navigation Company, and the Oregon and California Railroad Company."[2] Through distribution of rail passes, financial contributions, and business relationships, Oregon's political

---

* Mitchell was senator until 1897 and again from 1901 to 1905. Simon reached the pinnacle of his long political career when the Republican Legislature elected him to the U.S. Senate in 1898, where he served until 1903. Joseph Dolph was Oregon's first two-term senator, 1885-97.

leaders and state officials were indebted to and identified with the interests of the railroad companies. Lawmakers were not about to bite the hand that fed them: no important railroad regulatory legislation would be passed in Oregon.

The 1882 campaign had resulted in the reelection of Melvin C. George to the state's single seat in the U.S. House of Representatives (a first for a U.S. Representative from Oregon). Voters also elected wool exporter and former House speaker Zenas Moody as governor. The legislature remained solidly Republican.

When the legislature convened in September 1882, it needed to elect a senator because Democrat LaFayette Grover was nearing the end of his six-year term. Republicans vowed to replace him with one of their own. The leading Republican candidate was Portland attorney Joseph Dolph, Sen. John Mitchell's former law partner. For the duration of the 40-day session, legislators voted over and over, failing to arrive at a majority for Dolph (or anyone else). Dolph was finally elected after 75 ballots on the last day of the session, approaching midnight.[3]

Weeding Out Political Corruption

Responding to rising public pressure, Congress passed the Pendleton or Civil Service Act in January 1883, establishing a three-person Civil Service Commission that was empowered to draw up and administer competitive examinations to determine who was qualified to hold a federal job on the basis of merit. The purpose of the competitive examination system was to stop politicians from giving government jobs to friends, relatives, and political supporters. The act also prohibited the practice of requiring federal officeholders to make campaign contributions to the politician who got them their job. The Pendleton Act didn't apply to state governments and initially applied to only 10% of federal employees, but it was an important first step in reforming the American political system. Oregonians were delighted with the Pendleton Act. For the next 25 years, political and governmental reform was to remain at the top of Oregon's "To Do" list.

On September 11, 1883, most Portlanders welcomed the arrival of the first transcontinental train to reach the city. A holiday was declared and the *Oregonian* reported that excited townspeople put on "the greatest display ever witnessed in this city."[4] After 24 years in the Union, Oregon was now linked by rail to the rest of the nation. Oregon's days of acute isolation were ending.

Oregonians voted Republican in the 1884 election. James G. Blaine of Maine took 51% of the Oregon vote, but lost the presidential contest to New York's conservative Democratic governor, Grover Cleveland.

The Legislature of 1885

The Legislature of 1885 was hopelessly divided: who would be Oregon's next U.S. senator? Come March, the U.S. Senate seat held by Democrat James Slater would be open. The Republican Legislature would see that the job went to a Republican, but both Solomon Hirsch, president of the state Senate in 1880, and John Mitchell wanted the seat. Slater had replaced Mitchell when his term ended in early 1879, but now John Mitchell wanted his Senate seat back. Legislators cast 69 ballots during the session; neither Hirsch nor Mitchell could muster a House or Senate majority. So the session ended with no new senator; until November 1885, Oregon had only one. Governor Moody called the legislature into special session to fill the vacancy. Mitchell was ready this time. He knew that the Republican minority (the Corbettites) would never vote for him. So he turned to the minority Democrats. With money allegedly supplied by the Southern Pacific Railroad, Mitchell bribed 17 Democrats, buying himself a second Senate term.

A freshman Republican state representative from Portland, Jonathan Bourne, Jr., participated in both the regular and special legislative sessions of 1885. A recent transplant from Massachusetts, Bourne was wealthy, ambitious, mercurial, and capable of being as ruthless as any politician in Oregon. A loyal Mitchell ally in 1885, Representative Bourne was destined to break with Mitchell in 1897 and to lead a movement to keep Mitchell from returning to the Senate. Bourne's political star was bright and rising fast in 1885. By 1906, he would be one of Oregon's most powerful politicians.

From 1885 on, strong party unity in Oregon was a faraway dream. Railroad politics influenced both parties at all levels. Spreading money about liberally, the Southern Pacific and other railroads made local and state politicians, farmers, and businessmen believe that their interests should line up with those of the railroad, since the railroads could do more for them than any political party.[5] With dozens of politicians feeding out of its cash-filled trough, Oregon government remained in the grip of railroad money and political graft remained the rule of the day. The Southern Pacific was the state's most influential lobby and Senators Joseph Dolph and John Mitchell were its willing mouthpieces. Most Oregon legislators happily helped their Southern Pacific friends any way they could.

Governor Grover and the Chinese Issue

A new outbreak of nativism had appeared in Oregon in the early 1870s and this time whites aimed their hatred at the Chinese. Although only a few dozen

Chinese lived in Oregon in the 1850s, the men who drafted a state constitution in 1857 included a clause denying "to all Chinese not residents of Oregon at the time of adoption the right to own mining claims or real estate."[6] In 1868, the United States and China concluded the Burlingame Treaty, which provided for free and reciprocal immigration between China and the United States. While many Oregonians hated this treaty, railroad barons welcomed this limitless pool of cheap and docile laborers. The Chinese replaced many Irish workers on railroad construction crews. What began as resentment slowly smoldered into hatred of the Chinese, who, in 1870, were the largest minority in Oregon, 3,300 out of 91,000 people.

Unlimited Chinese immigration quickly became Oregon's hottest political issue in 1870. Democratic Governor LaFayette Grover blasted the Burlingame Treaty in his inaugural address and he was greeted with lusty applause when he said he favored an immediate end to further Chinese immigration. Throughout his tenure, Governor Grover used the Chinese issue to his political advantage, becoming the public symbol of white resistance to all things Chinese. The arrival of so many Chinese came at a time when labor organizers were trying to bring white workers together in unions. Desirous of improving wages, working conditions, and job security, union men hated the Chinese because they were willing to work for lower wages and took jobs away from whites. Unions couldn't succeed if there was a steady supply of cheap workers to take the place of workers trying to organize. In May 1879, a month following a large anti-Chinese meeting held in Portland, U.S. Senator James H. Slater of Oregon introduced a bill in Congress that allowed Chinese to live and travel in the United States but deprived them of the right to work.[7] Congress bowed to public pressure in 1882 and halted Chinese immigration to the United States for 20 years.

Sylvester Pennoyer Rockets into Power

Sylvester Pennoyer became a spokesman for Portland's anti-Chinese element in March 1885. Portland's white workers found a champion in Pennoyer, a successful lawyer-businessman who was blunt, opinionated, and charismatic. His colorful rhetoric excited and aroused his followers to action. Pennoyer won the Democratic nomination for governor in spring 1886 and the ensuing campaign was essentially a racist one: "The Mongolians Must Go!" Pennoyer was also an astute politician who knew how to frame issues so they appealed to a broad cross-section of citizens. Future governor Walter Pierce was 25 in 1886 when he met Pennoyer, who was campaigning for governor in Umatilla County. Pierce recalled that Pennoyer "talked the language that the people understand. He wanted the Northwest reserved as the home for the pioneers."[8] (Ironically, Pennoyer was a native New Yorker.)

Sylvester Pennoyer was the workingman's hero, and farmers especially liked him. He hammered away at monopolistic railroads, greedy bankers, and fat politicians. He told crowds that Oregon needed a leader who cared about ordinary people, who would not be cowed by big corporate leaders and complacent or corrupt legislators. Candidate Pennoyer presented himself as a fighter for the peoples' interests; he was a populist. A tireless campaigner, Pennoyer stumped the state, county by county, addressing more Oregonians than any other candidate in 1886. People appreciated his sincerity, intensity, and ability to put into words what they were thinking.

Pennoyer, a recent graduate of Harvard Law School, came to Oregon in 1855 to teach school in Portland, taught for several years, and was named superintendent of Multnomah County Schools, 1860-62. Pennoyer then went into the lumber business. He became editor and owner of the *Oregon Herald*, the

Sylvester Pennoyer

Sylvester Pennoyer was Oregon's first governor to serve two full terms. A man of keen intelligence, strong opinions, and freely shared prejudices, Pennoyer was mercurial, controversial, and charismatic.

COURTESY OF THE OREGON STATE ARCHIVES, GOVERNORS PHOTOS

Sylvester Pennoyer was born in New York in 1831, the youngest of nine children. He graduated from Harvard Law School in 1854 and soon departed for Oregon by steamer, arriving in Portland on July 10, 1855. He was hired to teach school in Portland (which he did for five years); he was appointed school superintendent in 1860. In 1862, Pennoyer went into the lumber business, and in 1868 he became editor of the state's leading Democratic newspaper, the *Oregon Herald*. The next year, Pennoyer bought the *Herald* and became a key spokesman for the Democratic Party.

In March 1885, Pennoyer was chosen as the spokesman for an anti-Chinese White Workers' Association. The issue of Chinese immigration had been a hot topic in Oregon and the nation for the previous 30 years. Governors LaFayette Grover, a Democrat, and Zenas Moody, a Republican, had made the Chinese presence a volatile political issue during their administrations. By early 1886, Pennoyer had decided to run for governor, making this his campaign slogan: "The Mongolians Must Go!" Pennoyer campaigned all over the state, arguing that Oregon must be kept as a home for the pioneers, a place where free white men had a chance to make a good living state's leading Democratic newspaper in 1868-69. *Oregonian* editor Harvey Scott disliked him, calling his opinions "unsound" and noting that "his appeal is never to intelligence or manliness, but always to ignorance and discontent."[9] Scott lampooned him for seeking the votes of the "oppressed," claiming his opinions were dangerous, that Pennoyer was a charlatan and a demagogue. Part of Scott's aversion to Pennoyer was purely political. As the editorial voice of the state Republican Party, it was Scott's job to criticize Democrats like Pennoyer. A born agitator, Pennoyer delighted in getting under the skin of two of Oregon's most prominent Republicans. Pennoyer was one of the most colorful, controversial, and charismatic politicians in Oregon history. Elected governor as a Democrat in a Republican state in 1886 by 3,700 votes over Republican T. R. Cornelius, Pennoyer pulled 51% of the vote. Running for reelection in 1890, Governor Pennoyer took 54% of the vote, defeating Republican David Thompson by over 5,200 ballots. Pennoyer was the first governor and only Democrat for the next one hundred years to serve two full terms.

without having to live near or work with unwelcome Chinese immigrants. Pennoyer's platform was racist and it worked; he was elected governor by 2,700 votes over his Republican foe, T. R. Cornelius, in 1886.

Pennoyer's election and reelection in 1890 occurred in an age when Oregon and the nation were torn by economic, social, and political forces dedicated to overturning the status quo. It was a time of protest and upheaval. Farmers, industrial laborers (and the budding labor movement), temperance forces, urban reformers, and women's rights and suffrage organizations were all active during this Gilded Age. Governor Sylvester Pennoyer's popularity was based on his advocacy of issues that appealed to farmers (reform of railroad shipping rates, for example), laborers, factory workers, small-shop owners, and craftsmen.

The governor was reelected in 1890 by 5,200 votes, with the backing of both the Democratic Party and a new, short-lived Union Party. In 1892, Pennoyer left the Democratic Party to join the new People's or Populist Party. Although Pennoyer's popularity remained high throughout his eight years as governor, his legislative accomplishments were few. In 1891, the secret ballot was adopted, after Governor Pennoyer and others had aroused an agitated electorate to push the legislature into backing this popular reform.

Pennoyer headed home to Portland after his term ended in January 1895. Within weeks, the former governor announced that he was running for the office of mayor. Pennoyer was elected despite the opposition of the Portland business establishment and a 3-to-1 Republican registration edge in Multnomah County. Pennoyer completed his two-year term in 1898. He died in 1902, age 70.

In his second term Governor Pennoyer became a leader in Oregon's powerful Populist movement, which swept through the state in the 1890s. He once told President Grover Cleveland to "mind his own business" and on another occasion he refused to meet President Benjamin Harrison at the Oregon-California border as Harrison traveled toward Salem on an official state visit. As host, Pennoyer insisted that Harrison call upon *him*, once the president reached the capital. This episode is classic Sylvester Pennoyer.

With his impressive gubernatorial victories in 1886 and 1890, Sylvester Pennoyer overcame a huge Republican edge in voter registration. Pennoyer knew that, despite their overwhelming Republican bias, Oregonians would vote for a candidate if they liked his character and personality. He virtually ignored the fact that he was a Democrat in his campaigns. He appealed to many people by forcefully stating his beliefs and taking stands on issues the majority of voters cared about. The voters were looking for a man who stood for something rather a man who stood simply as a representative of his party.[10] Pennoyer and other Democratic governors who followed him learned this lesson well.

Also in the June 1886 election, Republican Congressman Binger Hermann was reelected, replacing M. C. George. Hermann served eight terms in the U.S. House. Oregon Republicans ran on a party platform that focused on the contentious money issue. The GOP favored converting (or exchanging) paper currency into either gold or silver coins. Money, its value and metal backing, was fast becoming one of the hottest political issues in Oregon and the nation.

Regulation and Abuses

Public resentment of abuses in railway transportation led Congress to enact the Interstate Commerce Act in February 1887. The act created our nation's first federal regulatory agency, the Interstate Commerce Commission, and the law covered railroad companies whose track ran through more than one state. Such common practices as discriminatory rail rates, pooling, rebates, and unreasonable charges were now prohibited. Unfortunately, subsequent federal court rulings undercut the act's effectiveness.

The legislature of 1887 considered the question of state regulation of railroads and established Oregon's first regulatory agency, a Board of Railroad Commissioners. But the new board was given only token powers, so it accomplished little. For Oregon's farmers, however, the call for strict regulation of railroads remained an item of unfinished business.

The 1887 Legislature also enacted a law that later led to numerous land scandals in Oregon. The act authorized the sale of public lands, including the

best timber acreage, at a price of $1.25 an acre and it sparked a frenzy of specu-
lative buying. Because of the way the law was written, a few favored people
were able to form a land ring and levy tribute from buyers.[11] The resulting land
scandals reached a climax just after 1900.

Harrison Yes, Cleveland No

Oregon's male voters cast their ballots for Republican Benjamin Harrison for
president in 1888. Democrat Grover Cleveland was seeking a second term, but
took only 43% of the Oregon vote, down 4% from 1884. The Oregon GOP
criticized President Cleveland's tariff policy, which favored reducing import
taxes. Republicans wanted a protective tariff to shield American goods from
lower-priced imports. The tariff question was about to join the money issue as
one of the major political issues in both Oregon and the nation in the 1890s.

For one of very few times in the 19th century, the 1889 Legislature elected
a U.S. senator without crippling itself. John Mitchell was already in the other
Senate seat, so there was no cause for Republican disunity, and Senator Joseph
Dolph waltzed to a second term. Dolph's reelection was never in doubt, since
his law partner and protégé, Joseph Simon, was president of the state Senate.

Reformers in Oregon

A lean young man named William U'Ren moved to Oregon in 1889. A born
activist, U'Ren plunged into a campaign to convince voters that Oregon should
adopt the Australian (or secret) ballot* into law. U'Ren's baptism into Oregon
politics launched him into a brilliant political career. He would become the
father of the Oregon System and one of Oregon's most distinguished citizens.

1889 was a watershed year for reformers in Oregon. The public was fed up
with corrupt politicians, officeholders, and businessmen. Perverted by money
and power, Oregon government (especially the legislature) appeared to serve
only the narrow, selfish interest of railroad companies, land speculators, bankers, and mine owners. Laborers were unhappy with long work days, low wages,
and no job security. Farmers were burdened by low crop prices, high transportation costs, and heavy debts. Teetotalers, appalled by widespread alcohol
abuse, wanted to make Oregon sober. These feelings of frustration, of being
exploited and ignored, coalesced when a variety of reformers held a convention

---

* Before adopting the Australian ballot, Oregonians (and Americans everywhere) cast their ballot
in public, with the names of the candidates for whom a person voted being read aloud for all who
were present to hear.

William Simon U'Ren

William S. U'Ren was one of Oregon's most successful politicians, Yet, U'Ren held public office only once; he was elected to the state legislature in 1896 as a member of the People's Party, or Populists. U'Ren's stature as a political leader emanated from another place: he led the crusade to reform Oregon politics by persuading citizens to adopt the "Oregon System" early in the 20th century.

Bill U'Ren was born in Lancaster, Wisconsin, in 1859. In his teens, U'Ren trained to be a blacksmith. Working his way westward, the shy young man ended up in Denver, where he attended business college in 1878-79. U'Ren then studied law, passed the Colorado Bar, and practiced there for 8 years. In 1889, U'Ren moved to Oregon City and set up a new practice. He was 30.

While living in Denver, U'Ren had been an avid reader of a magazine called *The Arena*. This magazine, written by young scholars interested in reforming America's political institutions, fascinated him. The ideas that most intrigued him were those having to do with how to go about reforming state government. U'Ren saw the Oregon Legislature for what it was: the tool by which moneyed interests (railroads and land developers, for example) controlled the actions of state and city governments. Simply put, Bill U'Ren believed that what Oregon needed were these political reforms: the initiative (I), referendum (R), and recall, as well as the direct election of U.S. senators.

in Salem in August 1889. Grangers, Prohibitionists, and labor men attended the meeting. Delegates adopted a set of grievances and agreed to meet again the following month to further organize. They were upset that land grabbers had almost exhausted the public domain, and that "the corruption of the ballots has rendered our elections little less than a disgraceful farce. The dominant political parties have demonstrated their indisposition and their inability to effectively oppose these evils."[12] Delegates reassembled in September and took two important actions. First, they formed a new political group, the Union Party. Republicans and Democrats took note. Incumbent Gov. Sylvester Pennoyer was seeking a second term, and publicly stated his agreement with some of the new party's objectives. He was later endorsed by the Union Party, who gave him perhaps 5,000 votes. Pennoyer won reelection by a margin of 5,140. Second, the delegates adopted a platform containing a variety of planks. A prohibition law stood front and center. Farmers asked for national and state regulation of

Recognizing that few Oregonians knew anything about these political innovations, U'Ren set about to educate the public. He wrote articles, he made speeches, and he began to organize citizens who believed as he did: that it was high time that the people, the electorate, take control of their state and local governments. Power must be shared. The people's elected representatives should be working for the interests of all citizens. With the backing of the Grange, labor groups, newspaper editors, and the People's Power League (an organization dedicated to cleaning up Oregon politics by adopting the I and R), U'Ren moved closer to his goal.

Another political force was also afoot in Oregon in the 1890s: the national People's Party or Populists. Populism was most potent in the Midwest and Northwest. Thousands of Oregonians joined this reform party. In 1896, 13 Populists (including U'Ren) were elected to the Oregon Legislature. Because the Republican Party was, as usual, in disarray, the Populists were in a position to block or stall legislation. The infamous Hold-Up session of 1897 happened because the Populists, a handful of Republicans, and the few Democratic lawmakers kept the House from organizing. The Hold-Up meant that Sen. John Mitchell—who was not, then, a backer of the I and R—was not reelected. In 1902, Oregon voters approved the initiative and referendum by huge margins—the first time that the state constitution was amended. Voters approved the direct primary in 1904, the direct election of senators in 1906, the recall in 1908, and women's suffrage in 1912. This Oregon System became a model of political reform for the rest of the nation. Bill U'Ren had turned Oregon upside-down, changing, forever, how political power was distributed here. Preferring to work behind the scenes, William U'Ren, like all successful reformers, was tenacious in the pursuit of his goal. U'Ren lived until 1949, dying at age 90.

corporations, punishment of trusts, government support for agricultural associations, and a new land law.* Labor forces asked for government arbitration and assurance of fair wages. Another plank proposed an examination and 10 years of residence as a condition of citizenship and the right to vote.[13]

The Union Party held a state convention in April 1890. Besides endorsing the reelection of Governor Pennoyer, they readopted their September 1889 platform and added several planks. Among the additions they called for abolishing the nation's tariff system, a graduated income tax, direct election of U. S. senators, an eight-hour workday, and the adoption of the Australian ballot.

Governor Pennoyer was the only successful Union Party-backed candidate in the June 1890 general election. The party had also run their own candidates

---

* The proposed law asked that unused land grants be restored to the public for settlement, that the lands be subdivided into 160-acre homesteads, that railroad corporations be restricted to land they actually used, and that aliens be forbidden from purchasing these unused railroad lands.

for Congress and for the office of secretary of state,and their defeat shattered the party, causing various factions to separate, most notably the Prohibitionists. The Union Party faded fast. The Democrat-Union Party coalition was not, however, a total failure; the alliance it represented became the foundation for the bigger and more successful Populist Party in 1892.

Populism Takes Root in Oregon

The Farmers Alliance came to Oregon in 1890. Many who joined were members of the Grange, which, while fading in most of the nation, remained strong and influential in the Pacific Northwest. Leading the effort to organize the first Alliance chapter in Oregon were Seth Lewelling and his wife, Sophronia, of Clackamas County. The Lewellings had been long active in both the Grange and the Republican Party. The Lewellings' Milwaukie home was a hub of political activity for years. They also opened their home to young boarders, including William Simon U'Ren. A deep friendship developed between the older Lewellings and their young boarder. They shared U'Ren's zeal for political change. A political friendship was born that propeled Oregon into an era of unprecedented political reform.

A new third party, the People's Party (or Populists) was organized by 1,400 delegates meeting in St. Louis, Missouri, in February 1891. Greenbackers,* labor leaders, Grangers, and Alliancemen came together to build a party capable of challenging the established Democratic and Republican order. In July 1891, Populists held a nominating convention, selecting James B. Weaver of Iowa for president and James G. Field of Virginia for vice president.

The Oregon People's Party was founded at Oregon City in March 1892, led by Seth Lewelling and Bill U'Ren. Delegates adopted a wide-ranging and controversial platform. Some planks were simply lifted from the defunct Union Party. Populists favored an increase in gold and silver coinage, government ownership of railroads, telephones, and telegraphs, a 3% reduction of railroad rates, abolition of alien land ownership, reduction of corporate land holding to the ground actually used by the company, state publication of school books, restriction of county officials' salaries, women's suffrage, prohibition of liquor, an eight-hour

---

* Greenbackers were mostly farmers/debtors who favored more paper money (greenbacks) in circulation—but not currency backed by gold or silver (known as specie). They opposed the Specie Redemption Act of 1875, which, in essence, returned the nation to the gold standard while shrinking the supply of paper money in circulation. In 1878 the Greenback-Labor party formed and fielded scores of political candidates at the local, state, and national levels in the south and west. Fourteen Greenbackers were elected to the U.S. House in 1878.

workday, and restriction of Chinese immigration into the United States. They also addressed building an inter-ocean canal through Central America.[14]

Both Oregon Populists and the national People's Party crafted an umbrella platform so broad that it appealed to virtually every organized reform group in America. Nationally, Populism was mainly an agrarian protest and it claimed many followers in Oregon, who felt oppressed by the same conditions expressed by other farmers. The Union Party had already prepared the ground for Populism when it moved west. Populism incorporated the Union Party with its own forces resulting in a powerful Oregon third party that shook the old political structures.[15]

While Populist fever swept through Oregon, Bill U'Ren was talking about a little book: J. W. Sullivan's *Direct Legislation by the Citizenship through the Initiative and Referendum* (I and R). The idea of direct legislation is simple: provide the people with legal means to write their own laws, regardless of what their elected legislature does.* U'Ren was convinced that "with these measures as amendments to the Constitution, the legislature would be compelled to represent the voters who elected them, not the railroads or other interests."[16]

In 1893, William U'Ren organized the Direct Legislation League. The league subsequently put together a campaign to educate the public on the I & R and to lobby legislators. Over the next three years, Oregon's Populist surge made the political campaigns of 1892 and 1894 among the most colorful and contentious in state history. Exasperated by the national platforms of the Republican and Democratic parties, Gov. Sylvester Pennoyer bolted and joined the Populists in October 1892. Populists hoped to forge a winning combination with liberal Silverite Republicans and unhappy Democrats like Pennoyer. Despite their optimism, the Democratic-Populist fusion ticket had mixed success in the 1892 elections. Only a handful of Oregon Populists were elected. Many, however, ran surprisingly strong races, and, in some cases, outpolled their

---

* The initiative gives a citizen or a group the right to place a proposed law on the ballot for voters to decide. With a designated number of signatures on a petition, initiative sponsors can go directly to the people with a proposal. If a majority of voters approve the initiative measure it becomes the law of the state. The referendum kicks in when the legislature or a local government passes and then refers a proposed law directly to voters, letting them make the final decision. Over the past century Oregonians have used the initiative hundreds of times, and scores of initiatives have been approved by voters. The idea of the initiative and referendum and its adoption in Oregon first appeared in 1883-85 in an obscure newspaper called *The Vidette and Antimonopolist*. Representing "all toilers," *The Vidette* backed the initiative and referendum, as well as a six-hour workday, proportional representation, and woman suffrage. See Robert D. Johnston, *The Radical Middle Class: Populist Democracy and the Question of Capitalism in Progressive Era Portland, Oregon* (Princeton University Press, 2003).

Democratic opponent, losing by narrow margins to the Republican candidate. James Weaver, the Populist candidate for president, lost the election in Oregon to Benjamin Harrison by only 149 votes, 35,818 to 35,967. Four Populists were elected to the 1893 Legislature. For a party barely six months old, Populists were optimistic about their chances in the 1894 election.

The Campaign of 1894

Oregon's hotly contested governor's race in 1894 attracted plenty of attention. Many Democrats who had voted Populist in 1892 returned to their party and voted for William Galloway, but the Populist candidate, Nathan Pierce, ran ahead of Democrat Galloway 26,255 to 17,865. With Democrats and Populists sticking with their party candidates, Republican William P. Lord, Chief Justice of the Oregon Supreme Court, was elected governor with 47% of the vote.

Oregon gained a second seat in the U.S. House of Representatives as a result of the 1890 Federal Census. The new 2nd District essentially comprised the eastern two-thirds of the state, with the Cascades Mountains dividing it from the 1st. The two districts were not equal in population (as would be the requirement today). Republican W. R. Ellis was elected to the new seat in 1892. In the 1894 election, 1st District Republican Congressman Binger Hermann won a sixth term, defeating Democrat J. K. Weatherford and Populist Charles Miller (who, between them, exceeded Hermann's total by 1,200 votes). The results of the new 2nd District race were similar. There, victorious W.R. Ellis had 1,000 votes fewer than Democrat James H. Raley and Populist Joseph Waldrop combined. The legislative contests went overwhelmingly Republican, their candidates winning 82 of the 90 seats. Only seven Populists and one Democrat were elected to the legislature. But Republicans didn't represent a majority opinion in Oregon, since the combined fusion, Independent, and Populist vote was larger than the Republican.*

Mountains of Money

The 1895 Oregon Legislature was one of the most corrupt in state history, with money flowing like water into the pockets and down the throats of legislators. Many lawmakers had open palms whenever it was time for an important vote

---

* In 1894, the Populist candidate in Oregon's congressional District 1 took 27% of the vote, the same percentage captured by the Populist in the 2nd District. Populists did even better in 1896: 29% in the 2nd District and 40% in the 1st District.

in committee or on the floor. The year was a low point in Oregon's political history.

It was time for the legislature to elect a U. S. Senator. Two-termer Joseph Dolph wanted another six years. Joseph Simon, head of the Corbett-Dolph faction of the Republican Party, returned to the state Senate in January after sitting out one term. He was again chosen Senate president. Oregonians had two issues on their minds: the money question of gold vs. silver and political reform. Oregon was still feeling the effects of the 1893 economic depression. Many citizens demanded a cut in the salaries of state and city employees as a way to reduce taxes. Still in control of the Republican machine in Multnomah County, Senate President Joe Simon was not about to let the wages of Portland's city workers (his supporters) be cut. The bill to cut salaries never got out of committee. Meanwhile, William U'Ren's Direct Legislation League was gaining thousands of converts. With the clamor for the I & R, along with the direct election of U. S. senators, pressure was building on legislators to get aboard the league's train.

The money issue played prominently in the Senate election. Silver Republicans opposed Senator Dolph's reelection because he favored the gold standard. For six weeks the legislature balloted. On the last night of the session and the 60th ballot, Republican George McBride was elected senator and Joe Dolph was dumped. John Mitchell, Oregon's other senator, had blocked Dolph. Republicans were more bitterly divided than ever. To top it off, lawmakers passed no meaningful reform legislation. When rumors and newspaper accounts surfaced about mountains of money being spent in the Senate campaign,* the public grew more disgusted with their lawmakers. Their fury turned to contempt.

One bright spot appeared in the 1895 session: petitions with 14,000 signatures (there were 80,000 registered voters in Oregon) were presented to the assembly by the Direct Legislation League. The petitions requested that the legislature call a constitutional convention to incorporate the initiative and referendum into the state constitution. The assembly took no action on the petitions. So U'Ren and the league abandoned the idea of a convention in favor of a direct vote by the people. First, however, the legislature would have to be cajoled into approving the proposal as a constitutional amendment. Meanwhile, in 1895 U'Ren enthusiastically reported on the success of the league's educational

---

* The Northern Pacific spent $300,000 on Joseph Dolph's unsuccessful reelection bid. On the first of the 60 ballots, Dolph was only two votes short and the Northern Pacific offered $50,000 for two votes. Jonathan Bourne also admitted he spent $10,000 of his own money on George McBride's victory. (MacColl, *Merchants*, 322.)

campaign, "[N]o great reform ever made such strides before. Two years and two months ago not one man in a thousand in Oregon knew what Initiative and Referendum meant. Today I believe 3/4th of the voters understand and favor this revolution."[17]

Politically, matters worsened in Oregon over the next two years. The election of 1896 was probably the most corrupt in the state's history. In Portland and Multnomah County both Simon-Corbett and Mitchell wings of the Republican Party took part in ballot stuffing. They hired hobos to work in the primaries. Unbothered by the police, "they congregated in gangs about the polling places, turning away voters for the opponents and allowing repeaters to vote for their candidates."[18] "Ballot boxes were stuffed both during the election and the counting. Votes were regularly bought for $2.50 apiece. Judge [Leonard H.] McMahan reports that Simon, while boss of the state, colonized voters of the north side of the Columbia, and on election day, they were taken from polling

Jonathan Bourne, Jr.

Jonathan Bourne, Jr., was a paradox. He spent much of his personal fortune in Oregon rigging elections and buying legislators; on the other hand, he was an important player in the political reform movement led by William S. U'Ren. Ambitious and sometimes ruthless, Bourne was a wheeler-dealer, forever in the hunt for any advantage he could exploit for personal gain—whether in business or politics. Yet Bourne was also charming, a generous host who spent his fortune on good food and wine, on tailored suits, on the trappings of wealth.

Jonathan Bourne, Jr., was born in New Bedford, Massachusetts, in March 1855. His father was a wealthy textile manufacturer and owner of a fleet of whaling ships. As befitting a youth of his wealth and social position, Bourne was enrolled in Harvard University. However, the impetuous Bourne did not earn a degree—because he dropped out during his senior year.

Bourne arrived in Portland in 1878, age 23. He immediately dove into Portland society, making it a point to meet and befriend the city's business elite. Three years later, Jonathan Bourne was a founding member of Portland's most prestigious private men's club, the Arlington. Bourne passed the bar exam in 1881 and quickly realized that a law career was not for him. Instead, he began to invest in Portland real estate and banking, as well as in silver mines. Many of Portland's business leaders joined to form a Portland Stock Exchange in the late 1880s, choosing Bourne to run it. Bourne place to polling place, and were paid the [$2.50] price."[19] Even Harvey Scott, staunch Republican that he was, couldn't ignore the blatant examples of vote fraud in the Portland election. On June 8, 1896, he wrote in the *Oregonian* about a scene witnessed at the polls at the corner of Fourth and A streets. "There was a lively scene yesterday. Several men were arrested in that locality for buying votes, and great excitement ensued. The bribers were promptly bailed by Hon. Joseph Simon—who appeared to have charge of the proceedings. After that, a close watch was kept about the polls and vicinity, and the business of 'dealing' with voters in that quarter was materially diminished."[20]

The 60 Oregon House races were manipulated by Jonathan Bourne because his cohort, Sen. John Mitchell, would be seeking reelection in the 1897 Legislature. To assure Mitchell's victory, Bourne was chosen to influence the outcome of the House races to assure that a majority of Mitchell men were elected. With $225,000 from the Southern Pacific and $10,000 of his own money,

had early forged close friendships with Joseph Simon and his law partner, Joseph Dolph. Former U.S. Senator Henry Corbett, perhaps the wealthiest man in Oregon, was also counted amongst Bourne's friends.

During the 1895 election Bourne poured $10,000 of his own money into George McBride's Senate campaign. His money was spent on stuffing ballot boxes to assure the election of legislators who backed McBride's candidacy. Bourne also funneled $225,000 of Southern Pacific Railroad money into legislative races. He was instrumental in causing the Hold-Up session of 1897 when the legislature went home without conducting any business—and without electing a U.S. senator. Bourne spent $80,000 of his and his cronies' money entertaining fellow legislators; liquor flowed around the clock. In 1896 Bourne allied himself with populist William U'Ren, leader of the movement to reform Oregon politics. Bourne was a staunch supporter of U'Ren's drive to establish the initiative and referendum in Oregon. Bourne also backed the Direct Election Law of 1904. By 1903 it was known that Bourne wanted to be one of Oregon's U.S. senators. Indeed, Bourne spent so much money trying to influence legislators that he overdrew his bank account. Bourne's dream came true in the 1906 election when voters selected him as the "people's choice" for Senate and lawmakers elected him. Jonathan Bourne served a single term in the Senate, 1907-13. In 1910, Senator Bourne intervened in Oregon's gubernatorial campaign on behalf of Democrat Oswald West, in defiance of his party's nominee, Republican Jay Bowerman. Bourne's backing of West cost him dearly. His old friend and ally, Joseph Simon, turned on Bourne; with Bowerman, Simon blocked Bourne's candidacy for reelection in 1912. Bourne never returned to Oregon to live. He lived another 27 years, dying in Washington D.C. in 1940 at age 85.

Bourne proceeded to buy or fix (by stuffing ballot boxes) as many House races as possible. He offered candidates part of the $225,000 in return for a signed pledge to vote for John Mitchell for Senate in the 1897 session. The Southern Pacific locked these pledges in their corporate safe.[21]

Jonathan Bourne ran as a Multnomah County Silver Republican for a seat in the Oregon House. He won easily. He was joined in that chamber by freshman legislator William S. U'Ren, who headed a Populist slate of Clackamas County legislative candidates and led a 13-man Populist delegation into the 1897 session. No one had any idea that U'Ren was about to turn Oregon politics on its head.

The Hold-Up Legislature of 1897

Since statehood Oregonians had suffered through four decades of legislative shenanigans. The worst abuses had occurred when it was time to elect a U.S. senator. With each election the price of being elected went up. The highest bidder seemed always to have the advantage.* In Oregon, as elsewhere, Senate seats were for sale.

The drive for fundamental political reform in Oregon had been gaining steam for months. After the debacle of the 1897 Legislature, the tide for change would be unstoppable. Powerful forces were unleashed that party bosses and powerful interest groups couldn't contain. Nothing like it had happened before in Oregon.

The 1895 Legislature accomplished little, having tied itself in knots over the election of a U.S. senator. John Mitchell was the key figure in that fiasco. The same was true in the 1897 session. Senator Mitchell's reelection bid caused a deadlocked legislature. The House never officially organized. Consequently, the session of 1897 is known as the Hold-Up Legislature because no business was conducted (it was "held up").

This is the woeful story. Jonathan Bourne wanted to be House Speaker in 1897. Mitchell, a fellow Silverite Republican, promised Bourne the votes of his House supporters; in return, Bourne would deliver the necessary votes to assure Mitchell's reelection in the balloting for senator. Their deal was pure politics. But between the election and January 1897, when the legislature convened, the Republican Party held its national convention. In drafting a platform, the GOP adopted a gold plank, abandoning its former silver and gold position. William McKinley, Republican president-elect, also favored the gold standard. For several months Sen. John Mitchell tried to straddle the money issue. Finally,

---

* The obvious exception is Joseph Dolph, who spent $225,000 on his Senate bid in 1897 and lost.

he was summoned to meet McKinley and national Republican chairman, Mark Hanna. The duo told Mitchell that no Silver Senator could be elected in Oregon. The subject of patronage, the distribution of federal offices in Oregon, was also raised by Hanna. Mitchell got the point. To be reelected and to have any clout in the new Republican administration he had better play ball McKinley's way. Mitchell switched, abandoning his pro-silver stance in favor of the gold standard.

Jonathan Bourne was left out on a limb. How could he support Mitchell now that he was a gold standard man? Bourne, true to his pro-silver beliefs, broke with Mitchell—who then told his friends in the legislature not to support Bourne for speaker. Could Bourne exact revenge by preventing Mitchell's reelection as senator? Jonathan Bourne's powerbase was small: five silver Republicans and three Democrats in the House. Luckily for Bourne, Joe Simon also wanted to block Mitchell's election, since Simon himself might be elected if Mitchell was stopped.

Simon controlled nine gold Republicans in the House. Since Bourne and Simon's combined forces totaled only 17, they were extremely interested in a deal to gain the Populists' support. In exchange for backing Bourne for speaker and opposing Mitchell's reelection, Bourne and Simon promised support for Populist reforms: the initiative and referendum, a registration law, and a law providing for the election of judges. This set the stage for the "Hold-up of '97." With the Populist votes, the anti-Mitchell men totaled only 30 in the House and Mitchell's reelection seemed a certainty because his supporters were in a majority in the Senate. Bourne, Simon, U'Ren, and their followers were determined to block Mitchell's election and they took the extreme step of preventing the House from organizing. The leaders kept their 30 members from reporting to the House. Without a quorum (two-thirds of the members) the House could not organize, thus keeping the body from conducting *any* business in 1897. And it worked. The stalemate held throughout the session. The anti-Mitchell group would call off their "hold-up" only if Mitchell withdrew his candidacy. Mitchell refused and the legislative session ended with no laws passed by the House and no U.S senator elected.[22]

Through it all, Jonathan Bourne took good care of his people. Near the Capitol, he hosted an open house for legislators. Because the House never organized, members were not entitled to their $3 a day salaries. Host Bourne saw to it his followers were fed and bedded. Plenty of free drink and companionship was available. Most lawmakers had never seen tables heaped with trays of food—all of it provided by their friend, Jonathan Bourne. It was known as

Bourne's Harem and described as a den of prostitution and evil. Many representatives were kept intoxicated for days. Bourne admitted that the entertainment cost $80,000, but denied that the money bribed anyone. He described it as enticement. For several weeks he paid for the living expenses of a majority of House members, who entertained themselves so royally they forgot all about their legislative duties.

The funds for Bourne's activities came from various wealthy Portland men who "fondled senatorial ambitions" and were interested in Mitchell's defeat. Future governor Oswald West was a teller at the Ladd and Bush Bank in Salem at the time and gave conclusive evidence that Henry Corbett was foremost among these men. The people were indignant since, as candidates and party members, the legislators had repeatedly promised to make the 1897 Legislature a model of achievement. After three years of economic recession Oregonians expected better from their representatives. Reformers wanted to move the initiative and referendum and other direct legislation. Budget cuts were in order, too. Lean government was what voters wanted. Instead, "not a bill of any kind was passed that session, not even an appropriation for current expenses. For fifteen months the bills of the state had to be paid in warrants drawing interest of eight percent."[23]

With the Hold-Up Legislature, corruption in Oregon had peaked. As the people's contempt deepened, the forces of political reform grew stronger every day.

William U'Ren was one of the benefactors of the 1897 session. Although Populists were angered by U'Ren's deal making with Bourne, politicians saw him in a different light. U'Ren gained the respect of fellow legislators while making political bosses fearful. His newfound power enabled him to keep the I & R amendment moving through the 1899 and 1901 legislatures. The architects of direct legislation (including Jonathan Bourne, who had joined U'Ren's crusade) organized the Non-Partisan Direct Legislation League of Oregon in September 1897. When U'Ren and Seth Lewelling had begun the push for direct legislation five years earlier, one of their main obstacles had been the opposition of the Republican Party. With the founding of the non-partisan league, Republican stalwarts such as George Williams, Harvey Scott, and John Mitchell joined Jonathan Bourne as I & R boosters. U'Ren was now a giant step closer to achieving his goal.

Governor William Lord appointed his friend, Henry Corbett, to Oregon's vacant Senate seat. The U.S. Senate, however, refused to seat Corbett, ruling that Governor Lord had acted improperly because his power to appoint applied only where there was a failure of opportunity to elect. The opportunity, said the Senate, had existed with the 1897 Legislature. That body's failure to elect a senator meant the seat would remain vacant until a special session was called, or until the next regular session met in January 1899. Between March 1897 and October 1898, and for the second time since 1885, Oregon was represented in Congress by only one senator. The state and her people had again been denied their full Constitutional representation in the federal legislature. It was not fair, nor was it right. The time had come for Oregonians to take back their government from greedy, self-serving politicians, and the corrupting influence of special-interest money.

Joe Gets His Wish

Republicans, despite their part in causing the deadlocked 1897 Legislature, were overwhelming victors in the June 1898 elections. Theodore Geer of West Salem was elected governor, besting Fusion-Democrat William King by about 9,500 votes. Geer had been an active Republican since the early 1870s and had served four terms in the Oregon House, serving as speaker in 1891. A farmer and journalist, Geer was 48 years old and Oregon's first native-born governor. Twenty-four Republicans, three Populists and three Democrats were elected to serve in the 1899 Oregon Senate. In the House, 46 Republicans won seats. The remaining 14 slots were filled by men wearing different party labels: six were Democrats, four called themselves Union, three were Silver Republicans, and one, J. W. Virtue, said he was a Democratic-People's-Silver-Republican. The inability of the Democratic Party to identify and support viable legislative candidates added to their continuing political woes.

Gov. William Lord called a special session to elect a U.S. senator, which convened in Salem on March 26, 1898. Joe Simon presided over the Senate for his fifth and last time. The session lasted 20 days. Who would be Oregon's next U.S. senator? Portland's Henry W. Corbett wanted the job back. At 72, Corbett was rich, had powerful friends, and hoped to win the seat John Mitchell had lost in 1897.

When the special session began, Corbett was the leading candidate. His campaign manager was his old friend, Joe Simon. Corbett gave thousands of dollars to Simon to buy the votes necessary to assure his reelection to the Senate. But Corbett was seriously disliked by downstate Republicans, who resented his wealth and ties to big corporations. He could not expect to get their votes. Simon realized that Corbett was several votes short. So he and others convinced Corbett that he could not be reelected, and if he stayed in the race,

Joseph Simon

Joseph Simon was the "grand puppeteer" who pulled Oregon's political strings for over 30 years. As a power in the state Senate, a partner in Portland's most influential law firm, as a longtime Republican Party leader, as head of the Corbett-Simon faction of the GOP, as a U.S. senator (1898-1903), and as mayor of Portland (1909-1911), Joseph Simon was the political boss of Oregon.

Joe Simon was a boy of six when he arrived in Portland with his parents in 1857. Born into a Jewish family in Bechthelm, Germany, in February 1851, Simon spoke no English. Simon attended Portland public schools, where he was known for his keen intelligence, fierce ambition, and lofty goals. After high school, Simon went to work in the law office of Dolph, Mallory, and Bellinger, where he studied law. He passed the Oregon Bar in 1872 and joined Joseph Dolph's firm. He was 21. Simon then joined the Republican Party and dove into local politics. At 26, the young lawyer was elected to the Portland city council. A year later (1878) Joseph Simon was state chairman of the GOP and a newly elected state senator. Simon's meteoric rise in the city, party, and state politics was unprecedented—and he was only 29 years old. Joe Simon served in the state Senate from 1880 to 1891, and from 1895 to 1898. He was Senate president in 1889, 1891, 1895, 1897, and 1898, and Oregon's GOP representative on the Republican National Committee from 1892 to 1896.

the party might again rupture and deadlock. Reluctantly, Corbett withdrew. Joe Simon then declared his candidacy. With all 66 Republican legislators voting for him, Simon was elected Oregon's new U. S. senator, Oregon's most prominent Jewish politician and the first of his religion to represent Oregon in the U.S. Senate.* Simon's four-and-a-half-year Senate tenure was the highlight of his long and controversial political career. He did not seek reelection. Returning to Portland, Simon resumed his law practice. He returned as chairman of the Multnomah County Republican Central Committee. In 1909, Portland's establishment coaxed him to run for mayor. Simon won easily and served a two-year term, his last political office. Joe Simon lived until 1935 and age 83. Between 1880 and 1903 he was the most powerful man in Oregon politics—except, of course, for John Mitchell.

---

* Senator Richard Neuberger (1955-61) was Oregon's second Jewish Senator. Ron Wyden, a Portland Democrat, elected to the U.S. Senate in 1996 and reelected in 1998, 2004, and 2010, was the third.

Simon's political ascendancy matched his success as a young lawyer. Simon was assigned some of the firm's major accounts, most significantly the Oregon Rail and Navigation Company. Simon was soon the corporate secretary of the company. Indeed, throughout his political career, the public viewed Joseph Simon as a railroad attorney. Like him, Simon's political contemporaries, John Mitchell, Joseph and Cyrus Dolph, and Jonathan Bourne, Jr., were all known for their close ties to railroad company executives—and to the mountains of money these businessmen poured into Oregon politics.

Joseph Simon detested U.S. Senator John Mitchell. As a state senator, Simon was in a position to promote Joseph Dolph, his mentor and law partner, when it was time for the legislature to elect a new senator in 1882. Dolph's election and reelection (1889) to the Senate were direct results of his friendship with Joseph Simon. Ironically, John Mitchell was returned to the U.S. Senate by the legislature in 1885—and he served alongside Joseph Dolph, his longtime political foe.

As Senate president in 1897, Joseph Simon led a coalition to block Sen. Mitchell's reelection. Lawmakers went home without electing anyone to the Senate seat. The legislature was called into special session by Governor Lord in October 1898, to fill Oregon's vacant Senate seat. Guess who was chosen? Joseph Simon, president of the state Senate!

Simon served in the U.S. Senate from late 1898 until the term ended in March 1903. He did not seek reelection. Instead, Joe Simon returned to his Portland law firm, renewing his ties to the city's establishment. Forever ready to mix business and politics, Joseph Simon died in Portland in 1935 at age 84.

A Winning Strategy

Oregon's last legislature of the 19th century convened on January 9, 1899. The 90 male lawmakers had a loaded pistol at their heads. The people were in no mood for politics-as-usual. They would accept no more excuses, no more stalling, no more obstructionist tactics. The assembly had better produce or else!

William U'Ren and his Non-Partisan Direct Legislation League friends worked the Capitol halls, lobbying every solon on behalf of the proposed I & R amendment. Their careful planning, education campaign, and organization paid off. The measure sailed through both chambers by surprisingly large margins. However, before a constitutional amendment could be presented to the electorate for ratification the Oregon constitution required the approval of two consecutive legislative sessions.[24]

Lawmakers also passed a voter registration law. Now, election boards would supposedly have better control over who voted. Abuses such as repeat voting and voting under assumed names, long the scourge of Oregon elections, had triggered this election reform. The 1899 session also "passed a resolution advocating the election of senators by a direct vote of the people and asking representatives in Congress to use all honorable means within their power to accomplish that end."[25] This was 14 years before the 16th Amendment was added to the Constitution in 1913.

Republican dissension also played into U'Ren's hands. A growing number of Republican lawmakers had recently joined the Direct Legislation effort. With the tide running in favor of U'Ren's amendment, those Republicans who waited too long might miss the bandwagon. Finally, in April 1900, the Republican Party of Oregon joined Democrats and the nearly defunct Populists, and endorsed the Initiative and Referendum amendment. Had the tide finally turned for William U'Ren and the political reformers?

For nine years, William U'Ren and his army of political reformers had toiled to get the initiative and referendum adopted in Oregon. It had taken the legislature seven years to approve the constitutional amendment the first time. But before the proposal could go to voters it had to be approved a second time, by the 1901 Legislature. U'Ren and his Non-Partisan League didn't assume automatic legislative approval, nor did they intend to leave its fate to chance.

Studying the upcoming legislature, U'Ren grew uneasy. His goal was to get House and Senate approval of the I & R amendment. But the legislature needed to elect a U.S. senator. For U'Ren, this was of secondary importance. He feared that no other business would be transacted once legislators began balloting for senator. In the event of a deadlock, it was even possible the legislature could adjourn before acting on the amendment. If U'Ren was to achieve his goal, he needed the assembly to consider the amendment *before* they began balloting for senator. His strategy was simple, but brilliant.

He analyzed the composition of the new legislature. Republicans, as usual, dominated, but their numbers were declining: they held 56 of the 90 seats. The other seats were held by members elected under a variety of political labels, such as Fusion-Democrats, Regular Democrats, Silver-Republicans, Regular People's Party, and Union (or Citizens) Party. What all 34 had in common was their commitment to passage of the I & R amendment. But this minority could not get the amendment through the legislature. U'Ren would have to peel away some Republicans in order to get a majority of votes in the House and Senate. This was his strategy. Republicans were divided into two warring factions. One group stood behind John Mitchell's Senate candidate, incumbent George McBride. The Joe Simon wing of the party favored the aged Henry Corbett. Unless they could attract the votes of most of his 34 amendment backers,

U'Ren knew neither Republican faction could win and this was his trump card. If he wanted to win, Corbett couldn't antagonize the amendment supporters, nor could Mitchell and McBride. This essentially neutralized the opposition and the amendment passed.[26]

The U'Ren men also succeeded in pushing through the so-called Mays Law in 1901. This law was intended to take the Senate nomination out of the legislature's hands. Each party would nominate a Senate candidate to face off in the June general election. The winner of that contest would be considered the "people's choice." When the legislature next met, it was hoped that lawmakers would pick the people's choice. Unfortunately, there was nothing in the Mays Law that required the legislature to elect the people's choice candidate.

Lawmakers then turned their attention to choosing a senator. Balloting seesawed between Corbett and McBride. After 40 ballots everyone knew that neither man could win. Then, on the last regular day of the session, State Senator George Brownell, a Republican Party leader of Clackamas County, nominated John Mitchell. After 25 ballots (and with the votes of 11 Democrats), Mitchell was elected. "Democrats were supposedly promised positions on the Portland police and fire boards and some county offices if they would support Mitchell." One Portland house member "was allegedly given $100 every time he voted for Corbett, plus a slug of whiskey in the [House] cloakroom. One observer noted that the Southern Pacific money beat the Corbett money."[27] So, off to Washington, D.C., went John H. Mitchell—for the fourth and last time. Would the new Mays Law finally do away with the many abuses associated with how Oregon elected U.S. senators?

The Vote for Women?

Oregon men had voted in 1884 for the first time on whether to amend the state constitution to give women the vote. Abigail Scott Duniway headed the campaign to pass the amendment. With her brother, Harvey Scott, editor of the *Oregonian*, heading the opposition (which also included liquor interests and other powerful adversaries), the amendment was doomed: 28,176 against adoption, only 11,223 in favor. Sixteen years would pass before the question of women's suffrage would again appear on the ballot in June 1900.

Duniway and her legions of dedicated followers had devoted years preparing for the vote. The suffragists "arranged a systematic network of private correspondence that directed thousands of timely letters to strategic destinations. They took pains to dissociate themselves from the cause of prohibition, perceived as a liability. They worked closely with the Red Cross Society. They received endorsements from the Oregon Pioneer Association, the Oregon State Grange, the local chapter of the Grand Army of the Republic, and leading male citizens. They courted the support of several labor unions [and] they distributed an immense quantity of leaflets and varied papers."[28]

Buoyed by the surge of political reform then in vogue in Oregon, the suffragists believed victory was near. But, at the last minute, Harvey Scott launched a withering attack on the suffrage measure; on June 4, 1900, it lost by fewer than 2,200 votes (26,265 in favor, 28,402 opposed). The measure carried in 21 counties and gained over 48% of the vote. The amendment reappeared in the elections of 1906, 1908, and 1910—and was defeated each time by increasingly large margins.

The Oregon System Is Born

The election of 1902 was one of the most significant in state history. The electorate passed the I & R amendment to the Oregon Constitution by a 12-1 margin. Oregon had joined Wisconsin in the forefront of political reform in the United

Abigail Scott Duniway

Abigail Scott Duniway was the quintessential pioneer woman; her trials and tribulations were those faced by many frontier women. She was born on the family farm in Illinois in 1834, one of 12 children. Possessing a keen mind, Abigail was basically self educated. As a girl she developed her lifelong interest in writing, books, and ideas.

Abigail's large extended family, in wagons, trekked to Oregon in 1852. The trip was marred by the death of Abigail's mother. Once in Oregon, the Scotts scattered, most of them starting farms near Salem. Abigail became a teacher. A year later Abigail married Benjamin Duniway; she was 18. The couple had six children. Working from dawn to nightfall, Ben and Abigail lived on the edge, beset

OREGON HISTORICAL SOCIETY, #NEG 62620.

by unpaid bills and deepening debt. They lost their farm to creditors. And in 1862, Ben Duniway was seriously injured in a wagon accident; he would be an invalid for the rest of his life. Abigail Scott Duniway became the family breadwinner.

In 1871, the Duniways moved to Portland. There, Duniway started a reformist newspaper, *New Northwest*, featuring articles about women's suffrage, temperance, education, and women's legal rights, which she published until 1886. Over the years, *New Northwest* was the official voice of the women's suffrage movement in the

States. The initiative and referendum were the cornerstones of the "Oregon System" consisting, also, of the direct primary (1904) and recall of public officials (1908). Oregon's adoption of these political reforms was dramatic proof of the high level of popular discontent with the old order of things. Voters felt the government was getting away from them and they wanted more direct control in the making and enforcement of laws. The legislature hadn't responded to voter demands and voters were fed up with coaxing and pleading to secure the desired legislation.[29] Time had run out and Oregon voters weren't waiting any longer for the legislature to act on society's problems. The adoption of the initiative and referendum in 1902 and the granting of the vote to women in 1912 are the two most important political reforms Oregonians have ever made.

George Chamberlain Steps Up

George Chamberlain, the 1902 Democratic nominee for governor, was optimistic about victory despite a huge Republican registration edge of 3-1. A very able politician, Chamberlain's persona appealed to both Republicans and

Pacific Northwest. By the mid-1880s Abigail Duniway was recognized both regionally and nationally as one of America's pre-eminent leaders of the women's suffrage movement. She met Susan B. Anthony in 1871 when the latter visited Portland. They remained friends and allies until Anthony's death in 1906; at times, however, their friendship was strained, as the women disagreed over policy and tactics.

By the time she was 45, Abigail Duniway had raised her children, cared for her ailing husband, paid the family bills, owned and run a business, founded and published a newspaper, and made hundred of speeches throughout Oregon, Washington, and Idaho on behalf of suffrage; she was the first woman to address the Oregon Legislature (1872), and to have a novel published in Oregon (1895). In short, Abigail Duniway was a dynamo.

Used to being in charge, Duniway often clashed with other reformers. Her caustic tongue, single mindedness (some said "obsession"), her fierce independence, and insistence on doing things her way often undercut her efforts. Four times she led the effort to get the suffrage issue on the ballot in Oregon. Every time, Oregon men rejected the measure. Finally, in 1912, women's suffrage passed, making Oregon the 7th state to give women the vote. Though other, younger women had taken over leadership of the suffrage cause in Oregon, Duniway was acknowledged as the "mother" of the movement. In 1912, Abigail Scott Duniway was the first woman to register to vote in Oregon. She was 78. Abigail Duniway had made women's suffrage the focus of her life for the previous 41 years. As the stubborn voice for women's rights, Duniway became the most prominent woman in the state's history. She died in 1915, aged 81.

Democrats. One acquaintance attributed his bipartisan following to the way he represented his ideas with minimal partisanship and maximum appeal to the masses. A shrewd politician, he wasn't an early agitator but knew how to pick up reform ideas when the electorate's intentions became clear. Walter Pierce, later governor and congressman, described George Chamberlain as "a born politician, one of the most genial, affable, companionable men I ever knew."[30]

Republicans bloodied themselves in 1902. They dumped their respected governor, incumbent Ted Geer, in favor of William J. Furnish, former sheriff of Umatilla County. Like Chamberlain, Furnish stumped the state, working hard to touch voters, but he was not a good speaker. Chamberlain was a more polished speaker, though not charismatic. His effectiveness rested on the popularity of the issues he raised, and on working the audience before and after each speech. Always friendly, Chamberlain greeted people with a warm smile, pumping handshake, and lots of back-slapping. His campaign message centered on the adoption of the I & R amendment, calling it the "only salvation for the mass of the people" and exhorting Oregonians to vote for it regardless of party affiliation.[31] Other issues Chamberlain campaigned on were "municipal control of public utilities, state anti-trust legislation, and programs to benefit organized labor. Above all, he sought to eliminate machine politics in Oregon and to protect public rights in the management of state-owned lands."[32]

With over 91,000 votes cast, Chamberlain defeated Furnish by 246 votes—the closest gubernatorial election in Oregon history. Thousands of Republicans abandoned Furnish to vote for Chamberlain. From 1902 to 1920, George Chamberlain was Oregon's most important political leader.

In victory, Chamberlain followed the formula established by Democratic Gov. Sylvester Pennoyer. Downplay your Democratic party label. Stress non-partisanship. Talk about yourself and where you stand on issues. People want to know who you are and what you believe. Voters care more about these things than about whether you are a Republican or a Democrat. Chamberlain was the epitome of non-partisanship, a trait that helped him get reelected governor in 1906, and elected U.S. senator twice, in 1908 and 1914.

Like Pennoyer, Chamberlain also exploited disunity in the Republican Party. While one wing fought the other, able Democrats like Chamberlain and, later, Oswald West and Harry Lane, crafted campaigns that led to victory in an overwhelmingly Republican state.

Oregonians wanted reform in 1902. Chamberlain's ability to present himself as a reformer had a lot to do with his stunning victory; people reasoned that a vote for him was a vote for a better Oregon. The legislative races of 1902 produced impressive Democratic gains. Sixteen Democrats were elected to the House and six to the Senate. Thirty years would pass before Democrats again held as many as 22 legislative seats.

The gubernatorial contest and the initiative and referendum issues were the centerpieces of Oregon's June 1902 election. The third important question on the ballot was who would be the people's choice for U.S. senator? The Mays Law had empowered political parties to pick a nominee for the Senate seat. Democrats nominated C. E. S. Wood of Portland. Denied renomination as governor by his Republican Party, Gov. Theodore Geer sought the U.S. Senate seat. By petition, he succeeded in getting his name on the June ballot to face Wood. In what was essentially a popularity contest, Ted Geer defeated Wood by over 12,000 votes. The people had spoken: they wanted their outgoing governor to be their next senator. Voters expected the 1903 Legislature to rubber-stamp their choice. Why, Oregonians reasoned, take the time to choose a Senate candidate if the legislature did not follow the electorate's lead?

Chapter 6
George Chamberlain and the Os West Express, 1903-13

More Disappointment

Oregon bubbled with optimism as the 1903 Legislature convened in Salem. The 1902 election had produced a ringing mandate of change. Male voters passed the initiative and referendum amendment, elected a reform governor, and picked Theodore Geer as the people's choice for U.S. senator. Surely, they thought, legislators shared the public's enthusiasm for reform. The time had finally come for Oregon to remedy its most pressing social and economic ills. The session, however, turned out to be a mixed bag, legislators as often as not ignoring public opinion. There were, however, bright spots.

Electing a U.S. senator was at the top of the legislative agenda. The public held its breath. For the past 40 years, electing the state's two U.S. senators had been the main cause of political corruption in Oregon. Senator Joseph Simon, an old machine politician, was retiring. Would legislators honor the "people's choice" candidate, former governor Ted Geer and elect him senator? No, they would not. House and Senate Republicans "simply laughed at the people's choice. Geer had a few friends, but the Republican machine was determined to elect another man to the Senate."[1]

Lawmakers knew they were under siege: voter approval of a Direct Primary Law was on the horizon (and was likely to pass), the initiative and referendum were now law in Oregon, William U'Ren and his legion of People's Power League supporters were pushing for the direct election of U.S. senators, and the state's Republican majority had just elected a reform Democrat as governor. So, in 1903, the heavily Republican legislature decided it was time to take a stand: they and they alone would decide who Oregon's next senator would be.

Six prominent Republicans vied for the seat: Jonathan Bourne, Charles W. Fulton (state Senate president), Judge Henry McMinn, *Oregonian* editor Harvey

Scott, state Senator Franklin Pierce Mays, and Theodore Geer. On the fortieth ballot and last night of the session, Astoria's Charles Fulton was elected, beating back a last-minute attempt to elect Harvey Scott. The usual money and promises of federal jobs were traded for votes. Bourne spent so much he overdrew his bank account. Legislator Walter Pierce was offered $10,000 just to make a speech on Bourne's behalf; he refused the offer, and remarked that "the selling, the corruption, the trading was astonishing."[2] After State Senator John D. Daly of Corvallis promised to vote for Fulton, he later became surveyor general of Oregon on Senator Fulton's recommendation.[3] Nothing had changed. Lawmakers were going to continue to elect Senators their way.

But Fulton's election sparked an immediate backlash. Using their newly won right to the initiative, William U'Ren and the People's Power League circulated petitions to place a Direct Primary Law on the 1904 ballot.* Oregonians passed the Direct Primary Amendment 56,285 to 16,354 in 1904, using the initiative route, which confirmed William U'Ren's unflagging faith in the initiative's value. With the initiative they now had the means to chip away at the legislature's powers and change the entire system.[4]

Governor George Chamberlain's inaugural address was laced with reform proposals. He called for a reform of local taxes relating to lack of uniformity among county property assessments. He called for an inheritance tax. Chamberlain also favored compulsory arbitration of labor disputes. The governor favored increased state aid for poor school districts and a plan to consolidate districts. Despite the legislature's refusal to give up its power to elect U.S. senators, much of his program was enacted in the 1903 session. Major new acts included one that made railroads liable for worker injuries—even when the injury was caused by the negligence of another employee. Women and children gained new protections under Oregon's first statute regulating child labor, and a second which limited a woman's workday to no more than 10 hours. Oregon's first State Board of Health and State Bureau of Labor were established. The passage of Oregon's first county library law set another precedent. A provision in the recently adopted I & R amendment provided that arguments pro and con on initiative measures could be submitted to the secretary of state, who was then required to post them in a pamphlet distributed to all voters describing

---

* The Direct Primary Nominating Election Law was designed to abolish the old convention system, which was mainly responsible for the perversion of state government and the entrenchment of special privilege. Under the Direct Primary Law the people would both nominate and elect candidates.

the measures.[5] With this package of legislation, Oregon joined Wisconsin as a national leader of Progressivism at the state level.

What's in It for Me?

How could the 1903 Republican legislature, meeting in the wake of voter approval of the initiative and referendum, approve, on one hand, so much of Gov. Chamberlain's progressive agenda, while, on the other hand, ignoring the voters' mandate to elect the people's choice candidate for U.S. senator, Ted Geer?

Approving George Chamberlain's legislative package was the popular thing to do. Chamberlain, a former legislator, prosecutor, district attorney, and attorney general, had many friends and allies in the House and Senate. Although a Democrat, Chamberlain approached most issues in bipartisan fashion; he convinced lawmakers that working together they could advance the interests of all Oregonians. And his friendliness and personal charm made it easier for lawmakers to back his proposals, some of which had been around for years.

The question of why lawmakers ignored the people's choice nominee for U.S. senator is best answered this way: The framers of the U.S. Constitution had given the legislative branch in each state the power to choose their state's senators. It was a prerogative that state lawmakers did not want to give up. There were, after all, many potential benefits to being wooed by prospective senators and their backers: the promise of personal gain (jobs, contracts, even cash bribes). An even more selfish reason was this: more often than not, the Oregon legislature chose a member of the state Senate to be U.S. senator.

So, by playing along, an ambitious lawmaker might, over time, work his way into a position where *he* might end up as a viable Senate candidate. The 1903 Legislature simply did not want to part with this important power. There was just too much in it for them to let the public decide who their U.S. senator would be.

Oregon's Infamous Land Fraud Trials

Land fraud was an abiding example of post–Civil War corruption in Oregon. For over 40 years hundreds of Oregonians (and outsiders, as well) had defrauded the state and federal government out of millions of acres of public land. Fraudulent land titles came through various methods, including: bribing government officials, paying a person to file a claim (on land they never intended to live on or develop), filing a claim under a false name, or by illegal exchanging of tracts of public land. Oregon's school reserve lands were also plundered along with public domain lands. The Oregon land law of 1887 had removed virtually any

George Earle Chamberlain

Most Oregonians have never heard of George Chamberlain. Yet over a period of 30 years, 1891-1921, he was the most successful and influential politician in Oregon.

George Earle Chamberlain was born in Natchez. Mississippi, on July 1, 1854. The son of a physician, Chamberlain graduated from Washington and Lee University, where he earned a Bachelor of Arts and Law degree in 1876. Later that year, Chamberlain headed for Oregon, settling in Linn County. He immediately landed a job as a teacher and was admitted to the Oregon Bar in 1877. Chamberlain plunged into community service: as an organizer of Albany's first temperance society, as deputy clerk of Linn County in 1878-79, and as a young attorney in an established law practice. Elected to the Oregon House, Representative Chamberlain served two terms, 1880-84. Chamberlain also found time to edit a small Democratic newspaper, serve as a district attorney, 1884-86, and, in 1890, he chaired the Linn County Democratic Central Committee.

The office of attorney general was created by the legislature in 1891; Governor Sylvester Pennoyer appointed George Chamberlain to the post, and he was elected to the job in 1892. Chamberlain left the AG's office in 1895 and moved to Portland where, in 1900, he became district attorney for Multnomah County, a job he held until his inauguration as governor in January 1903.

The challenge facing Chamberlain as the Democratic nominee for governor had seemed insurmountable. For every one Democratic voter in Oregon there were at least three registered Republicans. Chamberlain campaigned as a non-partisan, rarely mentioning his Democratic affiliation. Instead, he talked about issues and about what he wanted to do as governor. A strong supporter of the Initiative and Referendum, Chamberlain attracted enough Progressive Republican votes to win the governorship; his margin of victory was only 246 votes out of over 112,000 votes cast. As governor, George Chamberlain clamped down on fraudulent land practices, pushed prison reform and salmon restoration, and democratized politics by supporting the Oregon System then taking hold in the state.

George Chamberlain liked people, moved easily through crowds, was an engaging speaker, and enjoyed campaigning. His honesty and sincerity always came across. Gov. Chamberlain ran for reelection in 1906, facing Republican James Withycombe; the governor was reelected by 2,500 votes. Chamberlain resigned on February 28, 1909, to become a U.S. senator. He was reelected by direct vote of the people in 1914, serving in the Senate until 1921. He then remained in Washington, D.C., as a member of the U.S. Shipping Board. Chamberlain died on July 9, 1928, age 69. He was buried in Arlington National Cemetery.

restraint from the sale of state lands, actually urging fraud. Between 1893 and 1905, 1.4 million acres of state lands were sold—one third of the state's grant lands. Bogus applications were filed and approved, and settlers were paid from $200 to $300 for copies of the deeds. Agents like S.A.D. (for Stephen A. Douglas) Puter and Franklin Pierce Mays then sold the fraudulent claims to the timber companies and took their commissions. Federal and state land officials were bribed to process the dummy applications quickly, before they handled the bona fide ones. From 1897 to 1903, while past and future Oregon Congressman Binger Hermann was commissioner of the U.S. Land Office in Washington, D.C., he reputedly approved thousands of bogus claims for a price.[6]

These illegal practices were so common that there was scarcely an Oregonian who did not know something about them. Hundreds of individuals and dozens of corporations had lined their pockets by defrauding the government. Some made huge fortunes doing it. How was such a racket allowed to go on for so long? For one, there were too few government land agents, and agents were often buried under mounds of paperwork. Bribes were common. Slipping an agent $10 or $20 to process a filing quickly, with minimal scrutiny, was a standard practice. A man beholden to a politician for his job wasn't likely to ask questions if one of them or their agent filed a suspicious land claim. The sentiment of "Keep your mouth shut, look the other way, do as you are told and you will keep your job and make everybody happy" infected Oregon for half a century.

Land fraud wasn't confined to any particular administration or political party. Democrats were as guilty as Republicans.* Farmers, doctors, ranchers, merchants, mayors, city councilmen, lawyers, politicians, laborers—all were involved.

All this changed when George Chamberlain became governor in 1903. Candidate Chamberlain had promised to stop the land scams and within months of taking office Governor Chamberlain appointed a new state land agent named Oswald West.

Os West was 30 when Governor Chamberlain hired him. Intelligent, enthusiastic, and honest, West took his job as custodian of state lands very seriously. After a yearlong investigation he submitted a report of his findings to Governor Chamberlain, who had earlier quietly notified top officials in the United States

---

* But recall that, after 1880, Republicans controlled the Oregon Legislature and both U.S. Senate and House seats. Thus, the greater opportunity for wrongdoing by them. All the politicians convicted in Oregon's Land Fraud Trials in 1905 were Republicans.

Department of Interior that West was unearthing dozens of examples of criminal activity. Justice Department staff began investigating behind the scenes. A federal grand jury heard testimony in Portland in early 1904. A second jury met from November 1904 through April 1905 and initially issued 26 indictments, affecting 100 persons. The indictments produced a wave of incredulity in Oregon because there were some big fish in the net. President Theodore Roosevelt appointed a Special United States Prosecutor, Francis J. Heney, and sent him to Portland to try the government's cases against the 34 persons indicted (one of whom was a woman). Included were three Oregon state senators (Franklin Pierce Mays, Robert Booth, and Winlock Steiwer); a state representative (Willard N. Jones); both of Oregon's congressmen (John N. Williamson and Binger Hermann); United States Attorney John Hall; former United States Deputy Surveyor Henry Meldrum; and Stephen A. Douglas Puter, the alleged "King of the Oregon Land Fraud Ring." The biggest fish of all was Oregon's senior United States senator, John Mitchell. Oregonians were stunned and many rallied to Mitchell's defense.

Senator Mitchell came out swinging. On January 17, 1905, he addressed the Senate, delivering an angry rebuttal and denying all allegations of wrongdoing. "I deny, in the most absolute and unqualified terms, that S.A.D. Puter ... offer[ed] money, or [gave] me the sum of $2,000 in two $1,000 bills, as an inducement to use my influence with Binger Hermann, then Commissioner of the General Land Office, to induce him to pass to patent twelve certain homestead entries."[7] Mitchell was indicted two weeks later, on February 1, 1905.

Senator Mitchell's Portland trial began on June 20 and ended on July 3, 1905. His friends competed for space in the crowded courtroom. Journalists from all over took copious notes. Mitchell proclaimed his innocence. The jury saw it differently. "After deliberating seven-and-a-half hours, [the jury] returned at 11 o'clock that night, while the din of firecrackers and the blare of skyrockets were heralding the approaching [July] Fourth, with this verdict: we find the defendant guilty as charged."[8] There it was: John Mitchell was guilty of bribery and perjury. A collective gasp rolled through the packed courtroom. After 22 years as an Oregon senator and 43 years as a Republican Party boss, John Mitchell had fallen. The judge sentenced the senator to six months in the Multnomah County jail and fined him $1,000. John Mitchell didn't serve his sentence. He died on December 8, 1905, after slipping into a diabetic coma following dental surgery.[9]

Of the 34 federal indictments handed down in the land scandals, 33 persons were convicted. Stephen A. Douglas Puter fled Oregon but was captured and returned to Portland. Convicted of conspiracy to defraud the government, he was sentenced to two years in the county jail and fined $7,500. He served eighteen months in jail and was pardoned by President Roosevelt on December 31, 1908. Congressman Binger Hermann escaped conviction on a technicality. State Senator Steiwer was convicted of conspiracy after pleading guilty. He received no sentence. State Rep. Willard Jones was sentenced to one year at McNeil Island Penitentiary and fined $2,000. State Sen. Franklin Mays was convicted of conspiracy to defraud the government and sentenced to four months in jail and assessed the largest fine, $10,000.

The public was relieved. Forty-five years of political abuse were ending. It was a new day for Oregon government. Oregonians wouldn't forget George Chamberlain or Oswald West for helping end a half-century of corruption and land fraud schemes. But there was more to do. Women must be enfranchised, and voters needed the power (the recall) to remove corrupt, incompetent officeholders who were unwilling to represent the views of their constituents.

Reform Continues with the 1905 Legislature

Prodded by grassroots lobbying from William U'Ren and the People's Power League, the legislature in 1905 passed even more reform legislation than it had in 1903. Governor Chamberlain's popularity also made it tough for lawmakers to ignore his legislative wish-list. "The hottest battle of the 1905 session revolved around the Wet-Dry issue. The Dry forces fought to sustain the local option law passed by the people under the initiative in 1904."[10] The local option law permitted voters in a precinct to decide whether or not to ban alcoholic consumption and sales within their precinct—even though their county might be Wet.

With no U.S. senator to elect, the legislature got down to business. Dozens of important laws were enacted, including the establishment of a state library commission. Cornelia Marvin of Wisconsin was hired as the first secretary of the commission. Miss Marvin induced women's clubs all over the state to open subscription libraries. She set up traveling libraries and a system of lending books by mail order and without charge—the first such system in the United States.[11] Country folk had no electricity in 1905 and few had telephones. Thousands of Oregonians lived isolated, lonely lives. With books by mail, rural Oregonians were better connected to the outside world.

Other important legislation included acts for the care of dependent, neglected, and delinquent children, as well as for the rehabilitation of wayward girls; a parole law; and creation of a commission to establish an institution for epileptic and retarded children.[12] A comprehensive food and drug law was enacted and the 1903 child labor law was strengthened. At Governor Chamberlain's urging, the assembly also approved a bill to provide whipping posts for wife beaters, with a maximum punishment of 20 lashes. Lawmakers also enthusiastically passed a resolution expressing confidence in Sen. John Mitchell, recently under federal indictment for bribery and conspiracy.

Enter Dr. Harry Lane

Portland experienced another significant event in the summer of 1905—the June mayoral election. Lane, grandson of General Joseph Lane, was elected mayor. Lane was a medical doctor whom Gov. Sylvester Pennoyer had appointed superintendent of the State Insane Asylum in 1887, and later to the new State Board of Health (1903). Harry Lane won election on June 5, 1905, by 1,200 votes and his election closed an era in Portland's history. Lane was reelected in 1907, making him Portland's first two-term Democratic mayor. During his time as mayor, Portland made strides in confronting long-ignored municipal problems.[13] Oregon now had an honest and dedicated reform mayor in its largest city and a man of like qualities in the governor's chair. The People's Power League was also gaining strength and it had a long list of reforms it intended to introduce via the initiative.

Chamberlain Gets Another Four Years

Oregon's 1906 campaign season was unusually contentious. The featured contests were Governor Chamberlain's reelection bid, and selection of the people's choice candidate for U.S. senator. Chamberlain's reform record and leadership style were major issues in the race. He campaigned vigorously in favor of the Oregon System and for further political and social reform. His opponent was Republican James Withycombe, a veterinarian, educator, and agriculturalist. Withycombe was not a seasoned politician. Chamberlain crisscrossed Oregon in his campaign. Newspapers were the primary source of news, and he was a master at wrangling interviews with the local editor. A feature story on his speech and interview normally made the front page of the next edition.

The *Oregon Statesman* noted that registered Republicans outnumbered Democrats in Oregon in 1906, 62,230 to 23,753. Always mindful of the odds against a partisan Democrat, Chamberlain distanced himself from his party label. Non-partisanship and discussion of the day's issues were his campaign focus. Voters reelected him in June (Chamberlain, 46,000; Withycombe, 43,500). George Chamberlain remained Oregon's most popular politician.

Voters also turned their attention to 11 state ballot measures whose subjects ranged over divorcing public utilities from politics, prohibiting free passes on railroads, and levying a gross earnings tax on refrigerator and oil cars, on Pullman sleepers, and on express, telephone, and telegraph companies.[14] Voters learned quickly to use the initiative to accomplish reform. The public realized that the old, cozy ties between big railroads such as Southern Pacific and Northern Pacific and Oregon legislators kept the legislature from regulating railroads. With the initiative the people did not have to wait for the legislature to act—they could pass their own laws.

Testing the Direct Primary Law

Voters tested the 1904 Direct Primary Law on April 20, 1906, when they held the state's first nominating election. The days of machine-controlled conventions and hand-picked candidates were over. Now, any man who met the qualifications and secured the necessary number of signatures was eligible to file as a candidate. Republicans, Democrats, and third parties would choose a nominee for each state, county, and local office, as well as for U.S. senator, to represent their party in the general election. The Direct Primary Law allowed candidates for the legislature to sign a pledge known as Statement Number One agreeing to always vote for the candidate for U.S. senator who received the popular majority. There was, however, no requirement to sign the pledge, and there was no penalty for breaking it, other than voter displeasure.[15]

The Direct Primary Law had its enemies and U'Ren and the People's Power League wanted it to have a fair trial. To assure that the measure worked as intended, its backers wanted a Senate candidate who would build his campaign on the Direct Primary Law. The office of U.S. senator was the biggest prize in the political basket and U'Ren didn't want "to take any chances that, through failure of the Senatorial provision in the primary law, it would be put back on the legislative auction block."[16] U'Ren had trouble finding a candidate willing to run for senator with Statement Number One as a platform.

U'Ren was rebuffed by several prospective Senate candidates. He then asked Jonathan Bourne, Jr., to run for the office. For years, Bourne had been closely associated with the Joseph Simon wing of the Republican machine. When John Mitchell double-crossed Bourne in 1897, Bourne had joined U'Ren to produce the infamous Hold-Up session. Bourne continued working with U'Ren for the initiative and referendum and was a key player in the 1904 Direct Election campaign. For nearly a decade Bourne was one of Oregon's premier reformers, an architect of the Oregon System. Yet, he was an enigma who carried the torch of reform in one hand and a bag of campaign cash in the other. In the last 20 years Bourne had pumped tens of thousands of his own dollars into Oregon campaigns. As an old-school wheeler-dealer politician and one of Oregon's most important political reformers, he had a foot in both the past and present. He hardly seemed to be the man reform-minded voters were looking for.

Had William U'Ren lost his senses? Why did he think Bourne was the best Senate choice? Bourne, like U'Ren, wasn't wedded to a political party label. He didn't believe in party lines or regularity and most of the time he was off on his own pursuing his individual goals. He was smitten with the game of politics and since his family's fortune gave him a generous income, he wasn't in it for monetary gain. U'Ren turned to Bourne because he both liked and trusted him. He knew Bourne was intelligent, intensely aggressive, and dedicated to popular government. Most important, Jonathan Bourne was committed to making the Statement One provision of the Direct Primary Law work. There was immense educational work to do throughout the state to instruct voters in the new methods. Most of that instruction would "have to be done through the mails, and postage used on such a scale was expensive. Bourne was just the man to make the campaign. His record would hardly bear close scrutiny, but he was sympathetic with the scheme of giving the government back to the people, and that was what would count in this campaign."[17] Long-time Mitchell-Republican and prominent Portland attorney Harold M. Cake challenged Bourne for their party's senatorial nomination. Running on a "Popular Government" platform, Bourne made Statement One the single issue of the primary election. In the minds of voters, Bourne's name and Statement One were linked. The public shared his desire that Statement One should work as intended. This time around, Oregonians expected their people's choice senator to be elected by the 1907 Legislature. A vote for Bourne was seen as a vote for the Direct Primary Law. A victory for Jonathan Bourne would be a victory for the people.

Candidate Bourne edged Cake for the Republican Senate nomination on April 20, 1906. In June, he faced the Democratic nominee, John M. Gearin, who had been appointed to fill Mitchell's seat after his sudden death in December 1905. As he had in the primary, Bourne scored a narrow victory, defeating Gearin 42,538 to 39,417. Despite continued opposition from key Republicans, Bourne was elected to the Senate by the 1907 Legislature. U'Ren's plan had worked perfectly. By making the commitment to Statement One a qualification for nomination and election to the legislature, Bourne, U'Ren, and the People's Power League succeeded in binding legislators to honor their statement pledge and, thus, to vote for the people's choice for Senate. Senator Bourne did everything he could to promote political reform. For an old machine politico, his metamorphosis was miraculous.

The Campaign and Election of 1908

Oregon was awash in politics in 1908. Three elections were scheduled: the April primary (when Republicans and Democrats would choose their party nominees for the legislature, statewide offices, U.S. senator, and House of Representatives); the June general election (when voters would decide who their state legislators and state officials would be, the people's choice for U.S. senator, and who would represent Oregon in the U.S. House of Representatives, as well as the fate of 19 ballot measures; and the November federal election for president.

With hundreds of volunteers, the People's Power League funneled various reform proposals to voters. The legislature even referred three constitutional amendments to the ballot. Controversy still swirled around Statement One. Would lawmakers balk when it came time to honor their statement pledge and ignore the people's choice for Senate? Or would they follow the lead of the 1906 Legislature and honor the people's candidate? Would enemies of Statement One succeed in weakening it?

The 1908 Senate election was the hottest political contest. Charles Fulton, Oregon's last machine-picked senator, stood for reelection. Portlander Harold Cake challenged Senator Fulton. In February, William U'Ren stirred things up when he announced that he, too, was a Senate candidate. Was he really interested in being a senator? Or was he merely using his candidacy as a platform to promote the four People's Power League initiatives on the ballot? U'Ren's true motive was to defend Statement One from its enemies.

Most critics of the pledge were old-guard Republicans like Harvey Scott. Legislative leaders hated the pledge because it effectively stripped them of their power to elect senators, a loss they deeply resented. U'Ren submitted an initiative measure in the 1908 election designed to strengthen Statement One by making it more difficult for legislators to ignore the people's choice for U.S. Senate.* Foes of Statement One saw the measure as an opportunity to convince

---

* U'Ren's measure was intended to put more teeth into the Statement One pledge by making it a direct instruction to the legislature. A legislator who had taken the pledge should feel obligated to vote for the people's choice candidate for U.S. senator. The problem was that even if a legislator signed the pledge he was not obligated to honor it; but one who failed to do so knew that he would likely face the wrath of voters, thousands of whom belonged to U'Ren's grassroots organization, the People's Power League. That's what happened in the April 1908 primary: two dozen Republican legislative candidates who refused to sign Statement One were defeated. 1906 was the last year that the legislature refused to elect the people's choice. It was a different story in 1908. An angry electorate

the public to kill the pledge once and for all. Their campaign included these arguments: the pledge weakened political parties; the constitutional rights and duties of legislators were violated; and the pledge had forced Oregon to abandon the representative form of government that was guaranteed to every state by the Constitution of the United States.[18] Their opposition energized the state's political reformers to organize a potent statewide campaign. U'Ren's Statement One measure was overwhelmingly approved, 69,700 to 21,150. Voters sent a clear message that they wanted to choose their U.S. senators and they expected their legislature to rubberstamp that choice.

U'Ren didn't trust Fulton, whose recent claims to now favor the direct election of senators didn't wash with U'Ren. When Harold M. Cake announced on February 29, 1908, that he approved the primary law and favored Statement One, U'Ren withdrew from the Senate contest.[19] He endorsed Cake and urged his followers to do the same.

On March 14, 1908, Gov. George Chamberlain was the last candidate to enter the Senate race, agreeing to be a candidate if Democrats nominated him in the April primary (which they did). The governor reiterated his strong support for the Direct Primary Law and commitment to "electing only candidates for the legislature who are willing to bind themselves to vote for that candidate for U.S. Senator receiving the highest number of votes."[20] He made Statement One the centerpiece of his campaign.

The Fulton/Cake Republican contest was tense and divisive. Trying to neutralize a late tirade of bitter speeches by Fulton, Cake resorted to heavy newspaper advertising. His message was direct: "For two years I have fought the efforts of the old machine to wrest from the people their right to elect their own Senator and to restore the old corrupt system which had brought disgrace upon the whole state."[21] The bruising campaign ended with a 3,000-vote victory for Cake on April 17, 1908. Reform Republicans had ousted a member of their party from his Senate seat, confirming the GOP as a two-headed dragon which fed upon itself. Democrats nominated Governor Chamberlain as their Senate nominee.

Republicans outnumbered registered Democrats 3-1, so Chamberlain faced an uphill battle in June. Yet he won the people's choice nomination for senator by a margin of 1,500 votes out of 112,000 cast. It was the third time Chamberlain had overcome huge odds to take a major political office away from a Republican.

---

was watching. This time, lawmakers honored the people's choice, electing Democratic Governor George Chamberlain to the U.S. Senate.

What was Chamberlain's appeal? His ability to portray himself as a true non-partisan, as a man who believed that issues and ideas should prevail over blind party loyalty, had broad appeal. Other explanations for his success include his incumbency: he had a record to run on. He was a champion of reform and a tireless cheerleader for his ideas; Oregonians knew where he stood on issues. In speaking his mind, Chamberlain didn't offend people. He never criticized an opponent's personal qualities, always focusing on issues and the differences between his position and his opponent's.

Senator Jonathan Bourne also played a critical role in Chamberlain's victory. Bourne was Oregon's highest-ranking Republican officeholder. He rushed home from Washington, D.C., when he was warned that Statement One might be in trouble in the upcoming election. Upon his return, Bourne campaigned vigorously to make the Statement One pledge binding. As old-guard Republicans shuddered, Bourne also said Chamberlain was the best qualified candidate to be senator. In endorsing Chamberlain, he put his reform wing of the Republican Party into the governor's corner. The savvy Bourne saved the best for last: he invited Republican President Theodore Roosevelt to visit Oregon to endorse Democrat George Chamberlain's candidacy. During his visit, the president urged the next legislature to honor the people's choice, electing George Chamberlain to the Senate. Roosevelt's endorsement of Chamberlain and the Oregon System was far more popular with voters than the cries of stalwart Republican legislators who hated both Statement One and the thought that they might have to vote for Democrat Chamberlain for the Senate.

The last factor explaining Chamberlain's broad appeal was his link with the People's Power League. Even though William U'Ren endorsed Harold Cake, the rank-and-file leaguers were likely drawn to Chamberlain. The governor's strong stances favoring the Oregon System and work of the league sat well with that group.

An aroused public watched with special interest the convening of Oregon's 25th Legislative Assembly in January 1909. Would this Republican body honor their Statement One pledges and elect Democrat George Chamberlain to the Senate? Jay Bowerman presided in the Senate and C. M. McArthur in the House. Balloting for the Senate occurred on January 19 and backroom bargaining continued up to the hour of the vote. Many reluctant Republicans searched for a way out of their Statement One pledges. Surely, there must be some technicality, some way to keep from voting for a Democrat! But, when balloting began, Chamberlain's victory was confirmed. The governor got 19 of 30 Senate votes and 34 of 60 House ballots, and became Oregon's first Democratic senator since

LaFayette Grover left the office in 1883. Chamberlain's election reaffirmed the national precedent Oregon had set in 1906—electing a United States senator by a direct vote of the people. Again, Oregon led the nation down the path of political reform. Nebraska, Nevada, Colorado, and seven other states adopted some version of Oregon's plan of pledging legislative candidates to vote for the people's choice for Senate. The rest of the country had to wait for ratification of the 17th Amendment in 1913 before they, too, got the right to elect their U.S. senators directly.

William Jennings Bryan, for the third and last time, was the Democratic nominee for president in 1908. Back in 1896, Bryan nearly carried Oregon over William McKinley. (Allegations of vote tampering in Multnomah County suggest that Bryan may, in fact, have won Oregon.) But by 1908 things had changed. The money question had faded as a political issue. And Theodore Roosevelt had been president for seven years. Roosevelt's popularity remained high in 1908. The fact that he had visited Oregon twice (in 1903 and 1908) had endeared Roosevelt to voters; consequently he had taken 67% of the Oregon vote in 1904. Six years into its own remarkable political transformation, the state welcomed the president's Progressive policies and reforms. When Roosevelt stepped aside in favor of his Secretary of War William Howard Taft for president, Oregonians dutifully voted for TR's choice. Democrat Bryan took only 34% of the Oregon vote in 1908, down from the 48% he had carried here in 1896.

Voters had considered 19 amendments to the Oregon Constitution in the June election. Measure 13, recall of public officials, passed by nearly 2-1. Oregonians now had a tool with which to remove an elected officeholder. The three cornerstones of the Oregon System were finally in place: the initiative, the referendum, and the recall. Another important amendment changed the state's June general election date to November, a practice followed to this day. For the first time voters had decided an issue brought to the ballot via the referendum. Two other ballot measures passed in June were a Corrupt Practices Act designed to eliminate election day vote fraud and the People's Power League initiative to bind legislators to elect the people's choice for United States senator. For the fourth time, Oregon men defeated the proposed women's suffrage amendment, 58,670 to 36,858. "The total number of measures and amendments passed was greater than the number submitted in any previous election—or subsequent election until 1920."[22] Popular government was ablaze in Oregon. Other envious Americans watched what Oregon was doing to change its political and social landscape. The Oregon System had taken Oregon to places few states had been.

The Contest for Governor

Chamberlain resigned the governorship on February 28, 1909, to take his Senate seat. Republican Secretary of State Frank Benson became governor on March 1. Benson's poor health kept him in California hospitals most of his term. He resigned on June 17, 1910, and state Senate President Jay Bowerman became temporary governor.

Early one morning in late July 1910, Oswald West returned to his Portland hotel room on Washington Street. He had paid a late-night visit to the Sellwood home of Harry Lane, former Portland mayor. He'd tried to persuade Lane to be the Democratic candidate for governor and left the doctor's home with the understanding that Lane would call him within the hour with an answer. The weary West nervously waited for Lane's call.

> I ate a banana and crawled into bed. Lay awake hoping for a call from Dr. Lane, but none came. I again surveyed the field for a suitable candidate. As the time neared 2 a.m., I decided to become a candidate myself. So, I arose, dumped the remaining bananas out of the bag; split it down the sides; flattened it out and wrote a gubernatorial platform; crawled back into bed; cried and fell asleep. In the morning, I caught an early train for Salem; borrowed the required filing fee from my fellow [railroad] commissioner Tom Campbell, and thus became the Democratic candidate for Governor and—strange as it may seem—was elected.[23]

A bruising contest between Oswald West and Republican Jay Bowerman followed. The men were two of the rising stars in Oregon politics; West was 36, Bowerman 33. Both campaigned nonstop. To West, every town, no matter how small or remote, was an important destination. He trudged into fields, barber shops, banks, mining and lumber camps to talk to voters. No man ever worked harder to get elected. Wherever there was a solitary voter, Os West tried to reach him; he was in constant motion.

The stakes were high in 1910. Bowerman opposed the Statement One pledge and rested his campaign on that issue. And there was another issue, which the astute West was quick to exploit. Jay Bowerman became his party's nominee in a series of controversial party "assemblies." West claimed the assemblies were an attempt to return Oregon to the old days when a handful of party bosses—not individual party members—picked the candidates for office. These assemblies were merely resurrected state party nominating conventions with a new name—and they were an attack on the 1904 Direct Primary Law. To Os West, Bowerman's candidacy was an assault on the Oregon System itself. His campaign for governor thus was a mission to protect Oregon's infant political reforms.

Harvey Scott had been a leading critic of Oregon's Direct Primary Law since 1906 and he opposed it for two reasons. First, the law allowed virtually any adult male to run for public office. Scott was convinced that the direct primary "opened the way to demagogues and political adventurers, men without party responsibility or backing."[24] Second, Scott believed the direct primary weakened the two-party system. He and other Republican Party leaders were dedicated to weakening the direct primary system and returning Oregon to the old way of choosing party candidates in conventions. On July 14, Harvey Scott wrote: "Those [candidates] who take Statement One should understand that every effort will be made to beat them in both the primary and general election. Against all pretend Republicans who take Statement One 'the knife' will be used with the utmost vigor and to the hilt."[25]

Twenty-four of these assembly-picked Republican legislative candidates were defeated in the primary election. All had campaigned against Statement One. If there was any "knifing" of candidates in 1910 it was not at Harvey Scott's hand, but, rather, at the hands of the friends of Statement One, said William U'Ren, speaking for the People's Power League.

Os West was fond of reciting this line about his opponent: "Bowerman is running away from his record, and I am running on mine."[26] At Heppner, in northeast Oregon, West said: "This is a contest not between men but between principles. There is a great question, a mighty issue, which confronts the people of the state. It is the question of whether the people or the corporations shall run this state. It is a question for the people to decide on November 8, whether they will rule themselves, or whether they will surrender their government into the hands of big business and machine politicians."[27]

Two of Oregon's best-known leaders jumped into the governor's contest on West's behalf. Senator George Chamberlain returned from the Capitol to campaign for his protégé. And the man West had tried to persuade to run for governor, Harry Lane, also joined in. Lane pounded Bowerman and the Republican leadership in a series of speeches, charging that they believed "the people are too ignorant to rule themselves, [that] we must forget party lines—we must stand for ourselves."[28] Republican Sen. Jonathan Bourne, true to his Progressive colors, also campaigned for West. Republican leaders were incensed by Bourne's abandonment of Bowerman—and they would not forgive or forget it.

Jay Bowerman faced other obstacles. His party, as usual, was in disarray. Many Republicans disagreed with Harvey Scott and resented his attempt to

Oswald West

Although Os West governed a century ago his name is often mentioned today. West is remembered as the politician responsible for preserving Oregon's Pacific coastline as a public beach. Modern governors Tom McCall and Robert Straub often invoked the memory of Os West and his environmental legacy. Indeed, in 1967, McCall cajoled a reluctant legislature to enact Oregon's Beach Bill, reminding lawmakers that it was their chance to build upon West's great achievement.

West was born into a family of seven children in Ontario, Canada, in 1873. His family immigrated to Oregon when he was a small boy. Educated in Salem public schools, West dropped out at 16 to work as a bank messenger. Three years later, West was a teller, a job he did until 1889. When the Klondike Gold Rush got underway, he headed to Alaska; six months later, West was back in Salem, no richer than when he had left. In 1903, Oregon's new governor, Democrat George Chamberlain, appointed Os West as state land agent. In that role, West established a reputation as an honest and hard-working public servant. He went after crooked land speculators who had fraudulently secured over 900,000 acres of Oregon school lands. West's diligence in getting the acreage returned to the state did not go unnoticed. In 1907, West was appointed to the Oregon Railroad Commission, a regulatory agency that had been given little authority to change anything. Os West, however, took this job seriously too. So he began to walk along hundreds of miles of rail line, inspecting the tracks and talking with farmers and ranchers as he met them. Rail company practices had turned public opinion against

impose his will on the party. Some didn't favor the assembly idea. Others were committed to the direct primary and Statement One. Bowerman was on retainer to the Southern Pacific Railroad Company and many were suspicious of his corporate ties. Another hurdle was of his own making. He had earlier publicly blasted Statement One and, as Senate president, had voted for a bill that would have made it a misdemeanor to take the Statement One pledge.

Oswald West ran his campaign on a shoestring and relied on the generosity of citizens to provide him free housing, meals, and transportation. Local supporters usually rented the hall in which West spoke. Ben Olcott (his brother-in-law and future governor) printed and distributed thousands of handbills. In one, West promised that if elected, "no corporation nor individuals, nor machine nor combination of men, will have the slightest claim on me."[29]

the railroads; indeed, the railroads were a target of the Populist uprising of the 1890s, and Progressives in the early 19th century. Oregonians appreciated West's work on the commission and his advocacy for tighter regulation of the industry. In 1910, West decided to run for governor. Because Republicans outnumbered Democrats 3-1, he followed Gov. Chamberlain's example by campaigning on a non-partisan platform. West visited dozens of small towns, talking with individuals, civic groups, and local newspaper editors. West won, defeating acting governor, Republican Jay Bowerman, by 6,000 votes.

Faced with an overwhelmingly Republican legislature, West knew that he could not advance his reform agenda without reminding lawmakers that, as governor, he had the power to veto bills. During the 1911 session, Gov. West vetoed 63 bills, about one-fourth of all measures enacted. Things were different for West in the 1913 session. With support from the few Democrats and a handful of Progressive Republicans—along with the threat of the veto—West found that lawmakers were willing to play ball with him. West, a champion of direct legislation via initiative petition, also bypassed the legislature, working, instead, with citizen groups who were backing dozens of initiative petitions. During his tenure voters passed women's suffrage and set up a workers' compensation system, while the legislature (with West's blessing) established the office of state forester, a bureau of forestry, and a fish and game commission. But West's major achievement was a 1913 bill (written by him) making Oregon's entire Pacific coastline public property. It was this act of 1913 that Tom McCall and others built upon in the 20th century. West did not seek reelection in 1914. He did, however, challenge Republican Charles McNary in the 1918 U.S. Senate race. West lost badly. Later, West earned a law degree, practiced law, became a lobbyist, and remained active in the Democratic Party. Always controversial, Os West lived until 1960, dying at age 87.

The final tally showed a decisive victory for West, 54,850 to Bowerman's 48,750; Socialist W. S. Richard pulled 8,000 votes. For the third consecutive election, a minority Democrat had been elected governor.

On November 10, the Medford *Mail-Tribune* carried a "thank you" statement from the governor-elect on its front page. West promised "As governor, I shall not be the representative of any class, faction or clique, but shall be the public servant and active agent of all the people." The editor, in the same edition, wrote something with which many historians have agreed: "Mr. West will make the best governor Oregon ever had."[30]

Harvey Scott, *Oregonian* editor, didn't live to see Bowerman's defeat. One of the fathers of the Oregon Republican Party and the two-party system, Scott died in August 1910. Oregonians had been treated to his pen and opinions since 1865.

Heightened voter interest in 1910 was due to the exciting race for governor and also to one of the longest ballots in state history, with 34 state and county races featuring 131 candidates. There were also 32 state ballot measures, including several constitutional amendments. A measure prohibiting the sale and consumption of alcoholic beverages in Oregon aroused the most interest. The Prohibition measure lost by 25,000 votes. The question of woman's suffrage appeared on the ballot for the fifth time and Oregon men defeated it again. Voter turnout in 1910 continued at about 75%, in line with most elections held in Oregon between 1904 and 1910.

Governor Oswald West

Oswald West was 38 when he was inaugurated Oregon's 14th governor on January 10, 1911. His meteoric rise to the governorship had been extraordinary; only eight years earlier he was a junior bank clerk in Astoria. When his term ended in 1915 he stepped aside, satisfied with what he had accomplished. Building on the Progressive foundation laid by his mentor and predecessor, George Chamberlain, Governor West was about to take Oregon on an unforgettable ride through a choppy sea of reforms.

West was a complex man, a bundle of paradoxes. He was widely considered to be a champion of the people, a fighter for the rights and interests of ordinary people. He often condemned big corporations, believing them to be greedy and indifferent to the welfare of both their employees and the greater community. West believed that businessmen generally had low ethical standards. Yet, after he left public office in 1915, he established a lucrative law practice in Portland, and took utility companies for clients. He even became a utility lobbyist.

Oswald West followed a set of basic personal principles. What he said and did was generally consistent with these principles. One of West's enduring principles was his steadfast belief in public service. "I was taught to believe that a public office was a public trust and that political dishonesty, extravagance and waste should not be tolerated," said West.[31] Yet, on one occasion as governor, West ordered the speaker of the Oregon House locked in his office so West could get a pet bill passed. A fiscal conservative, West scrutinized legislative appropriation bills and regularly cut funds he believed wasteful, unnecessary, or unaffordable for the state. He was notably single minded and his "strong sense that what he was doing was right, led him to employ methods that were often bizarre, sometimes devious, and even at times autocratic, but always colorful and bearing the stamp of his personality."[32]

As a Progressive, Governor West believed government could produce a more orderly and humane society. Government should help people in need. He trusted the people to make wise decisions, provided they had access to accurate information. An impatient man, he wanted to get things done and he sometimes resented those who disagreed, or who stood in his way. He wasn't interested in power for the sake of status or personal prestige. Power was the tool through which he could make the sweeping changes he believed the people of Oregon had elected him to make. He believed he was in a race against time to get something done.

Os West hated liquor. He was a proud prohibitionist and an active and outspoken leader in both the 1909 and 1914 campaigns to make Oregon a "dry" state.

Os West always kept in mind that he was elected to protect and extend the Oregon System. He believed his job was to "do everything in my power to forestall any attempts of the legislators to tamper with the laws enacted by the people."[33] As governor, he was the guardian of all the Progressive reforms dating back to 1902. As a seasoned politician, he was aware of the pitfalls awaiting him as a reformer (and a minority Democrat) facing a Republican legislature. But he loved a good fight and was fond of saying that he was "born to stir up trouble."[34] Consequently, Governor West had more than his share of confrontations.

West and Bowerman Lock Horns

Governor Oswald West worked with the 1911 and 1913 legislatures, both overwhelmingly Republican. The 1911 House consisted of 57 Republicans, two Democrats, and one independent. The Senate had 26 Republicans, three Democrats, and one independent. Yet there were 15 to 20 reform-minded lawmakers West could occasionally count on for support. The 1911 session produced little significant legislation. It was a classic confrontation between a popular and aggressive new governor and a legislature dominated by conservative Republicans. West and his gubernatorial rival Jay Bowerman were at loggerheads, with Bowerman making West's life miserable.

When West arrived in Salem, corporate lobbyists and the old guard politicians were there in force. One reporter wrote: "You can't take a step without walking upon the toes of some lobbyist, so thick are they oozing through the State house in crowds; those who want appropriations; those who want bills defeated and those who want bills passed. The corporations are well represented: telephone, telegraph, railroad, power and light all have agents. Sometimes the rotunda resembles the director's meeting of a $20 million plant—there is such a plentitude of corporation lawyers."[35]

Jay Bowerman led the obstructionists—those legislators bent on blocking and embarrassing the West administration. West's foes were mainly in the Senate, though Bowerman had supporters in the House, as well. Together, these foes posed a serious obstacle to West's legislative agenda. But Governor West fought fire with fire. He announced: "that if they persisted in killing all his measures, then he would veto any bill they favored without even reading it, whether it had merit or not." The veto, or the threat of it, turned out to be one of the most potent weapons in his arsenal. Fortunately for West, there was a friendly legislative minority often strong enough to sustain his vetoes. Forced by circumstances to live up to his threat in the 1911 session, West piled up a record 63 vetoes.[36] The 1911 Legislature was a captive of this tug-of-war between a strong-willed governor pledged to reform and an equally tough former Senate president dedicated to blocking those reforms. "It was no clean business. It was dog-eat-dog," said West.[37]*

When the session adjourned after 41 days, on February 18, neither West nor the legislature had much to show for their efforts. The *Oregon Journal*, the state's leading Democratic newspaper, said legislators passed "peanut bills" and concerned themselves with trivial matters. The editor went on to write: "There are many good men in the body. It was their misfortune [that] certain holdover senators were bent more on playing politics than legislating for the state. These circumstances created two legislative factions—and with Bowerman's crowd playing for obstruction—the hands of men anxious to serve the state were tied."[38]

The Woman Suffrage Victory of 1912

The Progressive Era in Oregon—as embodied by the administrations of governors George Chamberlain and Oswald West—reached its zenith in 1912 and

---

* A fine example of West's struggle with the legislature was the controversy over the state printer bill. West introduced a bill to put the printer on a flat salary. Since its establishment in territorial days, the office of printer had been controversial. The printer took his salary from the fees he charged for each printing job—and there was no limit on what he could charge. West thought the practice invited corruption and often produced an extravagant expenditure of public money. On the last day of the 1911 session West's bill sat in a House committee, having already passed the Senate. Without warning, the bill was passed out of committee and indefinitely postponed by a House vote. The governor's bill appeared to be dead. Only a suspension of House rules would permit a vote to reverse its earlier action. Speaker John P. Rusk refused to allow such a vote. When Rusk went to his office, West had him followed. Once he was inside, the speaker's door was locked from the outside, trapping him. With Rusk out of the way, West's friends suspended the House rules, lifted the bill from postponement, and passed it. With an irate Rusk shouting from his locked office, Os West got his way. See Case, "The Oregon System," 143, 146.

1913. For the sixth time the question of woman's suffrage was on the Oregon ballot. The measure's crushing defeat in 1910 was still fresh in the public's mind. But things were different in 1912. Abigail Duniway, still the titular head of the woman's suffrage movement in Oregon, was elderly and ailing. The torch had been passed to new, younger, women, notably Esther Clayson Pohl Lovejoy, a physician and public health official, and Josephine Mayer Hirsch, wealthy social leader and activist. Mrs. Hirsch was president of the Portland Equal Suffrage League. Joining Pohl Lovejoy and Hirsch was W. M. "Pike" Davis, president of the Men's Equal Suffrage Club of Multnomah County.

Women in all of Oregon's border-state neighbors had the vote by 1912: Idaho (1896), Washington (1910), and California (1911). Consequently, there was a heightened sense of urgency to adopt woman suffrage here in 1912. A host of non-suffrage organizations were active in the campaign: the Women's Christian Temperance Union, the State Federation of Labor, the Oregon State Grange, and the Socialist Party of Oregon backed the amendment's passage.

1912 was a good year for woman's suffrage to be on the Oregon ballot. Also on the November ballot were two important political contests featuring prominent progressives. Three progressive candidates were vying for the presidency: Woodrow Wilson, New Jersey's reform governor; Theodore Roosevelt, the Progressive Party nominee; and Eugene Debs, labor leader and Socialist Party candidate. Five of the six candidates to be the people's choice for U.S. Senate were also reformers. "For Esther Pohl Lovejoy, the important thing about the suffrage victory in November 1912 was not that the initiative passed with only 52% of the vote, a margin of only 4,161. Rather, it was the impressive increase from the 37% who supported suffrage in 1910, illustrating the ability of Oregon suffragists to reverse the results of earlier campaigns. This powerful result, this positive application of the Oregon initiative system, and this impressive victory for equality was due, in her view, to the strength that came from diverse organizations."[39]

Abigail Scott Duniway, age eighty and in failing health, cast her first ballot in the November 1914 general election. Her life's work as a political and social reformer, begun in 1858 as a young letter writer, had come full circle. Fifty-six years had passed. The leadership of Oregon's woman's suffrage movement was now in the hands of women half her age. Duniway, the most important woman in Oregon's political history, died in October 1915. She had changed Oregon forever.

The 1913 Legislature: A Shining Star and a Punch

The 1913 Legislature was one of Oregon's most successful. Jay Bowerman did not return to the Senate, nor did several of his old-guard cronies. In general, a large number of legislators appeared to be willing to cooperate with the governor and show a stronger progressive attitude.[40] In a candid welcoming address, House Speaker C. M. McArthur noted that the public had lost confidence in their legislators. The people had turned to the initiative and referendum in frustration, bypassing the legislature. "The time has come for the legislature to reassert itself by wholesome legislation and rigid economy of appropriations. There is no necessity for the wholesale use of the initiative and referendum. Let us stay here and work honestly on every issue without ill feeling, and it is to be hoped that we will go through the session with very little of it."[41] The governor, the press, and the public welcomed the speaker's conciliatory tone. Could partisan bickering be behind them? It did not take long to find out.

Legislators balloted for U.S. senator early in the session. In only ten minutes the people's choice nominee, Democrat Harry Lane, was elected. The *Oregon Journal* commented: "Statement No. 1 is no longer an issue. It is an institution, an established order of the free government of Oregon."[42]

During the early weeks of the 1913 session lawmakers devoted most of their time to reconsideration of the many bills vetoed by Governor West after the adjournment of the 1911 Legislature. Most vetoes were overridden. Now the opposition (mostly in the House) came out into the open, and West was engaged in another struggle.[43] With nine days to go until the forty-day session adjourned, only thirty-one of 939 bills introduced had been passed. Most of West's legislation was stalled. When the state's newspapers began to snipe at the lawmakers, pressure began to build on them to be more productive. The law-making pace quickened. As before, Os West threatened to use his veto liberally. With strong allies in both the House and Senate, West's proposals began to move through the legislative maze.[44]

As the days of the session ticked off, Governor West got into a fistfight. For several weeks Frank Perkins, a Portland *Evening Telegram* reporter, had criticized the governor. Some of his comments were personal and West resented them. Apparently the governor had promised himself that if ever Perkins spoke to him, he would punch him in the nose. On the evening of February 14 (Oregon's birthday), West came out of an office into the Capitol corridor. Perkins was talking with several legislators. West thought Perkins was talking to him. He stopped and asked Perkins if he was, and the reporter said, "No, sir, I was not."

West retorted, "I do not want people who write lies about me speaking to me," and told him that he was never to speak to him. Perkins was about to respond when the governor lost control, slugging Perkins in the face and knocking him down. West jumped on Perkins, striking and kicking him. As the pair rolled around the onlookers rushed to separate them. The governor stood, straightened his suit and coolly exited the scene.

The House met all day and much of the night of February 25, considering 79 bills and passing 59. Governor West had mixed feelings when the legislature finally adjourned on March 4 after 51 days. He was pleased that most of his proposals had passed, but unhappy that lawmakers had created a number of new government offices and run up costs to pay for them. Twenty-five of the 40 bills West vetoed were of this kind. West was simply not convinced the offices were needed—at least when balanced against their cost to taxpayers.

Progressive Reforms

The 1913 Oregon Legislature took Progressivism to its ultimate peak. More important reform laws were passed in this session than in any other prior to the late 1960s. The bulk of these measures were either introduced by Oswald West or were strongly backed by him. The extraordinary success of this session had much to do with the governor's ability to guide his program through a reluctant Republican assembly. The legislators of 1913, among Oregon's most forward-looking lawmakers of the 20th century, deserve credit for enacting West's far-reaching proposals. The 1913 reform package basically falls into four categories: prison and criminal justice, worker and labor, natural resources and environment, and child welfare.

The most important prison/criminal justice reforms included establishment of a State Board of Parole and stricter laws to regulate liquor traffic and to control prostitution. By executive order, Governor West established several new prison practices relating to convict treatment and rehabilitation. Until George Chamberlain became governor in 1903, Oregon had had a reputation for having one of the nation's most inhumane and brutal prison systems. West built upon penal reforms made by Chamberlain, including more rehabilitation, altering the spartan and oppressive prison environment, abolishing the dehumanizing striped suits and the traditional practice of lockstep that forced prisoners to hobble like disciplined, shuffling human columns. There was no more flogging and West restricted the ways in which convict-made goods could be sold to the public so they would not compete with free labor.[45] West developed an honor system for prisoners; cooperative and nonviolent prisoners could work outside the prison, sometimes without guards. "Progressive prison reform typically sought means to maximize the prisoners' self-respect and sense of self-determination, through such methods as indeterminate sentencing laws and the institution of probation and parole procedures, all of which were enacted in Oregon during Chamberlain's and West's administrations."[46]

West's honor system was controversial because it was a radical departure from traditional prison practice. Many citizens feared its consequences. Had the governor gone too far? Was the public in danger? West's response was to back an initiative petition on the 1912 state ballot to validate his practice. The public backed their governor and his honor system, passing his initiative by a margin of 73,800 to 37,500.[47]

Oregon workers and labor benefited from legislation that West backed, including the establishment of an Industrial Welfare Commission "to regulate wages, hours, and the safety, health and welfare of workers. The commission promptly established a minimum-wage requirement for factory and store employees."[48] Corporate interests challenged the law. The supreme courts of Oregon and the United States ruled the law constitutional. Another act set an eight-hour work day for state employees, and another set a maximum ten-hour workday in certain manufacturing businesses along with a provision for over-time. The Assembly of 1913 also established a state Child Welfare Commission, and increased appropriations for state institutions caring for homeless and abandoned children.

Os West Saves Oregon's Beaches

On the environmental front, the legislature established a State Department of Forestry, created a Fish and Game Commission and a State Highway Commission. But the most important legislation enacted in 1913 was an act that Os West fathered to place Oregon's 400-mile Pacific Ocean coastline under public ownership. Oswald West is best known for this act. As state land agent, he'd authored a similar bill, one that reserved to state ownership the beds and the land below the low-water mark of Oregon's streams.[49] The consequences of these acts on the future of Oregon's waterways and beaches cannot be overstated. Oswald West recognized the pressing need to preserve Oregon's scenic ocean coastline and inland waterways from development. Because of him, Oregon's ocean beaches belong to the people.*

---

* In West's honor Oswald West State Park on the Oregon coast south of Cannon Beach was named for him.

Governor West's keen interest in preserving Oregon's environment and scenic beauty did not go unnoticed. In 1911, Theodore Roosevelt said "In Governor West of Oregon I found a man more intelligently alive to the beauty of nature, more eagerly desirous to avoid wanton and brutal defacement and destruction of wild nature and more keenly appreciative of how much this natural beauty should mean to civilized mankind, than almost any other man I have ever met holding high political position."[50]

Oswald West decided early in his term not to seek a second term as governor. He accomplished what he had set out to do, he said. When the 1915 Legislature met, West showed up as a special political reporter to write a regular column in the *Oregonian*. He moved his family to Portland and established a law practice that lasted until 1947. In 1918, he came out of retirement to challenge Republican Charles McNary for U.S. Senate; West lost to McNary, 82,360 votes to West's 64,300.

For a time, West served as Democratic National Committeeman for Oregon. Otherwise he practiced law, was a utility company lobbyist and, rather loudly, observed Oregon politics for the next 45 years. West's position as a utility lobbyist meant that he was an opponent of the development of public power. The issue of public vs. private power development was a main reason why Oregon's Democratic Party could not come together as a cohesive unit in the 1930s and '40s. West and others successfully exploited the issue, using it as a wedge, to keep younger, more liberal (pro-public power) Democrats from either taking control of the party, or from getting their candidates nominated. Consequently, West was always in the corner of the more conservative, old-guard Democrats. He was a prolific letter-writer, for decades sending hundreds of letters to newspaper editors in all parts of Oregon. Always ready with an opinion, he continued as one of Oregon's most controversial and beloved citizens. When he died at age 87, in 1960, the eulogies were many and heartfelt. Oswald West was acknowledged as one of Oregon's great leaders. Numerous tributes appeared in the August 23,1960, *Oregonian* on the occasion of his death. Republican Governor Elmo Smith called him "one of the giants of Oregon history. He was the greatest Oregon Democrat." Congresswoman Edith Green said, "Os West was one of Oregon's authentic great men. His courage was limitless, his passion for justice was unlimited; his wit, his integrity, his understanding of the purpose of democracy will be sorely missed." Governor and U.S. Senator Mark O. Hatfield said, "I know of no single individual whose administration has made more of an impact in Oregon history."[51]

America 1912-13

The year 1912 was the high-water mark of Progressivism in America. New Jersey's reform governor, Democrat Thomas Woodrow Wilson, was elected president. His victory was partly due to a divided Republican Party. Former President Theodore Roosevelt challenged President William Howard Taft for the Republican nomination, which Taft won. Roosevelt then ran as third-party candidate, heading the Progressive or Bull-Moose Party ticket. Most of the Progressive wing of the Republican Party ended up in Roosevelt's camp. Eugene Victor Debs, labor activist and leader of the American Socialist Party, also ran as a third-party candidate. In 1912 Roosevelt, Debs, and Wilson all ran on reform platforms, which shows how deeply Oregon and the nation were committed to change.

Wilson won in November with 42% of the national vote; Roosevelt got 27%, Taft 23%, and Debs 6%. The Oregon returns showed much the same outcome. Wilson carried Oregon (the first Democrat to do so since Horatio Seymour in 1868), but with only 34% of the vote. Roosevelt edged Taft in Oregon, 27% to 25%. Debs took about 10% of the state vote.

Dr. Harry Lane, former Democratic mayor of Portland, won the people's choice nomination for U.S. Senate. Lane, a Progressive, edged Portland Republican Benjamin Selling. The 1913 Legislature went along with the people's choice and elected Lane to the Senate, where he joined Democrat George Chamberlain, the first time since 1883 that two Democrats held Oregon's U.S. Senate seats simultaneously.

Chapter 7
Oregon During World War One, 1914-20

The Great War, known today as World War One, broke out in central Europe in August 1914. President Wilson immediately issued a proclamation of American neutrality. As the war dragged on, a reluctant United States was drawn into the fray. By early 1916 the war had become the country's leading political issue.

Governor James Withycombe

In 1914, Republicans were elected to all of Oregon's top political offices; James Withycombe (the first Republican to hold office since 1903) was elected governor by a margin of 27,000 votes and Ben Olcott was elected secretary of state. The legislature remained lopsidedly Republican. The 1910 Census had given Oregon a third U.S. House seat in 1912 and Republicans won all three congressional seats in 1914. The only major office won by a Democrat was George Chamberlain's Senate seat; he defeated Republican R. A. Booth by 23,500 votes, and was Oregon's first senator to be elected by a direct vote of the people. The 17th Amendment to the U.S. Constitution, ratified in early 1913, removed state legislatures from the Senate-election process. Third-party candidates Progressive William Hanley, Prohibitionist H. S. Stine, and socialist Floyd B. Ramp took over 18% of the Oregon Senate vote.[1]

James Withycombe's election as governor in 1914 came on the heels of 10 years of political activism and reform in Oregon. Beginning with the Oregon System, Oregon had been on a roller-coaster ride, adopting and implementing many important reforms. Withycombe, an honest man and able administrator, was elected governor partly because voters wanted a rest after a decade of feverish political and social change; he had proposed no significant changes. It seemed to be a campaign fought without issues.[2] During the 1914 campaigns the *Oregonian* warned readers that "Oregon must avoid getting a radical reputation." There was worry that 20 years of reformist agitation was giving the state a reputation for innovation and radicalism that indicated political and

economic instability to some. That instability might discourage future investment in Oregon. "If cautious conservatism was what Oregon needed and
wanted, then Withycombe was the correct choice [for governor]." Two veteran political observers, conservatives Henry M. Hanzen and C.C. Chapman,
agreed with the *Oregonian*: Withycombe's tenure as governor was "four of the
most uneventful years Oregon ever had."[3]

Oregon's First Women Legislators

The opportunity for women to run for the legislature finally came after Oregon
men approved the woman's suffrage amendment in 1912. Marian Towne, a
Jackson County Democrat, won a seat in Oregon's House of Representatives
in the 1914 election, the first woman elected and the first to serve in the
Oregon Legislature. Towne was one of only four Democrats in the House.
One newspaper described her as a "very womanly woman, with not the least
hint of manishness, which she couldn't have with her barely five feet of stature
and fascinating smile. She possesses a bright mind. Miss Towne went to the
University of Michigan and studied law, the only woman in the law school. She
is admitted to the bar in Oregon and expects to engage in the practice of law."
A Represenative Scheubel "announced himself hostile to the idea of women's
service on juries. He declared women are to blame for the double standard of
morality that now prevails."[4] Midway into the 1915 session, Kathryn Clark of
Glendale defeated two men for a vacant Senate seat to become Oregon's first
woman state senator. She joined the other 27 Republicans and two Democrats
in the senate. She was known for "reading her remarks as to pending bills and
crocheting during sessions."[5]

In December 1916, Umatilla, Oregon, situated on the Columbia River
northwest of Pendleton, made election history. Forty townspeople cast ballots for mayor, city council, recorder, and treasurer. All positions were won by
women. Umatilla elected a "Petticoat Government." It was the first all-female
government elected in Oregon. Until January 21, 1921, the mayor's office and a
majority of city council seats were held by women.

The Election of 1916

Woodrow Wilson stood for reelection in 1916 with the campaign slogan "He
kept us out of war." Supreme Court Justice (and former Republican governor
of New York) Charles Evans Hughes opposed Wilson. Oregon was breaking
in one of its recent political innovations: the presidential preference primary.
Under this plan Oregon's secretary of state prepared a ballot with names of

both declared and possible presidential candidates from both parties. If a prominent national Republican's name surfaced on a regular basis in Oregon, even if he hadn't announced his candidacy, the secretary of state could exercise his prerogative and include that prospect's name on the party's ballot. That is how Justice Hughes got his name on Oregon's Republican ballot in 1916. He refused to have his name entered in other primaries, but under Oregon's unique election law he "could not prevent his name from going before voters. Oregon had the last primary before the Republican convention and Hughes won impressively. Influenced by the Oregon vote, the Chicago convention nominated Hughes on the third ballot."[6]

Oregon was the only Far West state to vote for Hughes in the general election. Nationally, the presidential contest went in Wilson's favor. Hughes carried Oregon with 48% of the vote to Wilson's 46%. Wilson's national total was 49%; Hughes took 46%. The electoral vote total was Wilson 277 and Hughes 254— the closest election in the 20th century. There were 293,000 registered voters in Oregon in 1916, 92% of whom voted for president. Voter turnout in Oregon was very high from 1910 to 1916: 98% in 1910; 90% in 1912; and 85% in 1914 (the first election in which Oregon women voted). Voter registration in Oregon jumped from 160,000 in 1912 to 305,000 in 1914, reflecting the new women's vote. Voter turnout nearly doubled from 1912 to 1916, with women voting.

An Issue of Race

The issue of race was also on the 1916 Oregon ballot. Voters defeated an amendment (by a margin of only 674 votes out of 200,728 cast) to bring Oregon's constitution into conformity with the 15th Amendment to the U.S. Constitution. Passed in 1870, the 15th Amendment granted the vote to Negro men. Oregon's Constitution of 1857 had a provision denying the vote to Negroes, a provision that was still part of the state document in 1916. Despite what Oregon's outdated constitution said, Negro citizens in Oregon could, in fact, vote in 1916. Oregon voters were asked to amend their constitution so it was no longer in conflict with the U.S. Constitution. Some thought the defeat silly, while others said it smacked of racism. C. C. Chapman, longtime editor of *Oregon Voter* magazine, wrote: "Prejudice against colored races was mainly responsible for the negative vote. Some authorities ascribe the 100,700 'nos' to crass ignorance. To our knowledge many voted 'no' in protest, realizing full well that the vote could have no effect on the citizenship status of the Negro."[7] This vote reveals a certain perverse nature among Oregon voters, a trait that has reappeared throughout Oregon's political history.

The 1917 Legislature

The 1917 Oregon Legislature was liberally sprinkled with men who would go on to higher office. State Senators Albin W. Norblad and Walter Pierce would become governors. Millionaire Robert N. Stanfield, speaker of the Oregon House, would become a U.S. senator, as would state Senator Fred Steiwer from Umatilla County. State Senator Robert Butler would go on to the U.S. House of Representatives. Mrs. Alexander Thompson of The Dalles was the only woman legislator in the 1917 session.[8] The average legislator was 46. The youngest, Dr. Goode of Portland, was only 21. Nine lawmakers were over 60. A third were lawyers and 18 were farmers. Thirty-one of the 90 members were native Oregonians.

Governor James Withycombe, in his Opening-Day address to the assembly, made several controversial proposals, including one that called for the sterilization of the unfit*, more power for the governor and less for members of the Board of Control, consolidation of boards and commissions, and a statewide prohibition on alcoholic beverages. Withycombe gave his official blessing to increased road funds for matching federal grants. He also recommended a three-man, unsalaried highway commission.[9]

Prohibition took center stage in the 1917 session. Oregon had adopted "bone dry" amendments making it illegal to sell liquor in Oregon in 1914 and 1916. Now the 1917 Legislature needed to enact the necessary laws to put these amendments into effect. The Senate passed the enabling law unanimously. The House, by a vote of 53-7, did the same. To celebrate, the ladies of the Women's Christian Temperance Union's "dry committee" served half-pint bottles of loganberry juice to legislators. On February 2, Governor Withycombe signed the enabling bill, making Oregon an officially "dry" state. The loganberry toast was then repeated. The "Noble Experiment" (which is what Prohibition was called in the United States, 1919-33) had begun in Oregon.[10]

Senator Harry Lane Votes Against War

While Oregon's lawmakers wrestled with these issues in 1917, the United States broke diplomatic relations with Germany on February 3. Leading the opposition to President Wilson's policy was Wisconsin Sen. Robert La Follette. Senator Harry Lane sided with La Follette. When the Senate voted on Wilson's resolution to declare war on Germany (on April 4), Harry Lane was one of six senators to vote no. Lane and others argued that the United States was not forced

---

* Governor West endorsed this earlier. It passed and was declared unconstitutional.

into war by treaty obligations nor was it directly threatened. Lane steadfastly opposed American entry into Europe's war. Wilson criticized Lane, a fellow Democrat, and called the other dissenters a "little group of willful men."[11] The late teens were a time of mindless jingoism in America. A federal judge in Texas said the six senators should be lined up and shot for defying the president. In Oregon, recall petitions that denounced him for treason were circulated against Senator Lane by wealthy and well-organized forces. Thousands of signatures were collected. The *Oregonian* editorialized: "Next to being ashamed of Harry Lane for what he has done, the people of Oregon are ashamed of themselves for having sent Harry Lane to the United States Senate."[12] A recall campaign was started. Senator Lane was devastated by the wrath heaped on him. "Deeply hurt by the venom of his critics, Lane suffered a nervous breakdown and died on May 23, 1917, two months after his dissenting vote."[13]

Four years and four months into his Senate term Harry Lane, age 62, was dead. The responsibility of filling Senator Lane's seat fell to Republican Governor Withycombe, who appointed Republican Charles McNary. McNary's brother John encouraged Charles to take the post, declaring, "It will be a nice experience and it will not last long."[14] McNary took the seat. In 1918 he ran for the position and was elected to a full six-year term, trouncing Oswald West, 82,400 to 64,300. John McNary's prediction was wrong: Sen. Charles McNary served for the next 26 years, until his death in 1944.

Oregon, the Great War, and Unbridled Patriotism

The declaration of war generated the most intense patriotism that American society had ever encountered. The Wilson administration moved swiftly to set up a war propaganda machine. Most newspapers and magazines portrayed the German empire and its leader, Kaiser Wilhelm as the devil incarnate. The Germans became "Huns" who "were bent on destroying freedom, motherhood and everything else that was sacred to life." Oregonians closed ranks behind President Wilson and Congress. A wave of fierce patriotism swept through the state, as Oregonians came together to oppose any individual or group who criticized any aspect of American policy or involvement abroad. Patriotic organizations sprang up everywhere. Led by fundamentalist Protestant clergy, these patriotic organizations focused on two aspects of the war. First, people were asked to make personal sacrifices and to do what was necessary to assure Allied victory. Activities included food-collection drives and recycling basic materials such as metals and cloth; urging men to volunteer for the armed forces; and purchasing Liberty bonds to finance the war. Second, the state and nation must be made safe from within. Oregon went on a hunt to silence anyone perceived as unpatriotic or dangerous to the American cause. Approximately 85% of the state's residents in 1919 were native born. With one of the most homogeneous populations in the country, Oregon was overwhelmingly white, Anglo-Saxon and Protestant (WASP).[15]

Pacifists were scorned and Socialist pacifists were deemed even lower.[16] Oregon patriots directed their enmity against any individual, organization, or group that didn't fit the dominant WASP mold. This meant that Catholics, Jews, Negroes, Japanese, Chinese, persons of German ancestry, pacifists, and radical labor leaders were singled out as the targets of Oregon's rabid patriots. Many businesses, schools, colleges, and government at all levels reflected Oregon's hyper-patriotism. Politics in Oregon between 1917 and 1923 became the captive of intolerance masquerading as super-patriotism.

Intolerance Runs Amok

The most celebrated cases of Oregon's war-time intolerance included a German-born Portland businessman named J. Henry Albers; Floyd Ramp, a prominent Socialist-farmer from Eugene; medical doctor Maria Equi; and Miss Louise Hunt, assistant to Portland's city librarian.

Albers was an esteemed Portland businessman and president of Albers Brothers Milling Company. While returning from a business trip to San Francisco by train, Albers had too much to drink and started singing German songs. For this he was "arrested, jailed and convicted for seditious conduct by a German alien. He was given three years in a federal penitentiary and fined $10,000."[17] Albers appealed his case all the way to the U.S. Supreme Court in 1921. The U.S. Solicitor General withdrew Albers' case on the day the Court was to hear it, saying the government had erred. Shortly afterward Albers had a paralytic stroke and died.

Floyd Ramp was involved in an incident in September 1917 that led to his arrest, conviction, and 18-month federal prison term. On his way to deliver a wagon of wood to Roseburg, he came upon a train being loaded with soldiers. Mr. Ramp stopped and asked the young men "if they knew what they were fighting for. Then [he] told them they were fighting to protect John D's [Rockefeller] money."[18] That brief encounter got him a prison term for violating the Espionage Act.

Dr. Marie Equi was an outspoken Portland radical and feminist. She described the Great War as "The Big Barbecue." Her utterance got her a 10-month prison term in San Quentin, California, for sedition. Louise Hunt,

Portland librarian, chose not to buy war bonds. Rufus Holman, chairman of the Multnomah County Board of Commissioners, joined William F. Woodward, a Portland druggist, Republican Party leader, and a member of the Library Association Board, in publicly criticizing Hunt's unpatriotic stance. The Library Board stood up for her, but the clamor for her removal continued. Reluctantly, Louise Hunt resigned and moved out of Oregon.[19]

Since the beginning of the Great War the Catholic Church had come under fire from a small but growing group of outspoken journalists, politicians, and Protestant clergymen. The Catholic Church was seen by some as a menace to America's free institutions because the Church was led by an absolute ruler in the Pope; some Protestant ministers in Portland began to warn their flocks of suspected Catholic treachery.[20]

The American Patriotic Association, American Patriotic League, and the Oregon Federation of Patriotic Societies, fielded a slate of candidates to run in the May 19 Oregon primary. The election came in the middle of the last year of the Great War. Nearly two million Americans were in or on their way to Europe. People believed the war was nearly over. Anticipating victory, Oregonians shared the nation's heightened patriotism. Now was not the time for any dissent that could prolong the war. Oregon's patriotic societies in 1918 favored free and compulsory education for all Oregon children in public schools. Catholics knew these groups wanted to abolish parochial schools in Oregon and weaken Catholic influence. This compulsory school issue played a part in most legislative races. While it is unknown just how much influence these patriotic societies had on the election outcome, we do know that between 1916 and 1922 over half of the successful Multnomah County Republican legislative candidates got support from at least one patriotic organization.[21]

Oregon's commitment to the United States' war effort was extraordinary. In spite of a small population (700,000 in 1917), Oregon did more proportionally than most states to assure an Allied victory. Oregonians dug deep, reaching 92% of their quota for men and women military volunteers, a higher percentage than any other state. They bought war bonds in record numbers. And they were generous in their contributions to the Red Cross and other relief organizations. Oregonians were asked to give $2 million to support the Red Cross and other relief organizations. They subscribed $3.148 million or 55% more than requested.[22] Oregonians proudly met and exceeded their nation's call for help.

The Armistice ending World War I came on November 11, 1918. This didn't put an end to the internal tensions that had been building up over the past three years. Rumors of diabolical, radical conspiracies against the government and the institutions of the United States were spreading. Even in Oregon, there were fears that a Communist revolution might begin, patterned after the Bolshevik revolution in Russia in November 1917. The local press fanned such fears during a time when the labor movement was in turmoil, heightening public fear of revolution.[23]

A Republican state representative named Kasper K. Kubli rode the anti-Catholic, pro-American wave in the 1918 election. Kubli was a Portland attorney and owner of a stationery store and he was an outspoken super-patriot. Between 1919 and 1923 he was one of Oregon's most influential politicians. A shrewd opportunist, he was very successful in exploiting the fears, bigotry, and hatred many Oregonians felt during and after the war. When a resurrected Ku Klux Klan made a grab for power in Oregon in 1922, Kubli (initials K.K.K.) was issued Klan membership card number 1. In 1923, Klansman Kasper K. Kubli was elected speaker of the Oregon House.

Oregon's November election brought a second term to Gov. James Withycombe, who defeated Democrat Walter Pierce 81,000 to 65,400. Ben Olcott was reelected secretary of state. Charles McNary, Senator Lane's replacement, won his own six-year term, defeating Oswald West. McNary didn't personally campaign in Oregon, preferring to remain in Washington to work on the war effort. He followed this pattern in his four reelection campaigns from 1924 to 1942.[24]

Oregon's 30th Legislature

Oregon's 30th Legislative Assembly met in Salem on January 13, 1919. Seymour Jones, a farmer and one-termer, was elected House speaker. W. T. Vinton, an attorney, was elected Senate president. Lawmakers considered several war-related issues. State Senator Walter Pierce introduced a veteran's benefit bill, which voters approved as Measure 8 in the special election of June 1919. The ballot measure provided financial assistance to war veterans who wanted to enroll in college or trade school. A small tax on all Oregon property generated the revenue to pay for the program. By 1922 over 6,000 veterans had gone to school on these benefits. Oregon's veteran's bill was the first adopted in the United States to aid returning soldiers and sailors.[25]

The legislature also ratified the 18th Amendment (prohibition of alcoholic beverages) and passed a labor reform law by which the principles of the Clayton Anti-Trust Act of 1913 were adopted as Oregon law. This act legalized strikes and boycotts and prohibited injunctions against picketing. Many hailed the bill as Oregon's "labor Bill of Rights."[26]

The assembly turned its attention to Bolshevism and terrorism. Kasper K. Kubli and Sen. Walter A. Dimick of Clackamas County sponsored what were called anti-syndicalism bills. The bills made it a crime to engage in or advocate sabotage or violence as a means of changing industrial ownership or effecting political change. The bills passed into law and were designed to suppress the International Workers of the World, (IWW). Founded in 1905 by Bill Haywood and others, the IWW (whose members were often called Wobblies) wanted to unite all industrial workers in the world into one body committed to the end of capitalism. In the West, miners, railroad men, metal and migratory workers belonged to the IWW. During the Senate debate, senator B. L. Eddy of Douglas County called the Bolshevik movement "a deadly ferret clutching at the throat of the American eagle, the worst menace that has ever faced civilization."[27] Senator Walter Pierce stood against the Kubli-Dimick bills, arguing that the best way to limit Bolshevism was not to use force, but to change the conditions causing desperate people to embrace the ideology. Pierce urged full employment, good wages, improved living conditions, and adequate food as the best ways to combat Bolshevism's appeal. His argument made no impact; his was the only vote against the bill in the Senate. The House approved the bill with four dissenting votes. As soon as Governor Withycombe signed the bill, Portland police cracked down. Socialists, labor leaders, and even newspaper vendors were arrested. Literature was confiscated or burned, offices were broken into and furniture was destroyed. Oregon, like the rest of the country, was into its own "Red Scare." Several years later, voters (using the initiative petition) overturned the Dimick-Kubli bill. Oregonians believed the legislature had gone too far.

One of the most controversial bills of the 1919 session came before the house on February 20. Sponsored by Rep. John B. Coffey of Multnomah County, the bill would have banned discrimination against Negroes in hotels, restaurants, resorts, and theaters. A motion to postpone the bill indefinitely failed. Mrs. Thompson, the only woman to serve in the 1919 session, ridiculed Republicans for opposing Coffey's bill, reminding them that they were members of the party of Abraham Lincoln, the Emancipator. But Representative Coffey's bill was defeated. With five members absent, 31 representatives voted "no" and 24 voted "yes." A Representative Lewis locked himself in a committee room to avoid voting on the bill. He was returned by the sergeant at arms. He voted against the bill, saying it was the business of Congress, not Oregon, to deal with the issue of Negro rights. Mrs. Thompson also cast a "no" vote. With rare candor she declared that her Kentucky roots had led her to grow up with strong racial prejudices toward Negroes. In light of her feelings she could not support the bill. The fact that a Negro equality bill had been introduced and voted on by the legislature was remarkable for that time. Most states didn't bring up the issue. Considering Oregon's traditionally strong dislike for Negroes it was, indeed, a noteworthy event. With a population over 98% white, and with fewer than 2,000 Negroes in the state, the fact that 24 of 55 state representatives voted for the bill shows that not all Oregonians shared the pervasive intolerance that gripped Oregon during the war.

Violence By and Against Labor

Four days after the legislature adjourned on March 4, 1919, Gov. James Withycombe suddenly died. At 65, he was seven weeks into his second term. Secretary of State Ben Olcott, a Republican, succeeded him as governor.

Labor strife and outbursts of violence marked the remainder of 1919. Two events occurred in the Northwest that reinforced the paranoia many Oregonians were feeling that year. A powerful bomb was sent in the mail to Seattle's outspoken Mayor Ole Hanson, an anti-labor Red-hater. Fortunately, the device was discovered before it exploded.

Another violent episode occurred on November 11 in Centralia, Washington, 80 miles north of Portland. Centralia was the coal-mining center of the Northwest. Local American Legion chapters had organized an Armistice Day parade through the streets of Centralia, Washington, for November 11, 1919. Centralia's mineworkers, who were members of the IWW, were on strike (part of a national stoppage involving 400,000 miners). The Legionnaires and Wobblies did not like one another. When local Wobblies found out that the parade route would pass their meeting hall they prepared for trouble. Wobblies, armed with pistols, were stationed in the hall; others with rifles were on the roofs of several nearby buildings and an adjacent hill. When a contingent of Legionnaires halted in front of the IWW Hall, shots were fired at them, killing two marchers. Angry Legionnaires stormed the hall, and two more of them were shot and killed.

That night a mob overran the city jail and dragged a Wobbly into the street, where they tortured and mutilated him, tied a rope around his neck, and threw him off a bridge. Eight Wobblies were indicted for the killing of the Legionnaires; four were convicted and sentenced to prison terms of 25 to 40 years. In 1931-32 three of the men were paroled. No one was ever indicted for the murder of the Wobbly.

Fear of more violence swept the region. Would Oregon be next?[28] While Oregon and Washington suffered labor jitters, President Wilson arrived in

Portland on September 15, 1919, promoting his League of Nations proposal. Thousands lined the streets to welcome him. Charles McNary was one of the few Republican senators to endorse Wilson's idea. Ten days after his Portland visit, Wilson fell ill and was rushed to Washington, D.C., where he had a paralytic stroke. Months later, the Republican Senate rejected the League and Versailles Treaty. An embittered Woodrow Wilson lived out his life in Washington, D.C., dying there in 1924 at age 67.

A Special Session

Governor Ben Olcott called a special session of the legislature in early January 1920. Meeting for six days, the legislature went on a bill-passing spree. It increased workmen's compensation benefits, and ratified the 19th Amendment (which gave women the right to vote nationwide). It referred an act to restore capital punishment to the people, authorized a $10 million bond issue for roads contingent on voter approval, doubled the tax for the veterans' education bill, and levied additional state taxes for elementary schools, the University of Oregon and Oregon State Agricultural College (OSU today), and Oregon's teacher training colleges. The law of succession was changed, putting the president of the Senate rather than the secretary of state first in succession for governor.[29]

The 1920 Senate Race

Democrat George Chamberlain wanted a third term. He'd been elected twice as a non-partisan Democrat and his appeal to progressive Republicans had helped elect him in 1908 and 1914. But could he do it again in 1920? His first obstacle was in the Democratic Party. An influential group of party leaders were tired of Chamberlain's lukewarm ties to the party. Some were angry with the senator for recommending so many Republicans to federal offices in Oregon and resented Chamberlain's strong ties to the state's Republican business establishment. Finally, party leaders were upset because Chamberlain had deserted President Wilson, a fellow Democrat, when the senator voted against the Versailles Treaty. Chamberlain had also criticized Wilson for running a slipshod wartime government. Nonetheless, Chamberlain won renomination 2-1.

Republicans nominated Robert N. Stanfield to face him in November and worried about Chamberlain's strength with Republicans. The November vote was close. George Chamberlain, Oregon's most prominent politician since 1902, lost to Robert Stanfield 100,100 to 116,700, though he got 17,000 more votes than there were registered Democrats in Oregon. Running against the gigantic Harding-Republican tide sweeping the state and nation in 1920, George Chamberlain's long political career was over. Oregonians wanted a new face to represent them in the Senate. Voters, of course, had no way of knowing they had made a big political mistake when they elected Stanfield.

Chapter 8
The Election of 1922, the Ku Klux Klan, and Governor Walter Pierce, 1921-27

The 1920s was Oregon's Republican decade. In ten years, Democrats won major offices only twice: Governor Walter Pierce and U.S. Rep. Elton Watkins in the 3rd District in 1922. Republicans won every other major federal and state elected office in the 1920s, keeping firm control of the legislature. Over the decade (with 28% of voters registered as Democrats) Democratic presidential candidates didn't carry a single county.

No Oregon governor's race has sparked as much controversy as the 1922 campaign. Democrat Walter Pierce scored a record 34,000-vote victory over Gov. Ben Olcott. Pierce's acceptance of the endorsement and support of Oregon's rejuvenated Ku Klux Klan is what made the contest so controversial.

The Klan in Oregon

The Ku Klux Klan was the single most powerful force in Oregon politics from 1922 to 1924. The Klan dominated and set much of the 1923 legislative agenda and a majority of lawmakers were either Klansmen or sympathizers. Oregonians are often amazed that an organization like the Ku Klux Klan, historically associated with racial violence and with fomenting religious and racial hatred, could have taken hold in Oregon. In three years the Oregon Klan grew so quickly that it easily controlled many local school boards, some city and county governments, and the Republican Party of Oregon. The Klan also enjoyed a following among many Protestant church congregations. Most politicians either joined the Klan or sought its support and only a handful had the courage to criticize the Klan. How did the Klan, in such a short time, become so influential in Oregon? The chief explanation rests with the prevailing economic, social, and political order of the post-Great War world.

The Great War lasted for 51 months in Europe and wrought profound changes. Russia, originally an Allied Power along with Great Britain and France, withdrew from the fighting in November 1917. The country was in convulsions as the Bolshevik Revolution spread throughout the land. Russia plunged into a five-year civil war. When the fighting stopped, Vladimir Lenin's Communist forces were in control of the government and most of the country. Preoccupied with their part in the Great War from 1917 to 1918, Americans paid little attention to Russia. But when the war ended, Americans took more interest in Russia's internal strife. After all, a revolution was underway in the world's largest country with a whole new political, economic, and social order evolving. Lenin's Russia was anti-capitalist, anti-Western, and anti-democratic. The United States perceived Marxist Russia as a threat to democratic, freedom-loving peoples everywhere. The U.S. government refused to allow Americans to trade with Russia; nor would it grant diplomatic recognition to the new government in Moscow. American policy isolated Russia, treating it as an outcast nation.

As the Bolsheviks tightened their hold on Russia, American opinion makers became concerned that Marxists were preparing to infiltrate the United States. Many Americans thought that Lenin's goal was to promote class warfare in the United States, too. Americans equated organized labor agitation in this country with the Russian plan to spread Communism everywhere. By 1919, many Americans were in an anti-Bolshevik frenzy. Attorney General A. Mitchell Palmer's infamous Red Raids of 1919-20 were part of this festering hysteria. When labor strikes and bombings occurred in various corners of the United States, many believed Russian Communists were responsible.

At home, the war had produced its own social tensions. When the country threw itself into war production in 1917, its factories and mines needed large numbers of new workers. In large northern cities like Chicago, Detroit, and New York, the demand for labor drew hundreds of thousands of rural folk northward. During 1917-19 huge numbers of southern Negroes flocked to these urban centers, seeking the higher wages and job opportunities these cities afforded. With the influx of so many Negroes, social tensions grew.

The growth of cities and suburbs came at the expense of small towns and rural life. Old roots were being ripped out of familiar ground as people moved away, severing ties with family, friends, and community. These city-bound people experienced a kind of loneliness and isolation they had never known. Where was America headed? Why were traditional roles and values under such strain? For many there was a deep anxiety that something was deeply wrong with America. In this confusion the Ku Klux Klan sprang back to life—only this time, the Klan's tentacles reached outside the Deep South into the Midwest and Far West, to places like Indiana and Oregon.

In 1920 there were no more than 5,000 Klan members scattered throughout the South. That same year a recently organized public relations firm, the Southern Publicity Association, took on the KKK as a client and made the Klan the fastest-growing organization of its type in the country. A national recruiting drive began that trained organizers and sought converts wherever conditions seemed best. When an organizer came to town he carried a recruitment kit that included a list of those who were considered likely recruits such as "Protestant clergymen, police officers, local officials, politicians and ordinary citizens who had been associated with similar hate movements."[1] Oregon's first Klan was organized in Medford in January 1921 by Maj. Luther I. Powell. By November the Klan was a hot item in Pendleton. Portland organized next. When Portland's Rev. Reuben E. Sawyer of the East Side Christian Church addressed an enthusiastic crowd on December 22, Klan memberships were snapped up by the dozens. Fred L. Gifford, a Portland electrician and employee of the Northwestern Electric Company, was the Grand Dragon of the Oregon Klan. From their bases in Medford, Pendleton, and Portland, the Klan quickly spread into the hinterland, emerging in the Tillamook, Astoria, and La Grande areas. The Klan was most successful at recruiting in Portland and Multnomah County, the state's most urban area. The Klan was known for its opposition toward Negroes, Catholics, Jews, and immigrants. Basing its philosophy on hatred and bigotry, the Klan played on peoples' fears and worked to achieve its goals through fear mongering, violence, intimidation, and ostracism.

The Oregon Klan, like Klans everywhere, was composed largely of Protestant white males. Most members were of Anglo-Saxon heritage. The Klan saw itself as a powerful adjunct to the Protestant Church and, since they viewed the United States as a Protestant nation, they believed that they were the soul of Americanism and the spirit of Protestantism. Klan leaders saw their movement as a crusade to save America from a variety of evil forces. They believed the "stability of American society was threatened by a combination of lawlessness, illiteracy, disrupting strife and controversy [racial and labor tensions, for example], propaganda and economic inequality." By banding together they sought to preserve local control over their communities and homes. "If social controls were tightened, local communities might be insulated from undesired intrusions from media and other secular [nonreligious] influences." The organization focused on individual morality and wanted sober, God-fearing, church-going Protestant family men in its ranks. Thus, the Klan tried to enforce prohibition on its members and their communities; and they opposed gambling, prostitution, and cheating on one's wife. Urban Klansmen were afraid of change. "The Invisible Empire provided a way of facing change in a spirit of ethnic and social solidarity . . . Oregonians were particularly ripe for such appeals because of [their] strong identification with a pioneer past that celebrated individual virtues, American nationalism, and Protestantism. It was the feeling of belonging that attracted followers in Oregon in the 1920s."[2]

Many Oregonians welcomed the Klan as a patriotic organization: these were loyal Americans keeping Oregon safe from corrupting influences from outside and from within. The Klan's appeal was irresistible for the thousands who joined the crusade. The Ku Klux Klan was part of a nativist outburst in the post-war United States. Its rapid growth occurred at a time of increased immigration of non-Protestant people to the United States. Klan venom was regularly aimed at Oregon's Catholics. At a Salem Konklave, the Rev. J. R. Johnson announced that "the only sure way to cure a Catholic is to kill him." Klansmen were told not to patronize Catholic-owned establishments, not to hire Catholics, and above all, not to vote for Catholic candidates.[3]

A favorite Klan activity was to disrupt a Protestant church service by the appearance of robed and hooded visitors. One Sunday in May 1922 18 Portland congregations were disrupted this way.[4] In 1922 the Klan turned its attention to politics. It infiltrated and took control of the Republican Party of Multnomah County. Then the Klan began to recruit and back candidates for the county commission and the Portland City Council. The Klan also looked at legislative candidates. Slates of Klan-endorsed candidates ran in Oregon's May Primary and a large majority of the Republican nominees for the legislature were either Klansmen or Klan sympathizers.*

Klan violence and intimidation flared in several Oregon locations in 1922. In Medford, Klansmen on three occasions staged phony hangings. In one case a white man, piano merchant J. F. Hale, was lured from his home and driven at gunpoint in a caravan of 10 cars to a secluded spot outside of town. Klansmen were going to teach Hale a lesson for his moral laxity (he allegedly consorted with several 16-year-old girls). When a noose was placed around Hale's neck he feigned a heart attack. Panicked, the Klansmen drove him back to town and disappeared. Hale later filed kidnapping charges against his captors. A sensational trial of six Klansmen ensued. All were found innocent. The jury foreman was a cousin of one of the defendants. The judge, C. M. Thomas, had recently been elected with Klan support.[5] During the summer, Klansmen in Portland burned several crosses on Mount Tabor. The same Klan had earlier tried to organize a

---

* In the West, the Klan worked within the Republican Party because it was the party in power.

consumer boycott of Meier and Frank Co., part of an anti-Semitic campaign against Julius Meier, one of the store's proprietors, a prominent Jew, and future governor. Reverend Doctor Sawyer spoke to a Portland Klan audience, saying "Jews are either Bolsheviks, undermining our government, or are Shylocks in finance or commerce who control and command Christians as borrowers or employees. It is repugnant to a true Christian to be bossed by a Sheenie [Jew]."[6]

The Klan and the Governor's Race of 1922

The Klan endorsed an obscure state senator named Charles Hall for governor in the May primary. A Coos Bay Republican, Hall was also a Klansman. His main opponent was Republican Governor Ben Olcott. Olcott had been chief executive for nearly four years, but this was his first time running for governor. Some criticized him for lavish spending, saying his administration was too quick to spend the public's money.* Ben Olcott was a moderate. He was honest, ran a scandal-free administration, and had a good deal of tolerance for all types of people. His term had been relatively quiet until the Ku Klux Klan began to grow in Oregon in 1921. He was horrified by what he saw the Klan doing, particularly its acts of terror aimed at individuals, groups, and communities. He believed that when a man puts on a mask, he divests himself of a large part of his sense of responsibility. On May 13, 1921, Governor Olcott issued a proclamation denouncing the Klan in blistering terms. He noted that there were statutes on the books that made it unlawful for masked citizens to go on the streets, and he expected the local authorities to enforce them.[7]

Olcott's stance against the Klan stirred up a hornet's nest. His advisers told him he was committing political suicide. The governor's forthright and courageous stand drove thousands of fellow Republicans into the arms of his opponent, Charles Hall. Olcott believed most citizens were fair, tolerant, and peace-loving. Unlike many civic leaders, he chose not to ignore what the Klan stood for. The Klan was wrong for Oregon and Olcott said so.

There were also four lesser-known candidates in the Republican race, so the public assumed the election would be close. Governor Olcott won the GOP primary, besting Charles Hall by 500 votes out of 116,000 cast.

Klan activity in the May primary also focused on the legislature and on the 2nd and 3rd District Congressional contests. As a Roman Catholic, five-term Nick J. Sinnott, Oregon's 2nd District Congressman, was on the Klan's

---

* During Olcott's term, Oregon embarked on its modern highway construction program. Public demand for better roads grew with the sale of each car, so the Legislature and Olcott responded by undertaking an ambitious and costly road-building program.

political hit list. Congressman Clifton N. McArthur, a four-term Republican in the 3rd District, was also targeted for defeat by the Klan, who thought him too independent. Yet McArthur won renomination in May. So, instead of backing McArthur, the Klan threw its weight behind the Democratic candidate, Elton Watkins, a Mississippi-born former assistant U.S. attorney. His stand on key issues was attractive to the Klan: strict immigration limits, a veterans' bonus, and (announced late in his campaign) support for the Klan's Compulsory School bill. Watkins was not a Klansman but he certainly accepted their support.

The Compulsory School bill was initially sponsored by the Scottish Rite Masons fraternal order in 1920. The bill was aimed at church-affiliated schools, and would require all Oregon children to attend a public school. The Masons wanted to weaken the Catholic Church's hold on the 7-8% of the state's children who attended its schools. In addition, the Masons believed the surest way to fuse various elements of the population was to require all religious faiths, races, and social classes to attend public school together. Klan leader Fred Gifford made the Compulsory School bill the centerpiece of the Klan's 1922 political campaign. A candidate who supported the bill usually got the Klan's endorsement; the Klan worked to defeat candidates who opposed the bill.

Democrats chose Walter Pierce, former state senator and 1918 gubernatorial nominee as their candidate for governor. Pierce was an old-time Populist-Democrat from La Grande, and a charismatic speaker known for his ability to reduce an audience to tears. His main pursuit in life, besides politics, was cattle ranching. While sometimes assuming the character of a country bumpkin (farmers loved him), Walter Pierce was a shrewd political animal.

Klan support for mostly Republican candidates in the May primary election worked against party unity. Many Republicans were appalled by the Klan's coziness with Republican officeholders and candidates. Some worried that the Republican-Klan association hurt the party's image. How could a loyal Republican, a member of the party that had sponsored the 13th, 14th, and 15th amendments to the Constitution, along with Negro emancipation, and the Civil Rights Acts of the late 1860s, square this party tradition with the Ku Klux Klan, an avowed enemy of Negroes? Walter Pierce decided his chances for victory in November were not as hopeless as many thought.

The Klan and its ally, the Federation of Protestant Societies (FOPS), wanted Ben Olcott defeated in November, so they turned to Walter Pierce's candidacy. Where did Pierce stand on the Compulsory School bill issue? What was his position on another Klan-FOPS-backed bill to prohibit public school teachers from wearing religious garb to school? Did Pierce favor spending public money to support private and/or religious schools? Could he be counted on to support legislation to prohibit Asians from owning land or property in Oregon? The Klan-FOPS forces cared very much about these issues—and they were hoping that Walter Pierce saw things their way. Grand Dragon Fred Gifford went to La Grande to have a conversation with Pierce, hoping to extract a pledge of support for the Compulsory School bill in return for the Klan's endorsement and active support in November. The results of the meeting were inconclusive. Gifford went away believing that Pierce was in the Klan's corner. Pierce, however, denied he made any agreement with Gifford; he was likely playing the Klan leaders for his own purposes.[8] On September 12, Pierce said that tax reform—not the Klan, and not the Compulsory School bill—was the main question facing voters. Then he issued a statement announcing his support for the Compulsory School bill. "I did not bring religion into this campaign. It is not the issue. I am in favor of and shall vote for the Compulsory School bill. I believe we would have a better generation of Americans, free from snobbery and bigotry, if all children up to and including the eighth grade, were educated in free public schools of America."[9] Pierce also announced his support for the sectarian garb bill for teachers as well as his opposition to spending public money for private or sectarian purposes. Within days the Oregon Klan endorsed Walter Pierce for governor. It *appeared* a political bargain had been made.*

As he campaigned, Walter Pierce tried to push the Compulsory School bill into the background. His primary interest was in tax reform. A gutsy and tireless campaigner, he estimated that he spoke to 75,000 voters (most of them farmers and residents of smaller cities and towns) between May and November. But his campaign was a lonely one. "He had no organization, and other Democratic leaders, including Oswald West, were largely silent. Most Oregon newspapers either opposed Pierce or ignored him. Less than a half dozen of the states' dailies backed him."[10]

Governor Ben Olcott campaigned against the Klan and the Compulsory School bill. Most newspapers lined up for Olcott. In endorsing Olcott, some editors attacked Pierce's record as a legislator. George Putnam, the longtime editor of Salem's *Capitol Journal* wrote that Pierce had consistently voted for expenditure bills and called him a hypocrite, saying that he talked out of both sides of his mouth. Campaigning on a platform of tax reductions and tax reform, as a lawmaker Pierce had voted to spend money and raise taxes. Putnam

---

* The issue of whether or not Pierce made a deal with the Klan has never been resolved. Pierce said no deal was made nor was he ever a Klansman; no records exist which say otherwise.

Walter Marcus Pierce

COURTESY OF THE OREGON STATE ARCHIVES, GOVERNORS PHOTOS

Democrat Walter M. Pierce was elected governor in 1922, defeating the incumbent, Republican Ben Olcott, by about 35,000 votes. Like Olcott, Walter Pierce had been born in Illinois (May 30, 1861).

Pierce left Illinois when he was 22, finally settling in the tiny Oregon town of Milton in northern Umatilla County in 1883. Pierce was hired to teach school and farmed on the side. In 1886, Pierce became superintendent of Umatilla County schools, a post he held until 1890. Like several of Oregon's early governors, Walter Pierce began his political career as a county clerk: he was elected to that position in Umatilla County in 1890 and reelected in 1892. Pierce and his young family made a temporary move to Evanston, Illinois, where he earned a law degree from Northwestern University in 1892. The family resettled in Pendleton and Pierce set up a law practice, speculated in land, owned/operated a small electric company, and bred cattle. Pierce was elected to the Oregon state Senate in 1902, but was defeated for reelection in 1906.

Pierce, however, remained a highly visible public figure. He was president of the State Taxpayers' League, was a founder of the Oregon Farmers' Union and Public Power League, and he served on the Board of Regents of Oregon Agricultural College (Oregon State University today), 1905-27. Walter Pierce was also an early advocate of producing cheap hydroelectric power by building dams on the Columbia River.

and other editors also raised the question of the Compulsory School bill's cost to taxpayers. What if the bill passed? Would it mean that several thousand Catholic children would be forced to attend public schools—at an additional cost of one million dollars?

Olcott was swept out of office on election day. Walter Pierce captured 57% of the vote, the highest winning percentage since Addison Gibbs was elected governor in 1862 with 67%. Elton Watkins, with Klan support, defeated incumbent Clinton McArthur in the 3rd District, 36,690 to 35,696, the first Oregon Democrat elected to Congress since 1879. His tenure, however, was short (he lost his re-election bid in 1924 to Republican M. E. Crumpacker by over 11,000 votes). Like Sylvester Pennoyer, George Chamberlain, and Oswald West before him, Walter Pierce had overcome the nearly 3-1 Republican advantage in voter registration. Pierce didn't campaign as a non-partisan nor did he put his party affiliation at arms length. Stressing issues, particularly taxes, he won because of his positions. The national press generally credited the Klan with Pierce's

Low-cost electricity would, Pierce knew, be a boon to agriculture in semiarid northeastern Oregon.

Pierce's interest in politics was a driving force though his life. He sought (and lost) the Democratic Party nomination to the U.S. Senate in 1912, was elected again to the state Senate in 1916, and in 1918 lost a bid to become governor when he was defeated by the Republican incumbent, James Withycombe. But Pierce was elected governor in 1922. His victory was controversial because he had supported a proposed compulsory school bill backed by the state's resurgent Ku Klu Klan. Pierce's main interest, however, was tax reform, including the idea of establishing an income tax in Oregon. Pierce also attracted voters because he favored laws to deny aliens (Japanese, for example) from owning land in Oregon. Walter Pierce was also a champion of prison reform, a longtime supporter of prohibition, and the state's leading advocate for public ownership and development of hydroelectric power.

Pierce angered many fellow Democrats when he endorsed Progressive Robert M. LaFollette for president in 1924. His backing of LaFollette was in keeping with the governor's lifelong advocacy of issues important to farmers, ranchers, and laborers.

Governor Pierce lost his bid for reelection in 1926. And in 1928 he was defeated for a seat in the U.S. House of Representatives. In 1931, however, Pierce rode the long coattails of Democrat Franklin D. Roosevelt: he was elected to Congress in Oregon's 2nd District. He was 71 years old. Pierce was reelected four times. Pierce returned to Oregon in 1943 and settled near Salem. He died in 1954, two months shy of his 93rd birthday. Walter Pierce is the only former governor to be later elected to the U.S. House, and he lived longer than any other Oregon governor.

victory and the passage of the school bill. But the school issue undoubtedly split both major parties in the 1922 election. "Pierce lost nearly as many votes as he gained by declaring for the school bill. Thousands of Democrats deserted to Olcott while Republicans in even greater numbers left their party to support Pierce, many because they liked his tax emphasis. The school bill was only one factor in the Pierce triumph. The other decisive elements were farmers' discontent over high taxes and low prices, and the bitter primary that had divided the Republican Party."[11]

The irony of Walter Pierce's victory and Ben Olcott's defeat has not faded with time. Walter Pierce was unwilling to publicly condemn the Ku Klux Klan. His failure to do so makes it appear that he believed in the Klan, or, at the very least, that if elected he would have no trouble working with the Invisible Empire. Pierce's support of the Compulsory School bill (which passed by about 12,000 votes) helped more than hindered his chances of winning. Ben Olcott, on the other hand, believed that the Klan was misguided and wrong for Oregon.

And he said so, over and over. Olcott condemned the Compulsory School bill as un-American, as an act of intolerance and prejudice. Unwilling to do what was politically safe, Olcott spoke against the tide of blind patriotism and bigotry sweeping Oregon—and it helped cost him the governorship.

Democrats increased their members in the Oregon House from two to nine.* Their Senate representation jumped from one to four. The *Oregon Voter* noted that more inexperienced men would be members of the legislature than at any other point in Oregon history and that the new members were "in the main beholden to some secret organization for their election."[12]

The vote on the controversial Compulsory School bill was close. The initiative passed, 115,506 to 103,685, even though it lost in 21 of the 36 counties.† All the Republican candidates from Multnomah County for seats in the Oregon House won re-election and most were Klan-endorsed. "Klansman K. K. Kubli was speaker-designate of the house. In the state senate the Klan expected to control one-half the members. Oregon had become an adjunct of the Invisible Empire. Though no one realized it at the time, this was the Klan's high point. Henceforth it would begin to wither as rapidly as it had grown."[13]

What attracted so many Oregonians to the Klan, to Klan-endorsed candidates and legislation? Many "middling" Oregonians (members of the lower middle and working class) probably voted for the Compulsory School bill because they hoped "the school bill would create a more democratic society by eliminating the ability of elites to educate their children in exclusive schools." In short, what many voters wanted "was a school system capable of giving an equal and classless education to all children." Urban areas appear to have provided the bulk of votes for the bill.[14]

Walter Pierce Is Inaugurated

Walter Pierce, a man with a suitcase full of ideas and legislative proposals, was about to get the chance of his political life. As governor, could he, as a Democrat, achieve any degree of legislative success with a top-heavy GOP Legislature? Could he duplicate the remarkable success that Democrat Os West had with the Republican Legislature of 1913?

Dapper in a three-piece suit, bow-tie, and new cream-colored Stetson, Walter Pierce strode toward the Capitol. It was mid-morning of January 8, 1923. The day was overcast and showery. Some legislators arrived late in Salem. Flood waters

---

* Only one of the nine Democrats elected to the House in 1922 was reelected in 1924.
† The Supreme Court of the United States ruled Oregon's Compulsory School law unconstitutional in 1925.

reached far into the low plains along the Willamette River that winter, the worst since the disaster of 1890. Pierce was the first governor since Zenas Moody to come from east of the Cascades. A familiar face in Salem, Pierce had been a state senator in the 1903, 1917 and 1919 sessions. Pierce carried a copy of his inaugural address in his coat pocket, expecting to be sworn in about noon, after the House and Senate organized. But there was a hitch. The Senate was squabbling over who would be president. Prineville's Jay Upton and Roseburg's L. B. Eddy were vying for the post. Eddy's backers knew their man was short of the 16 votes needed. So they decided to stall until Eddy himself arrived from the south. They remained hidden, denying the Senate a quorum. Senator Eddy finally arrived in mid-afternoon. But the Republicans chose Jay Upton as Senate president, 16-13. Senator Eddy cast his ballot for Mrs. Kinney, the lone female senator.

After dinner, Walter Pierce took the oath of office and his inaugural address followed the simple ceremony. His main theme was taxation. "He recommended shifting at least half of the existing state tax burden from farms and homes by means of a graduated income tax." He also touched on the need for a severance tax on the one-third of Oregon timber standing in national forests. He proposed the consolidation of some state commissions and departments within the executive branch. He recommended setting up a paid state highway commission and proposed a higher gasoline tax and increasing license fees on high-priced cars as ways to pay for construction. Pierce talked about the plight of Oregon's farmers, suggesting ways to address their problems of heavy indebtedness and high taxes. He touched on the question of land ownership by Asian emigrants and asked for legislation to prohibit the sale or lease of land to Asians. In conclusion he said that the people's high expectations of the legislature would end in disappointment "unless the executive and legislative branches carry out their duties in harmony."[15]

Oregon's newspapers generally approved of his address. Governor Pierce knew he faced an uphill battle. He was governor by a landslide, but would the Republican Legislature go along with the people's choice? The overwhelmingly Republican Legislature—26 to four in the Senate and 51 to nine in the House—made it immediately apparent that they planned to fight Pierce's program.[16]

The "Yellow Peril"

With Kasper K. Kubli, a Ku Kluxer, in the speaker's chair and a Klan-approved Senate president, Jay Upton, the 1923 Legislature got to work. The Klan acted on their agenda quickly. A bill banning the wearing of religious apparel (such as a nun's habit) by teachers in public schools was passed unanimously in the

House. Only two votes were cast against the bill in the Senate. Pierce signed the act without hesitation. Other Klan-sponsored anti-Catholic legislation fared less well. Bills to eliminate Columbus Day as a state holiday (a slap at the Knights of Columbus) and to prohibit the importation of wines for sacramental purposes passed the House and failed in the Senate. "A bill to tax church property failed in the house by a vote of twenty-four to thirty-five."[17]

Another issue in the recent campaign had been the "Yellow Peril," the fear of Japanese Americans. Both Pierce and Olcott had favored a law prohibiting Asians from owning or leasing land in Oregon. The issue had flavored Oregon politics for years. The gubernatorial elections of 1870 and 1886 had rested on the issue of Chinese immigration; Governor Sylvester Pennoyer was elected in 1886 on a platform to "Keep the Mongolians Out." A bill denying the right to own property to Asians had died in the three previous legislatures (1917, 1919, and 1921). When Japanese families settled in the Hood River Valley prior to and during World War I, area legislators had sponsored a bill to keep the newcomers from competing with whites for land ownership.

Hood River was not alone in its racial fears. Wherever pockets of Japanese settled there was likely to be an ugly racist outburst. A typical anti-Japanese rant appeared as an editorial in the *Central Oregonian* newspaper in January 1922: "The Japs' good points have been dwelt upon recently, and the fact that he pays his bills, is reasonably law-abiding and works hard is the sum of his total assets. But a Jap's a Jap. The melting pot never even warms him. He considers that he is a superior race and has no desire to lower himself by becoming Americanized— were such a thing possible."[18] Medford citizens were horrified in March 1923 when news circulated that 40 Japanese workers were on their way to work in a nearby orchard. The Medford Elks Lodge, a local American Legion post, and the Medford *Mail-Tribune* led the charge, and the California company importing the Japanese workers caved in to public pressure. The Japanese workers never showed up. In 1925, in the coastal town of Toledo, an angry crowd of locals took action against a band of recently arrived Japanese. Thirty-five Japanese men, women, and children had come to Toledo to work at the Pacific Spruce Corporation's mill. "A loud and agitated mob of about 300 men, women, and children met and paraded en masse to the Japanese quarters, where they routed the sawmill workers from their homes, loaded them on trucks, and forcibly evicted them from town."[19]

The Alien Land bill zoomed through the 1923 session. The bill passed unanimously in the Senate. A single lawmaker voted against it in the House. Governor Pierce, who noted in his inaugural address that "European and

Asiatic civilization cannot amalgamate and we cannot and must not submit to the peaceful penetration of the Japanese and Mongolian races,"* promptly signed the bill.[20] Most Oregonians were relieved.

Other "Americanism bills" passed, as well. A bill prohibiting aliens from operating businesses such as rooming houses and hotels was enacted. A literacy test requiring those registering to vote to read a passage of the state constitution and write at least ten words in English was made law. Pierce also signed a bill requiring that the United States Constitution be taught in both private and public schools. Another bill prohibited the use of any textbooks that "spoke slightingly of the founders of the republic or men who preserved the union, or which belittle or undervalued their work. It passed the house but failed in the senate."[21]

Walter Pierce Hammers Away at Tax Reform

From 1922 to 1930, when voters approved an income tax referendum, tax reform dominated Oregon politics. In seven consecutive statewide elections prior to and including 1930, Oregonians kicked the issue around. The law they finally passed in 1930 remained Oregon's basic income tax law until 1953.[22]

As Oregon's head cheerleader for tax reform, Walter Pierce was the person most responsible for selling the graduated income tax as a replacement for the state's increasingly unpopular tax on property. The governor was convinced that the property tax was killing Oregon's farmers. Pierce was acutely aware of how the property tax worked against agrarians. In 1921, the average net income for a typical Oregon farmer was $463, with taxes averaging $303. Tax delinquencies were increasing all over the state and in remote Malheur County tax delinquency reached 34%. As wheat and livestock prices slumped to new lows in the post-war depression, comparable figures were recorded for other eastern Oregon counties as well. Pierce's inaugural address made tax reform the paramount goal of his administration. With his landslide victory as leverage, he waited patiently for the 1923 Legislature to take meaningful steps to confront Oregon's tax issue. It quickly became apparent to Pierce that legislators wouldn't touch the issue and many were dead set against an income tax. At the halfway point of the 40-day session, the governor began to turn up the heat. "I told them [legislators] that I would

---

* Oregon's Alien Land Law didn't reduce land purchases among the Japanese. Ways were found to legally circumvent the discriminatory land law. Some had trusted Caucasian friends hold or lease land back to them, but many purchased land in the names of their American-born children, who were citizens. See Barbara Yasui, "Nikkei in Oregon," *OHQ*, 76,2 (1975): 247.

veto appropriations without regard to the necessity if they failed to provide the funds. I took strong ground that the income tax should be graduated, bearing more heavily upon the wealthy and powerful, and lightly upon those with small incomes."[23]

Near the end of the session a compromise tax bill was passed, including a clause referring it to voters at the next state election. Pierce disliked it, and believed that the tax was too low, that it would raise too little revenue. Reluctantly, he signed the act, convinced that a weak income tax law was better than no income tax law, establishing an income tax precedent and laying a foundation for the next legislature. The 1923 income tax law was a first step. It began to shift the tax burden off of property. Many newspapers endorsed the tax proposal. Governor Pierce devoted most of his time to working for the referendum's passage. With only 35% of registered voters casting ballots, the referendum passed by 516 votes out of over 117,000 cast. Pierce had won.

The governor and his pro-tax reform allies had no time to savor their victory. Within days, Portlander C. C. Chapman* filed an initiative petition to repeal the new tax law. Oregonians would have another chance to vote on the income tax in November 1924, but in March the state began collecting the new personal income tax. The $3 million collected far exceeded the original estimate of $800,000, to the delight of Governor Pierce. With its new income the state then lowered property taxes by over $2 million, substituting the income tax revenue for the lost property tax money. Approximately 58% of individual income tax payers, with a new combined income over $50 million, owned no real property since their money was invested in stocks, bonds, or in bank accounts. For the first time they were directly paying a state tax.[24]

Chapman criticized the income tax, fearing it discouraged out-of-state investors from coming to Oregon; without this precious investment capital, Oregon's industrial base would stagnate, he believed. With a $52,000 war chest, he waged an aggressive campaign to repeal the income tax. The anti-tax forces put $15,000 into newspaper advertising, a new tactic in Oregon politics. With 25,000 unhappy citizens paying a direct tax for the first time, coupled with the repeal committee's money, and the cynical mood of voters, Oregonians passed Chapman's measure (123,799 yes to 111,055 no). Walter Pierce's precious income tax had lasted only one year. The *Oregonian* went so far as to conclude that "the principle [of the

---

* Chapman was editor and publisher of *Oregon Voter*, a weekly political news magazine, a staunch Republican, and outspoken critic of Walter Pierce. From this position Chapman was to shape public opinion in Oregon for the next forty years.

income tax] is dead in Oregon."[25] Pierce disagreed and he vowed to keep fighting until voters reversed themselves—no matter how long it took.

Pierce and the 1925 Legislature

Governor Pierce delivered two messages to the 1925 Legislature. The first was his State of the State address on January 12. His second was a special written message he released to the assembly and the public on January 29. Together these documents encompassed the governor's vision for Oregon. He laid out what he thought the state's present and future problems were or would be and proceeded to outline a score of solutions. Few governors, either before or since, have taken as analytical, as visionary, a look at Oregon as Walter Pierce did in 1925. He shared with the citizens of Oregon that 1923 state records disclosed that 25,000 Oregon taxpayers who had enjoyed a total net income of $67 million had paid total property taxes of only $327,000—less than one-half of 1%. Farmers, whose net incomes totaled a little less than $11 million, had paid $6.38 million, almost 60% of their incomes, in property taxes. This unequal tax distribution was slowly confiscating the property of many people of this state. Pierce said that land ownership in the state should be entirely free from state taxes and millage levies of all kinds. For immediate relief he suggested a wide variety of other taxes, some old and some new: a gross earnings tax on public utilities; a severance tax on timber and other natural resources; a tax on insurance companies; professional and occupational taxes; taxes on cigarettes and motion pictures; and an increase in the gas tax. [26]

Governor Pierce's special message of January 29 touched on a host of other topics including high telephone rates and hydroelectric power development, including the construction of power plants and dams on several rivers (including the Columbia, where McNary Dam is today). Pierce also proposed higher taxes on timber and more emphasis on reforestation. He opposed highway billboards, proposed changes in child labor laws, and urged job programs for the unemployed. But there was little response to his call to action.[27]

Governor Pierce delivered his special message to the people by radio, making him the first Oregon governor to use that medium. The message had little impact on legislators. With only seven Democrats in the 90-member assembly, Pierce had little chance of advancing his proposals. Frustrated, he became even more vigilant about protecting the interests of ordinary people. He vetoed 31 bills passed by the 1925 Legislature. He used his single-item veto power on numerous appropriation bills. He had a few Republican allies in the legislature, most notably George Joseph, a progressive Republican from Portland.

A dynamic, mercurial state senator, George Joseph was also Oregon's leading advocate of hydroelectric power development. Senator Joseph was joined by several other progressives and the few Democrats, who, on occasion, formed a band of legislators large enough to sustain some of the governor's vetoes.

In spite of an obstinate legislature, Walter Pierce held his ground, even though his "plea for a child labor amendment was turned down, his compulsory industrial accident insurance proposal was buried, and his renewed proposals for consolidation of state commissions and agencies received short shrift." Salem's *Capital Journal* wrote that Governor Pierce had out-guessed and out-maneuvered Republican house and senate leaders at practically every turn.[28]

Yet the legislature still knew how to throw a curve or two. Foes of the income tax, emboldened by their defeat of the 1923 tax law, had a new plan. Why not make the problem of new taxes go away? Why not amend the Oregon Constitution to prohibit the passage of another income tax? When the 1925 Legislature met, it approved the Dennis amendment, which prohibited the adoption in Oregon of either an inheritance tax or another income tax prior to the year 1940.* Voters would decide the issue at the November election. The remainder of 1925 saw Walter Pierce campaigning against the Dennis amendment and he kept to a heavy schedule of speeches.

Pierce was still very popular with many Oregonians and his attention now focused on 1926 and his political future. He eyed two political races: the U.S. Senate seat held by the inept Robert Stanfield, and a second term as governor.

The 1926 Senate Race

Governor Pierce rejected a 1926 run for the Senate and decided to run for a second term as governor. Democrats fell to squabbling over the party's Senate nominee. With the approach of the campaign, Democratic leaders were unusually optimistic. Republican Sen. Robert Stanfield had been an embarrassment to the party and state since early in his term. A heavy drinker, he consorted with prostitutes, and partied often and hard. The D.C. press called him Oregon's "Playboy Senator." Stanfield refused to listen to Oregon's GOP leaders who told him that his rowdy behavior had discredited him with voters at home. In fall 1925, the reckless Stanfield was arrested in Baker, Oregon, charged with drunk and disorderly conduct, resisting arrest, using profanity, and threatening to kill the arresting officer.

---

* The amendment was named after Bruce Dennis, publisher of the LaGrande *Observer,* who had defeated Pierce for a state Senate seat in 1920.

Fred Steiwer, longtime Republican leader and former legislator, challenged Stanfield for the Republican nomination in the 1926 primary. Steiwer, a strong backer of prohibition, was supported by the Anti-Saloon League and endorsed by the *Oregonian,* and in May he was nominated for the Senate. But Stanfield was not finished. In August, he re-entered the Senate race as an independent. His candidacy split the Republican Party down the middle. Democrats nominated Bert E. Haney, a prominent Portland attorney and former member of the U.S. Shipping Board. But Haney's victory caused a rupture in the Democratic Party. His opponent was former Congressman Elton Watkins. Haney had close ties to George Chamberlain and for Democrats sick of the domination of their party by the Chamberlain-West faction, Bert Haney was hard to like. The resulting schism killed any chances Haney might have had to win the Senate seat. The vote was close. Republican Steiwer won with 40%, followed by Haney's 36%, and Stanfield's 23% of the vote. Steiwer beat Haney by 7,700 votes.

Isaac Patterson

Walter Pierce faced Republican Isaac "Ike" Patterson in the governor's race. Patterson was a Polk County fruit grower, a former state senator who had held a federal post as Collector of Customs. He had long desired the office of governor. With 211,000 registered Republicans behind him (compared to 82,000 Democrats), Patterson conducted a cautious campaign and rejected Pierce's offer to debate. They had served as state senators together, and Patterson knew Pierce well and appreciated his potent public speaking skills.

Pierce was the first Oregon politician to campaign on the radio. He appealed to voters over a Portland radio station on the night of October 31, 1926. He cited the reduction in costs of state government and the partial redistribution of taxes he achieved. He sought to tie Patterson to special interest groups, calling him a politician of the old reactionary type.[29] The Patterson campaign outspent Pierce 10-1 and business was solidly in Patterson's corner. Both candidates were longtime Drys, so neither was endorsed by the Anti-Saloon League. Only the farm bloc remained loyal to Pierce. But it wasn't enough. In November, Ike Patterson rolled over Walter Pierce 120,000 to 93,500. Pierce pulled nearly 40,000 fewer votes than he got in 1922. Still, his total exceeded the number of registered Democrats in the state. He carried 11 of 18 eastern Oregon counties and won Patterson's home county of Polk, but Patterson carried Multnomah County by a large margin.[30]

Pierce's record as governor had been unimpressive. His place in Oregon history as an outstanding public figure came mostly from his imaginative anticipation of future social needs. He realized that real property could not go on paying the major costs of government and recognized that people would expect more and more from their government, which would inevitably mean larger governmental expenditures.[31] Pierce's "dedication, vision, and political courage in the field of tax reform were among his greatest contributions to Oregon."[32]

Approaching age 66, it looked like Walter Pierce was leaving public office for good in 1927. Not so. In 1932, he was elected to the U.S. House of Representatives from eastern Oregon at the age of 72, the oldest person ever elected to his first term in the House. He served for 10 years and staunchly supported President Franklin Roosevelt's New Deal in Congress.

In the same election, Oregon voters rejected the Dennis amendment, with a vote of 121,973 opposed and 59,442 in favor.[33] Undaunted, the 1927 Legislature again passed the Dennis amendment and referred it to voters. The measure was again crushed in Oregon's special election of June 28, 1927, by a vote of 84,700 no to 19,400 in favor. Thinking that the third time might be a charm, the 1929 Legislature re-passed the Dennis tax ban, and again referred it to the people. This time (a year after the stock market crash and onset of the Great Depression), C. C. Chapman and the Republican Legislature were not disappointed. In November 1930, voters approved the Dennis amendment 105,200 to 95,207 opposed. The new tax ban would remain in effect until 1953.

Chapter 9
Two Deaths: 1927-33

The oldest man ever elected governor of Oregon, Isaac Patterson, was 67 years old when he took office on January 10, 1927. A veteran politician, he loved farming and worked several hundred acres in Polk County. Independent and conservative, Ike Patterson was his own man. He was not a reformer. Committed to honest, efficient, and thrifty government, he was more concerned about making government work better than in adding to its size. Tall, silver-haired, and erect of posture, Patterson exuded confidence. Known for his integrity, kindness, and dedication to lean government and hard work, he was respected by both political insiders and the public.

Governor Patterson's inaugural address contained no surprises. The *Oregonian* remarked that the speech "presents nothing sensational or revolutionary, was businesslike in tone and conservative in recommendation."[1] After his inauguration he drove to Portland and delivered his 38-minute inaugural address over radio station KGW to a statewide listening audience. Like his predecessor, Walter Pierce, Patterson effectively used radio as a valuable new tool of communication. Slowly, the fundamental practice of Oregon politics was changing.

Oregon and the nation were riding a wave of prosperity in 1927. Yet serious problems faced the state. Tax reformers continued to push for change, urging adoption of a personal income tax to replace the hated state property tax. Farmers struggled with low commodity prices and rising debts. But Oregon continued to grow and with growth came new demands: more schools, highways, bridges, jails, courts, health services, electric power-lines, and telephones were needed.

Many New Faces

Oregon's 1927 House of Representatives was notably inexperienced. Twenty-six members were rookies and 19 were serving in their second session. Only eight of the 60 members had served three or more terms. Among the newcomers was Earl Snell, an Arlington automobile dealer and future governor. Attorneys

(19), farmers/stockraisers (17), and bankers (8) dominated the House. Fourteen lawyers sat in the 30-member state Senate, as did seven farmers and five bankers. Portland Republican Henry Ladd Corbett, grandson of former U.S. Senator Henry Winslow Corbett, Harvard educated, and heir to one of Oregon's largest family fortunes, presided over the 1927 Senate. Corbett was respected for his intelligence, honesty, and fairness. Medford's John H. Carkin, an attorney, was House speaker and serving his fourth term. The session fit the pattern of conservative, business-oriented Republican legislatures associated with Oregon's first half of the century.[2]

Voters in the 1926 election had defeated a referendum put forth by the 1925 Legislature, the so-called "tithing bill," which would have raised additional money for state government by requiring 5% of all fees collected by state boards and commissions to go to the State General Fund. Backers of the tithe had hoped to raise over $300,000 each biennium. Governor Patterson was an outspoken supporter of the tithing bill. He was convinced the state would need the money to balance the next biennial budget. He made passage of a new tithing bill his top legislative priority in 1927. As a popular governor, Patterson used his prestige and keen political skills to guide the tithing bill through the Republican House. But the Senate killed the measure. Patterson's tenacity in pushing the tithing measure alienated some key legislators. Numerous newspapermen also took exception to Patterson's insistence on advancing a measure voters had resoundingly defeated in the previous election. In short, Patterson's crusade cost him precious political points in 1927.

But aside from the tithing bill, Governor Patterson pretty much got his way with the 1927 Legislature. What he didn't like he vetoed—42 bills in all. Faced with a budget deficit of about $4 million, the governor wielded his veto axe on appropriation bills totaling $1.3 million. Higher education took the biggest hits. The State Board of Control was strengthened by a Patterson-backed bill to make the board the central purchasing agency for all state departments, boards, and commissions, and the 11 state institutions, including the penitentiary and state hospital.

The governor signed a bill to close the Willamette River and its tributaries to commercial fishing. In addition, he approved a measure defining a person convicted of three felony crimes as a habitual criminal, who could then be sentenced to a life term in the penitentiary. Proposed salary increases for state employees and county assessors did not pass the session due to Patterson's longtime opposition to them. Most newspaper editors scolded the governor for opposing the pay hikes, saying that they were both fair and overdue.

A Special Election

A special statewide election on June 28, 1927, resulted in a fifth defeat (since 1922) of a proposed state income tax. Voters rejected the measure, repudiating the state's business leaders, newspaper editors, politicians, and governor, all of whom backed the tax. Voters were in no mood to approve any kind of tax in 1927. As a result, most tax increases and bond issues at both the state and local level were defeated. C. C. Chapman, writing in his *Oregon Voter*, speculated that the defeat of the proposed state income tax was due to the fact that voters "construed the bill as favorable to larger incomes and unfavorable to smaller incomes, and therefore discriminating."[3]

Voters also rejected state Senator George Joseph's resolution to raise the per-diem pay for legislators from $3 to $10. The obsolete provision of the Oregon Constitution forbidding Negroes and Chinese from voting was finally overturned in June. Fifty-seven years after ratification of the 15th Amendment, Oregonians brought their constitution into conformity with the U.S. Constitution. Oregon was like most states, reluctant to assure full political rights to minorities.

Mr. Smith, Mr. Hoover, and the Election of 1928

With the 1927 June election behind them, Oregonians joined the rest of the country as it geared up for the campaign of 1928. With the colorless, though popular, Calvin Coolidge out of the presidential picture, Herbert Clark Hoover (formerly of Newberg, Oregon) appeared to have a lock on the Republican nomination. For Democrats, the 1928 race was anything but certain. After the crushing defeat of their presidential candidate, John W. Davis, in 1924, Democrats in Oregon and across the land searched for a candidate who would reunite the party and lead it to a November victory. The National Democratic Party, like its Oregon counterpart, was in disarray in 1928. Yet, with no incumbent president, Democrats were optimistic about capturing the presidency. Governor Alfred E. Smith of New York was the leading Democratic contender. Smith was a Wet—he favored the repeal of Prohibition. And he was a Roman Catholic. Long associated with the powerful New York City political machine controlled by Tammany Hall Democrats, Smith was despised by most southerners and by many westerners.

Former Governor Oswald West, a staunch friend of Prohibition, led the Oregon opposition against Smith. He persuaded Senators James Reed of Missouri and Thomas Walsh of Montana to run against Smith in Oregon's May 1928 Democratic primary. Appealing to Oregon's large bloc of prohibitionists,

West attempted to defeat Smith solely on the alcohol issue. Still influential in Oregon, Os West gave a series of fiery speeches against Al Smith throughout the state, urging Oregon Democrats to "kick the booze hounds in the slats and send them back to their night clubs with their tails between their legs."[4]

Nonetheless, Governor Smith's backers effectively blunted West's assault; Smith easily won the Democratic nomination. Os West pouted from his lofty perch as Oregon's Democratic National Committeeman. Instead of promoting party unity and backing Smith's candidacy, West refused to attend the Democratic National Convention that summer. When the fall general election rolled around, West sat on the sidelines, refusing to work for his party's presidential nominee.*

Al Smith had no real chance of carrying Oregon in 1928. While he polled 34% of the vote (up from John Davis's anemic 24% in 1924), Smith was crushed by Herbert Hoover's 64% of Oregon's November vote. Nationally, Hoover won 58% of the vote to Smith's 41%. Bruised and contentious, Oregon's Democrats emerged from the 1928 campaign seemingly more impotent than ever. Long a minority, Democrats appeared incapable of overcoming their chronic differences. The continued internal strife sapped what little vitality the organization had. Underfunded, poorly locally organized, paralyzed by an abiding distrust between rural and urban members, the Democratic Party appeared destined to everlasting mediocrity.

Wall Street Trembles

Prior to its collapse in the fall of 1929, most Americans mistakenly believed that the New York Stock Exchange was the barometer by which to gauge the nation's economic health. As the exchange went so went the country. The exchange's dizzying and unprecedented 1927-29 climb only reinforced the public's belief that the economy was sound and would continue to boom. But for those willing to look under a patina of misguided optimism, dozens of festering problems could be found. In Oregon's heavy industries (the building trades and lumber production), unemployment began to grow in the early part of 1927. Agricultural prices were weakening. By 1927, ten giant utility systems were in the process of absorbing nearly 75% of the nation's total electric light and power business, and Oregon's private utilities were enmeshed in the financial web.[5]

---

* Two years later, in the 1930 spring primary, Democrats stripped Os West of his committeeman post, rewarding his disloyalty with defeat. Former governor Walter Pierce was elected to replace him (Pierce endorsed Senator Walsh in the 1928 primary. Once Al Smith won the Democratic nomination, Pierce backed him). From this new position, Pierce launched his successful bid for a seat in the U.S. House of Representatives in 1932.

Several major financial institutions in Oregon went bankrupt between 1927 and 1929. The Northwestern National Bank of Portland closed its doors and liquidated its assets beginning in March 1927. The Bank of Kenton collapsed two years later, preceding the closure of Overbeck and Cooke Company, a pioneer stock brokerage house in Portland.[6] In short, several of the fundamental causes of the Great Depression, including the concentration of wealth in the hands of a few, high unemployment, depressed lumber and farm prices, along with bank failures, were evident in Oregon and elsewhere before Wall Street collapsed in October 1929.

The Legislature of 1929

When Oregon's 1929 Legislature met for 50 days, from January 14 to March 4, the state hadn't yet been staggered by economic collapse. Consequently, the worsening economy had only a minor impact on what lawmakers did. There was nothing extraordinary about the makeup of the 1929 Senate. All thirty members were male, virtually all were Republicans, and the majority were legislative veterans. Again, banker Henry Ladd Corbett of Portland was Senate president. The majority of senators were either lawyers or agriculturalists. Senators Gus Moser, Charles Hall, Albin Norblad, and E. L. Eddy, along with Corbett, wielded most of the power. The Senate was pretty much a comfortable old boys' club.

The House was more unsettled than the Senate. Fifty-four of the 60 members were rookies or still learning the legislative ropes. The days of a House dominated by a dozen grizzled power-brokers were finally gone. Among the House freshmen were two members of special note. Both represented District 18 of Multnomah County. Forty-one-year-old Swedish-born Gust Anderson was secretary of the Multnomah County Central Labor Council. A machinist by trade, Anderson was the first labor leader elected to the Oregon House. Joining Anderson was a California-born Portland attorney named Dorothy McCullough Lee. Only 28 (but appearing much younger), Lee was the only woman to serve in the 1929 Legislature.*

Republican Scramble

Governor Isaac Patterson died unexpectedly on December 21, 1929, at age 70, opening a huge political chasm in Oregon. Patterson was popular and

---

* Lee served three terms in the House before being elected to the Senate in 1939. Appointed to the Portland City Council in 1943, Lee was elected the city's first woman mayor in 1948; she was defeated for reelection in 1952.

it was widely assumed that he would have sought, and likely won, a second term. Six prominent Republicans threw their hats into the ring to replace him. Suddenly, the upcoming May 1930 primary got very interesting. Albin Norblad, an Astoria lawyer, was president of the state Senate and first in the line-of-succession to replace Patterson until the election. The Swedish-born Norblad, age 48, took the oath as governor on December 22, announcing that he would seek election to the office the following year. Norblad's naked political ambition, expressed before Isaac Patterson was buried, offended many Oregonians. He was by no means a shoo-in for the Republican nomination. Opposing him were three state senators: former Senate President Henry Ladd Corbett of Portland, Charles Hall of Coos Bay, and Jacob J. Jeffery, a perennially unsuccessful candidate. Most observers believed the contest was between Corbett and Norblad, with Hall given only an outside chance. Yet Hall had made an impressive showing in the 1922 Republican gubernatorial primary and couldn't be entirely dismissed.*

Al Norblad grabbed the headlines with his campaign slogans "Pull for Oregon or Pull Out" and "Hats off to the past. Coats off for the future." An aggressive booster of Oregon, Norblad hoped to appeal to the over one hundred thousand young men and women who had reached voting age in Oregon in the 1920s. He backed President Hoover's public works program as a means of putting thousands of workers back on the job. His positions on boosting Oregon agriculture, reducing taxes "through careful supervision of the state's budget and expenditures"[7] and his tough stance against lawbreakers were the usual positions taken by Oregon politicians in the 1920s.

Henry Ladd Corbett was an honest and dependable public servant, a bearer of two of the state's most prominent political names and a safely predictable Portland senator. He was the choice of much of Oregon's business establishment. Corbett's campaign slogan, "Economy, efficiency, and progress," while reassuring to some, failed to capture the imagination of most voters. His positions were a rehash of the slogans Patterson had run on in 1926. Among his political opponents, he was highly respected as a person whose word was always good. "But to the progressives, Corbett had three political liabilities: his inherited wealth, his sympathy with private utilities and his lack of personal charisma."[8]

Until March 1930, the GOP campaign was a sedate, gentlemanly contest between Norblad, Corbett, and Hall. None of them had yet generated much

---

* Charles Hall had challenged Gov. Ben Olcott in the GOP primary. Olcott had blasted the KKK, while Hall endorsed the Klan (and was endorsed by them). Olcott defeated Hall by only five hundred votes.

public enthusiasm. That all changed dramatically on March 3. A board of referees recommended to the Oregon Supreme Court that former state Senator George W. Joseph of Portland be disbarred for life from the practice of law because of "slanderous and unprovoked charges against Justices Rand and McBride of the Oregon Supreme Court and for conduct unbecoming a member of the bar." Ten days later, George Joseph announced that he was seeking the Republican nomination for Governor of Oregon.[9]

A Crusading George Joseph

Who was George W. Joseph, Sr., and why did his overnight candidacy so startle and shake Oregon's political foundations? He was a prominent Republican attorney in Portland* and a progressive Republican. In his first and second sessions as a state senator, in 1911 and 1913, he was a key backer of many of the reforms advanced by Democratic Gov. Oswald West. Joseph returned to the Senate in 1921, continuing until 1928. Throughout the 1920s, Joseph was Oregon's leading advocate for the development of cheap hydroelectric power in Oregon. Outspoken, fearless, and aggressive, he hated machine politics and those who practiced them. Witty, highly intelligent, uncompromising, and sometimes unforgiving, he was a formidable political personality in Oregon. Though he was an urban politician, Joseph's advocacy of cheap hydroelectricity endeared him to farmers and small businessmen in rural Oregon. As a state senator, he condemned Oregon's major utility companies for blocking his efforts on behalf of public power development. In so doing, the maverick Joseph made a lot of powerful political enemies. Some prominent business leaders thought he was a dangerous and unpredictable radical. His biting sarcasm and love for practical jokes made him feared by friend and foe alike.

When George Joseph dramatically entered the governor's race in spring 1930, he did so, in part, to vindicate himself. Believing he had been grievously wronged and unjustly condemned for his remarks about and actions against Justice Rand, Joseph decided that the governor's contest gave him a forum for gaining public support. Throughout his stormy campaign, candidate Joseph talked about the "dirty deal" he had got. He painted himself as the underdog, as a victim fighting to save his good name and reputation.

---

* In 1895, at age twenty-three, Joseph had formed a law partnership with a young man named Julius Meier, a recent law school graduate at the University of Oregon. A year later young Meier went to work in his family's business, the Meier and Frank Company. Meier, however, maintained his law partnership with Joseph (until 1910). The two remained lifelong friends and political allies. Joseph was hired as the attorney for Meier and Frank.

The Oregon press had a heyday with Joseph's candidacy. The *Oregonian* called him reckless, saying he needed to admit his errors in professional judgment, and to conduct himself in a more restrained, positive manner. The Medford *Mail-Tribune* wrote "no citizen in his right mind could believe for a moment that [Joseph] is qualified [to be governor]." Yet the more the newspapers criticized George Joseph, the more steam his candidacy picked up.[10] The country slipped daily into a worsening economy while "a rising tide of protest that was reminiscent of the Populist and Progressive eras" surfaced in Oregon.[11] George Joseph happily rode that buoyant tide.

On May 16, George Joseph was chosen as the Republican nominee for governor with 50,400 votes. He beat Governor Norblad by a margin of over 4,150 and Henry Corbett trailed with 33,900 votes. Rolling to a huge lead in Multnomah County (Joseph's 27,570 votes exceeded the combined vote of Corbett and Norblad), Joseph overcame his losses outside his home county. Edward Bailey, a young Junction City attorney, got the Democratic nomination.

How did George Joseph do it? The answer is that he successfully linked his candidacy "with the interests of the common people, the consumers."[12] Another factor was Joseph's ability to exploit the divided Republican vote; he won with 30,000 fewer votes than the combined vote of Norblad and Corbett. Within days of his victory he was back on the campaign trail. Delivering dozens of speeches throughout the state, Joseph quickly drove himself to a physical collapse. One day in June while walking with his close friend and advisor Henry Hanzen, he slumped to the sidewalk by Portland's Multnomah Hotel. Refusing medical treatment, Joseph admitted to Hanzen that he had probably had a heart attack. He promised to take a vacation to California as soon as he tied up a few loose ends. "Joseph journeyed with Colonel W. C. North to Camp Clatsop on Sunday. On Monday morning he ate breakfast with North and Major George C. White of the National Guard. After the hearty meal he mounted a horse and rode to the drill ground where he watched the troops. Dismounting, he began to talk with some officers. Suddenly, with a smile on his face, he stopped talking and fell backwards. A doctor was summoned. George W. Joseph had died of a heart attack at 8:57 A.M., June 16, 1930. He was fifty-eight-years old."[13]

Oregonians were stunned. Many were still mourning the death of Gov. Isaac Patterson. Now, George Joseph, the man Republicans had chosen to replace Patterson, had himself fallen. Would GOP leaders pick an old-guard Republican to replace George Joseph, or would they choose a reformer like Joseph?

A "Rich Boy" for Governor?

Julius Meier, a lifelong Republican, shared his friend George Joseph's progressive vision for Oregon. After the special Republican state convention met and chose Portland hotelman Phil Metschan to replace Joseph, Meier thought of running for governor as an Independent. With strong backing from his family, business associates, and Joseph's legion of followers, Julius Meier decided his chances of election were better than Metschan's. He officially entered the campaign after Metschan rejected Joseph's platform. "The convention that nominated Meier was as wildly enthusiastic as any in the state's history. Meier endorsed the Joseph platform, literally word for word, and promptly received the backing of the State Federation of Labor and the Oregon Grange."[14] Republicans again found themselves a badly divided majority. Could "Big Ed" Bailey, the Democratic gubernatorial nominee, slide into the governor's chair while the more numerous Republicans fought each other? Bailey conducted a low-profile campaign, hoping that Metschan and Meier would so bloody each other that he would be elected. But Bailey's party was also fractured and squabbling. A proposed "initiative measure providing for the creation of People's Utility Districts by majority vote of the people residing in such districts" added spice to the fall campaign.[15]

The 1930 campaign quickly focused on the personal differences of the two major candidates. Metschan emphasized his early pioneer life with slogans like "Native Son of the Old West!" And in several statewide radio broadcasts, Metschan called Meier a greedy big businessman. In the November 1, 1930 issue of the *Oregon Voter*, the Republican State Central Committee ran a full-page ad that concluded: "Revolutionaries are springing up everywhere. Property is being nationalized and destroyed. Don't play with fire, but play safe. Mark your ballot for Phil Metschan."[16] *Oregon Voter* also featured a series of derogatory political cartoons lampooning Julius Meier. Unparalleled in the history of Oregon political journalism, the cartoons depicted Meier as a *Little Lord Fauntleroy*-like character, dressed in knee britches, ruffled collar, black patent leather shoes, velvet jacket and beribboned sailor's cap. The implication was obvious. Meier was a spoiled rich boy used to having things his own way, a man who would not hesitate to buy whatever he wanted, including the governorship of Oregon. The *Voter* cartoons were vicious and unusually hard-hitting. These cartoons also played to the nativist inclinations of many Oregonians. The Ku Klux Klan's influence on Oregon politics in the early 1920s was fueled, in part, by anti-Jewish prejudice. The *Oregonian* endorsed Phil Metschan. Downstate, however, Meier got the support of the Salem *Capitol Journal* and the Medford *Mail-Tribune*.

Julius Meier swept to victory in November, pulling 56% of the vote, besting Democrat Ed Bailey by over 72,000 ballots. Bailey surpassed Republican Phil Metschan by a margin of over 15,000. Metschan took only about 19% of the vote, or 46,800 ballots. Oregonians decisively elected George Joseph's heir-apparent by one of the biggest margins in state election history. Julius Meier was the first elected Jewish governor of Oregon. Only eight years earlier, back in the Klan-dominated election of 1922, candidates at all levels ran on anti-Catholic and anti-Jewish platforms. Perhaps Oregonians were tired of the charges and insinuations launched from all corners of the country that they were a racist, bigoted lot. Their emphatic support for Julius Meier helped to put to rest that infamous chapter of Oregon's political history.

Other Results in 1930

The controversial Public Utility District (PUD) initiative, Measure 13, which was backed by Meier, passed by about 30,000 votes. A similar measure was approved in neighboring Washington.

The 1930 campaign also featured two other races: the U.S. Senate contest between incumbent Charles McNary and Democratic challenger Elton Watkins, and the battle in the 3rd Congressional District. Senator McNary was seeking a third consecutive term, something no Senate candidate had ever accomplished in Oregon. The moderate McNary had attained a key Republican leadership role in the Senate and since 1924 had been one of the nation's leading spokesmen for agricultural reform. His positions made him popular with farmers everywhere, particularly in the West. For several months in 1928 he was a possible vice-presidential nominee on the Republican ticket. Democratic one-term (1923-25) Congressman Elton Watkins, was no match for the popular McNary, who took 58% of the tally, drubbing Watkins 137,000 to 66,000. With his landslide, Charles McNary continued as Oregon's most powerful politician and biggest vote-getter.

The 3rd District U.S. House race featured the ascent of a new political star in Oregon: General Charles Martin. A conservative Democrat, Martin was a 47-year army veteran. Martin moved to Portland to retire with his wife in the fall of 1928. Though a lifelong registered Republican, General Martin permitted his name to be written in as a last-minute Democratic candidate on the May ballot. He won his new party's nomination with 705 write-in votes. In November, the distinguished political novice swept to a resounding victory over Republican Franklin F. Korell. Considering that Multnomah County was still a bastion of Republicanism, Martin's 55% vote total was impressive. At a ripe age of 67, Charles Martin was beginning a short but spectacular political career.

Oregon Slips into the Great Depression

When Julius Meier took office as governor in January 1931, Oregon's economic picture was bleak. Several prominent Oregon banks either failed, were forced to merge, or were in shaky condition in the early 1930s. The Hibernia Bank closed in December 1931. Governor Meier had the American National Bank, in which he was an owner, sold to the First National Bank in June 1933.[17] Oregon's fragile financial institutions, like those everywhere, reflected the deepening national depression.

Sectors of the Oregon economy had been stumbling since 1927, notably lumber and wood products. Lumber mills were operating at 45% of normal. The volume of Oregon business dropped 20% in 1930. Logging employment had dropped 48%. Twenty-four thousand heads of families were unemployed in Portland, representing about a third of households.[18] Over 30,000 were jobless in Multnomah County in early 1933, about one-third of the state's total unemployed. Several prominent Oregon banks either failed, were forced to merge, or were in shaky condition in the early 1930s. Thousands of men and women who had worked full-time in 1928 had either no job or a position cut back to part-time work at greatly reduced wages. With the wages of most Oregonians plummeting, there was growing public pressure in 1931 to cut the wages of public employees to bring them in line with salaries in the private sector.

Against this grim backdrop Gov. Julius Meier and the legislatures of 1931 and 1933 were expected to keep state government afloat. The state general fund had a deficit of over $3 million. To make matters worse, out-going Gov. Albin Norblad left a budget which recommended spending $1.6 million more than the state estimated it would take in as income in 1931-32. Governor Meier knew that his first order of business was to slash the state's budget deficit.

Oregon's First Depression-Era Legislature

Republicans maintained their decades-old grip on the 1931 Legislature. But their popularity was slipping and they knew it. Voters seemed poised to knock the Republicans out of power—if they failed to right Oregon's sagging economy. The legislature convened in Salem on January 12. Senators picked Albany lawyer Willard L. Marks, to be their president. Portland attorney Frank J. Lonergan became House speaker. Neither Marks nor Lonergan had had long legislative careers. For the second consecutive session, Dorothy M. Lee was the only female legislator.

Governor Meier got most of what he wanted from the legislature. His personal legislative agenda was short and there was no real organized opposition to it. Meier didn't push any major reform legislation of his own. Instead, he concentrated on trying to keep the pending 1931-32 state budget from going deeper in debt. The governor tried to convince lawmakers to balance the budget. He failed. When legislators adjourned their 54-day session on March 6, they had produced a budget with a deficit of $2.25 million. Governor Meier got out his veto pen and carving knife. He vetoed $600,000, $500,000 of which was from higher education, leaving $1.65 million in excess expenditures. Added to the state deficit from previous administrations, this gave him a total state deficit of $4.5 million to pass on to the 1933 Legislature.[19]

Through selective salary cuts of state employees and getting reduced bids on state purchases, Meier further reduced the deficit. The legislature had enacted a law requiring the relatives of institution inmates to pay some of the costs for their upkeep. This measure was expected to bring in another $150,000 to the general fund.

After the legislature adjourned, C. C. Chapman, editor of the *Oregon Voter*, blasted lawmakers for accomplishing so little. He blamed the lack of legislative accomplishment on the failure of a cohesive majority to take charge in either house, attributing this failure to poor leadership. Chapman assigned the legislature's lack of forceful leadership and purpose to the recent November elections. The overwhelming repudiation of Republican nominee Phil Metschan, coupled with the resounding victory of Julius Meier running as an Independent, had a lot to do with the severe case of caution affecting legislators. Meier's role as both a new political face and the candidate who had run on the anti-utility/pro-hydropower platform of the deceased George Joseph added to the confusion and uncertainty most legislators felt in 1931. Voter approval of the Public Utility District (PUD) initiative only reinforced the mood in Salem that voters were angry, unpredictable, and wanted certain changes. Oregon's economy was in shambles and this was the overriding factor in determining what legislators could and couldn't do in 1931: members were keenly aware that their only choice was to cut existing programs and services. Lawmakers' failure to balance the 1931-33 state budget reveals their reluctance to cut too deeply into the muscle of state government. They left it up to the governor to make many of the toughest decisions to cut programs. It was simple politics: let the governor take the heat, let him face an angry electorate—so legislators could creep unnoticed back into their districts.

Politics Undergoes Fundamental Change

American politics were profoundly changed by the presidential election of 1932, the most important election in 20th-century American politics. The vote was a referendum on the Hoover/Republican handling of the Great Depression. This watershed election produced several notable outcomes, including an end to Republican domination of the American presidency, as signaled by Franklin Roosevelt's election and three-time reelection. With the two terms of Harry S. Truman following Roosevelt's twelve years in office, Democrats would hold the presidency from 1933 to 1953. This ended the Republican control of Congress and a viable two-party political system re-emerged. Franklin Delano Roosevelt became the pre-eminent American political leader of the century; and a fundamental re-alignment of American voting blocs occurred. A coalition of blocs attached itself to the Democratic Party, forming a new alliance that was to dominate national politics and government (with the exception of Dwight Eisenhower's presidency, 1953-61) during the middle third of the century, 1933-1969.

Oregon Democrats were unified and energized by the candidacy of Franklin Roosevelt. Democrats, long a third-rate power in Oregon politics, sprang to life as the state's most potent new political force. For only the third time in a presidential election, Oregon voted Democratic in 1932. Franklin Roosevelt took 58% of the state vote, slightly above his national percentage. Incumbent Herbert Hoover, who captured 64% of the 1928 Oregon vote, got only 37% in 1932.

Democrats also won two of Oregon's three seats in the U.S. House of Representatives. Incumbent one-termer Charles W. Martin was handily reelected in the 3rd Congressional District, besting Republican Homer Angell with 60% of the vote. Walter Pierce was elected to the first of five terms representing the 2nd District, the first Democrat elected in this congressional seat, a seat created back in 1892. Martin, nearly 70, and Pierce, 72, were two of the oldest members of the House. Democrats also made impressive gains in legislative races. They elected eight state senators, up from the single seat they held in 1931. Their numbers in the Oregon House jumped seven from the previous session to 17.

The Democratic victories happened because progressive Republicans crossed over to vote for the minority party. The *Oregon Democrat* observed: "The large number of progressive Republicans who voted the Democratic ticket, either in part or whole, are Democratic at heart and by a little progress of education in Democracy may be converted to our course."[20] Now, could Oregon Democrats maintain their coalition of progressive Republicans, farmers, industrial workers, and traditional Democrats that the party had forged?

Early in the New Deal, Democratic leaders were optimistic that they could do so. But unity was short lived. By 1937, their fragile coalition was unraveling. Returning to old habits, Democrats broke into two warring factions. In spite of their inability to remain unified, the Oregon Democratic Party made remarkable strides in the 1930s. For example, Walter Pierce held the 2nd District seat 1933-43. Charles Martin held the 3rd District slot 1931-35, and left Congress to assume the governorship in 1935. In 1936, Oregon elected its first woman to Congress, Democrat Nancy Wood Honeyman, in the 3rd District. Twice in the decade Democrats captured the Oregon House of Representatives, controlling the 1935 and 1937 sessions. The Democrats' victory in 1934 broke the 55-year-long GOP hold on the Oregon House. One-party rule of the legislature was temporarily broken.

Thousands of voters were registering as Democrats. Democratic registration climbed to a high of 48% in the 1930s. In Multnomah County, Democratic registration jumped from 25% of registered voters in 1930 to 53% in 1938. After Roosevelt carried Oregon in 1932, he captured the state easily in the presidential elections of 1936 (68%), 1940 (54%), and 1944 (52%).[21] Roosevelt's personal charismatic appeal, along with his New Deal legislative successes, had more to do with drawing voters into the Democratic fold than did any other factor. Without them it is doubtful whether the Oregon Democratic Party or the nation would have enjoyed the political renaissance that it did in the 1930s.

Oregon Is Dead Broke

Oregon's economic picture in January 1933 was a far cry from what it had been only two years before. The Great Depression had taken hold. Thousands of Oregonians lost their savings, their homes, farms, and businesses. Homeless men, women, and children, tattered and dirty, wandered from town to town, vainly searching for food, shelter, and work. So-called Hoovervilles or shanty-towns sprang up all over Oregon. Church and civic organizations tried to keep soup kitchens going to feed the many hungry. Thousands were desperate for relief aid. In 1934, Gov. Julius Meier summed up the general situation: "Oregon is dead broke."[22] The Depression was the dominant fact of American life in 1933, with millions of people suffering extreme hardships. One worker in four was out of work, both in Oregon and the nation. It was estimated that 34 million Americans, or a quarter of the population, were without an adequate income to live. As leaders looked ahead to the winter of 1933 they feared that as many as 25 million citizens would need some kind of assistance in order to survive the season. Coupled with over 5,500 bank failures (and with them the savings of millions of depositors), depressed farm prices, and high mortgage rates, the nation shuddered to think of what might be ahead.

Chapter 10
FDR, Old Iron Pants, and the Politics of Upheaval, 1933-38

FDR and the New Deal

The day dawned cold as winter lingered a little longer in March 1933. Great excitement was in the air. A happy throng assembled at the nation's Capitol to watch Franklin Delano Roosevelt take the presidential oath of office. Millions of Americans listened at home or at work, their ears glued to their radios. Roosevelt did not disappoint. His memorable first inaugural address ranks as one of the nation's great 20th-century speeches. The president radiated confidence and optimism. His stirring "We have nothing to fear but fear itself" forever summarized Roosevelt's upbeat message. The people were hungry for encouraging words. They yearned for a leader who conveyed genuine understanding and concern for their worsening lives. Would FDR deliver? Could he get the United States rolling again? Could he provide the immediate relief so many desperate Americans needed? Where would this millionaire New York patrician take them and their homeland? These were the critical questions on the minds of the people that Inauguration Day.

Americans were buoyed by Roosevelt's inaugural message. Action quickly followed. Congress was called into special session. When the session ended a hundred days later, 15 major bills had been enacted, including the creation of the Tennessee Valley Authority, the Civilian Conservation Corps (CCC), the Federal Deposit Insurance Corporation, the Agricultural Adjustment Act, and the National Industrial Recovery Act. Never had Congress passed so much critical and innovative landmark legislation with such dispatch.

Charles McNary, Oregon's senior U.S. senator, was a key figure in the 1933 Senate. Thirty-six Republicans elected McNary minority leader as well as the chairman of the Republican Conference, making him one of the most powerful Republicans in Washington. The press uniformly praised his abilities as a parliamentarian and political strategist. His honesty and integrity were beyond reproach. The senator's power and prestige were further heightened by his friendship and close working relationship with the new Democratic Majority Leader, Senator Joseph T. Robinson.[1]

Charles McNary endorsed most of President Roosevelt's early New Deal programs.* The Agricultural Adjustment Act, one of the cornerstones of FDR's First Hundred Days, was patterned on the senator's McNary-Haugen bill, first introduced in Congress in 1924. Putting partisanship aside, McNary was one of FDR's most ardent Republican supporters. He enjoyed "having a president who was politically flexible and more interested in results than philosophical purity. Roosevelt and McNary were pragmatists who believed politics was the art of the possible. McNary admired Roosevelt's devotion to the common people and his refusal to let political and governmental traditions stand in the way of helping victims of the Depression."[2] An enduring friendship developed between the Oregon senator and the president. Roosevelt appreciated McNary's frank criticisms, wit, intelligence, and political acumen. This friendship helped Charles McNary to be a pivotal player in guiding to passage the Northwest's most important New Deal legislation: over $30 million to build Bonneville Dam on the Columbia River.[3]

The early New Deal rested on the 15 acts passed by the Congress of spring 1933. Many of these programs were revolutionary in concept and design, adopting a whole new philosophy of government (and its proper role). Such fundamental change, of course, sparked much controversy. Critics of the New Deal, and there were many, believed that the New Dealers went too far in their attempts to bring about relief, recovery, and reform in the country. Big Government, they argued, endangered individual property rights, robbed people of their incentive to work, and created a too-expensive new federal bureaucracy. Many Americans still subscribed to the values espoused by Calvin Coolidge and Herbert Hoover. Government should not intrude unnecessarily in peoples' lives. It should be thrifty and small. Government was not responsible for manipulating the national economy. Let the natural laws of economics, such as supply and demand, and the tenets of laissez-faire capitalism, continue to determine how the nation conducts its business. FDR's "artificial priming" of the economy, said his critics, was both dangerous and a threat to free-enterprise, unregulated capitalism.

---

* The label "New Deal" was adopted by F.D.R. and the Democratic Party as the name of their package of legislation designed to bring the nation out of the Great Depression by providing relief, recovery, and reform.

This philosophical disagreement over the New Deal had a profound effect on politics at all levels. In Oregon, these differences helped tear apart the Democratic Party. There was a contest between liberals and conservatives for domination of the party. When Roosevelt was elected in 1932, conservatives were in control, but liberals announced their intention to assume command. Liberals said there was no need for the Democratic Party to exist in Oregon unless they advocated and executed radical changes. The conservative wing eventually opposed Roosevelt and the programs of the New Deal. Voters in Oregon who were behind the national administration viewed the state Democratic Party and its leaders as reactionary. In an attempt to secure the benefits of the New Deal (such as patronage), Republicans and Democrats frequently exercised an independence of party and non-partisanship reminiscent of the Progressive era.[4]

Democratic Party unity was also undercut by labor tension, which was high throughout the nation in the late 1930s. Rivalry between the older American Federation of Labor (AFL) and the newer Congress of Industrial Organizations (CIO) also caused politicians to take sides. If one was pro-AFL, one was viewed as anti-CIO and vice versa. Oregon's conservative Democratic leadership, headed by Gov. Charles Martin, had little sympathy for labor's aspirations. This meant pro-labor Democrats were unwelcome in the party. Another obstacle was the party's inability to identify and back politically able and credible candidates for office. Conservatives refused to support liberal-backed candidates; liberal Democrats returned the favor when conservative candidates ran for office. The failure of these warring sides to compromise explains why the Democratic Party in Oregon didn't realize even more electoral success than it did in the 1932-38 period. "[T]he major obstacle to Democratic success during the New Deal was the failure of party leaders to support the administration's public power program and, most specifically, the power program as interpreted by the Oregon Grange and the State Federation of Labor. This issue, above all others, became the chief source of schism in the Democratic Party."[5] The fight between the proponents of inexpensive, federally owned and generated electricity and the backers of privately owned electricity colored Oregon's politics throughout the 1930s. The issue divided consumers and utility companies, as well as Republicans and Democrats.

The Ugly Reality of Deepening Depression

Republican Fred B. Kiddle of Island City was elected president of the Oregon Senate in 1933. Arlington's Earl Snell served as speaker of the Republican-controlled House. A decidedly rural view dominated the session. Julius Meier, in fragile health because of a bad heart, was beginning the second half of his term as governor. Legislators found themselves between a rock and a hard place. Faced with the ugly reality of the deepening depression, lawmakers had no choice but to tread water in 1933. Severely shrinking government revenues forced them to try to maintain the status quo as best they could. There was no money to start new programs, nor were there enough funds to pay for existing services. Paradoxically, the people were looking to their legislators to provide some sorely needed relief. Surely their representatives and senators would help the many homeless and jobless. City and county governments, like the state, were hurting, too. Courts and police were hard pressed to keep up with spiraling crime rates. Yet with the loss of revenue (as assessed property values dropped and property taxes went unpaid) local governments were unable to add police or to set up new relief programs. Those most in need had to look elsewhere. This explains why so many people, in Oregon and nationally, saw FDR and his New Deal administration as their only savior. Many expected the federal government to do what churches, private charities, and state and local governments could not do.

An aroused public turned its attention toward Salem as the Legislature of 1933 convened.* The people were anxious to know how far the assembly would go to soften the Depression's impact. Almost a quarter of Governor Meier's budget was meant to eliminate the deficit carried over from the 1931-32 biennium. *Oregon Voter* speculated that a general sales tax would have to be passed "to finance some of the items left off the Meier budget, and to finance some state relief for the destitute"[6] and protested proposed cuts in the higher education budget— a 37% drop from 1929-30.[6] Lawmakers chopped the state general fund budget to just under $6 million, down from $7.74 million in 1931-32. State employees took a 25% salary cut in 1933. Even judges, whose salaries, by law, could not be reduced, took salary cuts.[7]

Lawmakers joined Gov. Julius Meier in referring a measure to the people for a July 21, 1933, vote. The measure proposed establishing a state sales tax, which most politicians believed was the only way to generate new state revenues. But the referendum was ill timed. How could lawmakers ask for a sales tax when so many citizens couldn't afford basic foods and necessities? The tax was rejected, 45,600 in favor, to 167,500 opposed. Lawmakers also referred a constitutional

---

* Oregon lawmakers set a precedent in 1933 by holding three sessions. A five-day special session met in early January before the regular session convened; another special session met in late November.

amendment permitting voters to decide whether or not to continue Prohibition. Voters ended the Noble Experiment in Oregon 143,000 to 72,700.

State Sen. Henry Corbett's bill to amend the controversial criminal syndicalism bill passed the legislature. Now the government had the powers it needed to deal with those who deliberately plotted to overthrow by violence or sabotage for revolutionary ends.[8] Senators defeated SB 329, which would have limited the work week to 48 hours for any hotel, restaurant, or mercantile establishment.[9] Opponents thought the bill was too radical. A move to abolish the so-called Moser Law of 1915, which required that women teachers should receive equal pay with men, was defeated. C. C. Chapman bristled at the idea that, in times of such economic hardship, a woman should hold a teaching job when a man (probably a breadwinner) went unemployed. It didn't occur to him that a female teacher might need the job as much as a man.[10]

Election of 1934; General Martin Runs for Governor

Fall 1933 found Oregon's journalists and political pundits trading rumors about whether or not Gov. Julius Meier would seek reelection. Some were sure that the governor's fragile health would force him to withdraw. If Meier did run, would he return to the Republican Party, or again campaign as an Independent? State Treasurer Rufus Holman was touted by some as a viable threat to Meier, if the governor ran as a Republican. Could Oregon's feuding Democrats come together long enough to select a credible candidate to challenge either Julius Meier or his stand-in? In early 1934, citing failing health, Governor Meier announced he would not seek reelection. His exit opened the door to hopeful Republicans. The gubernatorial contest of 1934 was a colorful and divisive campaign.

The challenge facing Republicans in 1934 was: could they re-unite? Could they bind the wounds inflicted by the bloody campaign of 1930? Party leaders knew defeat was likely if they failed to patch up their differences. After Julius Meier's withdrawal, five candidates entered the Republican primary, and three were considered serious contenders: state senators Sam H. Brown and Joe E. Dunne, and Treasurer Rufus Holman. Brown and Holman had worked in the Joseph-Meier campaign of 1930, and sought nomination on the basis of a public-power platform. Both announced support for an Oregon Grange-sponsored initiative that would empower the state to build transmission lines from Bonneville Dam to distribute low-cost power to domestic consumers.* Dunne was cautious

---

* Construction of Bonneville Dam began in 1934; electricity generation began in 1939.

on the power issue. He supported cheap power but was careful not to specify for whom. His ambiguous position along with his refusal to endorse the Grange measure seemed to class Dunne as an opponent of cheap hydroelectricity that might compete with private utility companies.[11] Brown and Holman shared identical platforms and it was evident both were vying for the same bloc of voters. Hydropower supporters feared that the candidates would split that bloc, thus boosting Dunne's chances of winning the nomination. Brown and Holman got a lot of heat for one of them to withdraw; neither man budged, which did result in a victory for Dunne, who won the Republican primary with 30% of the vote. Brown and Holman, combined, took 40% of the vote, each man taking about 20%. For Republicans it was 1930 all over again: this time Joe Dunne, a foe of cheap, publicly owned hydroelectricity, like Phil Metschan in 1930, won the gubernatorial nomination because the party was so badly divided over the power issue. The Joseph-Meier-Holman-Brown Republicans, staunch friends of hydropower, found themselves in the same position as in the summer of 1930 after the death of George Joseph: they had no candidate who represented their views. The question was, could they accept their fate and back Joe Dunne in 1934?

Prior to FDR's election in 1932, Oregon Democrats had long been a bedraggled, second-rate party. That changed in 1933-34. Roosevelt's bold and innovative leadership, backed by several New Deal successes, energized Oregon Democrats. Suddenly, they were a vibrant, enthusiastic, and optimistic bunch. Democrats in 1934 now believed they had as much chance as the Republicans to win the governor's chair.

Charles Martin announced his candidacy for governor on February 3, 1934. Portland's *East Side Post* noted that "Republicans are puzzled, Democrats are dumbfounded, by the *Oregonian's* support of Congressman Martin. Like the Democratic *Oregon Journal*, it is throwing support to the general."[12] Martin was an outspoken backer of Bonneville Dam and the great hydroelectric power it would generate; both Democrats and Republicans who believed in public power considered Charles Martin a friend. These forces were wary of the *Oregonian's* support of Martin, because the newspaper had consistently endorsed the position of Oregon's major utility companies: that inexpensive, publicly owned hydroelectric power must not compete with higher-priced energy produced by private utilities. Did the *Oregonian* know something about Martin's position on the power issue that the public didn't? Why were they endorsing a Democrat for governor?

Charles Martin's true position on public power was soon exposed in the state's press. "The suspicion that Martin was no friend of public power was confirmed by [Os] West's role as an instigator of Martin's candidacy. The *Oregon Statesman* reasoned that Martin was a puppet of West, who in turn was the political representative of utility interests."[13]

Public-power Democrats, most of whom were from the liberal wing of their party, determined to block Martin's nomination. Supporters of hydro-power development saw cheap electricity as a necessity if Oregon was to climb out of the Depression. Bringing cheap electricity into all parts of Oregon would help diversify and accelerate the state's economic recovery. Who would step forward to challenge Charles Martin in the May primary? When none of the big-name Democrats came forward, Willis Mahoney, mayor of Klamath Falls, threw his hat into the ring. The fiery, quirky Mahoney ran on a "platform identical with the positions of [Republicans] Sam Brown and Rufus Holman on public power." Mahoney, however, went further with his positions: "He advocated several social and economic reforms: federal old age pensions, a 50% tax on incomes and inheritances in excess of $50,000, increased benefits under the Workman's Compensation Law, and redistribution of wealth."[14] The Walter Pierce-Bert Haney wing of the Democratic Party agreed with Mahoney's stand on public power. On other issues they disagreed. Willis Mahoney's spirited campaign against Congressman Martin came up short. The general beat the mayor, with 58% of the Democratic vote.

Public power people were not happy. Neither Republican Joe Dunne nor Democrat Charles Martin was a friend of low-cost hydropower. When Republican State Senator Peter Zimmerman, a Yamhill County farmer, entered the governor's contest as an Independent, they were ecstatic. Zimmerman was philosophically a left-wing populist-progressive. Many thought him a Socialist. Whatever his political stripes, Peter Zimmerman posed a serious threat to both Joe Dunne and Charles Martin.

Zimmerman was a dedicated Grange man.[15] His popularity among farmers alarmed both Republican and Democratic leaders. Zimmerman adopted Mahoney's planks favoring increased taxes on income and inheritances. He also came out in favor of old-age pension reform. Worried about losing liberal votes to Zimmerman, Martin declared his support for old-age pensions, unemployment insurance, and tax reductions, and also tempered his position on public power development. He noted that the federal government would build transmission lines from Bonneville to supply domestic consumers with inexpensive power, which made the Grange initiative for state construction of transmission lines an unnecessary and unwarranted expenditure of state funds. Republican Joe Dunne stood firm on his original platform, which stressed his "loyalty to

Charles Henry Martin

Charles Martin, known as "Old Iron Pants," was one of Oregon's most colorful and controversial governors. Martin served during the last half of the Great Depression, 1935-39. Oregon (like most states) was beset by labor woes, featuring strikes, lockouts, and on occasion violent clashes and even arson occurred. Gov. Martin, a retired career Army general, was a staunch supporter of law and order. He was outspoken and hypercritical of people whose actions (or words) threatened public peace and order. Charles Martin shot from the hip. And he was no friend of labor; he intervened in several labor disputes, always on the side of owners/managers.

Charles Henry Martin was born in Illinois in 1863. He was a graduate of West Point Academy (1887), and his Army career spanned 40 years. Martin reached the rank of major general in 1919. His long military service took him all over the world: from Fort Vancouver to China (during the Boxer Rebellion), the Philippines (during the Aguinaldo insurrection), to the Mexican border in 1915, to France in World War I, and, finally, the Panama Canal Zone. No other Oregon governor had travelled as extensively as General Martin. When he retired from the Army in 1927, he and his wife (who was born in Portland) moved to the Rose City. Though he was a lifelong Republican, General Martin was persuaded to run as a Democratic write-in candidate for Congress in the 3rd District in 1930. Martin won

the Constitution, his opposition to Communism, and the fact that he was the Father of the $5 auto license."[16] He was crushed in November, carrying only 29% of the vote. Democrat Charles Martin won by 21,000 votes with 39% of the vote over Independent Peter Zimmerman, who received 32%. Once again, a Republican schism boosted Democrats to victory.

So, as Oregon and the nation slipped deeper into the Great Depression, voters chose a career military man to run their state. At an age (71) when many men were fishing, hunting, or splitting wood to pass time, Gen. Charles Martin, former military governor of the Panama Canal Zone, was ready to take charge of state government as a minority Democrat. Would Governor Martin work effectively with the legislature? Would he forge ties to the Roosevelt administration? Did Martin have the temperament to compromise, to listen, to share, or would his chain-of-command, top-down style impede or help him be an effective governor?

the House seat with ease. He was 67 years old. Congressman Martin won reelection in 1932, drubbing Republican Homer Angell, 74,397 to 40,650. In 1934, Martin was cajoled by Oswald West and others to run for governor.

The central issue of the '34 campaign was hydroelectric power development. Martin favored hydropower development by private utilities. Republican candidate Joe E. Dunne straddled the fence, assuming an ambiguous position on the issue. State Senator Peter Zimmerman, a passionate progressive and a longtime leading proponent of cheap electricity from hydroelectric dams financed by the federal government, was so disgusted with Dunn's and Martin's stances that he entered the race as an independent. The public power issue caused a rupture in Oregon's Republican and Democratic parties. Charles Martin was elected governor with only 39% of the vote. Together, Dunn and Zimmerman had a combined total of 182,442 votes. Martin drew only 116,677 votes, but it was enough to make him Oregon's next governor. Martin was 71, the oldest person ever elected governor in Oregon.

"Old Iron Pants" had a stormy term as governor. Between his criticism of labor, his stance on hydroelectric power development, and his bitter denunciation of several popular New Deal programs, Martin tore Democrats apart. Indeed, Monroe Sweetland remembered Martin "as a caricature of a military dictator in an American uniform." Martin, however, wanted a second term. In the May primary of 1938, Martin was opposed by State Senator Henry Hess. With the blessing of the Roosevelt administration, Hess waged a winning campaign, toppling Martin 59,620 to 52,642. Old Iron Pants had lost his first political campaign. Martin retired to Portland where he died in 1946, four days before his 83rd birthday.

Portland's 1934 Dock Strike

Congress, in June 1933, enacted the National Industrial Recovery Act (NIRA), one of the cornerstones of FDR's New Deal program. The act allowed workers the right to organize and bargain collectively through their chosen representatives and prohibited employers from any interference, restraint, or coercion of the process. The NIRA was felt nationwide, especially among dock workers and longshoremen on the Pacific Coast. For the first time, unions received official recognition, sanctioned by federal law. The right to strike became a basic American freedom.[17] Portland had experienced a protracted strike by the International Longshoremen's Association (ILA) back in 1922. Local shippers broke the strike with an army of strikebreakers and eastern money, gutting the union. Passage of the NIRA breathed new life into Portland's ILA. By fall 1933, over 1,100 men belonged to the union's local chapter. The Longshoremen, under the terms of the NIRA, requested that their bosses (the shipping company executives) sit down with them to confer about wages, hours, and working conditions. The executives refused to meet. In exasperation, Portland's ILA set a strike date of May 9, 1934. This resulted in the most devastating work stoppage in Oregon's history. The 82-day strike wreaked havoc on Portland's economy. Maritime commerce ground to a halt. Over 3,000 waterfront workers were affected and 50,000 other Oregon workers lost employment, including 12,000 to 15,000 in Portland. Almost all the lumber mills ceased export production and the grain export business dried up. It was estimated that $30 million were lost before the strike ended on July 31, when city leaders and national labor mediators intervened.[18] The victorious ILA extracted its hard-won concessions, but many Oregonians developed a smoldering, general resentment toward labor.

The Portland strike of 1934 was a taste of the future. Over the next five years Oregon and the nation were rocked by labor unrest. Nationally, control of the American labor movement was at stake. The two giants, the AFL representing mostly skilled workers and the CIO representing mostly semi- and unskilled workers, were locked in a bitter turf war to attract millions of unorganized workers into their respective unions. With most of the nation's conservative business establishment doing whatever it could to defy and blunt the thrust of the new labor unionism, turbulent days awaited Oregon and the nation.

Relations between Governor Martin and Oregon labor were chilly and often rancorous. Martin considered himself a super-patriot and was sure that labor leaders were conspiring to overthrow American institutions. To Martin most labor agitation was an assault on the American way of life. In failing to distinguish between honest, law-abiding labor leaders and those who were not, the governor erred. By 1936, "Old Iron Pants," as Martin was known, regularly referred to Oregon's labor leaders as "goons" and "racketeers," lumping them all together. He ordered the chief of Oregon's new state police to give him weekly written reports about labor activities in the state. Much of the public liked his tough stance, but his indiscriminate verbal assaults on union leaders alienated the rank and file of Oregon labor. As labor turned against Martin, so did the liberal or New Deal wing of Oregon's Democratic Party. Governor Martin's handling of Oregon's labor disputes became his Achilles' heel.

Oregon's Second Depression Legislature

The 38th Legislative Assembly convened on January 14, 1935. Portlander Henry L. Corbett was elected Senate president and Toledo's John E. Cooter was speaker of the House. After a 55-year hiatus, Democrats had taken control of the Oregon House in the November election of 1934 with a comfortable majority of 38 seats. The Senate remained Republican, 17 to 13. The majority of House members were first-termers and inexperience made for a rocky House session. Out of about a thousand bills introduced, 557 were passed. Responding to pressure caused by the recent Portland dock strike, lawmakers granted the state police power to patrol and intervene in industrial disturbances. Public employee pay cuts made in the 1933 session were continued in 1935. Legislators took on natural resource issues, and passed a bill to halt certain salmon-catching practices that seriously depleted fish populations. Despite attempts by Governor Martin and several key legislators to hold the line on state spending, the 1935 Legislature increased the 1935-37 budget by $3.3 million, raising the state total to $14.8 million.

On April 25, six weeks after the session adjourned, the Oregon Capitol burned to the ground. A spectacular nightlong fire drew thousands of fascinated onlookers. The great Capitol dome, added in 1893, which loomed 250 feet above the Willamette Valley, collapsed early. The venerable building, which opened in 1876 (the cornerstone was laid in 1873), was a total loss. Departmental offices that had been housed in the Capitol building were set up in various buildings around Salem.[19] Oregon was without a capitol building for the next three and a half years. Governor Charles Martin called the legislature into special session to make plans for a new capitol. A 20-day session convened on October 21, 1935. The House assembled in the Salem Armory, while the Senate met at the Marion Hotel. The special session was led by Democrat Howard Latourette of Portland, who presided over the House, and Republican Henry L. Corbett, who continued as Senate president. Lawmakers approved the construction of a new capitol and enacted several bills to make Oregonians eligible for benefits created by the recent congressional passage of the Social Security Act.

Labor Strife Resumes

Labor unrest erupted in Oregon again in May 1935, and continued unabated for several years. It was Charles Martin's fate that this happened throughout his tenure as governor. Martin's first serious labor crisis as governor occurred at the Stimson Lumber Company mill in Gaston, in western Washington County. A force of state police and Washington County deputies dispersed an assemblage of 250 to 300 striking Stimson employees on May 23. There was little violence, but mill managers convinced Martin that drastic action was needed to protect mill property. Acting on the owner's request, the governor declared martial law in Washington County. The Oregon National Guard took control of the mill. Governor Martin took similar action at Astoria in August. There were other labor disputes at lumber mills in Tillamook (June 1935), Cottage Grove (January 1936), Bridal Veil Lumber Company in east Multnomah County (in 1936), and Dallas (in May 1936). Similar lumber mill boycotts or strikes continued into 1937. Trouble flared again at the Stimson Lumber plant in Gaston in July 1937. The mill had been closed for nine weeks when AFL-affiliated employees asked Governor Martin for police protection so they could go back to work.[20] The State Federation of Labor, an AFL affiliate, had earlier condemned Governor Martin for ordering the National Guard into the plant in May 1935. Many in the labor movement bitterly resented Martin's interference, believing that his actions were pro-business and anti-labor. The Stimson Lumber dispute was typical of the jurisdictional struggle between the AFL and CIO. Nowhere was this confrontation more apparent that in Oregon's lumber industry.

Labor unrest hit the Portland waterfront again in July 1937, Newport and Toledo in August, and Coquille in September. 1937 was the high-water mark of labor disputes in Oregon. Labor violence, in the forms of shootings, arson, destruction of property, as well as fist-fights and beatings, spread through western Oregon. There were more than 250 recorded acts of violence in the state. "Industries attacked in Portland, along the Willamette Valley, in other parts of Oregon, and across the Columbia River, included lumber mills, shipping facilities, breweries, farming and gardening enterprises, dry-cleaning establishments, laundries, bakeries, restaurants, and barber shops."[21]

A year of labor violence and strikes in Oregon came to a head on November 29, 1937, when arsonists burned the Salem Box Factory plant in west Salem. The public was outraged. The press and Governor Martin condemned the violence. A police investigation discovered the arsonists and those who hired them. Police arrested Al N. Banks, a former secretary of the Salem district of the Teamsters' union. Banks confessed his part in the arson. He explained "that the fire was set because the owner wouldn't make his enterprise a union operation."[22] Governor Martin proclaimed the Salem Box fire to be the last straw. In March 1938, he swung into action against labor violence and took the bold and unusual step of appointing Ralph E. Moody, Assistant Attorney General of Oregon (and grandson of former governor, Zenas Moody), as a special prosecutor to conduct a comprehensive investigation of the previous year's labor strife. Martin's critics immediately charged him with playing politics. With the May primary approaching, many saw his action as an appeal to anti-labor voters. Moody's investigation culminated in a detailed report, complete with a list of recommended legislation to better regulate labor disputes. Moody's recommendation that an anti-picketing bill be drafted resulted in an initiative petition drive. The measure carried by nearly fifty thousand votes in November 1938, 186,500 yes to 137,700 no. The public, for the time being, was fed up with labor strife.

The Election of 1936

President Franklin Roosevelt ran for reelection in 1936. Oregonians, like voters everywhere, paused to focus on FDR's race against Alf Landon, governor of Kansas. The president's popularity was high and his political coattails were long. Roosevelt continued to attract thousands of new voters into Oregon's Democratic Party. One outcome of this party resurgence was one of Oregon's closest U.S. Senate contests ever. Incumbent Republican Charles McNary withstood a vigorous challenge by his Democratic opponent, Willis Mahoney. President Roosevelt's 64% victory in Oregon nearly carried Mahoney into the Senate. The tense contest resulted in a razor-thin victory for incumbent McNary, 199,332, to 193,822 for Mahoney, a margin of only 5,500 votes. Two other significant results of the 1936 election were the election of the first Oregon woman to Congress, Democrat Nancy Wood Honeyman (daughter of Oregon lawyer and man of letters C. E. S. Wood) in the 3rd District, and the victory of 38 Democrats to the Oregon House, which assured continued Democratic control of that body in 1937. Republicans gained a seat in the Oregon Senate, upping their total to 18 of 30 seats. Honeyman bested two major opponents, Republican William Ekwall, and Independent John A. Jeffrey, taking 78,624 votes or 53% of the total.[23]

Man Is a Fighting Animal

Charles Martin's direct, shoot-from-the-hip style was a source of constant friction with the public. Martin was always in someone's political doghouse for something he said or did. A forthright military man, he wasn't tactful and if he thought someone was doing something against the public interest, he let the public know about it.[24] The nickname "Old Iron Pants" suited Charles Martin— considering his crusty, sharp-tongued, opinionated, and generally irascible demeanor. The general liked to say that "man is a fighting animal."[25] Martin was always more prepared to fight than he was to say nothing, to compromise, or to retreat. Though he was honest, conscientious, and dedicated to public service, his words and deeds steadily eroded his effectiveness and support as governor.

The governor was not without compassion and humanity. His words and acts, however, often demonstrated otherwise. It was suggested that the aged and feeble-minded wards of the state should be chloroformed and Martin thought it a fine idea. He noted that if 900 of the 969 inmates at the Fairview Home in Salem were "put out of their misery" it would save the state $300,000. He asserted that the able-bodied unemployed should not be given federal or state assistance. Fearing the state legislature was about to adopt a sales tax, a group of farmers petitioned Governor Martin to veto any such legislation. He told the group that what the legislature did was "none of their business " and added, "Go home and listen to the birdies sing." Martin often ignored the economic and social plight of Oregonians during the 1930s while he zealously emphasized law and order. "At the height of the depression, he declared that the most pressing problems of the day was sterilization of persons convicted of sex crimes. That Martin's attention should be occupied by such a peripheral problem must have seemed curious to those who were concerned with employment and survival in an era of economic collapse."[26]

Martin angered many in the labor movement when he branded some leaders as "pestiferous peewees." Martin reportedly advised law enforcement officers to "beat the hell out of" labor leaders, boycotters, picketers, and strikers.[27]

Governor Martin's relationship to the Roosevelt Administration was controversial. The governor considered himself a genuine New Dealer, generally subscribing to FDR's progressive policies. But there were areas of serious disagreement between Salem and the White House. Martin became increasingly critical of what he believed was the administration's pro-labor stance. Old Iron Pants thought the National Labor Relations Board and its employees were so pro-worker that their intervention in labor disputes worked against the interests of both the public and the employer. He publicly criticized the NLRB, as well as Secretary of Labor Frances Perkins. The governor also clashed with Roosevelt's people over the public power issue. Martin had been instrumental in obtaining federal funding for the construction of Bonneville Dam in 1933, but his belief that cheap hydroelectric power should go primarily to the development of heavy industry was at odds with those who saw cheap electricity as the way to both electrify rural Oregon and drastically cut rates for consumers. When New Dealers in the administration and Oregon proposed a Columbia Valley Authority (CVA), a federal power program patterned after the Tennessee Valley Authority, Martin balked. Congress didn't pass the CVA bill, but Martin's opposition to it was seen as unfriendly by public power advocates in Oregon and the administration.

Old Iron Pants further alienated the administration and Oregon's liberal Democrats when he declared that the New Deal's social security program was driving the country into national socialism. Regarding his opposition to federal relief, Martin claimed he was a "Hoover Democrat" and asserted that democratic nations had lost their moral force through pampering their people.[28]

Despite their policy differences, the president and Eleanor Roosevelt, hosted by a beaming Governor Martin, rode in an open touring car to Mount Hood on September 28, 1937, to dedicate Timberline Lodge. Built by the Works Progress Administration, a federal relief agency, the lodge was one of Oregon's most impressive New Deal projects. Employing hundreds of men, Timberline Lodge was constructed largely of native stone and wood. From the south-facing second-floor balcony, President Roosevelt delivered a short address to a crowd of thousands. But within months of his visit, President Roosevelt and Governor Martin had a final falling out.

By spring 1938, Charles Martin had burned many of his political bridges. His deepening opposition to New Deal programs as well as his fundamental disagreement with FDR's New Deal philosophy of government proved to be one more nail in the governor's political coffin.

Charles Martin Out, Charles Sprague In

Charles Martin's reelection bid was in deep trouble by spring 1938. The governor had made enemies in a host of powerful voting blocs, including the Grange, labor (both the AFL and CIO), liberal, New Deal Democrats, progressive Republicans, and public power advocates. Martin's Democratic Party was badly divided. The pro-Martin conservatives continued their party battle with the younger New Deal Democrats, who were led by Richard Neuberger. Since the previous spring, Oregon's liberals had joined forces by creating the Oregon Commonwealth Federation (OCF). The federation declared itself a nonpartisan league of progressives with Democrats, Republicans, and Socialists. The founders included "Republican Peter Zimmerman; Ben Osborne, executive secretary of the State Federation of Labor; Monroe Sweetland, a young Socialist-activist, and several prominent leaders of the Grange."[29] The OCF's chief plank was public power; it was Oregon's leading advocate for cheap hydroelectric power development until its demise in 1942. Martin despised the federation, claiming it was a subsidiary of the Communist Party. He ordered Charles Pray, chief of the Oregon State Police, to compile Reports of Communist Activities on OCF's doings. In addition to these foes, Oregon's two Democratic congressional members, Nan Wood Honeyman and Walter Pierce, turned against him in the May primary. The *Oregon Democrat* asserted that "by word and deed Charles H. Martin has demonstrated that at heart he is not a Democrat, that he never was a Democrat, and that his endorsement of Democratic principles was pretense and sham."[30]

Even FDR got into the defeat-Martin campaign. Secretary of Interior Harold Ickes wrote an endorsement letter to Martin's Democratic opponent, former state senator Henry Hess of La Grande, which was widely publicized.[31] The feisty governor conceded nothing to his opponents and put up a valiant fight. But he was doomed. Old Iron Pants lost the May Democratic primary 52,642 to 59,620. His enemies said that he "dug his political grave with his own tongue."[32] After four years, the public had grown tired of their salty, acid-tongued governor. Born at the beginning of the Civil War in 1861, Martin seemed more and more out of step with the challenges facing 20th-century America. By 1938 he'd worn-out his welcome and by the time Old Iron Pants left office in January 1939, most Oregonians were glad to see him go.

Republican Resurgence

The election of 1938 was a triumph for Oregon Republicans. Democrats lost virtually all their post-1934 political gains. Henry Hess lost the November gubernatorial contest to Salem Republican Charles Sprague, longtime editor of the *Oregon Statesman* newspaper. Generally regarded as a progressive, Sprague endorsed the administration's public power program and proved far more friendly to FDR than Martin had.[33] For the first time since 1926, Oregon's dominant Republican Party elected a governor.

Besides Charles Martin, there was another major Democratic casualty in November: 3rd District Congresswoman, Nan Wood Honeyman. Having served as one of her bridesmaids when Eleanor Roosevelt married her distant cousin, Franklin Delano Roosevelt, in 1905, Honeyman was a close friend of the First Lady. Representative Honeyman became embroiled in Oregon's nasty labor disputes and sided with the CIO and its newest affiliate, the International Woodworkers of America, formerly the Lumber and Sawmill Worker's union under the AFL. As she stood for reelection in 1938, Nan Honeyman was opposed by both a hostile AFL and State Federation of Labor. She also faced the enmity of Gov. Charles Martin and his loyal backers. Honeyman joined Oregon's other Democratic congressman, Walter Pierce, in backing Henry Hess over Charles Martin for the Democratic gubernatorial nomination in May. After his loss, Martin actively campaigned against both Hess and Honeyman. She lost her seat in Congress after a single term to Republican Homer D. Angell, 66,498 to 69,049. Governor Martin's personal feud with fellow Democrats did more than rupture the party, it led to a GOP sweep in 1938.

Republicans recaptured the Oregon House. A new era of Republican domination of the legislature was beginning. Republicans continued their hold on the other statewide offices, secretary of state, treasurer, and attorney general. Oregon had returned to its essentially Republican stripes, though the decades of one-party control were gradually ending. The huge, four-decade-old gap in voter registration between parties was closing fast. It would be another dozen years before Republicans lost their numerical majority over the state's Democrats.

A New Capitol Building

Oregon's new Capitol building was dedicated on October 11, 1938. Lame-duck Governor Charles Martin presided at the dedication ceremonies in one of his last public appearances as governor. On January 9, 1939, Martin delivered a farewell message, reviewing his achievements, to the 40th Legislative Assembly. He was proud of reducing the state's bonded debt from $52 million to $42 million and noted the completion of five major bridges on the Coast Highway. The Capitol and state library building had been completed. There were new budgeting controls to provide constant supervision over expenditures; and a state commission for the blind.[34] Charles Sprague took the oath of office, and the era of Old Iron Pants was over.

Chapter 11
How the War Changed Oregon, 1939-48

Governor Charles Sprague

Charles Sprague was 50 when he entered the governor's race in spring 1938 and had never run for political office. He was a moderate Republican with a liberal position on human rights. He campaigned on a plank to "sustain civil liberties and broad racial and religious tolerance." On the volatile labor issue, Sprague's stance was middle-of-the-road, but firm. He believed in protecting labor's legal rights, but was quick to add that he would tolerate "no organization, labor or employer, to override the authority of the State."[1] One editor noted that as an employer, Sprague had dealt fairly with labor and was well-regarded and respected because of it."[2] Candidate Sprague took the Progressive Republican position on the hotly debated issue of Bonneville power and campaigned on a plank to "preserve Bonneville power as a public benefaction free from private exploitation and political racketeering."[3] As a campaigner, Sprague came across as earnest, businesslike, and highly principled. Throughout his campaign he painted himself as a non-politician, a political outsider, a fearless, frank, and honest observer of public affairs.

Republican Sprague's landslide victory in November over Democrat Henry Hess, 60 to 40%, came at the head of his party's rout of the Democrats. Nationally, the GOP gained 77 seats in the House of Representatives as well as eight Senate seats. Democrats, however, retained their majorities in both chambers.[4]

The 1939 Legislature

Oregon's 1939 Legislature convened in the new state Capitol on January 9 with an interesting mix of 90 members. Three were women—Dorothy McCullough Lee in the Senate, and Hannah Martin and Christina Munroe in the House. The 38 House Democrats of 1937 had been reduced to 13 in 1939. Twenty-two Republicans controlled the Senate, up from 18 in 1937. Hannah Martin, a Salem attorney, had served in three House sessions. Christina Munroe, a Hood River Democrat, was serving her second term in 1939. Born in Germany in 1867, the widow Munroe had run the family pear orchard business since the death of her husband in the early 1920s. A dedicated Grange member, Munroe was noted for her independence, intelligence, and common sense. C. C. Chapman, long-time editor of the conservative *Oregon Voter* magazine, was a freshman House Republican.

A total of 30 attorneys served in 1939, with 22 agriculturalists and seven insurance salesmen. Representative Osborne of Amity was a prune packer and Earl Fisher of Beaverton made horseradish. Clarence Ash of Astoria was a Columbia River bar pilot. Phil Brady of Multnomah County was a major Oregon labor leader. Henry Semon, a Klamath Falls Democrat, was known as Oregon's "Potato King." Senators George W. Dunn of Ashland and W. E. Burke of Sherwood traced their legislative careers back nearly half a century, to their first terms in 1895.[5] Robert M. Duncan, a Burns attorney, was Senate president.

The assembly wrestled with its usual number of varied and complex problems. The economic picture was brightening. Oregon and the nation had been gaining steam over the past two years. One of the major appropriations made by lawmakers in 1939 was the state's portion of relief dollars for Oregon's still many unemployed and needy elderly.[6] Legislators approved and Governor Sprague signed a state budget of about $25 million. Other legislative actions included: abolishing the State Bakery Board (a holdover from NIRA days); establishment of a crime laboratory in the department of state police; and an act "which lifted the mandatory minimum salary [for public school teachers] from $75 to $85 a month."[7]

The World Lurches Toward War

The 1939 Legislature was the last to meet prior to the outbreak of World War II in September. World events over the decade had slowly turned the attention of reluctant Americans toward the international arena. The emergence of totalitarian regimes in Italy, Japan, and Germany threatened world order and peace. Italy's vicious conquest of Ethiopia in northeast Africa in 1936, and neighboring Albania in January 1939, was widely condemned. More important than Italian dictator Benito Mussolini's actions were the aggressions of German Chancellor Adolf Hitler in central Europe, and Japan in East Asia. Hitler annexed Austria in a bloodless coup and western Czechoslovakia (the Sudetenland) in 1938. Japan's brutal invasion and bombardment of coastal mainland China in 1937-38 prompted cries of outrage from Western Powers. A keen observer of this

Charles Arthur Sprague

Charles Arthur Sprague, a moderate Republican, was elected governor in 1938, succeeding the controversial Charles Martin, a conservative Democrat. Sprague's early career was similar to that of several 19th-century Oregon governors (Sylvester Pennoyer, for example). Both Sprague and Pennoyer began their careers in education before graduating to newspaper publishing and editing.

Charles Sprague was born in Kansas in 1887. He earned a bachelor's degree from Monmouth College in 1910 and taught for a year before heading west to be superintendent of schools in Waitsburg, Washington. Sprague was then appointed assistant superintendent of public instruction for Washington, 1913-15. In 1915 he left education to pursue a new career in the newspaper business. He and his family moved to Corvallis in 1925 when he became business manager of the *Gazette Times*. In 1929, Sprague moved to Salem when he took a controlling interest in the *Oregon Statesman*. Sprague became sole owner and publisher of the *Statesman* in 1939, a position he held until his death in 1969.

Editor Sprague dove into politics in 1938. He won the GOP nomination for governor; with the Democratic Party in disarray (because of the policies and actions of Gov. Charles Martin, 1935-39), Sprague was elected, defeating seven other candidates.

deteriorating world order, FDR privately expressed his concerns for peace in Europe. He realized that an outbreak of war in Europe, North Africa, and East Asia would, ultimately, threaten the security of the United States. Roosevelt continued to push a naval buildup started the previous year, as well as order other forms of military preparedness.

The outbreak of war in Europe and Asia made Americans rethink their strong isolationist beliefs. Believing that Britain was the only obstacle to Hitler's war machine, in June 1940 the president approved the selling of surplus United States war materiel to Great Britain. In September 1940, Congress and the president ordered the first peacetime military draft in U.S. history. Roosevelt said the nation must be prepared to defend itself from possible Japanese or German attack.

1940 Election

1940 was a presidential election year. Franklin Roosevelt broke precedent by announcing his candidacy for a third term. Republicans nominated a moderate, Indiana's Wendell Willkie, a former utility company executive, for president.

Throughout his long career in newspaper publishing/editing, Charles Sprague was esteemed as one of Oregon's most important shapers of public opinion. A voice of moderation and temperance, Governor Sprague was known for his open-mindedness and fairness. Charles Sprague also had an independent streak, which eventually alienated the powerful conservative wing of his Republican Party. Indeed, Sprague vetoed so may Republican-backed bills that his opponents launched a statewide recall campaign to oust him from office. The recall failed.

Gov. Sprague's major accomplishments included the drafting of state regulations to ensure that logging practices would enhance efforts to protect and rehabilitate state-owned forests. Sprague also worked to reduce the state debt, and to organize Oregon's participation in World War II. While helping to organize Oregon's civil defense program, Gov. Sprague worked cooperatively with the Roosevelt administration in Washington, D.C. Sprague also worked to mend fences with Oregon's labor unions.

Gov. Sprague's moderate record rankled his conservative foes. In May 1942, the governor was challenged by longtime politician Earl Snell. Snell, who owned an automobile dealership in tiny Arlington, was secretary of state. Personable and outgoing, Earl Snell presented a sharp contrast to the more reserved, business-like demeanor and personality of Gov. Sprague. Only 30% of voters cast ballots in the spring primary. Snell toppled Sprague, denying him the GOP gubernatorial nomination for a second term. Charles Sprague returned to the *Statesman* in 1943, remaining there until his death in 1969, age 82.

Willkie's running mate was Oregon's senior senator, Charles McNary. With McNary on the GOP ticket, along with several hotly contested statewide races and nine ballot measures, Oregonians went to the polls in record numbers in November. The *Oregonian* predicted a turnout of 500,000 voters (479,000 did vote). From his Salem home, Senator McNary addressed the nation on the Columbia Radio Network. Willkie followed McNary with an address delivered from the East. Led by an 86% voter turnout in Multnomah County, FDR carried Oregon for the third time, but by only 40,800 votes. The Willkie-McNary ticket ran well in Oregon, but lost 217,555 to 258,415.

The 3rd Congressional District battle between Republican one-termer, Homer Angell, and Nancy Wood Honeyman was Oregon's featured political contest. Honeyman, whom Angell had defeated by 2,500 votes in 1938, lost by a similar margin in 1940, 80,900 to Rep. Angell's 84,300.[8] Honeyman, the first woman elected to Congress from Oregon, retired from elective politics.

Heated legislative contests, particularly in Multnomah County, saw the emergence of a young Democrat, State Rep. Richard L. Neuberger. The

Oregon Voter commented on Neuberger's victory: "He is sure to stir things up. Staunchly New Dealish, [he] likes to be called 'liberal,' is pro-labor, [an] ardent crusader for Public Utility Districts and/or any plan for public control of hydro-power. [An] able debater, interesting lecturer, outstanding writer; in the real *Who's Who*; one of the few national celebrities who has been elected to an Oregon legislature."[9]

Republican victories assured their control of the 1941 Oregon Legislature. They gained a seat in the Senate to make 25. But Democrats made impressive gains in the House, adding nine for a total of 22. The 1941 Legislature was led by Republican Dean Walker, a hop-grower and former college professor from Independence, who was Senate president, and Portland attorney Robert Farrell, Jr., speaker of the House.* Portland's Dorothy McCullough Lee was the only woman legislator.

A sales tax and unemployment compensation were at the top of the legislative docket. Representative Frank Lonergan introduced a sales tax proposal, suggesting that the new tax revenue should go 50% to property tax relief, 10% to education, and 40% to old age relief. The bill passed the House but died in the Senate. Lawmakers referred a cigarette tax to voters; proceeds were earmarked for public assistance, 60% to the state, the rest to counties.

Republican State Senator Rex Ellis, a Pendleton insurance man, introduced a controversial "Overthrow the Government" bill. The Ellis bill would punish anyone who advocated the use of force and/or violence to overthrow the U.S. government or any branch of it with up to ten years' imprisonment, a $10,000 fine, or both.[10] The Ellis bill reflected Oregon's growing concern for the deteriorating military picture in Europe and Asia as well as the desire to stifle any type of dissent. Though the United States was still officially neutral, her citizens were pro-British. The Ellis proposal was defeated at a time of swelling patriotism. Opponents argued that the measure likely infringed upon basic constitutional rights. Others said the bill was unnecessary because existing Oregon and federal law already protected against anyone who espoused the violent overthrow of the national government.

Lawmakers set a maximum highway speed limit of 55 miles per hour and approved a state budget of $25.8 million, up only $700,000 from the 1939-41 biennium. They also appropriated $250,000 to build a student union at the University of Oregon and a like amount for a similar facility at Oregon State College (now University).

---

* Farrell would step into the secretary of state's job in 1942.

Pearl Harbor!

By mid-1941, Oregonians were preoccupied with the war. Their newspapers blazed bold headlines about the fighting and radio broadcasters followed suit. In March, FDR signed legislation establishing the vital Lend-Lease program, which eventually provided $7 billion in military credits to the British (and, later, to the Soviet Union). Japan's surprise attack on the U.S. Pacific Fleet at Pearl Harbor, Hawaii, on December 7, 1941, catapulted America into World War II. On December 8, Congress declared war on Japan; on December 11 war was declared on Germany and Italy. Oregon Governor Sprague mobilized the National Guard. Hundreds of men rushed to enlist in the military. For the second time in 24 years, a reluctant American giant was forced into war. This war would be far more complex and bloody than the first. This time, the United States and her allies had two wars to fight, one in Europe and the Mediterranean, the other in Asia.

Frustrated Democrats

From 1932 to 1940, Democratic registration soared by 145,000 while Republican numbers dropped by 13,600. Democrats, only 32% of voters in 1932, had a 49.5% share of registration in 1940. In Multnomah County, where one-third of all voters lived, Democrats outnumbered Republicans 104,300 to 95,500 in November 1940. Democratic registration in the state's most populous county had skyrocketed from only 32% in 1932 to over 52% in 1940. A single Oregon county was Democratic in 1932; by 1940, 14 counties were Democratic—and three or four others were nearly even in registration.[11]

This Democratic resurgence did not translate into Democratic victories at the polls. Roosevelt's political coattails were short in 1940 and 1944; his narrow victory margins in Oregon did not appreciably boost the chances of Democratic candidates. The president's four victories in Oregon came from moderate-liberal Republicans; these Republicans, however, drew the line at supporting other Democrats. In all other major state races in the 1940s Republicans voted the party ticket. Walter Pierce's reelection to Congress in 1940 was the lone Democratic victory for major office in Oregon between 1940 and 1946. When Pierce sought a sixth term in 1942, at age eight-one, he was swamped by Republican Lowell Stockman. Why couldn't Oregon Democrats take advantage of recent increases in registration? What kept the party from capturing major offices in Oregon during the war years?

Democratic weakness came from several factors: the party was dominated by conservative, anti-New Deal leadership; Democrats didn't attract the labor vote; and the party was poorly organized and unable to recruit attractive candidates. There was a chronic shortage of money and great voter apathy. Over a third of the county chairmen failed to attend a 1942 statewide meeting to plan Democratic strategy for that year's election. Only 30% of the party voted in the primaries, and the Democratic gubernatorial candidate received just 22% of the vote in the general election.[12] Oregon Democrats stayed home in record numbers in the 1942 and 1944 elections. When they voted, they were as likely to vote Republican as Democrat. These were lean, discouraging years for Oregon Democrats.

Charles Sprague's Defeat

Oregon's May 1942 primary, five months after Pearl Harbor, took a back seat to the war and politics suffered. The campaign featured the Republican gubernatorial race between incumbent Charles Sprague and challenger Secretary of State Earl Snell. Republicans dumped Charles Sprague after one term, dumbfounding many Oregonians.

The Sprague administration was efficient, honest, patriotic, thrifty, often progressive, and scandal free. Charles Sprague was one of Oregon's most intelligent, articulate, well-informed, and tolerant governors. Yet fellow Republicans rejected him. Why? They found somebody they liked better: Earl Snell. Sprague had been only halfway through his term when rumors began to circulate about his chances of reelection. In January 1941 the *Oregon Democrat* speculated that "the bigwig Republicans have turned thumbs down on the Governor for a second term. The kingmakers are now feverishly beating the political bushes trying to take [out] the Governor in the primaries. Plenty of pressure is being brought on Earl Snell to be the candidate selected." In August, the *Democrat* noted that the Sprague-Snell campaign was "in full stride."[13] So, by spring 1942, the scene was set: would Republicans prefer Snell over Sprague? It was a tough choice.

The Eugene *Register-Guard* endorsed Governor Sprague. "He has those qualities of courage and character which are much more important than political charm [a backhand reference to Earl Snell] during the period when we are at war. Sprague [is] a scholarly man, a completely conscientious individual and therefore somewhat inept in the game of practical politics. He is easy to meet, makes it a point to listen to all who come to Salem, but makes up his own mind. His record is a good one, sound management, not spectacular, but reliable, and we have faith in him."[14]

Earl Snell was one of Oregon's best-known and most popular politicians. Entering the legislature in 1927, Snell rose quickly through the ranks, achieving the House speakership in 1933. Elected secretary of state in 1934, and reelected in 1938, he was a highly visible, active politician. Snell was an old school politician. He made friends and allies easily. He preferred the personal touch: a hearty greeting, handshake, and pat on the back were his trademarks. The late Cecil L. Edwards was Charles Sprague's chief-of-staff until the end of 1941. He relates that Snell "developed an intimate card file: names, including names of wives, children and pet dogs" were kept on civic leaders. "This card file plus his highly developed and sensitive social capacity were his assets in political progress. He was very informed, congenial and open. Upon meeting him you immediately felt that you had known him for life."[15]

Earl Snell campaigned on the ever-popular "cut taxes" plank. Charles Sprague, himself a fiscal conservative, countered Snell's tax-cut proposal by pointing out how he had kept the state budget lean.

Governor Sprague pulled 241,000 votes when he was elected in 1938—100,000 votes more than any man elected governor before him. Against Earl Snell, Sprague's supporters all but disappeared. In May, Snell trounced Sprague, 79,400 to 55,600 in the GOP primary. Charles Sprague was now a lame-duck governor. Meanwhile, Democrats nominated party stalwart Lew Wallace for governor.

The 1942 General Election

The *Oregon Democrat* moaned that in nine senatorial and 10 representative districts there were no Democratic legislative candidates. The Democratic Party had not identified or recruited viable candidates for office. Republican domination of Oregon government continued, partly by default. Lots of new blood would be flowing into the 1943 Assembly.

Seven ballot measures added spice to the 1942 fall campaign. The two most controversial ones were a proposal to increase legislators' pay, and one to add a tax on cigarettes. Oregon's lawmakers earned $3 a day when in session, the lowest legislative pay in the nation. The ballot measure, which passed 129,300 to 110,000, set lawmakers' pay at $8 a day. Voters had defeated similar proposals in the past. The cigarette tax measure lost, 127,400 to 110,600.[16]

The race between Republican Earl Snell and Democrat Lew Wallace drew the most voter interest in November. Portland's Democratic-leaning *Oregon Journal* suggested that voters "take your choice" on the gubernatorial candidates: "The *Journal*, not thrilled by either candidacy, believing that either one elected will give honest and industrious, if not outstanding, administration." Earl Snell crushed Lew Wallace. Snell's 78% of the vote (220,200 to Wallace's

62,600) was the most lopsided victory in Oregon gubernatorial history. His enormous popularity was affirmed at the polls. One journal remarked Snell's victory was a demonstration of his extraordinary vote-getting abilities "developed through years of consistent courtesy, consideration and kindliness, of a genial, friendly personality and sincere intent to do the right thing. Earl will go into the governor's office with more genuine affection than any one who had entered that office for many, many years. He is an extraordinary example of what sincere habitual friendliness can mean in political success."[17]

Republicans swept Oregon's four U.S. House seats. Population growth had given Oregon an additional House seat, which was filled for the first time in 1942. Republican Harris Ellsworth won the new 4th District seat with 60% of the vote, over Democrat Edward C. Kelly. The 1st District race featured conservative Republican James Mott, an isolationist, and Democrat Earl A. Nott. Mott beat Nott handily with 64% of the vote, for a sixth term.[18]

The War's Impact on Oregon's Economy

World War II had a profound effect on the Pacific Northwest. The region's economy and population were transformed. Portland became a major American industrial center and port. And never had demand for the region's agricultural and lumber products been so high. The production of ships and aircraft sparked a regional manufacturing boom. Shipbuilding became the region's main industry. Employment in the various aircraft, shipbuilding, and metals plants of the Northwest increased twentyfold. Boeing employed more than 40,000. Large and small manufacturing plants became part of the complex web of war production. New hydroelectric installations at Bonneville and Grand Coulee dams made for huge expansion of cheap electrical power. Over 72,000 workers swarmed into Portland in 1942-43.

Through their purchase of war bonds, Oregonians revealed themselves to be among the most patriotic Americans. They bought Series-E War Bonds in record numbers. By mid-1945, Oregonians had purchased $1.27 billion worth of war bonds—an impressive figure considering Oregon had only 1.3 million people.

Lawmaking in Wartime: The Legislature of 1943

American marines were in the final weeks of their six-month Guadalcanal offensive when Oregon's legislature convened in Salem in January 1943. With 78 of the 90 assembly seats, Republicans enjoyed the lopsided control that they'd had over most of the first half of the century. Three Democrats served in the

Senate, and nine in the House. Medford attorney William McAllister was speaker. Dorothy McCullough Lee, the lone woman senator, narrowly lost her bid to become state Senate president; senators chose W. H. Steiwer of tiny Fossil, Oregon. The assembly was, as usual, a virtual all-male club. Garibaldi's former postmistress, Anna M. Ellis, and North Bend's Stella Cutlip were the only female representatives. Twenty representatives were freshmen. The economic and social impacts of war shaped much of the session's agenda.

Lawmakers increased the budget for 1943-45 by $7.5 million. The nearly $35 million state budget included additional funds for the state hospital ($500,000), higher education (nearly $1 million), and state police ($450,000). The session broke all records for spending.[19] Lawmakers passed yet another sales tax measure and referred it to voters.

Oregon's Isolationists

Oregon, like all states, had its share of war critics, who represented divergent points of view. Some were longtime peace activists; some held strong religious convictions against war. More numerous were the isolationists, who opposed American participation in world politics. This group included prominent business and political leaders. Isolationists believed the United States should stay on its side of the Atlantic and Pacific oceans, disengaged from the bloodshed abroad. They also opposed the principle of the Atlantic Charter (1941) whereby President Roosevelt and Prime Minister Winston Churchill had agreed to work toward establishing a postwar international peace-keeping organization (the United Nations, founded in 1945).

Oregon's leading isolationists were Congressman James Mott and U.S. Senator Rufus Holman. Throughout the 1940s, fiery exchanges between Isolationists and war boosters/United Nations backers flavored Oregon politics. Former Governor Charles Sprague was a leading anti-isolationist.[20] In frequent speeches and editorials, Sprague kept a high profile during 1943. Senator Holman was up for reelection in 1944 and Charles Sprague wanted his seat. Using the editorial page of his *Oregon Statesman* like a lance, Sprague repeatedly jabbed Holman for his conservative views.

Senator McNary's Death

Senator Charles McNary, Oregon's United States Senator since 1918, died of a brain tumor on February 25, 1944. His death reverberated throughout the country. One of the most powerful leaders in the Senate, McNary was Oregon's best-known and most respected politician. Tributes and praise flooded into

Oregon. President Roosevelt wrote to McNary's widow Cornelia, that the senator "always put the national interest above blind partisanship and was ever free of rancor or intolerance." Senator Robert A. Taft declared: "The Senate and the Republican party cannot replace his judgment, his calm impartiality and able leadership."[21]

Salem's *Capital-Journal* credited McNary with being both of and in advance of his party, a leader with "the foresight to conceive new trends in government and the courage to espouse them." Richard Neuberger described him as one of the last progressives, observing that McNary led the struggle for forest conservation and had been responsible for protecting the nation's natural resources. "His efforts for farm relief focused attention on the problems of rural American and resulted in farm parity. He was the father of power development in the Columbia River that helped bring the Pacific Northwest into the modern era."[22]

More than a thousand mourners crowded into the Oregon State Capitol to pay their last respects to Senator Charles McNary. Twenty-six of his 95 Senate colleagues attended his funeral—a fitting tribute to a man so many said was the model of what a public servant should be.

Governor Earl Snell appointed Republican Guy Cordon of Roseburg to fill McNary's Senate seat, a widely praised choice in Oregon's press. Cordon, a lawyer and longtime Washington, D.C., lobbyist, was known as "able, aggressive, hard-working, resourceful, and honest."[23] Cordon had served as district attorney of Douglas County. Like Gov. Snell, he was a conservative, a "thoroughly conventional Main Street Republican."[24] His appointment was not a surprise to the state's political and print establishment. "Cordon, who by then also served as chief representative of the Interstate Association of Public Land Counties, already possessed an important state and Western constituency, had a solid (if heavily biased toward full-tilt commodity production) grasp of Oregon's important natural-resource issues, and knew his way around the Capitol."[25]

Republican Shuffle

With the May 1944 primary only weeks away, Guy Cordon faced a big decision. Would he seek the Republican nomination to fill the remaining five years of Charles McNary's Senate term? Cordon decided to run and he had company—Charles Sprague also filed for the Republican nomination. Initially, Sprague was far better known than Cordon. His bitter loss to Earl Snell in the 1942 GOP primary had tempered Sprague's hunger for elective office. With moderate and progressive backing, Sprague saw Charles McNary's death as an opportunity to serve in the U.S. Senate. He was considering challenging incumbent Sen.

Rufus Holman when Wayne Morse, dean of the law school at the University of Oregon, announced he would challenge Holman. So Sprague decided to go after McNary's old seat.

Wayne Morse was an expert on labor law with impressive academic credentials. He was an articulate and forceful speaker. At age 66, Rufus Holman was about 25 years older than Morse. Holman's political strength rested with "conservative Republicans, Townsendites, Grange members and [with] Republicans who do not like the Roosevelt administration."[26] Morse attacked Holman for his isolationism and frequent absence from the Senate. The *Oregonian* called Holman's absenteeism "the scandal of Congress." Holman's "record for racial and religious prejudice [was] undisputable" wrote the state's largest newspaper. Some of the senator's foes recalled his active membership in the Oregon Ku Klux Klan in the twenties. But Rufus Holman was a tough, effective campaigner and he fought back. The *Oregonian* reminded readers that Senator Holman "is no buffoon. He is a keen politician and indefatigable worker."[27]

Voters had a clear choice between Wayne Morse and Rufus Holman. Morse represented the progressive and youthful wing of the Republican Party. His vision of America's role in the postwar world differed sharply from Holman's. Morse saw the United States emerging from the war as an active and dominant leader in keeping world peace and order. Holman, by contrast, conveyed the values of older, more rural Oregonians. His strong isolationist bent appealed to voters who longed for a return to the days of America's disengagement in world affairs. Rufus Holman represented a fading past, while Wayne Morse symbolized a brightening future.

Oregon's other Senate contest between Republicans Guy Cordon and Charles Sprague was just as heated. Though he was well known in the state's business and political circles, Guy Cordon needed public exposure. Unlike Charles Sprague, he wasn't a household name in 1944. But with the backing of many Republican leaders, Cordon quickly overcame Sprague's advantage. Cordon's candidacy was also boosted by the popularity of Gov. Earl Snell, who had appointed Cordon to the Senate seat. Both candidates conducted vigorous campaigns, stumping the state, granting dozens of interviews, delivering radio addresses, and running scores of newspaper advertisements. Many who heard Cordon were impressed by his broad grasp of issues as well as by his knowledge of how things worked in Washington, D.C.

Most major dailies endorsed Sprague. Torn between the obvious merits of both men, the *Oregonian* sat out the May primary, making no endorsement, but the editors extolled Sprague's record as governor. "There is no question the

Republican Party owes him a debt; neither is there any question that the people of Oregon have reason to judge [Sprague] one of their best executives. Under his regime the party was rejuvenated. He fathered what is probably the most advanced forestry program of any state; his term saw an upping of pensions and an increase in unemployment compensation."[28]

The Allied invasion of Italy was underway when Oregonians trudged to the polls in May 1944. Both Senate races were too close to call. With 57% of registered Republicans voting, Wayne Morse defeated incumbent Rufus Holman, 68,800 to 58,000. Holman carried 20 of Oregon's 36 counties, but he lost the key counties of Lane (Morse's home) and Multnomah, where Morse defeated Holman by 8,200 votes. The Cordon-Sprague contest was much closer. Cordon edged the ex-governor by 5,000 votes, 66,600 to 61,600. Cordon's win was due primarily to his victory margins in Douglas (his home) and Multnomah counties. Save for a stint as an American delegate to the United Nations, Charles Sprague's political career was over.

Earl Wilcox Snell

Earl Snell was one of Oregon's most popular governors; his margins of victory have never been approached by any other candidate for governor. Earl Snell was a small-town boy from Gilliam County in eastern Oregon, and a veteran of World War I. Affable and conservative, Snell bought into an auto dealership in Arlington in 1915. He later expanded his business interests into banking and wheat ranching. At the tender age of 31, Earl Snell was elected to the Oregon House of Representatives; he served in the House from 1927 to 1935. Snell was House speaker in 1933. He was elected secretary of state in 1934 and reelected in 1938. In this role, Snell traveled widely throughout Oregon.

Earl Snell never forgot a face and he had an uncanny ability to remember a person's name. He also kept a huge collection of file cards on which he wrote the names of community leaders, their spouse's name, the couple's number of children, and even the name of the family dog! Whenever Snell visited a place he would consult his note cards beforehand. It was always "Hello, Don! How are things at the hardware store? How are Millie and the children?" No wonder that, over his eight years as secretary of state, Earl Snell built a network of friends in every corner of the state. As a politician, Snell seems to have always had his eye on one target: he wanted to be governor of Oregon.

Wayne Morse and Guy Cordon posted easy victories in the November general election. Cordon beat perennial Democratic candidate, Willis Mahoney, 260,600 to 192,300 (57 to 42%). Wayne Morse drubbed conservative Democrat Edgar W. Smith, 269,000 to 174,100 (61 to 39%). Morse carried all 36 Oregon counties and Cordon took 33, continuing the Republican monopoly of Oregon's Senate seats.

Dorothy McCullough Lee won a seat on the Portland City Council with 90% of the vote, one of the most lopsided elections in Oregon history. Voter turnout in November 1944 was over 81%.

Governor Earl Snell

War-weary Americans welcomed 1945, with good reason to be upbeat. The war was winding down. The Allied invasion of Western Europe was six months old. Soviet forces were pounding Germany from the east. Hitler's last-ditch stand at the Battle of the Bulge in eastern France was repulsed in January 1945.

In 1942, Snell's conservative backers convinced him that the May primary was the best time to take on fellow Republican, Governor Charles Sprague. With a voter turnout of only 30%, Snell defeated Sprague by a comfortable margin. Even though Charles Sprague had run an honest and efficient administration, Republicans decided that they liked Earl Snell better. Candidate Snell drubbed Democrat Lew Wallace in November, taking an unprecedented 78% of the vote. And Snell was reelected governor in 1946 with 60% of the vote.

Gov. Snell was blessed with a solidly Republican legislature. America was at war during Snell's first term in office. After victory came in summer 1945, thousands of Oregon men and women returned home and to civilian life. Gov. Snell proposed several programs to help veterans get back on their feet. A proponent of highway construction, the governor worked hard to corner federal grants to help pay for road projects. During Gov. Snell's tenure the legislatures of 1943, 1945, and 1947 approved hefty increases in the state budget. In 1945, the legislature, with Snell's blessing, established a public employees' retirement program (PERS). The 1947 legislature upped the state budget by 50%. Most of this increase went to the state's apprenticeship and training program, the state police, public welfare, county health departments, and to higher education.

On October 28, 1947, Governor Snell, Secretary of State Robert Farrell, Jr, and Marshall Cornett, Senate president, died in a plane crash in a remote area outside of Lakeview, Oregon, 4 miles north of the California border. Snell's death stunned Oregonians; Snell was 51 years old.

President Franklin Roosevelt was preparing to go to Russia in February, where he would confer with his two major wartime allies, Joseph Stalin and Winston Churchill, at Yalta, on the Crimean Peninsula. The Big Three would plan the final Allied offensive against Germany and Japan, and design the postwar peace.

Oregon's final wartime legislature convened in Salem in January 1945. Governor Earl Snell, more popular than ever, addressed the assembly. Over the past two years the governor had amassed enormous political clout. The Republican Party's wounds from the hard-fought gubernatorial campaign of 1942 and 1944 Senate battles were healed. Governor Snell's remarks to the 1945 Legislature were warmly received (83% were fellow Republicans). Much of his message focused on the postwar period. Snell endorsed a state-sponsored veteran's education-loan program and predicted that postwar construction spending by government would reach $400 million in Oregon. Anticipating the return of thousands of veterans and the lay-off of shipyard/industrial workers, Snell backed broad liberalization of employment benefits. Other issues addressed were the establishment of a state employee retirement system; setting up intermediate penal institutions for first-time youthful offenders; and tax revision to enhance private forestry ownership. Overall, the governor's program was forward-looking.

The Legislature of 1945

The 1945 Legislature was led by McMinnville's Eugene E. Marsh (no relation to the author) as House speaker, and Canby's Howard Belton as Senate president. With Dorothy M. Lee's departure from the Senate, that chamber was all-male. The House had two women members: Republicans Anna Ellis of Tillamook County and Rose M. Poole of Klamath Falls. House membership reflected that body's recent pattern of representing an ever-widening variety of occupations. The traditional dominance of lawyers-agriculturalists was ending.

Because of the unusual complexity of problems it faced, the session dragged on. Even the prospect of losing their $8 daily salary if they exceeded the 50-day session limit didn't deter lawmakers from meeting 19 additional days. The Senate was also disrupted by a small, vocal, insurgent faction led by W. H. Strayer, a veteran Democrat from Baker, and Republican Rex Ellis of Pendleton. This band resorted to stalling tactics and parliamentary gamesmanship. As the days passed, members became increasingly tired and irritable. Personality clashes erupted in public. One member called another "dumb." Yet once the session adjourned, legislators took pride in their work. Lawmakers approved a $9 million increase in state appropriations for 1945-47. They also

established a public employees' retirement system. Next came the establishment of a state civil service system. Other major actions included removing
the $40 monthly ceiling from old-age assistance so that individual grants could
be based on actual need; strengthening the enforcement powers of the Oregon
Liquor Control Commission; increasing the compulsory education age limit to
16; placing a dental college within the State System of Higher Education; and
implementing a county merger plan for local government.[29] The legislature did
not enact a bill to lower the voting age in Oregon to 18. Nor did it, as some
feared, go off on an anti-Japanese witch hunt. In late 1944, several prominent
Oregon journalists, notably C. C. Chapman, Charles Sprague, and *Oregonian*
editors, wrote or spoke about the strong anti-Japanese feeling that was gripping
the state. Chapman appealed to Oregonians to keep their prejudices and war-
time hatreds from coloring any actions that they might take against Japanese
Americans when the war ended: "We must make up our minds to adopt policies which will help make the world livable for other human beings as well as
for ourselves. We must adjust ourselves to the necessity of getting along with
people, races, and nations, so long as they keep the peace. We hope for an international order which will prove capable with dealing with any nation which
menaces our safety. Statesmanship, not political demagoguery, is what must be
built up and supported."[30]

The Nation's Leading Lumber State

Oregon's heady population growth continued into the post-war years, 1945-48.
By 1948 Oregon added another 114,200 citizens, bringing her population to just
under 1.5 million. The Portland area actually dropped by 13,000 residents after
the war, while the upper Willamette Valley grew by 45,000 to a population of
321,000. Southwestern Oregon also experienced a post-war population surge,
growing by over 46,000 to 172,000. In-migration accounted for most of the population increase in both regions. Leading the way in population growth were
Lane, Douglas, Jackson, Josephine, and Linn counties. What was responsible for
this postwar population surge? Lumber! America's postwar housing boom produced an enormous demand for timber and wood products. Dozens of Oregon
mills were built or refurbished in order to satisfy the country's insatiable appetite for wood products. Douglas County, as much as any county in Oregon,
benefited from these new lumber markets. Growing by 17,000 residents during
1945-48, Douglas and other lumber counties became the backbone of Oregon's
expanding lumber industry. With this new economic clout, Oregon's lumber
counties took on added political muscle, as well.

First District Congressman James W. Mott, originally elected in 1932, died in office on November 12, 1945. A special election was held on January 11, 1946, to fill Mott's seat. The Republican nominee, attorney A. Walter Norblad, Jr., son of former interim-governor, Albin W. Norblad, rolled over Democrat Bruce Spaulding to win the seat.

Oregon Elections of 1946

Oregon's 1946 May primary aroused little interest. Entrenched Republican incumbents sought re-nomination in three of the state's four congressional districts. In the 1st District, Walter Norblad, winner of the special January election, sought the nomination to a full two-year term. Popular Earl Snell was a shoo-in for the Republican nomination for governor. Democrat Carl Donaugh, a leader of the old guard faction of his party, had a clear shot at his party's gubernatorial nomination. Six local public utility district (PUD) measures added some interest in a few areas of the state. Otherwise, there were no statewide measures to consider in the primary. The spring primary was dull and the election uneventful with no surprises. Voter turnout mirrored the campaign's blandness. GOP turnout was 35% (99,200 of 281,000 registered voters cast ballots). Democrats did even worse; a meager 22% cast ballots on May 17. Only 56,400 of 259,000 registered Democrats bothered to vote.

The only Oregon politician to make headlines was rookie U.S. Senator Wayne Morse. Charles Sprague, in his *Oregon Statesman*, wrote "Morse thrives on gore and publicity," charging that the senator spent too much time on "his one-man crusade against Republican conservatives." The *Astorian-Budget* praised Morse for fast becoming a real influence in the Senate. Oregon City's *Banner-Courier* wrote a glowing Morse profile, noting the "respect and acclaim accorded him for his forthright, intelligent, electrifying oratory and courage."[31] Morse, though not a candidate in 1946, nonetheless stole most of the political spotlight.

The November general election featured no close races for either statewide or congressional office. In fact, the margins of victory for Gov. Snell over Democrat Carl Donaugh, 69 to 31%, and incumbent Secretary of State Robert Farrell over his challenger, David Epps, 73 to 27%, reveal how lopsided these contests were. Both Snell and Farrell carried every Oregon county. All four Republican representatives, Walter Norblad, Lowell Stockman, Harris Ellsworth, and Homer Angell, won reelection by margins similar to Snell's and Farrell's. In spite of these ho-hum contests, 59% of Oregon voters turned out on November 5. A bundle of controversial ballot measures were responsible for drawing many

Wayne Lyman Morse

Wayne L. Morse: sharp-tongued, fearless, controversial, fiercely independent, often brilliant, abrasive, and outspoken: a maverick. Wayne Morse was born in Wisconsin in 1900. He earned bachelor's and master's degrees at the University of Wisconsin and a law degree from the University of Minnesota (1928). In 1929 Morse took a job as assistant professor of law at the University of Oregon. By 1931, Morse was a full professor and dean of the small law school—a post he held until 1944. In spring of that year Morse challenged incumbent Republican U.S. Senator Rufus Holman in the GOP primary, and defeated him.

Morse quickly established himself in the Senate as a maverick Republican who did not always march in step with his GOP caucus. Elected to a second term in 1950, Morse left the Republican Party in 1954, and served as an independent before running (and being reelected) as a Democrat in 1956.

An early and vocal critic of America's involvement in the Vietnam War, Sen. Morse worked closely with Oregon Republican Senator Mark Hatfield, also an early critic of the war. Morse endorsed Hatfield's election in 1966, favoring him over fellow Democrat Bob Duncan. Always interested in agricultural policy, education, and labor relations, Morse cut a wide swath through Capitol Hill. Reelected in 1962 to a fourth term, Morse was instrumental in the passage of key federal education legislation during the presidency of Lyndon Johnson.

Sen. Morse was defeated for a fifth term in 1968, losing to Republican State Representative Bob Packwood by 3,200 votes. Morse, however, wasn't done. In 1974, he won the Democratic nomination for Senate. In July, at age 74, Wayne Morse died suddenly, not realizing his dream of returning to the Senate.

of these votes. By a margin of 162,000 to 133,000, voters removed an onerous provision in Oregon's 1858 Constitution: people of Chinese ancestry were no longer excluded from holding real estate and mining claims in Oregon.

The 1947 Legislature: Milestones Galore

1947 was one of Oregon's most memorable political years. First, the Forty-fourth Legislature set a record for longevity and spending. Second, Oregon's top three political leaders died in a plane crash on October 28. The Legislative Assembly counted 83 Republicans among its 90 members when it convened on January 13. The all-male Senate elected Marshall E. Cornett, a Klamath Falls businessman, their president. There were only five Democratic senators. John C. Hall, a Portland attorney, was House speaker. The House, with only two Democrats serving, had to deal with a sometimes confusing roll-call as there were three Bennetts, two Johnsons, two Wilsons and two Hills in the chamber.

The legislative docket was driven by issues related to Oregon's exploding population. Since 1940, Oregon had added 300,000 residents, a staggering 33% population increase, and the state faced pressing social and economic problems. Crime rates were up, schools and colleges were crowded, and traffic snarled an inadequate road system. In addition, Oregon's economy was undergoing fundamental change. Agriculture and fishing, the traditional mainstays of the economy, were waning in importance. Rapidly supplanting these activities was the state's expanding industrial sector. By 1947, half of Oregon's economy rested on industrial production, led by the lumber and wood-products industry, followed by food processing. Consequently, Oregon legislators were faced with folding these powerful new economic interests into the state's political equation. Everywhere lawmakers looked, the problems facing them carried huge price tags. Legislators increased the state budget for 1947-49 by 50%, reflecting the public demand for enhanced government services. State spending jumped from $46 million (1945-47) to $68.4 million (1947-49). So legislators decided the state needed more revenue. Their solution was to again propose another sales tax—set for a statewide vote on October 7, 1947.

The most dramatic action taken by the 1947 Assembly was to revolutionize how the legislature conducted its work. In a highly controversial move, legislators increased the legislature's own budget by 420% from $100,000 (1945-47) to $420,000 (1947-49). Most of these new costs went to pay the salaries of additional legislative staff and for more interim committee studies. Though the legislature continued the tradition of meeting biennially, its expanded staff assumed new day-to-day responsibilities, such as drafting legislation, gathering data, and preparing reports during the interim when the legislature was not in session. The 1947 Legislature forever changed how the assembly functioned. Lawmakers recognized that the time had come for basic governmental reform. Oregon was growing and changing rapidly, and the part-time citizen legislature needed new tools to help it keep up with the changing needs of the people.

Another legislative milestone was set when a landmark land-use planning act, Senate Bill 308, was passed. This act established county and local zoning-planning commissions. County zoning commissions were to be established in every county by the elected county commissioners. The act empowered the new commissions, intended for rural and growing suburban areas, to "institute zoning regulations only in areas where need for control exists and where there is a demand for them."[32] Lands used for agriculture, horticulture, grazing, or growing of timber were exempted. Foreseeing the need to control the postwar phenomenon of urban sprawl, Oregon's lawmakers had the wisdom to try to direct growth, displaying traditional Oregon values, including the need for order and planning, the protection of agricultural lands, and local control.

Exhausted lawmakers adjourned at 12:33 a.m., Easter Sunday, 1947. Their 83-day session exceeded by two weeks the longest previous legislature. They passed 596 new laws. The legislature "made major changes in Oregon's tax, school, welfare, and highway law. It increased funds to counties and cities, made some changes in veteran's legislation and adopted two bills designed to curb abuses of labor's right to organize; workmen's compensation benefits were also increased by an average of 50 percent."[33] Also enacted was "an amendment to the state constitution [to be voted on at the November 1948 general election] which would permit [the state to issue] up to $10 million in general obligation bonds for reforestation."[34] Voters approved the measure 212,000 to 209,300 in November.

Death on a Mountaintop

Late on Tuesday afternoon, October 28, 1947, a four-seat Beech-Bonanza took off from the Salem airport. Veteran pilot Cliff Hogue was at the controls and Senate President Marshall Cornett, Secretary of State Robert Farrell, Jr., and Governor Earl Snell were on board. The silver airplane, trimmed in red and blue, headed south to Klamath Falls. The men had dinner at Cornett's home, picked up some hunting gear, took off again to go east beyond Lakeview to a 20,000-acre ranch 8 miles north of Adel, Oregon. They wanted to get in a morning of duck hunting before returning to Salem late Wednesday afternoon. The hunters took off from Klamath Falls at 10:00 p.m. into an overcast, rainy sky. The ranch was about an eighty-minute flight from Klamath Falls. But the plane never made it to Adel. When Wednesday dawned, searchers scoured a huge area surrounding Lakeview. Late that afternoon, an airborne searcher spied what appeared to be plane wreckage at the 5,500-foot level of a rugged, piney, snow-frosted peak. On Thursday, a land party reached the crash site 15 miles west of Goose Lake and 4 miles north of the California border. All aboard were dead. The plane appeared to have taken a steep dive and crashed with great force into the mountain. "Their mutilated bodies gave grim evidence of suffering a terrific impact."[35] The grim news reached Salem in early afternoon.

Oregon's governor was dead. To complicate matters, the line of succession provided that the secretary of state would, in the event of the governor's death or incapacitation, be first to succeed him. Robert Farrell's death, of course, removed him from the picture. After Farrell in the line-of-succession was the Senate president, Marshall Cornett—but, he too, was dead. So, that left the third in line, Speaker of the House John H. Hall. The speaker was sworn in as governor at 3:09 p.m. Thursday, October 30, 1947. Governor Hall then proclaimed that Monday, November 3, would be a day of mourning and a legal holiday in Oregon.*

The state had never experienced a tragedy like this. Oregonians were stunned and grief-stricken. Governor Snell, for whom many felt genuine affection, was Oregon's most popular leader. After winning the office in 1942 with the greatest margin (either before or since) of any governor, Snell had been reelected the previous November with 69% of the vote. At fifty-one, Earl Snell's political future was bright. Robert Farrell, Jr., who was thirty-six when first elected secretary of state, had also won reelection in November, taking 73% of the vote. Many assumed Bob Farrell would succeed Earl Snell when the governor's second term ended in January 1951.

The *Oregonian* speculated on what the loss of Snell, Farrell, and Cornett meant to state politics: "The death of three high Oregon officials leaves this state with an unprecedented political situation. None of the three was near political retirement age, and each had strong voter support. Their loss means the way will be opened for new [Republican] candidates. Democrats will be inspired to new efforts, as well."[36]

Five thousand mourners crowded into and around the Capitol in Salem on November 3. Most listened to the memorial service via loudspeaker, as only 700 people could fit into the House chamber. Later that day, the new governor announced his appointment of State Senator Earl Newbry, Republican of Ashland, to succeed Robert Farrell, Jr., as secretary of state. Newbry, at 47, and Hall, age 48, were Oregon's rising political stars. Political analyst C. C. Chapman wrote in 1943 that Hall was "selfish, intolerant, caustic, an individualist, by sheer ability and keen intellectual power he vindicated the judgment of those who supported him." William M. Tugman, editor of the Eugene *Register-Guard*, wrote:

---

* C. C. Chapman, (*Oregon Voter*, November 1, 1947) argued that "Three precious lives were lost needlessly because Oregon failed to establish as policy a practice which many private corporations long ago insisted upon, that of forbidding two or three top executives from taking the same airplane at the same time. The loss to state government is too great a risk. Such is the lesson confirmed by this tragedy."

"John Hall is governor of Oregon—and on the spot, perhaps more so than any man since Al Norblad succeeded Ike Patterson [who died in office December 21, 1929]. It [the job of governor] came out of the blue. One man who knows him pretty well said: He's more aggressive than Snell. He's a fighter, but he doesn't always time his fights."[37] Earl Newbry, like Hall, had extensive legislative experience. Elected to the House in 1938, Newbry had served two sessions in the House and three (1943, 1945 and 1947) in the Senate. He had served as chairman of both the Senate tax and labor committees. A well-to-do businessman, he was known for fairness. A close ally of Hall's, Newbry was considered one of the legislature's experts on property and income taxes.

The Primary Election of 1948

In American politics, the year 1948 is remembered as the year President Harry Truman overcame great odds to defeat Republican Thomas E. Dewey. Oregon was the only western state to vote for Dewey over Truman, 260,900 to 243,150. Politically, spring 1948 was a trying time for Oregonians. The void caused by the deaths of three of Oregon's top leaders the previous October was temporarily filled by John Hall and Earl Newbry, but the uncertainty of who was to lead the state over the next four years weighed heavily on voters. Oregon's May primary was dominated by the race for the Republican nomination for president and John Hall's contest for the Republican gubernatorial nomination against Salem's Douglas McKay. Though little known to many Oregonians, John Hall had the prestige of being appointed governor in his favor. A sympathy factor also seemed to work to his advantage. Consequently, many believed that John Hall should be given the opportunity to serve a full four-year term of his own. Douglas McKay had been a state senator from Marion County since 1935. He was a successful businessman, owning Salem's Chevrolet dealership and a decorated veteran of both world wars. McKay, like Earl Snell, possessed a "spontaneous friendliness of manner that contributed to his popularity" and to his ability as a "natural leader."[38] McKay used such slogans in his campaign as "clean, vigorous, progressive."[39] The *Oregonian* praised Governor Hall as "one of the best minds Oregon has had in public service for a long time."[40] Yet, when endorsement time came, the *Oregonian* remained silent, endorsing neither Hall nor McKay. A 65% GOP turnout on May 21 gave Douglas McKay a narrow victory, after two days of uncertainty; McKay emerged the winner by 4,700 votes, 108,000 to Hall's 103,200. John Hall would be governor for only 14 months.

Oregon's Republican presidential primary "attracted exceptional attention, both in the state and in the nation at large. Oregon was the last state to select its delegates by popular vote prior to the national conventions." It was thought that victory in Oregon would "give a big boost to one candidate, and stagger the other. Governor Dewey won the May primary, defeating Harold Stassen 117,500 to 108,000. The primary attracted over 70% of the registered Republicans but only 49% of registered Democrats."[41]

The struggle for control of the Democratic Party of Oregon continued into the 1948 primary season. At odds were the older, conservative (and usually anti-New Deal) Democrats and their more liberal, issue-oriented rivals. Monroe Sweetland, one of the leaders of the liberal faction and a founder of the modern Democratic Party in Oregon, was elected national committeeman in May. Sweetland's victory was a watershed event. His election foreshadowed the rebirth of the Democratic as a viable political party in Oregon. An extraordinarily able party organizer and motivator, Sweetland quickly accomplished three important goals: restructuring the party, attracting many able young leaders into the fold, and allying the "new" Democratic Party of Oregon with the Truman administration in Washington, D.C. This link to the Truman government brought immediate benefits to Sweetland and his followers, including visits by ranking Democratic politicians (such as Sen. Hubert Humphrey), financial contributions, and federal jobs. "Sweetland also aided the drive to publicize the rebirth of the party by purchasing the *Oregon Democrat* in 1949. Under his editorship, the party's magazine became a forceful voice for liberalism in the postwar period."[42]

The nomination of Portlander Richard Neuberger to the state Senate was another important Democratic victory in the 1948 May primary; Neuberger led all Multnomah County legislative candidates in November.

Chapter 12
Oregon at Mid-Century, 1948-55

The Election of 1948

The intensity and excitement of the May Primary did not carry over into the fall general election. Even the addition of two splinter parties (the Dixiecrats and the Progressives) in the presidential campaign didn't arouse much new interest in politics.* A unified Republican Party predicted an easy victory for their presidential candidate, New York Gov. Thomas E. Dewey. Democrats, newly energized by Monroe Sweetland, attempted to patch together an organization capable of carrying President Truman to victory in Oregon; alas, Truman lost Oregon to Dewey by 17,700 votes.

Republicans retained all four congressional seats along with the offices of governor and secretary of state. Democrats, however, were optimistic about the future, for there were obvious cracks in the Republican Party's longtime grip on political power in Oregon. The election of Democrat Walter D. Pearson as state treasurer, coupled with the election of 20 Democrats to the legislature (where only seven had served in 1947), and a steady increase in Democratic Party registration were seen as signs that the Democrats, long out of power, might be on the verge of taking hold as Oregon's dominant political party.

In the race for governor, Salem Republican Douglas McKay defeated Democrat Lew Wallace by 45,000 votes, 271,300 to 227,000. Wallace had been the Democratic nominee for governor against Earl Snell in 1942. In that campaign, Wallace took only 22% of the vote, compared to 44% he drew in 1948. Voter turnout in 1948 was up nearly 50% over 1946. This huge increase in voter participation was due primarily to the resurgence of the Democratic Party, and to 1948 being a presidential election year. Another indicator of

---

* Dixiecrats were conservative states' rightists; they challenged anything that threatened white supremacy in the Deep South and were also foes of a strong federal government.

how a truly viable two-party system was emerging in Oregon was the election of Walter Pearson to the post of state treasurer. Pearson, a state senator from Multnomah County, edged Canby's Howard Belton, 242,000 to 239,000. Pearson was the first Democrat elected treasurer since G. W. Webb in 1886. In November 1948, there were 347,200 registered Republicans and 334,800 Democrats in Oregon.

The 1948 general election featured 11 statewide measures on the ballot. Five proposals were defeated, including one to grant a bonus to recent war veterans. A measure to create an Old Age and Disability Pension Fund was approved 313,200 to 172,500. It provided Oregonians over age 60 with a $100 monthly payment. Funds were to come from a new 3% tax on wages, salaries, farm sales, retail business, and earnings on investments and life insurance benefits above $100 a month.[1]

Oregon at Mid-Century

Oregon was a very different place in 1950 than in 1940. The population had grown by 40% to 1.5 million, over half of whom now lived in urban areas. The economy had moved away from a primarily agricultural-natural-resources-based model to a more diversified economy in which manufacturing played an increasingly important part. The state's labor force now included thousands of women workers, as well as several thousand African Americans.

A large industrial labor force had appeared and labor unions were now thriving. Most new Oregonians were white, Protestant, under age 40, and they came from all parts of the country. A majority of the newcomers favored the Democratic Party and in 1950 voter registration in Oregon tilted toward the Democrats for the first time since the early years of statehood. Though the number of registered Democrats looked good on paper, the figures disguised the fact that a vicious fight continued within the party. Lew Wallace, Howard Latouette, and others led the older, more conservative, and generally anti-New Deal Democrats. They were challenged by the younger, pro-New Deal, reform-minded, and issue-oriented liberals. Between 1946 and 1952 this intra-party struggle kept the party powerless in state politics.[2] Although it was losing its registration edge, Oregon's Republican Party continued to hold most of the political power in the state.

The Democratic Party suffered from a negative image with most Oregonians; it wasn't taken seriously. A lack of organization at the state and county level, underfunding, and the habit of nominating mediocre candidates for office undercut Democratic attempts to enhance their party's credibility.

Led by Monroe Sweetland and Howard Morgan, liberal Democrats, in 1946, had implemented a strategy to take control of the party. They identified and encouraged fellow liberals to seek control of their county central committees. Working through their new chapter of Americans for Democratic Action, Robert D. Holmes, a radio station manager, and James Goodsell, a reporter on the *Astorian-Budget*, took control of the central committee in Clatsop County, and recruited strong candidates to run for the legislature. Because of their efforts, in 1948 a Democrat (Robert Holmes) was elected to the state Senate from Clatsop County for the first time in the 20th century. Eugene attorneys Keith Skelton and Charles O. Porter led Lane County Democrats in a drive to wrestle control of the central committee away from the old guard. In Baker County, Al Ullman led a drive to take control of the party apparatus. In Multnomah County, union leaders George Baker (executive secretary of the AFL-CIO in Oregon) and Al Hartung (Longshoreman's Union) worked with John Broast, former U.S. Rep. Nancy Wood Honeyman, and Edgar Williams, Kelly Foster, and Ruth Flowers of Portland's African-American community to come together to rebuild the Democratic Party.[3]

These new Democratic leaders rejuvenated their party by developing a platform based on issues. They believed the Democratic Party should be a vehicle for improving society and promoting public service. Liberal Democrats urged the enactment of legislation to improve the social and economic well-being of Oregonians. They adopted President Truman's Fair Deal as a model for political action. The young reformers pushed programs such as "federal aid to education, public housing, increased social security benefits, national health insurance, repeal of the Taft-Hartley Act,* and a Columbia Valley Authority."[4]

Next, they focused their attention on farmers and industrial workers. The Grange and State Federation of Labor became the conduits liberal Democrats worked through as they sought to both revitalize their party and get strong Democratic candidates elected to public office. Monroe Sweetland, James Goodsell, Howard Morgan, Byron Carney (elected chairman of the state party in 1947), and others decided to make the establishment of a Columbia Valley Authority their main issue in the political campaigns of 1948 and 1950. The creation of another source of cheap hydroelectric power was a wildly

---

* The Taft-Hartley Act of 1947 was directed at organized labor: it outlawed the closed shop, which required a worker to join a union before they were hired. Section 14B legalized right-to-work laws by which states could forbid the requirement of union membership as a condition of employment. The law also provided for a cooling-off period before workers could go on strike.

popular idea with most farmers, especially those who farmed in arid eastern Oregon. This "bunch of young upstarts" (as Governor McKay called the liberal Democrats) focused on grassroots organization, precinct by precinct, county by county.

Finally, the liberals worked to enhance their party's image by purging it of politicians who had questionable reputations. Howard Morgan noted: "The [Democratic] party was not taken seriously because we had too many drunks, crooks, stumble-bums, has-beens, and never-wuzes."[5] The *Oregon Journal* wrote: "the Democratic donkey in Oregon had been a bewildered, frustrated split-personality critter without purpose, confidence, leadership or motive. There are signs [however] that the Oregon donkey is taking a new lease on life and showing some purpose about things that affect all people of the state."[6]

The Election of 1950

With the approach of the 1950 campaign season, Oregon Democrats were optimistic. Strong and active labor and farm backing made the new Democratic leaders believe they had a fighting chance to elect more than the usual handful of Democratic candidates. The key contests were the U.S. Senate seat of Republican Wayne Morse, the governorship, Oregon's four congressional seats, and the question of which party would control the 1951 Legislature.

The Senate race pitted Morse, a progressive, pro-labor Republican, against conservative Howard Latourette, who had been Democratic National Committeeman between 1936 and 1944. Latourette had captured his party's nomination in May, defeating Louis A. Wood, a professor at the University of Oregon, 81,200 to 71,000. Liberal Democrats were in a quandary. A friend of working men and women, and an outspoken champion of various social causes, Republican Wayne Morse was a far more attractive candidate to liberal Democrats than was their party's nominee; Latourette was convinced (for good reason) that Monroe Sweetland and his cronies, were out to scuttle his chances. Furious over the amount of campaign money he got from the Democratic National Committee (he had requested $6,400 but received $2,000), Latourette turned on his liberal foes. His old friend Oswald West also jumped into the campaign on his behalf.

Nationally, the election of 1950 was heavily influenced by world events (the beginning of the Korean War and the 1949 victory of Communist Mao Tse Tung in Mainland China) and by the rise of Wisconsin Senator Joseph McCarthy and his crusade to eradicate alleged Communists in the American military, state department, and intelligence community. Howard Latourette was the first Oregon politician to use the threat of Communism as a campaign tactic. He accused liberal Democrats of socialistic influences. Republican candidates picked up on Latourette's attempts to paint liberal Democrats as Communist sympathizers. Representative Harris Ellsworth of the 4th District portrayed his Democratic opponent, David Shaw, as a left winger with pink ideas. He said that campaign's main issue wasn't between Republicans and Democrats "but a contest between Communists and fellow travelers and the rest of us."[7]

Democrats parted company with Howard Latourette by the thousands. In November they crossed over and voted for Republican Sen. Wayne Morse, who won reelection with 75 % of the vote, crushing Latourette, 376,500 to 116,800. With over 378,000 registered Democrats in Oregon in 1950, Latourette's defeat was a sign that conservative Democrats were becoming a minority in their party. Morse proved a charismatic and effective campaigner and vote-getter. It seemed that, with the right candidate, the liberal wing of the Democratic Party was ready to carry the party to victory in the near future.

Three Democrats vied for the gubernatorial nomination in May 1950: State Senator Austin Flegel of Multnomah County, Lew Wallace, and State Treasurer Walter Pearson; it was one of the nastiest campaigns in memory. Flegel, a moderate-liberal Portland businessman, blasted Pearson and Wallace as "unfit to occupy the governor's chair."[8] The Democratic campaign got more and more negative and much of the public tuned out. Austin Flegel won the nomination, carrying 21 of Oregon's 36 counties and edging Wallace, 59,400 to 57,800; Pearson finished with 46,550 votes. In securing Flegel's nomination, the liberal Democrats showed their new political muscle. But their victory came with the high price of even more bitter party division.

Republicans nominated Gov. Douglas McKay for a second term, who, running unopposed, pulled 180,550 votes in the primary—17,000 more votes than the three Democrats combined. Republicans emerged from the primary united behind a popular governor. Though several Republican politicians and editors suggested that the Democrats were infected with left-wing and socialistic thinking, the governor's race was not as vicious as the Democratic primary had been. Governor McKay won reelection with 66% of the vote, 334,150 to Austin Flegel's 171,750 votes.

The 1950 campaign was a lopsided defeat for Oregon's Democratic Party. The internal feud had rendered it weak and ineffectual. This schism, coupled with the Republicans' ability to nominate candidates with broad voter appeal, kept Democrats from becoming the dominate party in Oregon in the early 1950s.

A Fistful of Stars

Extraordinary political talent served in Oregon's 1951 Legislature, which met for 116 days, the longest session ever. Three future U.S. senators (Mark O. Hatfield, and Richard and Maurine Neuberger) were members of the assembly. Representative Robert Y. Thornton would serve 16 years as Oregon's attorney general (1953-69). Hatfield and senators Robert Holmes, Paul Patterson, and Elmo Smith were future governors. Maurine Neuberger, Hatfield, and Thornton were freshmen House members. Mark Hatfield, at age 28, was the youngest of the 90 lawmakers. Maurine Neuberger was the only female representative and Marie F. Wilcox, a Josephine county Republican, was the only female senator. Twenty-eight members of the House were first-timers. Republican Paul Patterson, a Hillsboro attorney, was Senate president, and Salem's John Steelhammer was speaker of the House. Nine Democrats served in each chamber, a decline of two from their 20 seats in 1949. Republicans continued their overwhelming domination of the legislature.

When lawmakers convened on January 8, the United States was six months into the Korean War (1950-53). The economies of both Oregon and the nation were gearing toward war production. Inflation had also set in. Coupled with a growing population and demand for enhanced public services, including state funding of education, the legislature faced an uphill battle in deciding how to pay for all of it. Identifying new sources of state revenue was the major challenge.

One of the most hotly debated issues was legislative reapportionment. Armed with new statistics from the 1950 Federal Census, urban lawmakers vowed to change Oregon's legislative map to reflect the state's growing and shifting population. Senator Richard Neuberger wrote:

> Although the constitution of this state specifically orders a reapportionment every ten years, the Oregon legislature has not redistricted since 1910. Most state legislatures are supposed to be divided up on the basis of population. In other words, each House or Senatorial district must have the same number of people. This provision, strictly provided for in state constitutions, has been deliberately flouted in recent years. Oregon offers a case in point. Its constitution orders all legislative districts to be of approximately equal population. Yet one Senatorial district in Portland has 78,178 inhabitants, while a district in the sagebrush has 7,269 inhabitants. What does this mean? It means that each sagebrush voter possesses ten times the voice in the Senate of his fellow citizen in Portland.[9]

Dick Neuberger's argument was that Oregon's legislature, like those every-where, was still dominated by rural, agricultural districts. In Oregon, these dis-tricts were normally Republican and often anti-city in their views. These rural legislators were not likely to alter Oregon's legislative map in favor of shifting power to the northern Willamette Valley and to southwest Oregon. Despite intense lobbying from Oregon labor and Democratic Party officials and legisla-tors, the 1951 Legislature stood pat. No reapportionment plan was passed. This unwillingness to change Oregon's antiquated apportionment map was viewed as the single biggest failure of the 1951 Legislature.*

Lawmakers passed and referred six constitutional amendments to the November 1952 general election. They also increased state appropriations for 1951-53 by $12 million over the previous biennium. For the first time, the legis-lature appropriated over $100 million ($108 million) for the state budget. Higher education got the lion's share of the increase, nearly $5 million. An additional million dollars for military spending was also approved, reflecting the nation's growing commitment to winning the war in Korea. School district consolida-tion was one of the most time-consuming issues of the session (there were over a thousand school districts in Oregon). The State Board of Education was also reorganized—with nine members to be appointed by the governor.

The *Oregon Democrat* said the 1951 Legislature was "slovenly, criticizing law-makers for failing to pass a reapportionment plan, to follow up on a Grand Jury's recommendations to investigate a scandal involving the Oregon Liquor Control Commission (OLCC), and its unwillingness to enact a general civil rights act protecting religious and racial minorities from overt forms of discrimination."[10]

All in all, the 1951 Legislature was notable for several things: the number of bright political stars who served there; its record length; the unprecedented amount it appropriated; its failure to identify major new sources of state rev-enue; and its unwillingness to tackle reapportionment reform. To its credit was a long list of significant accomplishments, including an important highway building program, the reform of how the state conducted its financial business, and school district consolidation.

Richard and Maurine Neuberger

The Neubergers, Richard and Maurine, were the first husband-and-wife team to serve in the Oregon Legislature. Richard, a nationally known writer, was first

---

* Voters did, however, get a chance to vote on a reapportionment plan in November 1952. The measure, which got to the ballot via initiative petition, was passed, 357,550 to 194,300. Thus, it was not until 1953 that the legislature reflected this new reapportionment scheme.

elected to the legislature in 1940, serving a term in the 1941 House. Elected state senator in 1948, Neuberger had served in the 1949 session. Mrs. Neuberger, formerly Maurine Brown, was a longtime Portland high school teacher and writer. She married Richard in 1945.

Dick Neuberger was a popular public speaker and was already well known on the lecture circuit in Oregon. Neuberger had started out as a sports writer at the *Oregonian*, moving to be a correspondent at the *New York Times*. He had authored several books and was a regular contributor to popular magazines of the day. The couple was in the vanguard of Oregon's resurgent Democratic Party. As legislative candidates in 1950, the Neubergers "were able to cut deeply into Republican majorities in the heavy GOP precincts, while holding most of the Democratic vote [in Multnomah County] at the same time."[11] As Democrats, the Neubergers were members of the minority party in the legislatures of 1951 and 1953. As a team, they were among the best-known politicians in Oregon and their political stature far exceeded their power as members of the Democratic minority. Their ties as husband and wife seemed to add to their strength at the polls. They were asked to consider running for higher offices, Dick for the U.S. Senate (Senator Cordon's seat) and Maurine for Congress from the Portland district. "In 1950 and 1952 strong efforts were made to induce Dick to run for Congress, but he brushed [them aside], although leaving the door open for a different answer in the future. Dick's popularity is untested outside Multnomah County, but it takes no crystal-gazer to know that his strength is state-wide. There is not a more popular speaker in the state in either party."[12] Their political stars were shining brighter by the day.

Oregon and the Nation in 1952

The year 1952 found the United States in the middle of the Korean War. In Washington, D.C., Wisconsin Senator Joseph McCarthy was knee-deep in accusations and investigations of alleged Communist activity in both the Truman Administration and the U.S. Army. America was rife with fears of Communism and the danger it seemed to pose to the Free World. The Cold War was underway. Fighting alongside United Nations forces in South Korea, the United States found itself dedicated to a foreign policy of containment—that is, doing whatever was necessary to keep Soviet and Chinese Communism from expanding into non-Communist areas. With the establishment of the North Atlantic Treaty Organization (NATO) in 1949, the United States, Canada, and their European allies had successfully halted further Soviet aggression in central Europe. The Cold War was the dominant fact of life in the world in 1952—and it was to remain so for the next forty years. Oregonians weren't immune to these world tensions. In fact, politics in Oregon were quite influenced by the Cold War, particularly the fighting in Korea.

Oregon had plenty of tensions of its own in 1952. The dramatic population growth of the previous decade had profoundly changed the state. Though the population growth rate dropped to 16% during the 1950s, Oregon was forced to wrestle with dozens of critical problems directly caused by the swelling population. Education, race relations, industrial mechanization, demand for better roads and state highways, and a slowing national economy were among the critical issues facing Oregonians and their elected leaders in 1952.

The 1952 presidential election dominated the campaign season in Oregon. With Democrat Harry S. Truman leaving the White House, Republicans, who had been out of power since Democrat Franklin Delano Roosevelt took office in 1933, were determined to regain the presidency.

The face of Oregon's electorate was changing quickly. Most newcomers were under age 45. Many were labor-union families. Several thousand were African-Americans. And the majority were Democrats. Politics were undergoing a radical transformation in traditionally Republican Oregon. Oregon Democrats made their own history in the 1952 primary by voting in the highest percentages ever (53% of those registered, nearly 202,000 votes).[13] In populous Multnomah County, 66% of registered Democrats voted. While Democrats voted in record numbers, Republicans did ever better: 68% voted (down from 70% in May 1948).

Oregon Democrats favored Tennessee Sen. Estes Kefauver for president in the 1952 primary. Kefauver swamped Supreme Court Justice William O. Douglas (although he did not seek the Democratic nomination, Douglas got 29,500 votes). Former Illinois Gov. Adlai Stevenson was third (with 20,350 votes). In addition, 9,000 Oregon Democrats wrote in Gen. Dwight Eisenhower's name as their choice for president. Oregon Republicans were nuts about Eisenhower, casting 172,500 votes for him in May. California Gov. Earl Warren ran second with 44,034 ballots. Later that summer, Democrats chose Adlai Stevenson as their presidential nominee, and Republicans tapped General Eisenhower as their candidate.

Dwight Eisenhower, commonly called "Ike," campaigned on a slogan of "Korea, Communism and corruption." Republicans everywhere embraced Ike's slogan. During the campaign Eisenhower promised that, if elected, he would personally go to Korea to do what he could to break the stalemated peace talks there. With 83% of registered voters casting ballots in November, Eisenhower carried Oregon with 60.5% of the vote, 5% ahead of his national vote. Democrat Adlai Stevenson did better nationally than he did in Oregon, where he took only 39% of the state vote, compared to 44% in the country.

The rest of the Oregon ballot included the state's four U.S. House seats, legislative races, a hotly contested race for attorney general, and 18 state ballot measures. The November election included a greater number of candidates than any election ever held in Oregon and a greater number of measures than in any recent election.[14]

Riding Eisenhower's long coattails, Oregon Republicans swept into office. In spite of their dynamic new party leaders and growing registration, Democratic candidates did poorly in legislative elections. Only four Democrats (including Richard Neuberger and Robert Holmes) were elected to the Oregon Senate and 11 to the House. In October, Sen. Wayne Morse had announced that he was leaving the Republican Party; for the time being he would serve in the Senate as an independent. Conservative Republicans rejoiced in Morse's departure—and they began searching for a conservative candidate to challenge Morse when he ran for reelection in 1956.

One-term Democratic State Rep. Robert Y. Thornton won the office of Oregon Attorney General, which was being vacated by George Neuner, a Republican. Thornton, a Portland native and a Stanford University and Georgetown University Law graduate, was one of the bright new faces in Oregon's resurgent Democratic Party.*[15] Portlanders Richard and Maurine Neuberger easily won reelection to the Oregon Senate and House in 1952. Both pulled more votes than Dwight Eisenhower in Multnomah County.

Republican committees spent over $315,000 in Oregon's 1952 elections while Democrats spent only $29,000. Outspent 11-1, Democrats continued to struggle to get elected in Oregon.[16]

Mr. McKay Goes to Washington

A week before Christmas 1952, Gov. Douglas McKay resigned. Incoming president Dwight Eisenhower had picked McKay to be his Secretary of Interior. The vacancy in the office of governor was filled by Republican State Senate President Paul Patterson. Patterson took the oath of office on December 27. Governor

---

* In 1962, Thornton was the Democratic nominee for governor opposing Republican Mark O. Hatfield. He lost to Hatfield by only 35,000 votes. In 1970, he was elected to the Oregon Court of Appeals. He was elected to a second six-year term on the Court in 1974. Thornton's public career spanned thirty-two years, making him one of the longest-serving politicians in Oregon history and one of only three men to be elected to all three branches of Oregon government.

Patterson was a former Hillsboro city attorney and deputy district attorney in Washington County. Like McKay, he was a conservative Republican. The 52-year-old Patterson served the last half of McKay's term (to January 10, 1955).

The 1953 Legislature

Oregon's 47th Legislative Assembly convened in Salem on January 12, 1953. A week later the inauguration of President Dwight D. Eisenhower and Vice President Richard M. Nixon took place in the nation's capital. Two months later Soviet dictator Joseph Stalin died in Moscow.

Oregon and the nation were sliding into a period of declining economic growth. In the last six years of the Truman presidency, 1947-52, the annual rate of economic growth in the nation was 4.3%. During the Eisenhower years, 1953-1960, it was only 2.5%. Oregon had the highest unemployment rate in the country by the end of 1953. As a result, the state's welfare rolls were bulging. But the new legislature hardly seemed to notice. Rushing to get its work done, the Legislative Assembly went home after 100 days (on April 21).

Republican Rudie Wilhelm of Portland was speaker of the House in 1953. His Senate counterpart was Republican Eugene E. Marsh, a McMinnville attorney. Democrats, numbering only four in the Senate and 11 in the House, had little influence. With only two women among the 90 legislators (Republican Representative Dorothy Wallace, a Portland secretary and Maurine Neuberger, a Portland Democrat), the legislature took on its usual middle-aged, white male complexion. Working in tandem, the House and Senate pushed through a remarkably large package of significant legislation in barely three months. Of the 747 bills enacted, only five were vetoed by Governor Patterson. Lawmakers approved a whopping budget (for 1953-55) of $193.2 million. Legislation on a broad front was enacted, including Oregon's first anti-discrimination law guaranteeing racial and religious minorities the use of most public accommodations with violators subject to a $500 civil suit. Eight million dollars was set aside for a state building program, most of it earmarked for Oregon's public college campuses. Acts were passed allowing counties to use voting machines. Working parents were allowed to deduct $300 for babysitter expenses from their state taxes. Courts were given the right to order blood tests to determine disputed parentage. Lawmakers helped consumers by enacting a law requiring public hearings when electric utilities proposed to raise rates.[17] A sweeping bill revising state laws going back 94 years passed. Lawmakers avoided school district reorganization and ignored labor's request to extend unemployment insurance to all employees.

Wayne Morse Talks On, and On, and On . . .

One of the hot issues in both Oregon and nation in the 1950s related to the question of how to best develop the country's energy resources. The development and ownership of both hydroelectric power and offshore oil reserves was of primary interest. Oregon had a huge stake in public power-resource issues, with its heavy reliance on Columbia River dams and the hydropower and vital irrigation provided by the dams.

The Eisenhower administration jumped right into the public power/resource development issue. With Oregon's Doug McKay serving as Ike's point man, the administration tried to push several controversial measures through the 1953 Congress. Blessed with GOP majorities in both the House and Senate, President Eisenhower introduced a controversial tidelands oil bill in Congress. The bill proposed to transfer the authority to develop offshore oil reserves away from the federal government to the individual states. Some Senate Democrats (and most of Oregon's new Democratic leadership, along with Sen. Wayne L. Morse) decided to fight the Eisenhower plan. Many Democrats (and Morse) believed underwater (offshore) lands "could be better preserved and more prudently managed by federal agencies, which would be more resistant than the states could be to the massive pressure for development exerted by the oil companies."[18]

On April 1, 1953, Morse joined a handful of Democrats in a Senate filibuster against the proposal. The filibuster was still in full swing three and a half weeks later. On April 24, Wayne Morse took his turn in the debate rotation. Morse spoke for 22 hours and 26 minutes, breaking (by five hours) the filibuster record set in 1908 by Morse's lifelong hero, Sen. Robert La Follette of Wisconsin. During his filibuster, Morse didn't sleep, eat a meal, sit down, or go to the toilet. For 16 hours he spoke without notes. Morse's feat made newspaper headlines all over the country. But the filibuster failed and Eisenhower got his bill.

Wayne Morse's stand revealed a lot about him. He would do whatever was humanly possible to steer America in the direction he believed best served the public interest. If it was an issue Morse felt passionately about, he would be the last person standing in the debate. He was a fearless fighter, a man willing to personally take on the popular new Eisenhower administration by himself, if necessary. The filibuster revealed his iron constitution (the man was blessed with a seemingly bottomless reservoir of energy). Morse's leadership on energy and conservation issues reflected both his personal beliefs and what he believed most Oregonians wanted, as well. The upcoming political campaigns of 1954 and 1956 in Oregon would spotlight these very issues.

1954: A Year to Remember

By the end of 1954, state politics had experienced a radical transformation. Oregon's anemic Democratic Party was on the rise and the Republican hold on power was slipping; a true two-party system had revived in Oregon.

The year started off with a flurry of political activity. Two Republican contests, both fiercely fought, dominated the spring campaign. In the 3rd District (basically Portland and Multnomah County), eight-term, 79-year-old Republican Homer Angell was seeking a ninth House term. His opponent in the May primary was journalist and radio-TV commentator, Tom Lawson McCall, age 41. Homer Angell had been elected to the House of Representatives in 1938 and he'd never been seriously challenged. Rep. Angell, a one-armed Portland attorney, was a progressive Republican in Oregon's most urban and Democratic congressional district. Angell's success as a politician rested on his broad appeal to a cross-section of voters. He was a rare pro-labor Republican (as was Wayne Morse during his first two Senate terms). Tom McCall conceded that the congressman "had a tremendous relationship with organized labor. He nearly always won the endorsement of all the unions. This enabled him to persevere in one of the strongest union and Democratic districts in the west."[19] A backer (in the 1930s) of a plan to provide a fixed government income for the elderly, Angell was popular with senior citizens. Angell "also spoke up for black protection in Oregon."[20] He favored increasing the low salaries of federal workers and continuing housing and education benefits for veterans, as well as giving away surplus government food supplies to needy Americans. Angell's platform appealed to both moderate and liberal Republicans as well as Democrats.

Challenger Tom McCall was a prominent figure in the Portland media market (where he worked at KGW Radio). McCall was Governor McKay's executive secretary from 1949 to 1952 and well known in Republican inner circles as a McKay man. McCall was apprehensive about challenging Angell, a respected fellow Republican. But a group of influential Portland Republican leaders believed Angell's day had passed, that it was time to elect a younger Republican to Congress. McCall wrote: "we were just trying to find out if Republicans wanted Angell to go on—or have some new blood. It was a very gentle campaign."[21]

Homer Angell campaigned on a platform of continuing to work with President Eisenhower "to stamp out Communism and wasteful spending and to maintain prosperity based on [a] peace economy, not war."[22] Appealing though this platform was to many voters, it didn't address public power, the key issue of the campaign. McCall focused on dams and power development as the dominant issues. He pushed a plan for regional corporations that gave

Oregon independence in power and multi-purpose dam development. Angell supported a high dam built by the federal government instead of the traditional Republican position favoring small, privately built dams in Hell's Canyon on the Snake River. "That issue was so volatile that if you didn't take the traditional Republican position in the primary, you couldn't get nominated. And if you took the Republican position in the primary, you probably couldn't win in November because the Democratic and Republican positions were diametrically opposed. Angell was taking the Democratic position."[23] The issue seemed to work in McCall's favor. He defeated Homer Angell by nearly 14,000 votes. Party leaders and the press called Angell's defeat one of the major political upsets in the nation.

Tom McCall's future in politics looked bright. Now, the only thing that stood between Tom McCall and a seat in Congress was Democrat Edith Starrett Green.

Another Republican primary race featured Earl Newbry, Oregon's popular secretary of state, against Gov. Paul Patterson, for the gubernatorial nomination. Patterson had been governor for only 16 months, having replaced Douglas McKay when the latter resigned to join the Eisenhower cabinet. Patterson had never run for statewide office. Could he defeat the better-known Newbry? Both candidates promised to further streamline state government to provide efficient service at less tax cost. Republicans stayed with Paul Patterson and he scored a narrow victory over Earl Newbry in May. Democrats nominated Joseph P. Carson, Jr., mayor of Portland (1933-41), to face Governor Patterson in November.

Colliding Titans

With the divisive May primary behind them, Oregonians turned their attention to the featured political contest of 1954: the U.S. Senate race between incumbent Republican Guy Cordon and Democratic State Senator Richard Neuberger. The race turned out to be one of the 20th century's most important political contests in Oregon. Guy Cordon had been appointed senator by Governor Snell in March 1944 on the death of Charles McNary. In a 1944 special election, Senator Cordon was elected to serve the remaining four years of McNary's term. Cordon easily won a full term in 1948. In 1954, he'd been Oregon's U.S. senator for a decade.

Rarely in Oregon political history had voters had a chance to pick between two such different candidates. Guy Cordon and Richard Neuberger had almost nothing in common. Former Governor Charles Sprague compared the two candidates:

Cordon is of slight build, modest in demeanor; Neuberger is pretty husky, and aggressive. Cordon is taciturn, rarely speaking in public or in the Senate; Neuberger is vocal and amazingly fluent as a writer. Cordon doesn't like to campaign, has avoided speechmaking tours of the state. Neuberger is gregarious and provocative; both his interests and his occupation as a writer have taken him to all nooks and corners of the state. Cordon is a lawyer, and his mental processes are those of the lawyer; Neuberger is a journalist and publicist. Both are men of integrity and principle. Both believe that their own policies are best for Oregon and for the country.[24]

Monroe Sweetland remembered Guy Cordon as "slow-spoken, almost inarticulate, a small-town lawyer from Douglas County. Cordon was not tuned to the temper of the times." Republican Tom McCall, recalling his own 1954 candidacy for Congress, said that running on the same ballot as Cordon was "a handicap. He [Cordon] was probably the most conservative member of the Senate. He was a pro-McCarthyite, an isolationist, as bad on race as there was." The *Oregon Democrat* criticized Cordon for his "extreme isolationist" views. Calling him one of the die-hards against NATO, the *Democrat* sniped at the Senator for wanting to impose high import tariffs in order to protect American products from outside competition.[25]

Cordon was the last old guard Republican from Oregon to serve in the U.S. Senate. His voting record was generally to the right of the Senate's "Mr. Conservative," Ohio's Robert Taft. Cordon believed that the federal government was both too big and too expensive. Yet, when it was time to protect and enhance Oregon's economic interests, he saw to it that federal dollars flowed into the state for timber-access roads, county timber subsidies, and electric power development, among other things. "Cordon was the sole Pacific Northwest senator to vote against the 1949 North Atlantic Treaty, saying the country simply could not afford something as big as NATO. Cordon's positions revealed him as a typical Taft-wing, pro-business, small government isolationist."[26]

Since his college days at the University of Oregon, Neuberger had made a good living as a writer, often writing on conservation and natural resource issues. He and his wife, Maurine, were Oregon's most famous political couple. Monroe Sweetland recalled that Dick Neuberger was the rising star of the Democratic resurgence in the late 1930s, '40s and '50s.

He was the consummate liberal-journalist candidate for the progressive forces in Oregon politics. All Democratic leaders and deep into the party ranks believed Neuberger's election to the Senate would be the ultimate test of the Democratic Party. Dick Neuberger had never run a statewide race. He was strong with both the American Federation of Labor (AFL) and the Congress of Industrial Organizations (CIO), and with liberals and moderates on college campuses. He was Jewish. Grange leaders like Neuberger. He was a friend of Robert Marshall, founder of the Wilderness Society, part of the budding environmental movement then current in Oregon and the United States in the mid-50s.[27]

Dick Neuberger benefited from a united Democratic Party in 1954. Party commitment to his election was unusually well focused and organized. A tireless campaigner and charismatic speaker, he crisscrossed Oregon, giving dozens of speeches. He also had strong assistance from Sen. Wayne Morse. Morse had been Neuberger's teacher and mentor in the early 1930s when Neuberger was a student at the University of Oregon. Although officially an independent, Morse raised thousands of out-of-state dollars for Neuberger's campaign and contributed hundreds of his own dollars to Neuberger's fund. More importantly, Morse made over 60 speeches throughout Oregon on Neuberger's behalf.

Morse drew large audiences and regaled them with witty stories. Neuberger focused his campaign on public power issues, particularly those relating to the Columbia River. The Democrat favored construction of a hydroelectric dam on the Snake River at Hell's Canyon. Unlike Cordon, who wanted such a dam to be owned by a private utility company, Neuberger believed that a Hell's Canyon dam should be built, owned, and operated by the federal government. He insisted that hydroelectric power rates should be kept low to promote industrial expansion as well as affordable electricity and irrigation water to farmers in arid eastern Oregon. Neuberger attacked Cordon for his chummy ties to large utility companies, calling him "Senator Giveaway" for favoring corporate interests over those of ordinary citizens. Neuberger pounded away on this issue, taking the slogan of "Stop the Giveaway!" as the centerpiece of his campaign. Cordon was blasted for his isolationist views. Neuberger said that "my opponent has had a voting record for eleven years of opposition to most of the policies, domestic and foreign [such as the creation of NATO], which have been designed to protect America in world affairs and to provide a better and more humanitarian life for all citizens at home."[28]

Oregon's press overwhelmingly endorsed Guy Cordon's reelection. *Oregon Voter* wrote that "Senator Cordon, by industry and character has won the highest standing in the U.S. Senate, and, by his initiative and ever-increasing influence had made himself intensely valuable to Oregon, both in the field of appropriations and in legislation." About Dick Neuberger, the *Voter* said: "He has made himself well-known by his writing, oratory partisanship, and authorship of numerous measures of much public appeal and little or no practical value. He was entirely ineffective [as a state legislator] in relation to any important legislation."[29] Republican leaders underestimated Richard Neuberger and the resurgent Democrats. The GOP thought Guy Cordon was unbeatable.

Oregonians went to bed on election night not knowing who their senator would be. Early the next morning, a subdued, exhausted Dick Neuberger phoned his old friend and advisor, Monroe Sweetland, thinking he had lost and wanting to concede. Sweetland cautioned him to wait and be patient. Late votes from working-class districts in North Portland were still not tabulated, nor were votes from pockets in Clackamas and Coos Counties.[30] For Neuberger and the Democrats, the wait was worth it.

Richard Neuberger won the Senate seat. With 70.5% of registered voters (but only 50% of registered Democrats) casting ballots, incumbent Guy Cordon lost to Dick Neuberger by 2,462 votes. How had Neugerger done it? First and foremost, he carried his home county of Multnomah by a margin of nearly 17,000 votes (90,900 for Cordon and 107,700 for Neuberger). A 74% voter turnout in Multnomah County helped him immensely. He carried only 10 counties, yet he won. His strong stance on hydroelectric power development along the Columbia River gave his candidacy a boost in northeastern Oregon and in Multnomah, Clatsop, and Columbia counties. His strong foreign policy positions favoring American commitment to NATO and the United Nations also distinguished him from the isolationist Guy Cordon. Richard Neuberger was the first Democrat in 40 years to be elected to the U.S. Senate from Oregon.

Guy Cordon's loss to the liberal Neuberger was a stunning defeat for the conservative wing of Oregon's Republican Party. Oregon was changing. Demographic changes, underway since World War II, were having a profound effect on the state's social order, economy, and politics. The continuing diversification of the Oregon economy, reflecting the state's changing demographics, meant that economic and political power was shifting away from more rural timber counties to the greater Portland metropolitan area.

Indeed, Cordon's defeat was a two-edged sword, marking both the decline in the influence and popularity of the conservative wing of the state GOP and the corresponding rise of influence/popularity of the moderate-progressive wing of the party, as evidenced by the long careers of moderate-progressives Mark Hatfield, Robert Packwood, and Tom McCall.

A second major political shift underway in Oregon in the 1950s was, of course, the re-emergence of a true two-party state, as evidenced by the explosion of voters registering as Democrats and the emergence of politicians like Richard and Maurine Neuberger, Wayne Morse, Edith Green, Al Ullman, Robert Holmes, and Bob Straub.

Edith and Tom

The other key political race in November 1954 pitted Democrat Edith Green against Republican Tom Lawson McCall in Oregon's 3rd Congressional District race. It was a memorable political campaign. Edith Green had lost a close race for secretary of state in 1952 to Republican incumbent Earl Newbry. Green had run the best Democratic campaign for secretary of state since 1874, when Stephen Chadwick was the last Democrat elected to that office.

Tom McCall and Edith Green had a lot in common. They were both exceptional public speakers, tireless campaigners, well informed on issues, were highly intelligent, and both had exceptional political instincts. And they were relatively fresh faces on Oregon's political landscape. Green was a former Salem teacher. She had also been a lobbyist for the Oregon Education Association. "Bright, and excellent with crowds, Green could go into a union hall and convince the men of her positions. She was one of the first politicians in Oregon to speak out on women's issues, particularly the need to get more women involved in politics and government."[31] With strong labor union backing, and the support of many teachers and women, Edith Green put together a well-organized campaign. She campaigned on an income exemption for working mothers and low-to-medium-income families. She believed that atomic power should be developed for peace and industry. She took traditional Democratic positions on such issues as improved social security, and old age and welfare benefits. She endorsed the United Nations and spoke in favor of reforming America's antiquated civil rights laws.

In the last days of the campaign, McCall delivered a controversial speech, written by one of his advisors, in which he pictured Green as a puppet, controlled by "labor bosses pulling the strings that made this little lady dance and flip."[32] He later regretted making the speech, but the damage was done. Many voters saw McCall as a bully. In heavily Democratic and pro-labor Multnomah County, his remarks about Green's ties to labor worked against him. With the high turnout in Multnomah County, and the popularity of fellow Democrat Richard Neuberger on the ballot, Edith Green defeated Tom McCall (104,000 for Green, 94,350 for McCall). So began the 20-year House career of Edith Starrett Green, who became the most powerful Oregon woman to ever serve in Congress.

Republican Governor Paul Patterson was elected to a four-year term, clobbering Democrat Joseph Carson, 322,500 to 244,000, taking 57% of the vote. Democrats were victorious in 25 House contests, more than doubling the 11 seats they held in the 1953 Legislature. Republicans maintained a six-vote majority in the House (for the 1955 session). Democrats fared less well in their state Senate races, gaining only two seats (bringing them up to six). But Richard Neuberger's and Edith Green's election to Congress marked a turning point in Oregon's political history. The Republican stranglehold on political power was beginning to loosen. The state's spiraling population growth, that included tens of thousands of new, younger, independent, and Democratic voters, and a rejuvenated Democratic Party (which focused on bread-and-butter issues) resulted in the beginnings of a fundamental power shift in Oregon. A century of one-party Republican domination was coming to an end.

Growing Pains

Oregon's booming population (up 55% in 15 years) created new demands on state and local governments. The public wanted more government services. With a youthful population and high birth rate, Oregon was having difficulty building and paying for public schools. Higher education was also hard pressed to keep up with the need for modem classroom buildings, libraries, and dormitories. Many rural roads and state highways were in disrepair and overwhelmed by heavier traffic. The number of registered automobiles in Oregon had shot up from 408,000 cars in 1945 to over 739,000 in 1955.

Oregon lawmakers also had to face the state's high unemployment rate and swollen welfare rolls. Legislators were in a catch-22. Where was the money to come from to pay for a bigger state budget?

The 48th Legislature was, as usual, controlled by the Republican Party. Almost half the House (27) were freshmen. Republican Rep. Edward Geary, a Klamath Falls seed grower, was elected speaker. There were four women members in the House, all Democrats: Katherine Musa of The Dalles, and Jean Lewis, Kay Meriwether, and Maurine Neuberger of Portland. The Oregon Senate had no female members in 1955. It did, however, have three future governors: Republican Elmo Smith of Ontario/John Day, Mark O. Hatfield of Salem, and Robert Holmes, an Astoria Democrat. Portland Republican Rudie Wilhelm, who was speaker of the House in 1953, had won a Senate seat in November, as had 32-year-old Mark Hatfield. Joining them was Milwaukie's Monroe Sweetland, the national committeeman of Oregon's Democratic Party. Both Elmo Smith and Sweetland were small-town newspaper publishers.

Five weeks into the session (on February 17), Wayne Morse, Oregon's senior U.S. senator, walked into the Lane County Courthouse and registered as a Democrat. Twice elected as a Republican, Morse had left the party in 1952, preferring to sit in the Senate as an independent. For the past three years, Democratic Party leaders Howard Morgan and Monroe Sweetland repeatedly invited Morse to join their party, and Morse finally relented. His announcement delighted most Democrats and galled most Republicans. Wayne Morse's political future now rested with Oregon's rejuvenated Democratic Party. Would voters punish Morse in 1956 for abandoning the Republican Party?

The Legislature of 1955 lasted 115 days. Legislators passed 774 bills out of 1,132 introduced. Here are the highlights: Workmen's Compensation rates were increased; a new State Water Resources Board was created to coordinate water conservation throughout Oregon; Portland State College became a four-year liberal arts college in the State System of Higher Education; funds were appropriated for a new state mental hospital to be located within 20 miles of downtown Portland; and a law passed making it unlawful for an employer to discriminate between the sexes in the payment of wages for work of comparable character. Lawmakers also killed a sales tax proposal.

Most of the tough decisions related to the state budget. Lawmakers increased the budget for 1955-57 by $24.6 million (to $217.8 million). The largest amount went into Basic School Support: $6 million more, raising the state's share of public school costs to $72.2 million. Because appropriations (expenditures) were projected to exceed revenues (income) by $61.5 million, lawmakers were forced to pass several hefty tax increases. Two-thirds of the $61.5 million shortfall would be made up by a $41.2 million increase in personal income taxes. A three-cent cigarette tax would raise $8.8 million and an increase in liquor prices (in state-owned liquor stores) would yield another $3.8 million. Lawmakers had bitten the bullet and faced up to the political reality of the day: raising taxes was the only way they could pay for the expanded services the public was demanding from their state government.

Rising Racial Tensions

America's budding civil rights movement continued to make headlines in 1955. In Montgomery, Alabama, Rev. Martin Luther King, Jr., took over the leadership of a coordinated boycott by African American citizens against the racially segregated city-owned bus system. The Supreme Court, following up on its earlier ruling in *Brown**, determined that racial segregation in America's public schools must end, that the integration of the races must proceed "with all deliberate speed." The court's rulings caused racial tensions to rise all over the country, especially in the Deep South. But, de facto segregation was also the custom in Portland and her nearby suburbs. Blacks regularly faced job and housing discrimination in metropolitan Portland.

Portland Public Schools (PPS) had always been desegregated. But, because of restrictive housing policies—promoted by realtors and city officials— Portland's Negro population had been squeezed into an area just east of the Willamette River called Albina. Consequently, the public schools in Albina had high numbers of Black students. So, in fact, by the late 1950s, Portland had a handful of predominantly Black schools. To an outsider, PPS appeared to practice racial segregation, though no such policy existed. The *Brown* decision caused the PPS to declare that "it had a policy of equal education and that it would take no action regarding segregation in Portland Public Schools."[33] So, for the time being, things did not change in Portland. Pressure from the NAACP and Black citizen groups increased in the 1960s. Various reports and studies made recommendations for improving schools with top-heavy Black populations. But change was slow and tensions between Portland's Black community and school district officials were often tense over the next two decades. Meanwhile, most Oregon legislators (like their constituents) buried their heads in the sand, pretending that racial politics wasn't really an issue here.

---

* In 1954, the Supreme Court, in *Brown v. Board of Education of Topeka*, ruled that racial segregation in America's public schools denied black children their equal protection rights provided in the 14th Amendment. In essence, the *Brown* decision said that America's public schools must be racially integrated.

Chapter 13
Raging Bulls, 1956-59

A Silent Death

On January 28, 1956, Gov. Paul Patterson announced he would seek the Republican nomination for U.S. Senate in Oregon's May primary. Party leaders had been cajoling him to do this for months; finally, the governor relented. GOP leaders were still smarting over the loss of Guy Cordon's Senate seat to Richard Neuberger in November 1954 and they ached to put a Republican back in the Senate. On the evening of January 31, Governor Patterson went to Portland's exclusive Arlington Club for a meeting with his campaign advisors. Seated on a couch in an upstairs lounge, without warning, the governor "silently slumped back on the couch, unconscious. Before a hastily summoned physician could administer effective aid, Patterson died."[1] The GOP's best hope to defeat Wayne Morse was gone. Oregonians were shocked by Patterson's sudden death, the second time in nine years that a Republican governor had died in office. The next day, Republican Elmo Smith, president of the Oregon Senate (next in line of succession to the governor) was sworn in as the state's new chief executive.

Two prominent Republicans were recruited within weeks to fill the void in the Senate race caused by Patterson's death: Philip S. Hitchcock and Lamar Tooze, a Portland attorney. Phil Hitchcock was a moderate-progressive Republican reputed to be one of the legislature's most persuasive speakers. He'd recently resigned his state Senate seat to take an administrative position at Portland's Lewis and Clark College. His supporters believed that the popular urban Republican would give Wayne Morse a strong race. Hitchcock appealed to many of the same interest groups as Morse, notably labor, public power advocates, and students.

Phone Calls in the Night

About 2 a.m. on Friday, March 9, Phil Hitchcock and Lamar Tooze were awakened by back-to-back phone calls. The mysterious caller was Douglas McKay.

McKay had served in the Eisenhower Cabinet as Secretary of the Interior, for the previous three years. At 62, the popular former governor was the titular head of Oregon's Republican Party. On Monday, March 5, journalist A. Robert Smith had spoken with McKay in Washington about whether he was considering a run for the Senate seat held by Wayne Morse. McKay told Smith that, no, he would leave such a tough race to a younger man. Within hours McKay was summoned to breakfast with a couple of Ike's top advisors. "So, two days before the Oregon [primary] filing deadline, Sherman Adams [Eisenhower's chief-of-staff] gave McKay a poll which showed that McKay's support among Oregon voters was in the mid-40s [percentile], Morse's in the mid-30s."[2] Adams was adamant: the party needed him to go after Wayne Morse. McKay listened, then told his colleagues he would go home and sleep on the idea.

Twenty hours later, 11 a.m. Thursday, Doug McKay conferred with President Eisenhower about the Oregon Senate race. McKay, the loyal party man, said he would leave the administration to run for the Senate. That afternoon, using a false name, McKay boarded a plane for Portland. Under the cover of darkness, he quietly checked into the Multnomah Hotel in downtown Portland, also under an assumed name. Hours later, Doug McKay made his phone calls to Phil Hitchcock and Lamar Tooze, asking them to meet with him in his suite for breakfast. Both agreed to do so. During breakfast, McKay told them that he was driving to Salem that afternoon to file for the Republican nomination for the U.S. Senate. Tooze agreed to pull out of the race. Hitchcock told McKay he was staying in the race and if he was going to win the GOP Senate nomination he'd have to go through Phil Hitchcock to do it.

Republican leaders swung into action. Wendell Wyatt, chairman of the Republican Party of Oregon, along with William L. Philips of Salem, McKay's closest political advisor, tried to talk McKay out of running. Jess Gard, Republican National Committeeman, disagreed, arguing for McKay to stay in the race. The resulting Hitchcock-McKay contest drove a wedge right down the middle of the Republican Party. Phil Hitchcock's supporters were incensed. They were angry with the White House for meddling in Oregon politics. His friends resented the way Doug McKay had snuck into Oregon at the last minute. To them, Phil Hitchcock had been stabbed in the back by his conservative rivals.

Hitchcock had an uphill battle on his hands. He had never run for statewide office but he ran a spirited campaign against the better-known, better-financed McKay. Hitchcock pulled nearly 120,000 votes in May, but it was not enough. Douglas McKay won the GOP Senate nomination with 123,000 votes, 46% of the tally (two minor candidates drew 26,700 votes in addition to Hitchcock's total). After a bruising, divisive campaign, could Republicans now launch a unified campaign against Oregon's premier politician: Sen. Wayne Lyman Morse?

The Campaign of 1956

Oregon Democrats turned out in record numbers in the May primary. Over 225,000 Democrats cast ballots, about 56% of those registered. Republicans saw a sharp fall in their turnout—down to about 58% (a 70% turnout was normal). Would Democrats be able to retain the momentum which had carried Edith Green and Richard Neuberger to victory in 1954?

After Labor Day Oregonians paid more attention to the fall campaign. There were many exciting political contests to attract voters. Besides the McKay-Morse Senate race, the governor's campaign between interim Governor Elmo Smith, a conservative Republican, and Democrat Robert Holmes also drew attention. Smith and Holmes were vying for the right to complete the last two years of Paul Patterson's term. The candidates knew each other well, having served together in the state Senate. Elmo Smith was a small-town newspaper editor and publisher and former mayor of Ontario. Bob Holmes "used his [Astoria] radio station as a bully-pulpit. He had a liberal, pro-labor constituency. Holmes was also a close friend of Dick Neuberger and Wayne Morse. Like most leading Democrats, Holmes had a good relationship with the press. He made a good impression—he was intelligent and well-dressed."[3] In assessing the governor's race, the *Oregon Democrat* wrote: "in this contest the personalities and issues are in strong contrast. Holmes, dean of Democrats in the State Senate, is thoroughly familiar with state government problems and the needs of the people of Oregon. In the State Senate Smith distinguished himself by faithful adherence to the conservative wing of the GOP. Elmo Smith has opposed federal development of dam sites and favored the Hells Canyon grab reflecting his support for the Eisenhower administration. Smith had voted against: teacher salary raises, making Portland State a four-year college, and unemployment compensation for workers. He was the only state senator to vote against endorsement of the United Nations."[4]

The secretary of state contest between 34-year-old Republican Mark O. Hatfield and State Senator and Democratic National Committeeman Monroe Sweetland was an important race, as the office of secretary of state was historically a launching pad for those seeking the governorship. Hatfield was dean of students and an associate professor of political science at Salem's Willamette University. He'd entered the legislature in 1951, serving two terms in the House before his election to the state Senate in 1954. Monroe

Sweetland's legislative tenure was nearly identical to Hatfield's. Sweetland recalled his race against Hatfield as "brisk, but inexpensive. It was a civil campaign with no belligerence and a minimum of personal hostility. We had served together in the House and Senate and were good, congenial personal friends. Hatfield and I were in sharp agreement on many issues, including public education, the rights of ethnic groups, especially blacks and Native Americans, and issues of pacifism. We found ourselves in disagreement on those issues in which his conservative friends were interested, such as banking and railroad regulation."[5] Along with lively federal and statewide races, voters also faced competitive campaigns in almost every legislative district. Never had the Democratic Party recruited so many attractive and qualified candidates to run for public office.

Senate Showdown

The 1956 Senate race between Wayne Morse and Douglas McKay set several precedents. Wayne Morse, twice elected to the Senate as a Republican, was seeking a third term—as a Democrat. Never in the history of the U.S. Senate had a person been elected as a member of one party and later reelected as a member of another party. The race also set precedents with its cost; it was likely Oregon's first million dollar political campaign. Morse reported spending $266,400, McKay $230,000. Because of "the huge quantities of unaccounted for cash that flowed through both offices, it is likely that the reported figures were grossly understated." A third precedent was set when President Eisenhower, a sitting president, campaigned for Douglas McKay. Ike hoped his personal popularity in Oregon would help McKay topple Morse. Eisenhower had reason to go after Morse: the outspoken Democrat was Ike's harshest congressional critic, calling Eisenhower "politically immoral." Vice President Richard Nixon came twice to speak at McKay rallies. Senator Morse also invited prominent Democrats to Oregon. Adlai Stevenson, the Democratic candidate for president, and former First Lady Eleanor Roosevelt addressed a Morse rally. The *New York Times* wrote that the "Oregon Senate seat is a top priority of both parties this year. Each has invested more prestige, high-level effort, and possibly even more cash, in the Oregon outcome than in any other senatorial race in the country."[6] With these high stakes, the Morse-McKay race turned into a donnybrook.

The Morse camp was happy to have McKay as the senator's opponent. "As Secretary of the Interior, McKay had been on the front line defending administration natural-resources policies, many of which were unpopular in

Oregon. This provided Morse with ammunition he could use against McKay, and, it also gave him an opportunity to begin his campaign on the attack. Morse's people regarded McKay as an easy mark, as a man who was wooden, quite inept, and not too bright, a small man in every sense, with no personal appeal."[7]

Douglas McKay was short and silver-haired. He was not a forceful speaker and on occasion, he was inarticulate, mincing and dicing words in awkward ways. But he was a warm, friendly man. He loved to chit-chat and swap stories. A *New York Post* reporter wrote that McKay was a man "with the benign and agreeable air of a small-town druggist."[8] Doug McKay came across as a cheerful, down-to-earth man (he was actually a wealthy Chevrolet-Cadillac auto dealer). In contrast, Wayne Morse was "stern, humorless, even evangelistic. Apparent to all was the zealot in his nature, as he lectured voters with a relentless gleam in his eyes deeply set beneath bristling, dark brows."[9] To Morse, politics was the most serious of callings. He was fiercely combative. And he always played to win.

Wayne Morse had a sharp, often caustic tongue; consequently, he made lots of political enemies. Many Oregonians thought the senator was arrogant and self-righteous to a fault. Others admired his candor. Morse's reputation as a political maverick—who followed his conscience first—was like an aphrodisiac to thousands of voters. But he was almost impossible to love, and at times difficult to even like. Often controversial, Wayne Morse backed down to no one.

Morse blasted out of the gate, taking the offensive against McKay. From the start, Doug McKay was on the defensive, back-pedaling, reacting to Morse's relentless verbal blows. Morse attacked McKay as a "tool" of the Eisenhower administration, the one responsible for carrying out natural resource, conservation, and economic policies that were unpopular in Oregon. The administration's anti-inflation tight-money policy caused a slump in Oregon's lumber industry. "The Administration also opposed increases in social security benefits, as well as in the minimum wage to protect Oregon labor from cheap labor in the Southern states. McKay's Hells Canyon decision would mean high profits for the utilities and higher electric bills for Northwest consumers and industry. The choice for the Senate [said] Morse, was [a question of] public interest vs. private interest."[10] Douglas McKay's main constituencies were mainline Republicans including business and industrial elements. Monroe Sweetland remembered that "McKay was allied with private power companies at a time when the issue of private versus public power development was the hottest political topic in

Oregon. Because of his pro-private power stance, McKay was unpopular with farmers, particularly in eastern Oregon."[11]

The senator's base of support was broad, consisting of organized labor, conservationists and environmentalists, advocates of public power, educators, college students, minorities, and farmers. "He knew how to touch a rural audience—partly because he was widely known for his interest in horses and cattle. He could identify with the interests of voters wherever he was talking."[12] Morse also benefited from the help of the Neubergers, who delivered speeches all over Oregon for him. In addition, Dick Neuberger's position on the Senate Interior Committee made him a useful conduit for providing valuable information against McKay.[13]

During the campaign McKay ridiculed Morse for being a "left-winger," a leader of Oregon's "left-ward drift." He declared, "I represent the American free enterprise idea, Morse represents the left-wing socialist idea."[14] Morse reminded voters that McKay was part of the Washington establishment, which was willing to trade away what was important to ordinary Oregonians in order to boost the profits of their powerful corporate friends. Morse's message resonated across Oregon.

The number of Oregon registered voters on election day (November 6) climbed to an all-time high. The Democratic Party stretched its recent lead in voter registration to about 37,500 over the Republican Party (451,200 to 413,650). Wayne Morse won a third term, defeating Doug McKay by 61,000 votes (54 to 46%). Douglas McKay's long career of public service was over.

Other 1956 Election Results

Happily for Bob Holmes, Wayne Morse had long coattails in 1956. In the race for governor, Democrat Holmes squeaked out a narrow victory over Oregon's Republican governor, Elmo Smith. Holmes defeated Smith "with vigorous support from Oregon teachers, labor, and from Senators Morse and Neuberger, and Congresswoman Edith Green during the final week," by 7,600 votes, 369,400 to 361,800.[15] The Holmes-Smith race was the closest gubernatorial contest in Oregon since Democrat Oswald West defeated Republican Jay Bowerman by 6,100 votes in 1910. Robert Holmes was the first Democrat to be elected governor since Charles "Iron Pants" Martin in 1934.

The race for secretary of state between Mark Hatfield and Monroe Sweetland was also close. "Youthful Mark Hatfield cut into the Democratic lead, particularly in Multnomah County, where Hatfield's excellent TV concentration was centered, overcoming Sweetland's strength in eastern and southern Oregon counties."[16] Hatfield carried 21 counties and won the election by 18,500 votes (368,100). Monroe Sweetland prevailed in 15 counties and got 349,500 votes (49% to Hatfield's 51%).

Except for Republican Congressman Walter Norblad's reelection victory in the 1st District, and Sig Unander's win over Democrat Wiley Smith in the state treasurer's race, Hatfield's victory was the only major win by a GOP candidate in a statewide contest in 1956. Democratic candidates won every other major office.

The U.S. House races in Districts Two and Four were nail-biters. In the end, Democratic challengers won both seats, defeating incumbent Republicans. In the 2nd Congressional District (eastern Oregon), Democrat Al Ullman beat one-term Republican Sam Coon (53,200 to 51,800). Ullman had lost to Coon in an equally close race in 1954. This time, Ullman won. His election marked the beginning of a 24-year-long career in the U.S. House. By the end of his tenure, Congressman Ullman of Baker City was among the most powerful men in Washington, D.C.

In the 4th District (southern Oregon), Eugene attorney Charles O. Porter, a Democrat, defeated Harris Ellsworth, a seven-term Republican. Porter won by 4,500 votes. Meanwhile, up north in District 3, one-term Democrat Congresswoman Edith Green of Portland won reelection, rolling over her Republican opponent, Phil Roth, by over 55,000 votes. Walter Norblad was the only Republican to retain his U.S. House seat in 1956. Norblad, representing a heavily Republican area centered in Washington County, handily defeated Salem Democrat Jason Lee by 18,800 votes. A political precedent was set with the victories of Edith Green, Al Ullman, and Charles Porter. For the first time in state history Democrats had been elected to a majority of Oregon's U.S. House seats. Between 1858 and 1954, 115 U.S. House elections were conducted in Oregon. Of these congressional elections, Republican candidates won 97, Democrats 18. Never before had two Democrats held an Oregon congressional seat at the same time. Since 1858, Republicans had won 84% of the state's U.S. house races. Indeed, between 1880 and 1930, only one Democrat (Elton Watkins, in 1922) was elected to the U.S. House from Oregon.

President Dwight Eisenhower carried Oregon again in 1956; his margin of victory was 77,000 over Democrat Adlai Stevenson. Ike's popularity in Oregon had slipped since 1952. Adlai Stevenson pulled 59,000 more votes in Oregon in 1956 than he had in 1952.

The election of 1956 returned Oregon to the fold as a true two-party state. For most of the previous 75 years, Oregon had been dominated by the Republican Party. 1956 changed all that.

Trouble Ahead

When the new Congress convened in the nation's capital in January 1957, Democrats held five of Oregon's six seats. Back in Oregon, Democrat Robert Holmes was sworn in as the state's new governor, and Democrats were taking control of both houses of the legislature. On the surface, the Democratic Party appeared to be stronger and more unified than ever. But that was about to change.

Oregon Democrats were thrilled to have both Senate seats and they knew that they had a well-regarded and outstanding delegation. Wayne Morse was known as a fearless maverick and Richard Neuberger, who was seen as a Morse protégé, quickly made a name for himself as a bright light and a legislator to watch. But by the late 1950s their respect and admiration had curdled. While they formerly appeared so close that "the press referred to them as Morseberger, the two senators were now openly at each other's throats, attacking one another almost daily.... The two men were now locked in the most extraordinary public feud between two senators from the same state, a feud all the more remarkable in that it involved two senators from the same wing of the same political party."[17] Although Oregon Democrats had achieved so much, they were starting to feel demoralized.

Dick Neuberger had known Wayne Morse for 25 years. After Morse was elected to the Senate in 1944, he became a frequent subject of Neuberger's articles for national magazines. When Neuberger ran for the Senate in 1954, Wayne Morse worked for his election. Since Neuberger had entered the Senate in January 1955 many had seen him as Morse's alter ego. But, after two years in Wayne Morse's controversial shadow, Dick Neuberger wanted to create his own identity in the Senate.

There was no single event that set into motion the breakup of the Morse-Neuberger friendship. There were, however, a series of occurrences that drove the men apart. Morse, who always took things personally if you disagreed with him, did several things that disturbed Neuberger. Morse had publicly blasted President Eisenhower as "politically immoral for accepting gifts for his Gettysburg [Pennsylvania] farm, from trees and shrubs to cattle and farm machinery."[18] For this and other actions, Richard Neuberger realized that his close relationship with Wayne Morse was making *him* look bad. Neuberger decided that it would be best for his political future to put some distance between himself and Wayne Morse.

At Edith Green's urging, Oregon's congressional Democrats met weekly for breakfast in early 1957. Problems, issues, and legislation relating to Oregon and the Pacific Northwest were reviewed and discussed in these meetings.

Despite the growing rupture between Neuberger and Morse, the delegation met throughout 1957.

Neuberger by this time imagined Morse in collusion with Green, at least in part because of his own relationship with Morse was beginning to break down, personally and politically. Morse had opposed the Eisenhower administration on a number of key bills—for which Neuberger voted the other way. But it was the indirect effect of a domestic policy dispute that accelerated the deterioration. One day on the Senate floor, Morse charged his usual allies with "parliamentary expediency" and "phony liberalism" for their handling of a 1957 civil rights bill. Neuberger took Morse's remarks personally, especially when Morse sent copies of these charges to many of their Oregon constituents. Neuberger retaliated by asking Illinois Senator Paul Douglas to write a letter to Oregon voters praising Neuberger's civil rights record, a letter that pointedly excluded any reference to Senator Morse's civil rights work. Morse was livid, and let Neuberger know about it in writing. Thus began a series of exchanges that saw the two Senators, separated only by one floor and at opposite ends of the same building, firing charge and countercharge almost daily via missives carried by messenger to each other's office.[19]

During August 1957, Morse and Neuberger fired letter after letter at each other. The letters quickly got personal. Each impugned the other's integrity. After a couple of weeks the senators agreed to tone it down, returning to their customary friendly relationship. For several months both men tried to curb their harsh rhetoric toward the other. But the damage was done. Never again would either man fully trust the other. Their troubled friendship was over. By the summer of 1958, Morse and Neuberger were no longer speaking to each other. Their feud was exposed in national magazine and newspaper articles.

The infamous Neuberger-Morse feud of 1957-60 bred disunity and distrust among Oregon Democrats. Edith Green, Charles Porter, and Al Ullman remained loyal to Wayne Morse. Their relationship with him continued to be open and professional. Dick Neuberger and his wife, Maurine, were now estranged from the rest of Oregon's Democratic delegation in Congress. The relationship between Edith Green and the Neubergers had always been cool. Congresswoman Green suspected that the Maurine Neuberger had an eye on her 3rd District House seat. The Neubergers believed that Edith Green coveted Dick Neuberger's Senate seat.

Looking at the long association between Wayne Morse and Dick Neuberger it is apparent that the seeds of their feud had been there all along. Even when they worked closely and effectively as a Senate team in 1955-56, the two did not trust each other. There were personality factors in both men that eroded their friendship. In many ways, they were alike. Both were bright, highly articulate, and strongly opinionated. Both liked to be in charge and had towering egos. Each loved the spotlight and relished their senatorial powers. They were combative, aggressive, and ambitious. Each insisted on having the last word. "Despite the early political success of their alliance, Wayne Morse and Dick Neuberger were at one another's throats. Perhaps this was inevitable. Both men were ardent self-expressionists, unaccustomed to following anyone else's lead, intense by nature, and equally capable of rubbing others the wrong way."[20] Considering their personalities it is a wonder that Wayne Morse and Richard Neuberger had been friends and political allies for as long as they had.

The late Travis Cross, a Republican leader with close ties to Mark Hatfield, characterized Richard Neuberger as "likeable, but not loveable."[21] Robert Y. Thornton, Oregon's Democratic attorney general, said that Neuberger "always wanted to be the only pebble on the beach."[22] The aging Wayne Morse became less tolerant of anyone who disagreed with him and his well-known self-centeredness often worked against him. Sadly, Morse ignored the sage advice that a Democratic leader had once given him: "Wayne, it's okay not to be right all the time."

Once the feud boiled into public view by August 1957, neither man would back down. They were simply too proud, too pig-headed, to extend a hand of reconciliation. A new series of press releases, public disavowals, and heated personal letters between Morse and Neuberger appeared in early 1958. Even after Dick Neuberger was diagnosed, operated on, and treated for a testicular malignant tumor in August 1958, the hostile rhetoric continued between them. In April 1959, Senator Morse announced that Richard Neuberger was not worthy of reelection, adding that he would campaign against his colleague in 1960. For the remainder of Neuberger's term, Oregon's Democratic "bulls," horns locked, snorted, and grunted, and pushed each other all over the political arena as Oregon and the nation watched, transfixed and disgusted. Newspaper editors throughout Oregon generally blamed Wayne Morse for the breakdown of the relationship. J. W. Forrester, Jr., longtime editor of the Pendleton *East Oregonian* newspaper, wrote about Morse in the fall of 1958: "The strange and shifting career of this brilliant but misguided Senator—this man who, almost by rote, questions the integrity of all who disagree with him. How tragic that a mind so incisive should be devoted almost wholly to negativism and abuse." William Tugman, editor of the Eugene *Register-Guard*, writing in a similar vein, likened Wayne Morse to a figure out of a Greek tragedy—"a hero destroyed by a fatal fault of character, his own insatiable ambition." Eric Allen, editor of the Medford *Mail Tribune*, faulted Morse for his arrogant pride. "His arrogance has led him to castigate those who, while in general agreement with his beliefs, have dared to criticize him on one point. Morse's independence, his determination to place principle above politics are both admirable in themselves. But he has carried both to a point where he has alienated honest, sincere people of every political shade, by his implication that anyone who disagrees with him is either stupid or hypocritical.[23]

Unless Morse and Neuberger mended their fences, it was apparent to everyone that the approaching Senate election of 1960 was going to be ugly. The idea that Richard Neuberger—a senator by a margin of only 2,462 votes—would be facing a hostile Republican opponent, a divided Democratic Party, and the enmity of Wayne Morse campaigning against him, might have caused a person of lesser ability to consider whether his reelection was worth it. But not Dick Neuberger, who eagerly awaited the 1960 campaign. He was certain that he would both defeat his GOP foe and repel the assault that Wayne Morse was preparing against him.

Governor Robert Holmes and the Legislature of 1957

The 49th Legislative Assembly convened in Salem on January 14, 1957. For the first time in 75 years, Democrats controlled both the House and Senate. Portland Democrat Pat Dooley was elected speaker of the House. Only 39 and a war veteran, Dooley had served in the 1953 and 1955 sessions. The House dove into its work. The Senate, however, was stalled. With a 15-15 party split, senators couldn't agree on who would be president. Senators were lined-up behind either Republican Warren Gill of Lebanon or Democrat Walter J. Pearson of Portland. For 10 days (and 288 ballots) the Senate was deadlocked. On the 11th day and 289th ballot, Democrat Boyd Overhulse, a compromise candidate, was elected. Overhulse was a conservative Democrat from Madras, described as an "able, studious, cooperative, non-splurging legislator, a good talker and analyst, who had lots of common sense."[24] He was the first Democratic Senate president since 1878. Slowed by the Senate's rocky start, the 49th Legislature set a record for longevity—128 days.

The third key player in the 1957 Legislature was Democratic Governor Bob Holmes. With his prior senatorial service, Holmes had many friends in the legislature and he was blessed with a Democratic majority. The governor proposed a sweeping package of programs. His proposed 1957-59 state budget increase could be paid for without passing any new taxes because Oregon's economy was booming, and there was a projected budget surplus (the result of a huge

45% increase on personal income passed by the Republican Legislature of 1955) of over $30 million to fold into the equation.

Governor Holmes' legislative proposals weren't revolutionary and several had kicked around Salem for years. He favored hiring a full-time, paid administrator for the State Board of Parole; he proposed establishing the office of lieutenant governor; and he wanted to abolish the State Liquor Control Board. Holmes opposed capital punishment and wanted it abolished in Oregon. He favored amending the state constitution to allow the legislature to meet in annual sessions. All of these proposals took a back seat to his primary goal of increasing state spending on public education. Holmes proposed increasing the state's share of local school costs from $80 to $120 per pupil (for 1957-59) to help local taxpayers support their schools. The governor wanted to raise the salaries of professors and teachers in Oregon's public colleges and those of all other state employees. The most popular proposal was his call to repeal the hated 45% surtax on personal income passed by the 1955 Legislature. Overall, Governor Holmes' legislative package was cautious and safe; he wanted the legislature to pass his proposals.

The 49th Legislative Assembly adjourned just before midnight on Tuesday, May 21, 1957. Legislators passed a general fund budget of about $275 million for the 1957-59 biennium. The governor had convinced lawmakers to increase state spending by about $57 million over the 1955-57 budget. Most of this budget increase went to the programs favored by the governor: $15 million more for Basic School Support (a figure well below the governor's recommended $40 million); and $15 million for salary raises for both state employees (including the governor) and college professors/teachers.

The governor's proposals for annual legislative sessions and the office of lieutenant governor were not acted on. The legislature addressed the abolition of capital punishment by passing it on to the voters in the form of a referendum to be decided in the November 1958 general election. It was one of 12 statewide measures referred to the 1958 election.

What to Do with $70 Million?

Scarcely five months after the regular session adjourned, the legislature was called back into special session on October 28, 1957, by Governor Holmes. For the tenth time since 1859, the legislature met in special session. Acting on the recommendation of Republican State Treasurer Sig Unander, the governor had called the special session to decide what lawmakers wanted to do with an unanticipated budget surplus of over $70 million. Governor Holmes wanted legislators to pass two bills: "one to return $9.5 million of income taxes a year to the taxpayers, and one to use $5 million a year to increase state Basic School Support, leaving about $50 million (of an anticipated $70-$74 million surplus) to start the new biennium in July 1959."[25]

Republican leaders came to the special session proposing to slash state income taxes by 30%, carrying over to 1959 a budget surplus of only $10-20 million. Two veteran Democrats, fiscal conservatives Ben Musa of The Dalles and Harry Boivin of Klamath Falls, joined 15 senate Republicans to cut personal income taxes above the percentage Holmes and Democratic leaders in the House and Senate wanted. Personal income taxes were cut by about 20%, midpoint between the governor's recommended 10% and the GOP's 30%. Income taxes on corporations were also lowered during the special session. And an additional $5 million went into the Basic School Support Fund. The budget surplus was now calculated to be closer to $31 million.

Legislators also enacted about a dozen other laws unrelated to taxes and the budget surplus. Considering how much grumbling there had been (mainly from Republican leaders and the state's daily newspapers) about the need for calling a special session, the nineteen-day affair wasn't as rancorous or divisive as many pundits had predicted. Some Democrats left Salem predicting that the Republicans had gone too far, that a $31 million surplus was too small. These Democrats forecast gloomy days ahead for Oregon, predicting that a new tax increase was inevitable if the next legislature was going to balance the biennial budget for 1959-61.

The Campaign of 1958

The big issue facing voters in May 1958 was who would be Oregon's next governor. Democrat Robert Holmes seemed to be a shoo-in for his party's nomination. His opposition in the primary was the perennial candidate Lew Wallace. Never a popular vote-getter, Wallace was an easy hurdle for Holmes to overcome. Governor Holmes won a lopsided victory, 128,800 votes to 59,800. Most assumed that Sig Unander, Oregon's state treasurer, would be the GOP candidate. But barely a year into his term as secretary of state, Mark O. Hatfield surprised voters by announcing that he would seek the Republican gubernatorial nomination. The Unander-Hatfield contest featured two of Oregon's rising young political stars. Joining Unander and Hatfield in the Republican primary was State Senator Warren Gill of Lebanon. Mark Hatfield won the primary with 105,500 votes to Unander's 64,700 and Gill's 40,100.

The November 1958 general election featured the governor's contest, the state's four U.S. House races, and the issue of which party would control the legislature. Democrats wanted to retain their hard-earned majority in the House; their target in 1958 was to win outright control of the Senate. There were also 13 ballot measures, 12 of which had been referred to voters by the 1957 Legislature. Two controversial measures looked at the abolition of capital punishment in Oregon and whether legislators ought to have a salary raise.

The governor's race between incumbent Robert Holmes and Mark Hatfield took center stage. Hatfield, young, handsome, focused, articulate, and confident, drew enthusiastic crowds wherever he spoke. Holmes and his Democratic supporters tried, mostly unsuccessfully, to pin Hatfield down on key issues (particularly Eisenhower administration policies that were unpopular in Oregon). Hatfield proved adept at dodging the Democratic broadsides. His campaign focused on conveying the impression of an attractive, intelligent, reasonable, vigorous man with fresh ideas. He wanted to provide better service for fewer taxes. Neither man seemed to misstep. Both candidates conducted themselves in gentlemanly fashion, never attacking the other personally until the last week of the campaign. Experts believed that Hatfield was ahead, though not far enough to anoint him the victor on election day. Then Senator Wayne Morse jumped into the governor's race and sealed Bob Holmes' defeat. Here's the sorry story.

Wayne's Big Blunder

Five days before the November 4 election Wayne Morse made a speech in Klamath Falls. He introduced the facts of an unfortunate incident from 1940. The incident involved the Republican candidate for governor, and in raising the incident Morse was attempting to persuade voters that Mark Hatfield was unfit to be governor of Oregon.

In late spring 1940, Mark Hatfield, then a 17-year-old high school senior, was driving his mother's car to a school band practice about 7 p.m. On his way into South Salem, he struck and killed a seven-year-old girl. According to court testimony, Hatfield said that he never saw the child, that she simply darted into the road while trying to rejoin her sister, who was waiting for her on the other side of the street. Marion County authorities didn't file criminal charges. The child's parents, however, did file a suit against Hatfield for civil damages. The case came up for trial in October 1941. It was a routine damage suit. Testimony focused on whether Hatfield could have seen the child. The county court awarded the parents $5,000 in damages. Hatfield's lawyers appealed the case to the Oregon Supreme Court. The Court's opinion confirmed the lower court's ruling.[26]

Governor Holmes and his campaign manager had known about the Hatfield incident for some time, but chose not to use the incident in the campaign. Morse had a copy of the secret report on the Hatfield incident. He was convinced that, because of his court testimony, Hatfield was an unworthy candidate for governor. Over Holmes' objection, Morse decided, in the final days of the campaign, to make the accident a campaign issue. In his Klamath Falls speech, and in addresses in Riddle, Portland, and Baker City, Morse assailed Hatfield as one who "cannot be believed under oath as a witness." The next day, in Medford, Morse repeated his attack on Hatfield. After his talk, Morse was approached by a woman who asked him "Why did you do it?" "I do not intend to let a man run for public office who lies to a jury. I don't intend to let a man lie to a jury and get away with it," was the Senator's curt reply.[27]

Morse's last-minute attack on Mark Hatfield unleashed a wave of indignation across Oregon. Many people viewed Morse's assault as a smear tactic—designed to boost the candidacy of Governor Holmes. Virtually every Democratic leader in the state disavowed Morse. Holmes scrambled to stem the damage. Appearing on Portland television with Congresswoman Edith Green, Holmes told viewers that if "such techniques as the personal attack on Hatfield were necessary to be reelected, then I do not want to be governor that badly.[28]

The public outrage caused a backlash that destroyed Governor Holmes' reelection chances. Hatfield was swept into office 331,900 (55%) to 268,000 for Holmes (45%). As Holmes' defeat became apparent, Morse telephoned the governor to tell him, "I lost the election for you, I lost the election."[29] In fact, Hatfield's victory was expected, regardless of Wayne Morse's blunder.

There was significant drop-off in voter turnout in the November 4 general election compared to 1956. Voters had cast 731,000 ballots in the 1956 governor's contest. In 1958, only 600,000 votes were cast in the Hatfield-Holmes race. Holmes got 268,000 votes in 1958, compared to 369,500 in 1956. His political base had eroded enough in two years that he lost Multnomah, the state's largest Democratic county: Holmes 92,650 to Hatfield's 107,000. Although Hatfield defeated Holmes by nearly 64,000 votes, Hatfield's total was actually 30,000 votes below the 362,000 ballots that GOP candidate Elmo Smith pulled in 1956.

Democrats retained their majority in the Oregon House in 1958 and, for the first time since 1880, they gained a majority in the Senate, winning 19 seats. New faces in the 1959 Legislature were future governors Robert Straub (Democratic Lane County state senator) and Victor Atiyeh (Republican Washington County state representative). Voters approved eight of 13 statewide measures. Oregonians refused to abolish capital punishment, 276,500 no to 264,400 yes.

The issue of capital punishment remained a hot political topic in Oregon for the next 20 years. Voters rejected, by a huge margin, a measure to raise salaries for state legislators.

The Legislature of 1959: Oregon's 50th

Walter J. Pearson, a fixture in Oregon politics, was elected president of the Democratic state Senate in 1959.* Democrat Robert Duncan, a Medford attorney, was speaker of the House in 1959. Democrats Alice Corbett, a Portland businesswoman, and Portland attorney Jean Lewis were the only female senators in 1959. Eight women (six Democrats and two Republicans) served in the House.

Oregon's 50th Legislature convened on January 12. Oregon was preparing to celebrate its centennial. In his inaugural remarks, "Governor Hatfield in typical methodical detail, gave the Legislature his bold program, well spelled out, and Democrats and Republicans alike were brought up short—and unexpectedly—by it." Noting that Oregon was on the cusp of a second century, the new governor said, "[L]et the Oregon taxpayer, in the spirit of the pioneers of a century ago, decide: Is this essential or merely desirable; and if it is only desirable can I afford it?"[30] Several themes cut through Governor Hatfield's address. He wanted to modernize state government, hoping to make it more efficient and less costly by eliminating some Oregon boards and commissions. Hatfield also urged better cooperation between Republicans and Democrats in the House and Senate, and between the legislative and the executive. As an educator himself, Hatfield recommended a bevy of educational and social reforms: more efficient use of public school buildings (implying a longer school year); providing more state financial assistance so more young adults could afford to go to college; enlarging the State Board of Higher Education from nine to 12, and the State Board of Education from seven to nine members; assisting low-income senior citizens by exempting them from paying property taxes up to $7,500 a year; and prohibiting job discrimination because of age.

The legislature got off to an orderly start. Speaker Duncan and President Pearson prepared for the session by having their Legislative Counsel staff begin drafting bills a couple of weeks before the assembly convened. The session began without the rancor and disorganization which had plagued the 1957 Legislature. But Governor Hatfield's call for better working relations between

---

* A Portland insurance man, Pearson had been a prominent Democrat since his election to the Oregon House in 1942 (he served in the 1943 session). Elected to the Senate in 1944, Pearson served in the 1945 and 1947 legislatures.

the legislature and his office fell on deaf ears. Within two weeks, Democrats were openly criticizing the governor for not having come up with his own tax plan for them to consider. Democrats also criticized Hatfield for his hands-off approach to working with the legislature. State Senator Monroe Sweetland

Mark Odom Hatfield

In the pantheon of Oregon political leaders Mark O. Hatfield stands above all other public figures. Mark Hatfield's political life spanned the last half of the 20th century, 1950-1997. No citizen has served the people of Oregon longer than Mark O. Hatfield.

Born in Dallas, Oregon, in 1922, Mark Hatfield grew up there and in Salem. A Navy veteran of World War II, Hatfield earned an undergraduate degree at Willamette University and a graduate degree from Stanford University. Hatfield joined the Willamette faculty in 1949. He was elected to the Oregon House of Representatives in 1950 and re-elected in 1952; he was elected to the state Senate in 1956.

Mark Hatfield, a Republican, was elected secretary of state in 1956, and governor in 1958, when he was 36 years old, defeating Governor Robert Holmes by 64,000 votes. Gov. Hatfield was reelected in 1962, defeating Democratic Attorney General Robert Y. Thornton by 35,000 votes.

Hatfield's eight-year tenure as governor spanned the era of the late Eisenhower, Kennedy, and early Lyndon Johnson presidencies. In short, Mark Hatfield was governor at a time when the United States was torn by its military involvement in Southeast Asia, civil rights struggles at home, and a roller-coaster state and national economy. The Cold War was in high gear as evidenced by the Soviet-U.S. Missile Crisis in Cuba in 1962. Oregon's population was growing at a moderate rate with suburban sprawl continuing at a brisk pace, particularly in metropolitan Portland. Oregon's lumber industry was becoming increasingly automated, producing basic changes, including a steady decline in timber-related jobs. The spiraling cost of public schools and universities was also an issue that faced Hatfield as governor.

Mark Hatfield's meteoric rise in Oregon politics reached its zenith in 1966 when he was elected to the first of five terms in the United States Senate. Hatfield's 30-year Senate career exceeded that of Republican Charles McNary, who had served in the Senate for 26 years. Senator Hatfield's stature grew over the decades. For six years, he served as chairman of the Senate Appropriations Committee, thus making him one of the most powerful politicians in Washington, D.C. Finally, in 1999, at the age of 74, Mark Odom Hatfield retired from politics and came home to Oregon for good. He died in August 2011.

called Hatfield's leadership "lackluster." Consequently, the Democratic legislature went its own way, doing pretty much what it wanted, ignoring the governor, working, instead, from the budget proposals left by Governor Holmes and the reports of its interim committees.

The legislature adjourned on May 6, after 115 days in session. Lawmakers passed a general fund budget of about $310 million for 1959-61, $11 million above what outgoing Governor Holmes had recommended. The biggest increase in the state budget ($8 million) went to the State Board of Higher Education for repair and construction of buildings on Oregon's college campuses. Because of the opposition of Senate President Walter Pearson, the Basic School Support Fund got no additional money for 1959-61. Lawmakers enacted landmark legislation when they established both a community college system in Oregon and a State Scholarship Commission. And funds were increased for special education programs for the mentally challenged, gifted students, and handicapped children.

The legislature made several major and controversial efforts to change Oregon's tax structure. Governor Hatfield proposed a capital gains tax, the loss of income to the state from such a lowered tax to be offset by a two-cent cigarette tax. Oregon was one of only two states that didn't tax cigarettes. The Senate, Democrats and Republicans alike, substituted a sales tax toward the same end, but neither passed. The legislature enacted a property tax relief program for needy senior citizens.

Eighty-nine years after the 1870 Legislature refused to ratify the 15th Amendment to the U.S. Constitution (which guaranteed voting rights to all citizes), the centennial session ratified the amendment. Another vestige of racism was removed from Oregon law with passage of HB639, which eliminated the statutory prohibition of whites marrying Negroes or Mongolians (meaning Asians of Oriental blood).

Lawmakers approved state funds for the construction of a new bridge across the mouth of the Columbia River, connecting Astoria to Washington State. The completion of the bridge subsequently boosted commerce and tourism, opening both states to the ease and convenience of direct auto travel.

Lawmakers commemorated Oregon's (and the legislature's) hundredth birthday by donning costumes and re-enacting the meeting of the state's first legislature at Oregon City in 1859.

Overall, the 1959 session was cautious, orderly, and efficient. Governor Mark Hatfield kept a low profile, and was more of a bystander than an active participant in hammering out budgets. With a coterie of conservative

Democrats and Republicans holding the balance of power, nothing terribly bold came out of the session.

Chapter 14
When Tom Blew the Whistle, 1960-62

An Untimely Death

In 1960, President Dwight Eisenhower's second term was ending and the nation was about to elect a new president. Would Vice President Richard M. Nixon, a Californian, become president? Would Democrats choose a new face after nominating Adlai Stevenson in 1952 and 1956? A handful of Democrats jockeyed for position as seven state primaries got underway. With a May election at the end of the scheduled primaries, Oregon would be in the national political spotlight—if only briefly.

Two days before Oregon's March 11 filing deadline, tragedy struck. Richard Neuberger, Oregon's junior United States senator, died of a cerebral hemorrhage in Portland. Diagnosed with testicular cancer in summer 1957, Neuberger had undergone an operation and lengthy cancer treatment. While his health steadily deteriorated, he had continued to meet his rigorous Senate schedule. In spite of his continuing feud with Sen. Wayne Morse, Neuberger was optimistic and looking forward to running for reelection in 1960. With his popularity at an all-time high, it had seemed a certainty. Working through their shock, Democratic Party leaders scrambled to find a last-minute replacement for Senator Neuberger. Democratic officials convinced Maurine Neuberger, Dick's widow, to run in her husband's place. Though Representatives Edith Green and Charles Porter rushed home to Oregon to test their own possible Senate candidacies, both quickly stepped aside when Mrs. Neuberger said she would run for her husband's seat.

Senator Neuberger's funeral, conducted at Portland's Temple Beth Israel, was somber and sad. "Neuberger's friends arose to speak a last farewell. Those who followed the rabbi included Governor Hatfield, Sen. Lyndon Baines Johnson, former Gov. Robert Holmes, U.S. Supreme Court Justice William O. Douglas and others."[1] Conspicuously absent was Senator Wayne Morse.

257

Maurine Brown Neuberger, a former state representative from Portland, and her husband's closest political confidante, was a household name in Oregon. With a sympathy factor also working in her favor, she was a formidable candidate. Meanwhile, as candidates and their parties campaigned for the May primary, Republican Gov. Mark Hatfield appointed Democrat Hall M. Lusk, an Oregon Supreme Court Justice, to complete Richard Neuberger's term until voters elected a new senator in November.

John Fitzgerald Kennedy

Oregon's May election attracted national attention because of the uniqueness of the state's open presidential primary law. According to Oregon statute, the secretary of state could place the names of any potential Republican and Democratic presidential nominee on Oregon's primary election ballot. This meant that a potential candidate (who might even protest his or her inclusion on Oregon's ballot) could sit back, and with little effort or money spent, find out if he or she could generate enough grassroots support to become a viable presidential candidate.

Only Vice President Nixon was listed on the GOP primary ballot. The Democratic primary was quite a different story, with five prominent candidates: Senators Lyndon Johnson (Texas), Stuart Symington (Missouri), Hubert Humphrey (Minnesota), John Kennedy (Massachusetts), and Wayne Morse of Oregon, whose name appeared on the ballot as a favorite-son candidate.* Six state primaries had taken place prior to Oregon's May election and John Fitzgerald Kennedy had won all six. As the Democratic campaign swung into Oregon, Kennedy had the most and the least to lose of the Democratic candidates. If Kennedy lost in Oregon, he would go to the Democratic National Convention as a recent loser. If he won Oregon, Kennedy would go to the convention as the favorite to win the nomination for president. But John Kennedy was Catholic and the only other Catholic presidential nominee was New York Governor Alfred Smith in 1928. Smith was crushed by Republican Herbert Hoover. A generation later, the Democratic Party faced the question of whether JFK was electable. Would the "Catholic issue" doom his chances? Oregon has always

---

* A favorite-son candidate is typically a prominent state politician whose name is placed on a state ballot or in nomination at the national convention as a courtesy. When Oregon's secretary of state added Senator Wayne Morse's name to the list of Democratic candidates for president in May 1960 it was an acknowledgement of Morse as a Democrat of national stature. When a state delegation casts all or part of their votes for their favorite son they are turning the political spotlight both on their state and on the candidate.

been a Protestant state. During the early 1920s, when Oregon was gripped by an anti-Catholic surge led by a rejuvenated Ku Klux Klan movement, citizens had voted to abolish all parochial and private schools. Had Oregon changed over the decades? Was there enough of an anti-Catholic vote to hurt Kennedy at the polls?

Kennedy pulled out all the stops in Oregon. He brought his mother, Rose, his wife, Jackie, and his brothers Bobby and Teddy into the state to campaign and he outspent his chief rival, Senator Morse, $54,000 to $9,000. Kennedy helped his candidacy immeasurably when he convinced Portland Rep. Edith Green to leave Hubert Humphrey's campaign to join the Kennedy team as its state chair. Representative Green's political stature was immense; to have her in his camp was a real coup. Kennedy scored an impressive victory on May 20. "The final count gave Sen. Kennedy 143,000, Sen. Morse, 90,000. Morse had been trounced in his own home state. His presidential bid was over."[2] Kennedy now strode confidently toward his party's nominating convention.

The Contest for the Senate Nomination in 1960

Maurine Neuberger defeated several minor Democratic candidates, easily winning her party's nomination to fill both the short-term (caused by her husband's death) and the long-term (to succeed her husband by serving her own six-year term in the Senate) position. With 253,000 Democrats casting ballots in the Senate race in May, nearly 200,000 (or 80%) of them voted for Maurine Neuberger. In the Republican Senate primary former Governor Elmo Smith was pitted against three minor candidates. Smith, with 173,000 of the 228,000 Republican votes, won the GOP nomination with ease.[3]

Smith and Neuberger were diametric opposites. Smith was from the conservative right wing of the GOP while Neuberger represented the left, or liberal, wing of the Democratic Party. Voters would have no trouble telling the differences between the candidates. Neuberger was the first woman to be nominated by a major political party for a seat in the U.S. Senate. With a tight contest for president between Republican Richard Nixon and Democrat John F. Kennedy also on the ballot, Smith and Neuberger anticipated a high voter turnout in the fall.

Nixon, Neuberger, and Appling

By November 1960, Oregon, still wedded to a natural-resources-based economy tied to lumber, wood products, and agriculture, had passed through ten years of rather flat economic growth. The stale economy was responsible for the state's small population increase between 1950 and 1960. Oregon added only 247,000 people (to 1.768 million) during the decade. There were 900,616 registered voters in Oregon in November 1960. With the spirited Nixon-Kennedy and Neuberger-Smith races on the ballot along with 15 state measures, legislative races, and tight contests for attorney general and state treasurer, Oregonians were motivated to vote in November and 86.5% did. Oregon was once again a national leader in voter participation.

The presidential contest between Nixon and Kennedy was close all over the country. For the first time, the candidates participated in a series of face-to-face live nationally broadcast television debates. The lesser-known Kennedy appeared well informed, quick witted, and self deprecating. Handsome and charismatic, JFK captivated millions of viewers. To many Americans, Nixon, though a seasoned debater, with first-hand knowledge of world affairs, seemed humorless, uncomfortable, and defensive. Though it is impossible to know how these debates influenced voters, it is generally believed that they gave Senator Kennedy an edge among the millions of undecided voters. In one of the closest presidential elections in history, Kennedy won the popular vote by a margin of 119,000 out of 68.335 million votes cast. In the Electoral College, Kennedy took 313 ballots to 219 for Nixon. Fifteen electoral votes were also cast by Southern electors for Sen. Harry F. Byrd of Virginia.

Both Kennedy and Nixon campaigned in Oregon. True to their traditional Republican inclinations, Oregonians favored Nixon, who polled 408,000 votes in Oregon to Kennedy's 367,400. Vice President Nixon won 52.6% of the Oregon vote, while nationally he got 49.6%. Nixon carried Oregon by winning all parts of the state, including heavily Democratic Multnomah County, where he defeated Kennedy by 3,000 votes.

Republican businessman Howell Appling, Jr. (appointed secretary of state in 1959 by Mark Hatfield when he became governor) clobbered Democrat Monroe Sweetland 415,400 to 343,500 in the secretary of state contest. In southern Oregon, Republican State Senator Edwin Durno upset Democratic Congressman Charles Porter of Eugene in Oregon's 4th Congressional District. Incumbents in Oregon's other congressional districts were reelected with ease: Edith Green in the 3rd District, Walter Norblad in the 1st, and Al Ullman in the 2nd District. In legislative races, Republicans cut into the Democrats' control of the House, reducing their majority to 31 of the 60 seats. In the Senate, Democrats held a 20-10 majority.

The outcome of the Maurine Neuberger-Elmo Smith Senate contest was not close. Neuberger won about 55% of the vote, defeating the former governor by 70,000 votes, 412,800 to 343,000. Maurine B. Neuberger was the first woman elected to the U.S. Senate from Oregon. She was the third woman elected to Congress from Oregon, joining Rep. Nancy Wood Honeyman and Edith Green. The Neuberger-Smith Senate campaign was a low-cost affair. Both candidates spent under $100,000.[4]

The 1961 Legislature

Speaking to a packed House chamber and gallery, Mark Hatfield delivered a 40-minute address. The governor continued to believe in the need to reorganize, streamline, and make state government more efficient. He proposed a General Fund Budget for 1961-63 of $359 million, including $15.55 million for constructing state office buildings. As in 1959, Republican Hatfield would have to work with a Democratic legislature. The new legislature, however, would be far kinder to Hatfield's proposals than the 1959 session had been. With a conservative Democrat-Republican coalition controlling the Senate, along with a nearly equally divided House, Gov. Hatfield was hopeful that more of his legislative package would be enacted in 1961 than had been in 1959.

Harry Boivin, a conservative Klamath Falls Democrat, was elected Senate president by a vote of 19-10. The choice of Boivin ripped apart the majority Democrats and the split between urban, liberal Democrats and rural, conservative Democrats (who allied themselves with the 10 Republican senators to elect Boivin) would continue to the end of the decade. Democrat Robert Duncan of Medford was reelected House speaker. Despite holding a slim one-vote majority, Duncan made little effort to include the Republican minority in leadership positions. "Some Republicans were chagrined and possibly embittered when Speaker Duncan appointed only one Republican to chair one of the twenty house committees; and Duncan appointed only five Republicans to vice-chairmanships, although some of these were important committees."[5] Six women served in the 1961 Oregon House.

The legislature dragged on for 124 days, making it the second-longest session ever. Adjourning at 8:01 p.m. on May 10, 1961, the assembly concluded its business in spite of the threat posed by the badly divided Democratic Senate. What did lawmakers accomplish? As usual, the biennial state budget took center stage. Governor Hatfield's 1961-63 budget passed Democratic scrutiny. Lawmakers passed a state general fund budget of $366.78 million, about $8 million more than the governor had proposed. Basic School Support was increased to 38%. Counties received a new source of revenue that they would share with cities, in the distribution of state liquor tax revenues. Critical environmental legislation was enacted. The State Sanitary Authority (which was later replaced by the Department of Environmental Quality or DEQ), established in 1938, was strengthened, and granted power to clean up polluted waters in Oregon. This landmark legislation was a new beginning for Oregon. For the next 20 years environmental concerns were among the leading issues debated in Oregon. In fact, the flurry of environmental laws passed over the next two decades placed Oregon among the world's leading environmental reformers.

Morse Ascending and the Election of 1962

Senator Wayne Morse was up for reelection in 1962. Did Oregonians want their maverick senator to represent them for a fourth term? Or were they fed-up with Morse's frequent pettiness, his angry outbursts aimed at foe and friend alike? Had he simply burned too many political bridges?

Since 1954, when Morse changed his party affiliation to Democrat, the senator had generally worked against the Republican administration of President Dwight Eisenhower. The election of John Kennedy in November 1960 changed things in Washington, D.C. With Democratic control of both the White House and Congress, Wayne Morse, with 17 years of Senate seniority, was catapulted into Washington's inner circle of power. As chairman of the Senate Subcommittee on Education, Morse was now one of the president's main point men in Congress: the fate of JFK's education program rested with Oregon's Wayne Morse and with Congresswoman Edith Green, chair of the House Committee on Education. By summer 1962, Wayne Morse's stature had grown dramatically—in the Senate, the White House, and Oregon.

Nevertheless, a private poll in December 1961 showed that Morse trailed his chief Republican rival, Sig Unander. In early 1962, writer A. Robert Smith published his long-awaited biography of Wayne Morse, *The Tiger in the Senate*. Smith's balanced account of Morse showed him warts and all. Morse, with his usual thin skin, took Smith's criticisms as a personal attack, describing the book "publicly as a 'premeditated character assassination' sponsored by 'political enemies' who wished to see him defeated in the fall."[6] The book and Morse's reaction to it received enormous press coverage, putting Morse in the center of Oregon's political spotlight.

The Oregon primary was set for May 18, 1962. With only one Democratic opponent, Morse ignored the primary campaign. Running on his incumbency, superior campaign organization, and $19,000, he easily won his party's nomination with about 75% of the vote (183,400 to 46,200). The Republican primary went as expected. Sig Unander, with lots of family money and name familiarity, defeated five opponents. His chief rival was one-term Congressman Edwin Durno of southern Oregon, who pulled 73,000 votes to Sig Unander's 107,000. Unander's total was barely 50% of the GOP vote of 213,000. Compared to Morse's 183,000 votes and a Democratic registration edge of 73,000 in Oregon, Sig Unander had a big mountain to climb if he was to topple Wayne Morse.

Sig Unander was a stolid man. Tall, broad-shouldered, dark-haired, with tortoise-shell glasses and tailored suits, Unander looked like a banker. Reserved and cautious, he presented a sharp contrast to the more fiery, in-your-face style of Wayne Morse. Throughout the summer and early fall, the Senate contest remained close. Morse held his slim lead in the polls. Still, Unander dogged Morse's steps.

Morse had a solid standing with the timber industry, which was part of his strength. He knew that Oregon's health and that of the timber industry were joined. "Early on, Morse chose to ally himself with the smaller operators, usually the buyers of timber, rather than such giants as Weyerhaeuser, Crown Zellerbach, and Georgia-Pacific, each of which owned or controlled many thousands of acres of lucrative forest and considered Morse their enemy. By 1962, however, most of the smaller operators had become aware of how valuable Morse had been to them."[7]

On October 22, just two weeks before the general election in Oregon, the United States was plunged into the Cuban Missile Crisis. For six days, Kennedy stared down Soviet Premier Nikita Khrushchev. For a week it seemed the United States and the Soviet Union might go to war in America's backyard. When the crisis began, Wayne Morse (a ranking member of the Senate Foreign Relations Committee) had immediately returned to Washington. His sudden departure reminded Oregonians just how important their senator had become in the nation's capital. In May, he was elected to a fourth term in the Senate. Morse rolled over Sig Unander, 344,700 to 291,600.

Incumbent Gov. Mark Hatfield shared top billing with Morse on Oregon's 1962 primary ballot. Hatfield took 80% of the GOP vote and again headed for the November election. The Democratic gubernatorial primary featured two of the state's best-known politicians, Attorney General Robert Y. Thornton and former Oregon Senate president and state treasurer, Walter Pearson. Thornton represented the liberal wing of the party, Pearson the conservative. Thornton won 148,000 to 61,500.

The contest in the 4th District was Oregon's most interesting congressional race in 1962. Two years earlier, Charles O. Porter, a two-term Eugene Democrat, had been upset by Republican Edwin Durno, who had given up his House seat to run for the Senate in 1962. Consequently, the seat had no incumbent. Three prominent Democrats vied for the nomination: Robert Duncan, speaker of the Oregon House, State Senator Robert Straub of Eugene, and former Congressman Charles Porter. All three were liberal Democrats. Duncan won the primary, edging Porter (18,750 to 17,650). Straub was third with 14,450 votes. State Representative Carl Fisher, running unopposed, won the Republican nomination to face Bob Duncan in November. Duncan defeated Fisher with 54% of the vote (Duncan: 83,700, Fisher: 71,500). All three incumbents prevailed in Oregon's other U.S. House races.

The governor's race between incumbent Republican Mark Hatfield and Democrat Robert Y. Thornton was closer than expected. Hatfield's ability to get Democrats to vote across party lines resulted in his narrow victory in November (345,500 to 310,400), overcoming the Democrats' big edge in voter registration. Hatfield outspent Thornton $90,000 to $13,000.

The 1962 Oregon legislative races featured lots of close contests. Democrats held onto their 31-29 majority in the House. A young Portland attorney named Robert Packwood was elected to the House, as were two other future leaders of note: Democrat James Redden (future Oregon attorney general and federal judge) and Republican John Dellenback (future U.S. congressman). Democrats increased their grip on the Senate, where they would hold a 21-9 advantage in the 1963 session.

Tom McCall Makes a Big Splash

On the night of November 21, 1962, viewers settled down for an evening of television. Portland's Channel 8, KGW-TV, was airing a documentary special and thousands of citizens tuned in to watch. The program, *Pollution in Paradise*, produced by KGW, had an immediate and stunning effect on viewers. Portland's Tom McCall, a commentator and reporter at KGW since 1956, researched, wrote, and narrated the one-hour documentary about air and water pollution in Oregon. Never had a local TV station produced a documentary like *Pollution in Paradise*. Working with Tom Dargan, program director at KGW, McCall had devoted most of the year to producing the documentary. The film touched on a range of environmental issues, including the use of chemical fertilizers and pesticides, smokestack emissions from lumber mills and pulp and paper plants, water and air quality, and the impact of pollution on plant and animal species, particularly fish (and especially salmon). The central theme of the film was the Willamette River. Since the earliest days of settlement in Oregon, the Willamette had been the region's lifeline. All of the largest cities in western

Oregon were situated on its banks. For 130 years the Willamette had been a river highway for agricultural goods, people, and livestock. It generated electric power for Eugene and Oregon City. Farmers drew water from the Willamette to irrigate their crops and water their livestock.

Unfortunately, the river was also used "as a trough for raw municipal sewage and industrial wastes." Slaughterhouses dumped animal waste and manufacturing companies dumped in used chemicals. Pulp mills, the worst offenders, flushed their wastes into the Willamette. The cocktail of chemicals and raw sewage fed the algae that eventually "covered the river like a tepid green sheet."[8]

The issue of pollution in the Willamette had been around since the 1920s. The city of Portland conducted research studies of the river and by the early 1930s the culprit had been identified. The Willamette's deplorable condition was largely caused by the five pulp mills operating on or near the river. In 1933, Portland voters approved a $6 million bond measure to build sewage-treatments plants along the river. They were never built.

By 1938, the Willamette's polluted state produced a serious health hazard. Scientists found E. coli bacteria. Scientists monitored the river over the next 25 years. Because of legislative inaction and a veto by Gov. Charles Martin, Oregonians in 1938 (by initiative petition) passed a statewide ballot measure establishing the Oregon State Sanitary Authority, empowering the agency to clean up Oregon's rivers. But the authority did little to alleviate pollution in the Willamette. With few enforceable pollution laws in Oregon, and being underfunded, understaffed, and susceptible to lobbying pressures from the pulp mill owners, the Authority accomplished little over the next two decades.

Tom McCall began to investigate the record of the Sanitary Authority in late 1961 and quickly concluded that, despite the Authority's claim that the Willamette was cleaner than it had been in 20 years, the river was as polluted as ever, and the Sanitary Authority had not done its job. Trailing a KGW cameraman, McCall set out to photograph examples of pollution and environmental degradation in Oregon. "We started filming way up with the cleanest water and the smallest rivulet contributing to the Willamette River system. Then, we showed what happened to this water, how it had become one of the most polluted rivers in the West. It was unfit for swimming. Indeed, it was so filled with wastes during the fall that salmon could not move upstream. The oxygen level of the water at the mouth of the river was nearly zero."[9] Besides blowing the whistle on the biggest polluters (Crown-Zellerbach and Georgia-Pacific), McCall pointed at the legislature, claiming that it had repeatedly failed to pass laws to give the Sanitary Authority the necessary tools to clean up the Willamette and its tributaries.

Pollution in Paradise was a sensation, a call to arms. Radio and television commentators, along with leading newspapers, discussed and wrote about the film's significance. At work and on the street, in classrooms and barber shops, Oregonians talked about it. The people (as McCall and Dargan had hoped) were aroused to action. They demanded that the Willamette be cleaned up, that environmental laws be passed to protect Oregon's fragile ecology and special beauty. Oregon would be forever changed by the forces unleashed by Tom McCall's film.

Tom McCall's face never appeared in *Pollution in Paradise*. Only his voice was heard. But what a voice it was. McCall was one of five children reared on a remote ranch near Prineville, Oregon. His parents were natives of New England. His maternal grandfather, Thomas William Lawson, was one of the richest men in America. Tom and his siblings were born at "Dreamwold," their grandfather's estate near Boston, Massachusetts. For half of his first nine years, Tom McCall lived at Dreamwold with his family, where they were attended by nannies, butlers, maids, and chauffeurs. McCall's paternal grandfather was Samuel Walker McCall, a 10-term Massachusetts congressman and governor of Massachusetts. McCall idolized his grandfather and proudly invoked his name throughout his life. From his mother, Dorothy Lawson McCall, Tom and his siblings developed their distinctly "not Western" accent. As a result, every time Tom McCall opened his mouth in public every Oregonian immediately recognized who it was. His distinct voice was a fundamental aspect of his celebrity.

Because of his regular exposure on KGW TV, Tom McCall was, by 1960, a well-known personality in Oregon. At 6 feet, 5 inches, with a large head, prominent nose, long, jutting jaw, and distinctive voice, Tom McCall was hard to ignore or forget. *Pollution in Paradise* changed his life. The documentary aroused the public like never before to the threat of environmental pollution. Oregonians were energized: environmental quality must be elevated to the top of Oregon's political agenda. The documentary created a new hero in Oregon, a new people's spokesman for environmental protection: Tom McCall. Two years after the broadcast of *Pollution in Paradise* Tom McCall was elected Oregon secretary of state; and two years after that he was elected governor.

Organized Confusion

The Oregon Legislature met twice in 1963: in regular session, January 14-June 3, and in special session, November 11-December 2. Both sessions were unusual.

Television cameras were present for the first time when Oregon's 52nd Legislature convened on January 14. Cameras, banks of bright lights, and miles of cable snaked through the main floor of the House, its side and upper viewing galleries. Symbolically, state government was further opening its doors to the public, welcoming citizens to become more informed and interested in how their elected leaders made decisions.

Mark O. Hatfield, Oregon's telegenic young governor, delivered his third Opening Day address, recommending a 1963-65 budget of $405.279 million He also proposed establishing a State Department of Commerce; a cigarette tax; fixed maximum speed limits for traffic; chemical tests for intoxication while driving; mandatory auto seat belts; additional basic school support; creation of an Oregon Port Authority; review of the Juvenile Code and establishment of a genuine public defender system; salary increases for state workers; consolidating the state boards of elementary and secondary education into one board; and the establishment of a committee to study property-tax reform with a report to the 1965 Legislature.[10] Ignoring the recent brouhaha caused by the TV broadcast of *Pollution in Paradise,* Hatfield said little about environmental issues. Finally, he appealed to the Democratic majorities to work with him in a spirit of cooperation.

The honeymoon between Gov. Hatfield and legislators did not last long. Indeed, the session turned out to be the longest to date as well as one of the most contentious and disorderly in recent memory. Senate and House Democrats couldn't get along with one another, either within or between chambers. Rural legislators believed that urban lawmakers were trying to set the agenda. Democrats held a slim 31-29 majority in the House. It took 22 ballots to choose Coos Bay's Clarence Barton as speaker. Barton knew that a single Democratic defection would paralyze the House and remove Democrats from power; he had to walk on eggs to keep his fractious caucus in line. Urban Democrats in the Senate were frustrated when a handful of fellow conservatives and the 10 minority Republicans joined to form a majority that made conservative Democrat Ben Musa Senate president. Finally, relations between Republican Mark Hatfield and Democratic leaders quickly soured, Hatfield calling lawmakers "meat axe" legislators and Senate President Musa labeling the governor a "spy," intent on intrigue and disrupting the Assembly.

New House and Senate Districts

New updated House and Senate district boundaries had been drawn in 1962. For much of Oregon's history, her legislative districts had been unfairly weighted toward the rural, less-populated areas of the state. For most of the 20th century, Oregon's urban-suburban areas had been underrepresented in the legislature. After re-apportionment in 1962, eastern Oregon lost four legislative districts, and those seats were shifted to the Portland suburbs and Willamette Valley, where the greatest population growth had occurred since 1950. Eight women, the most ever, served in the '63 House. Nine lawyers and 15 businessmen served in the House and the same number in the Senate.

The House frequently lapsed into turmoil. On one occasion, Speaker Barton, observing a lobbyist dropping notes to legislators from the upper gallery, stood on a chair and yelled at the lobbyist to stop such activity or he'd be banned from the chamber. Another time, Barton, trying to restore order, banged his gavel so hard that it broke. In the final days of the session, "the House, badly split and appearing leaderless, spent an hour in parliamentary confusion."[11]

The session bogged down early over the question of a state sales tax. Three different bills passed either the House or Senate—only to be rejected by the other chamber. Failing to reach a compromise, lawmakers gave up. Lawmakers devoted weeks to wrestling with the issue of salary increases for state workers and public-college employees. In a tense Sunday session, a compromise was reached, giving a raise to state police and other state employees, including the governor and other statewide elected officials.

Under intense public pressure, lawmakers passed a tough new environmental protection law. KGW-TV's Tom Dargan had earlier sent copies of *Pollution in Paradise* to school and community meetings around the state. Then Dargan scheduled and promoted a second broadcast in January 1963, just days before the new legislature was to meet. Lawmakers were inundated with letters and phone calls from thousands of aroused citizens. Ted Hallock, a rookie Portland senator, introduced a bill to give the state the power to close a polluting company. The bill passed and Governor Hatfield signed it, making it Oregon's most important attempt to that time to clean up the polluted Willamette River. "Passage of the bill signaled a change in Oregon politics. For the next 20 years politicians made the environment a high priority. Oregonians, they knew, wanted—and demanded—results."[12]

Legislators failed to refer a package of measures to revise the Oregon Constitution, as had been recommended by a blue-ribbon panel chaired by former governors Sprague and Holmes. Critics castigated legislators for their inability to move the recommendations to a public vote.

Lawmakers passed 653 bills in 1963. Hatfield vetoed nine and allowed 25 bills, including 19 with appropriations, to become law without his signature.

Lawmakers set a General Fund budget for 1963-65 of about $404 million, cutting $8 million for Basic School Support out of Hatfield's budget, but added $10.16 million for Higher Education. One big reality with which lawmakers had grappled was this: state spending in recent years had been growing faster that state revenue. The budget surplus of recent years was gone. Grudgingly, lawmakers referred a proposed increase in personal and corporate income taxes to voters in a special election set for October 15, 1963. The revenues from these new taxes were necessary to balance the state budget for 1963-65. Unfortunately for lawmakers, voters rejected the tax hikes, 103,700 yes, to 362,800 opposed. Consequently, Governor Hatfield called the legislature into special session on November 11, 1963, Veteran's Day.

When lawmakers convened in special session, Governor Hatfield told them that he favored cutting the budget rather than passing any new taxes. The Senate agreed, but the Democratic House did not. House Democrats proposed a number of new taxes. A bill to raise the tax on a pack of cigarettes by 4 cents did pass the House but died in the Senate. The House also passed a bill to cut legislators' monthly salaries from $250 to $200. The Senate buried it.

Dallas, November 22, 1963

The special session of the Oregon Legislature was in its 11th day, when, on November 22, 1963, TV news bulletins broke a terrible story: President John F. Kennedy had been shot in Dallas, Texas. News of the shooting and Kennedy's death was announced in the Oregon Senate by President Ben Musa just before noon, local time. Vice-President Lyndon Johnson took the oath of office as JFK's successor aboard Air Force One.

The special session of the Oregon Legislature recessed for nine days before reconvening on December 2. Legislators, reflecting the mood of the nation, conducted themselves with decorum and purpose. Lawmakers "gave authority to Governor Hatfield to cut the 1963-65 General Fund budget [by $43.5 million], down to $361 million, including cuts in school aid."[13] They also revised a $30 million bond measure for higher education construction they had passed in the regular session and referred it to the May 1964 primary ballot (in May, voters approved the bond measure 327,200 to 252,400 against).

The most controversial proposal coming out of the special session related to the creation of a Space Age Industrial Park at Boardman, a small town in northeastern Oregon (and within the district of Senate President Ben Musa). Governor Hatfield, an early backer of the Boardman project, proposed that the state lease (for 77 years) 100,000 acres of state land to the Boeing Company of Seattle for an industrial park at an annual fee of $60,000. After an afternoon of debate the House passed the bill 33-26 and referred it to the Senate, where it passed 20-10, all 10 urban Democrats voting against Ben Musa's pet bill. The special session then adjourned.

An Election to Remember

The May 15, 1964, Oregon presidential primary was notable because of the race for the Republican nomination, one of the most scrutinized, analyzed, wide-open, hotly contested, and expensive affairs in the history of Oregon politics. Six prominent Republicans were on the ballot: Governor Nelson Rockefeller of New York, Senator Henry Cabot Lodge of Massachusetts, Arizona Senator Barry Goldwater, former senator and vice president Richard Nixon of California, William Scranton, governor of Pennsylvania, and Senator Margaret Chase Smith of Maine.

"The campaign in Oregon, coming after the surprising Lodge victory in [the] New Hampshire [primary], was clearly a major test of the leading aspirants. Sen. Goldwater was well known in the state and was reportedly the personal favorite of most of the county chairmen."[14] Backers of Sen. Lodge also worked here to put together a viable organization for their candidate, but Lodge, Goldwater, and Nixon were busy campaigning in more populous states, and their backers relied heavily on mass mailings and commercials. Governor Rockefeller, with gobs of money, and a phalanx of volunteers and a statewide organization, did campaign and won the Oregon primary, pulling 33% of the GOP vote, 94,200 votes to Senator Lodge's 79,200.* Combined, the Republican candidates spent about $675,000 in Oregon, most of it attributable to Rockefeller's expenditure of $460,000—an amount exceeded only by Senator Wayne Morse's campaign against Douglas McKay in 1956. Rockefeller worked harder here than any of the GOP candidates—and it only cost him about $5 a vote to win the primary.

President Lyndon Johnson ran unopposed in Oregon's Democratic primary, pulling 272,100 votes. George Wallace, segregationist governor of Alabama, received 1,365 Democratic write-in votes.

The top GOP vote getter in May was Tom Lawson McCall, candidate for secretary of state, who pulled nearly 210,000 votes. McCall's TV documentary, *Pollution in Paradise*, had catapulted McCall and the protection of Oregon's environment to the front of Oregon's political agenda. Outspoken and controversial, McCall now had his sights on high elective office. His popularity seemed to cut across party lines, too. With Secretary of State Howell Appling, Jr., retiring, McCall had no incumbent to challenge him. And he had the blessing of Oregon's popular governor, Mark Hatfield, as well as Appling's. McCall crushed

---

* Senator Goldwater ran third with 50,100 votes (18%), just ahead of Richard Nixon's 48,300 ballots.

Portland appliance-store owner Dan Mosee in the primary, taking 79% of the vote. McCall's Democratic opponent in November would be State Senator Alfred Corbett.

The third notable race of May 1964 featured Democrat Bob Straub and two opponents seeking their party's nomination for state treasurer. Straub, a former state senator, Lane County commissioner, and state Democratic Party chairman, pulled 143,000 votes or about 55,000 more votes than his opponents combined.

The Republican National Convention met in San Francisco in the summer of 1964. Governor Mark Hatfield delivered the keynote address and served as the convention's temporary chair. It was a bitterly divisive convention, with liberal Nelson Rockefeller fighting for the nomination against conservative Barry Goldwater, who won the nomination. Many Oregon Republicans thought Goldwater was too far right to be elected. Mark Hatfield campaigned for Goldwater in both Oregon and California, but Tom McCall, GOP nominee for secretary of state, a liberal by conviction, and facing a Democratic registration edge of 512,000 to 402,300, made no public endorsement of Goldwater.

President Johnson rolled over Barry Goldwater in the general election in November, defeating him by over 16 million popular votes. With 85% of Oregonians voting, the president carried Oregon with nearly 64% of the vote, 501,000 to the senator's 282,800. However, "Oregon was the only state in the Union in which the Republicans were able to score a significant victory in 1964, winning 32-28 control of the House of Representatives, reversing the 31-29 Democratic edge of two years before."[15] The surprising GOP House victories are attributed to the efforts of two Republican leaders: Howell Appling, Jr., and young Robert Packwood, freshman legislator from Portland. Appling raised money so Packwood could recruit and train young Republican candidates and their campaign workers. Packwood sent recruits to canvass door to door, to conduct phone banks, place lawn signs in neighborhoods, and do target mailings. Bob Packwood introduced modern campaign tactics into Oregon politics. Six of the nine candidates recruited by Packwood won House seats, a couple in traditional Democratic districts. For the first time in 10 years, the 1965 Oregon House would be Republican.

Republican Tom McCall faced Democrat Alf Corbett in the race for secretary of state. Corbett was a highly regarded legislator, noted for his intelligence and integrity. And, like McCall, Corbett was liberal. McCall realized that he faced several potential obstacles: he was a Republican in a state with a Democratic registration edge of 77,000; a host of influential Republican Party backers were wary of McCall because of his withering criticism of corporate polluters; and party conservatives were miffed with him for having done nothing to help Barry Goldwater's candidacy for president. None of it mattered. In November, Tom McCall pulled 432,000 votes for secretary of state (150,00 more votes than Goldwater's Oregon total), cutting heavily into the Democratic vote—his total exceeded by 30,000 the number of registered Republicans in Oregon. Alf Corbett lost to McCall by about 96,000 votes. Overnight, Tom McCall had climbed into the upper echelon of Republican politicians in Oregon; suddenly, Mark Hatfield had a political rival he could not ignore.

Bob Straub won the treasurer's race against an aging incumbent, Republican Howard Belton, by less than 18,000 votes (389,100 to 371,600). Straub would be a fixture in state government for the next 15 years.

The featured congressional race in 1964 was in the 1st District, where nine-term representative Walter Norblad had died. First District GOP leaders picked Astoria attorney Wendell Wyatt to replace him. Challenging Wyatt was Democrat Blaine Whipple, a real estate developer who had run against Norblad in 1962. Voters had never elected a Democrat since the district was established in 1892. Whipple, boosted by Lyndon Johnson's long coattails, lost to Wyatt by about 14,000 votes, 122,000 to 108,000. There were no changes in Oregon's other congressional districts, where Democrats Al Ullman, Edith Green, and Bob Duncan were reelected with at least 65% of the vote.

The 1965 Legislature

The 53rd Legislature convened in Salem on January 11, 1965. Although Democrats controlled the Senate 19-11, a coalition of six dissident conservative Democrats, led by Ben Musa, Harry Boivin, and Debbs Potts, and the 11-member Republican caucus again took control. "The dominant figure in the Senate was Ben Musa, stubborn against change, except for such changes as he wanted."[16]

Republicans took charge of the House, 32-28. Charles Sprague, editor and owner of the *Statesman*, was impressed with the quality of House members and their leader, Speaker F. F. Montgomery. Sprague wrote, "Both political parties should turn to the House for their leaders, not to the moribund Senate. The voters will have their chance in 1966."[17] There were seven women representatives in 1965, including newcomer Betty Roberts, a high school social studies teacher. Another newcomer was a young Reedsport optometrist named Jason Boe. House Republicans were led by a diverse group of particularly able leaders: Speaker Montgomery, Stafford Hansell of Hermiston, John Mosser of Beaverton, John Dellenbeck of Medford, and Portland's Robert Packwood. This group represented a blend of conservative, moderate, and liberal inclinations—and they represented the new face of the Republican Party of Oregon.

The '65 session lasted 124 days, adjourning on May 14. Lawmakers approved a General Fund budget of $485 million for 1965-67, an increase of about $81 million over the previous budget and an amount $25 million above what Governor Hatfield had recommended.

Lawmakers revised Oregon's workers' compensation law, increased benefits by about 25% and extended coverage to include 200,000 additional employees; employers were given the choice of obtaining job injury insurance for employees from the state fund or a private firm, or to self-insure.[18]

The only new tax proposal to come out of the session was a cigarette tax, which lawmakers sent to voters as a state ballot measure. Voters passed the tax (4 cents per pack) in May 1966, 310,700 in favor and 182,000 opposed. The projected $4.5 million in new revenue was designated for local property tax relief and to cities and counties to fund local programs.

Other actions included the creation of a state corrections division to combine all the state's prisons into one entity; a bill to allow local school districts to provide free textbooks to poor students; and the requirement that persons arrested for drunken driving would be required to take a sobriety test, a bill pushed by Governor Hatfield as part of his enhanced traffic safety program.

But, there were failings, too, important decisions deferred. For example, a 1962 U.S. Supreme Court ruling had established the principle of one-person/one-vote, meaning that the number of people living in each congressional district must be approximately equal. Just how disproportional were Oregon's congressional districts as of May 1966? These are the figures: 1st Congressional District (northeast corner of Oregon), 517,678 residents; 2nd District (eastern Oregon), 265,164; 3rd District (Multnomah County), 522,813; 4th District (southwest Oregon), 463,032. The regular session ended, however, with no legislative action on either this ruling or the festering issue of revising Oregon's constitution.

The day after the regular session adjourned, Governor Hatfield called legislators back to Salem in special session on May 25. It took five days, but lawmakers did realign Oregon's congressional district boundaries to assure compliance with the court ruling. The bill passed 17-11 in the Senate and 35-24 in the House. Unfortunately, it had taken a U.S. Supreme Court ruling and the threat of federal court action to force Oregon's politicians to do what they should have done three years earlier. The task of redrawing Oregon's political boundaries (to reflect changes in population) often tied legislators in knots, causing partisan

Thomas William Lawson McCall

Few politicians have had as deep and lasting an impact on Oregon as did Tom McCall. Journalist, TV and radio commentator, top aide to Gov. Douglas McKay, legislative committee administrator, award-winning documentary film maker, secretary of state, and governor, Tom McCall was Oregon's quintessential public servant.

He was born on March 22, 1913, at Dreamwold, the estate of his maternal grandfather, Thomas William Lawson, one of the richest men in America. His paternal grandfather, Samuel McCall, was a 10-term Massachusetts congressman and three-time governor. His mother, Dorothy Lawson, was a beautiful Boston debutante who had a sharp tongue and an independent streak. Until he was nine, Tom and his siblings lived part of each year at Dreamwold, waited on by maids, butlers, nannies, and chauffeurs. Indeed, it was his upbringing in New England that shaped McCall's unusual Boston-like accent. The McCall children grew up in an atmosphere of wealth and privilege, politics and influence. From age nine to adulthood Tom's family lived on a remote ranch on the Crooked River near Prineville, Oregon. It was here that McCall developed his lifelong love of the land.

McCall graduated from the University of Oregon in 1936 with a degree in journalism. He moved north to Moscow, Idaho, to write for the *News-Review*, one of the town's two daily newspapers. Rail-thin and 6 foot 5, McCall became a local favorite. He married Audrey Owen of Spokane in 1939. In 1942 the couple left Idaho for Portland, where McCall took a job with the *Oregonian*, then as news-anchor for radio station KGW. After a stint in the Navy at the end of World War II, McCall returned to Portland in early 1946, landing a job as host of a nightly talk show on radio station KEX. As a radio personality, he was known by the name Lawson McCall.

bickering and, on occasion, dividing lawmakers and prolonging sessions. No wonder lawmakers deferred this onerous task, in the future letting the secretary of state or the courts decide where Oregon's legislative and congressional district boundaries would be.

Maurine Neuberger Leaves the Senate

U.S. Senator Maurine Newberger, remarried to a Boston psychiatrist, announced on November 1, 1965, that she would not seek reelection. She would leave Washington when her term ended in January 1967. Her announcement shook Oregon's political establishment. Who would run for the seat? Democrats Edith

McCall took up the cause of civil rights and the plight of the poor and unrepresented. Like his grandfather Samuel McCall, he was a maverick Republican, a populist-progressive at heart. In June 1949, McCall was hired as top aide to Oregon's new governor, Douglas McKay. For the next decade he became a fixture at the Capitol in Salem, returning from time to time to Portland as a political commentator for TV stations KPTV, and KGW. McCall's longtime dream to enter politics himself was realized in 1954 when he won the Republican nomination for the U.S. House seat in Oregon's 3rd District. But his opponent, Democrat Edith S. Green, defeated him by 9,600 votes.

In 1962, McCall wrote, produced, and narrated an award-winning documentary film, *Pollution in Paradise*, about the pollution of the Willamette River. The film, televised throughout the state, galvanized public opinion, awakening Oregonians to the need to clean up the Willamette. *Pollution in Paradise* made Tom McCall Oregon's leading crusader on behalf of conserving the state's environment. For the rest of his life, Oregonians considered him their voice in matters pertaining to the preservation and conservation of the state's forests, farmlands, rivers, and public beaches.

Tom McCall was elected secretary of state in 1964. Two years later, he was elected governor. As governor, McCall became one of America's best-known politicians. As an environmentalist, Tom McCall helped to shape the state and national debate favoring political solutions to conserve natural resources. During Gov. McCall's tenure, 1967-75, the legislature enacted several of Oregon's landmark environmental bills: the Beach Bill, to preserve the public beaches along Oregon's Pacific coast; Senate Bill 100, establishing statewide land-use planning; and the Bottle Bill, which placed a deposit on certain bottles to encourage their recycling.

Always controversial, the charismatic McCall dominated state politics from 1965 to 1975. In 1972, he developed prostate cancer and decided not to challenge fellow Republican, Senator Mark Hatfield, in the May primary. Tom McCall died of cancer in 1982, age 69.

The definitive biography of Tom McCall is Brent Walth's *Fire at Eden's Gate*, 1994. You won't find a better source about McCall and his colorful life.

Green, or Bob Duncan, or, perhaps, Al Ullman? For the Republicans, how about former governors Sprague or Elmo Smith? Oregonians did not have to wait long for an answer: Governor Mark Hatfield, a politician who had never lost an election, threw his hat into the ring. Walter Huss, a conservative Portland minister, would challenge Hatfield in the May 1966 GOP primary.

Two prominent Democrats filed for the Senate seat: Congressman Bob Duncan and Howard Morgan, member of the Federal Trade Commission, former legislator, Oregon Public Utility commissioner, and state Democratic Party chairperson. The Morgan-Duncan contest turned out to be a public debate on the escalating Vietnam War. Morgan was a "dove," a critic of American participation in the war; Bob Duncan was a "hawk," an outspoken supporter of President Lyndon Johnson's Vietnam policy. "Morgan, in spite of support from peace groups, from [Senator] Wayne Morse, and a last-minute endorsement from Edith Green, never seemed to develop an effective organization or campaign. Duncan commuted from Washington, hammered on the Vietnam issue, and won handily, carrying every county with a total of 161,200 votes to Morgan's 89,200."[19] Duncan's victory came in spite of his being outspent by Morgan $46,000 to $29,000.

Tom Makes His Move

With Mark Hatfield's term coming to an end, the office of governor was open in 1966. Tom McCall, in only his second year as secretary of state, filed in January for the Republican gubernatorial nomination; two political unknowns filed against him. State treasurer Bob Straub filed for the Democratic nomination; like McCall, he would face two minor candidates in the May primary.

There were 924,341 registered voters in Oregon in May 1966: 507,600 Democrats (50% voted in the primary), 399,200 Republicans (58% voted in the primary), and 17,440 "other." Tom McCall won the Republican nomination 216,000 to 30,300 for the runner-up, John Reynolds. Meanwhile, Bob Straub cruised to the Democratic nomination, besting State Senate President Ben Musa, 182,700 to 41,600.

A Republican Juggernaut

A Republican tidal wave swept across Oregon and the West in the November 1966 general election. Republicans won an additional 47 seats in the U.S. House, one of those in Oregon. The election of 1966 was one of the most significant in state history because it focused on the careers of two of Oregon's pre-eminent politicians of the 20th century: Mark Hatfield and Tom McCall.

The Hatfield-Duncan Senate race was a fiercely competitive, down-to-the-wire battle. In an era when close Senate elections were common in Oregon, the Duncan-Hatfield contest was a classic.* Mark Hatfield was the better-known candidate, having won three statewide elections. Duncan had never run statewide. But there were over 100,000 more registered Democrats in Oregon than Republicans. And Duncan had his position as a member of Congress along with the prestige and perks associated with that office.

---

* The Cordon-Neuberger race of 1954, the McKay-Morse contest of 1956, and the 1968 Packwood-Morse campaign were all hard-fought battles with narrow margins of victory.

Because he was an outspoken hawk, Duncan incurred the enmity of Senator Wayne Morse, a vocal critic of the Vietnam War. Morse endorsed Republican Mark Hatfield for the Senate. "Morse was supporting Hatfield for one reason: Hatfield opposed the war. Hatfield's statements on Vietnam could have been written in Morse's office; and with his election to the Senate, Morse would have a valuable anti-war ally in the upper chamber . . . If Oregon Democrats could not understand Morse's position on the election, then they could not understand how transcendent Vietnam had become to him." For Wayne Morse the Vietnam War was the single most important issue facing the nation. "From Morse's perspective, a vote for Duncan would be a vote to increase the blood quotient from Vietnam, and no Oregonian should cast a ballot for such a despicable purpose."[20]

The Duncan campaign was beset with problems. The congressman remained in Washington, attending to House business, when he should perhaps have been campaigning at home. Hatfield's campaign, in contrast, was a "model of near perfection Oregonians had come to expect from the governor and his able staff. [They] raised $374,000, placed 200,000 phone calls in Multnomah [County] alone; received the endorsement of 40 newspapers; inserted 600,000 flyers in state newspapers; secured endorsements from the Teamsters,' Musicians,' and Longshoreman's unions and many individual labor leaders . . . and generally pre-empted the middle-of-the-road."[21]

Voters elected Mark Hatfield their new U.S. Senator in November. But, it was close, the final results not known until the next day: Hatfield 354,400 to Duncan's 330,400. Hatfield won because he ran ahead in the Portland suburbs and in Duncan's home county of Jackson; overall, Hatfield carried 27 of Oregon's 36 counties.

The Governor's Race

The other high-profile race in 1966 was the governor's contest between Oregon's new state treasurer, Bob Straub, and new secretary of state, Tom McCall. The two had worked closely for the previous two years as members of the Board of Control and the three-person State Land Board. More often than not, they agreed on issues.

Publicly, McCall normally appeared as composed, forceful, and articulate. Behind the scenes, however, he was often nervous and worried about "what-ifs." Notorious for his thin skin, McCall did not always deal well with personal criticism directed at him in public. Fortunately, McCall hired Portland businessmen Ron Schmidt and Ed Westerdahl, both 28, to advise him and run his campaign. With their guidance, Tom McCall became the highly focused, successful, and popular politician that he was. McCall remarked about Straub's "amazing resiliency. Straub's candidacy would not be taken lightly. He was a strong person, physically. He could plod the campaign trail day and night and hold up. Moreover, he was running as the candidate of the party which had a great majority of the registered voters. I looked at him as solid-caliber competition."[22]

McCall and Straub were both progressives. They believed in planned, orderly change. Each had strong convictions about protecting Oregon's environment. Indeed, Straub's proposal to clean up the polluted Willamette River and to protect its banks from development, his Willamette River Greenway Plan, was hailed by McCall as a much needed reform—and McCall said so publicly, over and over. McCall said that it was time for Oregon to "draw a line in fighting pollution, even if it means saying to a major industry you cannot locate here if you are going to pollute our rivers and air."[23] As the campaign unfolded, Tom McCall continued to shape his image as a maverick, as a man who could not be bought or bossed. And voters loved him for it. Tom McCall, like his contemporaries Wayne Morse and Mark Hatfield, had developed his own constituency based on his own unique personality, not so much on political party affiliation. Because McCall was so popular with Republicans, Democrats, and independents, he was, to a large degree, able to function independently, and successfully as a politician, even though his liberal views often clashed with those held by many conservative and influential Republican leaders. Taking 55% of the vote, Tom McCall was elected governor in November, 377,300 to Bob Straub's 305,000. Bob Straub returned to his post as state treasurer, to await his next opportunity to run for governor.

Mr. Dellenbeck Goes to Washington

Bob Duncan's run for the Senate in 1966 meant, of course, that he'd had to give up his congressional seat in Oregon's 4th District. Republican John Dellenbeck, a two-term state representative, filed for the seat as did former congressman Charles O. Porter, a Eugene Democrat. Riding the Republican tide that swept Oregon that fall, John Dellenbeck defeated Porter, 94,100 to 56,000 votes. Dellenbeck would join Republican Wendell Wyatt and Democrats Al Ullman and Edith Green in the U.S. House.

The final Republican victory of 1966 came in the Oregon House, where GOP candidates won 38 of 60 seats. Democrats did, however, manage to retain control of the Senate, 19-11. But change was in the air. Tom McCall and Mark Hatfield were poised to step into their new positions in January. And Oregon would never be the same.

Chapter 15
The Tom McCall Years, 1965-75

Thomas (Tom) Lawson McCall was governor from 1967 to 1975. Despite the decades between then and now, Tom McCall's extraordinary influence remains part of who Oregonians are today. Tom McCall was an activist governor. Oregon has had few leaders like him.

Tom McCall was a journalist and television commentator by profession. A promoter, he appreciated the value of free media attention. He was a man who believed deeply in Oregon and the state's abundant natural beauty. He used the bully pulpit to champion his ideas and he was always in motion. With a flair for the dramatic, McCall attracted the media wherever he went. Oregonians expected to see their larger-than-life governor on the evening news.

At the core of Tom McCall's reputation was his passion for the natural environment. While McCall was governor the Oregon Legislature passed the Beach Bill, the Bottle Bill, the Bike Bill, and State-administered Land-Use Planning Bill (SB100), along with new state agencies to implement them, the Department of Environmental Quality (DEQ) and the Land Conservation and Development Commission (LCDC).

While not everyone liked Tom McCall, most people admired him for speaking out on a variety of issues, for rallying people to get involved in their government, to have an opinion, to take a stand. To care.

Goodbye Mark, Hello Tom

It was January 9, 1967. Bundled against the crisp morning air, hundreds of people trudged up the broad steps leading into the Capitol. Inside was a cacophony of sounds, of echoing voices reverberating in the great rotunda. Friends and acquaintances greeted one another, then climbed the west steps to the House chamber. Amid TV cameras, lobbyists, the press, legislators and their families, legislative staff, the Supreme Court, other major office holders, and former governors Sprague, Holmes, and Smith, Oregon's 54th Legislative Assembly got underway. After eight years as governor, Mark O. Hatfield delivered his farewell address. He was headed to Washington, D.C., as Oregon's new U.S. senator. After a standing ovation for Governor Hatfield, Clay Myers took the oath of office, replacing Tom McCall as secretary of state. Tom Lawson McCall then stepped to the podium and took his oath as governor. Governor McCall then gave his Opening Day address. McCall did not disappoint his audience. He expressed his gratitude to those who had elected him, and shared his plans for education, jobs, tax reform, and, most of all, the environment. Protecting the state was foremost in his plans. "Health, economic strength, recreation—in fact, the entire outlook and image of the state—are tied inseparably to environment. Water, air, land, and scenic pollution threaten these and other values in Oregon. The overriding challenge of the decade is the issue of the quality of life in Oregon," said McCall.[1] The governor endorsed the Willamette Greenway, an idea earlier proposed by State Treasurer Bob Straub. McCall said it was time to protect public access to all of Oregon's coastal beaches, urging legislators to make the issue one of their highest priorities.

Lawmakers listened attentively to their new governor's remarks. Seated near McCall were Senate President E. D. "Debbs" (named after Socialist and labor leader Eugene Debs) Potts, and F. F. "Monte" Montgomery, starting his second term as House speaker. Senator Potts was a conservative Democrat from Grants Pass and, like fellow conservatives Harry Boivin and Ben Musa before him, he had aligned with the senate's other Democratic conservatives and eleven Republicans to form a majority coalition to control the Senate. The 12 urban senators, who called themselves "Regular" Democrats, remained outside the inner circle of power. Speaker Montgomery, a Eugene insurance agent, had the luxury of presiding over a solidly Republican house, 38-22.

The 1967 Senate was all white and all male and included several bright stars, men destined for higher office: Victor Atiyeh, Berkeley Lent, and Edward Fadeley. The House also had its share of important future leaders, including Robert Packwood, Connie McCready, R. F. "Bob" Smith, Betty Roberts, Jim Redden, Jason Boe, Lee Johnson, Wallace Carson, Bill Stevenson, Phil Lang, and Stafford Hansell. There were five women representatives, three fewer than the 1965 session.

McCall Swings into Action

Not since the days of Oswald West (1911-15) had voters elected a leader like Tom McCall. West was, in fact, one of Tom McCall's heroes. The two men were alike in many ways. Both were idealistic. They believed life could be made better.

They were both fighters and when faced by a legislative obstacle were ready to appeal directly to the people, bringing public pressure to bear on reluctant politicians. Both were at times driven by anger and indignation, particularly when the public interest was jeopardized by greed or self-interest. Neither man tolerated injustice and both were willing to do the unusual or unexpected to draw public attention to a problem. They were impatient men who made things happen. Their strongest similarity rested on a deep appreciation and love for Oregon's unique natural beauty. For West and McCall the protection and preservation of Oregon's scenic Pacific coastline was imperative. Building on Os West's legacy, Tom McCall made environmental quality Oregon's number one political issue.

In March 1967 McCall set a precedent when, as a sitting governor, he testified before a legislative committee. He had been in office two months when he was invited to testify before the State Senate Air and Water Quality Committee. McCall wanted the legislature to help him draw a line against pollution. The anti-pollution bills before the panel included money for new sewer systems, tax credits for businesses that installed anti-pollution equipment, and new powers for the State Sanitary Authority. McCall insisted that, from now on, Oregon had an Eleventh Commandment: "Thou shall not pollute."[2]

Tom McCall had studied, written, and spoken about the sad state of the Willamette River for five years. As governor, he dedicated himself to cleaning up the Willamette. Armed with a new federal study highly critical of the Sanitary Authority's failure to restore the Willamette as a healthy waterway, McCall decided to shake things up. Since the authority had been established in 1938, one man had served as agency chairman; on April 17, 1967, he died. McCall promptly appointed himself chairman of the Sanitary Authority. McCall's action took everyone by surprise. The governor was letting the public know that the issue of environmental pollution was so critical that he would take charge of cleaning up the Willamette. McCall tolerated no more excuses for saving the Willamette from agricultural, industrial, and municipal pollution. The time had come to *do* something, and he intended to do it!

The second issue that Tom McCall tackled was the thorny problem of protecting Oregon's Pacific coast beaches from development. The Oregon coast had been a public highway since 1913, when Governor Oswald West pushed the law through the legislature. But a 1966 court decision threw the certainty of that splendid resource into jeopardy.[3] The issue of public access to coastal beaches came to a head in summer 1966 when a Cannon Beach motel owner erected a fence from the edge of his property seaward, extending out to the high-tide line. "Highway Department attorneys scoured the law and discovered the loophole in Os West's bill. The state could not order the motel fence down, because, simply, the state did not own the dry sands as everyone had assumed it did. So the state Highway Department proposed fixing the problem in the 1967 legislature with a bill that gave the state ownership of all the beach, from the wet sands to the vegetation line above the dry sands."[4]

Representative Sidney Bazett, a Grants Pass Republican, was chairman of the House Highway Committee in 1967. Bazett favored the Highway Department's beach measure, House Bill (HB) 1601. Governor McCall endorsed the legislation. But backers of the Beach Bill knew it was in trouble. Republican Majority Leader Robert Smith, a conservative Burns cattle rancher, opposed the bill. As a member of Bazett's committee, Smith was in a position to weaken or even derail the measure and succeeded in amending the bill in a way that actually narrowed public access to ocean beaches. The amended bill stalled in committee.

Deciding it was time to turn up the heat, McCall wrote a letter to Bazett (though the letter was meant for GOP leaders blocking the Beach Bill). He urged Republicans to protect the public interest by passing a Beach Bill that protected "the dry sands from the encroachment of crass commercialism." Next, the governor leaked the letter to the press, knowing that it would be the next day's headline. When the public became aware of what was at stake, they deluged House leaders with phone calls, letters, and telegrams. House Republicans were running for cover. McCall and his friends (in particular Ancil Payne, station manager at KGW TV in Portland) turned up the heat. An aroused public deluged Bazett's committee with 40,000 letters and phone calls. This prompted panic among those blocking the Beach Bill; they called for a new hearing on the measure. "The original bill proposed that the line of vegetation along the dry sands serve as a legal boundary, but everyone recognized that was an inaccurate and unreliable line. So House Republicans proposed that the state establish a survey line of seven feet above sea level as the boundary line of public ownership. McCall spotted the proposal as bogus; the Republicans' bill actually surrendered much of the state's claim, placing the boundary line closer to the ocean than the current law did."[5]

Tom McCall had a plan. Early on the morning of May 13, 1967, two helicopters swooped over the Coast Range and landed on the beach. McCall leaped out of the lead helicopter followed by reporters, scientists, and surveyors. Barking orders, the governor had the surveyors pound stakes in between the dry sands and the water. McCall announced that oceanographers at Oregon State University believed that the proper elevation line should be at 16 feet—not the 7 feet that Republican opponents wanted. "When the stakes were in, McCall walked to the stake highest on the beach. This stake, he said, marks where the public ownership should start. Then he marched to the second stake at the edge of the dry sand. 'This is where the state's ownership now ends,' he said. Then he took several long strides toward the ocean to a spot near the waves. This, he said, is where the Republicans want the line."[6] McCall now had both the public's and legislature's attention.

But did the state have the right to take land away from private owners? While the governor was grabbing headlines for his unconventional melodrama on the beach, lawmakers Jim Redden and Lee Johnson came up with a solution to the problem of private vs. public ownership of beachfront property when they realized "that the state did not need to own the beach; it just had to control it."[7] The young legislators wrote an amendment to HB 1601 which gave the state the power to zone any beach it did not own and to outlaw any development or construction not allowed by the state Highway Commission. With this amendment, the House passed the Beach Bill 57-3, and the Senate quickly followed suit. On July 6, Tom McCall proudly signed the Beach Bill into law—forever linking his name with the issue of environmental protection. The McCall credo of promoting preservation over development became the governor's most important political legacy to Oregon.

The Beach Bill wasn't McCall's only environmental triumph in 1967. The legislature enacted the largest package of water and air pollution abatement bills in state history. McCall proudly wrote: "The most singular accomplishment of the 1967 Legislature was its comprehensive program to curb air and water pollution. Unlike previous legislatures, this session faced the menace of pollution squarely and took decisive action to roll it back."[8] Lawmakers also funded McCall's proposal to establish the Willamette Greenway program—another popular environmental bill passed in 1967.

Tax Relief and the 1967 Legislature

Since late summer 1966, Oregon's economy had been in a slump, largely because of a decline in the nation's housing market. The demand for Oregon lumber had plummeted. As a result, state economists decreased the amount of revenue the state could expect to collect in 1967. During the session economists revised their forecasts downward three times; there would be less money to figure into the 1967-69 state budget.

McCall and legislators were on the spot, since they had promised to provide more property tax relief during the 1966 campaign. With the state facing an income shortfall, it was not a good time to enact a new tax relief program. The governor submitted a tax reform proposal to the 1967 session based on increasing the state's personal income tax. The House Tax Committee ignored McCall's plan. During the session, the House Tax Committee wrestled with drafting a property-tax reform plan and they passed a plan that included a proposed state sales tax—an odious idea to most voters. The Senate rejected the House plan. When the session adjourned on June 14, after a marathon 157 days, no tax relief plan had passed. The legislature's failure to enact tax relief was McCall's biggest legislative disappointment in 1967. Within weeks he announced that there would be a special session to address the property-tax issue in late October.

The governor prevailed when the 1967-69 state budget was set at $588 million, about $94 million above the 1965-67 budget (but still $30 million below McCall's recommendation). Lawmakers raised the minimum wage to $1.25 an hour, affecting 10,000 workers in the service industry; farmworkers were, however, left out of the law.

Despite its many impressive achievements, the 1967 Legislature failed on two fronts: it did not enact a tax relief program and the assembly couldn't agree on a comprehensive revision of the Oregon Constitution, programs that had been underway for five years. The House and Senate simply could not agree on a compromise. Thus, no action was taken to update the 1857 Constitution.

Celebrity

Tom McCall's popularity remained high throughout Oregon and his extraordinarily close relationship with the print and television media paid handsome dividends. McCall was so accessible to both the media and the public that he was rarely in his office. He preferred roaming the Capitol, talking with reporters in the press office, or buttonholing lobbyists, legislators, or citizens in a hallway or the coffee shop. Tom McCall loved people. The media liked working with one of their own, a man who understood what tidbit might make a good story. Consequently, McCall enjoyed a long honeymoon period, with the press portraying him in a favorable light. By the summer of 1967 he was riding a wave of popularity that only a few governors had experienced. Tom McCall had become "more than a political figure, he was a celebrity."[9]

His popularity did not always help him within the Republican Party. Conservative Republicans did not trust McCall. They resented his popularity. And some were irked because McCall had often worked outside, or around the party, to reach a goal. In the Beach Bill controversy he had embarrassed GOP leaders when he appealed directly to the people who, in turn, unloaded on Republican leaders. Tom McCall was unpopular with the conservative wing of the Republican Party throughout his two terms.

Tom McCall so yearned for the spotlight that being governor was not enough. Within weeks of taking office, he offered his support to beleaguered President Lyndon Johnson. Johnson's Vietnam War policy was under growing scrutiny and criticism by the American people. As the United States escalated its involvement in Vietnam, Johnson's critics became more strident, adding to the country's growing anti-war movement. In July 1967, President Johnson asked Governor McCall to serve on a task force of distinguished Americans going to South Vietnam to observe that country's upcoming election for president. In late August and early September McCall was in Vietnam. This foray into the national spotlight was the first of many occasions that added to McCall's growing reputation as a politician of national stature.

Wayne Morse Wants a Fifth Term

In July 1967, Sen. Wayne Morse announced the formation of a statewide reelection committee to run for a fifth term as Oregon's senior senator. A Portland television station aired twin showings in late June and early July of *Advise and Dissent*, a documentary on Senator Morse, which kicked off his reelection campaign. The films showed scenes from his public and private life and portrayed him as a hard-working, homey, and knowledgeable representative of Oregon, who, despite his role as a leading dissenter against the war in Vietnam, got things done for the state.[10] Morse told reporters that he expected former Congressman Bob Duncan to be his Democratic challenger in May. He assumed that the primary would be the key contest facing him in 1968—he believed he would win the November election, regardless of who his Republican opponent was. He scoffed at an October poll that showed him trailing Bob Duncan among Democrats 51 to 40%. Meanwhile, McCall's name began to surface in the Oregon press as a possible Republican Senate candidate.

On July 15, 1967, *Oregon Voter* magazine featured a story about 34-year-old state representative Bob Packwood, who was mentioned as a potential GOP candidate for U.S. Senate. "All signs point to his running. It appears Sen. Wayne Morse—if he defeats Congressman Bob Duncan [in the primary]—may have an even more formidable foe in November 1968."[11]

The Special Session of 1967

Oregon's economic picture didn't change much between spring and October 1967. When lawmakers returned for the special session on October 30, they faced the same financial problems they had encountered during the regular session. Their first order of business was to balance the state budget for 1967-69, which needed cuts of between $25 and $55 million.[12]

Governor McCall hoped that lawmakers would balance the state budget, as well as put together a tax-relief package for voters to decide. Legislators toiled for 23 days. They cut the state budget to avert a deficit but they didn't pass a tax-relief plan. The House and Senate, Republicans and Democrats, couldn't agree on a tax package. McCall was disappointed. He had even changed his mind in favor of a state sales tax—though Oregonians had repeatedly and overwhelmingly defeated such a tax. Tom McCall wasn't the only one disappointed by the legislature's failure to enact a tax-relief plan. The public realized that the issue was not going to go away. Either the legislature could come up with a tax plan that Oregonians would approve, or, if need be, the people could take matters into their own hands.

1968: Primary Politics in Oregon

1968 was a traumatic year for Americans. Violence rocked the nation, with political assassination, the continuing civil rights struggle, and growing civil unrest over Uncle Sam's deepening involvement in Vietnam, putting enormous strain on the nation's unity. America was in crisis. It was against this backdrop of war and domestic violence that Americans went about electing their political leaders in 1968. There were four important political races in Oregon. Two were part of the Democratic primary in May. The first race pitted Sen. Wayne Morse against Congressman Bob Duncan for their party's Senate nomination. The second contest featured Senators Eugene McCarthy and Robert Kennedy in Oregon's Democratic presidential primary. November featured the Senate race between Wayne Morse and his 36-year-old opponent, State Representative Robert (Bob) Packwood, and the presidential contest between Richard Nixon and Hubert H. Humphrey.

Bob Duncan had a score to settle with Wayne Morse. In 1966 Morse had helped keep Duncan from getting the Democratic Party's nomination for U.S. Senate.* Many Democrats resented Morse for helping Hatfield win a seat that

---

* Senator Morse was a leading dove while Bob Duncan was an outspoken hawk. For Morse, the idea of Bob Duncan becoming the Democrat's Senate nominee was unthinkable. Consequently, he intervened in the race, cajoling his friend and fellow dove, Howard Morgan, to challenge Duncan in the primary. Morse even raised money for Morgan. But Duncan prevailed, besting Morgan 159,000 votes to 88,000. When the Senate contest between Mark Hatfield, the Republican nominee, and Bob Duncan got underway, Morse endorsed Hatfield, because Hatfield was also a dove. Morse

Democrats (the Neubergers) had held for the previous twelve years. Bob Duncan waited, knowing that in two years Wayne Morse would seek reelection. And he intended to hit Morse head-on.

In June 1967 Democrat Phil McAlmond, a 39-year-old Portland realtor, announced that he would oppose Sen. Wayne Morse in the May 1968 primary. McAlmond went on a speaking tour, attacking Morse for his opposition to the Vietnam War. Morse ignored McAlmond and kept an eye on Bob Duncan.

Senator Wayne Morse's reelection campaign got a huge boost in January 1968. The aging chairman of the powerful Senate Labor and Public Welfare Committee announced his retirement. And Wayne Morse was first in line to be the next labor chairman, causing Oregon labor leaders to mend fences with the senator. The state AFL-CIO remained neutral in the Senate race, but most of the larger unions—the Longshoremen, Retail Clerks, Building Trades, Sawmill Workers, and the Teamsters—endorsed Morse, and poured thousands of dollars into his campaign. Early polls showed Duncan ahead of Morse, but with a huge campaign treasury at his disposal, Morse steadily gained on Duncan.

Bob Duncan hit Wayne Morse with everything he could and focused not on Morse's opposition to the Vietnam War but on the senator's advancing age (68). He hammered away at Morse's maverick status, claiming it hurt his ability to direct more federal dollars into Oregon. Fortunately for Morse the Oregon economy, as a whole, was growing. Personal income was up 9% in Oregon. The resurgence of the state's forest products industry was an important factor and lumber production was up over 12%. More people were working and the number of non-farm wage and salary workers increased. While Duncan made issues of Morse's age and maverick, go-it-alone style, McAlmond hammered Morse for opposing LBJ's Vietnam policy. He insinuated that Morse was disloyal, that his Vietnam stance undercut American efforts in Southeast Asia.

Morse won the Democratic nomination for a fifth Senate term in a close election; he won by 49 to 46% over Duncan, with the remaining support going to Phil McAlmond.[13] Turnout was high: 72% of registered Democrats voted. Senator Morse outspent Bob Duncan $294,000 to $90,000. Duncan lost by 10,300 votes (Morse, 185,000, Duncan, 174,800). Morse carried Lane, his home county, by over 7,200 votes. But the deciding factor in Morse's victory was not his incumbency nor his deep pockets: it was Phil McAlmond. It is assumed that most of McAlmond's 17,700 votes would have gone to

preferred to back a Republican who believed the Vietnam War was wrong. In November, Mark Hatfield (with Wayne Morse's blessing) defeated Bob Duncan by 24,000 votes, 354,000 to 330,000.

Duncan, because of their similar positions on Vietnam. Adding most of Phil McAlmond's votes to Duncan's would have given him about 190,000 votes, which might have been enough to unseat Morse. A poll conducted after the May primary showed that Senator Morse could be in trouble. "Of those who had supported Duncan in the primary, a whopping 50% said that they would vote for Packwood in the general election, while 31% felt that Morse had grown too old for the job."[14]

Robert Packwood had defeated a minor opponent by over 200,000 votes to win the Republican nomination. In November, Oregonians would choose between 68-year-old Wayne Morse and 36-year-old Bob Packwood. Morse entered the fall campaign with a bitterly divided Democratic Party. Bob Packwood, on the other hand, led a well-organized, statewide grassroots campaign; and his Republican base was united behind him. A confident Bob Packwood headed into the fall with momentum, optimistic that victory was within reach.

The second featured political campaign in Oregon in 1968 was the Democratic primary for president. There were three names on the May ballot: Senators Eugene McCarthy and Robert Kennedy, and President Lyndon Johnson. In March, after McCarthy, an outspoken opponent of the war, had scored a stunning upset in the New Hampshire primary, Johnson had withdrawn from the race. LBJ's withdrawal turned the Democratic Party upside-down. Senator Robert Kennedy, another dove, then entered the Democratic contest.

Kennedy and McCarthy each spent at least 10 days campaigning in Oregon. Senator McCarthy had an impressive grassroots organization, including hundreds of out-of-state volunteers. His greatest appeal was to suburbanites, independents, and college-age youth. Bobby Kennedy, blessed with the Kennedy charisma, also generated wild enthusiasm, particularly among minorities, the poor, and young. Edith Green, Oregon's most prominent woman politician, was Kennedy's state chair. The senators drew large, enthusiastic crowds wherever they spoke. Oregon's leading television stations and major newspapers covered the race like a blanket. The contest also captured national attention. Hundreds of reporters dogged the candidates, their stories snatched-up by an eager national press and television audience.

Eugene McCarthy won the Oregon Democratic primary, defeating Kennedy by 22,000 votes (164,000 to 141,600). He had outspent Kennedy, $381,000 to $291,000. President Johnson got 45,174 votes. In addition, Vice President Humphrey had his name written in by 12,400 Democrats. Of the 364,200 Democrats who voted in the May primary, 305,600 voted for McCarthy and Kennedy, the peace candidates. Together, the two senators drew 84% of the

Democratic vote in Oregon.

The 1968 GOP primary was also dominated by the the nomination for president. Former Vice President Richard M. Nixon won the Oregon primary, defeating Gov. Ronald Reagan of California. Nixon had always been popular in Oregon. In 1960, when he narrowly lost the presidency to Democrat John F. Kennedy, he had carried Oregon by 41,000 votes (52.5%). Nixon's popularity among Republicans did not, however, extend to party leaders Tom McCall, Mark Hatfield, and John Dellenback, who preferred New York Gov. Nelson Rockefeller. Governor McCall and Senator Hatfield worked behind the scenes to convince Rockefeller to run again in 1968. Rockefeller refused, leaving Nixon to face Reagan in Oregon's May primary.

Richard Nixon worked hard in Oregon. He had a large, paid campaign staff here. With lots of money, name familiarity, and thousands of loyal supporters, Nixon easily won the GOP primary (203,000 to 63,700), taking all 18 delegates to the Republican national convention. Nixon outspent Reagan $173,000 to $122,000. In addition, 36,300 Republicans wrote in the name of Nelson Rockefeller for president.

Murder in the Kitchen

Buoyed by his victory over Robert Kennedy in Oregon, Sen. Eugene McCarthy flew to California. The senators had one week before California's June 3 primary. Both men were under intense pressure. Their party's national convention was two months away. Gene McCarthy knew he was running out of time. A defeat in California would likely end his candidacy. Conversely, Bobby Kennedy knew that a California victory would make him the Democratic front-runner going into the convention.

The national media stormed into California. The three major television networks (ABC, NBC, and CBS) broadcast their nightly national news programs from the Golden State. The nation was watching. There was a huge voter turnout. The race was close. Just before midnight, Bobby Kennedy was declared the winner with 46% of the vote, to Gene McCarthy's 42% (Kennedy, 1.4 million votes, McCarthy, 1.267 million).

An exhausted but beaming Robert Kennedy, flashing his signature smile, made a short speech at the Ambassador Hotel in Los Angeles. He then exited through the hotel kitchen. Millions had stayed up to watch Kennedy's victory speech on television. A couple of minutes after the end of Kennedy's speech, popping sounds were heard. There was bedlam. Cameramen, pushing through the surging crowd, tried to focus their lenses on Kennedy. The senator was down. Rushed to Good Samaritan Hospital, Kennedy underwent brain surgery. Americans on the East Coast and Midwest awoke to the terrible news: Robert Kennedy was fighting for his life. With his wife, Ethel, his sisters, and sister-in-law, Jackie Kennedy, at his bedside, Bobby Kennedy died at 1:44 on the morning of June 6, 1968.*

Americans were stunned—Kennedy's murder came only weeks after Martin Luther King's assassination. Suddenly, a huge chasm opened up in the Democratic Party. With LBJ, Gene McCarthy†, and Bobby Kennedy out of the picture, who could the party draft to enter the campaign at such a late date? There was only one choice: Vice President Hubert Horatio Humphrey. A long-time Minnesota senator before becoming LBJ's vice president in 1965, Humphrey had a national following, and was respected as an honest, energetic, and dedicated public servant. So, as a last-minute replacement, Humphrey answered his party's call for help.

Richard Nixon won the presidential nomination on the first ballot at the Republican National Convention in Miami in August. In his acceptance speech Nixon pledged "to bring an honorable end to the war in Vietnam by putting party politics aside, to unite this nation, with the United States able to negotiate from strength rather than weakness."[15] Meanwhile, Democrats, meeting in Chicago, nominated Hubert Humphrey for president. George Corley Wallace, segregationist governor of Alabama, also ran for president in 1968. Wallace assailed "pointy-headed liberals" and demanded that state values should be allowed to prevail over the federal government's program to enforce equal rights laws. Because of his popularity in the Deep South, the Democratic Party feared that Wallace would siphon votes away from Humphrey in that region. Running under the name of American Independent Party, Wallace threatened to be a spoiler in November.

Tom and Monte

Tom McCall's first two years as governor (1967-68) fell far short of his expectations. He had scored big public points for his bold leadership in protecting Oregon's coastal beaches and his call to arms to save the Willamette River from further pollution. McCall used those two issues to reinforce his broad base of support among the people. But when it came to the Republican legislature,

---

* Arrested and later sentenced to life in prison was a twenty-four-year-old Jordanian named Sirhan Bishara Sirhan, a zealot who hated Israel. Sirhan fired eight shots at Kennedy, hitting him twice.

† McCarthy did not have nearly enough delegates to claim the Democratic nomination. His loss to RFK in California had stopped his momentum.

his record was a different story. The governor had crossed swords with both House majority leader Bob Smith and with Speaker F. F. Montgomery, whom McCall had embarrassed in 1967 when he caused a public outcry over the issue of public ownership and access to Oregon's coastal beaches. Now neither Smith nor Montgomery trusted McCall.

In March 1968, the relationship between McCall and Montgomery grew more sour, when McCall found himself at the center of two controversies, the first stemming from his endorsement of Clay Myers for secretary of state. McCall had appointed Myers to the office when he became governor in January 1967. Speaker Montgomery had wanted the job and he now feared that McCall's endorsement of Myers would hurt his own candidacy in 1968.

The second controversy involved the Oregon State Penitentiary (OSP). For months, conditions at the OSP had been deteriorating. After a riot there in 1953, a "get tough" warden had been hired to run the prison. Many archaic practices were still in effect, including one supported by the warden, the use of the Box, a dark, "6 x 8 foot cell furnished only with a hole for a toilet. Guards put naked prisoners into the Box, leaving them there for weeks without even bedding to keep them warm." By early 1968, tensions were rising at the OSP. The warden had cancer and could not perform his duties. Montgomery decided to make the situation at the prison a campaign issue and his staff leaked stories to the press about alleged conditions. He then attacked Clay Myers, who, along with Governor McCall and State Treasurer Bob Straub, was part of the three-person Board of Control that was responsible for the OSP. Coming to Myers' defense, Governor McCall fired off a letter to Montgomery, lambasting him for criticizing Myers and for making "reckless" statements that could worsen the situation at OSP. The governor charged Monte with "sowing the seeds of riot within the walls."[16] Then Tom McCall made a mistake he would deeply regret.

The March filing deadline for public office was only days away. Tom McCall was eager to again have Gov. Nelson Rockefeller (who had won Oregon's Republican presidential primary in 1964) on the GOP ballot in May. Rockefeller insisted he was not a candidate in 1968. McCall wanted to change Rockefeller's mind, so he (and a handful of other GOP leaders) planned to fly to New York to make a last-minute appeal. They were set to leave on March 9. Prior to his departure, the governor wanted to assure the press and public that everything was under control at the penitentiary. On March 8, McCall led a group of reporters on a tour of the OSP. The newsmen left the prison convinced that McCall had things under control and that conditions inside the prison were not as critical as candidate Montgomery claimed. The next morning, McCall flew to New

York. He had barely settled into his meeting with Governor Rockefeller when he received an urgent message: a riot had broken out at the OSP! Prisoners were on a rampage, taking over the complex and seizing dozens of hostages (mostly prison guards). Rioters torched four buildings. Because Governor McCall was absent, his chief of staff, Ed Westerdahl, immediately stepped in to negotiate an end to the riot. After all-night negotiations, the rioters agreed to end their rebellion the next morning. Thirty-one guards and prisoners were injured; no one was killed. Damage to prison property topped $1.5 million. Throughout the uprising Tom McCall was 3,000 miles away.

The OSP riot wrecked Montgomery's campaign for secretary of state. Governor McCall had earlier given the press a copy of the letter he had sent to Montgomery, in which he warned that his criticism of the prison was adding fuel to the fire. As far as the public was concerned, Montgomery's inflammatory statements about prison conditions were one cause of the prison riot. But there was plenty of blame to go around. Tom McCall was also culpable in his misreading of the situation. Had he allowed his personal ambition, his dream of being a national political figure, to interfere with his responsibilities as governor? Would voters hold him accountable?

Clay Myers easily defeated F. F. Montgomery in May for the Republican nomination for secretary of state. In backing Myers, McCall had continued to distance himself from the Old Guard wing of the Republican Party. And he'd made matters worse by trying to convince Rockefeller to run against Nixon in the Oregon primary. McCall remained cool toward Nixon and refused to endorse him in the November election. Conservative Republicans saw his snub of Nixon as an example of his petulance, vanity, and, disloyalty to the GOP. Would McCall's habit of burning his political bridges hurt his reelection chances in 1970?

The 1968 General Election

Oregon's November election was dominated by the U.S. Senate contest between newcomer Bob Packwood and Sen. Wayne Morse. Democrat Morse, a 23-year veteran of the Senate, was in trouble. The Democratic Party was in disarray. The primary contest between Morse and Bob Duncan had split the party. An August poll showed Morse with a 49 to 40% lead over the lesser-known Packwood. Morse decided to campaign by remaining in Washington, attending to Senate business—acting senatorial—and tried to mend his fences with labor. Most unions pledged their support, but they did so with less enthusiasm than usual. Many chose to work elsewhere, either for Humphrey for president or for labor-oriented candidates at the state and local levels.[17]

Wayne Morse and his staff were slow to realize that Bob Packwood was a serious threat. Not until late September did Morse begin to focus 100% on his campaign. Packwood had the advantage of his youth and financial backing. Money came from across the country, from donors concerned about Morse's position on the Vietnam War and energized by the possibility of adding a new Republican to the Senate. Packwood's strongest advantage may have been the years he had spent organizing the moderate wing of the Republican Party.[18] Relying heavily on residential lawn signs and radio and TV ads, Packwood concentrated on making his name known to voters all over Oregon. Packwood (like Bob Duncan in the May Democratic primary) criticized Morse for being out of touch with Oregonians, for being too old, and for being too much of a one-man band. It was time for a change, Oregon needed new leadership, said Packwood. Morse countered by stressing his seniority in the Senate and how he used his power to help Oregon. But many Oregonians weren't listening.

Bob Packwood then challenged Morse to debate him. Morse declined. Why give Packwood the spotlight? But then he changed his mind, agreeing to debate Packwood on October 25 at the Masonic Temple in Portland. The debate was telecast live in Oregon and excerpted nationally on CBS. The debate pulled a live audience of 800 sitting at crowded tables and two hundred standing spectators filled all the remaining spaces. Packwood's backers filled the ballroom, ready with rehearsed questions. Wayne Morse, with his silver hair and bushy eyebrows, wore a gray suit, which on television made him look old and washed out. Morse had agreed to a two-minute time limit to answer questions. Once the questions began, he floundered badly. He was used to giving detailed answers, and his answers were rushed and incomplete. Consequently, he seemed ill prepared and, worse, gave the impression he was trying to avoid answering the questions. By contrast, Packwood gave zingy 90-second answers.[19] The debate was the turning point in the election. Overnight, the underdog had emerged as Morse's equal.

Every indicator was that the election would be close. And so it was. Nearly 815,000 voters cast ballots, a record turnout. It took three days to arrive at the final tally. Bob Packwood had won! By a margin of 3,445 votes, the young state representative had toppled an Oregon political institution, one of the most powerful men in the federal government. A recount took until December 30, though the outcome did not change. Morse picked up 152 votes in the recount, shrinking Packwood's victory margin to 3,293 (Packwood, 408,600; Morse, 405,000). Morse outspent Packwood, $413,000 to $376,000.

Wayne Morse's long Senate career appeared to be over. Bob Packwood, a political unknown a year earlier, had scored one of the biggest upsets in the political history of both Oregon and the Senate of the United States. For the first time since 1952, both Oregon senators were Republicans: Mark Hatfield, only 46, and Robert Packwood, a mere 36.

Hubert Humphrey, the Democratic nominee for president, aroused little interest among party activists in Oregon. His campaign made scant effort to win the state, spending only $22,000, and conceding the state to Richard Nixon. Consequently, Nixon sailed to victory in November (408,000, to 359,000 for Humphrey). Third-party candidate, George Wallace, took 6% of the Oregon vote (about 50,000 ballots). Nixon was elected president with 43.4% (31.8 million) of the national vote, squeaking by Hubert Humphrey at 42.7% (31.1 million votes). Governor Wallace took 13.5% of the national vote (about 9.9 million ballots).

Bob Packwood

Robert ("Bob") Packwood was born in Portland in 1932. A graduate of Willamette University, Packwood graduated from law school in 1957 and embarked on a career in law in Portland. Elected to the Oregon House in 1962 (at age 30), Republican Packwood served in the 1963-67 legislative sessions.

COURTESY OF OREGON STATE ARCHIVES

In 1968, after several years of careful planning and organizing, Packwood won the GOP nomination for the U.S. Senate and the right to challenge Oregon's venerable senator, Democrat Wayne Morse. Morse was seeking a fifth term, and, at age 68, posed a striking contrast to the 36-year-old Packwood. Morse and his campaign took Packwood lightly at first. Meanwhile, Packwood was building a statewide organization and raising lots of money. A series of face-to-face debates did not go well for the under-prepared Morse, while Packwood came across as articulate and well prepared. The election was close. Indeed, the final outcome was not known for a month. Senator Wayne Morse was toppled in what was one of the most memorable political upsets in Oregon history.

Packwood, a moderate Republican supportive of abortion rights, proved to be a popular senator; he was reelected four times. Rumors, however, began to circulate in the early 1990s that Senator Packwood had a dark side: several women claimed that he had made unwanted sexual advances. Packwood scoffed at the rumors and Oregonians generally accepted his denials. Finally, a special committee of the Senate undertook a two-year investigation of an increasing number of formal charges against Packwood by over two dozen women. Finally, in September 1995, facing expulsion from the Senate, Bob Packwood resigned.

All of Oregon's U.S. representatives (Republicans John Dellenbeck in the 4th District and Wendell Wyatt in the 1st District and Democrats Edith Green in the 3rd District and Al Ullman in the 2nd District) were reelected in 1968. At the state level, House Republicans retained power, holding 38 of the 60 seats. Republicans also sliced into the Democratic majority in the state Senate, picking up three seats, giving the GOP 14 of the 30 slots in the upcoming legislative session. The only Democrat to win statewide office in 1968 was incumbent treasurer Bob Straub, who pulled 532,000 votes, 120,000 more than any other candidate on the Oregon ballot. But he was the exception in 1968. Otherwise, Oregon was a pretty solid Republican state.

Trouble in Paradise

Governor McCall was the first Oregon politician to sound the alarm about the consequences of rapid population growth. In his 1967 inaugural address, he had asserted that Oregon's "quality of life" was in jeopardy. Negative results of population growth included overcrowded schools, obsolete, overwhelmed local roads, overloaded sewer and water systems, more substandard housing, overworked local health and law-enforcement networks, and tacky roadside development (such as billboards). Between 1960 and 1970, Oregon grew by 323,000 residents (from 1.768 million to 2.091 million). Three-fourths of these newcomers (about 236,000) settled in the Willamette Valley, from Lane County in the south (over 52,000), to Marion in the central valley (over 31,000), to Multnomah in the north (over 32,000). The biggest increases occurred in the Portland suburbs. Between 1960 and 1970, Washington County grew by 68,000, followed by Clackamas with 53,000 new residents; between them, the two counties accounted for over 37% of Oregon's population growth during the 1960s.

A consequence of this new urban sprawl was the loss of prime Willamette Valley farmland. Between 1955 and 1970, one-fifth of valley land was taken out of agricultural use and converted to subdivisions and commercial development. Over 500,000 acres of Willamette Valley farmland was paved over for housing tracts, streets, highways, parking lots, shopping centers, and other commercial/ industrial uses. Tom McCall was appalled and concluded that "the only way to control growth was to protect the precious resource most at risk: the land." McCall understood better than any politician of his era that, in protecting its land, Oregon was protecting the natural resources it needed to survive. Progress was chewing at the edge of Oregon's natural resource base, and McCall decided to move Oregon toward statewide land-use planning. It evolved into his life's crusade. Tom McCall was convinced that "not only did the lack of strong land-use planning permit festering eyesores and contribute to pollution, it threatened the economic strength of the state."[20]

McCall concluded that what Oregon needed was a "wise-growth" policy. He knew that population growth was inevitable. The challenge was how to balance orderly, necessary economic growth against the need to conserve Oregon's most important natural resources. The governor realized that the best way to get on top of the sorry condition of local planning was for the state to take on the role of land-use planner. Throughout 1968 the governor's staff worked closely with a legislative committee to draft land-use bills for introduction in the 1969 Legislature. McCall's vision materialized in the form of Senate Bill (SB) 10. The 1969 Legislature didn't pass SB10 as drafted, but it did enact a watered-down version of it, requiring all city and county governments in Oregon to draw up a finished zoning plan within two years (by the end of 1971). The governor was given authority to take over local zoning if a local government failed to meet the deadline. Thus an important precedent was set: zoning and land-use planning are too important to be left up to local governments. Unfortunately, "legislators cut the funds intended to help cities and counties finish their zoning plans by the 1971 deadline. McCall feared that he had ended up with far too little—a symbolic step toward land-use planning, but little more. Too many legislators did not understand how land-use planning fit into McCall's larger plan to protect Oregon. McCall had failed to make his case, and the fierce opposition of industry lobbyists only stymied his effort."[21]

A Progressive Legislature

Oregon's 55th Legislative Assembly convened in Salem on January 13, 1969. Only 18 legislators were newcomers. Democrats held a slim 16-14 majority in the Senate. The Democrats were again divided—mostly along rural/urban and liberal/conservative lines. The 14 Republicans voted for conservative Democrat "Debbs" Potts for Senate president; urban Democrats also decided to back Senator Potts, thus unifying their caucus for the first time in several sessions. Betty Roberts, a Portland attorney, was the only woman in the 1969 Senate. The chamber was dominated by old timers. Eighteen senators had served in at least four regular senate sessions. Democrat Harry Boivin of Klamath Falls was attending his twelfth legislature.

Republicans held a solid 38-22 majority in the House. Robert "Bob" Smith, a cattle-rancher/businessman from Burns, was speaker. There were four female representatives. Speaker Smith tried to set a positive tone for the upcoming session when he remarked, "It is my hope that we will seek [solutions] in a setting of cooperation rather than bitter competition. It is my hope that we can work together in a spirit of unity."[22] Smith had extended the olive branch to senators, to Democrats, and to Gov. Tom McCall (who did not want to repeat the sour relationship he had had with GOP House leaders in 1967). Consequently, McCall agreed to be Bob Smith's point man on property-tax relief.

The defeat of a property-tax limitation measure on the November 1968 ballot gave legislators another chance to attack the thorny tax issue. GOP leaders wanted a sales tax. As a result, the first month of the 55th Legislature was consumed by the tax relief debate. Three tax plans were considered, one of them McCall's. The governor's plan was passed and referred to voters at a special statewide election set for June 3, 1969. The crux of the McCall plan was a 3% sales tax, with food and drugs exempt. The proposal "would freeze property taxes for persons aged 65 whose homes have a true cash value of $20,000 or less, and give income tax refunds to persons with low incomes."[23] The plan would reduce local property taxes by about 25% and the state revenue generated by the new sales tax would be deposited in the Basic School Support Fund. In other words, the state would return its new revenue to school districts. With more money coming from the state to help pay the costs of local schools, school boards could reduce local property tax rates by 25%.

Thousands of phone calls and letters from unhappy voters poured into the Capitol. Even before the passage of House Joint Resolution 8, House and Senate Republicans distanced themselves from the tax plan. To the governor's credit, he pretty much carried the tax-relief plan on his shoulders, taking the flak coming from the media and disgruntled voters. McCall knew that his tax plan was doomed. Since the 1930s, voters had repeatedly defeated every sales tax proposal referred to them. Half of registered voters cast ballots on June 3. McCall's plan was rejected eight to one (504,000 to 65,000).

The 1969 Legislature considered over 1,700 bills, adjourning May 23, after 131 days. Compared to the acrimonious, record-breaking 1967 session, the 55th Assembly conducted its business efficiently. Speaker Smith said that it was "one of the most productive and progressive session in the history of the State of Oregon."[24] Here are the highlights.

Governor McCall was most proud of the reorganization of state government, an issue that had been around for a decade. According to McCall "the 1969 Legislature shared my commitment to government reorganization. In addition to approving the Transportation Department, it adopted my recommendations for centralizing other departments. The Executive Department became the management agency for the state government, which merged budget, accounting, and data processing systems; and included the personnel division, the economic development division, and a Local Government-Relations Division. It marked the first time that local governments had been brought into the dialogue of state policy decision-making."[25] The Department of Human Resources was established to operate state institutions. The new department included Oregon's parole and probation agency, public welfare, vocational rehabilitation, and several smaller agencies. The Board of Control, established in Oswald West's administration in 1913, was abolished. The Department of Human Resources, now under the direction of the governor, received oversight responsibility.

To relieve an overburdened State Supreme Court, the 1969 session established Oregon's first Court of Appeals (consisting of five judges). It was expected to unburden the Supreme Court of 40 to 45% of its work load.[26]

Lawmakers also enacted a number of socially significant laws. The State Mental Health Division was empowered to prescribe the use of methadone and other synthetic drugs to treat addicts, especially heroin abusers. The legislature passed a law denying a tax exemption to any fraternal organization (Elks Club, Masons, for example) that restricted or limited its membership for reasons of race, color, national origin, or ethnicity. Oregon's abortion law was liberalized. The law allowed a pregnant woman to have a hospital abortion if her pregnancy was a danger to either her physical or mental health, or if the unborn child was liable to have serious mental or physical defects, or if the pregnancy was the result of rape or incest. Two physicians would have to consent that such a medical procedure was necessary and appropriate under this new statute.

"The 1969 session established a new and enlightened procedure and direction for Oregon's Correctional and Institutional programs. The new direction is away from incarceration and toward rehabilitation and treatment, with emphasis on work, counseling, and education outside of institution walls—all with the design to reduce the number of persons institutionalized by opening the door wider for community treatment and prevention."[27]

Recent campus unrest (some of it violent) at the University of Oregon, Oregon State University, and Portland State University resulted in a law granting expanded powers to the governor to deal with such public disturbances.

In setting the state's General Fund Budget for 1969-71, lawmakers pretty much stuck to the governor's recommendation. With a robust economy and higher revenue forecasts, McCall had proposed a 21% budget increase (or about $713 million). The State Sanitary Authority, which was renamed the Department of Environmental Quality (DEQ), was given new authority to control field and slash burning, with special emphasis on regulating the annual summer burning of thousands of acres of grass-seed fields in the Willamette Valley. The DEQ had the muscle to enforce its orders directed at industrial or agricultural polluters. The DEQ was also to develop auto and truck exhaust (emission) standards, which would be implemented by the Department of Motor Vehicles and the State Police. Legislators also created the Metropolitan Service District (MSD) to serve the greater Portland area (Multnomah, Washington, and Clackamas counties). The MSD had responsibility for regional sewage disposal, solid and liquid waste disposal, and flood control. Over the years, the MSD has added responsibilities, including air and water quality, Tri-Met, and the Oregon Zoo.

Too Many Eggs in One Basket

In spring 1969 Governor McCall launched a campaign to promote Oregon economic growth. Oregon produced 25% of the nation's lumber and its economy had remained heavily reliant on agriculture and timber production since the end of World War II. When the American economy was robust, Oregon's lumber industry prospered. However, when the national economy slowed down, Oregon's lumber market was early to feel the hurt and when Oregon's lumber market slumped, the state economy went with it. Tom McCall thought Oregon had put too many of its economic eggs in one basket and he hoped to change this. He wanted to diversify the economy, making it less dependent on lumber and wood products. He took on the roll of cheerleader, promoting Oregon as a haven for new business, believing that Oregon could "walk a thin line, encouraging economic diversity while controlling growth and making industries accountable for their pollution."[28] In out-of-state business recruiting trips, media interviews, speeches to business and environmental groups, and government conferences, Tom McCall promoted Oregon's economic growth. But he warned that growth came with a price tag: if a company was interested in locating here it must be willing to meet the state's strict environmental standards. Oregon, said McCall, was open for business—but not at *any* cost. Protecting the environment must take precedent over economic growth. By 1970, Tom McCall had become a symbol: he was the guardian of Oregon's environment.

Over the next five years, Governor McCall delivered the message across the nation that Americans must awaken to the threat of environmental degradation. The very quality of life on Earth was at stake. As a spokesman for environmental protection, Tom McCall became one of America's best-known and most controversial politicians.

Citizen Chambers

Among the hundreds of bills introduced but not passed in 1969 was one to help Oregon's environment. Known as the Bottle Bill, the measure was intended to reduce litter in Oregon. HB 1157 was sponsored by Republican Paul Hanneman, who introduced the bill on behalf of Richard Chambers, a Salem resident who owned a beach house in Hanneman's district. A hiker on Oregon's coastal and Cascade trails, Chambers carried bags so he could pick up litter along the way, much of it in the form of beverage cans and bottles. With each passing year, Chambers grew more agitated about the litter problem. Something had to be done.

In summer 1968, Rich Chambers had an idea. One way to reduce Oregon's litter problem was to require consumers to pay a deposit on every beverage can and bottle at the time of purchase (something then being tried in British Columbia). He explained his proposal to Representative Hanneman, who agreed to introduce such a bill in the 1969 Legislature.

Hanneman's Bottle Bill was ready at the session's opening. Speaker Bob Smith didn't like the bill, so he referred it to the State and Federal Affairs Committee, where Chairman Roger Martin would bury it. Hanneman approached Martin and, as a courtesy to a fellow Republican, asked him to schedule a hearing on HB 1157. Hanneman then went to Tom McCall's office, hoping that he would back the Bottle Bill. McCall agreed.

The hearing on the Bottle Bill drew a large audience. Richard Chambers testified by showing lawmakers samples of filthy bottles and cans he'd picked up on his rambles through western Oregon. Testifying against HB 1157 were some of the lobby's biggest guns: Reynolds Metals, International Paper, and Seven-Up Bottling Company.

Paul Hanneman convinced a fellow Republican who was a member of the State and Federal Affairs Committee to vote to pass the Bottle Bill (HB1157) out of committee—and that's what happened; by a 5-4 vote the bill went to the House floor. In a close floor vote Speaker Smith prevailed; the bill was returned to Martin's committee with a promise to amend the bill so that all interested parties could support it. Once it was back in committee, however, Martin buried the bill for good and the '69 session ended without enactment of a Bottle Bill. Hanneman and Chambers were disappointed that the governor hadn't gone to bat for the bill when they needed him. But McCall had changed his mind, deciding it was too soon to pass the Bottle Bill. McCall believed the bill would have a better chance if Chambers and Hanneman had more time to educate the public on the measure and its environmental benefits. Tom McCall's instinct proved to be right.

McCall Takes on the Establishment

In the span of nine months in 1969-70, two events occurred in Oregon that tested Tom McCall's leadership abilities. In December 1969, came Operation Red Hat, followed by Vortex in August 1970.

On December 1, 1969, the U.S. Army informed Governor McCall that the Pentagon was planning to ship nerve gas to Oregon for storage at the Umatilla Ordnance Depot near Boardman. The Army called it Operation Red Hat. McCall was told that the Pentagon would announce the operation the following day. Caught off-guard, McCall did not, at first, object to the shipment. But he quickly changed his mind when he "calculated that the nerve gas bombs headed for Oregon contained more that 7 billion drops of deadly liquids—more than double what it took to kill every human on earth."[29] Governor McCall decided to fight to protect the people of Oregon and Washington from the threat of lethal nerve gas: Red Hat must be stopped.

For the next six months, McCall fought the Nixon administration. The governor held press conferences, questioning why the Army needed the gas since President Nixon had signed a resolution denouncing the use of nerve gas as a weapon of war. McCall asked Senators Packwood and Hatfield as well as Warren Magnuson of Washington to join the protest—which all three senators did. The governor also collected (and sent to the White House) petitions and letters from over 62,000 Oregonians and Washingtonians opposing Operation Red Hat. McCall fired off letters to Secretary of Defense Melvin Laird, to President Nixon, and to Army Secretary Stanley Resor. Newspaper editors in Oregon backed McCall. The governor pleaded and cajoled. In April, McCall's defiant stand made national headlines. Tom McCall was a savvy politician and began to deliver speeches containing a more fundamental message: nerve gas is a symptom of what humans have done to their planet. "Man has fouled his nest. Man has squandered his resources. Man has treated his environment with cavalier abandon" said McCall.[30] Washington Gov. Dan Evans joined McCall in filing a suit against the federal government (the suit was quickly thrown out by a federal court). McCall reluctantly accepted defeat. He had failed to change the administration's position; nerve gas shipments to Oregon would begin on May 23, 1970. Then, Henry "Scoop" Jackson got into the fray.

Henry Jackson was Washington's senior U.S. senator—and the ranking Democrat on the Senate Armed Services Committee. Jackson, a hawk, had steadfastly backed President Nixon's war policies. But growing public outrage in Washington State over Red Hat got Jackson's attention. In late April, Senator

Jackson met with President Nixon and told him he opposed the nerve gas shipments to the Northwest. On May 23, Nixon told Jackson that he had changed its mind: there would be no nerve gas shipments to Oregon.

Scoop Jackson, who was running for reelection, immediately announced Nixon's reversal and took credit for changing Nixon's mind. The public, however, knew that the real credit for blocking Red Hat belonged to Gov. Tom McCall. Three days later, Tom McCall was re-nominated as the Republican candidate for governor.

Vortex

Vortex was the name of a state-sponsored rock festival held near Estacada, Oregon, on August 28-29, 1970. Thirty-five thousand (mostly young) people attended the concert on the banks of the Clackamas River. Governor Tom McCall's office had proposed Vortex—as a way to prevent potential violence in downtown Portland. Here's the background.

America was bogged down in the Vietnam War. There seemed to be no end to the killing and destruction. Consequently, millions of Americans were protesting the war. There were huge peace marches, editorials, nightly TV reports, and growing pressure on Congress and President Nixon. College campuses everywhere were in turmoil because of the war. There were sit-ins, marches, boycotts, clashes with police and soldiers, and even arson fires and bombings. In Portland, PSU students blocked downtown streets and took over the campus student center. Tensions were high. Then things got worse. The American Legion announced that it would hold its national convention in Portland on August 30. Legionnaires had invited Pres. Richard Nixon to address them. The FBI told Governor McCall that as many as 50,000 war protesters might be headed to Portland. McCall knew that something had to be done: Vortex, a free rock concert to draw potential protesters out of the city while the Legionnaires met in Portland, was his answer. The idea worked. Vortex was the safety valve that McCall hoped it would be. While Legionnaires paraded through downtown Portland, thirty-five thousand potential protesters were enjoying free food and music out in the country. Tom McCall's bold gamble had paid off. And the voters were watching very closely.

The Election of 1970

The Election of 1970 was unusual. For only the third time in the century there was no contest for president or U.S. senator in Oregon. Yet 56% of registered voters cast ballots in the May primary and 63% did so in November. Why the voter interest in an off-year election? The May primary focused on two main questions: who would be Oregon's next governor, and what did voters think about lowering the voting age to 19 in Oregon?

Measure 5, to lower the voting age, aroused the public. Voters felt so strongly that the proposal "drew 10% more votes than any other measure on the ballot; it also [attracted] 15,000 more votes than the total vote cast for the office of governor."[31] Measure 5 was soundly defeated on May 26. It did not seem to matter that hundreds of 18-, 19-, and 20-year-olds had already died in Vietnam.

In January 1970 State Treasurer Robert Straub announced that he would again seek the Democratic nomination for governor. He breezed to victory in the May primary, taking 66% of the Democratic vote. Meanwhile, Tom McCall hardly broke a sweat running for reelection. During the spring primary, McCall stayed close to the Capitol. Between his struggle to keep nerve gas out of Oregon and wrestling with a faltering state economy (and falling state revenues), McCall was plenty busy. As an incumbent, he had a record to run on. He ignored his opponents, campaigned little, and raised and spent $192,000 (mainly on TV ads). McCall took 74% of the GOP vote.

The governor's contest between Bob Straub and Tom McCall was the featured race in November. Bob Straub had an uphill battle ahead of him. Straub's first hurdle was Tom McCall's incumbency. McCall was charismatic, Straub was not. The governor raised and spent twice as much money. Bob Straub was also saddled with a badly divided party. The wounds inflicted by the acrimonious 1968 Senate race between Bob Duncan and Wayne Morse were still fresh and deep. As hard as Bob Straub tried, he could not find a hot issue to distinguish himself from McCall. No matter what tack Straub tried, he could not paint Tom McCall into a corner. He failed to hang a single controversial issue round McCall's neck.

Straub built his campaign on two issues: Oregon needed a leader who could achieve meaningful property tax relief and tougher laws to protect the environment. These were issues with which voters strongly identified but Straub was unable to convince voters that they should climb out of Tom McCall's boat and into his.

The success of Vortex at the end of August catapulted McCall into an insurmountable lead in November. Voters appreciated McCall for his bold, imaginative leadership and he was reelected by a majority of 76,000 votes: 370,000 to 294,000. McCall captured 55.5% of the vote, virtually the same number he got in 1966.

The Legislature of 1971

On January 12, the day the 1971 Legislature convened, Tom McCall appeared on CBS TV news. Governor McCall was being interviewed about Oregon's environmental movement. The reporter asked McCall how he proposed to regulate economic and population growth in Oregon. McCall's response startled viewers. With his prominent jaw thrust forward, Tom McCall answered the question in three short sentences. "Come visit us again and again. This is a state of excitement. But for heaven's sake, don't come to live here." Viewers watching McCall turned to each other. "Did he say what I think he said? What does McCall mean?"

The sight of the governor slamming the state's doors shut caught the media's attention. McCall explained the statement again and again, denying that people were unwelcome in Oregon. The three sentences would be taken out of context countless times and as newspapers across the United States and Canada (and even Europe) repeated McCall's statement, he had to defend it far and wide.[32]

Tom McCall did not back down. He preached the protection of Oregon's environment and scenic beauty for the rest of his life. For McCall, Oregon was special and he would do what he could to preserve and protect the state's unique qualities. Who wants to live in a state where uncontrolled population growth takes precedence over beaches, mountains, forests, rivers, and verdant farmlands? For those who understood what Tom McCall was saying, he became their hero all over again.

The mood was somber as Oregon's 56th Legislative Assembly gathered at the Capitol on January 11, 1971. In his second inaugural address, Governor McCall told lawmakers what they already knew: the session would be challenging and difficult. Oregon's economy had slowed dramatically over the past 18 months. The lumber market was flat. Thousands of Oregonians were out of work. Dozens of timber communities were suffering the effects of 15 to 20% unemployment rates. With so many people unemployed (and paying less state income tax) the state's income had shrunk. Governor and legislature were in a bind. Voters were in an uproar about their high property taxes. They wanted tax relief. And they expected the legislature to give it to them. In 1970 and early 1971, voters throughout Oregon defeated one local tax election after another, reminding legislators that property-tax relief was what they wanted.

House Speaker Bob Smith believed the new session could be the most difficult in history. "We are faced with a chronic shortage of funds for such things as education, property tax relief, and assistance to local governments," said Smith.[33] The House organized quickly and got to work. Speaker Smith, in an attempt to promote efficiency and cut costs, had reduced the number of House committees from 18 to 11.

The Senate got off to a shaky start. For the first 12 days the Senate was stalled while senators jockeyed to find the 16 votes necessary to elect a president. Finally, after 53 ballots, Democrat John Burns of Portland was elected president (with the backing of the 14 GOP senators and Democrat Debbs Potts). Burns immediately tried to repair his rift with fellow Democrats; he appointed 11 Democrats and seven Republicans to chair Senate committees.

One-third of Oregon lawmakers were newcomers in 1971. The Senate had two female members: Betty Roberts of Portland and Elizabeth (Betty) Browne of Oakridge. Twelve senators were businessmen and 12 were lawyers. The House, with 22 new members, had five female representatives: Democrats Nancie Fadeley of Eugene and Grace Olivier Peck of Portland, and Republicans Fritzi Chuinard of Portland, Norma Paulus of Salem, and Mary Rieke of Portland. The 1971 House was unusual because of the large number of educators who served. Seventeen members were either school teachers, administrators, former teachers, or professors. Educators were fast becoming a new political force in state government.

The 56th Legislature lasted 151 days, adjourning June 10, 1971. And it was one of the most innovative, productive, and forward-looking legislatures ever. The 1971 session launched Oregon onto the national and world stage as a leader in environmental protection legislation. Passage of the Bottle Bill was the session's greatest accomplishment. Of the hundreds of bills debated by legislators in 1971, none got as much attention as HB1036, the Bottle Bill, which was coming around a second time after a similar measure died in a House committee in 1969. HB1036 was the most controversial and hotly debated bill in 1971, attracting worldwide attention. Lobbyists representing bottlers, unions, aluminum can and bottle makers, and the soft-drink and beer industry flooded into the Capitol, intent on killing the Bottle Bill. Opposing them was an alliance of individuals and organizations. Principle supporters of the Bottle Bill included its originator, Richard Chambers of Salem, Rep. Paul Hanneman and Sen. Hector Macpherson, both coastal Republicans, and Oregon's popular governor, Tom McCall.

Beginning in January 1970, Tom McCall had repeatedly spoken in public about Oregon's growing litter problem and the need to pass a Bottle Bill in the 1971 Legislature. By focusing attention on litter, McCall helped to educate people about the problem. For the previous year Rep. Gordon Macpherson had chaired a legislative committee on litter. His committee had heard over 200 hours of public testimony on the subject. His group had concluded its work by drafting a bill for introduction in the 1971 session. Representative Paul Hanneman (who had introduced the original Bottle Bill in 1969) was also instrumental in the passage of HB1036. As members of the Republican majority in the house, Hanneman and Macpherson were part of the legislative power structure. Both used their clout within the GOP caucus to educate and influence their members to support the bill.

Industry's big guns descended on Salem to quash the Bottle Bill. Two dozen major corporations sent lobbyists (some from as far away as New Jersey, New York, and Chicago). These foes of HB1036 testified in committee, buttonholed lawmakers, and paid for full-page newspaper ads opposing the measure. The lobbyists argued that the bill was not needed; if Oregon had a litter problem, then just pass a tougher anti-litter law. Opponents claimed that hundreds of jobs were in jeopardy if HB1036 became law. The harder opponents pushed, the more certain lawmakers were that the Bottle Bill was good legislation. The House passed the bill 54-6, to the astonishment of the bill's foes.

HB1036 was assigned to the Senate Consumer Affairs Committee. Immediately, a rumor-mill surged through the Capitol. One rumor was that the foes of the Bottle Bill were making promises, including bribes, to senators. Democrat Betty Roberts chaired the Consumer Affairs Committee. One night, Senator Roberts received a phone call from a man who promised to give money to Democratic candidates if Roberts would bury the Bottle Bill in her committee. Roberts hung up on the caller. Senator Ted Hallock, another Portland Democrat, got a call similar to Roberts'. The next morning, May 27, Betty Roberts stood on the Senate floor and told about her nighttime phone call. The visitors' gallery stirred as the incensed Roberts sat down. Opponents knew they were sunk. The Bottle Bill would pass. And so it did, by a Senate vote of 22-8. A delighted Governor McCall signed the bill into law, announcing that a new day had arrived in Oregon. Tom McCall called the bill the "innovative highlight of my ten years in elective office.[34]

Tom McCall became the Bottle Bill's most ardent champion. He stumped the country, preaching the benefits of such a law. McCall addressed organizations, including the state legislatures of Michigan, Connecticut, Maine, Minnesota, Hawaii, Virginia, and Colorado. McCall's efforts paid off, as Michigan, Maine, and Connecticut passed their own bottle bills. Over time, the Bottle Bill has become one of Tom McCall's most enduring legacies.

The Bottle Bill was to go into effect on October 1, 1972. The bill's opponents went to court hoping to get it declared unconstitutional. A Marion

County Circuit Judge upheld its constitutionality. Undeterred, the plaintiffs took their suit to the Oregon Court of Appeals. On December 17, 1973, the court ruled that the Bottle Bill was, indeed, constitutional. Oregon's U.S. Sen. Mark Hatfield, backed by his colleague, Bob Packwood, introduced a national bottle bill in Congress. But the legislation was easily defeated in a Senate vote, 60-26, on June 30, 1976.

The 1971 Legislature enacted more ecology-friendly legislation than any session before it. Along with the Bottle Bill, lawmakers passed the Bike Bill, which set aside 1% of state highway funds so that the state, cities, and counties could build bike paths along the sides of roads or highways, through parks, along rivers, or wherever local groups lobbied for the construction of such paths. The Bike Bill was intended to get people out of their cars, promoting cleaner air, reduced traffic, and healthier citizens.

Oregon went nuclear in 1971. Construction began, near the Columbia River town of Clatskanie, on the state's first (and only) nuclear-fueled power plant. Named Trojan, the plant was controversial and became a political hot potato. Led by State Senator Ted Hallock of Portland, the legislature became embroiled in the Trojan controversy and wrestled with nuclear power issues for the next ten years. Some, like Hallock, wanted to stop the construction of Trojan. Failing in that, foes wanted to restrict where such facilities could be built. Senator Hallock sponsored three major bills relating to Trojan in the 1971 session. All died in committee.

A State Highway Beautification Act was passed. The bill called for the gradual elimination of billboards along state highways. The problem of air pollution was addressed in several bills. A bill was passed to improve urban airsheds by requiring automobiles to have approved emission-control systems. The DEQ was given authority to regulate vehicular traffic where high carbon monoxide or particulate content in the air could threaten human health.

Lawmakers enacted the Solid Waste Management Act of 1971. This bill revised statutes relating to solid waste, giving authority to cities and counties to regulate the placing and operation of solid waste sites throughout the state; all regulatory power relating to solid waste was transferred from the State Board of Health to DEQ.

1971 saw a sweeping overhaul of Oregon's Criminal Code—the first major revamping of the code in the 20th century. Several new state agencies were created, including a State Housing Division to provide low-cost housing, and the Children's Services Division to better coordinate and deliver services to underprivileged and disturbed children.

Spirited debate occurred when House Joint Resolution (HJR) 47 came up for a vote. The resolution called for Oregon to ratify the 26th Amendment to the U.S. Constitution: should the voting age in the United States be lowered to 18? Oregonians had recently defeated a similar ballot measure by a three to two margin. But the legislature approved HJR47, making Oregon the 31st state to ratify the Amendment, which was ratified by the required three-quarters of the states on July 5, 1971.

By making significant cuts in the proposed state budget for 1971-73, lawmakers squeezed out enough money to set aside $43 million for property-tax relief for homeowners, who would receive a tax refund from the state of between $100 and $400, depending on their income and amount of taxes paid. In addition, legislators added $200 million to the Basic School Support Fund, increasing the state's share of paying for public schools, K-12. The legislature also passed a 7% reduction in the state income tax rate.

At least one critical issue remained on the table when the assembly adjourned on June 10: the reapportionment of state legislative and congressional districts. Lawmakers did not attempt to redraw the political map of Oregon (as required every 10 years by the federal census). Reapportionment was a highly explosive issue, paralyzing some legislatures in partisan in-fighting. Legislative leaders punted reapportionment off to the secretary of state and the courts to decide. By so doing, lawmakers assured a more harmonious session by not letting reapportionment poison the proceedings. However, the legislature's decision not to deal with the issue was viewed as the session's most glaring failure.

The 1972 Oregon Primary

Oregon's primary election of May 23, 1972, occurred as the Nixon administration was trying to find a way to extricate the U.S. from the Vietnam War. Oregon Republicans were emphatic in their support of the president: he got 83% of the GOP vote in May.

Eleven prominent Democrats were on the primary ballot for president. Never had so many candidates for one office appeared on an Oregon ballot. All wings of the party were represented: Gov. George Wallace; Senators Henry Jackson, Edmund Muskie, Ted Kennedy, Eugene McCarthy, and George McGovern; U.S. Representatives Patsy Mink, Shirley Chisholm, and Wilbur Mills; Hubert Humphrey and lifelong Republican John Lindsay, mayor of New York City. The 1972 election was also the first time that two women were on a presidential ballot in Oregon. Senator George McGovern was the only Democrat to campaign in Oregon. A leading Senate dove, a critic of the Vietnam War, McGovern won with 50% of the Democratic vote (202,000; Wallace 80,500; Humphrey 50,500).

In the Republican Senate race incumbent Mark Hatfield scored a lopsided victory over three minor candidates with 61% of the vote. Three months earlier Hatfield's future had been much less certain. For weeks Tom McCall had acted as if he would challenge Hatfield. Despite pressure from the White House and other prominent Republicans, McCall was still considering a run at Hatfield right up to the March filing deadline. Then he said he did not have the stomach for a bruising campaign; Hatfield had told him that he would "shred" him if he challenged him in the primary.[35] Governor McCall knew that in two years his second term would end, and that Senator Packwood would be up for reelection; he would wait, knowing that he would have another chance to run for the Senate in 1974.

Six months later, during a routine physical examination, Tom McCall was told he had prostate cancer. After a week-long vacation and intense antibiotic treatments, his cancer was in remission. His health, however, would never be the same.

The Democratic Senate primary included Wayne Morse, Bob Duncan, and State Senator Don Willner. Morse won the nomination, defeating Duncan 170,000 to 126,500. Willner got 73,000 votes. The most hotly contested race in the 1972 primary was in the 4th Congressional District. Former congressman Charles O. Porter, a Eugene attorney, defeated James Weaver by 250 votes (out of 60,000 votes cast). In Portland, a young Democratic city commissioner named Neil Goldschmidt was elected mayor, winning 57% of the primary vote.

The 1972 General Election

Three weeks after the Oregon primary, a burglary occurred in Washington, D.C. On the night of June 17, 1972, five men were caught in the offices of the Democratic National Committee in the Watergate building. One of the burglars was James McCord, chief of security for CREEP, the Committee to Re-Elect the President (Richard Nixon). Reporters Bob Woodward and Carl Bernstein of the *Washington Post* began to dig into the story. They eventually found that there was a link between the Watergate burglary and the Nixon White House.

Americans didn't know about this connection when they voted in November. President Nixon was reelected by a landslide over Democrat George McGovern. Nixon won by 18 million votes, 61% of the national vote. Oregonians followed suit, giving Nixon 52.5% of the total, a 94,000-vote margin over Senator McGovern's 392,760 (42%). Eighty percent of Oregon voters cast ballots.

The Senate race between Republican Mark Hatfield and Democrat Wayne Morse was the featured contest in Oregon's November election. Senator Hatfield defeated Morse by 69,000 votes (494,000 to 425,000). Morse's age was a key reason for his defeat. Hatfield's impressive victory headed a GOP tide that, in general, swept through Oregon. The Republican surge of 1972 did not, however, include the Oregon Legislature, where Democrats won control of both chambers.

Changing of the Guard

Americans welcomed 1973 with trepidation. In March 1973, the last American troops and American prisoners-of-war left South Vietnam. Since 1965, 54,000 Americans had died in Southeast Asia. The war's impact, however, was still being felt across the U.S. Inflation was creeping upward. The federal budget was out of balance, and deficit spending and the national debt were soaring. Up to two million military personnel were preparing to re-enter civilian life. Military and veterans' hospitals were filled to capacity with tens of thousands of severely wounded soldiers. Clearly, Vietnam was still on America's mind, but the unraveling Watergate scandal was beginning to replace Vietnam as the day's topic. The U.S. Senate was preparing to conduct an investigation of President Nixon's role in the conspiracy. Was a constitutional crisis just around the corner? It was against this backdrop of domestic turmoil that Oregon's 57th Legislative Assembly met in Salem on January 8, 1973.

The legislature had a new look in 1973. Democrats had won control of both houses in November. Governor McCall, for the only time in his eight-year tenure, would work with a Democratic Assembly. Seven House members had won seats in the Senate. The House welcomed 28 new lawmakers, nearly half of the body. The 1972 election resulted in a drastic drop in the average age of a state representative. Five legislators were under 25, a dozen were under age 30, and 21 were between 31 and 40 years old. The House leadership consisted of 53-year-old Speaker Richard (Dick) Eymann; Phil Lang, 43-year-old speaker pro-tem; Les AuCoin, the 30-year-old majority leader, and Assistant Majority Leader Al Densmore, who was 26. There were nine women in the House, the most ever, and two women senators, Betty Roberts and Elizabeth (Betty) Browne. The first African American elected to the Oregon Legislature, William "Bill" McCoy, a Portland Democrat, won a House seat.[*]

---

[*] Two years later McCoy was elected to the state Senate, where he served for twenty years. Until Jim Hill's election in 1986, Bill McCoy was Oregon's only African American state senator.

Tom McCall Pushes Tax Reform

A noisy, expectant throng packed the House chamber as the 1973 Legislature convened on January 8. The crowd grew quiet when Governor Tom McCall began his Opening Day address. The governor's speech would set the tone for the session. McCall noted that a sweeping tax reform/school finance plan was his top priority—and it ought to be the legislature's, too. *Oregon Voter* wrote: "the interlocked school finance/property tax relief problem looms over the 1973 Session like a two-headed monster. Reducing property taxes will be easy, but raising other taxes to offset may well prove impossible, with the voters' anti-tax feeling. There is a lot of glib talk about raising income taxes, but there is no reason to think that the voters will have any part of it." McCall laid out an ambitious program including adoption of statewide land-use planning and lowering of the age of majority from 21 to 18.[36]

The session got off to a fast start. President Jason Boe (an optometrist from Reedsport) and Speaker Dick Eymann (a timber executive from Lane County) had asked lawmakers to submit bills before January 8. By getting this jump on the flow of legislation, Boe and Eymann were ready to refer 74 bills to committee on Opening Day.

The issue of tax relief and school finance reform had stalked the legislature for the previous six years like an 800-pound gorilla. In 1973, lawmakers wanted more than anything to get the gorilla off their backs. The tax issue was the first item on the agenda. Working in tandem with Governor McCall, Boe and Eymann were adamant about one thing: the legislature must craft a comprehensive tax relief/school finance package early enough to allow the people to vote on it before the legislature adjourned. If voters defeated the plan, lawmakers would then have time to write another proposal before the session ended.

Tom McCall, more than any other Oregon politician, had been committed to property-tax relief and reform. But things were different in 1973; for the first time in six years, legislative leaders wanted to work with the governor to fashion a tax program they all could get behind and sell to the public. McCall noted the irony in this: he, a Republican governor, had finally been united with two Democrats, Eymann and Boe, who believed in his tax plan as much as he did. This Democratic commitment explains why the legislature, for its first 10 weeks, devoted more time to the McCall Tax Plan than to anything else.

But when the bill reached the Senate it hit a stone wall. The bill was referred to the Senate Taxation Committee chaired by an irascible Democrat named Vern Cook. The mercurial Cook detested the McCall proposal, vowing that the McCall plan would only get out of his committee over his dead body. Jason Boe saw Cook's defiance as a direct challenge to his leadership. Boe did not hesitate: he removed Cook as chair of the Taxation Committee and appointed himself committee chair. One way or another, Jason Boe would get a tax measure out to voters.

Finally, on March 21, the McCall plan was ready for a Senate vote. Knowing there were problems, Jason Boe gave his gavel to another senator and took his place at his desk on the floor. From there, he led the debate on the tax plan. After a tense two-hour debate it was time to vote. The plan was defeated, 16-14. Four Democrats joined 12 Republicans to block the proposal. After a tense recess, a vote to reconsider the bill passed. This time, the plan passed 17-13. Three Republicans changed their vote: Victor Atiyeh, Hector Macpherson, and Dick Hoyt. All made it clear they did not like the bill but they wanted it to pass so voters could decide the issue. The next day, the House passed the McCall plan 39-21. The statewide vote on the tax plan would occur at a special election May 1, 1973.

Governor McCall campaigned nonstop for a month. He gave dozens of speeches to business, civic, and professional groups. He participated in radio and TV interviews and candid discussions with newspaper editors. McCall crisscrossed Oregon, talking to people on the street, confident they would trust and support him. Joining McCall in the campaign were all of Oregon's ranking Democrats: House Speaker Dick Eymann, Senate President Jason Boe, Treasurer Jim Redden, former Treasurer Bob Straub, and Wayne Morse. Other than McCall, no other prominent Republican campaigned for the tax plan.

The purpose of the McCall Plan was to change the way Oregon communities paid for their public schools. The governor proposed to shift the burden of paying for schools away from local property taxes and onto the back of state government. McCall wanted the state to pay 95% of local school costs. But where would the state get the millions of dollars needed? By raising taxes. The McCall plan would raise personal income taxes by 32% and hike corporate excise taxes from a flat 6% rate to a graduated rate up to 9%. In addition, the McCall plan included the establishment of two new taxes, one on profits earned by Oregon businesses, the second a statewide tax on the assessed value of income-producing property.

The *Oregon Voter* wrote: "In general the program is supported by big labor, liberal Democrats, and a handful of Republicans loyal to McCall. It is opposed by conservative Democrats, most Republicans and most business leaders. The alignment is natural because the McCall program is very similar to plans previously proposed by Democrats."[37] Associated Oregon Industries and the Oregon

Retail Council opposed the McCall plan, as did a group called Responsible Tax Relief. This organization included at least 37 legislators, led by Republican Stafford Hansell and Democratic Senator Vern Cook.

Things did not go McCall's way. The plan lost 358,00 to 253,700. McCall was so upset he threatened to resign. He'd been rejected as the people's leader. Though hurt and bitterly disappointed, Tom McCall did not resign.

Why did voters reject the McCall Tax Plan? Many people were unsure what the plan would actually do. Many voters were confused. And some rejected the plan because it didn't reduce taxes. Others feared that the plan was too much of a radical change all at once. A few days after the election the legislature went back to work on another tax program.

Dueling Democrats

Only days after the McCall plan's defeat, Senate President Jason Boe restored Vern Cook as chair of the Senate Tax Committee. While Boe tried to smooth out the discord within the Democratic caucus, Speaker Eymann wrestled with his own problems. Six conservative Democrats, led by freshman representatives Dick Magruder and Jeff Gilmour, butted heads with Eymann. Like Vern Cook, Magruder and Gilmour had opposed the McCall plan. The young lawmakers (Magruder was 26 and Gilmour 25) also criticized Eymann for a personnel decision he had made. Eymann reacted by stripping Magruder and Gilmour of their positions as chair and vice-chair of the House Consumer and Business Affairs. Rumors of a coalition between the six Magruder-Gilmour Democrats and the 27 House Republicans (to form a new House majority) floated through the chamber. But Eymann held on and the Democrats finished the session still in control, with the final weeks of the session more tense than usual.

The 57th Legislature dragged on for six months; at 180 days, it was the longest and most expensive session ever. Lawmakers wrote a second tax-reform plan and referred it to voters (at a special statewide election May 28, 1974). Legislators accomplished a lot in 1973. Thirty-seven new state departments and commissions were created, including a Department of Economic Development, a Health Commission, and a Transportation Commission. A host of controversial environmental bills also passed. The most important of these was the complex, emotionally charged Senate Bill 100, which established a precedent-setting statewide land-use planning law in Oregon. Senate Bill 100 is rated as one of the most important laws passed in Oregon in the 20th century; and it was the 1973 Legislature's most notable achievement.

A Landmark: Senate Bill 100

Senate Bill 100 established a comprehensive, state-run land-use law in Oregon. The bill was carefully prepared by a phalanx of dedicated Republicans and Democrats. With a national reputation as an advocate of land-use planning, Governor McCall had focused public attention on the issue for the past five years. Was the state ready for it?

McCall had three important allies in his quest to pass SB 100. Republican Senator Hector Macpherson, a Linn County dairy farmer, was concerned about the loss of prime farmland to development. Macpherson was the godfather of SB 100—he, more than anyone, was responsible for drafting the legislation. Another key player in the land-use drama was State Senator Ted Hallock, a Portland Democrat. Hallock chaired the Senate committee on Environment and Land-use Planning. Macpherson was a committee member. L. B. Day, a former state senator and labor leader from Salem, was McCall's third critical ally. Day was McCall's new director of the Department of Environmental Quality (DEQ) and one of Oregon's most colorful and controversial politicians. Known for his booming voice, keen intelligence, emotional outbursts, and dogged determination, Day was a man you wanted on your side. As an adversary, Day was clever, impatient, and strong willed—and he wouldn't take no for an answer.

Opposition to SB 100 included Associated Oregon Industries, Portland General Electric, Pacific Power and Light, Weyerhaeuser, Georgia-Pacific, and the Oregon Home Builders Association. Jason Boe also stood in Hallock's way because he believed that land-use zoning decisions should be left up to local governments. While Governor McCall despaired over the fate of SB 100, Ted Hallock hatched a plan to save it. A special task force of industry and farm representatives was appointed. And L. B. Day was put in charge. After many hours of intense negotiation, Day's task force produced a land-use bill and sent it to Hallock's committee, which passed the bill and sent it to the floor. The Senate passed SB 100 18-10. Hallock and Macpherson took the bill to the House, asking the Environment Committee to pass the bill without any changes. With SB 100 intact, the House passed it 40-20. A jubilant Tom McCall signed the bill into law. For the rest of the 20th century, SB 100 would be the land-use model most copied by other states and nations.

More Precedents

The 1973 Legislature passed a bevy of other precedent-setting laws. Oregon's first open-meetings law was enacted, requiring all public officials to conduct

their meetings in public, so citizens could observe and participate in the proceedings. The law applied to such entities as school boards, city councils, and
county commissions. Smoking tobacco in all public meetings was banned,
kicking off a 20-year crusade to prohibit smoking in all government buildings
(including schools), public places (such as shopping malls), and restaurants.
1973 also saw the passage of a revised shield law to protect members of the
news media from being forced to divulge the identity of their sources of
information.

Handicapped citizens rejoiced with the enactment of Oregon's first archi-
tectural barriers law. This act required that all new public buildings (as well as
those undergoing remodeling) be constructed with the handicapped in mind—
meaning that ramps, railings, and elevators be installed so that disabled persons
had easier, more open access to government buildings (including schools and
universities).

Catching Up with History

Representative Bill McCoy, a Portland Democrat and the only African American
in the 1973 Legislature, introduced HJR 13 to right an old wrong. The resolution passed both houses, overturning an action of the 1868 Legislature. In
January 1865, Congress had passed the 14th Amendment and referred it to
the states for ratification. The Amendment defined who qualified as a citizen
(all persons born or naturalized in the United States), and established the due
process and equal protection clauses. Oregon's Republican Legislature of 1866
ratified the Amendment. Two years later, Democrats, many of whom were
pro-Confederacy and against Negro equality, regained control of the legislature, and the 1868 session overturned Oregon's earlier ratification of the 14th
Amendment. Until 1973, the legislature had never ratified the Amendment.
Approval of Bill McCoy's resolution finally brought Oregon in line with the
rest of the states.

Issues of special importance to women resulted in the introduction and
passage of a number of bills in the session. The 11 women who served in the
1973 Legislature formed a women's caucus, led by Senator Betty Roberts,
a Democrat, and Republican Representative Norma Paulus, to push their
agenda. The caucus made ratification of the proposed 28th Amendment to
the federal Constitution, the Equal Rights Amendment (ERA), their priority.
A carefully planned strategy and the outspoken help of a number of male
legislators, including House Republican Roger Martin and Democrat Les
AuCoin, resulted in passage of Senate Joint Resolution 4, 23-6 in the Senate

and 50-9 in the House. Oregon had joined the growing list of states to approve the ERA.*

Betty Roberts, in her excellent memoir, writes:

> With the ERA passed only a month into the 1973 legislative session, our attention turned to bills that would bring Oregon laws into conformity with the new constitutional amendment. It may be hard to imagine today that women couldn't keep their birth names when they got married, couldn't get credit in their own names, couldn't stay in a motel alone, couldn't eat at certain restaurants at lunchtime, couldn't get insurance unless they had a husband, couldn't be admitted to some trade schools. It was shocking how fast the bills piled up. It was too big a task for one session, but we determined to make a good start.

Top priority, the women's caucus decided, were the bills that would affect the largest number of women. Those were the proposals prohibiting discrimination in public accommodation, allowing a woman to choose whether to keep her name upon marriage or to return to a former name if divorcing, and prohibiting discrimination in educational institutions and in insurance matters.[38]

Three important women's rights bills were enacted in the 1973 session. All were passed by wide margins. House Bill 2116 prohibited discrimination in public accommodations and housing, in securing credit and insurance, and denial of admission to vocational and trade schools based on gender. House Bill 2925 allowed a woman to keep her prior name when she married and would require a judge to allow a woman to change her name when she was granted a divorce. Senate Bill 74, sponsored by Senator Roberts, established a Children's Commission in the Department of Human Resources and included funding— to address the cost of adequate child care for working parents, as well as other vital services for children and families.[39]

Campaign and Elections of 1974

The Watergate scandal continued to unfold in the spring of 1974 while Oregon conducted its May 1974 primary election, impacting state and local politics. There was a voter backlash against Republican candidates (with a corresponding increase in support for Democrats running for office) and many voters

---

* The ERA was not ratified by the necessary two-thirds of the states, and did not become part of the federal Constitution.

stayed home on primary election day (voter turnout was only 47%). The race for governor and for U.S. Senate were the most important political campaigns in Oregon in 1974. Senator Bob Packwood's first term would end in January 1975 and he was early in announcing his candidacy for a second term. Wayne Morse was waiting and he ached to return to the Senate. Now, with the May 1974 primary approaching, Morse was back on the campaign trail. Jason Boe was running against Morse for the Democratic nomination. Morse, as always, was outspoken, controversial, and intense, glorying in the political fight. Jason Boe, in contrast, was a large, barrel-chested man with a deep and measured voice.

The years had taken their toll on Wayne Morse. At 74, he was thinner and grayer, a man of sharp, hard angles, his prominent nose, bushy eyebrows, and black-framed eyeglasses a cartoonist's dream. But with gravelly voice and piercing stare, he campaigned with the same vigor he always had. Everyone knew that 1974 would likely be Morse's last campaign. Democrats nominated him for the Senate (he won by 155,700 to 125,000 for Jason Boe). With only token opposition, Bob Packwood won the GOP Senate primary, amassing nearly 200,000 votes. It looked as if 1974 would be a repeat of the Morse-Packwood contest of 1968.

Because the Oregon Constitution prohibits a governor from seeking three consecutive four-year terms, Tom McCall's name for the first time in 10 years was not on the ballot. Ten Democrats, including three popular politicians, and five Republicans ran for governor in the May primary.

Bob Straub, seeking the Democratic nomination for the third time, was challenged by State Senator Betty Roberts of Portland and by State Treasurer Jim Redden. Straub was the best known of the three, having been on the November ballot twice as a candidate for state treasurer (1964 and 1968) and twice as Democratic nominee for governor (against Tom McCall in 1966 and 1970). Known as the father of the Willamette River Greenway and for taking the lead in saving the Nestucca Spit on the central Oregon coast from the realigning of Highway 101, Straub's pro-environment credentials were as strong as Tom McCall's. But despite his environmental record and eight years as an innovative state treasurer, the question of his electability as governor hung over his campaign. With 10 candidates in the field it was assumed that whoever won the Democratic primary would pull under 50% of the vote. Bob Straub won the nomination with only 33% of the Democratic vote (Straub: 107,200, Betty Roberts: 98,650, and Jim Redden: 88,800). Roberts and Redden between them drew over 187,000 votes, or 80,000 more than Straub's total. None of the seven lesser-known Democratic candidates got more than 5,000 votes.

The Republican gubernatorial primary featured veteran State Sen. Victor Atiyeh and Secretary of State Clay Myers. Myers was better known. Originally appointed secretary of state by Tom McCall in 1967, he was elected and re-elected in 1968 and 1972. Atiyeh was popular with the business community. Neither Myers or Atiyeh was flamboyant in the manner of a Tom McCall. They both exuded a quiet, businesslike approach to government and problem solving. Atiyeh won an impressive victory (144,500 to 79,000).

The May primary also featured an interesting congressional race for the 1st District seat of five-term Congressman Wendell Wyatt, who was retiring. Young State Representative Les AuCoin, a Forest Grove Democrat, won his party's nomination. His opponent was Republican Diarmuid O'Scannlain. A Democrat hadn't held the seat since its creation in 1892. Could Les AuCoin win in such a staunchly Republican district?

Wayne Morse's Senate campaign came to a sudden stop in mid-July. Felled by a serious urinary-tract infection, Morse was admitted to a Portland hospital. His condition worsened and on July 22, 1974, Wayne Lyman Morse died. Oregonians were stunned. For 30 years, Wayne Morse had been one of Oregon's most prominent, controversial, and powerful politicians. With his sudden death the Democratic Party was in a quandary—who could they find to replace Morse so late in the Senate campaign?

Into the spotlight stepped State Senator Betty Roberts. A lawyer, an articulate, effective legislator, a former high school teacher, and a leading feminist, Senator Roberts had lost a close election to Bob Straub in the May Democratic primary for governor. She was nominated to run for the Senate in Morse's place. Roberts launched a spirited last-minute campaign with the odds against her. Incumbent Sen. Bob Packwood had lots of money and an effective statewide campaign organization. A few days after Roberts' Senate nomination, President Nixon resigned. Oregonians wondered how the Watergate scandal would impact the November election. Would Watergate cause an anti-Republican backlash?

There were some surprises on November 5. Democrat Bob Straub won a landslide victory over Republican Victor Atiyeh for governor. Straub won 58% of the vote, pulling 445,000 votes to Atiyeh's 294,000. Voter turnout was up: 69% of registered voters cast ballots in November. Tom McCall had perturbed many Republicans when he backed Democrat Straub rather than Victor Atiyeh for governor.

Straub's easy victory was not the only political surprise in November. Prior to the election, Oregon's four U.S. House seats were held by two Republicans

(John Dellenbeck and Wendell Wyatt) and two Democrats (Edith Green and Al Ullman). Both Green (a 10-term incumbent) and Wyatt were retiring; therefore, Oregon would have at least two new representatives. In Wyatt's 1st District, youthful Democrat Les AuCoin broke the GOP's monopoly on that seat, defeating Republican Diarmuid O'Scannlain 114,600 to 90,000. AuCoin was starting his own nine-term career in the 1st Congressional District.

The 3rd District seat returned Democrat Bob Duncan to the U.S. House (Duncan had earlier served two House terms in Oregon's 4th District). In the 4th District, Democrat Jim Weaver upset four-term Republican Congressman John Dellenback, by almost 10,000 votes (97,600 to 87,000). Meanwhile, veteran Al Ullman won a 10th term in the 2nd District. The Democrats had done it— they had captured all four of Oregon's U.S. House seats.

The U.S. Senate race between Senator Bob Packwood and Democrat Betty Roberts was not close: Packwood, 421,000; Roberts, 338,600.

Democrats also swept through Oregon's legislative races, increasing their hold on the House, winning 38 seats. In the Senate, Democrats took 19 of the 30 seats. Among the newly elected representatives were future governor Ted Kulongoski and Attorney General Hardy Myers. Mary Wendy Roberts, a one-term state representative from Portland, was elected to the state Senate at age 30, making her the youngest woman ever elected to that body.

There were also several big upsets in the legislative elections. Republican State Senator Hector Macpherson, the father of Oregon's pioneering Senate Bill 100, was defeated by a young Democrat named John Powell. The second upset was even more stunning: Dick Eymann, Democratic speaker of the Oregon House, lost his seat to Bill Rogers, a Republican newcomer who grew hazelnuts and sold insurance. Eymann's defeat opened the way for seven-term Portland Democrat Phil Lang to become speaker. The face of Oregon politics was transformed by the 1974 election. The stench of Watergate had swept aside many Republican officeholders, replacing them with a phalanx of young Democrats who would shape Oregon government well into the 21st century.[*]

---

[*] The author was elected to the Oregon House in 1974 from District 5, Washington County.

Chapter 16
Bob Straub—Living in Tom's Long Shadow, 1975-78

Robert "Bob" Straub took the oath of office on January 13, 1975, as Oregon's 31st governor and the first Democrat in 16 years. This marked the end of a Republican era dominated by two of Oregon's most successful 20th-century politicians: Mark O. Hatfield and Tom Lawson McCall. At age 54, Straub had been a fixture in state government for the previous decade. As state treasurer, he'd worked closely with Governor McCall. They were allies on environmental protection and the preservation of Oregon's coastal beaches. As governor, McCall was a staunch supporter of the Willamette River Greenway Plan—an idea first proposed by Straub. Both men advocated statewide land-use planning (and its administrative arm, the Land Conservation and Development Commission, or LCDC). As Oregon's new governor, Bob Straub inherited the job of implementing the statewide planning goals being developed by LCDC. For the backers of land-use planning (notably the group 1000 Friends of Oregon), having Straub in the governor's chair was crucial, since the land-use laws were new and under attack by various groups throughout the state. One reason voters chose Bob Straub was because they believed he would continue the environmental work of Tom McCall.

Many Oregonians thought of Bob Straub and Tom McCall, both ardent environmentalists, as two peas in a pod. But though often linked philosophically, they were very different personalities. Garrulous Tom McCall hated being alone. He was an extrovert who relished being the center of attention and had a flair for the dramatic. Energetic and charismatic, he often appeared to be larger than life. He was a man impossible to ignore. Bob Straub was a friendly man who preferred the company of close friends and his large family (Straub and wife, Pat, had six children). Where McCall wore his emotions on his sleeve, Bob Straub was more deliberate, cautious, and reserved. Straub preferred to work behind the scenes and he didn't crave celebrity status. "Bob Straub was a doer, not a talker" said Victor Atiyeh.[1]

As public speakers, the two men were worlds apart. McCall's distinctive "Boston" pronunciation and colorful phraseology typically kept his listeners engaged. Straub wasn't flamboyant and spoke in a monotone voice; he came across as well informed, sincere, and concerned. McCall was sometimes stung by criticism and as easily upset by it, but Straub took it in stride. A self-effacing man, Bob Straub went about his work quietly.

A Democratic Legislature

Governor Straub was eager to get to work. The Oregon House welcomed 20 new members, the Senate nine. Eight women served in the House and three in the Senate. Phil Lang, a veteran Portland Democrat, was elected speaker of the House by his 38-member caucus. Jason Boe was reelected Senate president. The 58th Legislative Assembly was unusual for the large number of lawmakers who were related to one another. Three senators were named Roberts: Frank, Betty, and Mary Wendy. Frank was Betty's former husband; Betty had been Mary Wendy's stepmother, and Mary Wendy was Frank's daughter. Frank and Mary Wendy Roberts were the legislature's first father-daughter team. There were two Langs (Phil in the House and brother Loyal in the Senate), and two Fadeleys (Nancie was a representative; her husband, Ed, was a senator).

In his inaugural address, Governor Straub focused most of his remarks on the sad state of Oregon's economy. Oregon, like the rest of the nation, was mired in the worst economic recession since the 1930s. State unemployment climbed to near 10% and inflation near 12%. Oregon's timber towns, places like Coos Bay, Roseburg, Oakridge, and Springfield where the economies were based on the timber/wood products industry, were hit especially hard as climbing national interest rates caused a drop in home construction, and cut into lumber sales.

The high price of imported oil was one cause of the nation's economic distress. Gasoline prices had remained high for the previous 18 months, which ratcheted up business costs. Along with the sick Oregon economy, Governor Straub and the legislature faced frustrated, disgusted, and angry Oregonians soured by the residue of President Richard Nixon's resignation and the Watergate scandal. And there was more.

For the past decade, Oregonians had grown increasingly unhappy with rising local property taxes. One result of this voter frustration was a growing willingness to vote "no" on local tax levies for public schools and community colleges. In the May 1975 election, 31% of local school levies were defeated, up a few percentage points from the previous election. The issue of how to pay for public schools had led the 1973 Legislature (also controlled by Democrats) to produce the ill-fated McCall Tax Plan in spring 1973. A second tax plan was produced and referred to voters at the May 28, 1974, election, and defeated by more than 3-1.

Voters were weary. Eight years of charismatic, in-your-face Tom McCall had produced an electorate that wanted a "time-out" from being confronted year after year by so many challenging decisions (such as tax reform plans, growth and development issues, and environmental protection questions). Knowing the mood of the electorate, Governor Straub agreed with legislative leaders that the public needed a rest, time to cool off after rejecting the legislature's last two tax plans. There was no new tax-reform legislation in 1975. But Speaker Phil Lang wanted to take some of the pressure off property taxes by getting the legislature to increase the state's share of Basic School Support from 28 to 35% in the 1975-77 budget.

Speaker Phil Lang saw the challenge facing the '75 session this way: how do we craft a new budget in the middle of the inflation-recession whiplash, [while] stimulating the economy and providing help for those most severely affected by our economic woes? With a state unployment rate of 10% and an inflation rate of 12%, legislators knew the session would be both cautious and businesslike, with little room for expanding or starting costly new programs.[2]

A Full Plate

The 58th Legislature had a big agenda to wade through. Aside from needing to jump-start Oregon's ailing economy, legislators also wrestled with other issues that were controversial and potentially divisive, including: What was the best way to implement SB 100 and what should be the role of the new LCDC? Does Oregon need a Department of Energy to better plan and coordinate energy use and supply? Can the legislature find a better way to tax timber in western Oregon? Should a regional government be established in metropolitan Portland? How far should Oregon move toward establishing and funding public transit systems? Should the legislature modernize itself by expanding the Capitol to accommodate more staff while satisfying the demand for more meeting spaces? Should Oregon establish a state lottery? Could the state afford to increase the salaries of its employees? What could be done to reform state campaign-finance laws, including the limiting of campaign expenses?

Legislators also faced a number of environmental issues in 1975. What could be done to reduce smoke pollution caused by summer burning of grass-seed fields in western Oregon? Could Oregon do anything to help stop the depletion of Earth's ozone layer? Should the use of aerosol spray cans be banned in the state? Other environmental issues included solid waste disposal, recycling, conservation, and the development of alternative energy sources, such as geothermal and solar power.

The 1975 Legislature ground on for 153 days (January 13-June 14), the third longest to date. Senate President Jason Boe and Speaker Phil Lang ran their chambers tightly; neither man liked unnecessary delays and both were relentless in moving their agendas. Lang did this by "pigeonholing" bills (referring the draft to a specific committee to die). It wasn't a new practice, but Lang sometimes did it without input from the bill's sponsor or backers. Lang sometimes lost his patience, snapping at a representative or trying to cut him or her off by strictly enforcing House rules relating to the allotted time a member had to speak on a bill or resolution. Some representatives disliked Lang's style, considering him autocratic and inflexible.

The 58th Legislative Assembly didn't accomplish all it set out to do. Lawmakers failed to determine how best to tax timber holdings in western Oregon. The political hot-potato issue of Willamette Valley field-burning was relegated to more study; leaders saw that the issue had the potential to cause deep divisions in both chambers. The legislature's critics highlighted the failures with one pundit calling the session a "buck-passing" assembly, while others described it as "dull" and "workmanlike," concerned with "nuts-and-bolts." Secretary of State Clay Myers, a Republican, said the assembly was "lack-luster" and too much caught up on devoting "excessive time on special interest or trivial legislation." Glenn Otto, a savvy Democratic representative from Troutdale, characterized the 1975 session as "producing little new and dynamic legislation and rightly so—the session was probably only the lull between the McCall and the Straub years."[3] Otto, chair of the House Committee on Local Government and Urban Affairs, summed up the 1975 session when he noted that his committee's work, like the legislature's, "was one of cautious evaluation of where 1971 and 1973 acts had brought the state. Much of our committee work was concerned with correcting flaws in legislation from those years."[4]

Throughout his tenure, Governor McCall had worked with four legislatures to try to find a solution to the public's call for lower property taxes. He had worked closely with lawmakers to craft three different tax-reform plans and had been the state's most visible and outspoken advocate for the passage of each of these tax plans. Despite his prodigious efforts and broad popular appeal, McCall had failed to sell a majority of Oregonians on the merits of these tax proposals. When he left office in January 1975, both Governor McCall and the public were exhausted. This was the lull Representative Otto talked about; 1975 was a year for the governor and legislature to catch their breaths, a time to review, adjust, and study. It was not a time to enact major and controversial new programs.

Most observers agreed that legislators worked hard in 1975. Lawmakers considered 2,630 bills and enacted over 800 of them. Of these new laws, Senate Bill 771 will most likely be remembered. This bill was intended to draw public attention to a worsening environmental problem: the deterioration of Earth's ozone layer.* Recent scientific studies showed that one of the causes was the widespread use of fluorocarbon gas as an aerosol can propellant and as a refrigerant. While scientists and politicians worldwide debated the issue, the Oregon Legislature passed SB 771, banning the sale of any product that contained fluorocarbon propellant. Everyone recognized that Oregon's ban was symbolic. But because Oregon was the first government in the world to pass such a ban, the state again found itself the subject of news stories and headlines around the world. Several years later, Congress followed Oregon's lead.

Other Accomplishments of the 1975 Legislature

The 1975 Legislature provided some tax relief for Oregonians. State income taxes were reduced for those who earned less than $30,000 a year, which meant that 92% of households would save, collectively, $37 million in lower taxes. To help offset this loss of revenue, Democrats pushed through two tax increases, one that raised the personal income taxes of Oregon's wealthiest 8%, and another that increased the tax on corporations. Lawmakers also increased the school fund by 2% (to 30%), upping the state's share of public school costs to $427 million. With the state picking up more of the cost of schools, it was hoped that local governments or school boards could reduce local property taxes.

The 1975 Legislature established a State Department of Energy (a pet project of Governor Straub) to coordinate the supply, delivery, conservation, and cost of energy.

Lawmakers also tackled the problem of the rising cost of medical malpractice insurance. A new program required doctors to self-insure and to contribute

---

* The ozone layer is critical to our planet because it filters out the sun's potentially harmful ultraviolet rays. Another result of a deteriorating ozone layer is the greenhouse effect, whereby the temperature of Earth's atmosphere continues to climb.

President Gerald Ford with Oregon Congressional representatives Edith Green and Wendell Wyatt, and Sen. Bob Packwood, ca. 1974. *(Gerry Lewin Collection)*

to a state Medical Liability Excess Fund. The fund's money was intended to protect doctors against malpractice claims exceeding the limits of their malpractice insurance coverage.[5]

In enacting SB 381, the legislature tried to assert its power over the executive branch. The act gave the legislature authority to review the administrative rules of state agencies, to better ensure that the legislative intent of a law would be met when the rules went into effect.

Lawmakers referred a constitutional amendment to the voters. Should the legislature have the power to call itself into special session? Voters approved the amendment 549,000 to 377,300 on the November 2, 1976, ballot.

The Election of 1976

President Gerald Ford declared his candidacy for the Republican nomination for president in 1976. Hollywood movie actor and former governor of California, Ronald Reagan, also ran for the nomination. Oregon's 1976 May primary was a test of President Ford's electability; coming late in the spring campaign, the contest between Ford and Reagan would add momentum to the winner only weeks before the GOP National Convention. Because Reagan was from California, many assumed President Ford would have difficulty carrying the state's GOP vote.

The May primary invigorated Oregon's Democratic Party, which was looking for someone to give the Republican candidate a real race. Of eleven candidates listed on the Oregon Democratic primary ballot only three actively campaigned in Oregon: former Georgia Governor James "Jimmy" Carter, Governor Jerry Brown of California, and Idaho Senator Frank Church. Carter had built a formidable grassroots organization and, as a new face in politics and a Washington outsider, was arousing interest among Democrats. He had momentum coming into Oregon's May primary.* Senator Church, a charismatic speaker and longtime critic of the Vietnam War, was well known in the state and waged a spirited campaign, pulling support from prominent business leaders, youth, liberal Democrats, and farm interests. Handsome and outspoken Governor Brown attracted younger voters, environmentalists, and independents.

Nearly 300,000 Republicans voted in the May presidential primary. The outcome was close. President Ford edged Ronald Reagan by 13,500 votes (150,200 to 136,700) and went on to win the GOP nomination. Meanwhile, the spirited Democratic contest between Brown, Church, and Carter produced a huge Democratic turnout of over 431,000 voters. Frank Church won the state's Democratic presidential primary, drawing 145,400 votes to Carter's 115,300 and Brown's 106,800. Jimmy Carter ran a credible race in Oregon, since many Democrats were familiar with Church and his advocacy of such issues as salmon recovery, environmental protection, timber policy, and opposition to the Vietnam War. Jimmy Carter lost the Oregon primary, but went on to win the presidential nomination later that summer.

The political events of 1974-76 galvanized public opinion in both Oregon

---

* During the spring campaign, Carter's staff quietly approached Tom McCall, hoping for his endorsement. McCall considered Carter a friend and had worked with him when both were active in the National Governor's Conference. McCall preferred Carter over Ford, a fellow Republican. But to protect his job as a KATU-TV commentator in Portland, he endorsed neither. Walth, *Fire,* 412.

and the nation, heightening political interest and dramatically increasing voter registration in the state. Between 1974 and 1976 registration jumped from 1.04 to 1.42 million. Democrats benefited from the registration surge, going from 652,400 in 1974 to 794,000 in 1976. Republican registration grew by 58,000 to 497,300. The category of "other" (most of whom were independents) climbed by 77,500 (to 128,600), representing 11% of registered voters in Oregon. Democrats had a registration edge of nearly 300,000 in the state. In November 1976 74% of registered voters went to the polls in Oregon, compared to a national 53% voter turnout.

The Carter-Ford contest was one of the closest presidential races in 20th-century Oregon. The final vote tally took several days but, with over one million votes cast, Gerald Ford defeated Jimmy Carter in Oregon by 1,713 votes (492,120 to 490,407). However, Carter was elected president, taking exactly 50% of the popular vote and carrying the Electoral College vote 297 to 240. Jimmy Carter was the third man in the 20th century to defeat a sitting president.

The treasurer's contest in November between Republican Clay Myers (who had been Oregon's secretary of state for a decade) and Democrat Jewel Lansing (who was Multnomah County auditor) was a tight race. Lansing lost to Myers by just over fifteen thousand votes (478,600 to 493,700).

The campaign between Republican Norma Paulus and Democrat Blaine Whipple for secretary of state resulted in a landslide victory for Paulus (591,800, to 388,565). Paulus was the first woman elected to one of Oregon's top statewide offices.

Democrats won lopsided victories in all four U.S. House Districts: Les AuCoin in the First, Al Ullman in the Second, Bob Duncan in the Third, and James B. Weaver in the Fourth. Duncan was elected to the 3rd District seat for the first time in 1975, replacing longtime Congresswoman Edith Green.

Turmoil in Salem: The 1977 Legislature

Democrats won 36 House and 24 Senate seats in 1976, retaining their hold on the legislature. Democratic newcomer Wayne Fawbush of Hood River was called "Landslide" by his Democratic colleagues when he won a seat in the House by defeating incumbent Republican Paul Walden by 34 votes in the 56th District (8,303 to 8,269).

The composition of the 1977 Legislature reflected Oregon's changing demographics. Four members of the house were foreign born. As a child, Portland's Vera Katz had fled with her family from their home in Nazi Germany. Max Rijken of Newport was born in Java, Indonesia. Albany's Mae Yih was born in Shanghai, China, and Rep. Rod Monroe of Portland was born in British Columbia, Canada.

Nine women served in the House and three in the Senate. A wide age range separated the oldest House member (Republican Denny Jones, 67) and the youngest (Democrat Drew Davis of Portland, who was only 25). Democrat Debbs Potts, 67, was the oldest senator, while 29-year-old John Powell was the youngest. The Senate featured a band of veteran legislators: Vern Cook was in his tenth session, Richard Groener and Victor Atiyeh were in their ninth, Potts and Robert Smith were in their eighth. Speaker Phil Lang was the ranking member of the House, having served in eight regular sessions.

The 1977 Legislature was the second-longest session in history, dragging on for 177 days (January 10-July 5). One of the most contentious in memory, the 59th Legislature was dominated by intrigues, power plays, and deep, deep divisions. By the time the session ground to adjournment at 2:40 a.m., all semblance of decorum had vanished in the Oregon House. Members were at each others' throats. Honest debate on issues had been replaced by political posturing, personal attacks, bickering, and acute exhaustion. Many lawmakers were no longer on speaking terms, their personal animosities apparent to everyone, with acrimony replacing civility. Something had gone terribly wrong and the legislature had broken down.

The public had every reason to think the 1977 session would accomplish much. Yet divisions appeared immediately in the House, starting with a rift caused by the reelection of Speaker Phil Lang. Though blessed with a caucus of 36 members, Lang wasn't popular with all Democrats. A small group of them didn't want him reelected. Led by Representatives Dick Magruder and Jeff Gilmour, the disaffected group had had heated disagreements with Lang throughout the 1975 session. Whether Lang could muster the necessary 30 votes (in addition to his own) to be reelected speaker was questionable. Lang's troubles weren't confined to his Democratic foes: he was also challenged from outside his caucus. Twenty-two of the 24 members of the Republican caucus tried to form a coalition with the anti-Lang Democrats to form their own 31-vote majority—giving them control of the House and the power to elect one of their own as speaker. Fortunately for Phil Lang, only eight Democrats (led by Magruder) were willing to go along with Roger Martin, the House Republican minority leader. The Martin-Magruder coalition failed by one vote to take control of the House. And Lang's troubles were still not over. Within his Democratic caucus, Rep. Ed Lindquist, a firefighter from Milwaukie, challenged him for the speakership. Affable, approachable, and a moderate, Lindquist was liked by both conservative and liberal Democrats. Phil

Lang, by contrast, was businesslike and reserved, some thought distant and stubborn. The anti-Lang Democrats disliked his leadership and his legislative priorities. The conservatives thought he was a big-city liberal, who cared little about the problems of rural Oregon. Despite the challenge of both Ed Lindquist and the Magruder-led faction, Phil Lang prevailed, patching together 30 Democratic votes for reelection as speaker. While he was the sitting speaker, Lang was in a position to reach "understandings" with individuals about what coveted committee assignment might be expected in return for their vote for his speakership.

Once Lang was reelected, the conservative Democrats (nicknamed the Hornets for their propensity to sting without provocation), along with the rest of Ed Lindquist's backers, appeared to fall in line behind the speaker. The Hornets bided their time, waiting to see how the session progressed under Lang's leadership. Meanwhile, an uneasy truce existed within the Democratic caucus with the 36 members suspicious of each others' intentions and motives. Subsequent caucus meetings were rife with tension.

The Senate also got off to a rocky start. A group of Portland-area Democrats wanted to break Jason Boe's iron grip on the body and tried to block his election to a third term as president. They failed. Boe was reelected and the Democrats who opposed him were all denied a committee chairmanship. Except for this early power struggle, the Senate (compared to the house) ran relatively smoothly for the duration of the 1977 session.

Issues Facing the 1977 Legislature

Governor Bob Straub unveiled his legislative program during his Opening Day address. His proposals included Project Independence, a program to assist older Oregonians who, because of poor health or disability, needed outside assistance to remain in their own homes; an innovative community corrections program designed to help local governments better meet the needs of nonviolent offenders in community-based programs; increased state funds (revenue sharing) directed to local governments to assist them in paying for state-mandated services (such as courts and corrections); further clarifying and fine-tuning Oregon's controversial SB 100—statewide land-use planning and the role and authority of the LCDC, the administrative arm of the land-use law; putting more money into the state's Basic School Support Fund to help offset rising local property taxes; and more property-tax relief via Homeowner's/Renter's Property Tax Relief Program, commonly called HAARP.

Straub's legislative priorities generally meshed with the agendas of Speaker Phil Lang and Senate President Jason Boe. Senator Boe had a pet proposal that

Speaker Phil Lang and Rep. Vera Katz wearing T-shirts presented to them as House leaders in the 1977 session. Lang had been stripped of several key powers as speaker by a coalition of Republicans and conservative Democrats. The dissident Democrats were called "Hornets"; thus, Lang's shirt suggests the Hornets should buzz off, while Katz (one of Lang's staunchest supporters, was designated the Queen Bee, not a friend of hornets. *(Gerry Lewin Collection)*

he called "safety-net." He wanted to address a trend toward a growing number of annual local school budget elections. Boe also wanted to do something about stabilizing local school funding; to do this, he wanted to establish a "safety-net" for local schools, assuring that in the event that voters twice defeated a school budget, the local school board could automatically raise the budget by up to the statutory 6%, but not hold a third vote within that budget cycle. Boe made certain that his safety-net plan was the Senate's first order of business.

House Minority Leader Roger Martin (R., Lake Oswego) believed that the session's top priority should be the development of another school finance package. But in light of voter rejection of recent legislature-written school finance plans, Governor Straub and Speaker Lang were convinced that it was still too soon to send another proposal to voters. Both leaders believed that 1979 would be a better time for the legislature to tackle the contentious issue. With Oregon's economy on the rebound, economists were now projecting a revenue surplus of over $500 million at the end of the 1977-79 biennium. One of the big issues facing lawmakers in 1977 was what to do with this anticipated surplus. Speaking for his GOP colleagues, Representative Martin also proposed that the surplus be rebated to taxpayers, suggesting that two-thirds of what a person had paid in state taxes for 1976 be rebated. Speaker Lang identified Workmen's Compensation reform as a legislative priority. Also on the speaker's list was the continuing energy crisis; protection and enhancement of SB 100; the spiraling costs of Oregon's road and highway maintenance; and the special needs of aged Oregonians.[6]

The Senate got off to a fast start with over 150 bills referred to committee on the first day of the session. In spite of the Senate's preoccupation with accommodating President Jason Boe's school "safety-net" proposal, that body reported 51 bills out of committee by the end of the second week. The House moved more slowly. By March, House Republican leaders and the Hornets were grumbling about Lang's leadership. Roger Martin chided the speaker for not meeting with him on a regular basis, claiming that communication between his office and Lang's was very poor because Lang was uncooperative. Republicans also nursed hard feelings because Lang had appointed so few of them to committee leadership positions; only one Republican, Redmond's Sam Johnson, had been appointed to the powerful Joint Ways and Means Committee, and only three as committee vice chairs. As the days passed, the speaker became increasingly short-tempered because of what he perceived as challenges to his authority, including how he conducted daily sessions and referred bills to committee.

The May Rebellion

On May 4, like a slumbering volcano, the House erupted. Eighteen Republicans and 14 Democrats staged a rebellion. Nothing like it had ever happened in the Oregon Legislature. The new coalition was led by Republican leaders Roger Martin and Gary Wilhelms, and by Democrats Dick Magruder, Bill Grannell, Ed Lindquist (who was House majority leader), and future governor Ted Kulongoski. With a 32-vote majority, the new coalition amended House rules and stripped Phil Lang of most of his powers as speaker. Though Lang continued as speaker, his power was greatly diminished and he lost his authority to appoint committees and assign bills. Those powers were transferred to a new six-man Rules Committee (the men listed above), instantly dubbed the "Six-Pack." For the remainder of the session, the Six-Pack controlled where bills were assigned. They also set a timeline for when committee work would cease, set a tentative date to adjourn the session (June 17), and, finally, the group took control of the House's consent calendar.* The Six-Pack also took control of who would be appointed to House interim committees for 1977-78 and assumed responsibility for the staff of the House committees, as well as the employees of the speaker's office. The May Rebellion resulted in an unprecedented re-alignment of power midway through a legislative session. Lang was now a mere figurehead. Those who led the rebellion claimed they had acted with the public interest in mind. Republican leader Roger Martin said that "the committee was formed so that the best interests of Oregonians are served—in order that the house session begins moving in a positive direction. The whole idea of efficiency and working toward achievement underlies the committee's motivation. [It] was a bold decision that revived the legislature's sense of responsibility."[7]

The Author's Interpretation

Little has been written about the May Rebellion of 1977. As a member of the House during this time, the author is in a position to offer his observations about what happened and why. I believe that the May Rebellion against Phil Lang's leadership was a mistake, a blot on the history of the Oregon Legislature. To understand the dynamics of what happened, we need to review the facts leading up to May 4.

Phil Lang was freely elected to a second term as speaker by the required 31-vote majority (all Democrats). His reelection was unpopular with a handful of conservative Democrats. Republicans would have preferred one of their own to be speaker, but, with only 24 members, they knew they were a minority and had no legitimate claim to controlling the House. There was nothing unusual about this—this was the way it had always been: whoever had a simple 31-vote majority had the power to elect the speaker.

Lang made mistakes—some of which worked against him. His refusal to appoint more Republicans as committee vice chairs seemed arbitrary and unreasonable to most Republicans. He could also have improved his

---

* When a noncontroversial decision relating to routine business had to be made, the House was asked to approve (or consent to) the decision by a simple voice vote during a daily floor session.

communication with GOP leaders, though he might argue that, as the elected leader of the House, he wasn't required to consult with the minority about important decisions. Still, no one in a position of responsibility likes to be left out of the decision-making loop. Previous House speakers had done their jobs pretty much the way Lang did: controlling the direction the body took, including work pace, priorities, and which members would be appointed to run the 16 house committees. The crux of what Lang's opponents were unhappy about was that they disagreed with his priorities and, disliked his style of leadership. Some also didn't like Lang as a person. Most Republicans and some Democrats believed that Lang was unreasonably arbitrary and exclusive and that he simply did not care about what those who disagreed with him thought.

One of the most unfair criticisms of Lang was that the House moved at a glacial pace, that few laws of importance were getting passed. A record 2,812 measures were introduced by lawmakers in the 1977 session. Speaker Lang had no control over how many measures were introduced. Yet he was faulted for being inefficient, charged with letting the session wander without a captain at the helm. The speaker was expected to shepherd hundreds of bills through the legislative maze—and, when Lang did so, his critics said they did not like the way he did it. For many of Lang's detractors, he could do no right; some found fault with everything he did.

Speaker Lang had served longer in the House than any other member. His knowledge and experience were vast. Lang had been a productive speaker in the 1975 session. He was respected as an intelligent, hardworking, and capable lawmaker. None of this seemed to matter once his detractors had decided that, for whatever the reason, Phil Lang should no longer have the powers tradition-ally granted to the speaker of the House of Representatives.

Some of what happened to Phil Lang was the result of his own actions. But much of what occurred was not directly attributable to him. By joining in a coalition with dissident Democrats, the Republicans effectively embarrassed both the Democratic majority and the House's elected leader. The majority of Republicans who joined the rebellion (six did not) were, by gaining two seats on the powerful new Rules Committee, cutting themselves in for a big piece of the House leadership pie. By fomenting and joining the new coalition, the Republican leadership became part of the new House majority.

One can argue that what appears to be political opportunism had something to do with the rebellion. By joining the new coalition, Democrat Ed Lindquist, who earlier challenged Lang for speaker, gained himself a coveted seat on the

*Rules Committee, assuring himself a one-sixth vote in the all-powerful group. Republican Roger Martin, also a member of the Committee (and one of the architects of the May Rebellion), wanted to be Oregon's next governor.**

No Safety Net

Two weeks after the May Rebellion in the Oregon House, the special statewide election was held, on May 17. The cornerstone of the three-measure ballot was Senator Jason Boe's safety-net plan for public schools. Measure 1, "Safety-Net," was defeated 2-1, 252,061 opposed to 112,570 in favor, with only 25% of registered voters casting ballots.

Staggering to the Finish

The last month of the 1977 legislative session was a pressure cooker. Over 700 bills were passed in the last 30 days of the session, 500 in the final 20 days. Tension between the House and Senate only added to the problems in the fractious House. Nerves were frayed and tempers were short. Legislators and staff suffered from sleep deprivation. Numerous House-Senate conference committees met to iron out differences between two versions of a bill. As usual, there was lots of jockeying for advantage. There were off-hand threats that the House would hold up a Senate bill until that body agreed to pass such-and-such bill wanted by the House—and vice-versa. Finally, after 177 days, senators trudged over to the House chamber to join testy representatives to officially end the session. It was 2:40 a.m. Everyone was relieved to have the session over. Members had considered an unprecedented number of measures, passing 975 of them, also a record. Legislators hugged or shook hands, congratulating one another for what they had accomplished—much of it having been done under unusually strained circumstances.

A Record of Solid Accomplishment

Because of the state's weak economy and shrinking revenue in 1975, lawmakers had passed a "barebones" budget for 1975-77. This budget included cutbacks and deferred spending in several areas, including higher education, corrections, and human services. But things were different in 1977. Oregon's economy was improving. State economists projected a budget surplus of at least $500 million by July 1977. This big surplus gave legislators leeway to increase the state general

---

* In May 1978, Martin ran for the GOP nomination for governor—a race he lost to State Senator Victor Atiyeh.

fund budget for 1977-79 by $660 million. About $240 million of this increase was set aside for local property-tax relief. Another $295 million was added to the education budget, to be divided among Oregon's public universities and community colleges; the largest part of this money went into the basic school fund. The state general fund would pay 34% of local school costs in 1977-78 and 40% in 1978-79. Thus, "property tax relief was increased and supplemented by requiring a portion of the BSSF to be used to offset local property taxes."[8]

A severance tax (to be assessed at the time of harvest) on small-lot timber tracts was enacted. Oregon's state inheritance tax was also phased out over 10 years. Women and families were helped by SB 714, which added pregnancy to the list of "illnesses" that the state required insurance companies to include as a covered health benefit. Governor Straub's Project Independence was also passed, a plan still in effect that allows a person in poor health to remain in their home by providing drop-in, part-time nursing care.

A major reform of Oregon's Workmen's Compensation program was passed. The changes were designed to reduce recent runaway costs to employers and escalating workers' comp. premiums, as well as to make the delivery of benefits more efficient.

Legislators devoted much time to cost, availability, and conservation of energy. A weatherization bill was passed to require gas and electric companies to provide home weatherization services, including low-cost loans for homeowners and renters to weatherize. The hot-button subject of nuclear power continued to be an issue in the 1977 session. A controversial bill to prohibit the permanent storage of nuclear waste in Oregon was passed and signed by Governor Straub.

Straub Behind the Scenes

During the latter half of his term, Governor Bob Straub worked in concert with Portland Mayor Neil Goldschmidt and threw his weight behind an effort to quash a proposed new Mount Hood freeway to be routed through southeast Portland. Goldschmidt opposed the freeway in favor of a light-rail system. Congress had already appropriated $110 million for the freeway. Straub and Goldschmidt convinced the U.S. Department of Transportation to shift the freeway money into a fund to begin the construction of a light-rail system (MAX).

Economic Woes

Despite the budget surplus in 1977, 1978 found the United States (and Oregon) slipping deeper into economic trouble. The economy was weakened by a soaring rate of inflation, undercutting the value of the U.S. dollar. Industrial productivity continued downward. With passage of each new federal budget, the national deficit continued to grow. American consumers refused to curb their seemingly insatiable appetite for imported oil and gasoline; by 1979, 43% of petroleum products consumed in the nation were imported while domestic oil and gas production was declining by 10%. There were 117 million automobiles registered in the United States, 40% of all the cars on the planet. Americans were slowly forfeiting their economic vitality to the whims of international oil cartels that controlled both the supply and cost of crude oil. Oregon politics in 1978 played out amid these troubling economic indicators. Issues such as the availability of jobs, taxes, inflation, the spiraling costs of state and local governments, and the high price of energy (including electricity, natural gas, heating oil, and vehicle fuels) took center stage.

Politics in 1978

There were two featured political races in Oregon in 1978: the office of governor, and the U.S. Senate seat held by Mark Hatfield. Democrat Robert Straub was seeking a second term as governor and Senator Hatfield wanted a third term. Six Democrats challenged Governor Straub for their party's nomination in the May 23 primary. In a low-key campaign, Straub won the nomination, pulling 144,800 votes.

The Republican gubernatorial primary was a lot more interesting. Seven men sought the nomination: State Senator Victor Atiyeh, House Minority Leader Roger Martin, and 65-year-old former Governor Tom McCall were the main candidates. McCall, who had defeated Bob Straub for the governorship in 1966 and 1970, was trying for a political comeback in 1978. Though he'd remained in the public eye as a Portland TV news analyst, McCall's health and age were slowing him down a bit. Vic Atiyeh had been elected to the Oregon House in 1958 from Washington County. After three terms in the House, Atiyeh won a seat in the senate, where, for the past 13 years, he had served as the Republican minority leader. Atiyeh's ancestors had immigrated to the United States from Syria and the Atiyehs owned a rug business in Portland. Victor Atiyeh's reputation was as a successful entrepreneur, whose conservative pro-business values and commitment to controlling state government spending appealed to many voters. Roger Martin, in his early 40s, was the youngest of the three major GOP contenders. A forceful, sometimes caustic speaker, Martin was a new face on the statewide scene.

Early polls showed McCall with a big lead, but McCall had waited until February to announce his candidacy and was far behind Atiyeh and Martin in campaign organization and fund-raising. McCall self-destructed as the campaign unfolded. Slightly stooped, his eyes appearing watery and tired, he entered into a series of debates with Martin and Atiyeh. Martin attacked McCall's record as governor, blasting him for implementing policies that had hurt Oregon business. Atiyeh followed suit. McCall appeared weak, ill-prepared, and uncertain, and he seemed out of touch with the present day. Outspent 4-1 by Martin and Atiyeh (who spent a combined $390,000), McCall's $87,000 war chest was simply too small.[9] With the lowest GOP voter turnout in 30 years (barely 43%), the Republican gubernatorial nomination went to Victor Atiyeh. Tom McCall trailed Atiyeh by over 32,000 votes, 83,600 to 115,600; Roger Martin placed third with 42,600 votes. It was Tom McCall's last political hurrah—he never again ran for public office.

Republican Mark Hatfield won his party's Senate nomination with an easy victory over three minor challengers. State Senator Vern Cook of Gresham, a colorful, somewhat mercurial and controversial politician, won the Democratic nomination, like Hatfield defeating three minor opponents.

The fall campaign between incumbent Governor Robert Straub and challenger Victor Atiyeh was sedate and rather bland. With neither man a charismatic speaker, economic issues and Straub's record were the focus of the campaign. Republican Atiyeh emphasized his experience as a businessman and legislator who thought that state government had grown too big, too fast, and at too high a cost for average taxpayers to bear. Governor Straub took a stand against two November ballot measures—one to restore the death penalty and the other to limit local property taxes. Straub did not like to toot his own horn, so he failed to make a strong case for why he should be reelected. The governor simply didn't stir the public's imagination. Bob Straub had been in the political spotlight in Oregon for the past 13 years (as state treasurer and as governor). In 1978, Oregonians were ready to give the reins to someone else; with a 63% voter turnout, Victor Atiyeh was elected the 32nd governor of Oregon. Atiyeh defeated Robert Straub by 89,000 votes (498,450 to 409,000).*

With his defeat, Bob Straub retired from public office. He and his wife Pat continued to live on their farm in west Salem. Both remained involved in community service, including the founding of a low-cost housing program for needy families. Bob Straub lived until November 27, 2002, age eighty-two. Near the end of his life Straub was diagnosed with Alzheimer's disease—which he

---

* Four years earlier, Straub had defeated Vic Atiyeh with 58% of the ballots, pulling 445,000 votes.

announced to the public, hoping to cast more attention on this debilitating illness. The Salem *Statesman-Journal,* reflecting on the life of Bob Straub, wrote this about him: "Every time you walk on our beloved coastal beaches, you can thank Bob Straub for fighting to keep them open to the public. As you travel through Portland, you should be grateful that he helped kill the Mount Hood freeway project and instead embraced light rail. As you canoe or walk along the Willamette River, you can see Straub's vision for a Willamette Greenway to protect the waterway and adjacent land. As you worry about the waterway, you can credit Straub's legacy for helping prevent urban sprawl for three decades. If you receive home health care through Project Independence remember that Bob Straub founded the program."[10]

The U.S. Senate contest between incumbent Republican Mark Hatfield and his Democratic challenger, Vern Cook, turned out to be a stroll in the park for the senator. Cook was a poor campaigner. He was unable to put together a viable statewide organization and had even less luck raising money. Mark Hatfield won reelection by 209,000 votes, 550,000 to 342,000.

Another Democratic Legislature

There were some stunning surprises in Oregon's legislative races. Nine-term Democrat and two-time Speaker of the Oregon House Phil Lang of Portland was defeated by a political unknown, Republican Josephine (Jo) Simpson. State Representative Dick Magruder of Clatskanie, leader of the dissident Hornet faction in the Oregon House, had been defeated in the May Democratic primary by Garland Brown. Though he lost his own party's nomination, Magruder won (by write-in) the Republican nomination for state representative. However, state law barred Magruder from seeking the office as a GOP nominee because he had already lost his own party's nomination. In early summer, Dick Magruder was killed in a tractor accident on his farm. District Republicans then nominated Magruder's mother, Caroline, a Democrat. Thus, in November, two Democrats, Garland Brown and Caroline Magruder, faced each other. Magruder won the seat, 7,900 to 6,060.

Democrats maintained their hold on both the House and Senate in November. The Democratic majority, however, slipped by two seats in the House (down from 36 in 1977) and by one seat (to 23) in the Senate. Two freshman lawmakers elected to the 1979 Legislature were Republican Larry Campbell of Eugene and John Kitzhaber, M.D., a Roseburg Democrat.

Except for the election of Republican Victor Atiyeh over Democratic incumbent Governor Robert Straub, voters maintained the political status quo in

November 1978. Twelve statewide measures appeared on the ballot, including several controversial measures that boosted voter turnout on election day. The issue of abortion (Measure 7) generated the most interest. As proposed, the measure would prohibit state government from spending general fund dollars on programs or services to support abortion. The vote was close: those opposed to the ban on state spending prevailed, 461,500 to 431,600. Ballot Measure 8, to restore the death penalty for certain murders (which Straub opposed), was passed by a thundering 255,000 votes (573,700 to 318,600).

The End of an Era

With former governors Tom Lawson McCall and Bob Straub leaving politics, the year 1978 marked the end of an important political era in Oregon history. For the past 15 years, the state's politics had been dominated by Straub and McCall. Often working in tandem—because they had a shared vision for Oregon—the two leaders had steered their state into directions few thought possible. Building on the legacy of Oswald West, Bob Straub and Tom McCall spearheaded an environmental movement that changed Oregon forever.

Throughout most of his time in public office Bob Straub labored in the shadow of the more dynamic, more charismatic Tom McCall. He, unlike McCall, rarely sought the glare of lights and the whirring of TV cameras. Yet there were occasions when Straub would break out of character and seek publicity, as he did when he single-handedly stopped a re-routing of Highway 101 onto the Nestucca Spit on the Oregon coast in 1966.

McCall and Straub shared an unwavering love for the land and Oregon's scenic beauty. Together they led the drive to save Oregon's public beaches, protect the Willamette River, and preserve Oregon's farmlands, forests, rivers, and estuaries through state-coordinated land-use planning. Both men recognized (and actively promoted) the need for Oregon to shift its traditional economy away from heavy reliance on natural resources—toward a more diversified economy—one based more on manufacturing and computer technology. Tom McCall and Bob Straub were visionaries who had guided Oregon into new directions—and, in so doing, aimed Oregon straight at the 21st century.

Chapter 17
Governor Victor Atiyeh: Saving a Sinking Ship, 1979-86

Oregon's 60th Legislative Assembly convened in Salem on January 8, 1979. The 90 lawmakers assembled, as usual, in the crowded House chamber. Outgoing Democratic Governor Robert Straub made a short speech before Oregon's new governor, Republican Victor Atiyeh, was sworn into office. Governor Atiyeh's opening address focused on the familiar issues of taxes, property-tax relief, funding for public education, the condition of the state and national economy, and the need to balance the 1979-81 budget by invoking greater efficiency and cost cutting.

The Senate got right to work. With a lop-sided 23-7 majority, Democratic senators elected Jason Boe to an unprecedented fourth term as president. Republican L. B. Day of Salem, a local Teamster's Union official, was returning to the legislature following his service as director of the Oregon Department of Environmental Quality (DEQ). Day had made a name for himself as McCall's hard-nosed pointman on environmental issues. There were no women senators in the 1979 session.

The Oregon House had a terrible time getting started. Fractured along urban-rural lines, majority Democrats spent the first week squabbling over who their new speaker would be. The leading candidate for the job was Portland attorney Hardy Myers. The Hornets (what was left of them*) wanted key committee assignments in exchange for supporting Myers for speaker. Former Republican Minority Leader Roger Martin (another leader of the house rebellion of May 1977) had also left the House, vacating his seat to run

---

* Several key Hornets did not return in 1979. Gone was the head Hornet, Rep. Dick Magruder (who had lost his seat in the primary election in May 1978, and, shortly after, his life in a farm accident). Rep. Jack Sumner of Heppner, an ardent Magruder supporter, didn't run for reelection. Democrat Ted Kulongoski, one of the architects of the Democrat-Republican coalition that took power midway during the 1977 session, had moved over to the Senate to fill a vacancy in fall 1977.

for the Republican nomination for governor in May 1978. Also missing was nine-term Democrat Phil Lang, House speaker in 1975 and 1977, who had lost his seat in November to a Republican newcomer. Even with Magruder, Sumner, Lang, and Kulongoski gone from the House, the Democratic caucus was barely able to hold together as the session started. Hornets Jeff Gilmour, Curtis Wolfer, Drew Davis, and Max Simpson were back, as was Bill Grannell, a member of the notorious Six-Pack, and Rep. Mae Yih of Albany, a conservative Democrat.

At the end of the session's first week, Hardy Myers (a steadfast supporter of Phil Lang in 1977) was elected speaker. Several Hornets were rewarded for supporting him. Bill Grannell was appointed chair of the Revenue Committee; Drew Davis became chair of the Committee on State Government Operations; and Jeff Gilmour chaired the Agriculture Committee.

The Legislature of 1979

The issue of energy was high on the agenda. Bills were enacted to promote the refining and use of gasohol (a grain-alcohol plus gasoline blend) as auto fuel in Oregon. "Senate Bill 638 required electric utilities to guarantee that they would purchase any excess power generated by their private customers using such renewable resources as biomass, hydroelectricity, wind, solar, or steam."[1] The legislature also "broadened the conservation and weatherization programs established in 1977 to include manufactured homes, multifamily housing and business establishments."[2]

The public's continuing keen interest in the dangers of cigarette smoking resulted in a law to expand Oregon's smoking ban during recess in all public meetings (such as city councils, county commissions, school boards, and the legislature itself). All retail stores in Oregon (except tobacco shops) were also required to post signs noting that it is "unlawful to smoke in this store."

When it came to environmental legislation (one of the hallmarks of the legislatures of the 1970s), the 1979 session contented itself with fine-tuning existing laws; they did not enact any more precedent-setting legislation. Where to put solid waste (garbage) was an ongoing concern for Oregon's rapidly growing urban areas, particularly for metropolitan Portland. The major environmental bill passed in 1979 addressed the issue of where to site solid waste facilities. New authority was given to the Environmental Quality Commission (EQC) to decide where sanitary landfills were to be placed in five Oregon counties. Included in the EQC's authority was the option to use farmlands (under certain conditions) as dump sites.

In reviewing the actions of the 1979 Legislature, what really counted with the public was what lawmakers did about tax relief and the funding of public schools. Luckily for lawmakers Oregon's economy was robust. Legislators increased the general fund budget from $2.126 billion to $3.077 billion for 1979-81. The lion's share of this huge increase was set aside for property-tax relief. "Using surplus income taxes [lawmakers] promised to pay 30% of every homeowner's property tax bill up to a maximum of $800."[3] Legislators added $386 million or about 40% of the projected surplus revenue into this tax relief

Victor Atiyeh

COURTESY OF OREGON STATE LIBRARY

Victor Atiyeh was the only Republican elected governor between 1979 and 2011. A native Portlander, Atiyeh was a businessman and long-active Republican Party leader. Elected to the Oregon House in 1958 from east Washington County, Atiyeh served three terms before moving to the Senate in 1965. Atiyeh was Senate minority leader during three legislative sessions.

Atiyeh won the GOP nomination for governor in 1974 and faced Democratic State Treasurer Robert Straub in November. Straub defeated Atiyeh by a wide margin. Four years later, Governor Straub lost his reelection bid to Atiyeh. Governor Atiyeh served during troubled economic times in Oregon and the nation. A severe economic recession gripped Oregon between 1980 and 1984 causing the governor and legislature to hold 7 special sessions to cut the state budget by reducing programs and services. Atiyeh's first 5 years as governor were dominated by the state's economic and budget woes.

Governor Atiyeh worked closely with Democratic House and Senate leaders to guide Oregon through her troubled times. Atiyeh was steady, focused, and nonpartisan; his popularity soared, resulting in his reelection in 1982 with 61% of the vote.

In spite of Oregon's budgetary problems, numerous programs were instituted under Governor Atiyeh. Always a champion of economic diversification, Atiyeh actively promoted international trade and the sale of Oregon products, especially in Asia. He also pushed for reform of Oregon's land-use law and for federal protection of old-growth timber. Workers' compensation premiums were reduced under Atiyeh. And the governor was a vocal backer of Oregon Food Share, a critical program to assure that citizens in need got fed.

Governor Atiyeh left office in 1987, returning to Portland as a international business consultant and partner in his family's century-old rug business.

fund. The state's portion of basic school funding was maintained at 40% for 1979-81. Lawmakers jumped the education budget to $1.347 billion from $1.066 billion (an increase of $281 million); $800 million of the $1.347 billion was earmarked for Basic School Support. In addition, the 1979 Legislature set a critical precedent when it agreed to refund future state income tax surpluses. This tax refund was intended to be automatic and was soon known as "the kicker" (meaning that excess surpluses would automatically be "kicked back" to taxpayers in the form of a rebate).

The surplus gave lawmakers more options when it came to meeting the public's expectations, because the public wanted something done about taxes. For the second session in a row, legislators pumped over $660 million into programs to lighten the tax burden on citizens. For the time being the public was mollified. A move to establish a statewide property-tax limitation law (an idea which had been popular in some circles for a decade) was, again, headed off because of critical budget decisions made by the 1977 and 1979 legislatures. Many citizens, interest groups, and politicians wondered what would happen if Oregon's economy faltered and tax revenues dropped. Would the public continue to demand tax relief at a time when the legislature could not afford to give it? Time would tell.

The 60th Legislature dragged on for 178 days, making it the second longest session ever. The session ended just before midnight on July 4. Over 2,400 measures had been introduced. Nearly 600 bills were acted on during the last 20 days of the session. Governor Vic Atiyeh vetoed 19 bills (Governor Straub had nixed 20 in 1977). The usual rush to adjourn resulted in another political pressure cooker. Testy, exhausted legislators and staff welcomed adjournment at 11:25 p.m. as the last of the day's fireworks were set off outside the Capitol.

A Decade of Change

The year 1980 marked the end of a decade of prodigious population growth in Oregon. The state had grown by a staggering 25%, from 2.091 million to 2.633 million, an increase of 542,000 people. Oregon's explosive population growth had a lot to do with its changing economy, which went through fundamental changes in the 1970s. The state's traditional reliance on natural resources (including fisheries, timber and wood products, and agriculture) shifted toward the expanding sectors of the high-tech and manufacturing industries. The arrival of Hewlett-Packard in Corvallis and Intel to Washington County brought Oregon into the age of Silicon Valley—along with its thousands of high-paying jobs and hordes of spin-off companies and small suppliers.

The Election of 1980

1980 turned out to be a pivotal year in American presidential politics. Incumbent Pres. Jimmy Carter was challenged by Republican Ronald Reagan, a Hollywood film actor and former governor of California. Charismatic and a compelling speaker, Reagan was the darling of the now-dominant conservative wing of the GOP and ran as a Washington outsider, and opponent of Big Government. The American economy was in shambles in 1980. Soaring inflation and climbing interest rates undercut economic vitality, producing a deepening national recession. The festering Iran Hostage Crisis added to America's frustration and uncertainty. In Oregon, voters were preparing for their May 20 primary. Opposing President Carter for the Democratic presidential nomination were former California Gov. Jerry Brown, Jr., and Massachusetts Sen. Ted Kennedy. Carter didn't campaign, claiming that the Iran Hostage Crisis precluded his leaving Washington to stump the country. He remained popular with mainstream and conservative Democrats. More liberal Democrats were attracted to Kennedy and Brown. Heading the Republican presidential ballot in Oregon were Ronald Reagan and former congressman, CIA director, and ambassador, George Herbert Walker Bush of Texas. President Carter won Oregon's Democratic primary by a wide margin over Kennedy, 209,000 to 115,000. Governor Brown trailed with 34,500 votes. Ronald Reagan won the GOP nomination over George Bush, 170,500 to 109,200. Carter and Reagan went on to clinch their party's nominations later that summer.

Bob Packwood Goes for Another Term

The other featured political contest in Oregon was for Bob Packwood's U.S. Senate seat. Packwood, a two-term Republican, had a huge campaign chest as well as the advantages of an incumbent. He was popular and was considered a shoo-in for reelection. The Democratic contest for Senate was a spirited affair. Five candidates vied for the nomination: State Sen. Ted Kulongoski, former Congressman Charles O. Porter, and Jack Sumner, a former state representative, were the main contenders. Kulongoski raised the most money, garnered most major endorsements, and campaigned hard—and he won. The Eugene senator defeated Charles O. Porter by about 92,000 votes (161,000 to 70,000). Jack Sumner, a conservative Heppner wheat grower, was third with 46,000 votes.

A political upset occurred in the primary in Oregon's 3rd Congressional District. Two-term incumbent Robert Duncan was clobbered in the primary by young Ron Wyden, a co-director of the Oregon Gray Panthers, an advocacy group for senior citizens. Wyden defeated Duncan 56,000 to 37,000.

The November General Election

The November general election proved to be more attractive to Oregon voters than it did to Americans in general. Voter turnout in Oregon was 77%; nationally, it was 54%. President Jimmy Carter's popularity in national opinion polls had dropped to 26% in summer 1979. Meanwhile, candidate Reagan criticized Carter's indecisive leadership, playing to a feeling that many Americans shared, that the nation was adrift without a strong captain at the helm.

A minority of Americans were dissatisfied with the choice between Carter and Reagan. Consequently, Illinois Congressman John Anderson, a liberal Republican, ran as a third-party independent for president. Buoyed by a huge turnout of conservative, fundamentalist Christian voters, the Reagan ticket (with George H.W. Bush for vice president) rolled to an easy victory in November. Nationally, Reagan got 51% of the popular vote, compared to Carter's 41% and John Anderson's 7%. Reagan won a decisive victory in the Electoral College, besting Carter 489 to 49. Reagan won Oregon, though he won less than 50% of the Oregon vote (571,000 votes to Carter's 457,000, and John Anderson's 112,400 votes).

Meanwhile, Back in Oregon

Oregon's U.S. Senate race turned in favor of the incumbent, Republican Robert Packwood. Packwood ran ahead of his party's presidential ticket, as he got 23,000 more votes than Ronald Reagan. Democrat Ted Kulongoski pulled 502,000 votes, 45,000 more than his party's presidential nominee. But it wasn't enough—Bob Packwood rolled to a third term by a margin of 92,000 votes.

One of the biggest political upsets in Oregon history occurred in November. Twelve-term Congressman (1957-81) Al Ullman, one of the most powerful men in Washington, D.C. (as chairman of the House Ways and Means Committee), was narrowly defeated by newspaperman (and son of former Governor Elmo Smith) Denny Smith. Ullman, like several other influential, long-time Democratic members of Congress, was swept out of office by the conservative tide that propelled Ronald Reagan into the White House. Smith defeated Ullman by 3,700 votes, 141,800 to 138,100.[4]

Democrats prevailed in Oregon's other three U.S. House contests: newcomer Ron Wyden in the 3rd District, incumbents Jim Weaver in the 4th, and Les AuCoin in the 1st.

The general election also featured one of the most lopsided races in Oregon political history. Republican Norma Paulus, the incumbent secretary of state, defeated youthful John Powell, a Democratic state senator, by 462,000 votes

(766,000 to 304,000) to continue to serve in that position. Paulus remained the state's most visible female politician.

While Oregon voters jumped aboard the Reagan bandwagon in 1980, they preferred keeping Democrats in charge of the state legislature. For the fifth consecutive election, voters retained Democratic majorities in both the House and Senate, although the Democrats' hold on the House slipped by four seats (from 37 to 33 in 1981). The Senate remained solidly Democratic, 22-8. Voters elected a record nineteen women to serve in the 1981 Oregon House (including Barbara Roberts and Darlene Hooley). The Senate had only one woman member, Democrat Ruth McFarland of Clackamas County.

Governor Victor Atiyeh

Victor Atiyeh was the last Republican to be elected governor of Oregon in the 20th century.* His eight-year tenure was dominated by a sour state and national economy, by state budget deficits, and the fiscal crises that resulted. Oregon's economic woes were so severe that Atiyeh called the legislature into special session seven times in eight years.

The beginning of 1980 found Oregon in big trouble. As the months passed, things worsened. Oregon was in dire economic and budgetary straits. Not since the Great Depression of the 1930s had Oregon been in such a predicament. A combination of high interest rates, climbing inflation, soaring energy and fuel prices, and growing unemployment had brought the country to its knees. But because of a continuing dependence on lumber production, Oregon had been hit harder than most states, particularly after the bottom fell out of the home-construction sector. Unemployment rates in the timber/mill/wood products industry shot up to as high as 20% in some areas. The decline in lumber production had a severe ripple effect on the Oregon economy. Ironically, one reason Victor Atiyeh had wanted to be governor was because he believed Oregon desperately needed to continue to diversify its economy.

Atiyeh was convinced that as long as Oregon's economic base was so reliant on agriculture, tourism, and lumber production, the state would remain

---

* Between 1958 and 2010, only three Republicans were elected governor in Oregon. All were re-elected and served two full terms: Mark Hatfield, 1959-67, Tom McCall, 1967-75, and Atiyeh, 1979-87. Atiyeh was elected to a second term with 63% of the vote (against Democrat Ted Kulongoski in 1982). Neither Hatfield nor McCall ever pulled more than 55% when running for governor. Indeed, what Atiyeh did in 1982 was a rarity in Oregon politics. On only three previous occasions in the history of the governorship had a candidate pulled more than 60% of the vote: Republican Earl Snell got 78% of the vote in 1942, and 69% when re-elected in 1946; Republican Douglas McKay got 66% of the 1950 vote, followed by Atiyeh's 63% in 1982.

susceptible to every downturn in the American economy. Throughout his governorship, Victor Atiyeh kept this goal in mind: Oregon needed to work harder to establish a broader, more diverse economy by attracting new industries and businesses to the state.

As one of only a handful of states with no state sales tax, Oregon relied heavily on a single source of revenue: the personal income tax. In 1980, 72% of the Oregon budget was funded by state income taxes. But with so many Oregonians unemployed in 1980-82, the state's revenue dropped below projections by over $700 million. The predicament facing Governor Atiyeh and the legislature was how to bring the state's budgets for 1979-81 and 1981-83 back into balance. The need to constantly revise the state budget caused the governor to call the legislature into special session four times between 1980 and 1982.

The Specter of a Taxpayer Revolt

Since 1968, Oregonians had been increasingly upset about their escalating property taxes. A growing taxpayer revolt had caused the McCall administration (and the legislatures that met during the 1970s) to consider what the state might do to help reduce property taxes, leading to two sweeping tax-reform plans, which were rejected by voters in statewide elections. Despite other attempts, fundamental tax reform hadn't been achieved. Though the home-owner/renter tax-relief program was popular with voters (as was the kicker law), a string of well-intentioned legislatures had failed to come up with a new tax structure that voters would approve. A growing segment of voters continued to promote the idea that only a voter-initiated property-tax limitation law (which would set a maximum amount that local governments could assess on local property) would solve the problem. Of course, the revenue thus lost to local governments would have to be paid for out of the state general fund. The possibility of a voter-led local property-tax limitation law cast an ever more ominous shadow over the Atiyeh administration and the legislatures meeting between 1979 and 1987.

Victor Atiyeh had been a state legislator for 20 years. Every time lawmakers had tackled the issue of property-tax reform, Atiyeh was in the middle of the action. Atiyeh's years of experience working on the Senate Revenue Committee served him well as governor. While campaigning for governor in 1978, Atiyeh had hammered away at the issue of property-tax relief.[5] Governor Atiyeh was concerned about a growing citizen movement to limit property taxes. Frustrated Californians had recently approved a controversial property-tax limitation law—Proposition 13. With the prospect of a "Son of 13" being enacted in Oregon, Atiyeh redoubled his efforts to convince lawmakers to pass meaningful tax reform.

As a Republican governor working with a Democratic legislature, the pragmatic Atiyeh worked hard to keep partisanship at bay, and wouldn't allow it to sour his relationship with Democratic leaders. He typically met weekly with the speaker and president. In addition, legislators were welcome to drop by the governor's office to confer with Atiyeh about any matter of concern. The governor also appeared regularly to testify on bills or budgets before legislative committees. However, Atiyeh relied most heavily on the friendships he had developed over the years with lawmakers (particularly with senators) and drew on these friendships when trying to move his agenda along. When the state's gravest financial crisis hit hardest in 1982, Atiyeh's strong ties to the Senate helped enormously when he was forced to call lawmakers back into special session three times.

The 1981 Legislature

The 61st Oregon Legislature convened under a black cloud on January 13, 1981. Legislators had met in special session only five months earlier when Governor Atiyeh called lawmakers back to Salem to rebalance the budget because a new revenue forecast showed a shortfall of over $200 million by June. House Speaker Hardy Myers and Senate President Jason Boe working in tandem with Governor Atiyeh's office had already cut $204 million out of the 1979-81 state budget by reducing the budgets of various state agencies. Atiyeh agreed with legislative leaders that "budget cuts should be deliberate, careful, and selective; we tried, always, to protect the most vulnerable people."[6]

Legislators realized that the 61st Assembly would be a long and unusually difficult session. Jobless rates were high, business activity sluggish, the future, uncertain. State revenue forecasts were gloomy. All indicators were that Oregon had not yet hit economic bottom—bleaker days were ahead.

The new session remained Democratic. Portland attorney Hardy Myers, who had entered the house in 1975, was reelected speaker. This time, however, Myers had got his ducks in a row and there was no replay of the 1979 debacle when it had taken the fractious Democrats a week to choose a speaker. Myers appeased the conservative Democrats in his caucus by appointing most of them to leadership positions. Gone from the legislature was Senate President Jason Boe, a dominant personality of the past eight years.* Fred W. Heard, a

---

* Jason Boe had been an able administrator, often guiding the Senate through choppy waters. He, however, authored little important legislation during his long Senate tenure. Boe will be remembered for his efforts in support of Tom McCall's tax-reform plan in 1973 and, for his authorship of a "safety-net" plan to help stabilize local school budgets.

41-year-old moderate Democrat and educator from Klamath Falls, was elected president—without the political jockeying and delays that had frequently kept the senate from getting off to a smooth start.

Lawmakers faced a host of issues in 1981, including reforming Oregon's Workers' Compensation program and a controversial bill introduced by Rep. Jim Chrest and Sen. Ted Kulongoski regarding closure of manufacturing plants in Oregon, which would require a "one-year advance notice whenever an employer of more than fifty persons decided to close a plant or go out of business for any reason. It also provided for sizable payments to displaced workers as well as heavy reimbursements to the communities affected."[7]

Other issues included a challenge to the authority and scope of the Land Conservation and Development Commission (LCDC) and the reapportionment of Oregon's legislative and congressional districts, including the establishment of a 5th U.S. House District, a result of Oregon's steady population growth between 1970 and 1980. But the foremost issue was: Just how badly would the recession cut into state revenues? What would the next general fund budget look like? Every legislator had come to Salem knowing that crafting a budget (for 1981-83) would take center stage. Not until revenue forecasts were known in late spring or early summer would the governor and lawmakers know what funds would be available for the next budget. One thing was certain: lean economic times meant a bare bones budget. How were lawmakers going to balance a state budget when they had no way of knowing just how long and deep the economic recession would last? The result was the longest legislative session to that time: 203 days. The 61st Legislature dragged on from January 13 to August 1. The chief cause of this long session was a fundamental disagreement about how to offset projected revenue losses: should taxes be raised or state programs cut?

Victor Atiyeh remembered the session as a "cantankerous one," with contentious differences between House and Senate.[8] The session unfolded pretty much as expected. Legislators went about their committee work with attention to detail, moving at a snail's pace. As predicted, the economy remained depressed and interest rates high, consumer spending was down, inventories were growing, and manufacturing production was slumping.

Governor Atiyeh took a hands-on approach when it came to budget-making. Drawing upon his long legislative experience, Atiyeh understood, better than many governors, what had to happen behind the scenes to make the legislative system work. The governor's style was not to intimidate, threaten, or berate either the legislature, the Democratic majority, or individual lawmakers.

He saw the process of law-making as collaborative—it took teamwork to get things done.

Atiyeh's budget proposal for 1981-83 included deep cuts in state spending, coupled with modest increases in cigarette and alcohol taxes. Throughout every budget cycle when he was governor, Victor Atiyeh sat at the table with the Senate president and House speaker to reach agreement on what the new budget should look like.

After seven grueling months, legislators produced a budget that reflected dismal economic forecasts and falling revenue. Legislators decided, for the time being, to protect the popular homeowner/renter property-tax relief program. Lawmakers approved Atiyeh's proposal to cut 10%, or about $80 million, out of the Basic School Support Fund. Legislators reduced the budgets of Higher Education and Human Resources by 7% more than Atiyeh recommended.

The 61st Legislature enacted a record 998 bills (out of 2,533 measures introduced); Governor Atiyeh vetoed 17 of them. As exhausted lawmakers prepared to go home they knew that if the sour Oregon economy did not improve dramatically, they would likely return for at least two special sessions in 1982.

Three Special Sessions: Back to Salem

In 1982 the Oregon Legislature achieved a dubious record when they met three times in special session because of the state's continuing recession. As the year progressed, revenue projections continued to drop. In the eight months between January and September 1982, state revenue projections dropped by $565 million, or about 17% of the 1981-83 budget passed by the 1981 Legislature.

The first special session of 1982 lasted for 37 days (January 18-March 1), making it the longest special session in state history. Governor Atiyeh, believing that "a governor has to propose something, a bone for the legislature to chew on,"[9] addressed the special session on January 18. The governor proposed meeting the new $240 million budget shortfall by doing the following: a 10% across the board cut in state agency spending (worth $120 million), doubling beer and wine taxes, and tracking down delinquent taxpayers and forcing them to pay their overdue taxes. Atiyeh realized that his combined proposals didn't add up to $240 million; they were only a starting point.

By February 9, after 23 days of first one chamber, then the other, proposing and defeating plans to balance the budget, another revenue forecast arrived: the deficit had grown another $100 million (to about $337 million). Legislative leaders decided a short recess might help. Intense negotiations continued, as leaders sought to assemble a package of combined cuts and new tax revenues agreeable to 16 senators and 31 representatives. When the session reconvened on February 15, Governor Atiyeh floated "a new idea to the Assembly in the form of: a $37 million income tax increase for middle and upper income Oregonians, a $35 million reduction in property tax relief, $120 million in agency cuts, $21 million in less school aid, doubled beer and wine taxes."[10] Finally, on February 27, the House and Senate approved a package of bills to cut $337 million out of the budget. The House passed the package with no votes to spare: six Democrats voted against the plan. The remaining 27 Democrats and four Republicans joined forces to pass the bill, which included a one-year (1981-82) 7.9% income tax surcharge, $87 million in state agency cuts, and $16 million in reduced school aid.

Fourteen weeks elapsed before legislators returned to Salem for a second special session. Working closely with Governor Atiyeh, House and Senate Democratic leaders agreed on cuts to meet another budget deficit of $101 million. The session lasted one day (June 14). With Senate President Fred Heard and Speaker Hardy Myers leading the way, the governor's ideas were seamlessly blended into the legislative plan backed by the necessary majorities.

Scarcely eight weeks after the second special session, state economists declared that state revenue would drop another $87 million. So, for the third time in eight months, legislators returned to Salem to re-balance the 1981-83 budget. Oregon's general election was only two months away. The last thing legislators wanted was a special session that dragged on. When lawmakers reconvened at the Capitol on September 3, they stuck to a pre-approved script and passed Governor Atiyeh's plan to cover the latest budget deficit. The governor opened the session with an appeal not to make further cuts in state services. In a one-day, 10-hour session, legislators decided to borrow $81 million from the State Accident Insurance Fund (SAIF), in addition to another $10 million reduction in the state property-tax relief fund. Two months later, Victor Atiyeh rolled to a landslide victory and second term as governor. Democrat Ted Kulongoski, Atiyeh's November opponent again, had argued vigorously that the governor's "raid" on SAIF was illegal.

The Election of 1982

A combination of factors assured Victor Atiyeh's reelection (with 63% of the vote). The governor had been steadfast in the face of Oregon's worst economic recession in 50 years. Along with Democratic leaders Hardy Myers, Fred Heard, and Jason Boe, Atiyeh forged a bipartisan coalition that in the span of 25 months successfully conducted four special legislative sessions. Rarely had an Oregon governor faced as stern a test of leadership as the one Victor Atiyeh confronted during his first term. Voters were so impressed with their governor's steady, firm hand they chose to give him four more years in office. Victor Atiyeh's reelection by 265,000 votes (in a state where registered Democrats outnumbered Republicans by 200,000) was testament to the governor's popularity. With statewide voter turnout of 70%, Atiyeh carried all 36 counties in 1982, including Multnomah by 31,000 and Washington (his home county), by 42,000 over Kulongoski.

The November election featured an interesting addition to state politics. Because of rapid population growth in the 1970s, Oregon had gained an additional seat in the House of Representatives (the 5th Congressional District). The 2nd District of incumbent one-term Republican Denny Smith had been re-drawn so that he was now a resident of the new 5th District. Congressman Smith ran for the 5th District seat, facing Democrat Ruth McFarland, a state senator. McFarland ran a spirited campaign, raised lots of money, and gave Denny Smith all he could handle. But the better-known Smith won the new seat, 104,000 to McFarland's 99,000. Denny Smith's former 2nd District seat was won by another Republican, longtime state legislator Robert (Bob) Smith (no relation to Denny Smith), a conservative Burns cattleman-businessman. Democrats prevailed in Oregon's other congressional districts. Democrats also made gains in state legislative races, winning three additional seats in the House, giving them a 36-24 majority in the 1983 session. Republicans won an additional seat in the Senate, which Democrats hardly noticed, as they maintained a 21-9 majority in that chamber.

The 1983 Legislature

Oregon's 62nd Legislative Assembly met in regular session for 188 days, from January 10 to July 16, 1983. Two Eugeneans (Democrats Grattan Kerans and Edward Fadeley) were elected House speaker and Senate president, respectively, the third time in legislative history the speaker and president were residents of the same city. Their elections were hotly contested affairs. House Democrats caucused for eight hours, choosing Kerans as speaker on their 52nd ballot. The Senate took even longer to organize.

The gender balance in the 1983 Legislature was six women and 24 men in the Senate, 13 women and 47 men in the House of Representatives. Five of the six women senators had moved over to the Senate from seats they had held in the 1981 House: Republicans Nancy W. Ryles and Jeannette Hamby from Washington County, and Democrats Margie Hendriksen of Lane, Joyce Cohen of Clackamas, and Mae Yih of Linn County. The election to the Senate of five women was the first time in state history that so many female legislators had moved from one chamber to another in the same election.

The Death of Tom McCall

The legislature did not convene on time in January 1983. Former Governor Tom McCall succumbed to cancer after two months of rapidly declining health; he died on Saturday morning, January 8, 1983, two days before the 62nd Legislature was scheduled to convene. Several days of mourning ensued. McCall's body was placed in a simple pine casket and moved to Salem, where it was put on view in the Capitol Rotunda. Over 6,000 mourners filed past his casket, paying their respects to one of Oregon's most provocative, daring, and charismatic leaders. The legislature waited while lawmakers took time to participate in the period of mourning. On Wednesday night, January 12, a stately funeral was held for McCall in a packed House chamber. Former governor Robert Straub gave a stirring tribute to McCall, his life of accomplishment, and his unwavering love for Oregon. Governor Victor Atiyeh, with whom McCall had often disagreed, gave a gracious, emotional eulogy, calling Tom McCall a "genuine hero." Later that night, McCall's body was transported to Redmond for burial at the McCall family ranch.[11]

Strapping on the Boots

The legislature had a big mountain to climb. Oregon was still in the grip of a protracted recession. Oregon's unemployment rate reached its zenith in January 1983, a staggering 12.5%. The state's long-dominant timber industry was undergoing fundamental changes. In order to compete with cheaper foreign log imports (particularly from Canada), Oregon's timber companies had to find ways to cut costs. This meant investing in modernizing mills and new kinds of machinery in the harvesting of trees. Over the next three years, as Oregon's lumber production slowly climbed back to pre-1980 levels, the industry eliminated 30,000 jobs.

The bitter memories of 1982 were still fresh in the minds of lawmakers and the governor: huge state budget deficits and three special sessions of the legislature, coupled with the specter of a taxpayer revolt to limit the growth of property taxes. The House Democratic majority favored a sales tax plan, with Bend Democrat Tom Throop, chair of the House Revenue Committee, Salem Democrat Peter Courtney, and Corvallis Republican Tony Van Vliet leading the charge. The three men came to the session with the skeleton of a sales tax plan in hand.

Speaker Grattan Kerans opposed a sales tax, yet he believed that Oregonians should ultimately decide the question. So he stepped aside and allowed the House Revenue Committee to hold extensive hearings, while building a coalition of supporters. The speaker told Chairman Throop to hire whatever staff he needed to get a sales tax plan to the house floor for a vote. Kerans reminded Throop that he was personally "opposed to it, wouldn't vote for it, but wasn't going to stand in their way; [he] would take a detached view."[12] After weeks of hearings and drafting a sales tax plan, members of the Revenue Committee balked. The sales tax bill appeared to be dead. Kerans, true to his word, kept the issue alive; he appointed a special nine-person committee, headed by Throop, to act on the bill. By a vote of 7-2 the special committee passed the tax plan to the floor. After a heated, protracted debate, the House finally voted on the special committee bill: it was a tie! After several tense minutes, during which Speaker Kerans hesitated, Eugene Republican Larry Campbell stood and changed his "nay" vote to "aye." Thus did the House, in one of the most dramatic legislative votes of the decade, pass the sales tax plan by the barest possible majority of 31-29. Kerans signed the bill and referred it to the Senate for action.

Never Had a Prayer

The House sales tax bill never had a prayer in the senate. President Ed Fadeley opposed a sales tax. According to Kerans, Fadeley was "on a mission. He saw himself as a dragon-slayer, as the peoples' champion who would protect the interests of the common people over the interests of the corporate powers."[13] Fadeley thought that the sales tax was a bad idea, a tax repeatedly rejected by voters. He favored a different approach: a tax-limitation plan similar to one that Californians had passed as an initiative in 1978. House Democrats would have none of Fadeley's idea; for them it was a sales tax or no tax. Ed Fadeley, in turn, was just as adamant that his tax-limitation idea was the better option. A deadlocked legislature appeared likely.

As the session dragged on into July, Senate Democrats worked to get a tax limitation plan out of their chamber and over to the House for a vote. But Kerans, "with pandemonium reigning, adjourned the House before a tax limitation measure could come out of the Senate (where Fadeley had enough votes to get such a bill out of his chamber)."[14] This left the Senate unable to pass any further legislation. There would be no tax reform coming out of the regular legislative session. Lawmakers, in disarray, left Salem, knowing a special session was ahead—Governor Atiyeh had repeatedly warned legislators that if they failed to pass some type of major tax reform plan, he would call them back into special session.

Legislators returned September 14, 1983, and remained until October 21. The House passed a sales tax plan and sent it to the Senate. Ed Fadeley insisted that the House bill be amended. The House Democratic caucus was advised that Fadeley's amendment appeared to be constitutional. Both chambers passed the amended sales tax bill. When the Oregon Supreme Court reviewed the bill, it ruled the measure unconstitutional—because of Fadeley's amendment. Victor Atiyeh and Grattan Kerans believe that Fadeley (who had a brilliant legal mind and was a master parliamentarian) had inserted an amendment he knew was unconstitutional.

Lawmakers passed a state budget for 1983-85 of $3.15 billion, an increase of $173 million over the pervious budget. Governor Atiyeh pushed several bills, including one to re-establish the death penalty in Oregon (the legislature didn't act on it), one to toughen punishment for drunk drivers, and another to establish racial and religious harassment as a felony crime (these were passed into law). In keeping with his advocacy for Oregon to do more to promote job creation and economic diversification, the governor also requested (and was given) a doubling of the budget for Oregon's Department of Economic Development.

1984: Time to Elect a President

1984 was a presidential election year. In Oregon, the presidential campaign and the Senate race between Republican incumbent Mark Hatfield and Democrat Margie Hendriksen were the featured political contests. There were 736,600 registered Democrats, 527,000 Republicans, and 193,400 "other" (most of them independent) voters on the election rolls in spring 1984. Only 53% of registered voters cast ballots in Oregon's May primary.

In the presidential primary, Republican incumbent Ronald Reagan was un-opposed. Five Democrats vied for their party's nomination: former astronaut and current senator, John Glenn of Ohio; Sen. Gary Hart of Colorado; former Vice President Walter F. Mondale; Lyndon H. LaRouche, Jr.; and the Rev. Jesse Jackson. Senator Hart, handsome and telegenic, scored an impressive victory over Mondale, 233,600 to 110,400 in Oregon's Democratic primary, but it was Mondale who later got the nomination.

In statewide races, Democrat Barbara Roberts, a state representative from east Multnomah County, defeated three opponents for her party's nomination for secretary of state. Donna Zajonc, a state representative from Salem, easily won the Republican nomination for the same office.

Oregonians turned out in huge numbers (79%) to vote in November. Voters were energized by several close congressional races, competitive legislative contests, and the presidential election. Democrats outnumbered registered Republicans in Oregon by 200,000, yet President Reagan carried Oregon (as he had in 1980)—this time by almost 150,000 votes over Mondale (685,500 to 536,500)—and was re-elected by a landslide, taking about 59% of the vote. Democrat Mondale won 13 out of 538 electoral votes.

The U.S. Senate campaign featuring three-term incumbent, Republican Mark Hatfield, and newcomer Margie Hendriksen, a Eugene Democrat, resulted in a huge win for the senator. Hendriksen never knew what hit her. Unable to make an argument why voters should replace Hatfield, she took barely 33% of the vote, losing to the incumbent by 402,000 votes: 406,000 to Hatfield's 808,000.

Barbara Roberts, with a minority of the total votes cast, was elected Oregon's new secretary of state. She was the first Democrat elected secretary of state since Stephen Chadwick in 1874. Democrats Weaver, Wyden, and AuCoin retained their seats in Congress, as did Republicans Bob and Denny Smith.

There were no major political upsets in Oregon in 1984. Most voters split their ballots, crossing over to vote Republican and Democrat, depending on the office and the candidates involved. Democrats retained their majorities in the legislature. The assembly remained Democratic 34-26 in the House and 18-12 in the Senate, a three-seat pickup for the GOP.

Kitz and Katz and the Legislature of 1985

Two Democrats, one a community college administrator, the other an emergency-room doctor, were chosen by their caucuses to lead the 1985 Legislature. The era of Kitz and Katz had begun. Vera Katz, a six-term state representative from Northwest Portland, and Dr. John Kitzhaber, a six-year legislator from Roseburg, were elected speaker of the House and Senate president, respectively. Katz and Kitzhaber forged an alliance, bringing their chambers together in ways not previously seen. The partnership (quickly dubbed Kitz and Katz by the media) guided the legislature through six years (1985-90) of closely coordinated, mutual cooperation. For the time being the rancor and turf wars between the House and Senate faded.

Vera Katz was the first woman elected speaker of the Oregon House of Representatives. Born in Dusseldorf, Germany, she fled her homeland in 1933, with her Jewish parents and sibling, walking into France in 1940. Her family immigrated to Brooklyn, New York, where she grew up and attended college. Vera married artist-teacher Mel Katz and moved with him to Portland in 1964.

Vera Katz

Vera Pistrak was born in August 1933 in Dusseldorf, Germany, into a Jewish family. Her parents realized that under the regime of Germany's new chancellor, Adolf Hitler, they were at risk, so the Pistraks fled to France and, at night, crossed the Pyrenees Mountains into Spain. From there, the family emigrated to New York City, where Vera grew up. She earned BA and MA degrees from Brooklyn College and married Mel Katz, a budding artist. In 1962, the young couple moved to Portland. The presidential campaign of Robert Kennedy in 1968 motivated Katz to volunteer and, later, to become a political activist. In 1972, she was elected to the Oregon House as a Democrat, representing northwest Portland and a piece of eastern Washington County.

A vocal supporter of women's rights, gun-control legislation, and education reform, Representative Katz eventually ended up as a force in the powerful Ways and Means Committee and in the majority Democratic caucus. Katz was elected to nine House terms, serving from 1973 to 1991. She was elected the first woman speaker of the Oregon House in 1985, serving in that capacity for six years. And she was the first person to serve as speaker for three terms.

During her tenure as speaker, Katz formed a strong working relationship with Democratic Senate President John Kitzhaber, to advance programs they agreed on. The media dubbed the pair "Kitz and Katz." For several years Katz studied the problems of public education. Her bill, the Oregon Educational Act of the 21st Century, designed to establish career paths and stiffer educational requirements for students and teachers, was passed in the mid-1980s. Some of the ideas in the "No Child Left Behind" Act passed by Congress during the presidency of George W. Bush were drawn from Katz's education-reform law.

After leaving the legislature in January 1993, Vera Katz returned to Portland and was elected mayor, a post she held for the next 12 years. Her impact on city government and that city's quality of life rank her as one of Portland's most successful and influential political leaders ever. Indeed, Vera Katz ranks as the pre-eminent woman politician in Oregon between 1985 and 2005.

In 1972, Katz was elected to the Oregon House. Known for her hearty laugh, good humor, optimism, keen intelligence, strong work ethic, acute sense of fairness, and bold, colorful clothing, Vera Katz cut a wide swath through the legislature and state government.

Dr. John Kitzhaber had served a single term in the House followed by a four-year Senate term. Handsome, intelligent, and pragmatic, Kitzhaber was committed to a style of leadership that emphasized inclusion, compromise, and cooperation. An avid outdoorsman and angler, Kitzhaber's trademarks were blue jeans, a large silver belt buckle, cowboy boots, and tweedy sport coat. He attended high school in Eugene and graduated from Dartmouth College and the University of Oregon Medical School. He assumed the Senate presidency in 1985 at the age of 38.

The 63rd Legislative Assembly lasted for 159 days (January 14-June 21). It featured an interesting mix of people, including 18 women and 72 men (six women served in the Senate, 12 in the House); three legislators were African American and two had been born in Asia. Republican Paul Hanneman was starting his 11th term in the House, and Democrat Ed Fadeley was beginning his 22nd year in the Senate.

The 159-day session was the shortest in 10 years. Again, the issue of tax reform dominated the session. Republican Gov. Victor Atiyeh, a longtime foe of a state sales tax, did an about-face in 1985: in his Opening Day address he announced that he now backed a sales tax. Speaker Katz and President Kitzhaber agreed with Atiyeh. The session would be devoted to crafting yet another sales tax plan and referring it to voters. The plan legislators passed was proposed as an amendment to the state constitution to establish a 5% sales tax.The revenue would be used to cut property taxes by an average of 35% and to reduce a individual's income taxes by about 9.7%. The measure was referred to voters at a special statewide election set for September 17, 1985. Voters rejected the legislature's plan by a 5-1 margin, 189,733 in favor to 666,365 opposed.

Other significant legislation passed in 1985: the third Monday of January was designated as a state holiday to commemorate the life of Dr. Martin Luther King, Jr.; banking and election reforms were enacted; a three-person Public Utility Commission (replacing a single commissioner) was established; and a number of juvenile crime bills were passed, including a controversial measure to lower the age for a juvenile to be tried in an adult court from 16 to 15 if he or she was accused of a violent crime. Over 2,000 bills were introduced, 862 of which were passed. Governor Atiyeh vetoed 32 of them.

Lawmakers passed a $3.325 billion state budget for 1985-87, a 7.2% ($222 million) increase over the previous budget. Legislators balanced the budget by increasing the gasoline tax by 2¢ a gallon and made permanent a recent 27¢ increase in taxes on a pack of cigarettes. Legislators raised their own salaries from $700 to $895 a month and their daily expenses from $44 to $50 a day (while in session); their monthly expense accounts were increased from $300 to $400 (between sessions). Long-overdue salary increases for the state's top officeholders were also passed (for example, the governor's salary was raised from $55,400 to $72,000).

The 1985 Legislature was fortunate to meet at a time when Oregon's sluggish economy was on the rebound; there were no fiscal crises like those of the 1981 and 1983 sessions. Gone, for the time being, were the deep divisions and bickering associated with the previous five legislatures. The high level of cooperation between Speaker Vera Katz and Senate President John Kitzhaber paid dividends in the form of a shorter session and rising public confidence in the legislature.

The Campaign of 1986

In 1986 Governor Victor Atiyeh was nearing the end of his eight years in office. Who would succeed him? There were two other interesting contests as well: the race in the 4th Congressional District and Sen. Bob Packwood's campaign to win a fourth term. The May primary was dominated by these three contests.

Fourteen people entered the governor's race in May, seven Democrats and seven Republicans. Only two of the Democratic candidates were serious contenders: State Senator Ed Fadeley of Eugene and Neil Goldschmidt, former mayor of Portland. Goldschmidt was eloquent and charismatic, with legions of enthusiastic supporters in metropolitan Portland. A pro-business Democrat, he enjoyed support from the Jewish community and big-business contributors. Popular with college students, environmentalists, urban planners, and arts patrons, he was known as a man of bold vision who got things done. With a better grassroots organization and lots of money, Neil Goldschmidt won the primary, defeating Ed Fadeley by 133,000 votes (214,148 to 81,300). Secretary of State Norma Paulus topped the Republican slate of gubernatorial candidates. Oregon's first female secretary of state, Paulus hoped to become the first woman in state history to be the gubernatorial nominee of a major political party. She had no serious opponent in the GOP primary. The prospect of a Paulus-Goldschmidt campaign sparked widespread interest among voters. Both candidates were telegenic and articulate, and each was backed by organizations with lots of campaign money.

The race for Congress in the 4th District drew seven candidates, five of whom were serious contenders. Six-term Congressman James B. Weaver had not filed for reelection, opting instead to run for the U.S. Senate seat held by Republican Robert Packwood. Four Democrats vied for their party's nomination: State Senator Bill Bradbury of Coos Bay/North Bend, State Senator

Margie Hendricksen of Eugene, Peter DeFazio, a former congressional aide, also from Eugene, and Duncan Lindsey, an unknown. The Bradbury-DeFazio-Hendricksen contest turned out to be one of the closest races in years. DeFazio won the nomination with 22,530 votes, edging Bill Bradbury by 837 votes and Hendricksen by 1,735 votes (Bradbury: 21,693, Hendricksen: 20,795). The Republican contest was also a spirited affair. Longtime state representative Mary McCauley Burrows of Eugene opposed businessman Bruce Long for the GOP nomination. Long was victorious, defeating Burrows by 10,000 votes.

None of Oregon's other four U.S. representatives faced serious competition in the 1986 May primary. Incumbents Denny and Bob Smith, Les AuCoin, and Ron Wyden all cruised to easy victories against token opponents.

Incumbent Bob Packwood was opposed by conservative Joe P. Lutz, Sr., for the GOP nomination for U.S. Senate. Lutz put together a respectable grassroots campaign and gave Packwood a stiff challenge: Packwood defeated Lutz by 45,000 votes (172,000 to 126,300). Some wondered if Packwood was vulnerable in November. Three opponents faced Congressman Jim Weaver in the Democratic contest for U.S. Senate: perennial candidate Steve Anderson and state lawmakers Rick Bauman and Rod Monroe of Portland. Weaver, a longtime fixture in Oregon politics, was a populist with a shoot-from-the-hip style, and popular in his southern Oregon district. He won the Democratic nomination with 183,300 votes. Rod Monroe finished second with 44,553 ballots.

Despite his impressive showing in the primary, Jim Weaver was in trouble. Unknown to the general public, Congressman Weaver was being investigated by the House Ethics Committee for possible violations of federal election laws, relating to his alleged misuse of campaign funds. Weaver, apparently in an attempt to "grow" his campaign fund to better position himself against the well-heeled Bob Packwood, had invested several hundred thousand dollars of campaign funds in risky stock futures. Weaver's investment tanked and he lost most of the money. Facing increasing pressure from the Ethics Committee and the Democratic Party, Weaver agreed to withdraw from the Senate race. The Democratic Central Committee chose Rep. Rick Bauman to replace him. Bauman turned out to be a poor choice: unknown outside of Portland, with no statewide campaign organization, he had finished a distant third in the Democratic primary and he had little money. Bauman was a sacrificial lamb and he was doomed.

Neil or Norma? The Governor's Race

The fiercely contested governor's race between Republican Norma Paulus and Democrat Neil Goldschmidt had the electorate's attention in November. Paulus and Goldschmidt were well matched, both seasoned politicians and effective campaigners. Each had legions of enthusiastic and committed supporters, and both were good fund raisers. Paulus, because she had been secretary of state for eight years, had the edge in name recognition. Neil Goldschmidt had never held statewide office in Oregon. However, he had an impressive political resume, including service as U.S. Secretary of Transportation in the Carter administration. Dynamic, intense, and an often compelling speaker, Neil Goldschmidt was a formidable candidate.

Norma Paulus was a potent voter-getter. She was a popular politician, regarded favorably by both Republicans and Democrats. The governor's race was one of the most expensive in state history.* The bulk of this money was spent on TV advertising. Both campaigns also used door-to-door literature drops and phone banks. The candidates also appeared in several live TV debates. With 72% of registered voters casting ballots in November, Neil Goldschmidt was elected governor, defeating Norma Paulus by 42,500 votes, 549,456 to 506,986.

The United States Senate contest between Democrat Rick Bauman and incumbent Republican Bob Packwood resulted in a crushing defeat for Bauman, 376,000 to 656,000. Democrat Peter DeFazio won the 4th District Congressional seat vacated by six-term Democrat James B. Weaver, defeating Republican Bruce Long, 105,700 to 89,800.

Oregon's legislative races resulted in yet another Democratic sweep. Democrats retained control of the Senate 17-13. Democrats also kept their slim majority in the Oregon House 31-29.

Money, Money, Money

Political campaigns in Oregon (as well as in the rest of the nation) grew more costly every year. The average cost of a state representative race in Oregon's 1986 general election was $22,200, up from an average cost of only $3,450 in 1974. State Senate races were even more expensive (because twice as many people lived in a Senate district as in a House district): $34,800 in 1986 compared to $6,500 in 1974. In 1988, the average cost of a state Senate contest had climbed by another $15,000, to $49,250. The proliferation of special interest groups (and their political action committees or PACs) along with the addition of hundreds of new lobbyists at the State Capitol continued to change politics in Oregon.

---

* Goldschmidt had spent $1.277 million in the Democratic primary; Paulus had spent $676,000 to win the GOP nod. For the general election Paulus spent $1.435 million, to Goldschmidt's $1.602 million, for a total of just under $5 million.

With each new election, a candidate for the legislature, statewide, or federal office had to spend more time raising money. The $5 million dollar governor's race between Neil Goldschmidt and Norma Paulus in 1986 set the tone for what was ahead.

Victor Atiyeh's Legacy

Victor Atiyeh's tenure as governor ended with Neil Goldschmidt's swearing-in in January 1987. The Atiyeh era in state government, spanning three decades, was ending. Vic Atiyeh's eight years as governor were shaped by a four-year recession so severe that old-timers compared it to the Great Depression. Between 1980 and 1983, Governor Atiyeh led the way in cutting $750 million out of state budgets. Tough choices were made, as vital state services were cut to balance the budget.

Victor Atiyeh was a pragmatic businessman and a 20-year veteran legislator. As a Republican governor, he understood that if he was to accomplish anything he would have to work collaboratively with a Democratic legislature. The governor believed that state government worked best when people came together, when the legislative and executive branches shared ideas, debated openly, genuinely respected each other, and worked cooperatively toward common goals.

As Oregon's economy worsened in 1980-81, Atiyeh, like a good ship's captain, kept his grip on the wheel, eyes focused ahead. He was steady and dependable. Oregonians were impressed by Atiyeh's fairness, patience, civility, dedication, hard work, and his honesty and willingness to cooperate, share, and compromise. The governor preferred to do his job without fanfare, to work quietly behind the scenes to arrive at mutually agreeable solutions. Unlike some governors, Victor Atiyeh did not allow his ego to get in the way of doing his job as he saw it.

Some have faulted Vic Atiyeh for not being more of an activist governor. His agenda was too small, say his critics; he had no great vision, no grand innovation that he wanted to accomplish. Yet there is consensus that Victor Atiyeh was "a good steward, a more than adequate governor, an able custodian who served in bad times, a man who saw himself as a manager who brought a business perspective into government—who always had a balance-sheet in mind.[15] Vic Atiyeh was the first Oregon governor to appoint a woman as his chief-of-staff. And, Oregon's critical Food Share program was also established during his tenure.

Atiyeh believes that he was "a good governor and decent person, a governor that people would like to have, a man who loved and cared deeply about Oregon. I feel that Oregon was a better state because I was there. I was the right guy at the right time. My job was not to be a movie actor but, rather president of a company. We got through the recession with fairness and in fairly good shape."[16]

Victor Atiyeh is a modest man. He acknowledges that no landmark legislation (like a Bottle Bill, for example) was passed while he was governor. His goals were more modest. Atiyeh was interested in getting Oregon's economy back on its feet, working to diversify it, working to bring new industries into the state. To Vic Atiyeh economic development was vital. Even while the state staggered through its recession, he convinced legislators to double the budget of the Department of Economic Development and to establish an Oregon Economic Advisory Council. Under Atiyeh, the legislature established a full-time, staffed office of trade in Tokyo to promote the sale of Oregon products and services in Japan.*

On the environmental front, Governor Atiyeh was instrumental in convincing Washington State officials to join with Oregon, Idaho, and Montana to persuade Congress to pass a federal law to establish the Northwest Power Planning Council—part of whose mission would be to protect Columbia River salmon from extinction.

Governor Atiyeh made minority groups an important part of his legislative agenda. Three new state commissions were established, all of which Atiyeh actively promoted: Senior Services, Hispanic, and Black (African American) commissions. After learning about an incident of racial hatred directed at an African American man in Milwaukie, Oregon, Atiyeh ("I have always hated bullies") had a bill drafted (and for which he lobbied) to make racial harassment a felony crime in Oregon—a bill enacted by the Democratic legislature.

Victor Atiyeh was not interested in spending lots of taxpayer dollars. He wanted government to be more efficient and accountable. Even if he had proposed expensive new programs, there was no money to fund them. Because of the lingering recession, Atiyeh and the legislature were busy just trying to keep the ship of state afloat. What Oregon needed most in the early 1980s was a calm, experienced problem-solver—a leader who inspired confidence, a leader who understood what he had to do and how he had to do it. Victor Atiyeh was that person: the right man in the right place at the right time.

---

* To acknowledge his efforts to increase trade between Oregon and Japan the Port of Portland named the International Concourse at Portland International Airport for Victor Atiyeh. A life-size statue of Mr. Atiyeh greets passengers as they enter that concourse today.

Chapter 18
Neil and Barbara, Vera and John, 1987-94

Democrat Neil Goldschmidt became Oregon's 33rd governor on January 12, 1987. The 46-year-old Goldschmidt's close election victory in November generated widespread interest and excitement. In his meteoric political career, Neil Goldschmidt had left his imprint everywhere he'd been. Known by his supporters as "the boy wonder," or simply as "Neil," he was barely 30 when he was elected to the Portland City Council and became mayor at 32. Under Mayor Goldschmidt, Portland built a bus-transit mall in downtown, turning the central business district into a pedestrian-friendly haven; Portland's Tri-Met transit system reached far into the suburbs, pulling the metropolitan area together into a cohesive mass transit system. Goldschmidt joined Gov. Bob Straub in blocking the construction of a proposed Mount Hood freeway, which would have sliced through the heart of Southeast Portland neighborhoods. Goldschmidt believed that a public transit system of buses and light rail would better serve the needs of metropolitan Portland in the long run. Many Oregonians saw Goldschmidt as a man of vision, passion, and immense ambition, a man who was going places. Goldschmidt got things done. "[He] was a Democratic Tom McCall, an electric personality, who really got people excited; people believed in him."[1] Charismatic, telegenic, and an expert at attracting media attention, Neil Goldschmidt was admired by friend and foe alike. His style was intense, prodding, and provocative. He had ideas by the truckload. His energy was legendary. "He has two speeds, full-speed and crash."[2] A classic workaholic, Goldschmidt drove himself hard and expected the same from those who worked for him.

Back on Track

Goldschmidt took office in 1987, when the state's economy was picking up. Barbara Roberts (who would later become governor herself) commented: "Neil gave people hope and it was critical to the turnaround. ... The Oregon Comeback happened because people believed again."[3] Goldschmidt exuded confidence and optimism in his new job as governor. "His first months were a whirlwind of change. Goldschmidt handed the Legislature a sixty-day agenda of bills he wanted passed, reorganized several state agencies, and persuaded voters to pass a measure to keep schools from closing."[4]

Oregon's rebounding economy produced a projected state budget surplus of $286 million in 1987. State economists predicted an even bigger surplus in 1987-89. Goldschmidt was lucky: there would be money for long-neglected state programs. Republican Gov. Victor Atiyeh and four legislatures had had to slash budgets so severely that many state programs were harmed. Goldschmidt chose corrections, higher education, and economic development (particularly in rural Oregon) as priority programs for budget surplus money.

Goldschmidt had a Democratic legislature to work with. Vera Katz returned for a second term as speaker of the House as did John Kitzhaber, president of the Senate. Katz was a close friend and longtime political ally of Neil Goldschmidt. They had worked together on Portland city projects and their political philosophies were similar. With Katz in the speaker's office, Governor Goldschmidt believed the Oregon House would welcome his proposals. It was expected that Senate President Kitzhaber would follow suit, making Goldschmidt's term a productive one.

Oregon's 66th Legislature

The Legislature of 1987 lasted 168 days, January 12-June 28. A record 2,572 bills were introduced. Legislators passed 928 bills, 15 of which Governor Goldschmidt vetoed. There were 17 Democrats and 13 Republicans in the Senate, while the House continued to teeter on the sharp edge of a razor-thin Democrat majority of 31-29. Six women served in the Senate (the same number as in 1985) and 10 in the House.

"Budget repair" was Goldschmidt's primary goal in 1987.[5] Besides funneling more money into education, corrections, and economic development, the governor wanted to divert millions of dollars of new state lottery revenues to help rural Oregon grow its local economies. Goldschmidt believed that people should be empowered at the grassroots level to involve themselves with state officials to decide the best use of lottery dollars for economic development.[6] Another Goldschmidt priority was reforming Oregon's Workers' Compensation system. The issue of employer liability warranted attention and it would take Goldschmidt three years to achieve this reform.

From the moment Neil Goldschmidt took office he took charge. "He had ideas, he had a program—one which moved the state forward. The governor recognized that Oregon had pressing public safety needs. Therefore, Goldschmidt initiated a major program to expand the number of Oregon prisons, and, to establish new sentencing guidelines for felons." Governor Goldschmidt's dealings with the legislature were not always smooth. He made little effort to regularly communicate with rank-and-file members. Except for an occasional meeting with members of the Ways and Means subcommittees, he preferred to work through the chain of command, speaker Katz and president Kitzhaber's offices.[7]

The governor had a big agenda and he wanted to get things done quickly. Consequently, he was often impatient with the legislature's glacial pace. Accustomed to getting his way, he wanted to "shake things up, he wanted things to happen." His impatience was seen by some as disrespect for the legislature, while others saw Goldschmidt as often insensitive to the opinions and beliefs of others.[8] "Legislators grumbled that Goldschmidt didn't understand how they worked, didn't understand the rhythms of a legislative session. At times the ponderous bureaucracy frustrated Goldschmidt, as did the need to woo legislators before making a move. But in Salem, he was an outsider, the first to serve as governor in the state's modern history.[9] Governors Atiyeh, Straub, and Hatfield had all served in the legislature and all had been a part of state government for years.

What the Legislature Did

The governor got most of what he wanted in his proposed 1987-89 budget. The legislature approved $3.72 billion, an 11.3% increase over the $3.34 billion state budget for 1985-87. $32 million went for prison expansion, and $77 million was appropriated for new buildings on the campuses of Oregon's public universities. Corporations doing business in Oregon received a $20 million tax break. Poor and uninsured Oregonians benefited from a law forbidding hospitals from denying medical care to a person who was unable to pay.

The legislature also passed a bill allowing for the purchase and maintenance of a privately funded governor's mansion. Subsequently, Mahonia Hall, a 10,000-square-foot Tudor-style residence (complete with a ballroom) in the Fairmount neighborhood of South Salem was purchased to serve as the official residence of Oregon's governor.

Education continued to get the lion's share of the state general fund budget. The Education budget for 1987-89 was increased to $1.9 billion ($274 million), 51% of the general fund. The Human Resources budget was increased by $252 million to $1.093 billion, just under 30% of the state budget. Legislators returned excess revenue to taxpayers, upping tax relief from $159 million in

1985-87 to $313.6 million for 1987-89. The legislature was able to pay for these expanded programs because the state was taking in more revenue from rising personal income and corporate taxes. The state collected $2.455 billion in income taxes in 1985-87. And state economists were projecting that tax revenue would jump by $350 million in the next two years. This, coupled with an additional $38 million in corporate taxes, and a 7% increase in the state tax on cigarettes, paid for much of the expanded 1987-89 state budget.

One Cost of Rapid Population Growth

Oregon grew by 542,000 people between 1970 and 1980, causing many local school districts (especially in large suburban areas) to scramble to build schools and hire staff fast enough to keep up with the influx of new students. Oregon's public schools operated under a law that set a limit of 6% as the maximum amount a school board could raise taxes in a year without having to get approval from local voters. But what if a 6% tax increase was not enough? What if a school district needed an 8%, 9%, or 10% increase in order to keep up with rising costs? School districts could ask voters to approve a tax increase above 6%; the school board could decide to live within the allowable 6% tax increase; or the board could decide not to raise school taxes at all.

Any increase in school taxes (whether below or above 6%) meant that voters were being asked whether or not they wanted to raise their property taxes. Many school districts decided to live within the allowable 6% tax increase, which, in many cases, meant the district was actually falling behind in its ability to keep up with rising costs due to expanding enrollments, higher salaries, health insurance and retirement benefits, new school buildings, technology, books, remodeling and maintenance costs.

What about those school districts that asked voters to approve a tax increase above the 6% limit? In many cases, voters defeated these measures. School boards could hold two, three, or four elections in the same year, hoping voters would agree to increase property taxes.

Election Year 1988

As elections go, 1988 was not particularly memorable. None of Oregon's top three officeholders (governor and U.S. senators) were on the ballot. The presidential race dominated Oregon's May and November elections along with the statewide offices of secretary of state, treasurer, and attorney general. In addition, two-term Congressman, Republican Denny Smith, was thought to be in trouble in Oregon's 5th District, where he faced Democrat Mike Kopetski.

The names of six Democrats and three Republicans were on their party's presidential ballots. The GOP ballot was headed by Vice Pres. George Herbert Walker Bush. His challengers were televangelist Pat Robertson and Kansas Sen. Bob Dole. The Democratic ballot was headed by Michael Dukakis, governor of Massachusetts, and included the Rev. Jesse Jackson and four others. Governor Dukakis, a new face on the national scene, defeated Jackson in Oregon 221,000 to 148,200. George H. W. Bush won Oregon's GOP primary, defeating Bob Dole, 200,000 to 49,000. Like Governor Dukakis, Vice President Bush went on to win his party's presidential nomination.

Oregon's general election brought out 81% of registered voters (compared to 55% who voted in the primary). Eight ballot measures, the presidential campaign, legislative races, and Oregon's five U.S. House contests attracted the big turnout. Democrat Michael Dukakis carried Oregon, defeating Bush 616,200 to 560,100. Bush, however, was elected president with 53% of the national vote. Oregon was one of only 10 states (and the District of Columbia) to vote for Michael Dukakis in 1988.

All of Oregon's incumbent congressmen were reelected by hefty margins—except for Republican Denny Smith. Nearly 220,000 votes were cast in the 5th District between Smith and Democrat Mike Kopetski. Smith won by 665 votes, 111,229 to 110,564. Democrat Les AuCoin was reelected in the 1st District by over 100,000 votes; Republican Bob Smith was reelected by 50,000 votes in the 2nd District. In the 3rd District, Democratic Ron Wyden, without opposition, won another term. In the 4th District Democratic incumbent Peter DeFazio won another term by 66,000 votes.

Democrat Barbara Roberts was reelected as secretary of state, defeating her GOP opponent John Sheppard by nearly 450,000 votes. Republican Tony Meeker (who had been appointed to the job in 1987 by Gov. Goldschmidt) was elected to a full term as state treasurer and Republican David Frohnmayer won a third term as attorney general, pulling more votes (965,800) than anyone else on the November ballot. The legislature remained in Democratic hands, 19-11 in the Senate and 32-28 in the Oregon House.

Oregon's high voter turnout in November was also the result of keen interest in a bevy of ballot measures. Measure 4 provided for full sentences without parole or probation for certain repeat felony crimes. Voters passed the measure by a margin of about 4-1, 948,000 to 253,000 opposed. Measure 8 featured the issue of sexual discrimination. The state executive branch had, by administrative rule, banned discrimination against a person because of their gender or sexual orientation. Voters overturned the state ban, 626,750 to 561,350.

Measure 6 spoke to the volatile issue of cigarette smoking in public places. Oregon's Indoor Clean Air law (which had been widely copied by other states and cities) was under siege by smokers and tobacco companies. Measure 6 would have weakened the state's Clean Air Act. Because Oregon has one of the highest percentages of non-smoking populations, Measure 6 was defeated, 737,800 no, to 430,800 yes.

Kitz and Katz and the Legislature of 1989

The 1989 session lasted 177 days, from January 9 to July 4, passing a record 1,108 bills. The team of Kitz and Katz was back for a third time. Fourteen women served in the House, and seven in the Senate. Portland Democrat Vera Katz was the first person in state history to be chosen speaker for a third time. Two African Americans (Senators Jim Hill and Bill McCoy) were serving in the state Senate for the first time.

Goldschmidt enjoyed another remarkable legislative session in 1989, winning approval of an ambitious budget that included money to repair parks, programs, and agencies decimated by the recession of the early 1980s.[10] Prisons held much of the governor's attention. Oregon's severe prison overcrowding problem demanded bold action. "Goldschmidt spent more than $160 million to increase beds from about 3,900 to more than 7,000. He won legislation to override land-use laws to put prisons in Ontario, Baker, Portland, and North Bend."[11] The 66th Legislative Assembly was barely under way when Oregonians were shocked by a high-profile crime. Michael Francke, director of the Oregon Corrections Division, was stabbed in the heart at the north entrance of the Corrections Building in Salem on the evening of January 17, 1989. The Francke murder cast an ominous shadow over the 1989 Legislature—as well as over the second half of the Goldschmidt administration.

The session was dominated by the Ways and Means Committee, chaired by conservative Democrats, Rep. Jeff Gilmour of Jefferson, and Sen. Mike Thorne of Pendleton, and crafting a state budget for the next biennium. A record $4.53 billion general fund budget was passed for 1989-91—an 18% increase over the previous budget.

Another important achievement of the 1989 session was a bill to raise Oregon's minimum wage law, despite protests from business. The bill made Oregon's new minimum wage the highest in America. The issue of hate crimes was also addressed. The increased incidence and public awareness of these crimes had aroused groups (like the American Civil Liberties Union) to work with the legislature to amend state law. The result was a broadened state statute that made intimidation based on a person's sexual orientation a crime in Oregon.

A landmark healthcare reform bill was passed. Sponsored by Senate President (and Doctor) John Kitzhaber, the Oregon Health Plan provided state health insurance for poor Oregonians whose income was too high for Medicaid (the federal health insurance program for the poor).*

Speaker Katz also led a successful push for a tougher gun control law in Oregon. "The measure tripled Oregon's waiting time for gun purchase to fifteen days, required purchasers' fingerprints, and eased requirements for obtaining a concealed weapons permit."[12]

Governor Goldschmidt called the legislature into special session on May 7, 1990, a week before Oregon's primary election. Thwarted for three years in his attempts to move legislators toward making major changes in the Oregon's Workers' Compensation system, the governor called lawmakers back to Salem to wrestle with the issue. Goldschmidt had backed legislation to reform the system in the 1989 session and had been blocked by Democrat Grattan Kerans, chair of the Senate Labor Committee. Senator Kerans opposed the bill because he believed it was written by employer groups, to the disadvantage of injured workers. The one-day special session produced the reform legislation Goldschmidt wanted. "The new law was hailed by both business and labor and resulted in substantial savings to employers and better protection for injured workers."[13]

Goldschmidt Drops a Political Bomb

On February 9, 1990, Gov. Neil Goldschmidt announced that his 25-year marriage was in trouble and that he and his wife, Margie, were separating. As those assembled gasped, Goldschmidt then said that he would not seek reelection. This news rocked Oregon's political establishment to its foundation. For the remaining eleven months of his term, Neil Goldschmidt was a lame-duck governor.†

---

* What was unique about Kitzhaber's plan was that it ranked treatments according to which were most effective, both in terms of cost and improved medical condition. During those times when it was necessary to cut funds from the Plan, those treatments/medical procedures at the bottom of the prioritized list would no longer be covered by the Plan.

† One reason why Goldschmidt may have chosen not to seek a second term was that he had a secret. In 2004 the secret came out in a newspaper report telling of a sexual affair between then 35-year-old Mayor Goldschmidt and his children's 14-year-old babysitter. The affair, a felony crime, had been covered up for a decade. As the girl grew into adulthood, she experienced severe emotional and personal problems. Goldschmidt paid for the woman's psychiatric treatments and gave her $250,000 to help her establish a career and to protect their secret from ever becoming public. In May 2004, Goldschmidt publicly admitted to the affair and asked for the public's forgiveness.

During Goldschmidt's last year in office, the media and the public reflected on what kind of leader he had been. While his accomplishments were solid, there were many who thought that Neil Goldschmidt could have, should have, accomplished more. This governor was a dynamic and inspirational leader who fired off bold new ideas faster than reporters could write them down. In addition to his obvious leadership qualities, he was governor during a period of exploding prosperity (with huge state budget surpluses) and at a time when fellow Democrats controlled both chambers of the legislature. In reviewing Goldschmidt's governorship, *Oregonian* reporter Jeff Mapes speculated that "the governor lacked the patience and discipline to stick to that mantra of modern American politics: the simple, scripted message. [Goldschmidt] has raised expectations and forced people both in and outside state government to stretch. But not everyone wants to be stretched."[14]

In January 1988, Goldschmidt had unveiled a bold new idea called the Children's Agenda. The governor had exhorted public and private groups and state, county, and city governments to develop programs to help all children in Oregon. Goldschmidt claimed that, as a state, "We can do better." There was unnecessary duplication, waste, inefficiency, and gaps in the delivery of social services. Too many children lived in poverty, too many were hungry and too many lived in abusive homes. We need to do more to help children, said the governor. Goldschmidt talked about the needs of children in broad strokes, and lacked specifics. The Children's Agenda "was hard to explain to voters and even harder to demonstrate results. To the public, it became another unfulfilled expectation."[15]

Can Neil Goldschmidt be faulted for promising too much, for pushing an agenda that was too big, too ambitious to be achieved in only four years? Did he lead the public to expect more than could reasonably be delivered? An *Oregonian* editorial said: "Goldschmidt raised Oregonians' expectations of their state government. Surely, he as much as anyone regrets that those expectations were not fully met. But Oregonians will also remember Goldschmidt's call to expect more of themselves. In both cases, he knew the disappointment of expecting too much is still better than the despondency of expecting too little."[16]

Governor Goldschmidt will be remembered for leading Oregon into a period of unparalleled economic expansion. He brought unprecedented numbers of business leaders into state government to serve on boards and commissions and the state benefited from their talent, ideas, and expertise. Goldschmidt energized state government. He made average Oregonians look up and notice what their government was doing. He will also be remembered for leading Oregon through a period of unprecedented prison building. The number of available beds in Oregon's secure prisons increased by 75% under Goldschmidt. The governor also recognized that in deciding where to site the new prisons, the state had an opportunity to pump new life into Oregon's less populous areas, places like Ontario, Baker City, and North Bend, where new jobs were always scarce.

One of Goldschmidt's biggest failures was his inability to come up with a tax reform plan to answer the public cry for lower property taxes. Despite his notable leadership qualities and the support of a Democratic legislature, he fared no better than his predecessors, Tom McCall and Victor Atiyeh, in crafting a tax plan that shifted the burden of paying for public schools away from local property taxes. In later years, political writers would note, "Blame for passage of Measure 5, the property tax limitation [in 1990] cannot be laid solely on Goldschmidt's shoulders. But the governor's midterm withdrawal from the school finance-property tax relief issue and his later failure to ride vigorously into battle against the measure might have meant the difference between its narrow passage and its defeat."[17]

Oregon Changes Direction: The Election of 1990

The election of 1990 is memorable for two reasons. Oregonians elected their first woman governor, Democrat Barbara Roberts, and they passed Ballot Measure 5, a statewide property-tax limitation law.

Secretary of State Barbara Roberts defeated Oregon's attorney general, Republican David Frohnmayer, and independent Al Mobley with 46% of the vote to become governor. The conservative Mobley pulled 144,000 votes and it is believed his candidacy cost Dave Frohnmayer the election. Roberts led the field with 508,700 votes to Frohnmayer's 444,646 votes. The combined Frohnmayer-Mobley vote was 588,700, 80,000 more votes than Roberts got. Barbara Roberts carried her home county, Multnomah, by 67,000 votes. Her popularity with suburban women also helped her carry Washington County by 8,500 votes and Clackamas County by 9,200. Roberts also took Lane County, Frohnmayer's home county, by 4,700 votes. For the second consecutive gubernatorial election, over $5 million was spent by the candidates.*

---

* In the May primary Roberts raised nearly $600,000 (and spent $277,000). Dave Frohnmayer raised $2 million and spent $1.330 million in the GOP primary. In November, Democrat Roberts spent $1.54 million, compared to Frohnmayer's $2.1 million; Al Mobley spent $166,000. Together, Barbara Roberts and David Frohnmayer spent about $5.25 million in their primary and general election campaigns.

Ballot Measure 5

The issue of local property taxes had been a political hot potato in Oregon for over 20 years. For two decades, governors and legislatures grappled with the issue. In 1979 Californians passed Proposition 13, which set a limit on the tax rate that local governments could levy on a person's home or business. On five occasions, Oregonians had voted and rejected measures to establish a similar tax-limitation law in this state. But by 1990 voters wanted lower property taxes, so they approved Measure 5—which did not include a sales tax provision—by a 52,000-vote margin, 574,800 in favor to 522,000 against.

Measure 5 set a limit of 1.5% ($15 per $1,000) as the highest rate that lo-cal governments, combined, could tax a person for the assessed value of his/her property (this rate was to go into effect in 1995-96). Public school districts, city and county governments, community colleges, and other special districts (irrigation or flood-control districts, for example) would have to share every $15 collected in local property taxes. "At the end of a five-year phase-in, Measure 5 limits total school taxes to $5 per $1,000 of each property's real market value. All other local governments (not including school districts) would divide the remaining $10 among themselves."[18]

The second major provision in Measure 5 shifted most of the burden of pay-ing for public schools from local property taxes and onto the Oregon Legislature: by 1995-96 it was expected that the state would be obligated to pay for about 80% of the cost of schools ($3 billion more than the legislature paid for schools in 1991). When Oregonians passed Measure 5 they were saying they wanted the state, not their local property taxes, to pay for public schools. The big question for the governor and legislature was this: where were they going to find the billions of dollars they would need to pay for public education? Since 1991, the agenda of the Oregon Legislature has been dominated by this central question.

Kopetski vs. Smith

Senator Mark Hatfield sought a fifth six-year term in 1990—something only one man had done before: Republican Sen. Charles McNary, 1918-44. Hatfield had seen only token opposition in the May primary, while six Democrats had vied for their party's nomination. Newcomer Harry Lonsdale won the Democratic nomination for Senate by a 6-1 margin. Lonsdale was a millionaire Bend busi-nessman. With his silver hair, tailored suits, and speaking ability, Harry Lonsdale made a good first impression.

In November 1990 Oregon had 1.478 million registered voters. About 77% (1.133 million) of them cast ballots in the election. There were 692,100 registered

Democrats and 570,900 registered Republicans. Non-affiliated voters (most of whom were independents) numbered 161,000. Oregon's 3rd Congressional District (Multnomah County and part of Clackamas County) was the bastion of Democratic strength in Oregon with 158,500 registered Democrats compared to 90,200 Republicans.

A major political upset occurred in the November election: Republican Denny Smith lost his U.S. House seat in the 5th District to Democrat Mike Kopetski. The campaign turned ugly when Smith ran a TV ad (that drew national media attention) using the voice of Adolf Hitler to condemn Kopetski for being "soft," for being willing to appease Iraq's longtime dictator, Saddam Hussein. Many 5th District voters were disgusted with Smith's negative ad.

Mike Kopetski tried to run a positive campaign, focusing his remarks on such issues as improving the management of Oregon's timber resources, offering ideas for improving America's woefully inadequate childcare system, and making a commitment to be a team player, a co-operative and positive member of Oregon's congressional delegation. Building on the political base he'd established after losing to Smith in 1988, Kopetski had campaigned for two years, spending months with volunteers doing door-to-door canvassing, especially in vote-heavy Clackamas County. A nationally targeted contest, the Smith and Kopetski campaigns got lots of outside assistance in the form of money and technical staff from their national parties.

Many voters considered Denny Smith's positions to be extreme. Smith boasted that his independent, maverick style and constant criticism of congressional spending made him a more effective representative. Critics said otherwise: Smith alienated so many people (Republicans and Democrats alike) that he was a lone, isolated (and ineffective) voice in Congress. Meanwhile, Smith criticized environmentalists for attempting to halt logging in Oregon's old-growth forests—a sensitive issue that did not play well in the increasingly suburban 5th District.

Kopetski won the seat by 23,000 votes (124,600 to 101,650). Denny Smith—like his father, Elmo Smith—was very conservative. Kopetski, a moderate Democrat, successfully portrayed Smith as too extreme, out of touch with the mainstream, too conservative for a growing urban-suburban district.

Oregon's other congressmen were easily reelected. Meanwhile, Republicans ended 20 years of Democratic rule in the Oregon House of Representatives, winning four new seats, giving them a 32-28 majority in the House. Oregon was the only state in the union to change a Democratic House of Representatives to a Republican one in 1990. Democrats retained their hold on the state Senate, 20-10.

Governor Barbara Roberts, 1991-95

Barbara Roberts, Oregon's first woman governor, took office on January 14, 1991, the opening day of the 66th legislative session. Roberts was a familiar political name in Oregon.* Roberts had reached the governor's office after a long climb up Oregon's political ladder. Beginning as a school board member and county commissioner, Roberts was elected to the Oregon House of Representatives in 1980, where she served two terms. She was elected secretary of state in 1984. Reelected in 1988, she served in that position until she was elected governor in November 1990. Blessed with boundless stamina, Barbara Roberts was a master campaigner who enjoyed meeting people and mixing in a crowd. Her optimism and good cheer were infectious—qualities that attracted legions of enthusiastic supporters over the years. "The state's first woman governor brings to her new post refreshing directness and zest. Both her openness and enthusiasm were on display over the past week," wrote an *Oregonian* editor.[19]

Governor Barbara Roberts was a partisan Democrat, proud of her party and its traditions. She believed that "government could help people. It was that kind of ambition that drove her to politics to begin with."[20] Roberts' partisanship was well known, having been most evident in 1983-84 when she served as Oregon's first woman House majority leader. Her partisan slant did not sit well with Republican House Speaker Larry Campbell. Campbell and his Republican caucus had their own agenda—and it didn't necessarily mesh with what Governor Roberts wanted to get done. Partisan bickering intensified between House Republicans and Senate Democrats and between Larry Campbell and Barbara Roberts.

Governor Roberts set these goals: improving health care in rural Oregon; expanding Head Start and preschool programs; working on the state's shortage of affordable housing; providing more drug- and alcohol-treatment programs; reducing Oregon's climbing teen-pregnancy rate; improving race relations; welfare reform; addressing the problem of rising teen crime rates; protecting Oregon's environment by turning back efforts to weaken state laws; creating thousands of new jobs, especially by "encouraging greater processing of agricultural and wood products to squeeze more jobs out of the state's natural

---

* As previously noted, Governor Roberts' husband was State Senator Frank Roberts, a widely respected legislator and Democratic leader. Frank's daughter, Mary Wendy Roberts, was Oregon's longtime commissioner of labor. Betty Roberts, Frank's first wife, had a distinguished career in state government—as a legislator and as the first woman justice on the Oregon Supreme Court (1982-86). Between 1970 and 1995 the Roberts family was Oregon's closest thing to a political dynasty.

resources," and embarking on a major reform of Oregon's tax structure.[21] It was both an ambitious and expensive agenda, with estimates that—were everything on her list to be accomplished—the state budget would need to increase by $360 million. It turned out that Governor Roberts got only a fraction of her agenda through the 1991 and 1993 legislatures.

The Challenge Posed by Measure 5

When Roberts assumed the governorship she faced two important realities: she would have to work with a divided legislature, while she looked for ways to craft a state budget that implemented Measure 5 to pay for public schools. The governor and legislature had to figure out how much money public schools would need—and what the state could reasonably afford to pay—before lawmakers could decide how to pay for all other state programs/services. Governor Roberts had no choice but to submit a budget to the 1991 Assembly that included cuts in programs and staffing. By 1995 Measure 5 would require the state to pay for 75-80% of the cost of public education in Oregon, with a five-year phase-in of the 1.5% property-tax limitation. When Measure 5 passed in November 1990, many school districts in Oregon had tax rates above $15 per $1,000 of assessed value. So where was the difference between a tax rate of $15 or more and the Measure 5 limit of $5 (for schools) to come from?

Finding the estimated $663 million to add to the state's education budget for 1991-93 was the main problem for Governor Roberts and the legislature. Roberts had a two-pronged solution: cut existing state programs and staff, shifting those savings into the education budget and, second, convince Oregonians to pass a sales tax, the revenue from which would pay for public schools after 1993. It was estimated that, without a sales tax or any other additional revenue, the money available for state services other that education would shrink to as little as 15% of the budget.

The Democrats accused the Republicans of trying to cut their way out of the budget dilemma, while the Republicans said the Democrats were trying to tax their way out. "The reality is that the clock is ticking," said Senate Majority Leader Bill Bradbury, "and just making the cuts is not going to do it." Co-chair of the Ways and Means Committee Rep. Tony Van Vliet (R) agreed with Democrats that some kind of new tax would be necessary if other important state programs were to be maintained at current levels. "If people believe otherwise," he said, "someone has sold them a bunch of tooth fairies."[22]

Fortunately for Barbara Roberts and the 1991 Legislature, the Oregon economy was growing. Led by the high-tech explosion in Washington County and metropolitan Portland, the state's economy was quickly moving away from its traditional dependence on natural resources. But in general, there was a big disparity between the economic health of the Portland area and the rest of the state; many parts of Oregon continued to languish in the state's economic backwaters. For communities like Roseburg, Baker City, Oakridge, and Coos Bay/North Bend, the local economy was still in recession. In its attempts to curtail logging in national forests to protect habitats of endangered animal species (such as the Northern Spotted Owl), the federal government had caused more grief for these depressed local economies.

Like her predecessor, Neil Goldschmidt, Governor Roberts was concerned about the plight of those who lived in the timber towns. She advocated for economic diversification and job creation, improved rural health care, more affordable housing, and expanded preschool and Head Start programs. But Roberts also disagreed with those who blamed the spotted owl for their troubles, which angered many who made their livings as loggers, truck drivers, equipment operators, or mill workers. The governor's candor included remarks like "The logging industry is evolving as automation and foreign competition (and cheaper lumber) are cutting into Oregon's lumber market." Environmental concerns about animal habitat are legitimate public concerns, said Roberts.

The governor argued that both state and federal laws were intended to protect natural resources from over-cutting, over-grazing, and pollution. She understood, perhaps better than most politicians, the inherent conflict between traditional small-town outlooks and the point of view of an Oregon that was fast becoming a suburban-urban dominated economy. She had grown up in the tiny Yamhill County town of Sheridan, the economy of which was based on agriculture and, most importantly, on the large lumber mill in the town of Willamina, 5 miles away. In her youth, Roberts experienced first-hand what it was like for people to be laid off from their jobs, because the Willamina mill was struggling through another economic recession.[23] Although she sympathized with the plight of timber families, she would not back down in her criticism of those who blamed environmentalists for their predicament. This provoked rural Oregonians to spearhead three recall drives against Governor Roberts, all of which failed to reach the ballot due to an insufficient number of signatures.

Big Budget

Good news greeted lawmakers when they convened in early 1991: there would be a projected budget surplus when the 1989-91 budget expired on June 30. The legislature's staff also predicted big increases in personal incomes taxes

Barbara Roberts

Born in 1936, Barbara Hughey was raised in the small mill-town of Sheridan, Oregon. The mother of two sons, one of whom was autistic, Roberts got involved in the Parkrose School District as a concerned parent. Soon she was elected to the Parkrose School Board, followed by terms on the Multnomah County Commission and the Mt. Hood Community College Board. Barbara married state Senator Frank Roberts in 1974.

Elected to the Oregon House in 1980, she served in the 1981 and 1983 legislatures, rising to the position of House majority leader, the first woman in state history to hold that position.

In 1984, Barbara Roberts was elected secretary of state, the first Democrat in 110 years to be elected to that post. She was reelected in 1988. In 1990, Roberts won the Democratic nomination for governor. Elected in a three-person contest, Roberts was the first (and, to date, the only) woman governor of Oregon. Ballot Measure 5, the property-tax limitation proposal, was also approved by voters at the same election. With a Republican House and a Democratic Senate, Gov. Roberts had difficulty moving her programs through the legislature. Roberts set her sights on major tax reform; consequently, she held a series of public meetings throughout the state (called the Conversation with Oregon) to discuss state issues and her ideas about tax reform. The governor called the legislature into special session in July 1992 to draft a tax plan. The session adjourned after three days, unable to agree on an plan. The defeat of a Roberts-backed sales-tax plan in November 1993 (by a 3-1 margin) further undercut her effectiveness.

Governor Roberts' chief accomplishment was to get state government to adopt a management-by-objective program, designed to make government more efficient and accountable. The new procedure required the setting of goals and the measuring of outcomes in every state agency. The Oregon Education Act of the 21st Century was passed during Gov. Roberts' tenure and funding for public education was increased by over $1 billion. Oregon's Head Start program was expanded to include thousands more children. Public housing units were also dramatically increased under Roberts. And, as a woman, Roberts was an important role model for young females.

Handicapped by Measure 5's requirements, the governor found that there was little money for expanding the many human resources programs she favored. By the time Barbara Roberts left office in January 1995, her public approval rating was at an all-time low. Like her predecessor, Neil Goldschmidt, Roberts decided not to run for reelection.

and from higher-than-expected revenue from the state lottery. Altogether it was estimated that the state would reap $1 billion in additional income—allowing the governor and legislature to balance the 1991-93 budget and still cover the additional $663 million they would have to spend on public education.

The 1991 Legislature had the enviable task of deciding what to do with a $1 billion state surplus. When the session ended after 168 days (on June 30), lawmakers had increased the state budget to $5.6 billion, $1 billion over the $4.538 billion budget for 1989-91. No Oregon legislature had ever increased a two-year state budget by such a large amount. Public education was the chief beneficiary of the budget surplus. Legislators hiked the education budget from $2.177 billion to over $3 billion, an increase of $834 million. Education now consumed 54% of the general fund, up from 47.7% in 1989-91.

The 1991 Legislature was swamped by paper. Over 3,100 bills, resolutions, and memorials were introduced during the session (a record number). Only 967 bills were passed—12 of which Governor Roberts vetoed.

Lawmakers ended Oregon's short-lived (but popular) Homeowner's and Renter's Relief Program, but not before distributing a final payment of $22 million.

One of the most controversial bills passed in the late 20th century was enacted in 1991. The Oregon Education Act for the Twenty-first Century (HB3565) was the result of Rep. Vera Katz's determination to reform public education in Oregon. Since her arrival in the House in 1973, Katz had focused on improving public schools in the state. After a decade of preparation, HB 3565 was ready for consideration by the 1991 Legislature. As the recent three-term speaker of the Oregon House, Katz had clout. A master lawmaker, she carefully crafted a coalition of powerful education groups to assist both in the drafting of the bill and in the lobbying of legislators to back the reform. Katz involved the Oregon School Boards Association, the Oregon Education Association, the Confederation of School Administrators, the Department of Education, and private and public colleges and universities. HB 3565 had bipartisan backing and passed both chambers with ease and was signed into law by Gov. Barbara Roberts. The school reform law was designed to improve curriculum; channel all high school students into either a college preparation or a vocational education track; establish standards by which a student's mastery of certain skills and knowledge was to be regularly tested and evaluated; provide universal early childhood education; and to revamp the structure of the primary grades in public schools. These reforms were to be phased in over a decade. The act became a national model, parts of which were copied by a number of other states, and by George W. Bush's "No Child Left Behind" educational reform program implemented in Texas in the 1990s and nationally in 2001.

Several long-running environmental issues were also prominent in the 1991 session. Field burning, an incendiary issue since the early 1970s, was addressed. Willamette Valley field burning was reduced by 40%, down to 65,000 acres. In return, the state worked with the grass-seed industry by providing money for the development of alternatives to burning.

The Northern Spotted Owl was listed as an endangered species in 1990. Consequently, millions of acres of national forest land in Oregon was declared off limits to logging, a severe blow to the state's already depressed timber industry. Mill workers were laid off, and loggers and truckers left the woods, actions intended to protect spotted owl habitat. The 1991 Legislature enacted legislation providing low-interest loans to needy timber communities. Lawmakers also added $20 million in extended unemployment benefits to help affected communities.

The legislature passed a bill to require communities to adopt recycling standards for such materials as glass, scrap paper, newsprint, and plastic, maintaining Oregon's place in the vanguard of the national environmental movement. Water conservation was targeted by a bill to require the installation of water-saving toilets and showers in all new home construction in the state.

A popular "pro-family" bill was also enacted in 1991. A family-leave act permitted an employee to take unpaid leave in order to stay at home to care for an ailing family member, without facing the threat of losing her or his job.

Sales Tax?

Governor Roberts reminded the public that she was doing her part by submitting a leaner state budget and that she favored establishing a sales tax as the best way for the state to pay for public schools. She then announced that after the legislature adjourned she would travel around the state to have a "Conversation with Oregon." She would host town hall meetings in every part of Oregon so ordinary citizens could exchange ideas with her about state government, about taxes, and about how to best to prepare to implement Measure 5.

Senator Grattan Kerans, chair of the Senate Labor Committee in 1991, believed the governor's Conversation with Oregon went on too long and was too unfocused.[24] Nonetheless, Roberts returned from her town hall meetings convinced that the time was right to float another sales tax proposal to voters. She then called a special session of the legislature in July 1992 to consider a sales tax plan. However, the governor had not counted votes and had no way of knowing whether or not the legislature would pass her tax plan. "In the end, the plan was blown away because of a stubborn partisanship dispute over election dates."[25] Three days into the special session Republican House Speaker Larry Campbell declared that the sales tax plan would not fly and that the House would adjourn. The session ended abruptly with Barbara Roberts' political reputation irreparably damaged. "She had no political capital left. She had no ammo and no troops. Though she fought a good fight, she never had a chance."[26] Senate veteran Clifford Trow observed that "after the defeat of her sales tax package, Barbara was used up. She had no mandate." Roberts' relationship with the Republican house, and particularly with Speaker Campbell, deteriorated. "She ended up disillusioned, disappointed by both Campbell and [Democratic Senate President John] Kitzhaber's unwillingness to push her plans." [27]

The Election of 1992

In 1992, incumbent Pres. George H. W. Bush was defeated for a second term by Democrat Bill Clinton, governor of Arkansas. Record numbers of African Americans and women were elected to the U.S. House of Representatives. Almost twice as many women ran for election or reelection as state legislators as had a decade before. A record 49 Blacks ran for U.S. House seats, as did 30 Hispanic candidates.[28] Voters in Virginia, North and South Carolina, Alabama, and Florida elected African Americans to U.S. House seats, the first since Reconstruction. Oregon's northern and southern neighbors elected women to the U.S. Senate. In California, voters elected two women to the Senate: Representative Barbara Boxer and Diane Feinstein, former mayor of San Francisco. Washington State followed suit, electing "soccer mom" Patty Murray to the Senate. All three women were Democrats whose elections were boosted by the long coattails of presidential candidate Bill Clinton, who swept all three states in 1992.

In Oregon, Democrat Vera Katz, a 20-year veteran of the Oregon House and three-time House speaker, defeated Democrat Earl Blumenauer in a spirited race for Portland mayor. Katz and Blumenauer had served several terms together in the Oregon House and were philosophically close on most issues. Katz's victory, by a 3-2 margin, marked the first of three terms she would serve as mayor. For the next two years Oregon had the distinction among the 50 states of having both a woman governor and a female mayor of the state's largest city.

Other featured political campaigns in Oregon in 1992 included Bob Packwood's bid for a fifth term in the U.S. Senate against Democrat Les AuCoin, an 18-year veteran of the U.S. House, and the 1st District U.S. House race between Democratic newcomer Elizabeth Furse and Republican Tony Meeker. Furse, a co-founder and director of the Oregon Peace Institute, was born in Nairobi, Kenya. Her victory over Meeker was part of the Democratic and pro-woman tide sweeping across Oregon and the nation in November 1992. Another political milestone occurred when voters elected State Rep. Jim Hill, an African American, to succeed Tony Meeker as state treasurer. Hill was the first member of a minority group to be elected to a statewide office in Oregon's 133-year history.

A handful of ballot measures contributed to Oregon's 83% voter turnout in November. Two measures, in particular, aroused voters: Measure 9 was directed at persons who were homosexual, and Measure 3 proposed to set term limits on state legislators, Oregon's six statewide officeholders, and the state's U.S. House and Senate delegation.

The Packwood-AuCoin Senate Contest

With his 24 years of seniority in the Senate, Senator Packwood was a formidable opponent with piles of money ($8 million); a battle-tested statewide campaign organization; name familiarity; the perks of office at his disposal; and an impressive record as a wily, glib, tough-talking campaigner. Bob Packwood seemed unbeatable. But Packwood had liabilities. He was increasingly unpopular with the fastest-growing segment of his Republican Party, the conservative Christian element. His pro-abortion, pro-women's rights positions rankled the Republican right. Some voters simply believed that it was time for a change—Bob Packwood had been a senator long enough. In addition there were rumors, a growing undercurrent of sordid tales of Packwood's making unwanted sexual advances toward numerous women. Though vigorously denied by Packwood as merely the work of his political enemies, these rumors floated in and out of the edges of the campaign. Most voters gave their venerable senator the benefit of the doubt; the rumors were another example of "dirty politics."

Democrat Les AuCoin had barely survived the primary, after a costly battle with Harry Lonsdale. His May victory over Lonsdale (by 330 votes) cost him $1 million—money he had raised to run against Packwood. The primary seemed to take a lot out of AuCoin on a personal level; some political pundits said that AuCoin never regained his balance, that he was knocked off stride by Lonsdale's challenge. Oregon's Democratic leaders also realized that the AuCoin-Lonsdale race had caused divisions in the party.

A reporter characterized the Packwood-AuCoin race as "one of the most expensive and most savage in Oregon's history." A campaign in which Senator

Packwood had "battled back from a huge voter disapproval rating with a campaign of ferocity, cleverness and pure political muscle."[29] Robert Packwood campaigned hard on trade and environmental issues. The senator favored the North American Free Trade Agreement while Les AuCoin opposed it. AuCoin was convinced that NAFTA would result in American jobs flowing out of the United States and into Mexico. Bob Packwood said that it was time to amend the Endangered Species Act because it was crippling Oregon's timber industry. Les AuCoin disagreed and was adamant that federal forests needed to be better managed to protect both critical animal habitat and a lower, but steady, supply of logs. AuCoin also favored a middle-class federal tax break, to be paid for by increasing taxes on the wealthiest Americans; Bob Packwood disagreed. Senator Packwood had used his influence to block federal legislation to end a $100 million tax subsidy for American companies who exported raw logs. Les AuCoin favored the legislation, but was never able to turn Packwood's vote on the subsidy into a defining issue that he could use against him.

Between July 1 and October 14, Packwood pumped $1.8 million into his reelection campaign, while AuCoin spent $620,000. The senator had $2 million left for the final two weeks of the campaign, AuCoin was down to his last $209,000.

The election wasn't close, with Packwood winning by 78,000 votes (717,450 to 640,000). Packwood had outspent his challenger by at least 4-1. He blitzed TV with his campaign ads, while AuCoin's advertisements were few and far between. Packwood put AuCoin on the defensive, backing him into a corner and never letting him out. Packwood had the momentum and it propelled him to a fifth victory.

Elizabeth Furse Goes to Washington

Because of Representative AuCoin's run for the U.S. Senate, his 1st District U.S. House seat was vacant for the first time in 18 years. Tony Meeker, a longtime state senator and Oregon's current state treasurer, was the Republican nominee. Meeker had run for the position in 1986, losing to Les AuCoin by 54,000 votes. Elizabeth Furse was a face new to state politics. Her platform had broad appeal to Democrats and to women in particular. She was outspoken in her support of abortion rights, reduced military spending, health care reform, and enhancing the environment by insisting on vigorous enforcement of both state and federal laws designed to protect it. She took a forceful position against Ballot Measure 9, the anti-gay initiative. "Her stand [was] in sharp contrast to Meeker's hesitant disapproval, which seemed to be based partly on a desire not to alienate his conservative supporters. Meeker appealed to voters on the basis of a conservative fiscal and social agenda. That included opposition to abortion rights and opposition to a government-run-health-care system."[30]

The biggest challenge facing Elizabeth Furse was whether she was ready for national office. Did she have enough of a grasp on state, national, and international issues to be an effective representative? Furse campaigned hard. Voters were impressed by her common sense and willingness to speak out on controversial issues. Running ahead by a margin of two to one in the Multnomah County portion of the 1st District, Elizabeth Furse defeated Tony Meeker by 12,000 votes (152,900 to 141,000). Furse was the first woman elected to Congress from Oregon's 1st District.

President Clinton

The presidential campaign of 1992 was unusual because there was a serious third candidate for the office: Texas billionaire businessman, Ross Perot. Candidate Perot, who had never held public office, ran on a generally anti-government, anti-Democrat, anti-Republican platform. "It's time to sweep the rascals out," said Perot. The Texan's appeal was widespread and his participation in the nationally televised presidential debates with George Bush and Bill Clinton added much color and drama to the events. Perot regaled listeners with his folksy humor and no-nonsense approach to issues. He relished his role as a Washington "outsider" and "spoiler." Perot stunned his supporters in July when he suddenly withdrew from the presidential race. Weeks later, Perot announced that he was back in the race. With $60 million of his own money Perot saturated TV with political ads, including several in which he bought air-time and personally addressed the nation. Perot's campaign also distributed millions of bumper stickers, lawn signs, and lapel buttons.

Bill Clinton carried Oregon (and 31 other states) on November 3. What was surprising about Clinton's victory was that he carried the state by such a big margin: Clinton defeated President Bush by 145,000 votes (621,300 to 475,800). President Bush's campaign was undercut by Perot's presence on the ballot. Perot pulled 354,000 votes in Oregon, meaning that for every three people who voted for George Bush, two voted for Perot. Nationally, Perot got 19% of the vote, compared to President Bush's 37% and Governor Clinton's 43%.

Clinton won because he energized the traditional Democrat Party constituencies: labor, the urban vote, African Americans, and youth. Clinton carried the female vote 2-1; he also captured half of the independent vote and nearly 90%

of the African American vote. President Bush "ran best among fundamentalist Christians, Republicans and those making more than $75,000 a year."[31]

The 1992 Democratic tide didn't sweep away all Republican candidates. Republicans made headway toward winning back control of the Oregon Senate, cutting the Democrat's 1992 20-10 majority down to 16-14 for the 1993-94 term. With just two more seats, Republicans would recapture the Senate. The 32-28 Republican majority that had controlled the 1991-92 Oregon House held for 1993-94.

As if the presidential election and U.S. Senate race were not enough to arouse the Oregon electorate, the state's nine ballot measures grabbed everyone's attention. There seemed to be something for everyone among the nine measures.

The Ballot Measures

Measure 9 grew from a petition drive sponsored by a group called the Oregon Citizen's Alliance (OCA). Led by Lon Mabon, the OCA represented mostly conservative Republicans, many of whom were fundamentalist Christians. The *Oregonian* explained the OCA proposal: "Ballot Measure 9 is unprecedented in state and national politics. The sweeping, anti-gay initiative would amend the Oregon Constitution to label homosexuality as 'abnormal and perverse.' The measure would bar the state from extending civil rights protections to homosexuals. It also would prohibit government from promoting homosexuality and require schools and agencies to discourage it."[32]

Measure 9 galvanized Oregonians like few issues ever had. Thousands of citizens who'd never been politically active volunteered to help either the "Yes" or "No" on Measure 9 campaigns. All of Oregon's congressional delegation opposed the measure as did Gov. Barbara Roberts and former governors Atiyeh, Straub, and Goldschmidt. The chairs of the state Republican and Democratic parties came out against the measure, as did the Ecumenical Ministries of Oregon, the American Civil Liberties Union, the NAACP, League of Women Voters, Episcopal Diocese of Oregon, the AFL-CIO, Oregon Education Association, Oregon Medical Association, and the Jewish Federation of Portland. Most of those who endorsed Measure 9 were individuals (the OCA being the exception). The OCA's campaign caused widespread concern among voters and the electorate was deeply divided by the issue—anger, frustration, contempt, indignation, and recrimination pervaded the debate over Measure 9. Nearly a million and a half Oregonians (1.466 million) voted on the measure: 638,500 favored it, while 57% of the electorate voted against it (828,300).

Measure 5, to close Oregon's controversial Trojan nuclear-powered electric plant, on the bank of the Columbia River near the town of Clatskanie, Oregon, was defeated 874,600 against to 585,000 in favor. Measure 3, to limit the number of terms and years that a state legislator, statewide officeholder or member of Congress could serve, was passed overwhelmingly, 1.0 million to 439,700. Measure 3 was to take effect on December 3, 1992, but the courts ruled it unconstitutional.

How Measure 9 Changed Oregon

The election of 1992 was a turning point in the history of Oregon politics, with the issue of homosexuality causing a fundamental split in the Oregon electorate. "The 1992 election marks a great divide for Oregon. The landscape is changing. The battle over gay rights may be the biggest change. Homosexuality has become the key organizational issue for religious fundamentalists and the far right across the country."[33] The Oregon Citizen's Alliance and its conservative backers succeeded in polarizing Oregon's electorate like never before. Wielding the volatile social issue of homosexuality like a sledgehammer, the OCA drove a wedge between liberals, moderates, and conservatives, between rural and urban, north and south, east and west, Republican and Democrat. When the OCA headquarters was surrounded by police road blocks, and Director Lon Mabon wore a bullet-proof vest on election night, many Oregonians thought a siege mentality had overtaken politics. The OCA was on a crusade to purify Oregon culture by ridding it of what the OCA considered to be evil elements. The organization was dedicated to preserving "traditional western civilization" by sponsoring state ballot measures and working to elect like-minded politicians.

Responding to the defeat of Measure 9, Attorney General Dave Frohnmayer said: "We have to quit this stuff. We have to find a common ground of healing. I've never seen an election that was as ugly as this. This should never be the subject of an election again."[34] But Lon Mabon and the OCA weren't interested in healing; within months they were circulating another initiative petition to limit the rights of homosexuals (Measure 3, 1994). They remained a potent force in Oregon politics throughout the decade.*

---

* After the official demise of the OCA in November 2004, Oregonians passed Measure 36 to define "marriage" as between a man and a woman—an act intended to deny homosexual couples the right to marry and receive the benefits deriving from that union. The ghost of the OCA was still alive in Oregon—12 years after the defeat of Ballot Measure 9.

207 Days

The 1993 Oregon Legislature convened in Salem on January 11, minus two giants, Rep. Vera Katz and Sen. John Kitzhaber, both of whom had retired from
the legislature. Farewell to Kitz and Katz. The departure of Katz, House speaker
in 1985, 1987 and 1989, left a big hole in the House. Dr. John Kitzhaber's 12-year
Senate tenure had ended after he had served as Senate president for most of the
previous decade, spanning four regular and two special sessions. Respected by
Republicans and Democrats alike for his fairness, honesty, and willingness to
include all senators in decision-making, Kitzhaber left big shoes to fill.

The 67th Legislative Assembly was the longest on record. Lawmakers were
in session for 207 days, January 11-August 5, 1993. The new Senate president
was Democrat Bill Bradbury, an independent TV producer from tiny Bandon,
on Oregon's south coast. Republican Larry Campbell of Eugene returned as
House speaker. Bradbury and Campbell led by bare majorities.

The session started badly. House Republicans and Senate Democrats
couldn't agree on how to develop a biennial budget for 1993-95. Traditionally,
legislatures make budgets with members of both parties serving on the Joint
Committee on Ways and Means. The committee is headed by co-chairs, one
a senator, the other a representative. This was an arrangement followed since
statehood. But not so in 1993. Speaker Larry Campbell and House Republicans
insisted on drafting their own budget document apart from Senate Democrats.
For the only time in the history of state government, the 1993 Legislature
functioned with two Ways and Means Committees. Instead of working collaboratively to develop a budget, each body did its own thing. This arrangement
worked until it came time to resolve the differences between the two versions
of the budget. Conference committees (a typical way for the House and Ssenate
to resolve their differences over a bill) were appointed every time there was
a disagreement over a budget. This heavy reliance on conference committees
caused the 1993 session to drag on for an extra month.

The 1993 Legislature "was a long and difficult session—which appeared
to be unsuccessful." The budget was set at $6.35 billion, an increase of $848
million over the previous budget. Public education (K-12, community colleges
and public universities) got most of the additional money ($708 million), ac-
counting for 56% of the new budget. Human Resources got 27% and Public
Safety/Courts absorbed another 12%. With the addition of rising state lottery
profits to complement growing income tax revenues, lawmakers were able to
continue to phase in paying for public schools as required by the property-tax
limitation law passed in 1990.

The 1993 Legislature also cobbled together another sales tax plan and set a special election for November 9. The proposal featured a 5% state sales tax (to be dedicated to paying the state's share of public school costs); food and medicine were excluded from the tax. Nearly a million Oregonians voted on the measure. For the ninth time, voters rejected a sales tax (722,000 no, to 241,000 yes, a 3-1 margin of defeat).

Governor Barbara Roberts, who was particularly interested in Human Resources programs, had predicted in the days after the passage of Measure 5 that "people would die" as a result of cutbacks in state programs for needy Oregonians. The more money that was poured into education, the less there was for senior services, aid to dependent children, medicine and medical care for the poor and uninsured, state police, prisons, mental health services, and so on. Roberts' prediction proved to be right: over the next 10 years, people did die because the state was forced to curtail or eliminate services to some of its neediest citizens.

The budget Governor Roberts submitted to the 1993 Legislature reflected her desire to make government more efficient. Roberts "established new management practices in state government, including Management-by-Objective: setting goals and measuring outcomes in every state agency. For these innovations, Barbara Roberts received national recognition."

Legislators also reworked John Kitzhaber's Oregon Health Plan, addressing the issue of cost. Senator Cliff Trow recalled that in implementing the plan, they had a difficulty "related to the unwillingness of employers to step out, to help to better finance the new Health Plan." [35]

Legislators staggered to the last day of the grueling session, summer almost over. They had passed the biggest budget in state history—and poured more money into public education than any legislature before them. Lawmakers had enacted 831 new laws (out of 2,955 bills introduced), 12 of which were vetoed by Governor Roberts. They had tried a risky experiment to develop a state budget by having both a House and a Senate Ways and Means Committee. The experiment was time consuming and costly, causing unnecessary frustration, delay, and partisan bickering.

Packwood in Trouble

In November 1992, the *Washington Post* had reported that 10 women "had been the target of Packwood's sexual misconduct." In February 1993, the *Oregonian* noted that an additional 13 women had come forward to accuse Packwood of making uninvited and unwanted sexual advances. A February 8 public event in

La Grande attended by Packwood drew 100 protesters outside and 10 women inside walked out when the senator began his speech. When asked about the charges, Packwood refused to comment, saying only that he was looking forward to "a full and fair hearing before the Senate Ethics Committee."[36] Oregonians did not realize that the Senate's investigation of Bob Packwood's alleged misconduct would drag on for another two and a half years. Because of the investigation, Bob Packwood's job and reputation were under daily media scrutiny.

Barbara Bows Out

Barbara Roberts delivered the governor's annual address to the Portland City Club on Friday, January 14, 1994. She focused her remarks on Oregon's economy in transition and on her efforts to make state government leaner and more efficient. She talked about her target of reducing the size of state government by 4,000 employees—noting that 2,700 jobs had already been cut. The governor spoke about how Oregon's economy continued to diversify, moving away from its traditional reliance on timber and wood products. New jobs had been added (150,000), many of them in the high-tech industry. During her tenure, the governor claimed 13,000 newly built units of affordable housing. And at least 6,000 Oregonians were moved off welfare rolls. The governor also remarked on festering social problems, including the need for more services for the elderly poor, more school clinics to help reduce teen pregnancy, and tougher penalties and more jail space for juvenile offenders.

Roberts was in a spirited contest with John Kitzhaber for the Democratic nomination for governor. Since early fall, Kitzhaber had been campaigning to unseat Roberts. Because of the long illness and death (on October 31, 1993) of her husband, long-time State Senator Frank Roberts, the governor had hit the campaign trail late. A political poll conducted in January showed her lagging behind Kitzhaber, 2-1. The governor's sister and mother were also in poor health. Two weeks after her Portland City Club speech, Roberts called a press conference in the Capitol to announce that she was withdrawing from the primary campaign; she would not seek a second term. It was 14 weeks before the May primary.

Oregonian reporter Steve Duin wrote that Barbara Roberts had "interrupted a campaign that was wheezing along toward an unhappy ending with an unexpected, bittersweet farewell. Before she took her lumps in the Democratic primary, Roberts left friends and family with a lump in the throat."[37] Privately, Roberts' staff and family were relieved by her decision to stop campaigning. In

July, the governor had been hospitalized with chest pains. Her job was taking its toll on her both physically and emotionally.

Governor Roberts commented: "After three years—three tough years—of dealing with Measure 5, the timber crisis, reinventing and downsizing government, an exploding population and a changing economy, I know, beyond a shadow of a doubt, that this is a 24-hour-a-day job that requires full energy, total commitment and unwavering attention."[38] The governor announced that she would focus on a 1995-97 budget for legislative consideration, and on the thorny issues of teen pregnancy, juvenile crime, and state employee compensation.

With the governor's withdrawal from the primary campaign, John Kitzhaber now had a lock on the Democratic gubernatorial nomination. Stressing his legislative experience and his talent for building consensus, Kitzhaber won the Democratic nomination on May 17 with over 80% of the vote. Facing no serious opposition, he had raised $624,000 and spent $524,600 in the primary. The Republican race for governor was much livelier. State GOP chairman, Portland millionaire businessman Craig Berkman, was locked in a fierce struggle with conservative newspaper owner and former congressman Denny Smith. Berkman spent $1.049 million in the primary: Denny Smith spent $620,000. Smith won the Republican nomination, defeating Craig Berkman, 135,300 to 110,800.

Mike and Bob Come Home

With the incumbents retiring, the U.S. House races in Districts Two and Five were interesting. Six-term Republican Bob Smith was leaving politics (at least for the time being). And after only two terms, Oregon's 5th District Congressman, Democrat Mike Kopetski, had also decided to leave Congress.

Seven men filed for the seat being vacated by Bob Smith. State Senator Wes Cooley was opposed by Perry Atkinson of Medford and five others in the Republican primary. The race was very close. Cooley edged Atkinson by 940 votes (14,246 to 13,306). Jackson County Commissioner Sue Kupillas won the Democratic nomination over three opponents.

The 5th District primary featured five Democrats and four Republicans. Democrat Catherine Webber defeated former state representative and Clackamas County Commissioner Ed Lindquist, 21,900 to 17,175. The Republican nomination went to Jim Bunn, a state legislator. Oregon's other three incumbent U.S. representatives, Democrats Elizabeth Furse, Ron Wyden, and Peter DeFazio, skated to easy primary victories. Bill Witt, a conservative businessman, won the Republican nomination to face Congresswoman Furse in November.

A Republican Stampede

The American electorate was in a surly mood for much of the 1990s. Most voters were unhappy, dissatisfied with the status quo. Things weren't right and Congress, paralyzed by bitter partisan bickering, was a favorite target of the public's discontent. The exploding national debt bothered many Americans. Many believed federal taxes were too high, the bureaucracy too bloated, too expensive, and too unresponsive. Congress was calcified by too many longtime incumbents who were not interested in change. And the White House was to blame, too. Democratic President Clinton had made a clumsy attempt to protect the rights of homosexuals in the military, an exercise that aroused the ire of conservative Christian voters.

Voters lashed out in the 1994 general election. A huge "anti" vote swept across Oregon and the rest of the nation. This political wave was anti-Clinton, anti-liberal, anti-Democrat, and anti-incumbent. A Republican tide turned American politics upside-down. For the first time in 40 years, Republicans seized control of both the U.S. House and Senate. The Republican tide didn't stop with Congress—it continued through state capitals, sweeping aside 11 Democratic governors, and overturning many Democratic state legislatures and state officeholders.

Did the Republican juggernaut reach Oregon in 1994? Yes and no. Republicans captured the Oregon Legislature for the first time in 40 years. The Oregon Senate went from a 16-14 Democratic majority to a Republican majority of 19-11. Pendleton businessman Gordon Smith became the first Republican president of the Oregon Senate since 1955. The Oregon House remained Republican, 34-26. Bev Clarno of Bend was elected House speaker, the second woman (and first female Republican) to hold the job. But the Republican tide didn't produce a GOP victory in Oregon's governor's race. Democrat John Kitzhaber withstood a challenge by Denny Smith, winning by 104,000 votes (622,000 to 517,900). Kitzhaber had spent $1.7 million to Smith's $1.370 million.

The Republican stampede did impact Oregon's U.S. House races. Republican Jim Bunn won the 5th Congressional District seat; his victory over Democrat Catherine Webber (121,400 to 114,000) was attributed to the national Republican tide. But the real test of just how potent the GOP surge was occurred in the 1st Congressional District. There, Democratic Congresswoman Elizabeth Furse won reelection by an eyelash. Republican Bill Witt lost to Furse by 301 votes (121,147 to 120,846) out of over 250,000 votes cast. Wes Cooley, a conservative Republican, won the 2nd Congressional District seat, defeating Democrat Sue Kupillas by 44,000 votes. Ron Wyden was reelected in the 3rd

District by 118,000 votes and Peter DeFazio won a fifth term in the 4th District by an 80,000-vote margin.

Oregon's November ballot was full. In addition to the usual statewide, legislative, and congressional races, there were 18 ballot measures. Measures 13 and 16 grabbed the most attention. Measure 13 was another OCA-sponsored constitutional amendment intended to prohibit state and local governments from creating legal classifications based on a person's homosexuality. In other words, gays should not be granted legal rights already given to heterosexuals. Again, Oregonians defeated the OCA measure—but by only 38,000 votes (592,700 in favor of the amendment to 630,600 who opposed it). Measure 16 raised the idea of physician-assisted suicide (also known as Death With Dignity). The measure would allow terminally ill adults to obtain prescriptions for lethal drugs, which the individual could ingest in order to hasten death. Conservative groups and the Catholic Church assailed the measure. But, as they had done so many times before, Oregonians confounded the world when they passed Measure 16 by a margin of 32,000 votes, 628,000 in favor, to 596,000 opposed. Oregon was the second political entity on earth to provide for doctor-assisted medical suicide (Switzerland was the first).

Ballot Measures 11 and 18 also attracted a lot of attention in November. Measure 11 required mandatory sentences for specific felony crimes. The most controversial aspect of this measure related to the inclusion of juveniles as young as age 15. Many Oregonians thought this was too young, believing that the traditional approach of treating juveniles under age 18 differently from adult criminals was the best way to deal with young offenders. But the measure passed 788,700 to 412,800.

On the surface, Measure 18 seemed to be a pretty innocuous proposal. The measure banned the use of bait to hunt bears and the use of dogs to hunt cougars and bears. A barrage of TV ads quickly fanned public opinion in favor of the measure. Voters passed Measure 18, 629,500 to 586,000—to the howls of Oregon hunters.

Barbara Roberts: Too Tall a Mountain?

Barbara Roberts' term as Oregon's first woman governor ended in January 1995. Her tenure was a troubled one, an administration that experienced more lows than highs. Roberts' term was dominated by bitter defeats, frustration, rejection, and loss. Barbara Roberts acknowledged that she had failed to achieve her two highest goals: "correcting school finance while providing property tax relief through passage of a sales tax."[39] Some say that Barbara Roberts' governorship was "dead on arrival," that she had two strikes against her before she took office in January 1991: Ballot Measure 5 and an unhappy and unpredictable electorate. "It was there from the start. Always pressuring Roberts, always pushing her in a direction she didn't want to go. Measure 5. From the start, Barbara Roberts' governorship was strangled by an unrelenting Measure 5 and an unforgiving public." Democrat Peter Courtney, State Senate President from 2003 to 2012, said that because of the sour mood of the electorate "anyone who had been governor would have been in for an hellacious time. It's been a firestorm, it's been a tidal wave. Anyone would have caught holy hell with the public."[40]

Governor Roberts acknowledged that "there is a disillusioned, angry, frustrated public out there." She was disappointed that her efforts to communicate openly with voters (in her Conversations with Oregon), to involve them, had failed. Her attempts to "build a sense of confidence that government was an ally and not an enemy" had fallen short of re-engaging the public in a positive, "let's be part of the solution," dialogue. Suspicious of their government and leaders, much of the electorate was choosing not to trust them. "In many ways, the turmoil over Measure 5 only crystallized the growing voter disenchantment with all levels of government. Governors in a variety of states struggled with dismal poll ratings [Barbara Roberts included] as they have tried to balance the books while dealing with economic upheaval, crime, and troubled school systems."[41]

The Oregon economy grew while Roberts was governor. Though she can claim some credit for pursuing policies that promoted and sustained this growth, most of the forces driving the economy were beyond her control, the result of national trends and corporate decisions made elsewhere. Roberts did orchestrate a shrinking of state government: 2,700 state jobs were eliminated. Management-by-Objectives was instituted within the state bureaucracy, helping supervisors and legislators to better determine if money being spent was accomplishing what it was intended for. More women and minorities were hired as state employees and as members of various state boards and commissions under Governor Roberts. She was also a vocal opponent of the OCA's two anti-homosexual ballot measures that voters defeated in 1992 and 1994, campaigning against both. Over 13,000 units of affordable housing were built while she was governor. Most of the funds for this construction program were provided by federal grants, as were funds for the expansion of Portland's light-rail system.

But there were big failures, too. Roberts was convinced that a sales tax was the best way to generate the billions of dollars the legislature needed under the terms of Measure 5. Roberts courageously (and some say stubbornly) attached her star to this issue and put all her eggs in one basket. She was convinced that her plan would allow Oregonians to maintain all basic state programs while pumping billions more into public education.

Former State Senator Grattan Kerans believes that Governor Roberts was "done in by her staff. The governor's office was mismanaged."[42] Another prominent Democratic state senator thought that Barbara Roberts was "well-intentioned, personally warm and friendly. But she was frustrated by outside events and disillusioned by her efforts to bring the public along. She became defensive during the second half of her term as the Republican House grew less cooperative."[43]

The *Oregonian* wrote: "When at her best, Roberts [was] an effective, behind-the-scenes facilitator as Oregon made a transition from a natural resources-based economy to one fueled by the high-tech revolution. At her worst, Roberts failed to meet the high expectations that she and her supporters held for her as a leader and a problem solver. And she proved to be too partisan and uncompromising in her political philosophy to build the coalitions necessary to move her limited agenda along . . . Oregonians who value Oregon's high quality of life as much as she does will appreciate the battles she fought even though she won few wars."[44] Political writer Jeff Mapes put it this way: "Roughly speaking, she ran into a gale force of history that she didn't always understand and that was going the other way. It's how she will be remembered."[45] In short, Barbara Roberts had tried to ride a horse that was not going anywhere.

Governor Barbara Roberts and the Legislatures of 1991 and 1993 were faced with a great paradox: the state enjoyed a large budget surplus, a couple of billion dollars that could have been spent on some of Oregon's most pressing problems, such as economic development and job retraining, higher education, tuition, community mental health and drug-and-alcohol treatment and counseling programs, and ameliorating poverty and hunger as well as other root causes of juvenile crime. But legislators could spend only a fraction of the state's growing revenues on any of these programs. Instead, virtually all of the state's excess revenue could be spent only one way: to pay for public education.

So, in spite of a growing population, an expanding and diversifying state economy, and tens of thousands of new jobs produced by a thriving high-tech industry, because of Measure 5, the governor and legislature could not tap into this new prosperity. Consequently, 90% of the $2 billion that was added to the 1991-93 and 1993-95 state budgets went to pay for public schools—thus relieving homeowners and business people from having to pay high local property taxes. This has been the central challenge facing every governor and legislature since the 1990 passage of Measure 5.

Chapter 19
Choosing Senators, 1995-96

John Kitzhaber, M.D., age 47, took the oath of office as Oregon's 35th governor on January 9, 1995. The Kitzhaber-era in Oregon politics had begun in 1978 when the Roseburg emergency-room physician was elected to the Oregon House. After a single term in the House, Kitzhaber won a state Senate seat; he was elected to a second Senate term in 1984. Democrats elected Kitzhaber president in the 1985 session—and reelected him in 1987, 1989, and 1991.

Kitzhaber, an avid sportsman and fly fisherman, was keenly interested in environmental issues, particularly those related to fish habitat, hydroelectric power, and forest protection. "An environmentalist who wanted to protect natural resources, and a liberal who opposed a property tax limit and defended a woman's right to reproductive choices, Kitzhaber didn't hide his views from the largely conservative constituency." Voters were drawn to Kitzhaber because of his opinions. The doctor had lots of ideas, focusing on a variety of issues, including the quality and availability of health care and the rising cost of medical insurance. By the time Kitzhaber retired from the legislature in January 1993, he had been instrumental in the passage of legislation including "a bill to establish minimum stream flows; a hydroelectric policy that does not tolerate the loss of salmon and steelhead to development and electricity-producing dams; establishment of a statewide water plan; and a variety of contributions to both forest practices and land-use legislation."[1]

Kitzhaber's most notable legislative achievement was the Oregon Health Plan, which provided insurance coverage to more than 120,000 Oregonians without medical insurance. Senate veteran Clifford Trow, a member of Kitzhaber's Democratic caucus, observed that he was widely respected for his "fairness, his intelligence, and his knowledge. John Kitzhaber always looked for practical answers to problems. And, he was always willing to work both sides of the aisle to get things done."[2]

A Republican Legislature

John Kitzhaber was the first Democratic governor to serve two full terms since Democrat Sylvester Pennoyer (1887-95). Like Pennoyer, Kitzhaber served for eight years with a Republican legislature. Kitzhaber's effectiveness came from working collaboratively with Republican caucuses in non-partisan ways. Yet the governor was quick to remind legislators that, as chief executive, he had the power to veto legislation and the 1995 Legislature felt the sting of his vetoes. No governor since Oswald West in 1911 had vetoed so much legislation.

The 1995 Legislature was the first Republican-controlled session since 1955. The GOP had regained control of the House in 1990 after 20 years of Democratic rule and recaptured control of the Senate in 1994, ending 40 years of Democratic control. The 1995 Legislature lasted 153 days, January 9-June 10. Over 2,700 bills and resolutions were introduced, 851 passed, and 52 were vetoed by Governor Kitzhaber.

Republican Gordon Smith of Pendleton led the Senate. Senator Smith was a millionaire businessman who owned a large food-processing company. He was handsome, photogenic, an effective speaker, and he had his eye on Mark Hatfield's U.S. Senate seat. Consequently, Smith's term was marked by a moderating influence, as he tried to position himself as a middle-of-the-road Republican who, when appropriate, collaborated with Democrat John Kitzhaber.

The Folly of the Rule of Eighteen

The 1995 Oregon House was led by Speaker Bev Clarno, a Republican hay and cattle rancher from central Oregon. Clarno was the second woman and first Republican to be House speaker and she oversaw a 34-member Republican caucus. The caucus was deeply divided, with social conservatives often dictating the direction the party took on legislation and policy. At the beginning of the session the caucus adopted a controversial procedural rule, the so-called Rule of Eighteen, intended to keep too much power from concentrating in either the hands of the speaker or those of committee chairs. As applied, the Rule of Eighteen meant that 18 members of the 34-person caucus had to agree on a position before the caucus and House could move forward. The rule caused divisions within the caucus, weakened Clarno's ability to lead, and slowed down the progress of the House. Most importantly, the Rule of Eighteen put a small minority of House members in control of the body, as it took only 18 Republicans to decide important questions, thus, effectively bypassing the other 16 Republican caucus members (including Speaker Clarno) and the 26 minority Democrats. Eighteen of 60 House members could run the show. Democrats, along with much of the media, and some moderate Republicans, called it for what it was: rule by the minority.

The 1995 session was characterized by a re-alignment of leadership powers; the traditional authority vested in the speaker of the House and Senate president was transferred to what the majority of their caucuses wanted to do, thus restricting and reducing the powers of their chosen leaders. As the session unfolded a group of conservative Republicans used this control to hold captive the governor, the House Democrats, moderate House Republicans, the Senate, metropolitan Portland, and the state of Oregon.

An Interesting Mix

The 1995 Oregon House of Representatives had a diverse membership: 19 members were women (matching the record of 1991). Again, the House included two African American women, Portland's Margaret Carter and Avel Gordly (both of whom had served since 1991). Three representatives were gay or lesbian: Republican Chuck Carpenter and Democrats Gail Shibley and George Eighmey. Republican representatives Bill Markham and Denny Jones were serving their 14th and 12th terms, respectively. Republican Tom Brian of Tigard and (soon after) Salem's Kevin Mannix switched parties, both having originally been elected as Democrats.

The 1995 Legislature faced a mountain of tough decisions: school funding, as usual, took center stage. Included in this debate was what to do with a projected budget carry-over of about $300 million; should lawmakers refund this money to taxpayers? There were other equally contentious issues, including three of particular interest to pro-business Republicans: collective bargaining, public employee pensions, and the cost of Workers' Compensation Insurance. In addition, legislators had to implement (and pay for) three recently enacted statewide anti-crime measures that focused on lengthening prison terms for violent felons; required that prison inmates be involved in work programs; and remanded children age 14 and older to adult court if they were charged with murder or violent sex offenses. Another key issue was the cost of expanding the MAX light-rail network in metropolitan Portland.

"The most difficult vote I ever cast"

The eyes of the nation were on the Capitol Building in Washington, D.C. on Thursday, March 2, 1995. The Senate was voting on one of the key planks of the "Republican Revolution" of 1994: adding a balanced federal budget amendment to the Constitution. Led by Majority Leader Bob Dole, Senate Republicans spent weeks lining up the 67 votes they needed to pass the amendment. But one Republican senator told Dole that he could not, would not, vote for a federal balanced budget amendment. That man was Mark Hatfield, Oregon's senior senator. With a national TV audience watching, "with senators at their desks— a rare sight—Hatfield gripped the arms of his chair and stared straight ahead, his expression grim. Despite weeks of pressure, Hatfield stuck to his opposition to the proposed amendment, even when it became clear that he would cast the decisive vote against a key part of the Republican congressional agenda."[3] The amendment failed by one vote (Hatfield's), which unleashed a storm of bitter criticism from fellow Republicans. Some called Hatfield a traitor and demanded his expulsion from the Republican Party. Hatfield thought the amendment was a political gimmick. Standing on principle, Mark Hatfield cast "the most difficult vote in my thirty years" in the U.S. Senate. Though many Oregon Republicans joined the chorus of boos directed at Senator Hatfield, most Oregonians were not so critical.

Oregon Senate President Gordon Smith had visited Hatfield in Washington the day before the vote, urging the senator to back the amendment. But Hatfield would not yield. Smith then called reporters in Salem to tell them that he might challenge Hatfield—should the senator decide to seek a sixth term.[4] For the rest of the month Hatfield's Senate vote dominated the political news in Oregon; the activities of the 68th Oregon Legislature faded into the background while the furor over Hatfield's vote ran its course.

More Blood-letting

As the 1995 Legislative session rolled on, divisions among House Republicans deepened. Bickering, resentment, and mistrust took their toll on the GOP caucus. Through the Rule of Eighteen, the social conservatives took control of the caucus. Led by Representatives Bob Tiernan, Jerry Grisham, Eileen Qutub, and Cedric Hayden, the conservative Republicans caused havoc in their caucus, often clashing with moderates, such as Representatives Chuck Carpenter, Jane Lokan, Tom Brian, Ron Adams, house majority leader Ray Baum, and Speaker Bev Clarno. In early April, Rep. John Minnis was joined by a handful of Republicans who openly challenged the authority of Speaker Clarno. The mini-revolt ended quickly when Clarno stripped Minnis of his committee chairmanship and removed him from his other committee appointments. This turmoil in the House Republican caucus reminded some people of the 1977 rebellion within the ruling Democratic caucus. Bev Clarno retained her speakership in 1995, mostly because she remained loyal to her early commitment to her caucus that if it adopted the

Rule of Eighteen, she would abide by it as speaker. Her swift punishment of John Minnis in early April was a warning to the rest of her Republican caucus to fall into line behind her.

Clarno had made two other important promises when the session began in January: Republican leaders were committed to conducting as short a legislative session as possible, and they would not pass any new taxes. Both promises proved difficult to keep. Some observers wondered if Clarno hadn't painted herself into a corner. The last month of the 153-day session was dominated by partisan bickering, finger-pointing, backroom deals, personal attacks, and a race against the clock. "As the end of the session approached, the house teetered on the edge of political meltdown." House Minority Leader Peter Courtney warned: "There's a real danger of us going out of here hating each other and messing up badly." A Senate Republican put it this way: "Bev's not in charge . . . The cabals are in charge. What this means is that the thirty-four House Republicans have been split along several fault lines. Suburban vs. rural. Conservatives vs. moderates. Pro-lifers vs. pro-choicers. Freshmen vs. veterans. And that doesn't even begin to get into the personality conflicts." [5]

Senate President Gordon Smith criticized the House's Rule of Eighteen, saying that it had seriously hurt Clarno's ability to run the House. Smith likened Clarno's end of the Capitol to the movie *Animal House*. House Republican leaders blamed the Senate for slowing down the session, claiming that some of the disarray in the house was the result of a logjam of important bills stuck in the Senate.[6] More finger-pointing, more accusations to tear at already frayed nerves.

Knocking the Train off the Tracks

By June 9 the Oregon Senate was ready to go home. The House appeared to be stalemated: a single issue was keeping the Republican-controlled body from adjourning. Metropolitan Portland's MAX light-rail system had turned into a political football, further dividing House Republicans. Why the last-minute controversy? MAX was the key component in the Portland area's plan to reduce traffic gridlock (caused by a booming population). To supplement an even greater amount of federal transportation dollars, the region's voters had passed a series of costly public bond measures to build a state-of-the-art rapid transit light-rail system. By 1995, it was time to expand the MAX system further into the Portland suburbs. Working closely with civic leaders, area politicians, legislative leaders, and Senators Hatfield and Packwood, Gov. John Kitzhaber had requested that the 1995 Legislature approve $375 million as the state's share of the cost of expanding MAX southward into Clackamas County, and possibly northward, from Portland across the Columbia River to Vancouver, Washington. The Republican House split down the middle over the MAX issue. Speaker Bev Clarno and Majority Leader Ray Baum supported the funding proposal, as did longtime rural Republican Representative Denny Jones and a number of Portland-area Republicans. All Portland-area Democratic representatives endorsed the MAX plan, as did Salem's Peter Courtney and Pendleton's Gordon Smith. It was clear to everyone that most legislators wanted to approve the state's share of $375 million dollars to expand MAX. But there was a huge obstacle in the way: House maverick, Bob Tiernan (who some characterized as a "pitbull") and 17 other Republicans, invoking the Rule of Eighteen, blocked a final vote on the MAX proposal. The session ground to a standstill as Clarno and Smith watched the hours tick by. Finally, in concert with Governor Kitzhaber, Speaker Clarno and President Smith agreed to adjourn the regular session—with the understanding that Kitzhaber would call legislators back to Salem for a special session to reconsider the MAX plan. The session then adjourned.

Chuck Carpenter, a freshman legislator and member of the House Republican caucus, offered his assessment of how the session ended. Carpenter, a supporter of the MAX funding proposal, wondered how "the legislature could have so many people [in it] who hate government. You wonder if they have any business being in government."[7]

What Did the 1995 Legislature Accomplish?

Republicans ran the legislature in 1995 and, while GOP lawmakers wanted to cut taxes, political and economic reality had made it impossible to do so. The legislature had to appropriate enough additional money to pay the state's share of public school costs. Lawmakers increased the state budget for public education by $685 million (to $4.7 billion for the 1995-97 biennium). Public schools, K-12, would get $3.55 billion while higher education and community colleges shared the remaining $1.150 billion. Education consumed 57% of the state's 1995-97 general fund budget.

The total budget for 1995-97 was set at $8.2 billion, a 22% increase over 1993-95. In some cases, Republicans approved higher expenditures than Democratic Gov. John Kitzhaber had recommended. Legislators increased spending for prisons by $140 million (Kitzhaber had recommended $100 million). GOP leaders also supported a two-year extension of a special 10¢ tax on cigarettes.

The 1995 Legislature also passed these bills: a bill to provide a tax credit for employers who hired youths involved with gangs; SB 2 to make Oregon Health

Sciences University an independent public corporation; welfare reform, including passage of a Senate bill to require welfare recipients to search for work, setting a 24-month limit on receiving aid and requiring recipients to participate in work programs, job training, mental health and drug-addiction programs; and a bill requiring all school employees to be finger-printed so that individuals could be checked for any criminal history. The House passed several controversial bills that didn't make it out of the Senate: a bill to re-criminalize possession of marijuana and a bill to overturn Oregon's mandatory motorcycle helmet law. Legislators also rejected two highly controversial educational reforms: school vouchers and a charter school bill.

In addition, "some GOP legislators [had] wanted to put the screws to public employees' salaries, benefits and bargaining rights, but colleagues, union leaders, and Kitzhaber thought the proposals were too extreme. The governor and legislature compromised on money for a salary package, new pension criteria for new hires and changes in collective bargaining laws for public employees. The most significant change involves alterations to bargaining laws that tend to shift power to management."[8] Kitzhaber squeezed other compromises from Republicans. "A skilled negotiator, Kitzhaber worked with GOP leaders to reach agreements on such issues as workers' compensation, tort and education reform." It was Kitzhaber's threat of a veto that caused GOP leaders to moderate many of their positions. The *Oregonian* noted that "the Republicans faced many internal divisions as they struggled to accommodate everyone from members of the religious right to self-described Tom McCall moderates."[9]

Both new and veteran legislators were surprised by how bitterly partisan some House Republicans were.* Democrat Cliff Trow, who served 28 years

---

* Throughout the 20th century, as we have seen, the Oregon Republican Party typically consisted of two factions: the conservative and the moderate-progressive wings. Progressive Republicans in Oregon and Maine (and, sometimes, Wisconsin) often dominated their state parties. In Oregon progressive Republicans like Charles McNary, Robert Packwood, Tom McCall, and Norma Paulus held their positions for long periods. But with the election of Larry Campbell, a corporation lobbyist, as speaker of the House, the more conservative wing of the Oregon GOP came to dominate the legislature. The GOP nominees for governor in 1994 and 1998 were conservatives (Denny Smith and Bill Sizemore). This conservative trend in Oregon reflected what was happening to the GOP nationally. The congressional mid-term elections of 1994 resulted in a major re-alignment of power in the U.S. House, with an outspoken conservative, Newt Gingrich, as speaker. Since 1994, the national Republican Party has been dominated by the conservative wing, as was the case from the 1920s to the early 1950s.

The rise of Christian fundamentalists as a political force within the GOP over the past two decades is a fact of political life in America. A basic litmus test among Oregon (and national) Republicans today is whether a potential candidate for office fits the conservative mold—opposition to abortion, gay rights, restriction of gun ownership and use, and increased taxes; support for tougher in the Oregon Senate, believed that the growing influence of conservative Republicans within their party caucus had much to do with the legislature becoming more partisan, making it more difficult for individual legislators to work collaboratively with members of the other party. Democrat Trow, a longtime professor of history at Oregon State University, thinks the Oregon Legislature is a microcosm of national politics and recent cultural wars, evolving in the 1990s into an institution that became a captive of an anti-government, anti-urban, anti-progressive, and pro-conservative ideology. Narrow parochial interests, dominated by the agenda of right-wing Republicans, slowly eroded legislative traditions such as decorum, courtesy, honest debate, genuine respect, and the desire to befriend a colleague regardless of whether that person was a Republican or a Democrat. "Where," asked Professor/Senator Trow, "have all the moderate Republicans gone? Today, a moderate Republican is an endangered species in the House and Senate."[10]*

A June 1 *Oregonian* editorial castigated the legislature for being "careless" and "shortsighted." The editors criticized the 1995 Legislature for "a myopic view of the state's future" and noted that overall its work was undistinguished. "Bills and amendments were poorly drafted, inadequately aired, and dimly understood before being adopted or rejected; indeed, major policy changes were approved with virtually no public hearing at all, let alone any fine-tuning." The editorial described the Rule of Eighteen as an "especially grievous attack on the public process" and went on to say that it was "symptomatic of a session largely dominated by the House and Senate Republican caucuses rather than its leaders."[11]

Kitzhaber Calls a Special Session

Six weeks after the 1995 Legislature's adjournment, Governor Kitzhaber announced that he was calling lawmakers into special session on Friday, July 28. The previous Friday, the governor had vetoed 52 bills passed by the GOP-controlled legislature. Kitzhaber's announcement found conservative House Republicans in a foul mood.

The governor was under a lot of pressure to call a special session, particularly from Sen. Mark Hatfield's office in Washington, D.C. Hatfield needed

---

sentences for convicted criminals and tougher restrictions on immigrants. The most moderate Republican to be nominated for governor in recent years was Ron Saxton (in 2006)—and he lost to Ted Kulongoski by about 110,000 votes.

* The growth of the Democratic Party in Oregon and an increase in the number of independent voters have made it more difficult for Republicans—dominated by a conservative agenda—to be elected to major office in the state.

the legislature to approve the requested $375 million the state was being asked to pay as its share of the proposed $1.5 billion MAX light-rail expansion into Clackamas County. Failure to approve the funds could undercut Hatfield's ability to push through the federal funding (of $1 billion) for the MAX project. Republican Senate President Gordon Smith encouraged Kitzhaber to call a special session, telling him that the Republican Senate was ready to approve the MAX request. Smith made it clear that he favored the MAX bill and that he was a staunch supporter of public transit. With a possible U.S. Senate race in his near future, Gordon Smith was keenly aware of the political consequences if metropolitan Portland voters saw him as a foe of their popular light-rail system.

Speaker Bev Clarno laid her cards on the table, warning Governor Kitzhaber that calling a special session was risky, since a majority of her Republican caucus did not support the MAX request and they were "irritable" because of the governor's 52 vetoes.[12] Going into the special session, no one was sure what would happen. Would angry GOP conservatives focus on derailing the MAX funding request while trying to overturn some of the governor's 52 vetoes? What price would Democrat Kitzhaber, Senate President Gordon Smith, and Portland-area legislators backing MAX funding have to pay to get the Bob Tiernan Republicans to clear the way for passage of the MAX bill?

The session lasted only eight days, but it progressed like a theme park roller-coaster—it had so many ups and downs. At times, it appeared the session would end abruptly and lawmakers would go home without approving the state's share for Portland's MAX light-rail system. On August 1, the Senate got so fed up it adjourned and most senators left the Capitol. The next day the Republican House had a dramatic two-hour debate on the question of whether or not it, too, should go home. By a whisker (30-27), the House voted to remain in session when six Republicans from the metropolitan area joined 24 Democrats to defeat the motion to adjourn. These moderate Republicans were most responsible for saving the MAX funding bill from the legislature's trash heap. Just before midnight, August 3, the Oregon House finally approved a compromise bill by a healthy 40-17 margin. Thirty-nine minutes later (12:17 a.m., Friday, August 4) the Senate (which had reconvened) approved the same bill, 20-3. Metropolitan Portlanders and officials were ecstatic, as was Governor Kitzhaber—who had played a critical role in keeping the session going and in crafting the elaborate compromise bill that finally passed both houses.

The final compromise gave the Portland area the $375 million for MAX plus an additional $350 million for other statewide road projects, along with eight other provisions,* "including all or part of six bills that had been vetoed by Kitzhaber. None of them, however, would have huge policy impacts. For example, Kitzhaber sought to satisfy Republican critics of his pro-environment policies by agreeing to new limits on logging regulations for the next two years. The governor also resurrected a bill he supported during the session that tries to accommodate some regional differences in the state land-use program."[13]

The Republican House and Senate overrode two of Kitzhaber's recent vetoes, but House Democrats held together and denied Republicans the 40 votes they needed to override several other vetoes. One override was of a bill relating to local gun-control laws. The National Rifle Association and other gun groups lobbied lawmakers hard to overturn the bill barring local gun-control laws, intended to overturn a Multnomah County ordinance requiring assault weapons to be disassembled before being transported in the county. The override was passed, 46-13, in the House.

After a grueling week, the special session was over. The Republican Senate had got the ball rolling by proposing to add $375 million for road projects for the rest of the state. John Kitzhaber, with the support of a cohesive House Democratic caucus and a handful of moderate urban Republicans, coupled with Speaker Bev Clarno's patience and persistence, had forged an acceptable compromise. But these battles left festering wounds.

The Packwood Scandal

During the special session of the legislature, another significant political event was occurring: the worsening predicament of Oregon Senator Bob Packwood. Senator Packwood had been the subject of a two-and-a-half-year-long Senate Ethics investigation. Beginning with the publication of a *Washington Post* story at the time of his reelection in November 1992, Packwood had been under the Senate microscope. According to the *Post*, at least a dozen women had filed

---

* The eight minor provisions: establishing a regional problem-solving process for the state land-use program; a cap on logging regulations that reduce the value of timberlands by more than 10%; card-lock gas stations would be allowed to serve all motorists living 7 miles from a service station instead of the current 10 miles; establishing a fine for repeated unfounded complaints against animal feedlots; a ban on local pesticide ordinances; Portland-area communities would be forbidden from raising system development charges paid by real estate developers to help pay for the region's contribution to the rural transportation system; shooting ranges would be granted immunity from noise complaint; and, a $50,000 grant would be provided to protect salmon from cormorants on the north Oregon coast. See *The Oregonian*, Friday, August 4, 1995, A1.

complaints with the Ethics Committee, alleging Packwood made unwanted sexual advances toward them between 1969 and 1990. Most of the women alleged that Packwood had forcibly grabbed and kissed them (or attempted to do so). Several said Packwood had either groped or tried to grope their breasts and/or buttocks. The week before Oregon's November 3, 1992, general election, the *Post* notified Packwood that they were ready to print their story and asked him if he had any comment. Packwood quickly denied the accusations and issued a statement in which he apologized if his behavior had ever caused "embarrassment or discomfort" to any individual. Packwood told the newspaper he would sue them if they printed their story before the election. Having muzzled the *Post* (for the time being; they did publish a story after the election), Bob Packwood was elected to a fifth term, defeating longtime Democratic Congressman Les AuCoin by 78,000 votes.

In spring 1993, the Senate Ethics panel began investigating the growing number of complaints against Packwood. Seventeen women made 18 allegations of sexual misconduct. "The charges also accused Packwood of altering his diaries when he expected them to be subpoenaed by the committee and of asking lobbyists and others to obtain a job for his wife in order to lower his alimony payments when he divorced her."[14] Senator Packwood emphatically denied any wrongdoing throughout the Ethics Committee's investigation. He stalled, he obstructed, he denied, and he lied. The hotter the situation got, the harder Packwood worked to discredit the women, insinuating that they were unreliable or had personal or political vendettas against him. Meanwhile, more women came forward with their stories about Packwood's advances.

Senate Majority Leader Bob Dole and other GOP leaders saw that Bob Packwood's continuing presence was a growing liability—both to the Senate and to the Republican Party. On Wednesday, August 2, the full Senate Ethics Committee met and decided to release all documents collected during its investigation, "including relevant passages from the Senator's diaries and depositions from the women accusing him of forceful kissing and groping."[15] The committee would meet the following day to consider what punishment they would recommend to the full Senate.

When the ethics panel convened on Thursday, they were told that two more women had come forward earlier in the summer to file complaints of sexual misconduct against Packwood—that committee staff had, inadvertently, failed to report this information to the committee (eventually 29 women charged Bob Packwood with sexual harassment). Meanwhile, the unfolding scandal dominated TV and newspaper headlines in Oregon. Then the late-night TV hosts got into the act, skewering Packwood. Oregonians were mortified and embarrassed about the whole affair.

On Monday, August 7, 1995, the Senate Ethics Committee, by a 6-0 vote recommended that Bob Packwood be expelled from the Senate. Everyone (except Packwood) could see the writing on the wall: Bob Packwood had to go. While the public clamor for Packwood to resign grew, the senator, as he had for over two years, dug in, convinced he could weather the storm. Both the national and Oregon media criticized Packwood for remaining in office. With each passing day, Packwood's Senate friends deserted him. He became a pariah, a man to be avoided.

Exactly one month after the Ethics Committee had voted unanimously, the beleaguered Republican rose to address the full Senate. To a hushed chamber, Robert Packwood, Oregon's senator for the previous 26 years, said "It is my duty to resign." The powerful chairman of the Finance Committee was leaving the Senate. Oregonians were relieved. The nightmare was over. Packwood's resignation took effect on October 1, 1995.

Meanwhile, Oregon elections officials and politicians scrambled to prepare for a special election to fill his Senate seat. A party primary election, to be conducted by mail, was set for December 5. As voters began to focus on Packwood's replacement, Sen. Mark Hatfield, his voice heavy with emotion, announced that when his fifth term ended in January 1997 he would retire after 30 years in the Senate and 46 years in Oregon politics. Within the space of two months, Oregonians, who had not elected a new senator since Robert Packwood in 1968, would be electing two new senators.

The Campaign to Replace Bob Packwood

Between Bob Packwood's resignation and the special primary election to replace him on December 5 there were only nine weeks. This set off a wild scramble as 16 candidates filed for the office: 11 Republicans and five Democrats. Senate President Gordon Smith headed the list of Republican contenders, followed by former secretary of state (and GOP nominee for governor), Norma Paulus, and Jack Roberts, Oregon's new Commissioner of Labor and Industries; eight lesser-known candidates filled the ballot. Gordon Smith was a fresh face in Oregon politics. His youthful appeal, good looks, Mormon affiliations, and deep pockets made him a runaway choice among Republican voters. Meanwhile, two of the state's most powerful Democrats, Congressmen Ron Wyden and Peter DeFazio, squared off in their party's special primary. Three political novices were also on the Democratic ballot. Ron Wyden was the better-known candidate; voters in metropolitan Portland, the bastion of Democratic strength in Oregon (and Ron Wyden's home turf), were generally unfamiliar with DeFazio, who was from Democrat-rich Eugene-Springfield, and thought to have broader appeal in more rural areas of the state. Because the campaign was so short, those candidates with the most money had the advantage of saturating TV with their ads. In a statewide vote-by-mail election, Republican Gordon Smith and Democrat Ron Wyden won their primaries, Smith by a huge margin, Wyden by a much narrower one. Smith defeated Norma Paulus by 148,000 votes (246,000 to 98,100). "Smith, with armloads of cash and a conservative political agenda, beat the politically moderate Paulus by a 3-1 margin. Paulus raised about $300,000 and Smith about $2 million for the primary."[16] Democrat Peter DeFazio mounted a surprisingly strong challenge against Ron Wyden. The Portlander defeated DeFazio by just over 25,000 votes (212,500 to 187,400).

Fifty-eight percent of registered voters cast their mail ballots in the special election. With the primary over, voters now faced another brief campaign of only seven weeks before the special election between Ron Wyden and Gordon Smith, on January 30, 1996.*

Ron Wyden in a Photo-finish

The candidates spent millions on a barrage of TV commercials and mass mailings. Congressman Wyden based his campaign on the issues for which he had become best known: Medicare, Medicaid, and Social Security. He also focused on the environment, education, the budget and spending priorities of the Republican-controlled Congress, and Gordon Smith's conservative views, including the Republican's opposition to abortion. Smith favored federal tax cuts. "Wyden and Smith both came out swinging, and by Christmas both were hitting each other hard in their advertising. Both sides assumed the classic partisan positions: Smith called Wyden a tax-and-spend liberal, while Wyden said Smith was in cahoots with conservative extremists who wanted to gut social programs. Both had trouble wooing swing voters, making the race tough to predict."[17]

---

* In May, Democrats and Republicans would also decide on their nominees to replace Oregon's other senator, the retiring Mark Hatfield. In addition, the 1995 Legislature had changed the date when Oregon would hold its 1996 presidential preference election to March 12, advancing this election from its normal place as part of Oregon's May primary. Voters in Oregon's Third Congressional District (Multnomah County) also voted on April 2 in a special primary election to replace Congressman Ron Wyden (who was headed to the U.S. Senate). So, in a span of six months, Oregonians cast ballots in four statewide elections, while voters in Multnomah County did so five times.

The public was quickly disgusted with all the negative commercials. Wyden stumbled badly when, during the course of a TV station's current-events questionnaire, he was unable to locate the country of Bosnia on a world globe. Nor could Wyden answer another question about the price of a loaf of bread. Gordon Smith steadily closed the gap separating the candidates. The momentum seemed to be Smith's.

Then, three weeks before the election, Ron Wyden announced he would air no more negative TV ads. Wyden had listened to voters and responded accordingly: from now on he would conduct a positive campaign, one that focused on issues, rather than on tearing down Gordon Smith. With the active support of environmental and union groups, and a flood of money from out-of-state contributors, the Wyden campaign concentrated on grassroots organization, focusing their efforts on capturing the independent vote and the support of suburban Republican women, along with the traditional Democratic constituencies of senior citizens, students, environmental activists, labor, and pro-choice supporters.

Two issues came up during the campaign that hurt Gordon Smith. One involved his food-processing plant in Pendleton, which had been cited by the DEQ for polluting a nearby stream, killing hundreds of native fish. The issue played into Ron Wyden's charges that his opponent could not be trusted to safeguard Oregon's many precious natural resources. Smith was also hurt by an endorsement he received from the conservative Oregon Citizen's Alliance, headed by Lon Mabon, which had been prominent as the chief backer of several controversial ballot drives to deny legal rights to homosexuals. Smith didn't renounce the OCA's endorsement; but he made it clear that he did not approve of discrimination against any minority group. The issue became another reason for more affluent suburban/urban voters to reject Smith's candidacy.

Polls indicated the outcome would be close. The Wyden-Smith contest was the first time that a United States senator was elected by mail ballot. Nearly 66% of registered voters cast ballots in the special Senate election of January 30, 1996, a record.

The Senate campaign was one of the most costly in state history. Wyden spent over $3 million. Roughly half of his campaign contributions came from outside Oregon, about 20% coming from Washington, D.C., interest groups including pro-Israel groups (Wyden is Jewish), labor unions, and the health-care and financial industries. Another 20% of Wyden's treasury consisted of money he carried over from previous reelection campaigns. Gordon Smith spent over $4.3 million, $2 million out of his own pocket. Many of Smith's contributions came from lumber and business interests, and from conservative religious groups.

Election night went pretty much as expected. Early results were inconclusive. The votes from eastern and southern Oregon were solidly for Republican Smith. One county after another went into the Smith column. But everyone knew that the outcome rested basically on two factors: how big would Ron Wyden's margin be in Multnomah County (his home and the state's most populous county) and how well would the Democrat do in the big suburban counties of Clackamas and Washington?

By 10 p.m. it appeared Democrat Wyden was headed for a 1% victory, a final margin of only 18,220 votes out of 1.125 million cast. Wyden carried nine counties, Gordon Smith 27. But Multnomah, Washington, and Clackamas counties counted most. The final tally was: Ron Wyden, 571,700 and Gordon Smith, 553,500. About 30% of Wyden's statewide total came from Multnomah County. Ron Wyden was the first Democrat elected to the U.S. Senate from Oregon since Wayne Morse in 1962. Senator-elect Wyden would finish the remaining 35 months of Packwood's fifth term. After that, he would have to stand for reelection to a full six-year term in November 1998. With his wife, two children, and Oregon's senior Senator Mark Hatfield, at his side, Wyden took the oath of office as Oregon's new U.S. Senator on February 6, 1996.

Two days after the Wyden-Smith Senate election, the 1995 Oregon Legislature returned to the State Capitol for another special session—and Oregon's presidential preference primary was only six weeks away (March 12).

A One-Day Special Session

Governor John Kitzhaber and Republican leaders Bev Clarno and Gordon Smith had agreed that the legislature would meet early in 1996 to consider a corrections plan being developed by the governor and a panel of legislators and public officials. The community corrections bill was to cover a 20-year span and cost $94 million. It called for tougher sentencing standards for chronic property offenders. "Kitzhaber proposed housing felons with less than a one-year sentence in county jails rather than in state prisons. The plan would free about 1,500 state prison beds for violent criminals—by routing new money to pay for 1,486 county jail beds to absorb state inmates and fund treatment programs [at the county level]."[18] Legislators remained on task and the corrections plan was approved in what turned out to be a one-day special session.

Oregon Holds Its Presidential Preference Primary

The 1995 Legislature had enacted a law to separate Oregon's presidential primary from the rest of the traditional May primary ballot, setting the presidential vote for early March in the hopes of making the Oregon vote more important nationally. For several decades, the Oregon presidential preference primary drew national attention because it typically featured a wide array of potential presidential candidates and was held in May, several months before the national party conventions. Over the years, other states decided to hold their own presidential primaries, adopting dates in February, March, and April —making Oregon's primary less important. In deciding to move Oregon's presidential preference primary to March, lawmakers hoped to refocus national attention on who Oregonians thought would make a good president. March 12, 1996 was the new date for Oregon's presidential primary.

President Bill Clinton was seeking reelection in 1996. His was the only name on Oregon's Democratic ballot. Nine Republicans were listed on the GOP ballot. The top contender was Senate Majority Leader Bob Dole. Dole's chief rivals were commentator and political consultant Pat Buchanan and millionaire businessman Steve Forbes, publisher of *Forbes Magazine.* The March primary was conducted by mail—making Oregon the first state to conduct such an election in this way. President Bill Clinton took 95% of the Democratic vote (350,000). Senator Bob Dole won the Republican primary with 207,000 votes (51%), compared to Buchanan's 87,000 (21.3%), and Steve Forbes' 54,100 (13.3%). Dole faced Forbes and Buchanan in a score of later primaries with results similar to Oregon. President Clinton and Senator Dole secured their party's presidential nomination later that summer. The result of Oregon's earlier presidential primary didn't focus national attention on the state, nor did the outcome change the direction the Democratic and Republican campaigns took.

More Elections

Democrat Ron Wyden's election to the U.S. Senate had opened his 3rd Congressional District seat. A special primary election was set for April 2, 1996; everyone knew that whoever Democrats nominated would be elected in November (because the district was so lopsidedly Democratic). Two prominent Democrats opposed each other in April: 47-year-old Portland City Commissioner Earl Blumenauer and 70-year-old State Senator Shirley Gold. Blumenauer won the nomination by a 3-1 margin, 53,300 to 17,700.

The Oregon primary of May 21, 1996, was the fourth statewide election held in the past six months and voters were exhausted. Consequently, most boycotted the election; only 38% cast ballots.

The Battle for Mark Hatfield's Senate Seat

The featured political contest in May was the U.S. Senate contest to replace the retiring Mark Hatfield. Ten candidates, five from each party, vied for the nomination. The Republican ballot was headed by State Senator Gordon Smith—who had narrowly lost the special January Senate election to Democrat Ron Wyden. Smith was the heavy favorite to win the GOP nomination. Opposing Smith was the well-known, but widely unpopular, Lon Mabon, chairman of the Oregon Citizen's Alliance. Three minor candidates trailed.

The Democratic ballot featured Bend businessman Harry Lonsdale, State Senator Bill Dwyer of Springfield, Lane County Commissioner Jerry Rust, and Portland activist Anna Nevenich—who was on the ballot for the third time since

Ron Wyden

GERRY LEWIN COLLECTION

Ronald Wyden was born in Wichita, Kansas, in May 1949. He was reared in Palo Alto, California, and was a talented high school basketball player. A graduate of Stanford University, he entered the University of Oregon Law School, earning a degree there in 1974. Wyden founded an Oregon branch of the Gray Panthers, an advocacy and service organization for senior citizens, serving as director from 1974 to 1980.

In 1980, age 31, Ron Wyden challenged fellow Democrat Bob Duncan, Oregon's 3rd District U.S. representative, defeating Duncan in the May primary. He was elected to the House in November and reelected seven times, leaving the House after 15 years to run for the open U.S. Senate seat vacated by Republican Bob Packwood. Wyden defeated Republican Gordon Smith by a narrow margin in 1996 and went on to win full six-year terms in 2004 and 2010.

Wyden and Smith, who was elected to the Senate seat vacated by the retiring Mark Hatfield in 1998, formed a close working relationship to promote Oregon and Northwest interests. Wyden, a moderate Democrat, has been a national leader in health care reform and an outspoken advocate for tax reform. He has a reputation for hard work and a willingness to work both sides of the Senate aisle, sometimes voting with Republicans and co-sponsoring legislation with GOP members. In January 2012 Senator Wyden became the longest-serving member of Congress in Oregon history.

the previous December. The fifth Democratic candidate was Tom Bruggere. A face new to Oregon politics, Bruggere, age 50, was a self-made millionaire, co-founder of a software firm in Wilsonville. Most Democrats were familiar with Lonsdale because of his Senate runs in 1990 and 1992. Tom Bruggere had lots of money (much of it his) and concentrated on getting himself known to Democratic voters through mass mailings and heavy TV advertising. The Democratic race quickly turned into a two-man contest between Lonsdale and Bruggere.

Tom Bruggere scored a 2-1 victory over Harry Lonsdale, 151,300 votes to Lonsdale's 76,000. Gordon Smith flattened his four GOP challengers, defeating Lon Mabon by a 10-1 margin, 224,400 to 23,500.

Other Key Political Contests

First District Congresswoman Elizabeth Furse had barely won reelection in 1994. Furse ran unopposed in the Democratic primary. Six candidates vied for the GOP nomination. Bill Witt headed the GOP ticket, followed by former state representative and state treasurer Bill Rutherford, longtime legislator Stan Bunn, state representative John Meek, and newcomer Molly Bordonaro. As expected, the Republican vote was scattered all over the place. The better-known Bill Witt, for the second time, captured the Republican nomination, besting Bordonaro, 19,600 to 13,600. Stan Bunn got 10,500 votes. Elizabeth Furse pulled 48,000 votes in her uncontested Democratic primary.

Voters in Oregon's sprawling 2nd District were distracted by rumors that their enigmatic rookie congressman, Republican Wes Cooley, was under investigation regarding several possible crimes, including the legal status of his current marriage, perjury, lying under oath in a dispute with his former wife over a property loan, and whether or not a claim made by Cooley in the state *Voter's Pamphlet* about his military record was true. A defiant Cooley claimed that the rumors were nothing but dirty tricks by his political enemies. Fortunately for Cooley, he was unopposed in the GOP primary. Democrat Michael Dugan, district attorney of Deschutes County, won his party's nomination.

Meanwhile, voters in Oregon's 3rd Congressional District had two elections in spring, one a primary and the other a general election; the latter, of course, would normally be held in November. Both elections related to replacing Ron Wyden. The May general election would elect someone to fill the remaining seven months of Wyden's term. The primary election in April had decided who the Republican and Democratic nominees would be in the November general election—the winner of which would be elected to a full two-year House term, starting in January 1997. Democrat Blumenauer won both the May and November elections, becoming Oregon's new U.S. representative.

One-term Republican Jim Bunn had little trouble winning his party's nomination for the 5th District, but would face a stiff Democratic challenge in November from former legislator and Clackamas county commissioner, Darlene Hooley.

Controversial Measure 25, one of three measures on the May ballot, was passed 350,000 to 290,000. The measure amended the Oregon Constitution, requiring both houses of the legislature to obtain 60% majorities in order to enact any new law to raise taxes. The measure had been referred to the ballot by the Republican Legislature and was heralded by the GOP as a victory over high taxes and expensive government.

Wester Shadric Cooley

Wester Shadric ("Wes") Cooley had burst on the political scene in Oregon in 1992. From out of nowhere, he had knocked off longtime legislator Democrat Wayne Fawbush in State Senate District 28. Cooley's victory came in spite of the fact that he wasn't even a legal resident of District 28. In order to challenge Fawbush, Cooley had pulled a travel trailer into the district and run electricity to it with an extension cord. Cooley then claimed to be a bona fide district resident. When questions about Cooley's legal residence were raised, Secretary of State Phil Keisling looked into the matter. Keisling concluded that the "state lacked 'clear and convincing' evidence that Cooley did not live in the district. Keisling's decision leaned heavily on Cooley's promise to establish a legitimate residence in the district. Cooley won the election and never moved into the district."[19]

A majority of voters ignored troubling facts about Cooley's personal life, character, and public record. Wes Cooley was a liar who too easily conned his way into gaining the public's trust. "Cooley's life was filled with clues to the kind of man Republicans were backing. He claimed he was a government spy who killed men with piano wire. He lost his first race for office, for Placentia, California, city council, after telling voters that he had secret FBI files on his opponents." Cooley's personal life was also a shambles. Cooley had "agreed to support his ex-wife and children and then refused to turn over at least $56,000 in support payments."[20] And since 1977 Cooley and his common-law wife, Rosemary Herron, had claimed to be a married couple. As troubling as these facts were, it seemed only a few of Cooley's constituents were concerned about them.

When six-term Republican Congressman Bob Smith announced he would not seek reelection in 1994, Wes Cooley ran for the seat. Again, luck was on

Cooley's side. Six other Republicans also sought the nomination. Wes Cooley got only about 22% of the total—but it was enough to win his party's nomination. Cooley continued to spin myths about himself. He included at least two falsehoods in his 1994 *Voter's Pamphlet* biography. One lie was that he was a member of the prestigious Phi Beta Kappa honorary society. Another claim was that he had served in a special forces Army unit in Korea during that country's war, 1950-53. But his campaign struck a responsive cord with the conservative trends then sweeping Oregon and the nation. 2nd District voters elected Wes Cooley to the U.S. House in November—in spite of questions about Cooley's character and short political resume. Wes Cooley quickly established a reputation in Congress as a hard-working rookie. He irked the media and fellow politicians with his strident positions and his "in-your-face" style. Cooley became more arrogant and increasingly enamored with the mythical figure he had created for himself. Many of his constituents loved Cooley for his unorthodox ways, for his outspoken ridicule of environmentalists and government bureaucrats.

Oregon reporters, however, continued to dig into his past. In 1995, "news stories told of how Cooley and Rosemary repeatedly made false claims of marriage before their 1993 wedding; Rosemary's potentially improper collection of benefits as a veteran's widow; questionable tax deductions claimed by an employee; and misstatements Cooley made in his divorce from his first wife. But no story was as troubling to voters as an earlier report that Cooley could not substantiate his war record."[21] The controversy about Cooley's war record, his character, and his veracity began to take its toll. Oregonians were still smarting from Sen. Bob Packwood's resignation (three months earlier). Now, with the exposure of Wes Cooley's misdeeds, Oregon's political house was again in turmoil. Republican leaders, both in Oregon and Congress, pressured Wes Cooley to resign.* The GOP couldn't afford another scandal on the heels of the Bob Packwood fiasco. Cooley got the message.

Because Cooley had won the May 1996 primary he was the official GOP nominee for Congress in the 2nd District—his name would be on the November general election ballot. After he announced that he would not seek reelection, there was insufficient time between August and November to conduct a special election to choose a replacement. Under these circumstances, Oregon

---

* In December 1996, a special Marion County grand jury indicted Cooley on two counts of making false statements in the Voter's Pamphlet—each a felony crime. In March 1997 a jury found Wes Cooley guilty of lying about his military record. Cooley was fined $5,000 and sentenced to two years probation and one hundred hours of community service.

election law required that precinct committeemen and committeewomen meet and pick a party nominee. Eighty GOP leaders met in Bend and chose former Congressman Bob Smith.

The 1996 General Election

Oregon's November ballot was the most crowded ballot in 70 years. Not since 1926 (when 21 measures were on the ballot) had a state election featured so many ballot questions. The Oregon ballot was bloated by 23 measures.* The plethora of statewide measures boosted voter turnout (to 71.3%) in November. The ballot also featured a bevy of important races, including the presidency, a Senate seat, five U.S. House seats, the offices of attorney general, secretary of state, treasurer, and attorney general, as well as the makeup of the 1997 Legislature.

There were nearly two million registered voters in Oregon in fall 1996. The large registration edge enjoyed by Democrats for the previous 30 years was shrinking, though Democrats outnumbered registered Republicans 805,000 to 714,500. The surge in independent voters (to 400,000), coupled with the Republican tide sweeping the country, account for much of the Democrat's reduced registration margin. Interestingly, one in four Oregon Democrats lived within a few miles of each other in tiny Multnomah County.

Democrat Bill Clinton was seeking a second term in 1996. The president faced two major opponents in Oregon: Republican Robert Dole, longtime Kansas senator, and third-party candidate H. Ross Perot, nominee of the Reform Party. President Clinton swept the West Coast in November, carrying California, Washington, Nevada, Hawaii, Arizona, and Oregon. Not since Franklin Roosevelt was reelected in 1936 had a Democrat carried Oregon in two consecutive presidential elections.

The Smith-Bruggere Senate Race

Democrats were excited about the possibility of winning the Senate seat held for 30 years by Republican Mark Hatfield. Democratic leaders (locally and nationally) were pinning their hope on political novice Tom Bruggere. Bruggere's biggest challenge was to become known in every part of Oregon. To accomplish this, Bruggere campaigned non-stop. He spent heavily on TV advertising. But it was an uphill battle because Bruggere was not nearly as well known as Gordon Smith. Bruggere presented himself as knowledgeable, well prepared,

---

* There were thirty-two measures on the 1910 ballot, thirty-seven in 1912, and twenty-nine in 1914.

and intelligent. Bruggere's advantages were these: there were nearly 100,000 more registered Democrats than Republicans in Oregon; there were 400,000 independent voters to court; and popular Democratic President Bill Clinton was at the top of the ballot.

Bruggere and Smith knew the key to victory was to win the suburban vote in Washington and Clackamas counties. Both men concentrated their efforts in the northern Willamette Valley. For Bruggere, the task was to equal Ron Wyden's January vote in Democratic Multnomah County. He stressed two issues of particular importance to women: abortion rights and protection of the environment. He also "took a hard line on fiscal issues—he opposed tax breaks of any kind until the federal budget was balanced."[22] In addition, "ads from Bruggere and independent groups pummeled Smith for pollution problems at Smith Frozen Foods Inc., for manipulation by special interests and for budget-balancing plans that would harm the elderly and poor."[23]

Gordon Smith had several advantages in his campaign against Tom Bruggere. First, he had just completed a vigorous statewide campaign for Bob Packwood's seat, on which he had spent $5 million. Over 500,000 Oregonians had voted for Smith in his race against Ron Wyden. Consequently, Gordon Smith's name and face were instantly recognized across the state. The Republican also had a statewide organization in place when he made his second Senate bid.

Smith's strategy was to move toward the middle. Analysts had concluded that Smith lost to Wyden because many voters thought Smith was too conservative. Smith's opposition to abortion and his earlier endorsement by the OCA hurt him with moderate and independent voters as well as with suburban women. Throughout his campaign with Bruggere, Gordon Smith "pushed a message of moderation and common sense. Over and over Smith said he would represent Oregon with balance and consideration of all interests. He called himself a consensus-builder."[24]

About half of the 1.4 million votes cast were absentee ballots (678,000). As a result, a number of key races were in doubt until the weekend. The Senate contest between Gordon Smith and Tom Bruggere resulted in a larger victory margin than expected: in his second attempt, Gordon Smith won by 53,000 votes, carrying 31 of Oregon's 36 counties. The final tally was Smith, 677,300, and Bruggere, 624,400.

The U.S. House races in Districts One and Five were even closer than the Smith-Bruggere contest. First District incumbent, Democrat Elizabeth Furse, won a third term, again defeating Republican challenger Bill Witt (by 18,100 votes). The race had turned ugly near the end when Witt ran a TV ad accusing

Furse of securing a loan by using her position. Witt's last-minute salvo worked against him; the ad gave Furse the boost she needed to pull ahead of Witt in the final days of the campaign. Congressman Jim Bunn lost his seat to Democrat Darlene Hooley in the 5th District, 125,400 to 139,500.

Oregon's other three U.S. House races were blowouts. In the vast 2nd District, Republican Bob Smith came out of a short retirement to win back the seat he had held for 12 years. Democrat Peter DeFazio of Eugene won a fifth term in the 4th District. Finally, Democrat Earl Blumenauer, who had been elected to complete the last seven months of Ron Wyden's eighth term in the 3rd District, defeated his GOP foe by 100,000 votes.

The Clinton tide which swept the nation in 1996 impacted several key races in Oregon. Elizabeth Furse's tight reelection victory in the 1st District (where Clinton defeated Republican Bob Dole by 11,000 votes) was boosted by the president's popularity there. Democrat Darlene Hooley's defeat of Congressman Jim Bunn in the 4th District was also helped by Clinton's popularity in Marion and Clackamas counties.

A Democratic Sweep

Oregon's three major statewide offices (secretary of state, treasurer, and attorney general) were also on the November ballot. Incumbent Democrat Phil Keisling, Oregon's young secretary of state, was reelected by 300,000 votes. The state treasurer's contest between incumbent Democrat Jim Hill, Oregon's most visible African American politician, and Republican Bev Clarno resulted in a 101,000-vote victory for Hill. Clarno carried 22 counties, but lost where it counted most, Multnomah County, where Hill beat her by 86,000 votes. Democrat Hardy Myers, a Portland attorney and former speaker of the Oregon House, was reelected attorney general by 141,000 votes in what is typically a low-key campaign.

President Clinton carried Oregon with 47% of the vote to Bob Dole's 39%, and Ross Perot's 9%. The popular vote was: Clinton, 649,600, Dole, 538,100, and Perot, 121,200.

But Democrats did not have their way when it came to the 1997 Legislature. Democratic attempts to recapture control of the House and Senate fell short in November. Republicans retained control of the Oregon House, but only by the narrowest of margins, 31-29. The most hotly contested and watched House race was in District 24, the Lake Oswego area of Washington and Clackamas counties. There, the controversial Republican incumbent, Bob Tiernan, an obstructionist leader of the Rule of Eighteen cabal in the 1995 session, lost his bid for reelection to Democrat Richard Devlin, 11,550 to 12,557. The GOP strengthened their hold on the Senate, 20-10.

Stirring the Political Pot: Oregon's 23 Ballot Measures

Oregon's ballot measures sparked widespread interest in the fall. Sixteen measures were proposed constitutional amendments, only five of which were passed. Measures 31 and 47 in particular aroused intense debate and scrutiny.

Measure 31 was referred to the ballot by the 1995 Republican Legislature.* It was a rehash of Measure 19, which voters had defeated in 1994, and would amend the Oregon Constitution regarding free speech. "The Oregon Constitution says, 'No law shall be passed restraining the free expression of opinion, or restricting the right to speak, write or print freely on any subject whatever, but every person shall be responsible for the abuse of this right.' In its landmark 1987 decision in *State vs. Henry*, the Oregon Supreme Court interpreted those words to mean that obscenity is protected speech, making Oregon the only state to protect obscenity in its constitution. The *Henry* decision wiped out most of Oregon's anti-pornography laws, including Portland's ordinance governing the location of 'adult' businesses." Measure 31 proposed to add this phrase to the Oregon Constitution: "Obscenity, including child pornography, shall receive no greater protection under this Constitution than afforded by the Constitution of the United States." Passage of Measure 31 would give local governments authority to pass laws against expression as defined by federal law. "Cities could zone or prohibit businesses offering nude entertainment. Judges and juries could apply their own community's standards in determining what was obscene." [25]

Opponents of Measure 31 included the Democratic Party of Oregon, the Oregon Library Association, League of Women Voters, Oregon Education Association, and the American Civil Liberties Union. They claimed that "if adopted, 31 would allow every city and county—all 276 of them—to define obscenity differently. This would lead to a 'crazy-quilt' of conflicting laws across the state: What is legal in one town would be illegal in the next." [26] Voters rejected Measure 31 by 76,000 votes, 631,000 in favor, to 707,000 opposed.

The most contentious measure on the 1996 ballot was Measure 47, another property-tax limitation proposal. Measure 5, passed in 1990, had not produced the drastic lowering of property taxes that its sponsors had wanted. So Measure 47 (pushed by tax reformer Bill Sizemore and Rep. Bob Tiernan)

---

* One of the chief sponsors of Measure 31 was Salem Democrat Kevin Mannix. Soon after the 1996 election Mannix changed his party affiliation to Republican.

was on the 1996 ballot. The proposal would limit 1997-98 property taxes to what they were in either 1995-96 minus 10% or what those taxes were in 1994-95—whichever were lowest. The measure also limited the increase in property taxes to 3% a year.* The effect of the measure was to immediately cut property taxes throughout Oregon by $1 billion over the next two years (resulting in a loss of revenue available to school districts and other local government of about 20%). This loss of local revenue could only be replaced with state income tax money appropriated by the legislature or by local voters in the form of fees or special charges.

A powerful coalition of special interest groups opposed Measure 47. Governor John Kitzhaber, former governors Victor Atiyeh and Neil Goldschmidt, and Democratic legislators all opposed the measure. Extensive canvassing, the use of phone banks, mass mailings, and an avalanche of TV ads were all employed in the effort to defeat Measure 47. Most voters already had their minds made up—they wanted lower property taxes and were apparently less concerned about what lower taxes meant for local schools and other vital government services. Measure 47 passed with relative ease, 704,500 to 642,600, a margin of about 62,000 votes. Oregon now had one of the most restrictive property tax limits in the United States.

Voters also passed Measure 44 to increase the state tax on cigarettes and tobacco with the additional revenues to expand the Oregon Health Plan.

Money and PACs

Starting in the early 1970s, established groups were often reorganized into political action committees (PACs). Their purpose was to raise money to contribute to candidates seeking public office; to inform (or educate) the public about who they were and what their goals were (thereby attracting new members and their money); and to lobby politicians when it was time for them to make decisions. PACs, then, are political committees spawned by established interest groups. Today, most organizations have their own PAC.

The role of lobbyists and interest groups (PACS or Political Action Committees) continued to grow in Oregon as did the millions of dollars these

---

* Measure 47 also included a provision called the "double majority" rule, which applies to all local and state tax elections. For example, let's say that the Corvallis school district places a measure on the ballot to raise local school taxes. For the tax to be approved at least 50% of registered voters must cast ballots and at least 50% of those who vote must vote "yes." This is what is called a double majority. On November 4, 2008, Oregonians passed Measure 56, to amend Measure 47 of 1996, exempting tax elections conducted in May or November from the double majority rule.

groups poured into political campaigns. Legislative elections, which in 1974 cost an average of $3,400 per House candidate and $6,500 per Senate candidate, soared to $42,300 and $63,000 respectively in 1994. With each new election the cost of running for office only went up, up, up.

Oregon's 1996 legislative races were dominated by PACs, special interest groups (and their lobbyists), and by a handful of wealthy individuals who poured wheelbarrows full of money into their pet political campaigns. In addition, both Republicans and Democrats within the legislature formed party-caucus PACs and collected hundreds of thousands of dollars to funnel into their members' campaigns. Besides these caucus PACs, there was nothing to stop individual legislators from forming their own personal PACs. An example of the growing wealth, influence, and sheer numbers of interest groups is easily seen in the 1994 general election, when nearly $5.6 million was spent in Oregon House races alone. In 1996, Republican Gordon Smith spent over $8 million in his two campaigns for the Senate—while Smith's Democratic opponents, Ron Wyden and Tom Bruggere, spent over $5 million. Over $12 million was spent on November's 23 ballot measures. Add the cost of 75 legislative contests, the five congressional district contests, statewide offices, and scores of local contests—over $30 million was spent on political campaigns in Oregon in 1996.

Chapter 20
John Kitzhaber and the Republicans, 1997-99

Oregon's 69th Legislative Assembly convened at the Capitol on January 13, 1997. The challenges facing them would require prodigious effort. There was uncertainty about how much money would be available for public schools and universities. Would the robust Oregon economy continue to generate higher income tax revenues for the state? What about the so-called "kicker" fund, estimated to be about $385 million—should all or part of this money be rebated to taxpayers? How much money would there be for Oregon's unique Health Plan? Were recently adopted sentencing guidelines going to force the legislature to set aside additional millions for more jails and prisons? Were the session's two new leaders, Speaker Lynn Lundquist and President Brady Adams, ready to guide their chambers through the legislative maze? Would the inexperienced Lundquist succeed in holding together his fragile Republican House caucus? And what about the uncertainty caused by term limits (passed by the people in 1992 and due to go into effect at the end of the current legislative terms)?* Would the Republican Legislature forge a constructive working relationship with Democratic Gov. John Kitzhaber?

Governor Kitzhaber and legislative leaders agreed on their top priorities: implementing Measure 47 and increasing funding for public schools and universities. Other shared priorities were spending more money on both the Oregon Health Plan and on statewide road maintenance and repair. Improving water quality and salmon recovery were other shared concerns. There was agreement on Kitzhaber's proposal to hire 160 new case workers in the State Office for Services to Children and Families. Recent stories about the increased incidence of child neglect, abuse, and even murder had outraged the public, eliciting the governor's swift response. Though the governor and Republican leaders

---

* Twenty-four legislators (22 representatives and two senators) would be forced to leave office in January 1999.

generally agreed on these priorities, they disagreed about how best to attain these goals.

Republican leaders in both chambers wanted to reform election law, making it more difficult to file initiative petitions. Speaker Lundquist wanted to revise Oregon's term-limit law (though it was not a priority of Kitzhaber's). Senate Republicans wanted legislation to compensate landowners when environmental regulations reduced a person's property values—a political issue that would kick around for the next decade. The 29 House Democrats (in agreement with Governor Kitzhaber) focused most of their attention on protecting public education; they wanted the legislature to replace the $450 million that schools were about to lose due to the passage of Measure 47. And Democrats also wanted more money for Head Start.

The governor proposed a budget of $9.6 billion for 1997-99, a $1.4 billion increase over the current budget. The individual pieces of the governor's budget included setting aside about $3.96 billion (over 40% of the general fund) for K-12 education; expanding Head Start, a program for pre-kindergarten at-risk children; and freezing university tuitions.[1] The governor recommended $1.4 billion for public safety, including prison expansion, and $2 billion for human resources.

Republicans remembered how Kitzhaber outmaneuvered them in 1995. The governor had vetoed 52 bills—the most in 80 years. Now, Kitzhaber was proposing a huge budget increase and $800 million worth of new taxes to pay for it. House Democratic Minority Leader, Salem's Peter Courtney, suggested that "This time, Republicans are out to teach him a lesson. They're going to try to spank him."[2] Many wondered how long the "honeymoon" would last between the Democratic governor and the Republican Legislature.

Lynn Lundquist and Brady Adams

Speaker Lynn Lundquist was a 62-year-old Quaker farmer who had entered the House two years earlier. He had a reputation as a well-prepared, hardworking lawmaker. Low-key and self-effacing, Lundquist was a moderate Republican with a conciliatory style and desire to build consensus. Many hoped that his skills would help him keep a steady hand on a caucus that had broken apart and made war on itself in 1995.

Senate President Brady Adams' reputation as a tough negotiator and budgetary expert led to his election as Senate president. He presided over a senate in which Republicans held 20 of 30 seats. With this strong majority, Adams believed he could block or limit Governor Kitzhaber's boldest proposals. He agreed with

Kitzhaber about boosting funding for schools, but strongly disagreed with him about where the necessary new money would come from. Kitzhaber wanted to increase a number of existing taxes. Adams and the Republican Senate opposed *any* tax increases. Kitzhaber wanted the state to keep the budget surplus ($383 million)—which fell under the controversial kicker law. Adams and his GOP colleagues wanted kicker money rebated to taxpayers. While Kitzhaber touted budget growth by raising taxes and keeping kicker money, Adams preferred to trim budgets, shifting these savings to public education, corrections, and human resources. The 1997 session lasted 174 days (January 13-July 5). The number of lobbyists working the Capitol had continued to grow; 825 registered lobbyists worked the Capitol during the 69th Legislature.

Bill Sizemore in the Spotlight

The House Revenue Committee, chaired by Tigard Republican Tom Brian, devoted seven weeks to revising Measure 47 (which was poorly drafted and riddled with legal problems), intending to refer the revision to voters at the May 20 election. In early March, Brian's group started hearings to overhaul Oregon's antiquated property tax system. Knowledgeable people agreed that "the state's property tax system is a mess: It's a jerry-built contraption of limitations, exemptions, and mathematical calculations that even experts find impenetrable. Measure 47 didn't change any of that. Instead, it added 1,500 words of complexity." Brian's aim was "fairly limited: Keep the Measure 5 limits on property tax rates [that] voters imposed in 1990 and the Measure 47 limits on the size of everyone's tax bill, but make the system work better."[3] Brian invited Bill Sizemore into his inner circle. Sizemore, a conservative Republican, had been in the headlines for several years. As executive director of an organization called Oregon Taxpayers United, Sizemore had fathered Ballot Measure 47 in 1996.[*]

Bill Sizemore grew up in Montesano, Washington. In 1971, he enrolled in a Portland Bible college. Pursuing various business ventures, Sizemore plunged into local politics. He suffered big defeats in his bids for election to the legislature and to Portland City Council. His carpet business went bankrupt in 1987. A trail of defeat and failure had followed Sizemore up until 1993—when he was hired to head Oregon Taxpayers United.[4]

---

[*] Claiming about twelve thousand members, the OTU had been funded largely by a Washington, D.C.–based group called Americans for Tax Reform (which gave Sizemore's organization about $350,000) and by Oregonian Mark Hemstreet, owner of the Shilo Inns motel chain. See *The Oregonian,* March 3, 1997, A5, for details.

Oregonians voted on Measure 50, the legislature's revision of Measure 47, at a special statewide election on May 20. Sizemore had worked closely with the House Revenue Committee to revise the measure. Voters passed Measure 50 (as a constitutional amendment) by about 80,000 votes (430,000 to 341,800). Voter turnout was 42%. Measure 50 would cut taxes over the next two years by $870 million. The measure also required the legislature to replace the property tax money that schools would lose because of the new tax limitation.

"Blood will splatter"

A brouhaha occurred in the state Senate on May 20. During floor debate on HJR 85, the House Revenue Committee's proposed rewrite of Measure 47, Senate Democrats excoriated President Brady Adams for insisting on an amendment many feared could jeopardize the bill's passage. Adams wanted to add an $18 million tax break for the timber industry. He'd appointed himself to the Senate Revenue Committee to get his amendment added to the resolution. Clackamas Republican Ken Baker, chair of the Revenue Committee, had refused to provide the deciding vote in favor of adding the timber tax break, so Adams took his place.

On the Senate floor, HJR 85 passed 16-14. Four Republicans and all 10 Democrats voted no. "During debate Democrats attacked the timber industry for its greed and the Republicans for their subservience." Brady Adams exploded. He stormed off the podium, shoved his gavel into another senator's hand, and took a place on the floor, requesting to speak. "His voice trembled, and his face flushed redder and redder as he explained why he had broken from the House plan to rewrite Measure 47 and added a tax break for the timber industry. This was Adams unplugged. His outburst, articulate and provoked, surprised almost everyone. Some wondered if Adams could work effectively with the House, a separate but also Republican-controlled body."[5]

That afternoon, a Senate-House conference committee met and removed Adams' pet amendment, along with an exemption for a Portland pension fund, before unanimously re-passing the bill for final vote in the house and senate. On Friday, both chambers passed HJR 85 and referred it to the May 20 primary ballot for a statewide vote. Tom Brian's prediction that "Blood would splatter" (after the Senate's 16-14 vote) proved to be wrong. Brady Adams had acquiesced, knowing that his timber tax break would kill the measure and keep it from meeting the deadline to be referred to the May 20 ballot.

Confrontation at the Capitol

The Oregon House was in session near noon on Friday, April 18, when Margaret Carter, an African American lawmaker from Portland, rose to condemn what was going on in front of the Capitol. Several dozen protesters were gathered to criticize the state Office for Services to Children and Families, its policies, and its director, Kay Toran (who was African American). One of the more vehement protesters, a white man from Eugene named Lawrence Carver, had made an "effigy [of Toran]—a head that had been painted black, a black wig and a black plastic bag over crudely stuffed clothes—was hanging in a rope noose from a post in front of the Capitol. On the chest was pinned a hand-written sign that said 'Kay Toran.'" Rep. Carter called the protest "painful" and "disgusting." Democrat George Eighmey, a Portland attorney, rose to condemn the protest and called upon other representatives to join him, to go outside, and remove "the abomination, a disgrace to this Capitol." Most of the 60 representatives followed Eighmey and Carter out the front door. Representative Ron Adams, a West Linn Republican, approached the effigy, untied the rope by which it hung, and began to drag it away. Carver grabbed the figure and held it up over his head. Eighmey then stepped forward, slapped the effigy out of Carver's hand, and looked him in the eye, declaring: "You can protest all you wish, but you do not in this state Capitol desecrate a black woman in 1997." Governor Kitzhaber called the incident "outrageous" and went to Toran's office to speak to her about it. "Adams said that he went after the effigy because he saw it as a racist symbol."[6] Most Oregonians shared Adams' view. This clash between legislators (who were in session) and a group of protesters was unusual; nothing quite like it had occurred in the modern era of Oregon politics.

Governor Kitzhaber and the Republican Leadership

Governor Kitzhaber's proposed budget and spending priorities found a receptive audience in the Republican House. GOP Speaker Lynn Lundquist shared Kitzhaber's belief that as much money as possible should be funneled into public education. Lundquist, like the governor, believed that schools had suffered too many cutbacks since 1991, that the legislature needed to make up lost ground by investing enough money in schools to maintain present programs. The previous June, the Portland school district, because of insufficient state funds, had been forced to fire 300 teachers. Teacher layoffs had also occurred elsewhere in Oregon. The speaker put together a bipartisan House coalition, consisting of the 29 minority Democrats and a group of moderate Republicans, who also believed public schools needed a lot more money. Now Kitzhaber and the House worked together to push the governor's $9.6 billion budget.

Lundquist didn't agree with Kitzhaber on everything. Kitzhaber wanted to use the state's huge budget surplus (ignoring the kicker law) to fund a $1.2 billion budget increase. Lundquist believed that most of the surplus should be returned to taxpayers, but, that *some* of it could pay for part of Kitzhaber's 1997-99 budget.

The third partner in the legislature's behind-the-scenes budget negotiations was Senate President Brady Adams. Adams believed Kitzhaber's budget was too big, that state government should be leaner and not spend so much money. Adams wouldn't compromise on the issue of the kicker law and he had pledged not to raise taxes. By mid-April GOP leaders and Governor Kitzhaber had narrowed their budget differences to about $200 million. Negotiations then broke down. Brady Adams wanted to spend less on education than Lundquist and Kitzhaber. Adams decided to push his school budget through the Senate, putting the Republican House on the spot. Within days the Republican Senate passed a school budget of $4.11 billion and sent it to the House.

On Thursday, May 22, the Oregon House released its proposed 1997-99 budget. Lynn Lundquist set forth the details of a $9.66 billion proposal. He noted that the House budget was intended to end any further teacher layoffs, while providing a big increase in funding for the Oregon Health Plan for the poor. The Republican-Democratic House coalition that had crafted the budget wanted to funnel $80 million of the projected income tax surplus into paying for some of the 1995-97 budget.

President Brady Adams didn't blink or budge. He opposed the House-Kitzhaber budget, believing that the proposal was too high, with too much money going into education and social services. The House wanted to spend $250 million more on schools than Adams and his GOP caucus; Adams also wanted to spend $20 million less on Head Start and $40 million less on the Oregon Health Plan. Adams favored a Senate budget of $9.52 billion—$108 million below the House proposal. He believed that putting money into the pockets of the less wealthy was a better way to help them than developing new government programs. Adams and the Republican senators were branded "obstinate." One veteran senator speculated that Adams was a "captive of his conservative ideology of less government is best. He wanted to shrink the size of government but was forced to be more practical. Adams had a brashness and overconfidence which led him into difficulties, even within his own Republican caucus."[7]

On the same day as it released its proposed budget, the House also acted on two other important bills. First, by a vote of 36-17, the House passed a bill to establish vote-by-mail balloting for all Oregon elections. If the Senate agreed, the measure would be referred to the May 1998 primary election. Secondly, the House approved the $1.9 billion higher education budget passed by the Senate. The budget included a 10% increase in general fund dollars for higher education, or a total state contribution of $577 million for 1997-99. The bill included a two-year freeze on in-state tuition and a small salary increase for faculty. Slowly the wheels of government ground on, approving one budget after another.

Feuding Republicans

June 1 found Republican leaders Brady Adams and Lynn Lundquist at an impasse. Neither had yielded on the issue of the 1997-99 budget. Adams called Lundquist a runaway spender; Lundquist called Adams rigid and blind. Tension between the two leaders was palpable. Governor Kitzhaber thought Adams was isolating himself. A legislative stalemate looked more and more likely.

The Oregon House passed its $4.35 billion education budget by a lopsided vote of 53-6. Later that same evening, the Senate rejected the House's version, which was $250 million bigger than the Senate's, 16-14. Five Republican senators bolted their caucus to support the House's version. A conference committee would be appointed to find a compromise between the two bills. "Key to the Republican-Democratic bloc [in the House, which favored higher increased funding for schools] was Rep. Chuck Carpenter, one of the first members of his caucus to insist on a bigger allocation for education."[8] Carpenter had challenged his Republican colleagues in the Senate to get in line with the House.

Five days later (June 14) there was still no agreement on an education budget. President Adams talked about suspending floor sessions and closing key committees, to pressure the House to yield to his budget and end the session. "All session, Adams has uttered phrases such as 'dead on arrival' and 'off the table' about proposals from the House or Gov. Kitzhaber that require higher taxes and spending. Critics say Adams is being inflexible and confrontational, showing the House an in-your-face negotiating style that will prolong the session."[9] As typically happens at the end of a session, tensions between the chambers and within the caucuses resulted in emotional outbursts. Name-calling, blaming, and finger-pointing became routine.

The Senate session dragged on from 6:30 p.m. to midnight. As the night progressed tempers flared and bitter debates ensued. Republicans pushed through two supercharged bills: one to recriminalize marijuana, the other to slash money from the House-approved human resources budget. "Adams took the floor and lashed out at Democrats for trying to substitute a larger tax package on the floor. He said later the move hardened the will of conservatives who opposed any tax increase. 'They took out a stake and drove it right through the heart of the transportation package,' he said of the Democrats. Senator Randy Leonard, a Portland Democrat, accused Adams of displaying a 'spoiled brat attitude.' 'This guy is going to run the state into the ground,' Leonard said."[10] And so it went. Another week passed and there was still no education or transportation budget.

Breaking the Logjam

There were intense negotiations between Governor Kitzhaber and legislative leaders during the last week of June that allowed for some critical compromises. On Monday, June 30, the Senate passed the largest education funding bill in state history. The House quickly followed suit, passing SB5519 without debate, 53-3. Public schools K-12 would get $4.2 billion in state support for 1997-99. The next day, the Senate approved another record budget (of $1.87 billion) for the Department of Human Resources, including $800 million for the expansion of the Oregon Health Plan adding 47,000 Oregonians to the state plan. The issues of child abuse and foster care were also addressed: this part of the Human Resources budget was increased by 22%, earmarked for new case workers. In addition, the wages of the agency's care providers, including those working in group homes, were raised; services for developmentally disabled people were also expanded.[11] With the passage of both the education and human resources budgets, over 60% of the 1997-99 state budget was in place.

In just six years (1991-97), the Oregon Legislature had shifted the main cost of paying for public schools from local property taxes onto state government. Prior to the November 1990 passage of Measure 5, 65-70% of the cost of schools was paid for out of local property taxes. With the legislature's $4.2 billion education budget for 1997-99, over 70% of schools costs were now borne by state government (mostly paid for out of personal income taxes).

Lawmakers failed to find a way to provide stable long-term funding for state parks. Nearly $400 million in surplus state revenue was returned to taxpayers in the form of a tax rebate.

Doctor-Assisted Suicide

In late May, by a 32-26 vote, the House, which included more than a dozen social conservatives, passed HB 2954, asking voters to repeal doctor-assisted suicide.

On June 9, the Oregon Senate, by a vote of 20-10, passed HB 2954. Eighteen Republicans and two Democrats voted for the bill, while eight Democrats and two Republicans voted against it. The bill referred the question to the November 1998 general election.

The 1997 Legislature

The Oregonian rated the session "OK," saying it accomplished "a modest list of achievements." "The Senate was conservative and aloof, the House more moderate and scrappy. No sooner did the opening gavel bang than the quarrels began. Legislators put aside ambitious agendas. They skipped big tax changes. Instead, they coped. Perhaps more than any other legislature in this decade, members of the 69th session showed an ability to negotiate and respond."[12]

In the 1997 session, the governor had quickly discovered he could work with the Republican Speaker of the House Lynn Lundquist. Lundquist had to hold together a 31-member caucus that included a large number of social conservatives along with a band of moderate Republicans led by Chuck Carpenter. This latter group shared Lundquist's priorities—as did the 29 House Democrats and the governor. It was noted that Governor Kitzhaber "aligned himself with the more moderate House, a move that kept his influence in play. He played the House like a violin. Indeed, with Republicans often splintering on issues, Lundquist turned to alliances with Democrats."[13] The bipartisan solutions paid off, as the final budget looked a lot more like the one John Kitzhaber had recommended in December than the one Senate President Brady Adams pushed for most of the spring.

The relationship between Kitzhaber and Adams was cool. Worlds apart in personality and philosophy, the men seemed destined to clash. "Adams considered Kitzhaber a government sugar daddy and spendthrift. Kitzhaber thought Adams stubborn and naive. Whatever the adjectives, his persistence and his Republican majority spelled raw clout. But with the House aligned with Democrats and Kitzhaber, Adams found himself with insufficient forces to back up his power. He was left in the very frustrating position of being the odd man out."[14]

Oregon's surging economy and huge state income tax revenues allowed Governor Kitzhaber and the legislature to go on a spending spree in 1997. The $9.6 billion 1997-99 budget was a 19% increase over the prior budget. Conservative Republicans were appalled by Kitzhaber's big budget increase. Brady Adams believed the legislature needed to get control of spending.

The High Cost of Growth

There were forces in play that neither the governor nor legislature could control. Oregon's population kept growing. Between 1990 and 1996 Oregon grew by 339,000 people. In late 1993 Oregon reached 3 million and the population strained the state and local infrastructure. Along with these new stresses, voters toughened sentencing guidelines, which required the state to spend up to a billion dollars on more prisons and jails. City and county governments cried for more help from the legislature because of the drop in local government revenues caused by the passage of Measure 47.

The governor and legislature were between a rock and a hard place in 1997. Oregonians were demanding more state support for public schools. Some legislators (mostly conservative Republicans) wanted to hold spending in check and return the huge state budget surplus to taxpayers. Fortunately for Democratic Gov. John Kitzhaber the Oregon House, though nominally in Republican control, forged an alliance with the governor and built a budget based on Kitzhaber's blueprint.

The legislature was lucky. The Oregon economy was so strong in 1996-98 that lawmakers had enough money to pay for 70-75% of the cost of public schools. The 19% hike in the budget was widely applauded, in part, because so many state programs had been cut back over the previous six years. Many Oregonians were relieved when the legislature increased state spending by over $1 billion, feeling that Oregon had deferred paying for critical services long enough.

"Dr. No"

When he vetoed 52 bills passed by the GOP Legislature in 1995, Governor Kitzhaber had set a modern-day record. In 1997, Kitzhaber vetoed another 43 bills. The governor had started vetoing bills in April, while legislators were still in session. His vetoes continued until Friday, August 15, the last day that he could nix legislation approved by lawmakers. An irritated Lynn Snodgrass, Republican House majority leader, said: "Dr. No's at it again. [Evidently] the governor does not consider the Legislature to be an equal and competent partner in governing this state." President Adams said the governor used the veto with "reckless abandon. It is clear that the governor is not interested in constructive change but only in protecting the status quo."[15]

Kitzhaber's vetoes included a bill to give the timber industry a $25 million cut in taxes and another to give $4.8 million in subsidies to the horse- and dog-racing business in Oregon. Kitzhaber also killed a bill to overturn Oregon's motorcycle helmet law, and he nixed three bills to weaken land-use laws.

Republicans fumed, yet the governor knew his vetoes weren't in jeopardy. It takes a vote of two-thirds of the members of both the Senate and House to overturn a veto, and Kitzhaber knew it was unlikely that nine House Democrats would join the 31 Republicans to overturn a veto.

Doctor-Assisted Suicide: Round 2

Oregon held a special statewide vote-by-mail election on November 4, 1997, with only Measures 51 and 52 on the ballot. Both had been referred by the 1997 Legislature. Measure 52 was the $150 million State Lottery Bond program to assist public school districts with purchases of books, computers, and other necessary equipment. The measure roused little interest or debate and passed by 805,700 to 293,400. Measure 51 was a very different story and stirred widespread debate and community activism. Measure 51 was a referendum on the repeal of doctor-assisted suicide.

The issue had first appeared on the Oregon ballot in 1994 as Measure 16, and was approved by a margin of 32,000 votes. The 1997 Republican Legislature referred the issue to a second vote, bowing to pressure from the Catholic Church and Oregon Right to Life—both of which adamantly opposed doctor-assisted suicide. Joining the effort to pass Measure 51 were the Oregon Medical Association and numerous organizations representing hospitals, hospice groups, and senior citizens. Senator Mark Hatfield favored the repeal and was an active spokesman for Measure 51. Heading the opposition to Measure 51 was the chief sponsor of the original Measure 16, Barbara Coombs Lee, a nurse and lawyer. To a lesser degree, Governor Kitzhaber, a physician, spoke out against Measure 51, reversing his earlier stance against Measure 16. Kitzhaber said: "The ballot is an inappropriate place for a debate on moral issues."[16] The sponsors of Measure 51 raised and spent over $4 million.* Money came from around the country, mostly from Catholic organizations. The Archdiocese of Portland contributed $340,000 and Oregon Right to Life groups gave over $400,000 to support the measure. The opponents raised $1 million. George Soros, a billionaire financier and backer of progressive causes, made a $250,000 donation to the "No on 51" committee.[17] Outspent 4-1, the "No on 51" committee appealed to voters by questioning the motives of GOP lawmakers and their unwillingness to abide

---

* Only twice had a group spent more on a ballot measure than did the 1997 supporters of measure 51. In 1992, Portland General Electric spent $4.9 million to defeat two measures to close the Trojan Nuclear Power plant; in 1996, tobacco companies spent $4.85 million to defeat Measure 44 to raise tobacco taxes to support expanding the Oregon Health Plan.

by the earlier will of the people when they approved Measure 16. Many voters disliked being second-guessed by the Republican Legislature and the conservative organizations backing Measure 51.

The measure attracted attention from both the national and international media. The issue of doctor-assisted suicide was being debated in the American press and there was extraordinary interest in what Oregonians decided on November 4. The outcome surprised everyone. Oregonians defeated Measure 51, 666,300 opposed to 445,000 in favor, and retained the option of physician-assisted suicide for the terminally ill. A Harris Poll revealed that 68% of Americans supported reforms like Oregon's Death with Dignity Act. Now it was up to the Clinton administration and the courts to thrash out the destiny of doctor-assisted suicide.* The Death with Dignity Law, with the approval of the U.S. Department of Justice, was fully implemented in Oregon in 1998. During its first seven years (through 2004), 208 Oregonians ended their lives by following the procedures established in Measures 16 and 51.

The 1998 May Primary

Most voters snoozed through Oregon's spring primary season: only 35% of registered voters (a record low) cast their ballots. Two state contests got most of the attention: the governor's race, featuring incumbent John Kitzhaber, and the U.S. Senate seat held by Democrat Ron Wyden.

Governor Kitzhaber was popular, raised lots of money, and he had a solid record to run on. The GOP had difficulty finding a credible candidate to challenge him. Governor Kitzhaber ran a low-key spring campaign. He spent $345,000 facing two token opponents in the Democratic primary—whom he steamrollered by a 12-1 margin. Four Republicans vied for their party's gubernatorial nomination. Two were unknowns. The others were a conservative Portland pastor, Walter Huss, and Bill Sizemore, director of Oregon Taxpayers United. Sizemore was well known through his work on Measure 47 in 1996. He campaigned throughout the state, raising and spending $200,000. He won the GOP primary, defeating Walter Huss by 68,000 votes (108,000 to 39,200). Bill Sizemore won 52% of the GOP vote in May. But 24% of Republicans left their ballots blank, rather than vote for any of the GOP candidates. So, in a

---

* In 2001, then-U.S. Attorney General John Ashcroft, acting with the encouragement of the Bush White House, tried to overturn the law by threatening to punish doctors who prescribed federally controlled drugs to help terminally ill patients to die. In January 2006 the U.S. Supreme Court, 6-3, voted to uphold Oregon's Death with Dignity Law, arguing that Ashcroft had over-reached his authority.

primary election with the lowest voter turnout ever, Bill Sizemore's unknown opponents took 48% of the vote.[18]

Most Oregonians didn't take Sizemore's candidacy seriously. To many, he was a political gadfly who couldn't be considered a serious threat to a polished and accomplished politician like John Kitzhaber. One commentator speculated that the Sizemore-Kitzhaber race "will get a lot of attention, simply because there are a lot of groups terrified of Bill Sizemore."[19] Among those with whom Sizemore had tangled were the Oregon Public Employees Union and the Oregon Education Association—two of Oregon's biggest and richest political organizations.

Senator Ron Wyden, who had completed the last half of the unexpired term of former Bob Packwood, was on the ballot again in May. He was considered a shoo-in for renomination and drew only one challenger: a retired Portland city parks supervisor. Wyden raised a pile of money, ignored his opponent, and won the nomination by an 11-1 margin. Ron Wyden was a formidable candidate. He had the prestige of incumbency and gobs of money.

Republican voters nominated an obscure state senator named John Lim. Most Oregonians sensed that John Lim posed no threat to Ron Wyden.

Molly Bordonaro won the Republican nomination in the 1st District. An attractive young woman and a persuasive public speaker, Bordonaro drew a lot of attention in Oregon and in Washington, D.C. Money poured into her campaign; she defeated her opponent, John Kvistad, 35,000 to 17,800. David Wu won the Democratic nomination, defeating activist Linda Peters 29,100 to 23,900.

Seven candidates ran for the 2nd District congressional seat held by the retiring Bob Smith. The 2nd District covers over two-thirds of Oregon's land mass, comprising 20 counties, including all of eastern Oregon as well as Jackson and Josephine counties in southern Oregon. Four Republicans vied for the GOP nomination. One was disgraced former Congressman Wes Cooley. The contest became a two-man race between Greg Walden, a former state representative, and Perry Atkinson, a conservative Christian radio commentator from southern Oregon. Compared to his opponent's, Walden's positions were moderate. Walden raised the most money, campaigned hard, and won the GOP nomination by 15,000 votes over Atkinson, 37,000 to 22,200. Wes Cooley trailed with 6,150 votes.

Three Democrats were in the race for their party's nomination. The winner, Kevin Campbell, knew the odds were against him, as only two Democrats had held the seat.

PACs, Lobbyists, and Oregon Politics

American politics went through severe stress and change in the 1990s. At all levels of government, from the White House and Congress down to state governorships, legislatures, cities, and counties, the quest for and the exercise of power were fundamentally changed. Groups of people who shared common values and concerns continued to organize for the purpose of promoting their interests. The political goal of an interest group is simple: try to influence public officials when they're making decisions. Part of an interest group's quest for power is the aim of electing candidates who share your group's beliefs and goals.

A major PAC active during Oregon's 1998 political season was the Oregon Victory PAC, which represented Republican business interests. The Oregon Victory PAC raised $256,500 between September 1997 and April 1998, funneling its funds into GOP legislative races. The same was true for the Oregon Restaurant Association's PAC, the Oregon Nurses PAC, the Credit Union Legislative Action Fund, or Impact Oregon, Inc., a PAC set up by U.S. Senator Gordon Smith to direct contributions into the campaigns of Republicans running for state office. Just prior to the May primary, the state's 15 biggest PACs raised $2.2 million— most of it earmarked for legislative candidates or for gubernatorial candidates Bill Sizemore and John Kitzhaber. There were, of course, hundreds of more PACs in Oregon that were also raising money to contribute to political candidates.[20] National PACs also channeled money into Oregon. Individuals could contribute directly to a candidate or PAC. In others words, the $2.2 million raised by Oregon's 15 biggest PACs for the May primary was only the tip of a very large iceberg.

One of the best indicators of how "politicized" Oregon had become was the presence of over 800 lobbyists who worked the 1997 Legislature, spending over $15.6 million. These lobbyists were either full-time employees of their interest group, citizen volunteers, or consultants hired for the purpose of influencing legislative actions. Almost every group you can think of is represented today at the State Capitol: lawyers, doctors, electricians, handicapped or disabled, senior citizens, environmental groups, restaurant owners, Indian tribes, insurance sales, homosexuals, taxpayers, cattlemen, Catholics, veterinarians, veterans, school children, college faculty, police officers, state employees, commercial fishermen, nurserymen, lumber companies, and on and on.

The Rise and Influence of the Christian Coalition

In the early 1980s, a new national interest group began to coalesce: the Christian Coalition. Religious organizations had long been politically active at all levels of government, but the Christian Coalition was different. Various conservative Protestant and Catholic Church groups came together with one aim: to gain political power to take control of Congress, the White House, and state governments—by first taking over the national Republican Party.

Since 1990, the Christian Coalition had earned a reputation as the most powerful force in Republican politics, with victories ranging from local school board elections to "helping ensure Bob Dole's presidential nomination in 1996. Under the high-visibility leadership of Ralph Reed, the executive director, donations increased by an average of 40% per year." Reed radically reshaped the Christian right by "thoroughly integrating religious conservatives into the machinery of the Republican Party. The Christian Coalition was to be the Republican equivalent of the AFL-CIO in the Democratic Party, with a permanent and prominent place at the table."[21] Televangelist Pat Robertson was chair of the Coalition board of directors. The Coalition raised $26 million in 1996, much of it going to the Dole campaign.

Ralph Reed left his job in July 1996 to start his own political consulting firm. Portlander Don Hodel, a former official in the Reagan administration, took over Reed's job. When Reed departed, the Coalition bickered within. They disagreed on the issue of political strategy: what was the best way to get Coalition-endorsed candidates elected? One particular Coalition policy caused great dissension within the GOP. If a moderate Republican held a political office, do you leave him/her alone? Or, do you try to unseat that person in order to elect a Coalition-backed candidate? Ralph Reed said "the problem for religious conservatives is a practical one: We can stop the Republican moderates from winning. But they can also stop us from winning. We need to de-emphasize the divisions, to be team players, not kamikaze pilots."[22] In the late 1990s, Republicans at both the state and national level asked themselves these questions: What do we need to do to elect Republicans to public office? Is it time to bury the hatchet, to end the feud between conservative and moderate Republicans? Shouldn't our priority be to defeat Democrats? Indeed, these are the central questions that the Republican Party wrestles with to this day.

Wanted, Dead or Alive: Moderate Republicans

Oregon's 1998 Republican primary turned into an ugly inter-party war with conservatives going after members of their party who were too moderate. Conservative Oregon Republican groups purged their party of moderates: State Senators Jeannette Hamby of Hillsboro and Ken Baker of Clackamas, and State Representatives Lynn Lundquist of Powell Butte (speaker of the House), and Chuck Carpenter of Washington County. Carpenter had rocked many boats for the previous two years. He sometimes voted with House Democrats and espoused causes not supported by the Oregon GOP. Carpenter, a gay Republican, had sponsored an anti-gay discrimination bill during the 1997 session. With Democratic backing and a handful of moderate Republicans, he got his bill passed by the House, but the Republican Senate killed it, sparking a public outcry from Carpenter, who called President Brady Adams "a party hack."

The Republican Party of Oregon was dominated by conservatives, many of whom were either members of the Christian Coalition or were sympathetic with that group's positions. Republican State Chair Deanna Smith, the wife of former congressman Denny Smith, was one of the most conservative Oregon political figures to hold office in the last half of the 20th century. Chuck Carpenter had a target on his back, but some of his positions found favor with more liberal groups, many affiliated with the Democratic Party. Consequently, Carpenter amassed $239,000 for his May 1998 primary campaign. Conservative groups came after Carpenter with guns blazing. Bill Witt, a well-to-do businessman and avowed Christian, challenged Chuck Carpenter in the GOP primary. Witt had twice been on the ballot as the GOP nominee for Congress in the 2nd District. The Witt-Carpenter campaign was a memorable one, with money pouring into the candidates' coffers. The campaign was ugly as Witt and Carpenter assaulted each other, trying to convince Republican voters that "the other guy is not worthy of your vote."

Polls said the Witt-Carpenter race was a toss-up. Voter turnout was low, which probably hurt Carpenter more than it did Witt. With no Democratic opponent, the winner of the GOP primary would be the next state representative from the 7th House District. The returns came in slowly and the race seesawed back and forth. Final returns weren't announced until late in the week: Bill Witt had defeated fellow Republican Chuck Carpenter 3,375 to Carpenter's 3,329. A recount didn't change the outcome. The conservative campaign against a party moderate had succeeded.

GOP moderate Sen. Jeannette Hamby was in a similar battle with Charles Starr, one of the most conservative members of the Oregon House. A vocal Christian, Starr was a tough campaigner and his charge that Hamby was too liberal for the Hillsboro area resonated with many Republicans. Hamby had served in the legislature since 1981 and was widely respected for her intelligence, fairness, and good sense. None of it mattered. Charles Starr won the GOP Senate nomination 5,400 to Hamby's 3,500 votes.

Senator Ken Baker's district encompassed Clackamas County and part of Multnomah County. Another target of conservative Republicans, Baker was a moderate-conservative. Party conservatives backed former Rep. Jerry Grisham of Oregon City against him. Grisham's legislative record was somewhat more conservative than Baker's. Jerry Grisham defeated Ken Baker 4,750 to 3,500. Democrats nominated former Portland TV newscaster Rick Metsger to face Grisham. Veteran GOP Senator Tom Hartung (from Washington County) wondered if Grisham's conservative positions would assure a Metsger victory.

The last featured internecine battle among Republicans occurred in Central Oregon's House District 59. Conservatives wanted Republican House Speaker Lynn Lundquist out. The moderate Lundquist had worked with the Democratic caucus and Governor Kitzhaber during the 1997 session, infuriating the Republican right-wing. Millionaire businessman Mark Hemstreet, owner of the Shilo Inn motel chain, had been a major contributor to conservative Republican candidates in 1994 and 1996, giving at least $670,000 in these two elections. On March 27, 1998, Mark Hemstreet hosted a $50-a-plate fundraiser for conservative GOP contenders challenging incumbent Republicans that were considered too liberal. He supported Jerry Grisham and Charles Starr against incumbents Sen. Ken Baker and Sen. Jeannette Hamby. "Hemstreet [expressed] his desire to topple House Speaker Lynn Lundquist. 'I believe that Lynn Lundquist should be representing liberal Democrats, not claiming to be a conservative Republican.'" In the May primary, Hemstreet financed Grant County rancher Tan Hermens, Lundquist's challenger. He didn't say how much he planned to spend.[23] Yet Lundquist prevailed, defeating his opponent 4,100 votes to 2,550 and carrying all eight counties in the district. No Democrat filed for the office and Lynn Lundquist would return to the house for a third term in 1999.

In February, as Oregon's primary campaign season heated up, Rep. Bob Jenson, the only Democrat representing a district east of the Cascades, announced he was leaving his party to run as an independent. Democratic leaders were appalled since they had been chipping away for several years at the Republicans' hold on the Oregon House. Democrats had been optimistic that 1998 would see them win the two or three additional seats necessary for a 31-vote House majority.* It was a costly, frustrating situation for Democrats—who now had 28 House seats.

---

* Jenson's departure was the third time in the 1990s this happened (Kevin Mannix and Tom Brian both left the Democratic Party to become Republicans).

Turn Off the Spigot!

In November 1994, Oregonians had overwhelmingly passed Measure 9 to set spending limits on political campaigns.* The law was quickly challenged in the courts. In February 1997, the Oregon Supreme Court had ruled that the limits were unconstitutional because they violated the free-speech rights of Oregonians. Yet the court left certain incentives intact. If a candidate agreed to impose spending limits on his or her own campaign, this would be noted in the *Voters' Pamphlet*. Candidates agreeing to limit spending could promise contributors a $50 state tax credit for individuals and $100 for joint filers. Limits for the general election were $40,000 per nominee for a House contest, and $60,000 per nominee for a Senate seat. Not all candidates agreed to the spending limitations. The more competitive the race, the less likely candidates were to agree to the limitations. The Washington County House contest between Republicans Bill Witt and incumbent Chuck Carpenter—a race that cost over $400,000—was a classic example. The issue of costly political campaigns was on the mind of voters during the 1998 political season. Since some candidates tried to honor their pledge to live within the established limits, while others ignored them (by not pledging to limit their spending), most voters just ended up confused. The public liked the idea of less-expensive campaigns. The reality was that some races were more important than others, and scores of PACs wanted to pump their money into campaigns where they thought their candidates had the best chances of winning.

While the heat of the May primary cooled, various interest groups and their PACs busily prepared their pet ballot measures for the November election. With their backers having spent over $2 million gathering signatures, by mid-July 14 measures were ready for the ballot.

Yawn, Yawn, Yawn

Oregonians were not very interested in the fall political season. The state's two key contests were so lopsided in favor of the Democratic incumbents, Gov. John Kitzhaber and Senator Ron Wyden, that most voters paid them little heed.† Governor Kitzhaber's campaign manager said that "the more people know about Sizemore, the lower his vote total gets."[24] With the election three weeks away, these two high-profile races appeared to be over. But there were several

---

* An individual could contribute only $100 to a legislative candidate and $500 to a candidate for statewide office.

† One poll indicated that 44% of Republicans said they were supporting Kitzhaber over Sizemore, while only 37% said they were behind John Lim in his Senate race with Ron Wyden.

contests that did arouse public interest. And there were 14 ballot measures to lure voters into the campaign. At least $14 million had already been raised for the various campaigns by late September, most on behalf of the ballot measures, the contest for governor, and the congressional races.

Voter turnout in November improved dramatically over the May vote. About 60% of registered voters cast ballots in the general election, compared to 35% in May. Republican turnout was 66%, while 63% of Democrats and 41% of independents voted.

Kitzhaber's Landslide and Ron Wyden, Again

As expected, Democratic Gov. John Kitzhaber was reelected on November 3. He campaigned on a detailed agenda he called The Oregon Challenge, which focused on the issues of education, juvenile crime prevention, and protecting Oregon's unique quality of life. Republican Bill Sizemore focused his campaign on his usual issues; no new taxes, leaner government, reform of land-use laws, and mandatory sentencing for violent and repeat criminals. John Kitzhaber took 65% of the vote, 717,000 to 334,000 for Sizemore. The governor outspent his GOP foe, $840,000 to $375,000. Combined, the Kitzhaber-Sizemore contest cost over $1.2 million. Bill Sizemore's conservative positions didn't play well with the majority of Oregonians. Compared to John Kitzhaber's leadership abilities and experience, Sizemore (who'd never held a public office) was also seen as too inexperienced.

Senator Ron Wyden, seeking his first full term, had no difficulty defeating his Republican opponent, State Senator John Lim. Wyden's victory margin was 61% to 34%, 682,400 to 377,700, and he carried all 36 Oregon counties.

Congressional Races

The campaign for the 1st District U.S. House seat was a nail-biter. Incumbent Elizabeth Furse had retired, leaving the seat open. Republican Molly Bordonaro faced Portland attorney David Wu in November. Wu was new to politics and unknown to most voters. He made up ground fast, however, as he got lots of help and money from both the state and national Democratic Party. Bordonaro was a polished speaker, well prepared and persuasive. The election returns swung back and forth for several days. Finally, Wu emerged with a narrow victory, 120,000 to 112,800 for Bordonaro.

Voters in the huge 2nd District elected a new congressman in November: Republican Greg Walden. Democrat Earl Blumenauer won another term in the 3rd District. Democrat Peter DeFazio had become a political institution in southwest Oregon; he easily won a sixth term in 1998. As usual, the Republican Party had been hard-pressed to find a candidate formidable enough to challenge DeFazio. Congresswoman Darlene Hooley was seeking a second term in the 5th District; her opponent, State Senator Marylin Shannon, was a conservative Republican. Hooley's middle-of-the-road positions played well in Marion and Clackamas counties—where more than half of district's voters lived. Hooley defeated Marylin Shannon by 33,000 votes, 125,000 to 92,200.

Which Party Will Control the Next Legislature?

Democrats picked up three seats in the Oregon Senate in 1998. As a result, the 20-10 Republican majority in 1997 was reduced to 17-13 for 1999-2001. Jerry Grisham, a social conservative, lost to Democrat Rick Metsger in District 14, 21,800 to 16,900. Legislative veterans Democrat Clifford Trow of Corvallis and Republican Lenn Hannon of Ashland, won record seventh consecutive terms in the Senate.

Republicans increased their House majority in November to 34-25 (Rep. Bob Jenson was an independent). The strong Democratic minority of 29 in 1997 vanished. The November election featured two very close House races. In District 25, the Republican incumbent, Jane Lokan, a 77-year-old moderate, squeaked to a 100-vote victory over her Democratic challenger, Tom Civiletti, 8,357 to 8,257. In Salem, Democrat George Bell lost a tough race to incumbent Republican Kevin Mannix by 385 votes.

The Ballot Measures

Measure 67 was one of the most controversial and hotly debated questions on the November ballot. The measure would allow people who'd been diagnosed with cancer, AIDS, glaucoma, and other serious illnesses the legal authority to grow and smoke marijuana. A Southern California-based group called Americans for Medical Rights bank-rolled by billionaire George Soros was the primary financial backer of the measure. Measure 67 clashed with Measure 57, which made possessing less than an ounce of marijuana a misdemeanor, punishable by a maximum 30 days in jail and a $1,000 fine. Conservative Republicans (including Bill Sizemore) were behind Measure 57, while more liberal groups pushed Measure 67. Oregonians voted an emphatic "no" on Measure 57: 737,000 to 372,000 "yes." Voters approved Measure 67 by 611,000 to 508,000.

Measure 66 was a constitutional amendment to allow 15% of State Lottery profits to be spent equally on state parks and on protecting streams and wildlife habitat—issues the 1997 Legislature had failed to address. Led by the Nature

Conservancy's $58,300 contribution, backers raised nearly $282,000 for their campaign. Voters passed it by 380,000 votes, 742,000 to 362,200. Another political/governmental milestone occurred in November when Oregonians overwhelmingly approved Measure 60 to conduct all primary and general elections by mail ballot. The state had been experimenting with mail balloting for several years and most voters had grown fond of the convenience. Oregon became the first state to institute vote-by-mail: 757,200 favored Measure 60 and 334,000 opposed it.

Lynn Out, Lynn In

The Republican House caucus met on Monday night, November 9, to elect a speaker for the 1999 session. Speaker Lynn Lundquist was seeking a second term, opposed by Majority Leader Lynn Snodgrass of Boring. Snodgrass, a social conservative, had repeatedly locked horns with Speaker Lundquist over what direction the GOP agenda should take. After four ballots, neither Lynn could muster the 31 votes needed for election. Then three other Republicans made unsuccessful bids for the position. After twelve grueling hours, the Snodgrass Lynn defeated the Lundquist Lynn.[25] Another moderate Republican had been ousted by a conservative Republican. Would Snodgrass, the second Republican woman elected speaker, be able to hold together a fractious caucus? Would GOP divisions play to Democratic Gov. John Kitzhaber's advantage? Were there enough moderate Republicans who would occasionally vote with minority Democrats to form a 31-vote majority?

A week before Oregon's 70th Legislature convened, Gov. John Kitzhaber announced that he was going to sign an executive order designed to save every salmon run in Oregon, expanding his Oregon Plan, which had focused on coastal coho salmon and lower Columbia River steelhead. The Oregon Plan had been proposed as a way to prevent the federal government from listing Oregon salmon as endangered species. Kitzhaber was attempting to find an Oregon solution to rapidly falling numbers of native salmon before the federal government stepped in and told Oregon what to do and how to do it.[26]

The 1999 Oregon Legislature convened on January 11 at 10:30 a.m. in Salem. Senators joined representatives in the House chamber to witness the swearing-in of Governor Kitzhaber and to hear his inaugural address. The governor, dressed in his blue jeans, leather belt with large oval buckle, cowboy boots, white dress-shirt, tie, and dark jacket, delivered a ten-minute address. Kitzhaber scanned the audience. Twenty-five of the 60 House members were new. Three new senators were familiar faces: Democrats Tony Corcoran, Roger

Beyer, and Peter Courtney, because of term-limits, had been forced out of their House seats, and, subsequently, had run for and won seats in the Senate. Jackie Winters, a freshman representative from Salem, was the first Republican African American in state history to be elected to the legislature. The 1999 Legislature included 27 women—a record number. "Women make up 30% of the Oregon Legislature this year, a 10% increase over the last five sessions and a big increase over the 22% average nationwide."[27]

Kitzhaber's address focused on the importance of Republicans and Democrats working together in a genuine spirit of bipartisanship. He urged lawmakers to consider the importance of community as they went about their duties, and to guard against the bitter partisanship that was threatening the American presidency and eroding public confidence in government. In their inaugural remarks, Senate President Brady Adams and new House Speaker Lynn Snodgrass echoed Kitzhaber's plea for civility and bipartisanship. Unfortunately, these calls for more harmony lasted about as long as it took for the House chamber to empty after the ceremonies.

Governor Kitzhaber proposed a biennial budget of $10.7 billion for 1999-2001. He recommended that $4.6 billion of the budget pay the state's share of public education, K-12. Senate President Brady Adams suggested a budget very similar to Kitzhaber's, and agreed with the governor's $4.6 billion figure for schools. Speaker Snodgrass was more cautious, and suggested hammering out the education budget by late March.

There were other issues that threatened to undercut any chance of bipartisanship. Among these were Brady Adams' call for a tax cut amounting to $170 million, though he admitted that "there's a good probability that [we'll] have a declining revenue coming in."[28] Other hot-button issues were: a proposal for a 6¢-a-gallon gas tax increase along with a 33% increase in vehicle registration fees; parental notification when a young woman under 18 intended to have an abortion; charter schools; a possible push by social conservatives to overturn a recent appeals court ruling requiring state and local governments to offer health benefits to the domestic partners of gays and lesbians; scaling back the Oregon Health Plan; Kitzhaber's proposed $30 million program to combat juvenile crime; increased funding for public schools; a projected $26.7 million budget shortfall in the Portland School District and what, if anything, the legislature ought to do about it; adding more state police positions; siting of a proposed new women's prison in the Willamette Valley; and, finally, the issue of gun-control legislation. This latter issue, along with Governor Kitzhaber's juvenile crime package, was fresh on everyone's mind because of the May 1998 Thurston High School shooting in which a 15-year-old student named Kipland Kinkel took a rifle to school and killed two students—after murdering his parents in their family home. Some observers predicted a long, difficult, session ahead.

$$$ for Schools

On Monday, March 15, Kitzhaber announced his intention to be more proactive in seeking money for schools and more revenue for the state. Chair of the House Revenue Committee Republican Ken Strobeck noted that House Republicans had already gone beyond the governor's proposed $4.6 billion education budget. The governor then proposed $4.95 billion. Democrats were delighted. Speaker Lynn Snodgrass and GOP leaders said that they were looking at an education budget closer to $4.72 billion. Meanwhile, a coalition of parents and educators was pushing for an education budget of $5.16 billion. As the weeks passed, it appeared that a compromise figure between $4.72 billion and $5.16 billion would be the likely outcome of budget talks.

On Wednesday, March 24, Lynn Lundquist, chair of the Ways and Means Education Subcommittee, held a dramatic press conference. In a show of solidarity, the other eight subcommittee members stood with him. An ardent supporter of increased funding for public schools, Lundquist denounced his Republican caucus for holding the education budget in limbo and defiantly insisted that his committee was ready to pass out a $4.96 billion education budget. By insisting that Republicans support a higher figure for schools, Lundquist was suggesting that the GOP caucus was short-changing Oregon's school children. Speaker Lynn Snodgrass was not amused. To the speaker, Lundquist's press conference was a poke in the eye, and she acted quickly. The next day, the speaker removed Lundquist from the two committees on which he sat, removing any political clout the former speaker had. Capitol watchers wondered where Lundquist's demotion would lead. Would the uneasy truce between GOP conservatives and moderates hold together?

Locking Horns: Kitzhaber and the Republicans

In mid-April, Kitzhaber vetoed his first bill of the 1999 session—to be followed by 68 more vetoes, a record. Kitzhaber warned Republican leaders he'd veto any budget bill that exceeded his recommended spending levels. "And he also oppos[ed] a Republican charter school proposal, a prison siting bill, allowing adults to ride motorcycles without helmets, and changes to the minimum wage and family leave acts."[29]

Republican leaders criticized "Dr. No" for his inflexible and "autocratic" tendencies. Senate Majority Leader Gene Derfler said the governor was a poor communicator who had little respect for the legislature. But the governor had GOP leaders right where he wanted them: wary of his potential veto and aware that they had better work with him, otherwise every Republican-backed bill was in jeopardy. Columnist Richard Aguirre wrote: "The irony of the conflict is that Kitzhaber and Republican leaders seem more alike than they would like to admit: stubborn, clumsy at rallying public support, uncomfortable courting the news media and supremely self-confident."[30] Republican Kevin Mannix said the conflict between the governor and the Republican Legislature arose from deep philosophical differences and unwillingness on both sides to compromise. Kitzhaber and GOP leaders in the House and Senate were like two barnyard bulls, horns locked, heels dug in, pushing back and forth, unwilling to concede any ground to the other. And so the session ground on.

Snodgrass Backpedals

On Monday, May 17, the House Republican majority fractured over the issue of how much money to commit to public schools for 1999-2001. Speaker Lynn Snodgrass had scheduled a House vote on her caucus's $ 4.725 billion education bill. But she was forced to delay the vote at the last minute when the GOP caucus fractured. Five more Republicans announced that they wanted $4.96 billion for schools—the amount preferred by Governor Kitzhaber and Senate Republicans. It was clear to legislators that both sides would have to compromise. But a month later, budget negotiations had broken down. "Republicans and Democrats are so far apart on key budget issues that they have appointed a 19-member committee to meet privately. They even hired an outside facilitator at $1,200 a day to help them find agreement. The GOP leadership didn't produce a budget plan until Tuesday [June 15], despite already having approved some agency budgets. Neither the Republicans' budget nor Democratic Gov. John Kitzhaber's has the votes to pass the full Legislature unaltered."[31]

When a compromise was finally reached, neither side was happy. Public schools would get $4.81 billion in 1999-2001, a 10% increase. Oregon's public universities also got a huge infusion of cash, as the Higher Education budget was increased by over $500 million. One result would be a freeze on further tuition hikes.

What the 70th Legislature Accomplished

For once, an Oregon legislature did not end its session in the middle of the night.

The 70th Legislature adjourned at 3:15 on Saturday afternoon, July 24, 1999. The typical political intrigues, last-minute maneuvering, and arm-twisting went on as usual. House Republicans were especially active in the waning hours. The House passed a 5¢ per gallon gas tax increase—after defeating the bill twice in the previous two days. The three previous GOP legislatures had refused to pass a gas tax increase. Last-minute additions were made to the Human Resources budget including a controversial add-on to the Oregon Health Plan; $2.8 million was included for abortion and assisted-suicide programs—the result of efforts by Kitzhaber, Democrats, and moderate Republicans to push this money through the legislative labyrinth.

The 1999 Legislative Assembly had been dominated by: intense political bickering; crossed swords between Democratic Gov. John Kitzhaber and Republican House and Senate leaders (including the ever-present threat of the governor's veto): the presence of a large number of inexperienced lawmakers; and tight control of both chambers by conservative Republican leaders. The session lasted six and a half months, or 195 working days.

The media and most political analysts criticized the assembly for wallowing in partisanship, indecision, lack of vision, and its failure to tackle Oregon's most pressing problems including: stable funding for public education; fundamental reform of Oregon's tax system; environmental protection; health care; juvenile crime; and alcohol and drug abuse. Missed opportunities, critics called it.

Salem's *Statesman Journal* branded the session as "mediocre and irresponsible, a session mired in partisanship, a session with no major accomplishments, a Legislature with a miserable record."[32] Senate President Brady Adams conceded that he "counted GOP victories more by what he prevented than what he accomplished. Republicans slowed the growth of state government, Adams said, and they fended off Democratic pressure to raise taxes, except for a nickel-a-gallon gas tax hike."[33]

Social conservatives failed to pass most of their agenda into law. Among the GOP failures were attempts to bar legal marriage by gays, a requirement that parents be notified before their teenage daughter could get an abortion, and their goal to omit funding for abortion and assisted-suicide services through the Oregon Health Plan. GOP lawmakers had proposed dozens of tax breaks and tax cuts for various interest groups which would have lopped hundreds of millions of dollars from state revenues.

The state police budget included funds to pay for a hundred more troopers to patrol state highways. The legislature approved $20 million for Kitzhaber's youth crime-prevention program for at-risk and potentially violent teens.

Intense lobbying by city and county government officials had much to do with the bill's passage. A Republican bill to repeal Oregon's mandatory motorcycle helmet law for riders age 21 and older was defeated by one vote in the Senate, after passing the House 36-24. A bill to prohibit talking on a cellular phone while driving a vehicle died in the Senate.

House Bill 2581 was that rare measure passed by a unanimous vote in both the House and Senate—and signed by Governor Kitzhaber. The bill required insurance companies to provide coverage for prenatal and hospital childbirth care for dependent teens.

The Republican Legislature referred 21 ballot measures to the statewide elections of November 1999 and May and November 2000 and drew harsh criticism in the press for it. These 21 measures were just short of the 23 referred by the legislature in the previous 40 years combined. GOP leaders did an end-run around the governor's veto, passing controversial resolutions that didn't require the governor's signature and sending them directly to the people for a vote. Many of these GOP referendums were in the form of amendments to the Oregon Constitution. The avalanche of Republican measures drew a caustic response from Democrat Phil Keisling, Oregon's secretary of state, who said that the Oregon Constitution "is being turned into a cork-board with thumb-tacks and Post-It notes attached."[34] The *Statesman Journal* called this legislative trend irresponsible, as buck-passing. Some Oregonians grumbled that the $1.2 million for printing and mailing extra thick *Voters' Pamphlets* could be better spent on schools, hungry children, or on foster care.

Brady Adams and other Republican leaders had entered the 1999 session with a goal of reducing the size, cost, and clout of state government. Ironically, the GOP Legislature passed a record 1,169 bills and 205 resolutions and joint memorials in 1999.

The 1999 Legislature increased the state's General Fund Budget by $1.3 billion—from $9.35 billion (1997-99) to $10.64 billion for 1999-2001. A still-healthy Oregon economy and record personal income tax revenues allowed lawmakers to continue pumping more money into public education, universities, human resources, and the Oregon Health Plan. But there were warning clouds on the horizon: was Oregon in store for an economic downturn?

Dr. No: Round 3

On Friday, September 3, Gov. John Kitzhaber announced his vetoes of 25 more bills passed by the 1999 Republican Legislature. Added to the bills he had earlier vetoed, Kitzhaber had set a record of 69 vetoes. In announcing his last batch of vetoes, Kitzhaber claimed Republican leaders had played political games by enacting bills that they knew would never pass muster with him. Senate Majority Leader Gene Derfler faulted Kitzhaber for not doing more to improve his communication with Republican legislative leaders. Derfler asked: "Why blame somebody else for his inability to communicate with us?"[35]

Among Kitzhaber's vetoes were: Speaker Lynn Snodgrass's bill to require a doctor to notify parents before performing an abortion on a teenage girl; a bill to increase the speed limit on rural highways to 75 from 70 miles per hour; and a bill that would have prohibited counties and cities from suing gun manufacturers and dealers. In all, the governor vetoed 164 mostly Republican bills passed by the 1995, 1997, and 1999 GOP legislatures. Most of his vetoes, said Kitzhaber, reflected the deep philosophical differences which existed between Oregon Democrats and a Republican Party dominated by social conservatives. As long as John Kitzhaber was in office, Republican leaders should expect to make a convincing case for every bill they enacted to avoid the governor's veto pen.

Keisling Resigns

On Wednesday, September 22, 1999, Phil Keisling, Oregon's longtime secretary of state, announced that he would resign, effective November 8. Keisling had been appointed to the office in January 1991 by Gov. Barbara Roberts. He had won four-year terms in 1992 and 1996. He was widely respected for his abilities and accomplishments, and many lamented his departure from state government. During his tenure as secretary Oregon had adopted vote-by-mail in 1998, Keisling being the most vocal champion of this reform. He had won plaudits for streamlining how his office worked, making important changes in the Audits, Corporation, and Archives divisions, all of which are part of the office of secretary of state. He also converted the Elections Division to a fully computerized system. Secretary Keisling had most recently worked with lawmakers to propose reforms in Oregon's initiative system, believing that it should be harder for petitioners to get their measures on the Oregon ballot, and more difficult to amend the state constitution. Governor Kitzhaber surprised many people when he appointed Democrat Bill Bradbury secretary of state.

No Friend of Assisted Suicide

The Republican-controlled U.S. House of Representatives voted on Wednesday, October 27, to overturn Oregon's doctor-assisted suicide law. By a vote of 276 to 156, the House passed what it called the Pain Relief Promotion Act of 1999. The bill "would amend the Controlled Substance Act to prohibit the use of federally controlled drugs, such as morphine and sedatives, for assisted suicide. Doctors convicted for violating the law could lose their licenses to prescribe medication and face up to twenty years in federal prison."[36] The House vote prolonged the tug-of-war between the federal government and the state of Oregon over the issue. Would the U.S. Senate go along with the House? If it did, would President Bill Clinton sign or veto such a bill? Meanwhile, the House action did not stop terminally ill Oregonians from exercising their right to end their lives by ingesting a doctor-prescribed drug. This titanic struggle between Oregon and the federal government would go on for another six years, until January 2006—when the Supreme Court of the United States, in a 6-3 vote, upheld Oregon's assisted suicide law.

Looking Forward to a New Century and Millennium

Most Oregonians were happy to bid goodbye to the rocky decade of the 1990s and the 20th century. Dynamic change and the stresses associated with it had shaped the lives of Oregonians in new ways. Oregon had grown by nearly half a million people since 1990. Metropolitan Portland boomed, and the sprawl of suburban communities like Beaverton, Hillsboro, Gresham, and West Linn/Wilsonville extended into Clackamas and Washington counties. The arrival of Intel Corporation in Washington County in 1976 had sparked a high-tech boom unlike anything Oregon had ever seen. Salem/Keizer and Eugene/Springfield evolved into metropolitan regions with populations of over 300,000.

Oregonians had voted to change the way they paid for their public schools. Indeed, no event stands out more from the last decade of the 20th century than the decision to pass Measure 5 in 1990, establishing a limit on local property tax rates. For over 25 years Oregonians had told their political leaders that property taxes were too high. Governors and legislatures had wrestled with the problem, passing homeowner/renter property tax relief programs, and beefing up the state's Basic School Support fund.

The passage of Measure 5, and, later, Measure 11 (relating to tougher sentencing laws for felony crimes) caused fundamental changes in what Oregonians wanted out of their state government. Voters decided they would rather have most of the cost of public schools and community colleges come out of the state general fund budget—rather than out of the pockets of local property taxpayers. Because of Measure 11, Oregon continued building more prisons—with the result that the legislature had to shift billions more dollars into the Corrections budget, taking money away from other programs.

Oregonians adopted term limits for state officeholders in 1992. As a result, the Oregon Legislature went through considerable upheaval in the 1997 and 1999 sessions with longtime legislators denied further time in office. Years of experience and expertise were replaced by rookie lawmakers, most of them unfamiliar with the workings of state government. Oregon's growing interest groups stepped into this legislative vacuum along with their lobbyists, PACs, and millions of campaign dollars.

The 1990s heightened the glaring disparities between Oregonians who lived in the eastern two-thirds of the state and those who lived west of the Cascade Range. Less than one in five new residents who moved here, settled in eastern Oregon. Most of the best new jobs and economic opportunities followed these newcomers into the Willamette Valley: with Hewlett-Packard into Corvallis, with Intel into Washington County, and with Oregon Health Sciences University (OHSU) into metropolitan Portland. Except for the booming Bend area of Central Oregon, economically speaking most of Eastern Oregon remained off the beaten path in the 1990s. Yet some of Oregon's most powerful political leaders came from east of the Cascades, including House Speakers Bev Clarno (1995), Lynn Lundquist (1997), and Mark Simmons (2001), and Senate President Gordon Smith (1995).

Steady population growth in the 1990s added to Oregon's infrastructure woes. Public schools were crowded, as were universities, prisons, jails, and various hospitals. Oregon's roads and bridges were inadequate and deteriorating—due to age, delayed maintenance, and heavy use. And Oregon's population, like the nation's, continued to age, as the Baby Boomer generation moved into their fifties. The percentage of Oregon children living in poverty climbed from 14% in 1990 to 16% in 1998. Twelve of every 100 children in Oregon were known victims of abuse or neglect. The state's expensive foster-care program struggled to keep up with the demand to place thousands of children in alternative care. The methamphetamine drug epidemic swept into Oregon in the late 1990s and added to the foster-care crisis, as well as to other new pressures on community services, particularly on police forces, jails, and courts.

Oregon was leaving a troubling decade and dynamic century behind. Many longtime Oregonians were wary of the future, concerned about the deterioration of the state's quality of life. Environmental degradation was obvious to everyone. Crowded suburbs gobbled up thousands of acres of prime farmland. And 300,000 new commuters and thousands of heavy trucks clogged roads and highways, polluting the air with their emissions and relentless noise.

As concerned as most Oregonians were about their deteriorating natural environment, another issue stood, glaringly, head and shoulders above the rest: what would be the fate of Oregon's declining public school system? Many wondered how long Oregon could hold on, balancing quality-of-life issues against the fact that the legislature was having a harder and harder time coming up with the money to pay for even the most basic government services. Where would the 21st century take Oregon?

Chapter 21
Into the Future, 2000-11

"What is real is the future. And it is a future in which we—as individuals and as Americans—can achieve great things . . . Nothing like us ever was."

—*The Oregonian*, January 1, 2000

January 1, 2000: The Dawn of a New Millennium

People around the globe had been preparing for months for the new millennium. The 20th century was ending and, with it, the second millennium. A new century and a new thousand-year age was upon us. More than a million New Yorkers crammed into Times Square to welcome the new millennium. In Portland, 25,000 Oregonians squeezed into Pioneer Courthouse Square to celebrate the New Year.[1] For one day, at least, people everywhere were focused on the future and the promise of a better world.

Oregon was leaving one of the most dynamic decades in its history. Oregon's population was 3.28 million on January 1.* The state economy had undergone fundamental change. Oregon's high-tech industries had boomed, adding tens of thousands of new jobs and fostering dozens of tiny spin-off companies. Intel Corporation employed 14,750 Oregonians, while Nike provided 5,000 Oregon jobs out of a work force of 18,500. Thousands of more acres of farmland were covered by housing and industrial subdivisions, as suburbs crept 20 miles out in all directions from downtown Portland.

---

* Thirteen percent (439,000) of the population was sixty-five or older, while 823,000 (25%) were seventeen and under. A baby was born in Oregon every twelve minutes and someone died every eighteen minutes. Over 9,200 adults were incarcerated in Oregon's prisons. One in four Oregon adults was functionally illiterate. One in eight lived in poverty. 6,400 Oregon children were in foster care. And, nationally Oregon was forty-ninth in church attendance.

Exhausted Voters

One of the last things Oregonians had on their minds in January 2000 was that another political season was underway. In February, New Hampshire and Iowa would hold their presidential preference primaries. Oregon's primary was May 16, five months away. There was more controversy ahead: 32 measures were on the May and November ballots. Voter fatigue had set in.

Heading the May ballot were the presidential primaries, but both the Republican and Democratic presidential nominees were known weeks before the Oregon primary. Texas Gov. George W. Bush had locked up the GOP nomination and Vice Pres. Albert (Al) Gore, Jr. was the Democrats' choice. Consequently, Oregon's primary was humdrum.

Focus on Legislative Elections

Who would control the 2001 Legislature? Would Democratic Gov. John Kitzhaber face another GOP Legislature? Democrats knew their best chance was to gain control of the Senate, where they currently held 13 of the 30 seats. Fifteen Senate seats were up for election in 2000, only four of which were held by Democrats. Senate Majority Leader Gene Derfler, a Salem Republican, was in charge of the GOP Senate campaign. Derfler had only one session left before he would be forced out of office by Oregon's term limit law. And he wanted to be the next president of the Oregon Senate.

The Kitzhabers and Sen. Ron Wyden raised money to help Democrats running for the legislature. Republican Sen. Gordon Smith had funneled tens of thousands of dollars into Republican coffers since 1998. Political consultants predicted that the legislative races of 2000 would be the most expensive ever.

Candidates for the legislature spent over $4 million in May. Thirty would-be senators spent $1.4 million, while 153 House candidates shelled out $2.63 million. But this was a pittance compared to what candidates would spend in November.

Oregon's May 16 primary was the first of its kind in American history. Never before had a state conducted an all-mail-voting primary. Elections officials were delighted with the 51% turnout, the highest since 1988. Oregonians looked forward to America's first all-mail general election in November.

Poverty in Oregon

The Oregon Center for Public Policy issued a troubling report in early September 2000. The center's report noted that "the typical Oregon worker is no better off than ten or twenty years ago." Regardless of economic growth and government assistance (including welfare reform), over the last 20 years "Oregon's poverty rate has fluctuated between 10-14%." More than one in seven working families with children was poor. More than one in nine of all working households in Oregon sometimes ran short of food. The richest fifth of Oregon families held 38% of all income in the late 1970s; by the late 1990s that had increased to 48%. Low-paying jobs had increased.* The report could have been written in Martian. Except for a few newspaper editorials, no notice was taken of the poverty report. It never became an issue in the November general election. Not until the 2002 gubernatorial campaign was poverty raised as a political issue by Democrat Ted Kulongoski. Perhaps his personal history as an abandoned child growing up in an orphanage had sensitized him to what it is like to be poor.

The Fall Campaign of 2000

Most Oregonians put off thinking about the November 7 election as long as they could. There were 26 measures to consider. Not since 1914 had Oregonians voted on so many measures at one time; a handful of them aroused strong emotions. Eighteen measures came to the ballot via initiative petition, seven were legislative referrals, and one was a citizen referral of a law passed by the legislature. Petition sponsors spent $3 million to get their initiatives on the ballot. Seven measures were sponsored by Oregon Taxpayers United and led by the group's founder, Frank Eisenzimmer or by Bill Sizemore, the OTU's executive director. Lon Mabon and the Oregon Citizens Alliance (OCA) were also back on the ballot—with Measure 9, which would make it illegal for schools to encourage, promote, or sanction homosexuality. Other measures were sponsored by some of Oregon's biggest and richest interest groups including the Oregon Education Association (Measure 1, to ensure that schools were adequately funded); the Oregon Public Employees Union (Measure 99, to provide home care services); the League of Women Voters (Measure 6, to provide public funding to candidates who limit spending); and the Oregon Association of Hospital and Health Systems (Measure 4, to dedicate proceeds from the tobacco settlement to low-income health care). International businessman and billionaire, George Soros, was sponsor of Measure 3 (to prohibit forfeiture without conviction).

---

* In 1978, 30% of jobs in Oregon were classified as low paying; in 1998 it was 35%. Since the late 1980s the poverty rate had gone from 9.7 to 15.2%. Unions, which traditionally fought for higher wages, had lost clout. Oregon's rapidly growing high-tech industry was largely non-union and the number of part-time and temporary workers was on the rise. Employers passed more health insurance costs on to workers and cut back on pension benefits. There was also "a steady decline in manufacturing jobs, especially in the timber industry, and an increase in service sector jobs, including everyone from stockbrokers to movie theater ticket-takers."[2]

Many of these organizations were bitter political enemies—and they would spend as much money as they could to defeat each others' measures. There was simply no way to be a conscientious voter in Oregon without being drawn into the power struggles that characterized the fall campaign of 2000.

On September 3, the *Oregonian* set the tone for the campaign in a scathing editorial against Measures 8, 9, 91, and 93. These measures were sponsored, in order, by anti-tax activist Don McIntire, the OCA, and by OTU. *Oregonian* editors called these measures "monumentally bad, monumentally destructive." Measure 9 was called "a poisonous, hateful thing aimed at intimidating and stigmatizing one group of Oregon citizens. These measures offer a dark, ignoble vision of Oregon's future that community-minded voters should reject."[3] The ensuing campaign turned out to be one of Oregon's most gut-wrenching.

Who's In, Who's Out?

Some of the most fiercely fought campaigns in fall 2000 were for seats in the Oregon Legislature. A combination of factors (mostly term limits) meant that 25 of the 60 House seats had no incumbents. Republicans were optimistic about holding onto their majority. Ten races were considered too close to call. Democrats were counting on a big voter turnout—which always seemed to help their candidates most. They were focusing on winning GOP-held seats in Beaverton, Corvallis, Gresham, Damascus, Milwaukie and Salem.

Republicans barely retained control of the Senate. Democrats won an additional seat, giving them 14 to 16 for the Republicans. One of the featured races was in the Beaverton area of suburban Washington County. There, Senator Eileen Qutub, a Republican and a social conservative, was challenged by Democrat Ryan Deckert, a 29-year-old state representative. Deckert attracted lots of money and support from prominent Democrats, including the active involvement of both John Kitzhaber and his wife, Sharon. Senator Qutub was a vocal critic of the Oregon Health Plan and had pushed hard to cut plan funding. The race was the most expensive legislative campaign ever. Qutub had spent over $100,000 in her uncontested GOP primary and Deckert had expended $25,000 running unopposed in the Democratic primary. Deckert spent $312,000 on his campaign. In addition, he received in-kind contributions worth $165,000. Eileen Qutub spent $321,000 and got in-kind contributions worth $196,000. Together, they spent $633,000; adding their in-kind contributions, the campaign cost a staggering $994,000! Voters were dumbfounded that a lone seat in Oregon's 30-member Senate could cost almost a million dollars. Deckert defeated Qutub in November by 3,400 votes, 28,400 to 25,000.

The Deckert-Qutub race represented the new face of Oregon politics in which polling, professional campaign consultants, targeted mailings, TV ads, sophisticated fund-raising, and computer-generated materials had become the rule. And, of course, great mountains of money. There were 30 candidates for 15 Senate seats in November 2000. Together, they spent $3.54 million, an average of $118,000 per candidate, or $236,000 per Senate seat. The 125 candidates for Oregon's 60 House seats spent $7.76 million in the general election. The average amount spent by each candidate in 2000 was $62,100, or, combined, about $125,000 for every House seat. The cash expenditures for all legislative races combined were $11.3 million. This figure does not include the value of in-kind contributions nor separate expenditures made by PACs on behalf of candidates. When those expenditures are added into the mix, the cost of Oregon's 75 legislative races was closer to $20 million.*

The Contest for President

The presidential campaign between Republican George W. Bush, son of former President George H.W. Bush (1989-93) and Democratic Vice Pres. Al Gore was the most expensive in American history. And it was one of America's closest and most divisive elections.

Most Americans went to bed late on election night, November 7, not knowing who their new president was. The vote in Oregon and Washington was too close to call. Florida's 25 electoral votes were also in question as late returns indicated that Al Gore was close to overturning a small lead held by Governor Bush. Several states, including Oregon, were still counting ballots three days after the election. Finally, on Friday afternoon, Democrat Al Gore was declared

---

* The seven highest spending political interest PACs (those associated with a political party or with an elected politician) spent $3.35 million in cash and donated services and materials in the 2000 primary and general elections. The Senate Democratic Leadership Fund topped the spending list in this category: $750,500. Future PAC (supporting House Democrats) parted with $692,000, while Majority 2000, the House Republican PAC, poured $715,000 in cash and in-kind services into the two elections. Governor John Kitzhaber, and Senators Wyden and Smith also had their own PACs in 2000. Democrats Wyden and Kitzhaber, between them, funneled over $500,000 in cash into Democratic races and ballot measure campaigns. Senator Gordon Smith's Impact Oregon PAC gave $137,000 to Republican candidates.

   Interest group PACs poured more millions into the primary and general elections. Led by the Oregon Education Association's $794,000 (much of it in the form of in-kind contributions), the Oregon Victory PAC (Businesses for Republicans) and its $543,000 investment, Associated Oregon Industries ($505,000), Citizen Action by Public Employees ($504,000), and Oregon Right to Life ($444,000), the interest group PACs continued to be the major source of funding for the various ballot measure campaigns.

the winner in Oregon: 720,342 votes for Gore and 713,577 for Governor Bush, a plurality of 6,765 votes for the vice president.

Meanwhile, counting and recounting of the vote in Florida continued. On Saturday, December 9, the U.S. Supreme Court in a 5-4 ruling ordered an immediate stop to all vote counting in Florida.* On December 13, Albert Gore called George Bush, conceding that the governor had won the election. Electoral vote totals: Gore, 267, Bush, 271. George Bush was declared the winner of the Florida popular vote—by 537 ballots. Al Gore won the national popular vote by about 350,000. Commentators quickly dubbed the states that Bush won as colored red on the national political map; the states carried by Democrat Al Gore were colored blue. George Bush carried 30 "red states," while Al Gore won 20 "blue states" and the District of Columbia.

Eight of 10 Oregonians Voted

Secretary of State Bill Bradbury predicted an 80% voter turnout in November. Oregon's thick ballot and the presidential election, coupled with the fact that Oregonians could mark their mail-in ballots in the privacy of their homes, persuaded Bradbury that citizens would vote in near-record numbers. Bradbury was right: the turnout was 81%. Oregon's 26 ballot measures aroused great public interest and had much to do with the high turnout. All six of the Oregon Taxpayers United measures were defeated. Measure 8 (which would have capped state spending) and 9, respectively sponsored by conservative anti-tax activist Don McIntire and the OCA, were shot down. Measure 9 sparked the most controversy and resulted in an emotionally charged campaign involving thousands of aroused volunteers. "No on 9" bumper stickers blossomed all over the state, but especially in metropolitan Portland. Measure 9 was defeated by a margin of 86,000 votes, 702,500 yes, to 788,700 no.

---

* Thousands of disputed ballots, including many that had been improperly punched by voters, kept the Florida tally from being finalized. One county disqualified 19,000 ballots because they had more than one mark for presidential candidates on them. Democratic Party attorneys prepared to file lawsuits requiring that all ballots be tabulated. With each passing day it became more obvious that the final outcome in Florida would determine who the next president was. On Saturday, November 11, Democrat Al Gore was only eight electoral votes shy of the 270 needed to be elected. George Bush's electoral total stood at 246; he would have to win Florida and its 25 electoral votes if he was to win the presidency. For the next five weeks Florida was in turmoil as one lawsuit after another was filed. Some counties began to recount all of their ballots, some counties by hand, some by machine. Other counties started recounts and suddenly stopped them. On November 16, the Florida Supreme Court ruled unanimously that hand counting of paper ballots could go on despite legal efforts by Bush representatives to stop the tallying. The decision was appealed to the U.S. Supreme Court. Many Americans believe that Gore should have won the election.

Measure 86, referred to the ballot by the 1999 Legislature, would put Oregon's state income tax "kicker" law into the Constitution, though the legislature, by a two-thirds vote of both houses, could reduce or even eliminate the rebate in order to balance the state budget for two years. Voters were emphatic in their backing of Measure 86: 898,800 voted yes and 550,000 voted no.

State Senator Ginny Burdick of Portland was chief sponsor of Measure 5, one of the most emotional on the ballot. Burdick, a proponent of gun-control laws, had been stymied by the Republican Legislature, which had done nothing in 1999 after 15-year-old Kip Kinkel of Springfield murdered his parents and then went to school and killed two students and wounded a dozen others. Senator Burdick wanted to close a giant loophole in Oregon law: namely, that non-registered gun dealers were regularly selling guns to anyone who wanted to buy one at a gun show. Measure 5 would extend the requirement for criminal background checks to purchasers of firearms at gun shows as well as handguns sold through gun dealers, requiring that these records be kept for five years. The National Rifle Association led the charge to defeat Burdick's measure. Most Oregonians were appalled by recent gun violence; consequently, they passed Measure 5 by an emphatic 382,000 votes, 922,000 to 570,000.

Trying to Get Along: The Legislature of 2001

The tone of Oregon's 71st Legislative Assembly was set weeks before the session convened on January 8, 2001. The bitter partisanship of the 1999 session hadn't set well with Oregonians and in November voters had cut into the Republicans' House and Senate majorities. They now held 33 seats in the House, down from the 35 they had in 1999. Meanwhile, Senate Republicans saw their 17-13 majority slip to a bare 16-14 majority for 2001. Term limits and engaged voters pushed out many "partisan infighters, odd ducks and veteran leaders." Senators Eileen Qutub, Thomas Wilde, and Marylin Shannon were gone as were Reps. Ron Sunseri and Kevin Mannix and House Speaker Lynn Snodgrass and Senate President Brady Adams. "Their experience and knowledge may be missed, but not their fierce partisanship," wrote an *Oregonian* editor.[4]

Gene Derfler

Eugene Derfler, a 12-year legislative veteran, was chosen Senate president. Conservative and non-confrontational, Derfler was focused on conducting a harmonious session, where lawmakers worked diligently to agree on a state budget without the rancor that poisoned the previous session. Derfler was genial, goal-driven, pragmatic, and dedicated to making state government accountable and efficient. Nearly 77, Republican Gene Derfler was one of the oldest lawmakers to lead the legislature in the previous 100 years. "Leaders of both parties say Derfler is more interested in results than political grandstanding. 'My sense with Derfler is what you see is what you get,' said Democratic Sen. Tony Corcoran."[5]

Derfler also had a reputation for tackling tough issues, including energy deregulation, teacher tenure, and workers' compensation reform. He knew the session's biggest task was to balance the state budget when economic forecasters were predicting a $660 million revenue shortfall in the 2001-03 biennium. A key Derfler priority was to protect cheap hydroelectric power for Northwest consumers and industry.

Mark Simmons

Republican Mark Simmons was elected House speaker in 2001. Simmons was a 44-year-old heavy-equipment mechanic and union representative with Boise-Cascade Corporation who liked to remind people that "I'm just a regular guy who happens to be speaker of the house."[6] He prided himself on his low-key style, wasn't flamboyant, nor did he like the spotlight. In these attributes, Speaker Mark Simmons was a lot like Senate President Derfler. Because of the state's term limits law, Simmons and Derfler would serve as House and Senate leaders for only the 2001 session—both would be forced to leave the legislature in January 2003.

Simmons agreed with Derfler to conduct the session in an even-handed fashion, in a respectful manner. "There's no sense poking each other in the eye routinely. It's not productive to go looking for things we can fight about." Simmons claimed "his main goal for the session was to restore peace in a Capitol riven by partisan squabbling."[7] Simmons kept his cards close to his chest. He said little about his personal priorities in 2001. He did reveal that the legislature must continue to fund Project Independence so that senior citizens could live in their own homes.

Derfler and Simmons promised to work closely with Gov. John Kitzhaber to ensure that bills they passed had the governor's support. They announced that hot-button issues like abortion and gay rights were off the table in 2001. Simmons and Derfler knew that these issues (so important to social conservatives) had a lot to do with the polarization that had crippled the past two legislatures.

John Kitzhaber

The third key partner in Oregon's "Leadership Troika" was Governor Kitzhaber. He was entering the final two years of his second term and the 2001 session would be his last. Governor Kitzhaber agreed to talk regularly with GOP leaders. Was he perhaps wary of "going down in history as 'Dr. No' for his record number of vetoes"? He proposed to spend "more money on early childhood intervention and to boost rural economic development" which played into long-standing Republican goals.[8]

Kitzhaber released his proposed 2001-03 budget on December 1. He set a budget ceiling of $12 billion, with $5.2 billion going to public schools, K-12. Noting the state's projected revenue shortfall, Kitzhaber recommended scores of budget cuts. The governor proposed a spendy economic development program for rural Oregon. Included in his plan was money to expand roads and fiber-optic internet lines. Kitzhaber raised some eyebrows when he said he wanted to channel another $302.7 million into the budget of the Economic and Community Development Department to boost the economies of rural communities.[9] Always the ardent environmentalist, John Kitzhaber remained dedicated to implementing his Oregon Salmon Plan to clean up the Willamette River through water conservation, pollution prevention, and habitat protection. The governor wanted to establish watershed councils to bring river users together to restore fish habitat.

The Issues

The legislature's chief function is to decide on a two-year budget for state government. Governor John Kitzhaber's $12 billion budget—with $5.2 billion for public education—didn't spark the negative reaction he had faced during the session of 1999. The generally positive reaction to Kitzhaber's latest proposed budget lulled some legislators into thinking the session would be less fractious. Publicly, many lawmakers said they had the will to transcend partisan differences, to proceed without the rancor and nastiness that had characterized recent sessions. Would this be the "Kumbaya Legislature" that Sen. Rick Metsger called it?

There were plenty of tough issues. After several successful consumer lawsuits against the tobacco industry, lawmakers needed to figure out how to spend Oregon's portion of a nationwide tobacco settlement, expected to total $350 million in the 2001-03 budget period. Voters had rejected Measure 4, and the money went back to the Capitol.* Lawmakers also had to figure out how to distribute $115 million in new federal timber payments to counties with federally owned forests."[10] Despite these new revenues, a $660 million drop in state

---

* Gov. Kitzhaber recommended spending $246 million of the tobacco money, leaving $100 million in a health-care trust fund. Senate President Gene Derfler preferred to spend none of the tobacco money, but noted that his was probably an unrealistic idea. See "Smooth sailing expected," by Steve Law, *Statesman Journal*, January 7, 2001, Legislative Guide, 2.

income was anticipated, and figuring out where to make necessary budget cuts had the potential to rip the legislature apart.

Other issues were the Salmon Recovery Plan and Willamette River cleanup, a crying need to do something about Oregon's deteriorating roads, highways, and bridges, the expansion of the Oregon Health Plan, and the governor's recommendation to establish a rainy-day fund to help pay for public schools when Oregon's economy slumped. Any one of these issues had the potential to ignite a legislative donnybrook.

Oregon's controversial kicker law was another source of potential divisiveness. Although declining revenues were anticipated in the future, state economists predicted a $300-$400 million budget surplus at the end of the current 1999-2001 biennium. Voters had recently amended the constitution to require that a budget surplus that exceeded economic forecasts by more than 2% must be rebated to taxpayers (the kicker) unless two-thirds of the House and Senate decided to spend all or part of the surplus on other government programs. The governor wanted legislators to keep some surplus to spend on critical programs facing budget cuts. As the session progressed, President Derfler came to share Kitzhaber's position on the kicker rebate.

There was also the issue of reapportionment—the task of redrawing Oregon's political map to reflect population changes that had occurred since the 1990 Federal Census. A task fraught with tension, reapportionment was the political trap that brought the House of Representatives to its knees at the end of the session.

A Smooth Start—and Rebellion

The 71st Legislative Assembly got off to a smooth start with lawmakers making an effort to cooperate and stick to business. The leadership troika regularly talked to each other. Senator Lenn Hannon and Rep. Ben Westlund, co-chairs of the Joint Ways and Means Committee, got right to work, reiterating that they, too, were intent on keeping their committee together, that cooperation and civility mattered as they crafted a state budget. Hannon and Westlund were acutely aware of the breakdown of the traditional budget process in 1997 and 1999, undercutting public confidence in their elected lawmakers. Both were committed to keeping Ways and Means together no matter what.

Gene Derfler made an unusual move in mid-April when he appointed Democratic Minority Leader Kate Brown to the Ways and Means Committee. The move incensed several of Derfler's GOP colleagues. Derfler explained that he did not "have the votes of all of the Senate's sixteen Republicans and that a budget compromise—which includes kicker funds—must have Democratic support."[11] He hoped "Brown's presence on the panel will make it easier to craft bipartisan majorities to pass agency budgets about to come up for crucial votes."[12] For the remainder of the session, Gene Derfler had no choice but to work closely with both Democratic Governor Kitzhaber and Senate Democrats to move the Senate agenda forward.

The May Economic Forecast

On May 14, state economists released their forecast of where Oregon's economy was headed. State Economist Tom Potiowsky reported that the worst of Oregon's economic downturn would hit later in the year, probably in the third quarter, and that it might take longer for the economy to recover. "It's going to be a very tough year for Oregon before we start to see some improvement in 2002."[13] But the report was not as bleak as legislators feared. Lawmakers learned that they would have 20 million more dollars to spend than earlier forecasted.

Legislators continually found themselves marching around the same circle. Their two-headed dilemma was that they had to decide what to do with the projected $377 million surplus and then craft a new budget for 2001-03, when a recession was predicted and state revenues would drop. The economic forecast could have been worse. Legislators actually had several big pots of money at their disposal. The question facing them was: should they decide to keep (and spend) part or all of the $377 million budget surplus—reducing or eliminating the kicker rebates altogether?

Meanwhile, Governor Kitzhaber was busy preparing a revised budget proposal. Kitzhaber's priorities remained the same: more money for early childhood intervention and rural investment, enhancing reading programs in grade schools, and expanded health care for low-income Oregonians. While the governor kept floating out budget ideas, President Derfler's "biggest task is not figuring budgets but getting the majority needed to pass them."[14]

As if there weren't enough money issues for legislators to tackle, another one suddenly popped up. A new study warned that the Oregon's Public Employees Retirement System (PERS) could face billion-dollar deficits in the near future. Taxpayers at the local and state level would ultimately be responsible for covering these huge PERS shortfalls. The *Oregonian* warned: "The pension system is a huge shadow looming over Oregon's government and its taxpayers. It can't be ignored any longer."[15]

The Challenge of Redrawing the Political Map of Oregon

The House Rules Committee began hearings in early February on redistricting. The task of redrawing hundreds of political boundaries (to reflect changes in the populations of both state legislative and congressional districts) is always one of the most taxing and potentially explosive issues undertaken by lawmakers. Whatever plan the Republican Assembly came up with would have to be approved by Governor Kitzhaber. Failure to produce a new political-district map by June 30 meant the job would be passed on to the secretary of state, Democrat Bill Bradbury, which GOP leaders did not want to happen.

On Wednesday, March 14, the new U.S. Census figures were released. Lawmakers were acutely aware of what was at stake: "With subtle tweaking in a few critical places, the redrawn districts could solidify Republican control of the Oregon Legislature or give Democrats a greater chance at seizing control."[16]

Oregon had grown by 20% between 1990 and 2000. The biggest population changes occurred in metropolitan Portland (Washington County grew by 43%), Deschutes County in central Oregon (up 54%), Marion County (up 25%) in the northern Willamette Valley, and Jackson County (up 24%) in southern Oregon%.* It was in these areas where the most critical boundary changes would have to occur.

A skeptical Gov. John Kitzhaber said, "I think it's unlikely that the legislature will succeed. This is my third redistricting and I've never seen it succeed, but they'll give it a try and thrash each other around for a while."[17]

The Big Walkout

Tension in the Republican-led House grew to epic proportions in late June. Democrats and Republicans were in disagreement over redistricting. On Friday, June 22, Republican leaders announced their intention to ram their redistricting plan through the House and bypass the likely veto of Governor Kitzhaber. GOP leaders said they would pass their plan in the form of a resolution, not a bill. Kitzhaber had pledged to veto any redistricting bill without bipartisan support, but resolutions couldn't be vetoed. Democrats howled that the move was unconstitutional. On Monday, all but two of them played hooky, which kept the House from reaching the 40-member quorum needed to pass the resolution or conduct any other formal business.[18] This was a dramatic and unexpected

---

* Several counties (with small populations to begin with) actually had higher growth rates than those listed above. For example, Crook County grew by 36% (to a population of 19,200), Jefferson grew by 39% (but still had only 19,000 residents), and Morrow County was up 44% to 11,000 people.

move. The legislature hadn't witnessed a mass walkout by members of one party since 1971.

At the request of Secretary of State Bill Bradbury, the Department of Justice issued a written opinion. The Deputy Attorney concluded: "Resolutions do not have the force of law, and the assembly cannot unilaterally reapportion legislative districts by means of a resolution." The opinion was not binding on the legislature, though Bradbury was obligated to follow the legal advice.[19] The opinion emboldened House Democrats.

The House convened again on Tuesday. Thirty-three Republicans and two Democrats (including Minority Leader Dan Gardner) were present, but 25 Democrats were missing. Consequently, the House again couldn't conduct business. GOP leaders wanted state police to track down the absent Democrats and physically return them to the House chamber. The governor said that the use of force was out of the question. Wednesday, Thursday, and Friday passed without the 25 absent Democrats.

Finally, on Saturday, June 30, the longest walkout in legislative history ended. Democrats returned. Their five-day walkout had achieved what they intended it to do: stall the Republicans until Saturday, the deadline for the House to pass a redistricting plan. Now the task of redistricting would be turned over to Secretary of State Bill Bradbury, a Democrat. The Republican attempt to circumvent the intent of Oregon's redistricting statute was thwarted by the Democratic House minority.

The House had a lot of catching up to do. On Saturday, representatives passed 73 bills as members kept their emotions under wraps. Speaker Mark Simmons, who, on Thursday, had spent $2,000 to hire process servers in an effort to force the return of the wayward Democrats, worked hard to set a businesslike tone. Much of the legislation was uncontroversial. The most important bill allowed state agencies to continue operating, since the 1999-2000 budget cycle was ending that day. There was still much to do. Included on the list of pending bills was the budget for public schools (K-12), the human services budget, and the budget for early intervention programs for children at-risk. The house met on Sunday and every day thereafter until adjournment a week later.

Salem 2001: Grinding to a Halt

Legislators pulled an all-night marathon session on Friday. Lasting nearly 18 hours, the session finally ground to a halt at 5:15 Saturday morning—181 working-days after it had started. "In the final long day, lawmakers approved the revision of Kitzhaber's Health Plan so it could cover more low-income people.

They also approved the governor's Children's Plan, a statewide early intervention program that would help infants and families facing health and behavioral problems."[20] Early Saturday morning lawmakers passed the $12.1 billion state budget for 2001-03—a $1.3 billion increase over the previous budget. The biggest slice of the budget pie, $5.2 billion, went to pay the state's share of public school costs for the next two years. The new school budget was a $400 million increase, representing a 10% hike over 1999-2001 budget. Moderate Republicans in both the House and Senate joined the Democratic minorities to keep some of the budget surplus, thus reducing "kicker" income tax rebates.

John Kitzhaber said it was his best session as governor. Lawmakers had closely followed his budget proposal, including the ceiling of $12.1 billion and his target of $5.2 billion for public schools. Lawmakers also went for Kitzhaber's plan to spend $220 million to enhance elementary school reading programs, and to provide more money for the Oregon Health Plan. Except for the near-meltdown in the last week, the session ran smoothly. Republican House and Senate leaders Mark Simmons and Gene Derfler, along with Ways and Means co-chairs Ben Westlund and Lenn Hannon, had bent over backwards to keep the session focused and civil. They'd generally been successful in keeping volatile issues off of their agendas.

The *Oregonian* commended Gene Derfler for his "gutsy decision to support keeping part of Oregon's kicker refunds for spending on the elderly and higher education. That did more than any other single act to make this a successful session." The session was described as civil and solid, rather than grand and historic, and the most productive in the past decade. The establishment of the Oregon Cultural Trust to generate $200 million for arts, humanities, and historic preservation in the state was declared the session's most outstanding achievement. "Relying on private donations with tax incentives, this measure could be another Oregon landmark, right up there with the Bottle Bill."[21]

Despite their many achievements, lawmakers failed to tackle a number of serious problems. Little significant environmental legislation was enacted. And the issue of cleaning up the badly polluted Willamette River was virtually ignored. There was no reform of the Public Employees Retirement System; legislators passed the buck to the 2003 Legislature. Measure 7, the property compensation law passed by voters, was, for the time being, stalled by court challenges. Consequently, legislators did little to implement the law. Nor did they set up a rainy-day fund to soften the consequences of future economic recessions.

Legislators made a decision that would have dire consequences for the 2003 Legislature. They committed to over $500 million in state spending and $400 million in tax breaks that would create a budget shortfall of nearly $1 billion. The next legislature would have to deal with it, which was a huge gamble. The 71st Legislature was counting on a rebounding Oregon economy—and a resulting jump in state revenue—to cover the anticipated billion-dollar shortfall in June 2003. It was a risk that would lead Oregon down a dead-end road.

Perhaps the most important legacy of the 71st Oregon Legislature was that it regained some of the respect that earlier sessions had frittered away over the decade. Lawmakers knew a skeptical public was watching them. Oregonians were fed up with the partisan bickering, personal grudges, and costly delays so common in the 1990s.

John Kitzhaber, Politician

Governor John Kitzhaber cast a long shadow over the 2001 session. He'd already worked with three Republican Legislatures, some of which were particularly adversarial. But, more often than not, Governor Kitzhaber prevailed. He vetoed 181 mostly-Republican bills during his eight years in office. He threatened to invoke the veto on dozens of other occasions. Politically savvy and well prepared (with a detailed agenda and budget plan for legislators to consider), John Kitzhaber repeatedly outmaneuvered his four Republican Legislatures. Though his name is synonymous with the Oregon Health Plan—which provides medical coverage for 350,000 of Oregon's poorest citizens—his legacy extends to other areas, as well. For fifteen years, Kitzhaber was Oregon's foremost environmentalist, repeatedly warning Oregonians that their state couldn't continue its pace of growth without jeopardizing its carefully crafted land-use laws, clean air and water, and its ancient forests. Always a champion of Oregon's rivers, watersheds, and fish, Kitzhaber reminded people of the importance of vigilance, to act as stewards of these precious resources. Governor Kitzhaber was also a leading advocate on behalf of children, whether teenagers in trouble, children with no medical insurance, children struggling to learn to read in over-crowded classrooms, or families at risk due to poverty, neglect, or substance abuse.

During his second term, Kitzhaber focused on Oregon's transportation woes, and on the special needs of rural Oregonians, many of whom struggled to find good jobs, housing, and medical care. He said rural Oregonians deserved better highways and needed the state's help to bring computer services to all parts of Oregon.

John Kitzhaber was never short of ideas about what it took to keep Oregon unique. Though he lacked the flamboyant, in-your-face style of a Tom McCall,

Kitzhaber was no less passionate about what made Oregon special. He spent 22 years in state government telling people what he thought and why he hoped they would follow him into the future.

A Troubled 2002

2002 was dominated by the invasion of Afghanistan and the possibility of war with Iraq.* For Oregonians, there were other things to worry about, as well. A suddenly stagnant economy was causing a huge budget crisis in the state, which did not have enough income to pay for the programs approved for the 2001-03 state budget. The crisis became so acute the legislature was forced to meet in special session a record five times between February and September 2002. With each passing session, tensions increased between Democratic Gov. John Kitzhaber and the Republican-controlled legislature. The bipartisanship built during the 2001 session crumbled as partisan bickering again took hold.

Oregonians had a lot of things to worry about in 2002: war and the well-being of thousands of Oregon men and women serving in the armed forces; America's internal security; a state economy in shambles, featuring high unemployment rates;† projected state government budget deficits that climbed from $300 million to $600 million to $710 million to $846 million in four months; a fractious Republican Legislature dueling with a tough-minded Democratic governor through five special legislative sessions; and two major political campaigns, the May primary and the November general election.

Five Special Legislatures

State economists were predicting that unless the governor and legislature did something drastic to rebalance the 2001-03 budget, Oregon was facing a huge deficit. Just two months into the two-year budget the state faced a deficit of $208 million.[22] Governor Kitzhaber proposed raising taxes on cigarettes, beer, and

---

* Following the Al Qaeda attacks of September 11, 2001, American, British, and Afghan forces launched Operation Enduring Freedom in Afghanistan, to remove the Taliban regime, which had supported Al Qaeda. In March 2003, President Bush launched an invasion of Iraq, ostensibly to topple the regime of the Baghdad strongman Saddam Hussein, and to destroy what Bush called Iraq's arsenal of "weapons of mass destruction." Several Oregon Army National Guard units were among the first deployed to Iraq. Within a week, Hussein was toppled and the joint British-American invasion forces were left with the task of securing important installations while subduing thousands of loyal Hussein insurgents. Before long, over 130,000 American military personnel were deployed in Iraq. The president announced that his administration was dedicated to creating a new, democratic nation in Iraq and that U.S. forces would stay in Iraq indefinitely.
† Oregon's unemployment rate in October 2001 was 6.5%, compared to the national rate of 5.4%. The number of jobless Oregon workers had climbed by 45% during 2001.

wine, as well as making deep cuts in the existing budget. Republican legislative leaders, particularly House Speaker Mark Simmons, opposed increasing taxes, preferring to make budget cuts and withdraw money from available one-time sources. Through four special sessions, the governor and GOP leaders jousted, with the governor freely vetoing (or threatening to veto) Republican legislation. For nine months the two sides sparred, House and Senate Democrats typically supporting Kitzhaber, protecting his vetoes from override by the Republican majorities. On their fifth try, the legislature and the governor agreed on a course to rebalance the budget. Fierce partisanship reappeared along the way, particularly in the 32-member* Republican House, as Republicans blasted Kitzhaber for allegedly reneging on earlier agreements while the governor argued that Republicans were reckless and irresponsible, intent on using "smoke and mirrors" to balance the budget.†

Lawmakers established a precedent when, they, and not the governor, called the legislature into special session, the fifth session, in 2002. Oregon's economic indicators were growing even gloomier. "State officials said the gap between current obligations and projected income in the 2003-05 budget had ballooned to $1.5 billion."[23]

The Election of 2002

Democrat John Kitzhaber's eight-year tenure as governor would end in January 2003. Who would Oregonians choose to be their next governor?

The May primary campaign featured six major candidates: Republicans Ron Saxton, Kevin Mannix, and Jack Roberts, and Democrats Beverly Stein, Ted Kulongoski, and Jim Hill. The Democratic primary for governor was low-key. Neither Hill, Stein, nor Kulongoski was charismatic. Always civil, their emotions under wraps, the three Democrats conducted a series of debates around the state and on TV. The GOP candidates also held a series of regional TV debates. Republicans Saxton and Roberts were low-key personalities. Kevin Mannix was controversial and well known for his authorship of several popular ballot measures—which voters had approved—regarding stiffer penalties for convicted felons. His anti-abortion stance also endeared Mannix to the GOP's large conservative base. He was a tireless campaigner who gushed ideas, stirring

---

* State Representative Jan Lee of Clackamas County was originally elected as a Republican; after the 2001 session ended, Lee left the GOP and re-registered as a Democrat. So, when the legislature met in special session in 2002 the GOP House majority had slipped to 32.

† The legislature met in special session on these dates: February 8-11; February 25-March 2; June 12-June 30; August 16-20 and September 1-18 in 2002.

voters to think. And Kevin Mannix had a political sugar daddy, millionaire industrialist and backer of conservative causes, Loren Parks.

As late as mid-April, polls indicated that half of GOP voters were still unsure of who they would vote for. The *Oregonian* endorsed Ron Saxton and Democrat Ted Kulongoski.

Money, Mountains of Money

Democrats Hill, Kulongoski, and Stein raised and spent just over $3 million in the May primary. Bev Stein led the pack, spending nearly $1.3 million. Kulongoski, who'd been the Democratic nominee for governor in 1982, spent $885,000, followed by Jim Hill at $777,000. The three candidates also attracted $146,000-worth of in-kind contributions. Having served in all three branches of state government, Ted Kulongoski was the best-known Democrat. He'd been a fixture in state government since 1975, when he began his first term in the Oregon House. Kulongoski won the Democratic nomination by a healthy margin in a lackluster campaign: Kulongoski, 170,800, Jim Hill, 92,300, and Beverly Stein, 76,500.

The three major Republican candidates spent nearly $4.5 million in the primary and attracted $280,000 of in-kind contributions. Ron Saxton spent $1.844 million, followed by Jack Roberts at $1.6 million; Kevin Mannix, banking on his widespread name-familiarity, won the GOP contest, spending only $859,000. Mannix drew 117,200 votes, Roberts 98,000, and Ron Saxton, 93,500.

Seats in Oregon's legislature continued to rise in cost. Thirty-four candidates for the state Senate spent $1.314 million in May. For Oregon's 60 House seats, 140 candidates shelled out $3.178 million during the primary. Together the six candidates for governor and the 174 legislative hopefuls expended $12.4 million in the May 2002 campaign.

The campaign for governor between Republican Kevin Mannix and Democrat Ted Kulongoski turned out to be the most expensive in state history. Democratic leaders were intent on keeping the governor's office in Democratic hands. After 15 years, the GOP was anxious to elect a Republican chief executive. Ted Kulongoski was one of the best-prepared candidates to ever seek the governorship. He had served in both the Oregon House and Senate, been state insurance commissioner, attorney general, and a State Supreme Court Justice. He had been a statewide candidate four times. Kevin Mannix was a Salem attorney who had served several terms in the Oregon House as a Democrat before becoming a Republican. He served a short stint as an appointed state senator and had been an assistant attorney general in

Oregon (1975-77). A conservative with a headful of provocative ideas, Mannix was controversial and a relentless campaigner. Like Kulongoski, he had run for statewide office before. Mannix said that state government should be "re-engineered" to make it more efficient. He wanted to reduce the capital-gains tax and favored adding $100 million to Oregon's budget for elderly and other human resource programs. A social conservative, Mannix opposed abortion, same-sex marriage, and doctor-assisted suicide. Kulongoski supported abortion rights, Oregon's doctor-assisted suicide law, and Vermont's state law allowing civil unions for gays and lesbians. Kulongoski stressed improving Oregon's business climate (including streamlining business regulations). Putting the state's public schools on stable financial footing was also one of the Democrat's goals and he favored expanding the Oregon Health Plan to cover all children. He also wanted to reduce prescription drug costs through bulk purchasing.

The U.S. Senate campaign between incumbent Republican Senator Gordon Smith, and his Democratic challenger, Secretary of State Bill Bradbury, was duller than Smith's earlier Senate races. Bill Bradbury was unable to make a strong case for why he should be elected. It was a lackluster campaign, producing little real excitement among voters. Gordon Smith defeated Bill Bradbury by over 200,000 votes in November: Smith, 712,300, Bradbury, 502,000.

Another Democratic Governor

Ted Kulongoski and Kevin Mannix, between them, spent $8.7 million on their November campaigns. Mannix spent $4.1 million, outpacing challenger Kulongoski, who spent over $3 million. Kulongoski also benefited from in-kind contributions worth $335,000, while Mannix drew $227,400 worth of in-kind assistance. The vote was closer than expected. Democrat Kulongoski won by just over 36,000 votes, 618,000 to Mannix's 581,800.

Oregon's legislative races were also expensive. The 128 candidates vying for the 60 House seats in November together spent $7.48 million, while 33 Senate candidates spent $4.86 million. The election of 2002 continued the trend of big-money politics in Oregon. The Mannix-Kulongoski race and the six-dozen legislative contests cost about $20 million, on top of the nearly $12.5 million spent in the primary.

How would the flood of campaign money entering Oregon affect who ran for office and who, ultimately, would hold political power? Awash in money, Oregon seemed headed in the direction of her more populous and influential Pacific neighbors, California and Washington. Ten million dollar gubernatorial contests and million dollar campaigns for a single seat in the Oregon Legislature were now commonplace in Oregon, as were ballot measure proposals, often funded by out-of-state money, costing $5 million or more. As more citizens called for the reform of campaign finance laws, politicians, both at the state and national level, made empty promises about how they were committed to reform, while they spent even more time soliciting campaign funds from willing donors.

The Legislature of 2003

The 2003 Legislature lasted a record 227 days. Republicans had added three seats to their House majority in the 2002 elections. The House consisted of 20 women and 40 men. Karen Minnis of Troutdale was speaker and Deborah Kafoury of Portland was minority leader. Women also held leadership posts in the Senate (where eight of 30 members were female); Democrat Kate Brown and Republican Bev Clarno were leaders of their respective caucuses. Because the Senate was evenly divided, there was no majority leader. Salem Democrat Peter Courtney, who had served in the legislature since 1981, was elected Senate President in 2003 (and in 2005, 2007, and 2009-11).

Looking ahead to the new session, the *Statesman Journal*'s Dana Haynes wrote:

> When asked to name the top ten issues of the 2003 session, lawmak-
> ers and Legislature-watchers offered the same answer: the budgets
> are topics one through nine. Everything else—everything—takes
> second place to the 800-pound gorillas of finalizing a budget for
> 2001-03 and crafting a new state budget for 2003-05. The fate of
> Measure 28, which [goes] to voters on January 28, is the linchpin to
> all of the other budget discussions. The state faces a $2 billion short-
> fall in balancing an expected $11.4 billion budget. Ballot Measure 28
> [had come out of] the last of 2002's [five] fractious special sessions.
> The measure would raise income taxes to prevent cuts in 2001-03
> state services such as schools, colleges, social services and public
> safety. [24]

Voters defeated Measure 28 by a margin of 55-45%, which activated immediate cuts in the current 2001-03 budget. For example, $112 million in across-
the-board cuts in state government ordered by outgoing Gov. John Kitzhaber,
went into effect. The result was that 2,200 state government jobs were either
eliminated or left unfilled, including half of the positions in the State Police

(bringing them down to 201 positions, one-third of the department's force of 600 in 1980). Gov. Ted Kulongoski's budget also included further state job cuts of 400-500 as well as a freeze on state government salaries. The governor also pledged to cut his own salary by 5% (or $4,700). The defeat of Measure 28 triggered, altogether, $310 million in cuts to education, social services, public safety, and other programs.

Thus legislators spent much of the session's early days dealing with the state budget crisis (the 2001-03 budget, ending on June 30). It took until March for lawmakers to do this. Typically legislators beginning a new session are focused only on the *next* budget, the one for the following biennium. But the 2003 Legislature had inherited a budget mess left over from the 2001 session. The Oregon economy remained in a slump; as a result, the state was simply not taking in as much revenue as had been forecast two years earlier. Consequently, the governor and legislature had to keep slashing the budget until it was in line with the adjusted state income for the first six months of 2003.

The first bill signed by Gov. Kulongoski in 2003 was a critical one. Oregon's Public Employee Pension Fund had recently lost several billion dollars of its portfolio value. These losses threatened the long-term viability of the fund. Unless significant changes were made in the benefits that future retirees were entitled to, there might not be enough money left to pay them. Legislation to reform the pension system (PERS) was the first major bill enacted by lawmakers in 2003.

Gov. Kulongoski also guided through the session a $2.5 billion construction program to improve Oregon roads, highways, and bridges. Intended to boost the state economy by providing hundreds of high-paying jobs, the program would last for the next ten years; it was the biggest and most costly road program in state history. Other important actions taken during the '03 session included: a $5.2 billion budget for K-12 schools; new money pumped into the Oregon Health Plan (which restored medical services for about 65,000 single adults and childless couples); and restoring some of the positions cut in the Oregon State Police force.

How would these be paid for? A combination of moderate Republicans and Democrats came together in the House to pass a controversial three-year $800-million tax increase bill. By a vote of 19-11 the Senate concurred and Gov. Kulongoski signed the measure. Opponents vowed to overturn the measure via a referendum petition, but the following February voters approved the tax increase, thus assuring a significant boost in state revenue.

The 2004 Elections

Republican President George W. Bush ran for reelection in 2004; his opponent was Democrat John Kerry, longtime senator from Massachusetts. The election turned out to be just a divisive as the campaign of 2000. President Bush won a second term with 51% of the national vote. Oregonians continued to vote in higher percentages than the rest of the country. Eighty-four percent of registered voters cast mail ballots in Oregon in 2004, up from 80% in 2000. John Kerry, like Al Gore before him, carried Oregon with 51% of the vote.

There were no surprises in Oregon's five congressional races* and Senator Ron Wyden won another six-year term with a 64% plurality. The Oregon Legislature remained divided. Though Republicans lost two seats in the House, they retained a 33-27 majority for the 2005 session. Democrats, however, gained three seats in the Senate, giving them an 18-12 majority. Senate President Peter Courtney continued in that position in 2005, as did Republican Karen Minnis as House speaker. Legislative candidates spent $17.4 million in election year 2004.

Voter passage of Measure 37—which granted new property rights to landowners—caused new headaches for city, county, and state planners. Hundreds of millions of dollars in financial claims against county governments threatened agricultural and rural lands near cities, as well as Oregon's 40-year-old land-use planning system. In 2007, voters passed Measure 49, which modified the earlier measure, but legal challenges continued.

Oregon's economy began to rebound in 2004, after a severe two-year recession. The economy regained its vitality during 2005-06. Jobless rates continued to drop while personal income crept up for most Oregonians. Nonetheless, Oregon's political leaders grappled with the state's most serious problem: where to find the billions of dollars to fund public schools, K-12, as well as Oregon's chronically underfunded public university system. Oregon's jails and prisons remained full, her court dockets crowded. The scourge of methamphetamine continued to disrupt families and neighborhoods, the single most serious cause of crime in Oregon.

The Campaign of 2006

The year 2006 found Oregonians (and the American people) voting against Republican candidates. President George Bush's plummeting popularity hurt Republican candidates at all levels of government.

---

* All five congressmen were reelected: Democrat David Wu in the 1st District with 57.51 percent of the vote; Republican Greg Walden in the 2nd District with 71.63 percent; Democrat Earl Blumenauer in the 3rd District with 70.86 percent; Peter DeFazio in the 4th District with 60.98 percent; and Darlene Hooley in the 5th District with 52.86 percent.

Ted Kulongoski

Theodore ("Ted") Kulongoski's long career in public service is equaled by only a handful of Oregon politicians. Beginning in 1975 and continuing through 2011, Kulongoski served in all three branches of state government (something only one other governor in Oregon history, William Lord, has done).

Kulongoski, born in Missouri in 1940, was orphaned and grew up in a Catholic boys' home in St. Louis. He joined the Marines after high school and later earned his undergraduate and law degrees at the University of Missouri. He moved to Eugene in the early 1970s and, in 1974, was elected to the Oregon House as a Democrat. Ted served in the House in the 1975 and 1977 sessions before being appointed to a vacant state Senate seat in Lane County, where he served during the 1979-83 sessions. Senator Kulongoski was the Democratic nominee for governor in 1982, facing incumbent Governor Victor Atiyeh, who took 61% of the vote, a resounding defeat for the young legislator.

Governor Neil Goldschmidt appointed Kulongoski state insurance commissioner in 1987; in this role, Kulongoski led a drive to reform Oregon's Workers' Compensation program. Next, Kulongoski was elected attorney general (1992), where he led a move to reform the state juvenile justice system. Elected to the Oregon Supreme Court in 1996, Justice Kulongoski served on the court until his resignation in 2001 to run for governor.

Governor Kulongoski was narrowly elected in 2002, at a time when Oregon was slowly emerging from another economic recession. Reelected in 2006 by over 100,000 votes, Kulongoski was blessed to serve at a time when the legislature was controlled by members of his Democratic Party. A strong backer of increased state funding for education, Kulongoski also focused public attention on renewable energy, global warming, health care, hunger, transportation, and the need for the state to establish a rainy day fund to save surplus state dollars for use when the Oregon economy was in recession.

Of special note during his administration was that the governor regularly attended funeral services for Oregon soldiers who died in the Iraq and Afghanistan wars. As a former Marine, Kulongoski represented his office and the citizens of Oregon in commemorating the sacrifices that each dead soldier's family had to endure. He was the only state governor who honored his state's fallen soldiers in such a solemn and reverent way.

Oregon Democrats voted in large numbers during the mid-term election of November 2006: 576,000 cast ballots compared to 532,000 Republicans. Legislative races were hotly contested, as Democrats hoped to capitalize on voters' antipathy to Republican rule. The 10 most expensive legislative races in Oregon included eight House contests, highlighted by the battle in District 49, east Multnomah County. There, Republican House Speaker Karen Minnis faced a stiff challenge from Democrat Rob Brading. The contest quickly turned ugly, as both candidates resorted to mudslinging and character assassination. And money flowed like never before. Minnis outspent Brading 2-1; between them they spent $1.4 million, making it the most expensive legislative race in state history. Rep. Minnis was reelected by a couple of hundred votes. The Brading-Minnis campaign, along with the next nine most expensive legislative races cost $8 million. Although Minnis retained her seat she lost the speakership because Democrats gained a 31-29 House majority in November, ending 16 years of Republican control, and Portlander Jeff Merkley took over as speaker. On the national scene, all five of Oregon's incumbents (four Democrats and one Republican) won reelection; Democrats re-captured the House of Representatives, ending 12 years of Republican domination. Congresswoman Nancy Pelosi (D), was elected House speaker for 2007-09, the first woman in American history to hold that position.

Gov. Ted Kulongoski was reelected, defeating Republican Ron Saxton, a Portland attorney. Theirs was the most expensive governor's race in state history: Saxton spent over $9 million, Kulongoski over $5 million. Kulongoski's victory was part of the Democratic tide sweeping the country that fall, and he saw his reelection margin climb to 110,000, way up from his 36,000-vote victory in 2002.

And They Kept Coming

And people kept moving here. Oregon's population, like that of her Washington and California neighbors, grew steadily (to over 3.6 million by early 2007). The housing industry boomed from Washington County in the north to Ashland in the south to Bend in central Oregon. The competition for existing housing and undeveloped land drove prices up and up.

Issues linked to steady population growth presented new challenges to public officials and taxpayers. Rapidly growing areas struggled in 2006-07 to cope with overcrowded schools, felony crimes, overworked planning departments, congested streets, overburdened health delivery systems, and public construction projects. Public universities and community colleges were overcrowded and often beset by outmoded, poorly maintained campus buildings—even though tuition and related costs rose. Prisons and jails and youth detention facilities, court dockets, and the state's parole/probation system were pressed to keep up with caseloads and offender populations. Oregon's foster care system also struggled to stay current. And, always, there was the question of where the money would come from to pay for all of it.

But most parts of Oregon were not much impacted by population growth in the 1990s; 70% of the nearly 560,000 new residents who moved here in the decade settled in the Portland area. Oregon's population, like the nation's, continued to age. Oregon's over-65 population was predicted to be 20% of the state's total population by 2020. The implications of our aging population have not resonated with most Oregonians; in fact, only a few politicians ever talk about the issue. But an issue it will be.

In Oregon, as in the rest of the nation, wealth was concentrated in the hands of fewer and fewer people. The issue of the distribution of wealth, however, was rarely talked about. The state's poverty rate remained about 15%. Children and minority families headed by a single woman remained Oregon's most economically vulnerable citizens. One in four children under age six lived in poverty in the state.

The environmental issues that had been so important to Oregonians during the last third of the 20th century faded into the background after the year 2000. After Gov. John Kitzhaber, an outspoken environmentalist, left office in January 2003, the environment was essentially a non-issue in Oregon.

The Election of 2008

The Democratic contest for president featured a handful of prominent candidates, led by Senators Hillary Rodham Clinton and the junior senator from Illinois, Barack Obama. Obama won the Democratic nomination. Republicans chose 72-year-old John McCain, senior senator from Arizona as their presidential nominee. Candidate Obama attracted a crowd of 75,000 for a May rally at Tom McCall Waterfront Park in Portland, and he carried Oregon with 57% of the vote.

One of the nation's key Senate contests was in Oregon, where Democratic newcomer Jeff Merkley of Portland, riding Barack Obama's long coattails, defeated Republican incumbent Gordon Smith by over 50,000 votes; Smith was the last Republican senator on the Pacific Coast (excluding Alaska). Merkley joined fellow Democrat Ron Wyden in the Senate in January 2009, marking the first time since 1960 that Oregon had sent two Democrats to the Senate at the same time.

The congressional incumbents who ran for reelection all easily won their seats. In the 5th District, Darlene Hooley had announced in February that she would not run again; the seat was retained by the Democrats. Kurt Schrader defeated Republican Mike Erickson by 54% to 38%, though Erickson had outspent him by over $1 million.

The Democrats also succeeded in holding on to several statewide offices with open seats. The secretary of state's race was won by state Senate Majority Leader Kate Brown, with just over 50% of the vote. Attorney General Hardy Myers had served two terms and could not run again. The Democratic candidate, John Kroger, did not face a Republican opponent; in fact, he received enough Republican write-in votes to receive that party's nomination, and won with over 70% of the vote. Democrat Ben Westlund won in the race for treasurer over Republican Allen Alley by 51% to 45%.

Two of the measures on the ballot involved increased prison spending. Measure 57, a legislative referral, which passed, increased sentences for certain crimes. But to the relief of those concerned about Oregon's financial situation, Measure 61, which would have created mandatory minimum sentences for some crimes, received just under 49% of the vote, and failed.

Money Woes, Again

Money worries, as usual, dominated the 2009 Legislature (and the sessions of 2010 and 2011, as well). The national recession of 2008-10 hit Oregon hard, pushing unemployment rates above 10%. State economists predicted a huge revenue shortfall, causing the Democratic Legislature to slash budgets, shift money, tap federal stimulus funds, and refer two tax-increase measures to voters—Measure 66 to raise income taxes on higher-income households and Measure 67 to raise business taxes. After an expensive and bitterly contentious campaign, both measures passed. Meanwhile, the vicious cycle of Oregon's boom-or-bust economy continued to undercut the state's vitality, threatening funding for public schools, corrections, senior programs/services, families in crisis, and health care.

Oregon's Contest for Governor, 2010

Oregon experienced an unusual race for governor in 2010. Two-term former governor Democrat John Kitzhaber (1995-2003) came out of political retirement to challenge the Republican nominee, Chris Dudley, former center of the Portland Trailblazers professional basketball team. Dudley was a new face in Oregon politics—and he was seeking public office for the first time. The Oregon Republican Party thought they had a winner in Dudley. Not since 1982 had Oregonians elected a Republican governor. Kitzhaber stressed his extensive experience in state government, questioning Dudley's credentials and inexperience. The race was dreadfully expensive. Chris Dudley spent about $9.3 million

Six Oregon governors convened at the Capitol on December 18, 2002, for the memorial service of former governor Robert Straub (1975-79). Pictured left to right, standing, are: Mark Hatfield (1959-67), Neil Goldschmidt (1987-91), Barbara Roberts (1991-95), and Red Kulongoski (2003-2011). Seated, left to right, are Victor Atiyeh (1979-87) and John Kitzhaber (1995-2003 and 2011-).

to Kitzhaber's $5.8 million. Voter turnout was heavy and the final tally was unknown until late the next day: John Kitzhaber was elected to a third term, something no politician had ever done in Oregon. Kitzhaber's victory margin was slim—about 19,000 votes out of over 1.4 million cast. Taking 70% of the vote in heavily Democratic Multnomah County was the deciding factor in Kitzhaber's reelection.

With a state budget deficit of $3.2 billion dollars projected for the 2011-13 biennium, Gov. Kitzhaber and the Democratic Senate and the evenly divided House (30 Republicans and 30 Democrats, the first time in state history that the Oregon House has been evenly divided), the 2011 Legislature had a big mountain to climb to balance Oregon's biennial budget.

Where Is Oregon Headed?

As it was for all who have come before us, the future is cloudy and unknowable. Will we be crushed by the number and complexity of our problems? Will our state government and our elected and appointed leaders have the resolve, the imagination, and the necessary resources to deliver the basic services the public expects? Will we need to change or even eliminate some of our basic institutions? Will citizens continue to support our two-party political system and the way we choose our candidates for political office? Do Oregonians have the resolve to curb the huge amounts of money that threaten to overwhelm our campaigns and our political leaders' ability to make wise and prudent decisions to promote the common good?

None of us, of course, know the answers to these questions. Yet, if one takes time to learn and remember Oregon's history, where we have come from, one will realize that these types of challenges have always been with us. Human societies are, after all, highly complex and ever changing. Our ancestors worried about how they would pay for public schools and colleges, for roads and jails and sheriffs, and for judges and courts and markets for their products, for clean air and water . . . and their children's future.

Modern Oregon is no wilderness. Though our society and institutions have changed dramatically over five generations, our daily problems are often quite similar to the challenges our ancestors faced one hundred and fifty or ninety or thirty years ago. And they prevailed, as will we, somehow.

Oregon has changed dramatically since 1848, the year that the Oregon Territory was made part of the United States. In her early years Oregon was a remote and crude frontier, dominated by mud and rain, loneliness, deprivation, and back-breaking labor. Yet, people kept coming, walking the two thousand miles from America's Midlands . . . the promise of a better life compelling them ever westward to the Pacific Coast . . . and to Oregon. These Euro-Americans pushed aside the native peoples as they crossed the continent and settled here, creating new societies based on constitutions and laws and political institutions intended to promote order.

Oregonians, like Americans everywhere, have lived through peaks and valleys of prosperity and depression and war, each new generation being challenged to not only survive but to also protect and preserve the best that humans and Nature have provided them.

Notes

Abbreviations

OHQ   *Oregon Historical Quarterly*
OHS   Oregon Historical Society
PHQ   *Pacific Northwest Quarterly*
WHQ   *Washington Historical Quarterly*

Preface

1. Malcolm Clark, Jr., *Eden Seekers: The Settlement of Oregon, 1818-1862* (Boston: Houghton Mifflin, 1981), 58.
2. Robert C. Clark, *History of the Willamette Valley, Oregon* (Chicago: The S. J. Clark Publishing Company, 1927), 405.
3. Dorothy Johansen and Charles M. Gates, *Empire of the Columbia: A History of the Pacific Northwest* (New York: Harper and Brothers, Publishers, 1957), 290.

Introduction

1. Brent Walth, *Fire at Eden's Gate, Tom McCall and the Oregon Story* (Portland: OHS Press, 1994), 2.
2. John M. Blum, Edmund S. Morgan, Arthur M. Schlesinger, Jr., et al., *The National Experience* (New York: Harcourt Brace Jovanovich, 1981), 284.
3. Malcolm Clark, *Eden Seeker*, 5, 7.

Chapter 1: "Who's for a Divide?" The Oregon Country, 1834-49

1. Clark, *History of the Willamette Valley*, 270.
2. Ibid.
3. Ibid., 276.
4. Mirth T. Kaplan, "Courts, Counselors, and Cases: The Judiciary of Oregon's Provisional Government," *OHQ*, 62 (1961):121.
5. LaFayette Grover, The Oregon Archives—Public papers of Oregon, OHS Library, 1853, 11.
6. Grover, OHS Library, 14.
7. Charles H. Carey, *General History of Oregon* (Portland: Metropolitan Press, 1935), 330.
8. Grover, OHS Library, 13.
9. Clark, *History of the Willamette Valley*, 308.

10. Frederick V. Holman, "A Brief History of the Oregon Provisional Government and What Caused it's Formation," an address delivered at Champoeg, Oregon, May 2, 1912, printed in *OHQ*, 13 (1912), 134.

11. Leslie M. Scott, "First Taxes in Oregon, 1844," *OHQ*, 31(1930):1.

12. Clark, *Eden Seekers*, 208.

13. Harvey W. Scott, "The Formation and Administration of the Provisional Government of Oregon," an address given at the unveiling of the Champoeg Monument, May 2, 1901, published in *OHQ*, 2 (1901): 114.

14. Clark, *History of the Willamette Valley*, 448.

15. Ibid., 450.

16. Arthur L. Throckmorton, *Oregon Argonauts, Merchant Adventurers on the Western Frontier* (Portland: OHS Press, Portland, 1961), 100.

Chapter 2: From Territory to State, 1848-59

1. Johansen and Gates, *Empire of the Columbia*, 293.

2. *Guide to Oregon Provisional and Territorial Government Records*, Oregon State Archives, 1990, 81.

3. Clark, *Eden Seekers*, 230.

4. Clark, *History of the Willamette Valley*, 405.

5. Johansen and Gates, *Empire of the Columbia*, 291.

6. Clark, *History of the Willamette Valley*, 454.

7. Johansen and Gates, *Empire of the Columbia*, 291.

8. Leslie M. Scott, "Influence of American Settlement Upon the Oregon Boundary Treaty of 1846," *OHQ*, 29 (1928): 227.

9. Jesse S. Douglas, "Origins of the Population of Oregon of 1850," *PNQ*, 41 (1950):100.

10. Dan E. Clark, "Pioneer Pastimes," *OHQ*, 57 (1956): 333.

11. F. G. Young, "Financial History of Oregon," *OHQ*, 8 (1907), 140.

12. Thomas W. Prosch, "Notes from a Government Document on Oregon Conditions in the Fifties," *OHQ*, 8 (1907), 194. 11.

13. Charles Carey, *The Oregon Constitution and Proceedings of the Constitutional Convention of 1857* (Salem, Oregon: State Printing Department, 1926), 8.

14. Walter C. Woodward, *The Rise and Early History of Political Parties in Oregon, 1843-1868* (Portland, Oregon: J.K. Gill, 1913), 39.

15. Ibid., 40.

16. Florence Walls, "The Letters of Asahel Bush to Matthew P. Deady, 1851-63" (Reed College bachelor's thesis, May 1941) and Woodward, *The Rise and Early History*, 58 (footnote).

17. Ibid., vii.

18. David Alan Johnson, *Founding the Far West: California, Oregon, and Nevada, 1840-1890* (University of California Press, 1992), 57.

19. Ibid., 64.

20. Walls, "The Letters of Asahel Bush," xix and 20, and Woodward, *The Rise and Early History*, 84.

21. Woodward, *The Rise and Early History*, 5.

22. George Williams, "Political History of Oregon from 1853 to 1865," *OHQ*, 2 (1901): 4.

23. Woodward, *The Rise and Early History*, 66.

24. Ibid., 73.

25. Ibid., 90.

26. Ibid., 92.

27. Ibid., 93.

28. T. W. Davenport, "Slavery Question in Oregon," *OHQ*, 9 (September 1908): 226.

29. Woodward, *The Rise and Early History*, 94.

30. Ibid., 95.

31. Ibid., 102.

32. Ibid., 114.

33. Ibid., 114.

34. Ibid., 112.

35. Ibid., 116.

36. Charles Carey, "Oregon's Constitutional Proceedings, 1857," *OHQ*, 13 (1912): 27.

37. David Alan Johnson, 67.

38. Woodward, *The Rise and Early History*, 118.

39. Ibid, 119.

40. Robert Johannsen, *Frontier Politics and the Sectional Conflict: The Pacific Northwest on the Eve of the Civil War* (Seattle: University of Washington Press, 1955), 58.

41. Woodward, *The Rise and Early History*, 42.

42. Johannsen, *Frontier Politics and the Sectional Conflict*, 73.

43. Ibid., 77.

44. Clark, *History of the Willamette Valley*, 425.

45. Carey, "Oregon's Constitutional Proceedings," 53.

Chapter 3: Early Statehood and the Civil War Era

1. Johannsen, *Frontier Politics and the Sectional Conflict*, 131.

2. Ibid., 154.

3. Ibid., 203.

4. Scrapbook 58, OHS Collection, 207.

5. Woodward, *The Rise and Early History*, 232.

6. Scrapbook 112, OHS Collection, "Affairs in Oregon," *Oregonian*, September 29, 1868, 97.

7. Scrapbook 58, OHS Collection; "Half a Century Ago," *Oregonian*, March 24, 1864, 226.

8. Woodward, *The Rise and Early History*, 243.

9. William T. Fenton, "Political History of Oregon from 1865-1876", *OHQ*, 3 (1902): 49.

10. Ibid, 48.

11. Scrapbook 112, OHS Collection, "Letter from Oregon," *Oregonian*, October 3,1866, 76.

12. Woodward, *The Rise and Early History*, 255.

13. George H. Williams, "Political History of Oregon from 1853 to 1865," *OHQ*, 2 (1901), 1.

14. Woodward, *The Rise and Early History*, 256.

15. Ibid., 257.
16. Ibid., 262.
17. Charlotte Anna Chambers, "A Sectional Analysis of Political Parties in Oregon" (Bachelor's thesis, Reed College, 1939), 17.
18. Scrapbook 79, OHS collection, "Olden Days," 179.
19. Fenton, "Political History of Oregon," 53.
20. Lee Nash, "Abigail versus Harvey: Sibling Rivalry in the Oregon Campaign for Woman Suffrage," *OHQ*, Vol 98, Number 2, Summer 1997, 143.
21. Lauren Kessler, "A Siege of the Citadels," *OHQ*, 84 (1983): 116.
22. Ruth Barnes Moynihan, *Rebel for Rights: Abigail Scott Duniway*, (New Haven: Yale University Press, 1983), xv.
23. Kessler, "A Siege of the Citadels," 142.
24. Ibid., 140.

Chapter 4: John Mitchell and Other Tales of Corruption, 1868-73

1. E. Kimbark MacColl, *Merchants, Money, and Power* (Portland: The Georgian Press, 1988), 322.
2. Homer Owen, "Oregon Politics and the Initiative and Referendum" (Bachelor's thesis, Reed College, 1950), 2.
3. Ibid., 4.
4. Ibid., 5.
5. Ibid., 6.
6. MacColl, *Merchants*, 135.
7. Ibid, 136
8. Owen, "Oregon Politics and the Initiative and Referendum," 42.
9. Owen, "Oregon Politics and the Initiative and Referendum," 16.
10. Ibid.
11. MacColl, *Merchants*, 172.
12. Ibid.
13. E. Kimbark MacColl, *The Growth of a City* (Portland: The Georgian Press, 1979), 204.
14. Malcolm Clark, Jr., *Pharisee Among Philistines, The Diaries of Judge Matthew P. Deady*, (Portland: OHS Press, 1975), 154.
15. Ibid.
16. T. T. Geer, *Fifty Years in Oregon* (New York: Neale Publishing, 1912), 327.

Chapter 5: Money, Corruption, and the Reformers, 1882-1902

1. Evelyn L. Boese, "The Public Reaction to the 1906 Campaign of Jonathan Bourne, Jr. for U.S. Senate," (Bachelor's thesis, Reed College, 1951), 15.
2. Owen, "Oregon Politics and the Initiative and Referendum," 44.
3. Owen, "Oregon Politics and the Initiative and Referendum," 49.
4. MacColl, *Merchants*, 225.
5. Ibid., 248.
6. Malcolm Clark, Jr, "The Bigot Disclosed: 90 Years of Nativism," *OHQ*, 75 (1974): 123.
7. Ibid., 126.

8. Arthur Bone, *Oregon Cattle/Governor/Congressman: Memoirs and Times of Walter M. Pierce*, (Portland: OHS Press, 1981), 26

9. Harvey Scott, *History of the Oregon Country*, 74-77.

10. Robert W. Burton, *Democrats of Oregon: The Pattern of Minority Politics, 1900-1956* (Eugene: University of Oregon Press, 1970), 21.

11. MacColl, *Growth of a City*, 80.

12. Owen, "Oregon Politics and the Initiative and Referendum," 58.

13. Kingsley Trenholme, "Third Political Party in Oregon, from 1874-1892" (Bachelor's thesis, Reed College), 56.

14. Trenholme, "Third political party in Oregon," 59.

15. Boese, "The Public Reaction to the 1906 Campaign," 21.

16. Ibid. 5.

27. William S. U'Ren, *Direct Legislation Record*, 2 (June 1895): 15.

18. MacColl, *Merchants*, 322.

19. Owen, "Oregon Politics and the Initiative and Referendum," 53

20. Ibid., 55.

21. MacColl, *Merchants*, 322.

22. Thomas McClintock, "Seth Lewelling, William S. U'Ren and the Birth of the Oregon Progressive Movement," *OHQ*, 68 (1967): 213.

23. Boese, "The Public Reaction to the 1906 Campaign," 31.

24. Burton, *Democrats of Oregon*, 24.

25. Boese, "The Public Reaction to the 1906 Campaign," 35.

26. McClintock, "Seth Lewelling, William S. U'Ren," 213.

27. MacColl, *Merchants*, 345.

28. Lee Nash, *OHQ*, Vol 98, Number 2, Summer 1997, 135.

29. Boese, "The Public Reaction to the 1906 Campaign," 2.

30. Bone, *Oregon Cattle/Governor/Congressman*, 44.

31. Burton, *Democrats of Oregon*, 26.

32. MacColl, *Merchants*, 347.

Chapter 6: George Chamberlain and the Os West Express, 1903-13

1. Bone, *Oregon Cattle/Governor/Congressman*, 56.

2. MacColl, *Merchants*, 360.

3. Bone, *Oregon Cattle/Governor/Congressman*, 50.

4. Ibid., 58.

5. Ibid., 63.

6. MacColl, *Merchants*, 370.

7. S. A. D. Puter and Horace Stevens, *Looters of the Public Domain* (Portland: Portland Printing House, 1908), 183.

8. Ibid., 220.

9. MacColl, *Merchants*, 370.

10. Bone, *Oregon Cattle/Governor/Congressman*, 64.

11. Ibid.

12. Ibid.

13. MacColl, *Merchants*, 382.

14. Clark, *History of the Willamette Valley,* 700.

15. Russell G. Hendricks, "Election of Senator Chamberlain, the People's Choice," *OHQ*, 53, 2 (1952): 65.

16. Boese, "The Public Reaction to the 1906 Campaign," 45.

17. Ibid., 46.

18. Hendricks, "Election of Senator Chamberlain," 66.

19. Ibid., 71.

20. Ibid., 74.

21. Ibid.

22. Ibid., 77.

23. Oswald West, "Reminiscences," *OHQ*, 52 (1951): 153.

24. Chester Harold Case, "The Oregon System and Oswald West" (Bachelor's thesis, Reed College, 1952), 84.

25. Ibid., 89.

26. *Oregon Journal*, October 28, 1910.

27. Case, "The Oregon System and Oswald West,"106.

28. Ibid.

29. Burton, *Democrats of Oregon*, 31.

30. Medford *Mail-Tribune*, November 10, 1910, 1 and 4.

31. MacColl, *Growth of a City*, 489.

32. Case, "The Oregon System and Oswald West," 127.

33. West, "Battle for Life," October 3, 1937.

34. Case, "The Oregon System and Oswald West," 128.

35. West, "Battle for Life," *Oregonian,* October 3, 1937; Case, "The Oregon System and Oswald West," 137.

36. Case, "The Oregon System and Oswald West," 139.

37. Ibid., 130.

38. West, "Battle," October 3, 1937.

39. Kimberly Jensen, "Neither Head nor Tail to the Campaign," *OHQ*, Vol 108, Fall 2007, 373.

40. Case, "The Oregon System and Oswald West," 149.

41. Ibid., 157

42. *Oregon Journal*, January 22, 1913.

43. Case, "The Oregon System and Oswald West," 150.

44. Ibid., 153.

45. Ibid., 151.

46. Ward M. McAfee, "The Formation of Prison-Management Philosophy in Oregon, 1843-1915," *OHQ*, 91(1990): 272.

47. Ibid.

48. Ibid, 273.

49. Steve Neal, *McNary of Oregon: A Political Biography*, (Portland: OHS Press, 1985), 19.

50. *Oregonian*, August, 23,1960, 1.

51. Ibid.

Chapter 7: Oregon During World War One, 1914-20

1. Burton Onstine, *Oregon Votes: 1858-1972 Election Returns: By County, from Statehood to 1972 for U.S. President, Governor, U.S. Senator, and U.S. Representative* (Portland: OHS, 1973), 164.
2. George W. Joseph, III, "George W. Joseph, Sr.," (Bachelor's thesis, Reed College), 10.
3. Ibid., 11.
4. Scrapbook 58, OHS Collections, 169-73.
5. *Oregon Daily Journal,* January 9, 1915, 8.
6. Neal, *McNary of Oregon,* 30.
7. *Oregon Voter,* December 16, 1916, 211.
8. Bone, *Oregon Cattle/Governor/Congressman,* 99.
9. Ibid., 100.
10. Ibid.
11. Neal, *McNary of Oregon,* 31.
12. MacColl, *Growth of a City,* 137.
13. Neal, *McNary of Oregon,* 31-32.
14. Ibid.
15. MacColl, *Growth of a City,* 139.
16. Ibid., 140.
17. Ibid., 144.
18. Ibid.
19. Ibid.
20. Malcolm Clark, Jr., "The Bigot Disclosed: 90 Years of Nativism," *OHQ,* 75 (1974): 147.
21. Ibid., 155.
22. Clark, *History of the Willamette Valley,* 725.
23. MacColl, *Growth of a City,* 156.
24. Howard A. DeWitt, "Charles McNary and the 1918 Congressional Election," *OHQ,* 68 (1967), 140.
25. Bone, *Oregon Cattle/Governor/Congressman,* 126.
26. Ibid., 136.
27. Ibid., 131.
28. MacColl, *Growth of a City,* 159.
29. Bone, *Oregon Cattle/Governor/Congressman,* 138.

Chapter 8: The Election of 1922, the Ku Klux Klan, and Governor Walter Pierce, 1921-27

1. Clark, "The Bigot Disclosed," 151-53.
2. David Horowitz, "Social Morality and Personal Revitalization: Oregon's Ku Klux Klan in the 1920s," *OHQ,* 190:4 (1989): 367, 379.
3. Bone, *Oregon Cattleman/Governor/Congressman,* 151.
4. Clark, "The Bigot Disclosed,"165
5. Horowitz, "Social Morality," 383
6. Clark, "The Bigot Disclosed,"165
7. Ibid., 166.
8. Bone, *Oregon Cattleman/Governor/Congressman,* 168.

9. Ibid., 163.

10. Ibid., 168.

11. Ibid., 179.

12. Burton, *Democrats of Oregon*, 49 (footnote 30).

13. Clark, "The Bigot Disclosed," 174.

14. Robert Johnston, quoted in "The Paradox of Oregon's Progressive Politics: The Political Career of Walter Marcus Pierce," by Robert R. McCoy, *OHQ*, Vol 110, No. 3, Fall 2009, 1.

15. Bone, *Oregon Cattleman/Governor/Congressman*, 184, 186.

16. Ibid., 187

17. Ibid., 190.

18. Barbara Yasui, "The Nikkei in Oregon, 1834-1940", *OHQ*, 76, (1975): 225.

19. Ibid., 248.

20. Bone, *Oregon Cattleman/Governor/Congressman*, 192.

21. Ibid.

22. Ibid., 231.

23. Ibid., 231, 144.

24. Ibid., 229.

25. Ibid., 230, 231.

26. Ibid., 273.

27. Ibid., 274.

28. Ibid., 280.

29. Ibid., 319.

30. Ibid.,

31. Burton, *Democrats of Oregon*, 323.

32. Bone, *Oregon Cattleman/Governor/Congressman*, 231.

33. Ibid., 232.

Chapter 9: Two Deaths: 1927-33

1. *Oregonian*, Editorial, "The Governor's Message," January 11, 1927, 12.

2. *Oregon Voter*, January 1, 1927, 75.

3. Ibid., February 19, 1927, 4.

4. Ibid., July 2, 1927, 7.

5. Burton, *Democrats of Oregon*, 57.

6. MacColl, *Growth of a City*, 365-67.

7. *Oregon Voter* (quoting the Albany *Democrat-Herald*), February 22, 1930, 4.

8. *Oregon Voter*, January 25, 1930, 7, and February 8, 1930, 11.

9. MacColl, *Growth of a City*, 406.

10. Joseph, "George W. Joseph, Sr.," 38.

11. MacColl, *Growth of a City*, 405.

12. Ibid.

13. Joseph, "George W. Joseph, Sr.," Appendix, 2.

14. MacColl, *Growth of a City*, 406.

15. Ibid.

16. Ibid.

17. Ibid., 392.

18. *Oregon Voter,* November 1, 1930, 18-19.

19. MacColl, *Growth of a City*, 402.

20. *Oregon Voter*, March 7, 1931, 4.

21. Burton, *Democrats of Oregon*, 61.

22. Ibid., 64.

Chapter 10: FDR, Old Iron Pants, and the Politics of Upheaval, 1933-38

1. Neal, *McNary of Oregon*, 136.

2. Ibid., 141.

3. Ibid., 144.

4. Burton, *Democrats of Oregon*, 66.

5. Ibid., 71.

6. *Oregon Voter*, January 7, 1933, 5.

7. Ibid., January 21, 1933, 4.

8. Ibid., March 11, 1933, 10.

9. Ibid., March 18, 1933, 19.

10. Ibid., April 15, 1933, 6.

11. Burton, *Democrats of Oregon*, 76.

12. *East Side Post*, Editorial: "Martin Stock Begins to Drop," February 7, 1934, Charles Martin Papers, OHS collections, Box 8, campaign scrapbook.

13. Burton, *Democrats of Oregon*, 77.

14. Ibid., 78.

15. According to Robert Burton, "Zimmerman's campaign staff included the entire executive committee of the [State] Grange." See Burton, *Democrats of Oregon*, 81, footnote.

16. Ibid., 80.

17. MacColl, *Growth of a City*, 467.

18. Ibid.

19. William Allen Bentson, *Historic Capitols of Oregon* (Salem: Oregon Library Foundation, 1987), 15.

20. George S. Turnbull, *An Oregon Crusader: George Putnam* (Portland: Binfords & Mort, 1955), 175.

21. MacColl, *Growth of a City*, 468.

22. Burton, *Democrats of Oregon*, 82.

23. Turnbull, *An Oregon Crusader*, 180.

24. Onstine, *Oregon Votes*, 256.

25. William Josslin, Letter to Wesley Dick, December 11, 1967, Box 8, Charles Martin Papers, OHS Collections.

26. Burton, *Democrats of Oregon*, 70.

27. Ibid., and MacColl, *Growth of a City,* 484

28. MacColl, *Growth of a City*, 484

29. Turnbull, *An Oregon Crusader*, 232.

30. Burton, *Democrats of Oregon*, 84.

31. Ibid, 87.

32. William T. Josslin, "General Martin—Only Democratic Governor in 26 Years," MSS 708, OHS.

33. Burton, *Democrats of Oregon*, 87.

34. William T. Josslin, Mss. 704, Copy 1, page 2, Charles Martin Papers, OHS.

Chapter 11: How the War Changed Oregon, 1939-48

1. *Oregon Voter*, "Charles Sprague's Campaign Platform/Slogan," April 23, 1938,16.

2. Ibid., November 5, 1938, 12.

3. Ibid., April 23, 1938, 16.

4. *Oregonian*, November 10, 1938, 1.

5. *Oregon Voter*, December 31, 1938, 5.

6. Ibid., March 11, 1939, 11.

7. Ibid., April 15, 1939, 24.

8. *Oregonian*, November 5, 1940, 1.

9. *Oregon Voter*, January 14, 1941, 70.

10. Ibid., March 29, 1941, 9.

11. *Oregon Democrat*, January 10, 1941, 3.

12. Burton, *Democrats of Oregon*, 101.

13. *Oregon Democrat*, January 10, 1941, and August 4, 1941, 4.

14. Eugene *Register-Guard*, "The Candidates for Governor," May 10, 1942, 6.

15. Cecil Edwards in a letter to the author, January 22, 1992.

16. *Oregon Voter*, December 5, 1942, 4.

17. *Oregon Journal*, November 2, 1942, 2; Onstine, *Oregon Votes*, 88; *Oregon Voter*, November 9, 1942, 4.

18. Onstine, *Oregon Votes*, 257.

19. *Oregon Voter*, May 12, 1945, 22.

20. Ibid., March 13, 1943, 6.

21. Ibid., April 24, 1943, 8; Neal, *McNary of Oregon*, 234.

22. Neal, *McNary of Oregon*, 234; *Oregon Voter*, March 4, 1944, 7.

23. Neal, *McNary of Oregon*, 235.

24. Jeff LaLande, "Oregon's Last Conservative U.S. Senator," *OHQ*, Vol. 110, No. 2. Summer 2009, 5.

25. Ibid., 11

26. Medford *Mail-Tribune*, quoted in *Oregon Voter*, March 11, 1944, 6.

27. Ibid.; *Oregonian*, May 10, 1944, 10.

28. Ibid.

29. Ibid., May 23, 1944, 10.

30. *Oregon Voter*, December 16, 1944, 9, and December 9, 1944, 20.

31. Ibid., and December 16, 1944, 5.

32. Ibid, June 19, 1948, 6.

33. Ibid.

34. Ibid., April 5, 1947, 10.

35. Ibid., April 12, 1947, 10.

36. Ibid.

37. *Oregonian*, April 6, 1947, 20.

38. Ibid., May 18, 1948 (editorial)

39. *Oregon Voter*, May 15, 1848, 9.

40. *Oregonian*, May 18, 1948 (editorial).

41. Waldo Schumacher, "The 1948 Election in Oregon," *Western Political Quarterly*, March 1949, 121.

42. Robert Burton, *Democrats of Oregon*, 108, 109.

Chapter 12: Oregon at Mid-Century, 1948-55

1. *Oregon Voter*, October 5, 1948, 10.

2. Burton, *Democrats of Oregon*, 103.

3. Ibid., 106.

4. Ibid., 104.

5. Ibid.

6. Ibid., 113.

7. Ibid., 118.

8. Ibid., 116.

9. *Oregon Democrat*, September 1949, 13.

10. Ibid., May 1951, 6.

11. Ibid., January 1953, 47

12. Ibid., January 1953, 47.

13. Walter Dodd, *Oregon Democrat*, June 1952, 13.

14. *Oregon Voter*, December 13, 1952, 1.

15. Personal interview with Robert Y. Thornton, December 1999, Salem, Oregon.

16. *Oregon Democrat*, September 1953, 6.

17. *Oregon Blue Book*, 1954-55,122.

18. Mason Drukman, *Wayne Morse: A Political Biography* (Portland: OHS Press, 1997), 220.

19. Steve Neal, *Tom McCall: Maverick* (Portland: Binford & Mort, 1977), 34.

20. Monroe Sweetland interview, January 1998, Milwaukie, Oregon.

21. Neal, *Tom McCall*, 34.

22. *Oregon Voter*, March 27, 1954, 7.

23. Neal, *Tom McCall*, 35-36.

24. Charles Sprague quoted in *Oregon Voter*, September 18,1954, 7.

25. Monroe Sweetland interview, January 1998; Neal, *Tom McCall*, 39; *Oregon Democrat*, September 1954, 10.

26. LaLande, "Oregon's Last Conservative,"16.

27. Sweetland interview.

28. *Oregon Democrat*, May 1954, 10.

29. *Oregon Voter*, October 30, 1954, 1.

30. Sweetland interview.

31. Ibid.

32. Neal, *Tom McCall*, 41.

33. Ethan Johnson and Felicia Williams, "Desegregation and Multiculturalism in the Portland Public Schools," *OHQ*, spring 2010, 7.

Chapter 13: Raging Bulls, 1956-59

1. A. Robert Smith, *Tiger in the Senate* (New York: Doubleday, 1962), 308.
2. Ibid., 308, 309.
3. Sweetland interview.
4. *Oregon Democrat*, October 1956, 7.
5. Sweetland interview.
6. Drukman, *Wayne Morse, A Political Biography*, 228.
7. Ibid., 227.
8. Ibid., 232.
9. Smith, *Tiger in the Senate*, 317.
10. Ibid., 316.
11. Sweetland interview.
12. Ibid.
13. Drukman, 268.
14. Ibid., 231.
15. *Oregon Democrat*, Nov-Dec., 1956, 6.
16. Ibid.
17. Drukman, *Wayne Morse, A Political Biography*, 240.
18. Smith, *Tiger in the Senate*, 348.
19. Drukman, *Wayne Morse, A Political Biography*, 333.
20. Smith, *Tiger in the Senate*, 341.
21. Travis Cross personal interview, July 14, 1992, Portland, Oregon.
22. Thornton interview.
23. Smith, *Tiger in the Senate*, 370, 414.
24. *Oregon Voter*, January 26, 1957, 5.
25. Ibid., November 2, 1957, 3.
26. Smith, *Tiger in the Senate*, 373.
27. Ibid., 374, 375
28. Ibid, 376.
29. Ibid., 378.
30. *Oregon Voter*, January 17, 1959, 3.

Chapter 14: When Tom Blew the Whistle, 1960-62

1. Smith, *Tiger in the Senate*, 384.
2. Monroe Sweetland, "The Underestimated Oregon Presidential Primary of 1960," *OHQ*, 101 (2000); 329.
3. Drukman, *Wayne Morse: A Political Biography*, 330.
4. *Oregon Voter*, December 3, 1960, 5.
5. Ibid., January 14, 1961, 5.
6. Drukman, *Wayne Morse: A Political Biography*, 375.
7. Ibid., 377.
8. Brent Walth, *Fire at Eden's Gate* (Portland: OHS Press, 1994), 135.
9. Neal, *Tom McCall*, 60.
10. *Oregon Voter*, January 19, 1963, 4.
11. Ibid., June 8, 1963, 4.

12. Brent Walth, *Fire at Eden's Gate*, 147.
13. *Oregon Voter*, December 7, 1963, 3.
14. Donald G. Balmer, "The 1964 Election in Oregon," *Western Political Quarterly*, vol 18, 1965, 502.
15. Ibid, 507.
16. Charles Sprague, as quoted in *Oregon Voter*, May 22, 1965, 2.
17. Ibid.
18. *Oregon Voter*, May 22, 1965, 4.
19. Balmer, "The 1966 Election in Oregon, *WPQ*, vol 20, 1967, 595.
20. Mason Drukman, Wayne Morse, A Political Biography, *Oregon Historical Society Press*, 1997, 438, 441.
21. Balmer, "The 1966 Election, 595-96.
22. Tom McCall and Steve Neal, *Tom McCall: Maverick*, Binford and Morts, Portland, 1977, 68.
23. Walth, 161.

Chapter 15: The Tom McCall Years, 1965-75

1. Walth, *Fire at Eden's Gate*, 180-81.
2. Ibid., 182.
3. Neal, *Tom McCall*, 81-82.
4. Walth, *Fire at Eden's Gate*, 187.
5. Ibid., 188, 189.
6. Ibid., 190
7. Ibid., 191.
8. Neal, *Tom McCall,* 81
9. Walth, *Fire at Eden's Gate*, 202.
10. *Oregon Voter*, July 7, 1967, 3.
11. Ibid., July 15, 1967, 16.
12. Ibid., August 26, 1967, 7.
13. Drukman, *Wayne Morse: A Political Biography*, 444.
14. Ibid., 448.
15. *Oregon Voter*, August 17, 1968, 3.
16. Walth, *Fire at Eden's Gate*, 219, 220.
17. Drukman, *Wayne Morse: A Political Biography*, 449.
18. Joseph Allman, "The 1968 Election in Oregon," *Western Political Quarterly*, 22 (1969), 552.
19. Drukman, *Wayne Morse: A Political Biography*, 450, 452.
20. Walth, *Fire at Eden's Gate*, 243, 244.
21. Ibid., 248-49.
22. *Oregon Voter*, December 21, 1968, 6.
23. Ibid., February 22, 1969, 9.
24. Ibid., June 7, 1969, 5.
25. Neal, *Tom McCall*, 112.
26. *Oregon* Voter, June 7, 1969, 9.
27. Ibid, 7.

28. Walth, *Fire at Eden's Gate*, 249.

29. Ibid., 270.

30. Ibid., 276.

31. L. Harmon Zeigler and Barbara Leigh Smith, "The 1970 Election in Oregon," *Western Political Quarterly*, Vol. 24, 1971, 327.

32. Walth, *Fire at Eden's Gate*, 314.

33. *Oregon Voter*, January 1968.

34. Neal, *Tom McCall*, 204.

35. Walth, *Fire at Eden's Gate*, 346.

36. *Oregon Voter Digest*, June 15, 1971, 27.

37. Ibid., May 1, 1973, 5.

38. Betty Roberts, *With Grit and By Grace* (Oregon State University Press, Corvallis, 2008), 159. Roberts' book is an excellent source for anyone wanting to better understand the intricacies of how the Oregon Legislature works, including the function, operation, and power of committees and their chairs, how to involve the public in the consideration of pending legislation, the powers of the House speaker and Senate president, the role and influence of lobbyists, and, most important, the significance of personal relationships and friendships between legislators.

39. Ibid., 160-62.

Chapter 16: Bob Straub—Living in Tom's Long Shadow, 1975-78

1. Salem *Statesman Journal*, December 19, 2002, 2A.

2. "The 1975 Legislative Session," by Phil D. Lang, *Oregon Voter Digest*, August 15-September 1, 1975, 52.

3. *Oregon Voter Digest*, July 1, 1975, 4, 6.

4. Ibid., August 15-September 1, 1975, 59.

5. Ibid., 43.

6. Ibid., February 1977, 13.

7. Ibid., May 1977, 21.

8. Ibid., August 1977, 79.

9. Walth, *Fire at Eden's Gate*, 430.

10. Salem *Statesman Journal*, November 29, 2002, 10c.

Note: All election tallies included in this chapter were obtained from the Abstract of Voters, Office of Secretary of State, Salem.

Chapter 17: Governor Victor Atiyeh: Saving a Sinking Ship, 1979-86

1. Doug Heider and David Dietz, *Legislative Perspectives: A 150-year History of the Oregon Legislatures from 1843 to 1993* (Portland, OHS Press, 1995), 194.

2. *Oregon Voter Digest*, August 1979, 35.

3. Peter Wong, Salem *Statesman-Journal*, January 27, 2002, 5A.

4. *Abstract of Votes for Primary and General Elections*, Secretary of State, Salem. All election returns included in this chapter are taken from this source.

5. Personal interview with Victor Atiyeh, March 10, 2004, Portland, Oregon.

6. Ibid.

7. *Oregon Voter Digest*, February 1981, 43.

8. Atiyeh interview.
9. Ibid.
10. Peter Wong, Salem *Statesman-Journal*, January 27, 2002, 5A.
11. Walth, *Fire at Eden's Gate*, 469.
12. Personal Interview with Grattan Kerans, November 10, 2004, Salem, Oregon.
13. Ibid.
14. Ibid.
15. Atiyeh interview.
16. Ibid.

Chapter 18: Neil and Barbara, Vera and John, 1987-94

1. Grattan Kerans interview, December 13, 2004, Salem, Oregon.
2. Jeff Mapes, "Detour to Disappointment," Sunday *Oregonian*, July 22, 1990, "Northwest Magazine," 11. This quotation, as cited by Mapes, was made by Ginny Burdick, Neil Goldschmidt's press secretary when he ran for governor in 1986; later, Burdick was elected a Portland legislator.
3. Jeff Mapes, "An Uncertain Legacy," Sunday *Oregonian*, December 23, 1990, A-26.
4. Mapes, "Detour," 11.
5. Kerans interview.
6. Clifford Trow interview, December 9, 2004, Corvallis, Oregon.
7. Ibid.
8. Grattan Kerans interview, November 10, 2004.
9. Mapes, "Detour," 11.
10. Heider and Deitz, *Legislative Perspectives*, 204.
11. Mapes, "Detour,"12.
12. Kerans interview.
13. Ibid.
14. Mapes, "Detour," 12.
15. Heider and Deitz, *Legislative Perspectives*, 205.
16. Mapes, "Detour,"12, 14.
17. Kerans interview.
18. Ibid.
19. Jeff Mapes, "Three Tough Years," *Oregonian*, January 30, 1991, D12.
20. "Roberts' Opportunity," *Oregonian* editorial, January 13, 1991, D12.
21. Patrick McCormick, as quoted in *Oregonian*, January 30,1994, A-18. McCormick is a longtime political consultant and former Democratic staff member of the Oregon House.
22. Dan Hortsch, "Legislators expect smooth sailing," *Oregonian*, January 13, 1991, D-1.
23. Jeff Mapes, "State may face gridlock in government," *Oregonian*, November 8, 1990, C1.
24. John Terry, "Just a small-town girl," *Oregonian*, January 13, 1991, D-11.
25. Kerans interview, November 2004.
26. Steve Duin, "They say it's lonely at the top," *Oregonian*, January 29, 1994, 14.
27. Trow interview.

28. W. Dale Nelson, "Women, minorities make political surge," *Oregonian*, November 4, 1992, B3.

29. Jeff Mapes, *Oregonian*, November 1, 1992, B1.

30. Bill MacKenzie, "1st District voters give Furse AuCoin's old seat in Congress," *Oregonian*, November 4, 1992, A9.

31. Dee Lane, "Oregon, never was Bush country, lands strongly in Clinton Column," *Oregonian*, November 4, 1992, A9.

32. *Oregonian*, November 1, 1992, B5.

33. Foster Church, "Election brings turning-point in Oregon," *Oregonian*, November 8, 1992, C1.

34. Brian T. Meehan and Phil Manzano, "A great weight lifts from Oregon gays," *Oregonian*, November 4,1992, C3.

35. Trow interview.

36. Jeff Mapes, "Packwood ignores allegations," *Oregonian*, February 9, 1993, A1.

37. Duin, "They say it's lonely at the top," A1.

38. Roberta Ulrich and Foster Church, "Roberts faced tenure of high and lows," *Oregonian*, January 29, 1994, 15.

39. Jeff Mapes, "Barbara Roberts' collision with history," *Oregonian*, December 25, 1994, D1.

40. Jeff Mapes and Gail Kinsey Hill, "3 Tough Years," *Oregonian*, January 30, 1994, 1.

41. Ibid.

42. Kerans interview, December 2004.

43. Trow interview.

44. "Jury out on Roberts' legacy," *Oregonian* editorial, December 25,1994, D2.

45. Mapes, "Barbara Roberts' collision with history," D1.

Chapter 19: Choosing Senators, 1995-96

1. Dan Hortsch, "Kitzhaber's legacy built on consensus, persuasion," *Oregonian*, December 28, 1992, A9.

2. Senator Clifford Trow interview, December 9, 2004, Corvallis, Oregon.

3. Michael Wines, "GOP defeat won't end the deficit war," *Oregonian*, March 3, 1995, 1.

4. Ibid.

5. Jeff Mapes, "Session ending in divisions, turmoil," *Oregonian*, June 10, 1995, D1.

6. Ibid.

7. Jeff Mapes, "Vote still out on 68th Legislature's Deeds," *Oregonian*, June 12, 1995, A9.

8. "A look at the Legislature," *Oregonian*, June 12, 1995, A8.

9. Gail Kinsey Hill, Ashbel S. Green, and Jeff Mapes, "Legislature's goodbye is a special one," *Oregonian*, June 11, 1995, 1 and 12.

10. Senator Trow interview.

11. "A shortsighted session," *Oregonian*, June 11, 1995, E2.

12. Ashbel S. Green, "Kitzhaber calls session on light-rail," *Oregonian*, July 26, 1995, A1.

13. Jeff Mapes and Ashbel S. Green, "Votes highball light-rail funds to final approval," *Oregonian*, August 4, 1995, A1.

14. Dee Lane and Rose Ellen O'Connor, "New accusations delay action on Packwood case," *Oregonian*, August 4, 1995, A1.

15. Rose Ellen O'Connor, "Senate: No Packwood hearings," *Oregonian*, August 3, 1995, A1.
16. Jeff Mapes, "The Race: Smith vs. Wyden," *Oregonian*, December 6, 1995, 1 and 9.
17. Jeff Mapes, "Ron Wyden: The Next Step," *Oregonian*, January 31,1996, A1.
18. Ashbel S. Green and Phil Manzano, "Legislature warms up to catch Kitzhaber's pitch," *Oregonian*, February 1, 1996, E1.
19. Brent Walth, "Rep. Wes Cooley: An Issue of Trust," *Oregonian*, August 7,1996, A8.
20. Ibid.
21. Ibid.
22. Brian Meehan and Gail Kinsey Hill, "Smith, Bruggere wait for last votes," *Oregonian*, November 6, 1996, C3.
23. Gail Kinsey Hill, "Gordon Smith: the long road," *Oregonian*, November 7, 1996, A18.
24. Ibid.
25. "Measure 31: Restricting Obscenity," *Oregonian*, October 16, 1996, A10.
26. *Voter's Pamphlet*, Vol. 1, Phil Keisling, Secretary of State, November 5,1996, 213.

Chapter 20: John Kitzhaber and the Republicans, 1997-99

1. Gail Kinsey Hill, "The Hard Road Ahead," *Oregonian*, January 12, 1997, 1.
2. Ibid.
3. James Mayer, "Legislators get down to brass tax on Measure 47," *Oregonian*, March 3, 1997, A5.
4. James Mayer, "Sizemore enjoys new clout," *Oregonian*, March 3, 1997, A1.
5. Gail Kinsey Hill, "Adams' fiery outburst illuminates difficulty of leading legislators," *Oregonian*, March 21, 1997, D1.
6. Ashbel S. Green, "Black effigy angers lawmakers," *Oregonian*, April 19, 1997, 1.
7. Personal interview with Senator Cliff Trow, December 9, 2004.
8. Gail Kinsey Hill, "House approves $4.3 billion for schools," *Oregonian*, June 10, 1997, 1.
9. Ibid.
10. Steve Suo, and Ashbel S. Green, "Final weeks of the Legislature are no man's land," *Oregonian*, June 15, 1997, B1
11. Gail Hill, "Lawmakers OK record spending," *Oregonian,* July 2, 1997, 1.
12. "An OK session," an editorial, *Oregonian,* July 6, 1997, D4.
13. Ibid.
14. Ibid.
15. Jeff Mapes, "Kitzhaber tops 1997 vetoes with 26 more," *Oregonian,* August 16, 1997, 1.
16. David Broder, "Kitzhaber up front," *Oregonian*, October 8,1997, E13.
17. Jeff Mapes, "Measure 51 gathered late cash infusion," *Oregonian*, December 5, 1997, Metro section.
18. Jeff Mapes, "Independent voters show they're just that in Democratic primary," *Oregonian,* June 21,1998, C2.
19. Jeff Mapes, "It might be a hit show," *Oregonian*, February 15, 1998, G1.
20. See Campaign Finance Reports on file in the State Elections Division, Salem.
21. Michael J. Gerson, "The Christian Coalition falls to its knees," *Oregonian*, February 15, 1997, G1.

22. Ibid.

23. "News Update," *Oregonian*, March 29, 1998, C2.

24. Jeff Mapes, "Kitzhaber, Wyden lead easily," *Oregonian*, October 10, 1998, 1.

25. Craig Harris, "GOP bid to pick speaker stalls," Salem *Statesman Journal*, November 10, 1998, 1.

26. "Kitzhaber moves to protect salmon," Salem *Statesman Journal*, January 3, 1999, 1.

27. Kristen Green, "Issues split women legislators," Salem *Statesman Journal*, April 18, 1999, 1.

28. David Kravets, "Divergent issues converge," Salem *Statesman Journal*, January 10, 1999, 1.

29. Richard Aguirre, "Kitzhaber, Republicans wage war over governor's vetoes," Salem *Statesman Journal*, April 19, 1999, 3C.

30. Ibid.

31. "Legislature is making mess of budget work," an editorial, Salem *Statesman Journal*, June 17, 1999, 8C.

32. "Mediocrity ruled in third-longest session," an editorial, Salem *Statesman Journal*, July 25, 1999, 8C.

33. Steve Law, "Political bickering produced a messy, productive session," Salem *Statesman Journal*, July 26, 1999, 2F.

34. Chris Kenning, "Referrals risky legislative move," Salem *Statesman Journal*, July 26, 1999, 2F.

35. Keith O'Brien, "Kitzhaber scraps 25 bills," Salem *Statesman Journal*, September 4, 1999, 1.

36. "House vote attacks state's medical rights," an editorial, Salem *Statesman Journal*, October 28, 1999, 4C.

Chapter 21: Into the Future, 2000-11

1. *Oregonian*, January 1, 2000, A1.

2. Steve Mayes and Harry Esteve, "Oregon's poverty rate stagnant report says," *Oregonian*, September 3, 2000, D1.

3. "Pitfalls and Poison on the ballot," an editorial, *Oregonian*, September 3, 2000, F4.

4. "Oregon's new political landscape," an editorial, *Oregonian*, November 12, 2000, C4.

5. Laurence M. Cruz, "Derfler aims at change," Salem *Statesman Journal*, January 7, 2001, 1A.

6. "Speaker outlines his priorities," Salem *Statesman Journal*, February 19, 2001, 3C.

7. Lisa Grace Lednicer, "Simmons' cool style sets tone in House," *Oregonian*, March 4, 2001, 6A.

8. James Mayer and Lisa Grace Lednicer, "Budget cuts, quiet work may define 71st Legislature," *Oregonian*, January 7, 2001, A1.

9. Gail Kinsey Hill, "Kitzhaber wants to nearly double funds to prepare a base for lagging economies," *Oregonian*, January 7, 2001, B1.

10. Steve Law, "Diversity marks Oregon Senate," Salem *Statesman Journal*, January 14, 2001, 1A.

11. Lisa Grace Lednicer, "Lawmakers resolve to play nice," *Oregonian*, December 3, 2000, B1.

12. Steve Law, "Politician has bumpy month," Salem *Statesman Journal*, April 28, 2001, 1A.

13. Michael Rose, "Experts predict slow rebound for Oregon," Salem *Statesman Journal*, May 15, 2001, 1A.
14. Peter Wong, "Budget meetings open to the public," Salem *Statesman Journal*, May 20, 2001, 3A.
15. "A billion-dollar shadow," an editorial, *Oregonian*, March 4, 2001, 4G.
16. Steve Law, "Redistricting will shift representation," Salem *Statesman Journal*, March 15, 2001, 7A.
17. "Kitzhaber's final session presents a balancing act," Salem *Statesman Journal*, December 16, 2000, 3C.
18. Steve Law, "Democrats stage House walkout," Salem *Statesman Journal*, June 26, 2001, 1A.
19. Ibid.
20. Ibid.
21. "Salem 2001: Peace Train," an editorial, *Oregonian*, July 8, 2001, 4B.
22. Steve Law, "Budget unites Oregon leaders," Salem *Statesman Journal*, November 10, 2001, 2A.
23. Peter Wong, "GOP sidesteps Kitzhaber," Salem *Statesman Journal*, August 31, 2001, 1A.
24. "Oregon at a Crossroads," by Dana Haynes, *Statesman Journal*, January 3, 2003 (2003 Legislative Guide).

Index

A

Abernethy, George,12-16, 21
Adams, Brady, 421-24, 426-29, 436, 442, 445-46, 457
Adams, Ron, 398, 425
Adams, William, 29, 39
Alien Land Bill (1923), 156-57
Alley, Allen, 476
American Independent Party, 290
Anderson, Gust, 167
Angell, Homer, 175, 185, 192, 197, 210, 229, 230
Appling, Howell, Jr., 260, 270-71
Ash, Clarence, 195
Astorian-Budget, 210
Atiyeh, Victor, 3, 252, 280, 312, 318, 320, 328, 336-38, 342-43, 346-55, 358, 362-63, 365-66, 372, 385, 419, 473, 477
Atkinson, Perry, 390, 433
AuCoin, Les, 315, 318-19, 327, 340, 345, 360, 368, 381-83, 405
Australian Ballot, 85
Avery, J. C., 41

B

Baker, Edward Dickinson, 51, 53
Baker, George, 219
Baker, Ken, 424, 435, 437
Banner-Courier, 210
Barton, Clarence, 267-68
Baum, Ray, 398, 410
Bauman, Rick, 360-61
Beach Bill/beach protection, 122, 281-84
Bell, George, 440

Belton, Howard, 208, 272
Benson, Frank, 120
Benton, Thomas Hart, xii, 8
Berkman, Craig, 380
Bicycle Bill, 279, 307
Blumenauer, Earl, 381, 410, 413, 417, 439, 472
Boe, Jason, 272, 280, 311-13, 317, 321, 323, 329, 331, 334, 340, 348, 351
Boise, Reuben, 31
Boivin, Harry, 250, 261, 272, 280, 296
Bonneville Dam, 178, 181-83, 190, 194, 202
Booth, Robert, 111
Bordonaro, Molly, 412, 433, 439
Bottle Bill, 279, 300, 305-6
Bourne, Jonathan, Jr., 80, 92-95, 99, 106, 114-15, 118, 121
Bowerman, Jay, 93, 118, 120-23, 125-26, 128
Bradbury, Bill, 359-60, 376, 387, 447, 456, 463, 469
Brady, Phil, 195
Brian, Tom, 398, 423-24, 437
Brown, Jerry, 326, 344
Brown, Kate, 460-61, 470, 476
Brown vs. Board of Education (1954), 237
Browne, Elizabeth, 305, 310
Bruggere, Tom, 411, 415-16, 420
Buchanan, James, 36, 38, 49
Bunn, Jim, 390-91, 413, 417
Burdick, Ginny, 457
Burke, W. E., 195
Burns, John, 305

Burrows, Mary McCauley, 360
Bush, Asahel, 25, 28-32, 34-35, 37, 39, 41, 44, 54-55, 68
Bush, George H. W., 344, 368, 381, 384, 455
Bush, George W., 357, 380, 452, 455-56, 472
Butler, Robert 136

C

Cake, Harold, M., 115-18
California Gold Rush, 17
Campbell, Larry, 338, 354, 375, 381, 387, 401
Campbell, T. F., 61
Capital Journal, 160, 171, 204
Carkin, John, 164
Carpenter, Chuck, 397-98, 400, 427, 429, 436-37
Carson, Wallace, 280
Carter, James Earl, 326-27, 344-45
Carter, Margaret, 397, 425
Cayuse War, 16
Centralia riots (1919), 142
Chadwick, Stephen, 31, 60, 71, 356
Chamberlain, George Earle, 3, 76, 103-4, 107-10, 112, 117-18, 120-21, 123-24, 126, 129, 132-33, 143, 152, 161
Chambers, Richard, 300, 305
Chapman, C. C., 134-35, 158, 162, 165, 174, 181, 195, 209, 214
Chinese exclusion, 61, 80-82, 89, 211
Chisholm, Shirley, 308
Chrest, Jim, 349
Christian Coalition, 434-35
Church, Frank, 326
Clark, Kathryn, 134
Clarno, Beverly, 391, 396, 398-99, 403-4, 409, 417, 449, 470
Clinton, Hillary Rodham, 475
Clinton, William J., 381, 384, 391, 410, 415-17, 448
Coffey, John B., 141
Cohen, Joyce, 352
Columbia Valley Authority, 219
Compulsory School Bill, 150-51

Constitutional Convention (1857), 43
Cooley, Wes, 390-91, 412-15, 433
Coolidge, Calvin, 165, 178
Corbett, Alf, 271
Corbett, Henry, 58-59, 74, 93, 96-97, 100
Corbett, Henry Ladd, 164, 167-68, 170, 181
Cordon, Guy, 204-7, 230-31, 233
Cordon-Neuberger Senate Race (1956), 230-34
Cornelius, T. R., 83
Cornett, Marshall, 207, 211, 213-14
Courtney, Peter, 353, 393, 399-400, 422, 442, 458, 470, 472
Cross, Travis, 247
Crumpacker, M. E., 152
Curry, George, 33-34

D

Davis, Drew, 328, 341
Davis, John, W., 33, 165
Day, L. B., 314, 340
Deady, Matthew, 31, 41, 43, 75
Debs, Eugene V., 127, 132
Deckert, Ryan, 454-55
DeFazio, Peter, 360-61, 368, 390, 392, 406-7, 417, 439-40, 472
Dellenback, John, 264, 272, 278, 289, 295 319
Democratic Party of Oregon, founding of, 31, 44
   Democratic-Populists, 89
Democratic Standard, 40, 43
Democrats: Breckinridge-Lane, 50, 53, 56-57; Douglas, 49-50, 52, 57; National, 39, 45-46; Regular, 39, 44
Densmore, Al, 310
DEQ (Department of Environmental Quality), 279, 288-89, 299, 307
Derfler, Gene, 444, 447, 452, 457-61, 464
Devlin, Richard, 418
Dewey, Thomas E., 215-17
Direct Legislation League, 89, 91, 96, 99-100
Direct Primary Law, 2, 103, 114-15, 117, 120-21

Dole, Robert, 368, 405, 410, 415, 417, 435
Dolph, Cyrus, 78, 99
Dolph, Joseph, 73, 78-80, 85, 91
Donation Land Act (1850), xiii, 22, 26
Donaugh, Carl, 210
Dooley, Pat, 248
Douglas, Stephen A., 36, 49
Dred Scott Decision (1857), 38
Dryer, Thomas Jefferson, 27, 29, 34, 39, 43-44
Dudley, Chris, 476
Dukakis, Michael, 368
Duncan, Robert B., 211, 253, 261, 264, 272, 275-77, 285-88, 303, 309, 319, 327, 344
Duncan, Robert M., 195
Duniway, Abigail Scott, 55, 63-64, 101-2, 127
Dunne, Joe, E., 181-83, 185
Durno, Edwin, 260, 263

E

East Oregonian, 247
Eddy, B. L., 141, 155, 167
Eighmey, George, 425
Eisenhower, Dwight, D., 175, 225-27, 239, 244
Eisenzimmer, Frank, 453
Ekwall, William, 189
Elections (in state history): 1861, 54; 1866, 57-58; 1874, 61; 1882, 79; 1902, 102; 1906, 113; 1908, 116-17; 1910, 120-24; 1916, 133-35; 1922, 149-54; 1930, 171-73; 1932, 174-75; 1934, 185; 1936, 189; 1938, 192; 1940, 196-97; 1942, 200-202; 1944, 204-6; 1946, 210; 1948, 225, 217-18; 1950, 220-21; 1952, 225-26; 1954, 229-34; 1956, 240-44; 1958, 250-51; 1960, 259-61; 1962, 262; 1964, 270-72; 1966, 275-78; 1968, 286, 292-95; 1970, 302-3; 1972, 308-10; 1974, 316-19; 1976, 326-27; 1978, 336-39; 1980, 344-45; 1982, 351-52; 1984, 355-56; 1986, 359-61; 1988, 367; 1990, 372-74; 1992, 381-86; 1994, 391-92; 1996, 410-20; 1998, 432-33, 435-44;

2000, 453-57; 2002, 467-70, 2004, 472; 2006, 472; 2008, 475-76
Ellis, Anna M., 203, 208
Ellis, Rex, 198, 208
Ellsworth, Harris, 202, 210, 221, 244
Emancipation Proclamation, 54
Equal Rights Amendment (ERA), 315
Equi, Maria, 138
Eugene *Register Guard*, 200, 214
Eymann, Richard, 310-13, 319

F

Fadeley, Edward, 280, 321, 352, 354-55, 358-59
Fadeley, Nancie, 305, 321
Farmer's Alliance, 88
Farrell, Robert, 198, 207, 210, 213-14
Fawbush, Wayne, 327, 413
Field burning, 380
Fisher, Earl, 195
Flagel, Austin, 221
Flowers, Ruth, 219
Fluorocarbon propellant ban (1975), 324
Forbes, Steve, 410
Ford, Gerald, 325, 327
Franke, Michael, 369
Frohnmayer, David, 368, 372, 386
Fulton, Charles W., 106-7, 116-17
Furnish, William J., 104
Furse, Elizabeth, 382-84, 390-91, 412, 416-17, 439

G

Gaines, John Pollard, 27-30, 32, 35, 37
Gearin, John M., 115
Geary, Edward, 235
Geer, Theodore (Ted), 76, 97, 104-8
Gibbs, Addison, C., 53-54, 56, 58, 75, 152
Gifford, Fred L., 147, 151
Gill, Warren, 248, 250
Gilmour, Jeff, 313, 328, 341, 369
Gold, Shirley, 410
Goldbugs, 77

Goldschmidt, Neil, 309, 335, 359-62, 364-66, 369-72, 377-78, 385, 419, 477
Goldwater, Barry, 270-71
Gordly, Avel, 397
Gore, Albert (Al), Jr., 452, 455-56, 470, 473
Grannell, Bill, 341
Green, Edith, 131, 230, 244, 246, 252, 257, 259-60, 262, 272, 274, 276, 278, 288, 295, 325, 327
Green-McCall U.S. House race (1954), 234
Grisham, Jerry, 437-40
Groener, Richard, 328
Grover, LaFayette, 31, 46, 55, 60-61, 79, 81, 119

H

Hall, Charles, 149, 167-68
Hall, John C., 212, 214-15
Hallock, Ted, 306-7, 314
Hamby, Jeannette, 351, 435-37
Haney, Bert E., 161
Hanneman, Paul, 300, 305-6, 358
Hannon, Lenn, 440, 460, 464
Hansell, Stafford, 272, 280
Hanzen, Henry M., 134
Harding, Benjamin F., 31, 50, 54-55
Harrison, Benjamin, 84-85
Hartung, Tom, 437
Hatfield, Mark O., 131, 211, 222, 226, 236, 240, 243-44, 250-55, 257-58, 261, 263-64, 267-71, 273, 275-77, 280, 286, 289, 294, 307, 309-10, 320, 336-37, 346, 355-56, 366, 373, 398-99, 406-7, 409, 411, 415, 431, 477
Haywood, Bill, 141
Heard, Fred W., 348, 351
Henderson, J. H. P., 54
Hendriksen, Margie, 352, 355-56, 360
Hemstreet, Mark, 437
Heney, Francis J., 111
Hermann, Binger, 84, 90, 110-12
Hess, Henry, 185, 192, 194
Hill, Jim, 369, 382, 417, 467
Hirsch, Josephine Mayer, 127

Hitchcock, Philip, S., 238-39
Holladay, Ben, 66, 68-69, 72, 74-75
Holman, Rufus, 139, 181-83, 203, 205-6, 211
Holmes, Robert, 2, 219, 222, 226, 236, 240, 248-52, 257, 268
Honeyman, Nancy Wood, 176, 189, 191-92, 197, 219
Hooley, Darlene, 346, 417, 440, 472, 475
Hoover, Herbert Clark, 165-66, 168, 175, 179
Hornets, 329, 331
Hudson's Bay Company, 3
Hughes, Charles Evans, 134-35
Humphrey, Hubert H., 286, 288, 290, 294, 308
Hunt, Louise, 138
Huss, Walter, 275, 432
Hydroelectic power/public power development as a political issue: 160, 179, 183, 185, 191-92, 204, 229-30, 232

I

Independent Party, 61-62
Initiative. *See* Oregon System
International Workers of the World (IWW), 141-42

J

Jackson, Henry (Scoop), 302, 308
Jackson, Jesse, 355, 368
Johnson, Lee, 280, 283
Johnson Lyndon, 269-71, 285, 288
Johnson, Sam, 331
Jones, Denny, 328
Jones, Seymour, 140
Jones, Willard, 112
Joseph, George, 160, 165, 169-71, 174, 182

K

Kafoury, Deborah, 470
Kansas-Nebraska Act, 36, 38-39
Katz, Vera, 327, 330, 356-59, 365-66, 369-70, 379, 387

Keisling, Phil, 413, 417, 446-47
Kelley, Hall Jackson, xii
Kelly, James K. 54, 57, 60, 71-72
Kennedy, John F., 258, 260, 269
Kennedy, Robert, 286, 288-90, 357
Kennedy, Ted, 308, 344
Kerans, Grattan, 352, 354-55, 370, 380, 394
Kerry, John, 472
Kicker tax refund law, 343, 347, 460
Kiddle, Fred, B., 179
King, Martin Luther, Jr., 290, 358
Kinkel, Kipland, 443, 457
Kitzhaber, John, 338, 356-59, 365-66, 369-70, 381, 388-91, 395-96, 399-404, 409, 419, 421-23, 425-35, 438-39, 442-47, 449, 452, 458-59, 461-62, 465, 467, 470, 475-77
Know-Nothings, 34-35
Kopetski, Mike, 367, 374, 390
Kroger, John, 476
Kubli, Kasper K., 140-41, 154-55
Ku Klux Klan, 140, 145-57, 171-72, 205, 259
Kulongoski, Theodore (Ted), 319, 331, 340-41, 345-46, 349, 351-52, 453, 467-69, 471, 473-74, 477

L

Labor strikes, 187-88
LaFollette, Robert, 136, 153
Land Conservation and Development Commission (LCDC), 279, 349
Land scams, 66-67, 110
Land-use planning, 212, 279, 296, 313-14, 329, 342, 349
Lane, Harry, 104, 113, 120-21, 128, 132, 136-37
Lane, Joseph (Joe), 17-18, 20-21, 24-26, 29, 32, 35-37, 40-41, 46-45, 49-50, 53
Lang, Phil, 280, 310, 319, 321-23, 328, 330-33, 338, 341
Lansing, Jewel, 327
Latourette, Howard, 187, 218, 220
Lee, Barbara Coombs, 431

Lee, Dorothy McCullough, 167, 173, 194, 198, 203, 207
Lee, Jason, 8, 10
Legislative Assembly (sessions of):
1859, 47; 1860, 50-52; 1861, 54; 1865 (special session), 56; 1866, 58; 1868, 59; 1870, 60; 1885, 80; 1887, 84; 1895, 90-91, 94; 1897 (Hold-Up session), 87, 93-87; 1899, 99-100; 1901, 100-101; 1903, 106; 1905, 112; 1909, 118; 1911, 125-26; 1913, 128-30; 1915, 134; 1917, 136; 1919, 140; 1923, 155-58; 1925, 159-60; 1927, 162-62; 1929, 167; 1931, 173-74; 1933, 180-81; 1935, 186-87; 1939, 194-95; 1941, 198; 1943, 202-3; 1945, 208-9; 1947, 211-15; 1951, 222-23; 1953, 227; 1955, 235-36; 1957, 248-50; 1959, 253-56; 1961, 261-62; 1963, 266-69; 1965, 272-73; 1967, 279-84; 1967 (special session), 285-86; 1969, 296-99; 1971, 304-5, 307-8; 1973, 310-16; 1975, 321-25; 1977, 327-35; 1979, 340-43; 1981, 346-350; 1982 (special sessions) 350-51; 1983, 352-55; 1983 (special session), 355; 1985, 356-59; 1987, 365-37; 1989, 369; 1990 (special session), 371; 1991, 375-81, 394; 1993, 387, 394; 1995, 396-402; 1995 (special session), 402-4; 1997, 421-32; 1999, 441-47; 2001, 457-65; 2003, 470-71; 2009, 476
Leonard, Randy, 428
Lent, Berkeley, 280
Lewelling, Seth, 88, 96
Lewelling, Sophronia, 88
Lewis, Jean, 235, 253
Lim, John, 433, 438-39
Lincoln, Abraham, 49-56
Lindquist, Ed, 328-39, 331, 333, 390
Linn, Lewis, xii, 8
Logan, David, 41
Lokan, Jane, 388, 440
Lonergan, Frank, 173
Lonsdale, Harry, 373, 382, 412
Lord, William P., 90, 96-97
Lovejoy, Asa, 15, 21, 68
Lucier, Etienne, 10

Lundquist, Lynn, 421-22, 425-27, 429, 437, 449

Lutz, Joe P., Sr., 360

M

Mabon, Lon, 385-86, 408, 411, 453

Macpherson, Hector, 305, 312, 314

Maine Law (1851), 34

Mail Tribune, 123, 156, 170-71, 248

Manifest Destiny, 5

Mannix, Kevin, 397, 418, 437, 440, 444, 457, 467-69

Marks, Willard, 173

Marsh, Eugene, 227

Magruder, Caroline, 338

Magruder, Richard (Dick), 313, 328-29, 331, 333, 340-41

Mahoney, Willis, 183, 189, 207

Mapes, Jeff, 371, 394

Martin, Charles, 172, 175-76, 182-93, 196, 265

Martin, Hannah, 194

Martin, Roger, 300, 315, 328, 330-32, 334, 336, 337, 340

Marvin, Cornelia, 112

Matthieu, Francis X., 10

Metropolitan Area Rapid Transit (MAX), 399-400, 402-4

May Rebellion (1977), 331-34

May, Samuel E., 60, 71

Mays, Franklin Pierce, 107, 110-12

Mays Law (1901), 101, 105

McAllister, William, 202

McAlmond, Phil, 287

McArthur, C. M., 118, 128, 150, 152

McBride, George, 91, 93, 100-101

McCain, John, 475

McCall, Thomas Lawson (Tom): 3, 122, 229-31, 264-66, 271-72, 274-80, 299; 309, 320-21, 323-24, 336-37, 339, 346, 372, 404, 465; and Beach Bill, 281-83, 289; and Bottle Bill, 300, 305-7; death of, 353; and land-use planning, 295-96; and Operation Red Hat), 301-2; and OSP riot), 291-92; and Senate Bill 100, 313-14; Tax Plan (1969), 297; Tax Plan (1973), 311-13; and Vortex, 302;, ;

McCarthy, Eugene, 286, 288-90, 308

McCoy William (Bill), 310, 315, 369

McCready, Connie, 280

McFarland, Ruth, 346

McGovern, George, 308-9

McIntire Don, 454, 456

McKay, Douglas, 215, 217, 220-21, 226, 228, 238-39, 241-43, 346

McLoughlin, Dr. John, 3, 10

McMinn, Judge Henry, 106

McNary, Charles, 123, 131, 137, 143-44, 172, 189, 197, 203-4, 373, 401

Meek, Joseph, 10, 14, 16

Meeker, Tony, 368, 382-84

Meier, Julius, 149, 171-74, 176, 179-81

Meldrum, Henry, 111

Merkley, Jeff, 2, 474

Messenger, 41

Metropolitian Service District (MSD), 299

Metschan, Phil, 171-72, 174, 182

Metsger, Rick, 437, 440, 459

military road companies, 67-68

Minnis, Karen, 398, 472, 474

Missouri Compromise, 38

Mitchell, John H., 58-59, 66, 68, 70, 72-76, 80, 85, 87, 91, 93-96, 101, 111, 113-14

Mondale, Walter F., 355-56

Money issue, 77-78

Monroe, Rod, 328, 360

Montgomery, F. F. (Monte), 272, 280, 291-92

Moody, Ralph, 188

Moody, Zenas, 76, 79, 155

Morgan, Howard, 219-20, 236, 275-76, 286

Morse, Wayne Lyman, 2, 205-7, 210-11, 220-21, 226, 228, 232, 236, 241-43, 248, 251, 257, 259, 262-63, 275-77, 285-88, 303, 310, 312, 317, 409

Morse-Packwood U.S. Senate Race (1968): 288, 292-94

Mott, James, 202-3, 210

Munroe, Christina, 194-95
Murray, Patty, 381
Musa, Ben, 250, 267, 269, 272, 280
Musa, Katherine, 235
Muskie, Edmund, 308
Myers, Clay, 280, 291-92, 318, 323, 337
Myers, Hardy, 319, 340-41, 348, 351, 417, 476

N

Nativism, 34
Negro: race relations/rights, 12, 43, 56, 58-59, 135, 141-42, 237
Nesmith, James, 30-31, 51, 58, 74-75
Neuberger, Maureen, 2, 222-24, 226-27, 235, 257-59, 261, 274
Neuberger, Richard (Dick), 2, 98, 191, 197-98, 204, 222-24, 226, 230-33, 243, 248, 257
Neuberger-Morse Feud, 245-48
Newbry, Earl, 214-15, 230
New Deal, 177-79
Nixon, Richard, 257, 259-60, 270, 289, 294, 301-2, 309, 318
Norblad, Alvin W., 136, 167-68, 170, 173, 210, 215
Norblad, A. Walter, Jr., 210, 244, 260
Northern Spotted Owl, 380
Nott, Earl A., 202

O

Obama, Barack, 475
Offshore oil reserves/Tidelands oil bill (1953), 228
Olcott, Benjamin, 122, 133, 140, 142, 145, 149-53, 156
Oregon Boundary Question, 10, 15, 18
Oregon Capitol: burns, 187; dedication of (1937), 193
Oregon Central Railway Co., 68
Oregon Citizens Alliance (OCA), 385-86, 392, 408, 411, 416, 453-54, 456
Oregon Commonwealth Federation (OCF), 191
Oregon Country, 4, 14
Oregon Cultural Trust, 464

Oregon Democrat, 175, 200-201, 223, 231
Oregon Education Act for the 21st Century, 378-80
Oregon Health Plan, 370, 388, 395, 419, 426, 428, 442, 445, 460, 463-65, 469, 471
Oregon Journal, 126, 182, 201
Oregon Land Law (1887), 108
Oregon People's Party (1892), 88
Oregon Statesman, 28, 31, 41, 54, 56, 113, 192
Oregon System, 2, 87, 121, 125, 133: initiative and referendum: 2, 89, 91, 96, 99-100, 103, 119, 128; recall, 2, 119
Oregon Style (journalism), 29
Oregon Taxpayers' United: 423, 432, 453-56
Oregon Territorial Legislature (1849), 4
Oregon Territory, 19-21, 23-25
Oregon Trail, 11
Oregon Voter, 135, 171, 180, 198, 233, 285, 311-12
Oregonian: 27, 29, 41, 43, 55, 71, 74, 106, 123, 133-34, 170-71, 182, 205, 209, 214-15, 371, 375, 388-89, 394, 401-2, 429, 451, 454, 457, 461, 464, 468
Organic Law of 1843, 11-12, 14
Otto, Glenn, 323-24
Overhulse, Boyd, 248

P

Packwood, Robert (Bob), 211, 264, 271-72, 294, 307, 318-19, 325, 345, 359-61, 381-83, 389, 399, 401, 404-6, 414, 433
Packwood Scandal, 404-6
Parks, Loren, 468
Patrons of Husbandry (Grange), 62, 88
Patterson, Isaac, 161, 163-64, 167-68, 170, 215
Patterson, Paul, 222, 226-27, 230, 235, 238
Paulus, Norma, 305, 315, 327, 345-46, 359-62, 401, 406-7
Pearson, Walter, 217-18, 221, 248, 253, 263

Peck, Grace Olivier, 305

Pelosi, Nancy, 474

Pennoyer, Sylvester, 3, 81-84, 87, 89, 104, 109, 113, 152, 396

People's Power League, 87, 106-7, 112-13, 115-16, 118-19, 121

People's Transportation Company, 69-71

Perot, H. Ross, 384, 415

Petticoat Government, 134

Pierce, Franklin, 32-33

Pierce, Walter, 3, 81, 104, 136, 140-41, 145, 150, 152-60, 162-63, 175-76, 191-92, 199

Political action committees (PACs), 361, 419-20, 432, 455

Polk, James K., 24, 26

Poole, Rose M., 208

Popular sovereignty, 36-37

Populists / People's Party, 87-90

Portland dock strike (1934), 186-86

Porter, Charles O., 219, 244, 246, 257, 260, 263, 278, 309, 344

Pollution in Paradise, 264-66, 268, 270, 275

Potts, Debbs, 272, 296, 305, 328

Powell, John, 328, 345

Powell, Luther I., 147

Pratt, O. C., 38

Progressivism, 108, 126, 132

Prohibition / prohibitionists, 86, 136, 161, 165-66

Property tax relief, 283-84, 297, 321, 335

Public Employees Retirement System (PERS), 461, 464, 471

Public Utility Districts (PUD), 198

Puter, S.A.D., 110-11

Putnam, George, 151

Q

Qutub, Eileeen, 398, 454-55, 457

R

Ramp, Floyd, 138

Reagan, Ronald, 289, 326, 344-45, 355-56

Redden, Jim, 280, 283, 312, 317

Reed, Ralph, 435

Republican Party of Oregon, founding of (1856), 38-39, 41, 46

Rieke, Mary, 305

Roberts, Barbara, 346, 355-56, 364, 368, 372, 375-81, 385, 388-90, 392-94, 385, 388-90, 447, 477

Roberts, Betty, 272, 296, 305-6, 310, 314-19, 321, 375

Roberts, Frank, 321, 375, 389

Roberts, Mary Wendy, 319, 321, 375

Rockefeller, Nelson, 270-71, 289, 291

Roosevelt, Eleanor, 191-92

Roosevelt, Franklin D., 153, 162, 175-79, 184, 189, 191-92, 196, 203, 208

Roosevelt, Theodore (Teddy), 111-12, 118-19, 127, 137

Rule of Eighteen (1995), 396, 398-400, 417

Rutherford, Bill, 412

Ryles, Nancy W., 352

S

Salem Clique, 31, 33-34, 39, 44

Sales tax, 180, 190, 198, 203, 212, 268, 353-55, 358, 376, 378, 380-81, 388, 392, 393

Saxton, Ron, 402, 467-68, 474

Schrader, Kurt, 475

Scott, Harvey, 55, 81, 93, 96, 102, 106, 116, 121, 123

Selling, Benjamin, 132

Senate Bill 100 (1973), 313-14, 322

Shannon, Marylin, 444, 457

Shiel, George, 50

Silverbugs, 77

Silverite Republicans, 89, 91, 97

Simmons, Mark, 449, 458, 463-64, 467

Simon, Joseph, 78, 91-93, 95, 97-100, 106, 114

Sinnott, Nick J., 149

Sizemore, Bill, 401, 418, 423, 432-33, 435, 438-39, 453

Slater, James, 60, 80-81

Slavery (as a political issue), 37, 43, 59

Smith, Deanna, 436

Smith, Delazon, 46, 50

Smith, Denny, 345, 352, 356, 360, 367-68, 374, 390-91, 436

Smith, Elmo, 131, 222, 235-36, 238, 240, 243, 252, 259, 345

Smith, Gordon, 391, 396, 398-99, 403, 406-9, 412, 416, 420, 435, 449, 452, 469, 475

Smith, Robert (Bob), 282, 296-97, 300, 304, 328, 352, 356, 360, 368, 374, 390, 413, 433

Snell, Earl, 163, 179, 197, 200, 202, 204-8, 210, 213, 215, 346

Snodgrass, Lynn, 430, 442-44, 447, 449, 457

Soros, George, 431, 440

The Spectator, 15

Sprague, Charles, 3, 192-94, 196-97, 199-201, 203-5, 207, 209-10, 230, 268, 272

Stanfield, Robert N., 136, 143-44

Stark, Benjamin, 4

Starr, Charles, 436

Statehood Bill, 47

Statesman-Journal, 338, 445-46, 459

Stein, Beverly, 467-68

Steiwer, Fred, 136, 161

Steiwer, Winlock, 111-12

Steiwer, W. H., 203

Stevenson, Adai, 225, 244

Stockmarket Crash (1929), 166-67

Stout, Lansing, 46, 50

Straub, Robert (Bob), 3, 122, 252, 271-72, 277, 280, 291, 295, 303, 312, 317-18, 320-22, 324, 329, 331, 335-40, 342-43, 353, 364, 366, 385

Straub-McCall governor's race (1966), 277-78

Straub-McCall governor's race (1970), 303

Sumner, Jack, 340-41, 344

Sweetland, Monroe: 191, 216-17, 219, 231, 233, 236, 240, 243-44, 260

T

Taft, William Howard, 119, 132

Tax reform: 157-60, 163, 165, 311-13, 347

Temperance, 12, 34, 127

Thayer, A. J., 50, 55

Thompson, Mrs. Alexander, 136

Thornton, Robert Y., 222, 226, 247, 254, 263-64

Throop, Tom, 353-54

Thurston, Samuel Loyal, xiii, 21-22, 25, 29

Tiernan, Bob, 398, 403, 417-18

Toran, Kay, 425

Towne, Marian, 134

Trojan nuclear plant, 307

Trow, Clifford, 388, 395, 401-2, 440

Truman Harry, S, 175, 215-16

Tugman, William M., 214, 247

U

Ullman, Al, 219, 244, 246, 260, 272, 278, 295, 319, 327, 345

Unander, Sig, 244, 250, 262-63

Union Party (1860s), 49, 54, 56-57, 59

Union Party (1890), 86-87

U'Ren, William S., 3, 85-86, 88-89, 92, 94, 96, 99, 106-7, 112, 114-16, 118, 121

V

Van Vliet, Tony, 353, 376

Villard, Henry, 66, 72

Vinton, W. T. 140

Viva voce law, 35, 39

Vote-by-mail, 441

W

Walden, Greg, 432, 439, 472

Walker, Dean, 198

Wallace, George, C., 290, 294, 308

Wallace, Lew, 201, 207, 217-18, 221

Washington Post, 388, 404-5

Watkins, Elton, 145, 150, 152, 161, 172, 244

Weaver, James B., 309, 319, 327, 345, 356, 359-61

West, Oswald, 3, 93, 96, 104, 110, 112, 120, 122-26, 128-31, 137, 140, 151-52, 165, 169, 183, 220, 280, 339, 396

Westlund, Ben, 460, 464, 476

Whig Party of Oregon, 28, 30, 34-36

Whipple, Blaine, 272, 327

White, Elijah, 10

Whiteaker, John, 41, 44, 46-47, 50-51

Whitman, Marcus and Narcissa, 16

Wilhelm, Rudie, 227, 236

Willamette Falls Canal and Locks Company, 71-72

Willamette River Greenway Plan, 278, 280, 317, 320

Willamette Valley field burning, 323

Williams, Edgar, 219

Williams, George, 41, 43, 54, 59, 72, 75, 96

Williamson, John N., 111

Wilson, Woodrow, 127, 132-33, 135, 137, 142-43

Winters, Jackie, 442

Withycombe, James, 109, 113, 133-34, 136-37, 140-42, 153

Witt, Bill, 390-91, 412, 416, 436, 438

Wolf meetings, 10

Woman's suffrage, 63, 124, 127, 134

Wood, C. E. S., 105

Woods, George L., 57, 60, 67-68, 71

Wu, David, 433, 439, 472

Wyatt, Wendell, 239, 272, 278, 295, 318-19, 325

Wyden, Ron, 2, 98, 344, 356, 360, 368, 390-91, 406-411, 420, 432-33, 438-39, 452, 472, 475

Y

Yih, Mae, 327, 341, 352

Young, Ewing, 9

Z

Zajonc, Donna, 355

Zimmerman, Peter, 183-85, 191